TIDELOG®

2023

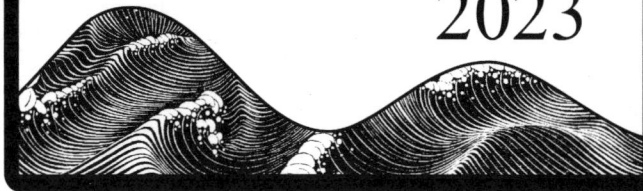

NORTHERN CALIFORNIA

Daily Tide Graphics
based on predictions by

National Ocean Service
U.S. Department of Commerce
National Oceanic & Atmospheric Administration

Astronomical Data
Courtesy of the United States Naval Observatory

Illustrated by
M. C. Escher
"Second Day of Creation"
© 2022 The M. C. Escher Company - Baarn Holland
All rights reserved.

Pacific Publishers, LLC
P.O. Box 2813
Tybee Island, GA 31328
912.472.4373
www.tidelog.com

TIDELOG 2023
GRAPHIC ALMANAC FOR NORTHERN CALIFORNIA

Including San Francisco Bay and Delta;
South to Monterey and north to the Nehalem River in Oregon

Tidelog brings the numbers to life!

TIDES: Daily graphics are based on official National Oceanic & Atmospheric Administration (NOAA) predictions for San Francisco, at the Golden Gate Bridge. Tide tables for Arena Cove, Port Chicago and Humboldt Bay, as well as NOAA's historical corrections and approximations for other locations, are in the back of the Tidelog.

Tide height is relative to the NOAA chart datum for mean lower low water (MLLW) which is represented by the x-axis of the daily graphic. Also indicated is mean higher high water (MHHW) shown as a horizontal white line at 5.84 feet showing the Great Diurnal Range, which is the difference in height between MHHW and MLLW.

CURRENTS: Time and strength of maximum currents and times of slack water are shown daily at San Francisco Bay Entrance and Carquinez Strait. Maximum current times are indicated by a " ∧ " while slack water intervals are indicated by a "⊣ ⊢" at the points between ebbs and floods.

Current tables for the Golden Gate Bridge, Benicia Bridge, San Mateo, Richmond and Oakland, as well as NOAA's historical corrections for other locations, are in the back of the Tidelog. For a comprehensive view of the tidal currents throughout San Francisco Bay, please see the **Tidal Current Charts** at the back of the Tidelog.

HOW TIDELOG BRINGS THE NUMBERS TO LIFE: the daily graphic below shows the tides, currents and astronomical movements to give you a visual picture for each day's conditions... at a glance!

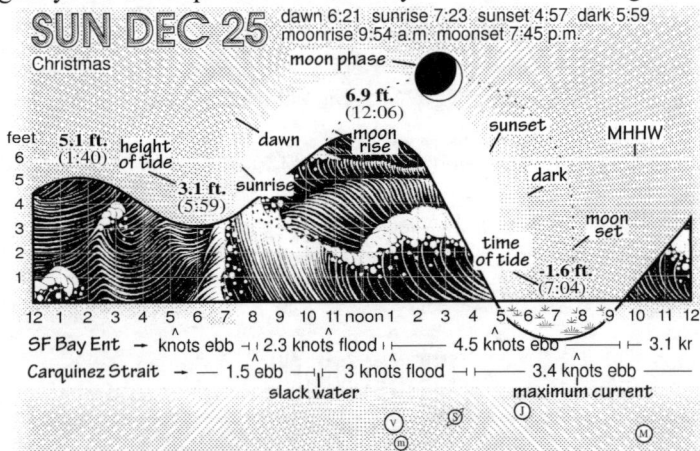

SUN DEC 25 — dawn 6:21 sunrise 7:23 sunset 4:57 dark 5:59 moonrise 9:54 a.m. moonset 7:45 p.m.
Christmas — moon phase

6.9 ft. (12:06)
feet — 5.1 ft. (1:40) height of tide — dawn — moonrise — sunset — MHHW
3.1 ft. (5:59) sunrise — dark — moonset
time of tide — -1.6 ft. (7:04)

12 1 2 3 4 5 6 7 8 9 10 11 noon 1 2 3 4 5 6 7 8 9 10 11 12
SF Bay Ent → knots ebb ⊣⊢ 2.3 knots flood ⊢ ⎯ 4.5 knots ebb ⎯ ⊢ 3.1 kr
Carquinez Strait → ⎯ 1.5 ebb ⊣⊢ 3 knots flood ⊣ ⊢ ⎯ 3.4 knots ebb ⎯
slack water — maximum current

MOON: The principal determinant of the tides is treated in detail, showing the interplay of the tides with the moon's phase, distance (apogee, perigee), and declination (north, south or over the equator).

The moon is shown in its current phase each day at the time it is highest. The dotted arcs indicate moonrise and moonset, and show which night times will have moonlight and which will be dark.

For an explanation of terminology and a brief outline of the forces which influence the tides and currents, see the next-to-last page of the Tidelog.

SUNRISE & SUNSET, DAWN & DUSK: Shown by the skyshading. The lighter band near the sun indicates the duration of nautical twilight, which determines "dawn" and "dark." Actual times are given daily.

DAYLIGHT SAVING TIME: All information in Tidelog is adjusted for Daylight Saving Time beginning on the second Sunday of March and ending on the first Sunday of November.

NOAA PREDICTIONS: Assume normal weather with normal seasonal variations. You must adjust the predictions for particular conditions. Heavy rainfall, low barometric pressure and strong onshore winds increase tides, while the opposite will decrease them.

We have made every effort to ensure that Tidelog's graphics faithfully depict NOAA predictions, but we cannot guarantee accuracy.

PLANETS: The five planets visible to the naked eye are shown at zenith, sized according to brightness as shown below:

ⓥVenus   ⓜMars   ⓢSaturn   ⓙJupiter   ⓜ Mercury

The planets move slowly, so they are shown only once a week in the panel after the Sunday daily graphic. Generally, a planet crossing overhead before noon is visible in the east before sunrise; a planet which is overhead after noon is seen in the west after sunset (Mercury, Venus, Saturn and Jupiter on the facing page); and a planet overhead near midnight may be seen all night. A planet whose zenith is within 45 minutes of the sun's is usually too close to the sun for observation, and is not shown until it is again visible.

METEOR SHOWERS, ECLIPSES: Noted when appropriate.

MON DEC 26

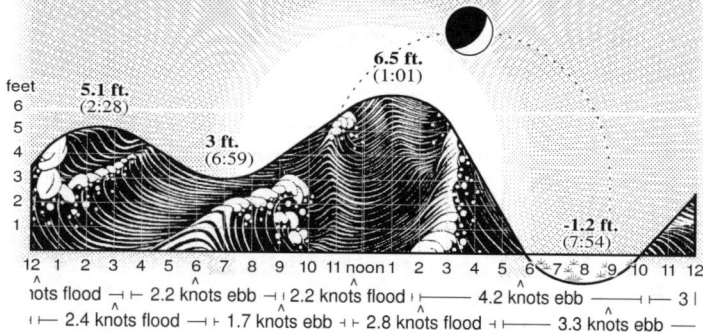

6.5 ft.
(1:01)

5.1 ft.
(2:28)

3 ft.
(6:59)

-1.2 ft.
(7:54)

feet
6
5
4
3
2
1

12 1 2 3 4 5 6 7 8 9 10 11 noon 1 2 3 4 5 6 7 8 9 10 11 12

nots flood ⊣ ⊢ 2.2 knots ebb ⊣ ⊢ 2.2 knots flood ⊦ ⊢ 4.2 knots ebb ⊢ 3 |
⊢ 2.4 knots flood ⊣ ⊢ 1.7 knots ebb ⊦ ⊢ 2.8 knots flood ⊣ ⊢ 3.3 knots ebb ⊢

TUE DEC 27

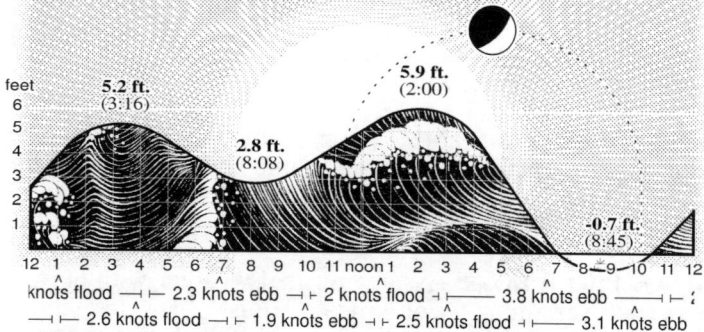

5.9 ft.
(2:00)

5.2 ft.
(3:16)

2.8 ft.
(8:08)

-0.7 ft.
(8:45)

feet
6
5
4
3
2
1

12 1 2 3 4 5 6 7 8 9 10 11 noon 1 2 3 4 5 6 7 8 9 10 11 12

knots flood ⊣ ⊢ 2.3 knots ebb ⊣ ⊢ 2 knots flood ⊦ ⊢ 3.8 knots ebb ⊢ ⊢ 2
⊢ 2.6 knots flood ⊣ ⊢ 1.9 knots ebb ⊦ ⊢ 2.5 knots flood ⊣ ⊢ 3.1 knots ebb

WED DEC 28

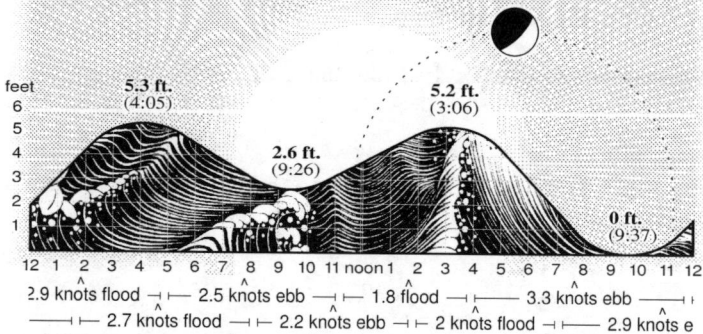

5.3 ft.
(4:05)

5.2 ft.
(3:06)

2.6 ft.
(9:26)

0 ft.
(9:37)

feet
6
5
4
3
2
1

12 1 2 3 4 5 6 7 8 9 10 11 noon 1 2 3 4 5 6 7 8 9 10 11 12

2.9 knots flood ⊣ ⊢ 2.5 knots ebb ⊢ ⊢ 1.8 flood ⊣ ⊢ 3.3 knots ebb ⊢
⊢ 2.7 knots flood ⊣ ⊢ 2.2 knots ebb ⊣ ⊢ 2 knots flood ⊣ ⊢ 2.9 knots e

THU DEC 29

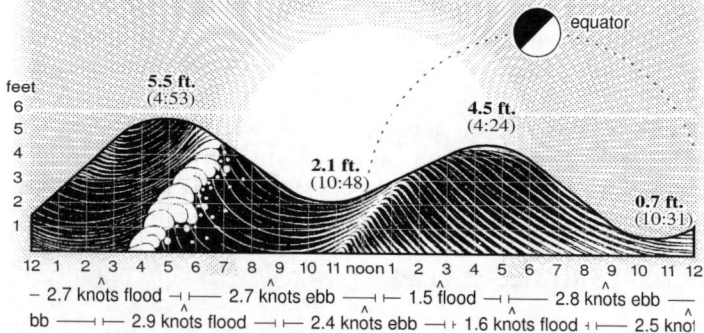

equator

5.5 ft.
(4:53)

4.5 ft.
(4:24)

2.1 ft.
(10:48)

0.7 ft.
(10:31)

feet
6
5
4
3
2
1

12 1 2 3 4 5 6 7 8 9 10 11 noon 1 2 3 4 5 6 7 8 9 10 11 12

– 2.7 knots flood ⊣ ⊢ 2.7 knots ebb ⊢ ⊢ 1.5 flood ⊣ ⊢ 2.8 knots ebb ⊢
bb ⊢ ⊢ 2.9 knots flood ⊣ ⊢ 2.4 knots ebb ⊦ ⊢ 1.6 knots flood ⊦ ⊢ 2.5 knot

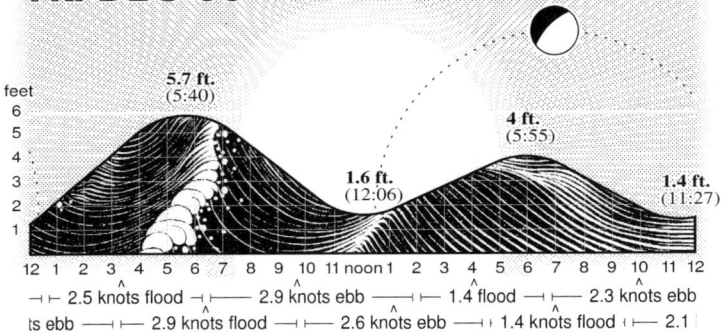

FRI DEC 30
dawn 6:23 sunrise 7:25 sunset 5:00 dark 6:02
moonset 12:31 a.m. moonrise 12:29 p.m.

5.7 ft.
(5:40)

4 ft.
(5:55)

1.6 ft.
(12:06)

1.4 ft.
(11:27)

feet
6
5
4
3
2
1

12 1 2 3 4 5 6 7 8 9 10 11 noon 1 2 3 4 5 6 7 8 9 10 11 12

⊣ ⊢ 2.5 knots flood ⊣ ⊢— 2.9 knots ebb —⊣ ⊢ 1.4 flood ⊣ ⊢— 2.3 knots ebb
ts ebb —⊣ ⊢— 2.9 knots flood —⊣ ⊢— 2.6 knots ebb —⊣ 1.4 knots flood ⊢ 2.1

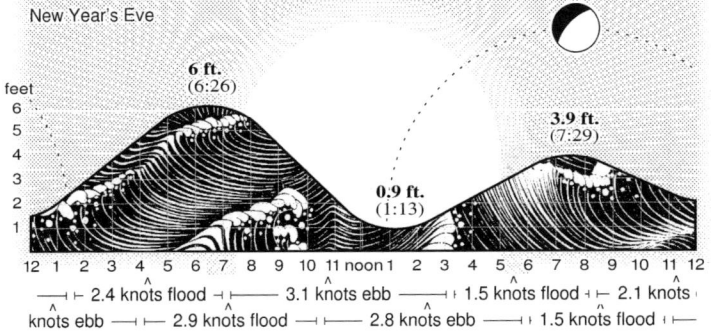

SAT DEC 31
dawn 6:23 sunrise 7:25 sunset 5:01 dark 6:03
moonset 1:36 a.m. moonrise 12:54 p.m.
New Year's Eve

6 ft.
(6:26)

3.9 ft.
(7:29)

0.9 ft.
(1:13)

feet
6
5
4
3
2
1

12 1 2 3 4 5 6 7 8 9 10 11 noon 1 2 3 4 5 6 7 8 9 10 11 12

—⊣ ⊢ 2.4 knots flood ⊣ ⊢— 3.1 knots ebb —⊣ ⊢ 1.5 knots flood ⊢ ⊢ 2.1 knots
knots ebb —⊣ ⊢— 2.9 knots flood —⊣ ⊢— 2.8 knots ebb —⊣ 1.5 knots flood ⊢—

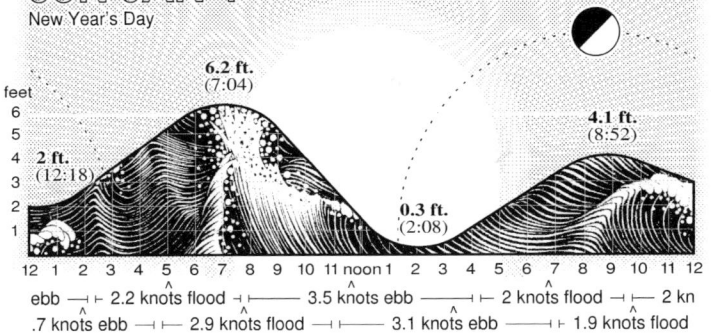

SUN JAN 1
dawn 6:23 sunrise 7:25 sunset 5:02 dark 6:04
moonrise 1:22 p.m.
New Year's Day

6.2 ft.
(7:04)

4.1 ft.
(8:52)

2 ft.
(12:18)

0.3 ft.
(2:08)

feet
6
5
4
3
2
1

12 1 2 3 4 5 6 7 8 9 10 11 noon 1 2 3 4 5 6 7 8 9 10 11 12

ebb —⊣ ⊢ 2.2 knots flood ⊣ ⊢— 3.5 knots ebb —⊣ ⊢ 2 knots flood ⊣ ⊢— 2 kn
.7 knots ebb —⊣ ⊢— 2.9 knots flood —⊣ ⊢— 3.1 knots ebb —⊣ ⊢ 1.9 knots flood

(V) (☿) (J) (M)

MON JAN 2
dawn 6:23 sunrise 7:26 sunset 5:03 dark 6:05
moonset 3:43 a.m. moonrise 1:52 p.m.

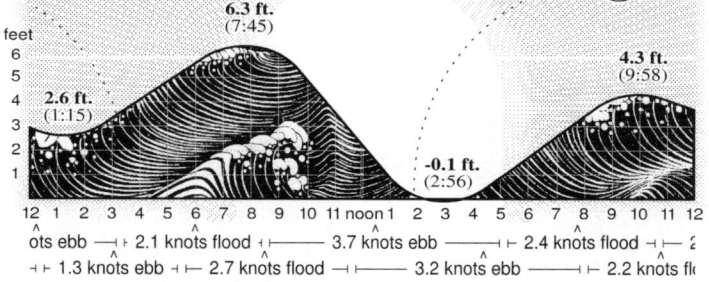

feet

2.6 ft.
(1:15)

6.3 ft.
(7:45)

4.3 ft.
(9:58)

-0.1 ft.
(2:56)

12 1 2 3 4 5 6 7 8 9 10 11 noon 1 2 3 4 5 6 7 8 9 10 11 12

ots ebb ⊣ ⊢ 2.1 knots flood ⊣ ⊢─── 3.7 knots ebb ───┤ ⊢ 2.4 knots flood ⊣ ⊢ 2
⊣ ⊢ 1.3 knots ebb ⊣ ⊢ 2.7 knots flood ⊣ ⊢─── 3.2 knots ebb ───┤ ⊢ 2.2 knots fl

TUE JAN 3
dawn 6:24 sunrise 7:26 sunset 5:03 dark 6:05
moonset 4:46 a.m. moonrise 2:27 p.m.

Quadrantids Peak

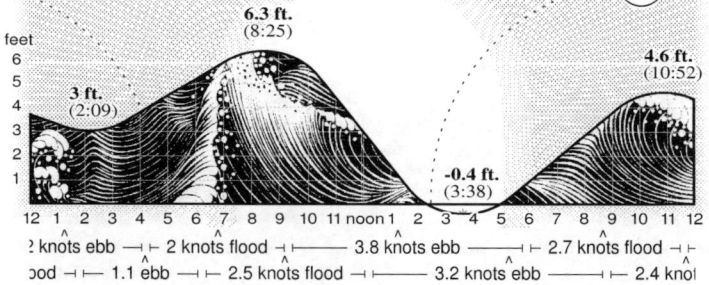

feet

3 ft.
(2:09)

6.3 ft.
(8:25)

4.6 ft.
(10:52)

-0.4 ft.
(3:38)

12 1 2 3 4 5 6 7 8 9 10 11 noon 1 2 3 4 5 6 7 8 9 10 11 12

2 knots ebb ⊣ ⊢ 2 knots flood ⊣ ⊢─── 3.8 knots ebb ───┤ ⊢ 2.7 knots flood ⊣ ⊢
ood ⊣ ⊢ 1.1 ebb ⊣ ⊢ 2.5 knots flood ⊣ ⊢─── 3.2 knots ebb ───┤ ⊢ 2.4 knot

WED JAN 4
dawn 6:24 sunrise 7:26 sunset 5:04 dark 6:06
moonset 5:48 a.m. moonrise 3:08 p.m.

Earth at Perihelion 8:17 a.m.

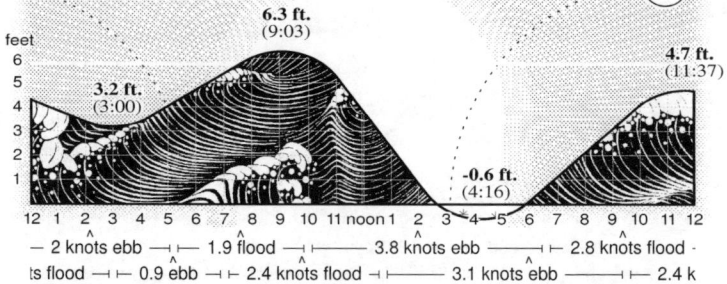

feet

3.2 ft.
(3:00)

6.3 ft.
(9:03)

4.7 ft.
(11:37)

-0.6 ft.
(4:16)

12 1 2 3 4 5 6 7 8 9 10 11 noon 1 2 3 4 5 6 7 8 9 10 11 12

─ 2 knots ebb ⊣ ⊢ 1.9 flood ⊣ ⊢─── 3.8 knots ebb ───┤ ⊢ 2.8 knots flood ·
ts flood ⊣ ⊢ 0.9 ebb ⊣ ⊢ 2.4 knots flood ⊣ ⊢─── 3.1 knots ebb ───┤ ⊢ 2.4 k

THU JAN 5
dawn 6:24 sunrise 7:26 sunset 5:05 dark 6:07
moonset 6:45 a.m. moonrise 3:56 p.m.

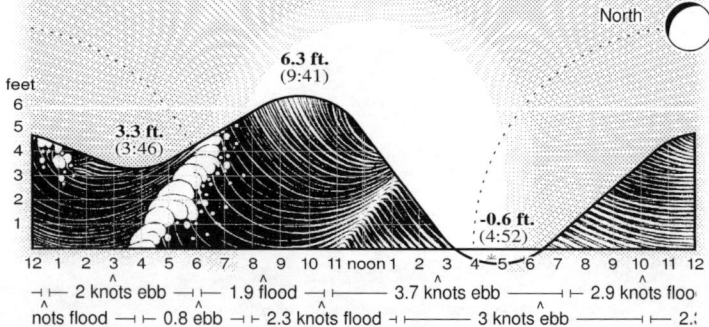

North

feet

3.3 ft.
(3:46)

6.3 ft.
(9:41)

-0.6 ft.
(4:52)

12 1 2 3 4 5 6 7 8 9 10 11 noon 1 2 3 4 5 6 7 8 9 10 11 12

⊣ ⊢ 2 knots ebb ─┤ ⊢ 1.9 flood ─┤ ⊢─── 3.7 knots ebb ───┤ ⊢ 2.9 knots floo
nots flood ⊣ ⊢ 0.8 ebb ⊣ ⊢ 2.3 knots flood ⊣ ⊢─── 3 knots ebb ───┤ ⊢ 2.

FRI JAN 6
dawn 6:24 sunrise 7:26 sunset 5:06 dark 6:08
moonset 7:36 a.m. moonrise 4:49 p.m.

Full Moon 3:08 p.m.

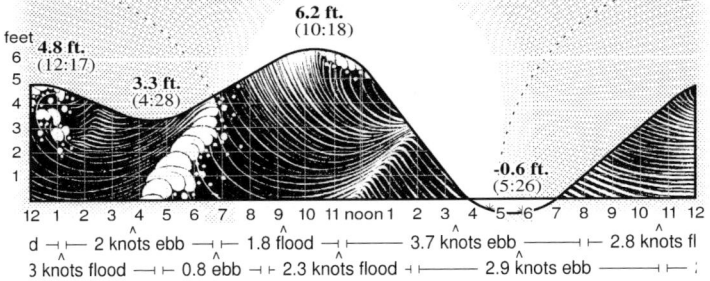

6.2 ft.
(10:18)

feet
4.8 ft.
(12:17)

3.3 ft.
(4:28)

-0.6 ft.
(5:26)

12 1 2 3 4 5 6 7 8 9 10 11 noon 1 2 3 4 5 6 7 8 9 10 11 12

d ⊢⊣ ⊢ 2 knots ebb ⊣ ⊢ 1.8 flood ⊣ ⊢——— 3.7 knots ebb ——— ⊢ 2.8 knots fl
3 knots flood ⊣ ⊢ 0.8 ebb ⊣ ⊢ 2.3 knots flood ⊣ ⊢——— 2.9 knots ebb ———⊣ ⊢

SAT JAN 7
dawn 6:24 sunrise 7:26 sunset 5:07 dark 6:09
moonset 8:21 a.m. moonrise 5:47 p.m.

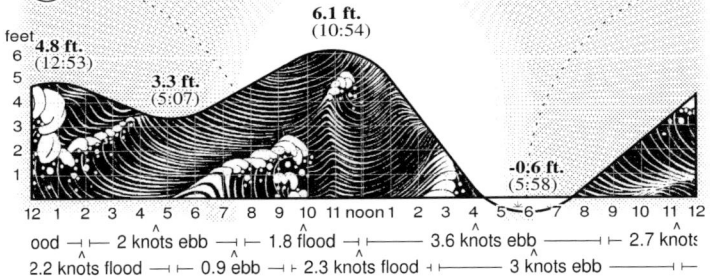

6.1 ft.
(10:54)

feet
4.8 ft.
(12:53)

3.3 ft.
(5:07)

-0.6 ft.
(5:58)

12 1 2 3 4 5 6 7 8 9 10 11 noon 1 2 3 4 5 6 7 8 9 10 11 12

ood ⊢⊣ ⊢ 2 knots ebb ⊣ ⊢ 1.8 flood ⊣ ⊢——— 3.6 knots ebb ——— ⊢ 2.7 knots
2.2 knots flood ⊣ ⊢ 0.9 ebb ⊣ ⊢ 2.3 knots flood ⊣ ⊢——— 3 knots ebb ———⊣ ⊢

SUN JAN 8
dawn 6:24 sunrise 7:26 sunset 5:08 dark 6:09
moonset 8:59 a.m. moonrise 6:47 p.m.

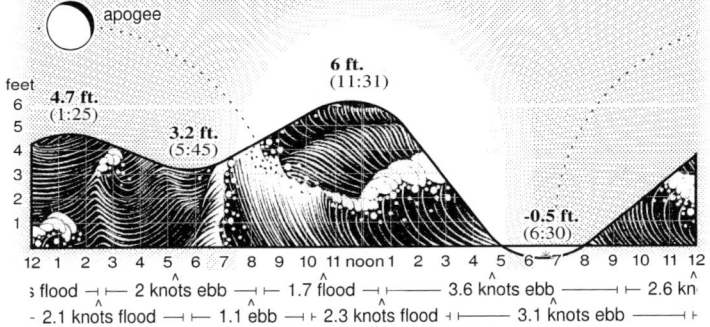

apogee

6 ft.
(11:31)

feet
4.7 ft.
(1:25)

3.2 ft.
(5:45)

-0.5 ft.
(6:30)

12 1 2 3 4 5 6 7 8 9 10 11 noon 1 2 3 4 5 6 7 8 9 10 11 12

s flood ⊢⊣ ⊢ 2 knots ebb ⊣ ⊢ 1.7 flood ⊣ ⊢——— 3.6 knots ebb ——— ⊢ 2.6 kn
⊢ 2.1 knots flood ⊣ ⊢ 1.1 ebb ⊣ ⊢ 2.3 knots flood ⊣ ⊢——— 3.1 knots ebb ———⊢

ⓥ ∅ Ⓙ

Ⓜ

Quadrantids Meteor Shower The Quadrantids run annually between Jan
1st - 5th with this year's peak the evening and morning of Jan 3rd & 4th.
This year the nearly full Moon will be high in the sky all evening, likely
washing out the shower. The Quadrantids, at peak, have produced up to 40
meteors per hour. The shower appears to radiate from the constellation
Bootes that on Jan 3rd will rise above the eastern horizon at 1:00 a.m.
Earth at perihelion at perihelion the Earth is at its closest to the
Sun than at any other time of year because the Earth's orbit is an
ellipse - slightly lopsided.

MON JAN 9 — dawn 6:24 sunrise 7:25 sunset 5:09 dark 6:10
moonset 9:31 a.m. moonrise 7:47 p.m.

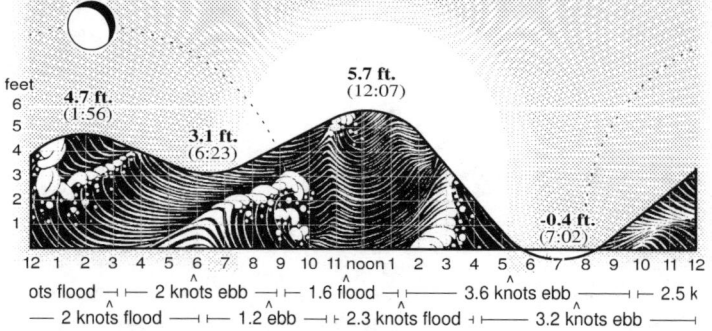

feet

4.7 ft. (1:56)
3.1 ft. (6:23)
5.7 ft. (12:07)
-0.4 ft. (7:02)

12 1 2 3 4 5 6 7 8 9 10 11 noon 1 2 3 4 5 6 7 8 9 10 11 12

ots flood → ⊢ 2 knots ebb → ⊢ 1.6 flood → ⊢ 3.6 knots ebb ——— ⊢ 2.5 k
— 2 knots flood — ⊢ 1.2 ebb → ⊢ 2.3 knots flood → ⊢ 3.2 knots ebb —

TUE JAN 10 — dawn 6:24 sunrise 7:25 sunset 5:10 dark 6:11
moonset 9:59 a.m. moonrise 8:47 p.m.

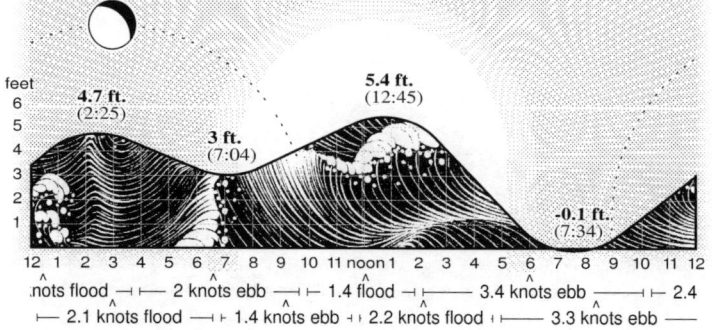

feet

4.7 ft. (2:25)
3 ft. (7:04)
5.4 ft. (12:45)
-0.1 ft. (7:34)

12 1 2 3 4 5 6 7 8 9 10 11 noon 1 2 3 4 5 6 7 8 9 10 11 12

.nots flood → ⊢ 2 knots ebb → ⊢ 1.4 flood → ⊢ 3.4 knots ebb ——— ⊢ 2.4
⊢ 2.1 knots flood — ⊢ 1.4 knots ebb → ⊢ 2.2 knots flood → ⊢ 3.3 knots ebb —

WED JAN 11 — dawn 6:24 sunrise 7:25 sunset 5:11 dark 6:12
moonset 10:24 a.m. moonrise 9:47 p.m.

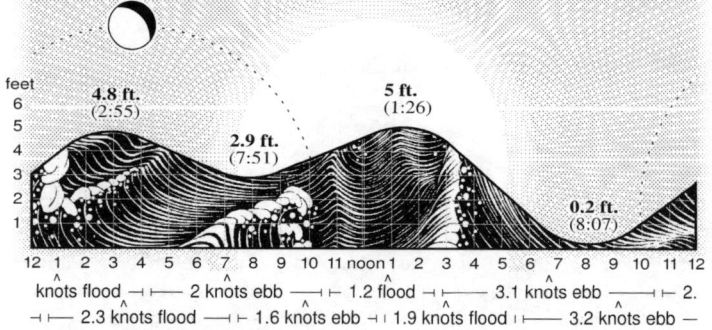

feet

4.8 ft. (2:55)
2.9 ft. (7:51)
5 ft. (1:26)
0.2 ft. (8:07)

12 1 2 3 4 5 6 7 8 9 10 11 noon 1 2 3 4 5 6 7 8 9 10 11 12

knots flood → ⊢ 2 knots ebb → ⊢ 1.2 flood → ⊢ 3.1 knots ebb ——— ⊢ 2.
→ ⊢ 2.3 knots flood — ⊢ 1.6 knots ebb → ⊢ 1.9 knots flood → ⊢ 3.2 knots ebb —

THU JAN 12 — dawn 6:24 sunrise 7:25 sunset 5:12 dark 6:13
moonset 10:47 a.m. moonrise 10:46 p.m.

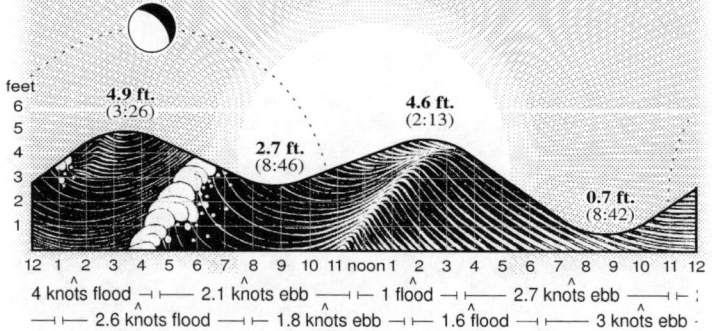

feet

4.9 ft. (3:26)
2.7 ft. (8:46)
4.6 ft. (2:13)
0.7 ft. (8:42)

12 1 2 3 4 5 6 7 8 9 10 11 noon 1 2 3 4 5 6 7 8 9 10 11 12

4 knots flood → ⊢ 2.1 knots ebb → ⊢ 1 flood → ⊢ 2.7 knots ebb ——— ⊢
→ ⊢ 2.6 knots flood — ⊢ 1.8 knots ebb → ⊢ 1.6 flood → ⊢ 3 knots ebb ·

FRI JAN 13

dawn 6:24 sunrise 7:25 sunset 5:13 dark 6:14
moonset 11:10 a.m. moonrise 11:47 p.m.

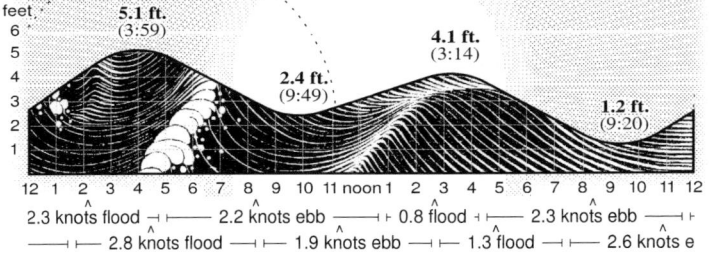

equator

feet
6
5
4
3
2
1

5.1 ft.
(3:59)

2.4 ft.
(9:49)

4.1 ft.
(3:14)

1.2 ft.
(9:20)

12 1 2 3 4 5 6 7 8 9 10 11 noon 1 2 3 4 5 6 7 8 9 10 11 12

2.3 knots flood ⊣ ⊢— 2.2 knots ebb ——⊦ 0.8 flood ⊣ ⊢— 2.3 knots ebb ——⊦ ⊢
——⊢ 2.8 knots flood ——⊣ ⊢— 1.9 knots ebb —⊣ ⊢ 1.3 flood ⊣ ⊢— 2.6 knots e

SAT JAN 14

dawn 6:23 sunrise 7:24 sunset 5:14 dark 6:15
moonset 11:33 a.m.

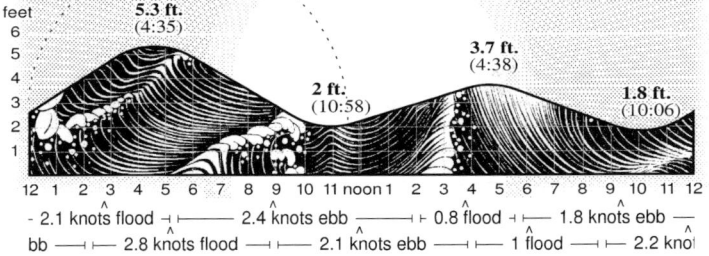

feet
6
5
4
3
2
1

5.3 ft.
(4:35)

2 ft.
(10:58)

3.7 ft.
(4:38)

1.8 ft.
(10:06)

12 1 2 3 4 5 6 7 8 9 10 11 noon 1 2 3 4 5 6 7 8 9 10 11 12

- 2.1 knots flood ⊣ ⊢——— 2.4 knots ebb ———⊦ 0.8 flood ⊣ ⊢ 1.8 knots ebb —
bb ——⊢ 2.8 knots flood ——⊣ ⊢— 2.1 knots ebb —⊣ ⊢— 1 flood ⊣ ⊢— 2.2 knot

SUN JAN 15

dawn 6:23 sunrise 7:24 sunset 5:15 dark 6:16
moonrise 12:50 a.m. moonset 11:59 a.m.

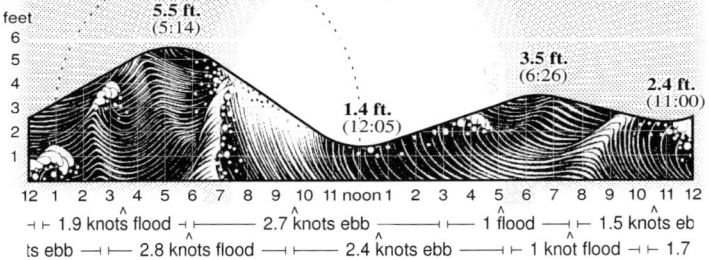

feet
6
5
4
3
2
1

5.5 ft.
(5:14)

1.4 ft.
(12:05)

3.5 ft.
(6:26)

2.4 ft.
(11:00)

12 1 2 3 4 5 6 7 8 9 10 11 noon 1 2 3 4 5 6 7 8 9 10 11 12

⊣ ⊢ 1.9 knots flood ⊣ ⊢——— 2.7 knots ebb ———⊣ ⊢— 1 flood ⊣ ⊢ 1.5 knots eb
ts ebb —⊣ ⊢— 2.8 knots flood ——⊣ ⊢—— 2.4 knots ebb ——⊣ ⊢ 1 knot flood ⊣ ⊢ 1.7

MON JAN 16

dawn 6:23 sunrise 7:24 sunset 5:16 dark 6:17
moonrise 1:57 a.m. moonset 12:29 p.m.

Martin Luther King Jr. Day

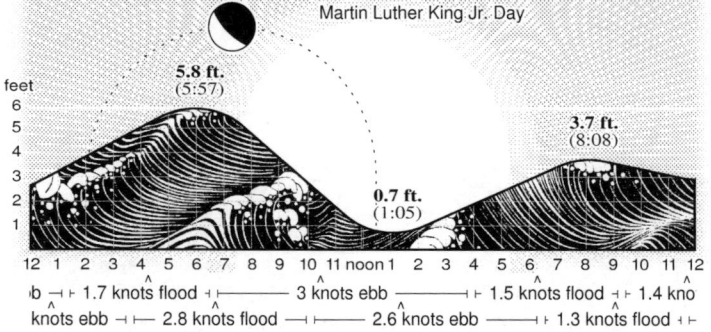

feet

5.8 ft.
(5:57)

3.7 ft.
(8:08)

0.7 ft.
(1:05)

12 1 2 3 4 5 6 7 8 9 10 11 noon 1 2 3 4 5 6 7 8 9 10 11 12

b ⊢ 1.7 knots flood ⊣ ⊢— 3 knots ebb —⊣ ⊢ 1.5 knots flood ⊣ ⊢ 1.4 kno
knots ebb ⊣ ⊢ 2.8 knots flood —⊣ ⊢— 2.6 knots ebb —⊣ ⊢ 1.3 knots flood ⊣ ⊢

TUE JAN 17

dawn 6:23 sunrise 7:23 sunset 5:17 dark 6:18
moonrise 3:07 a.m. moonset 1:05 p.m.

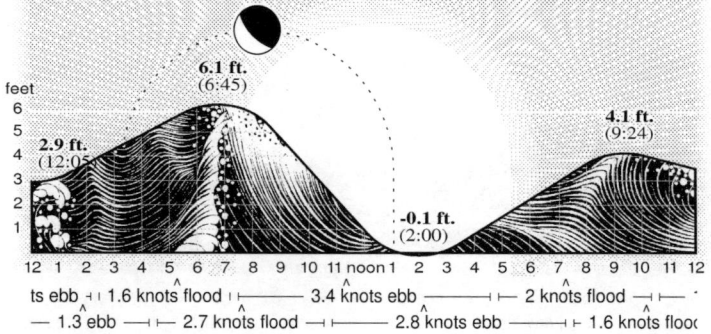

feet

6.1 ft.
(6:45)

2.9 ft.
(12:05)

4.1 ft.
(9:24)

-0.1 ft.
(2:00)

12 1 2 3 4 5 6 7 8 9 10 11 noon 1 2 3 4 5 6 7 8 9 10 11 12

ts ebb ⊣ ⊢ 1.6 knots flood ⊢ ⊢— 3.4 knots ebb —⊣ ⊢ 2 knots flood —⊣ ⊢·
— 1.3 ebb —⊣ ⊢ 2.7 knots flood —⊣ ⊢— 2.8 knots ebb —⊣ ⊢ 1.6 knots flood

---

WED JAN 18

dawn 6:22 sunrise 7:23 sunset 5:18 dark 6:19
moonrise 4:21 a.m. moonset 1:51 p.m.

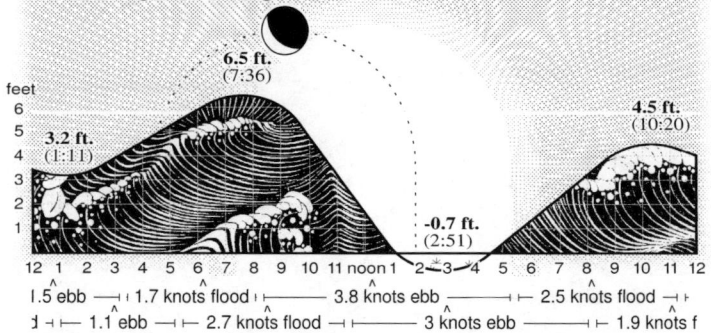

feet

6.5 ft.
(7:36)

3.2 ft.
(1:11)

4.5 ft.
(10:20)

-0.7 ft.
(2:51)

12 1 2 3 4 5 6 7 8 9 10 11 noon 1 2 3 4 5 6 7 8 9 10 11 12

1.5 ebb ⊣ ⊢ 1.7 knots flood ⊢ ⊢— 3.8 knots ebb —⊣ ⊢ 2.5 knots flood —⊣ ⊢
d ⊣ ⊢ 1.1 ebb —⊣ ⊢ 2.7 knots flood —⊣ ⊢— 3 knots ebb —⊣ ⊢ 1.9 knots f

---

THU JAN 19

dawn 6:22 sunrise 7:23 sunset 5:19 dark 6:19
moonrise 5:34 a.m. moonset 2:48 p.m.

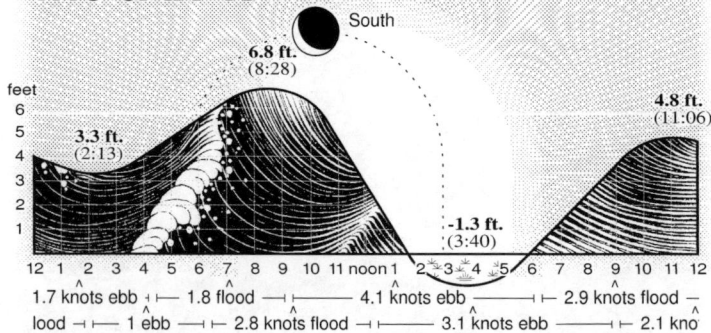

South

feet

6.8 ft.
(8:28)

3.3 ft.
(2:13)

4.8 ft.
(11:06)

-1.3 ft.
(3:40)

12 1 2 3 4 5 6 7 8 9 10 11 noon 1 2 3 4 5 6 7 8 9 10 11 12

1.7 knots ebb ⊣ ⊢ 1.8 flood —⊣ ⊢— 4.1 knots ebb —⊣ ⊢ 2.9 knots flood —
lood ⊣ ⊢ 1 ebb —⊣ ⊢ 2.8 knots flood —⊣ ⊢— 3.1 knots ebb —⊣ ⊢ 2.1 kno

FRI JAN 20

dawn 6:22 sunrise 7:22 sunset 5:20 dark 6:20
moonrise 6:41 a.m. moonset 3:57 p.m.

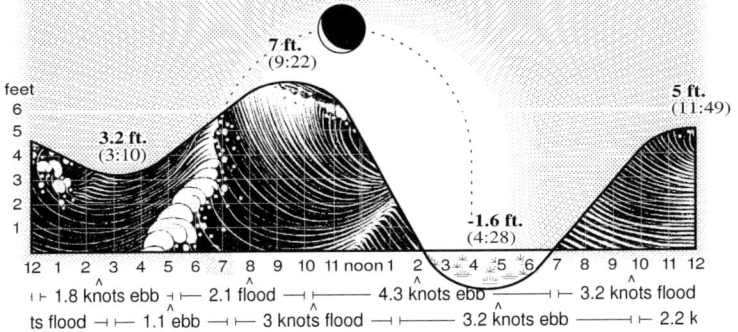

7 ft.
(9:22)

feet

5 ft.
(11:49)

3.2 ft.
(3:10)

-1.6 ft.
(4:28)

12 1 2 3 4 5 6 7 8 9 10 11 noon 1 2 3 4 5 6 7 8 9 10 11 12

⊢ 1.8 knots ebb ⊣ ⊢ 2.1 flood ⟶ ⊢ 4.3 knots ebb ⟶ ⊢ 3.2 knots flood
ts flood ⊣ ⊢ 1.1 ebb ⊣ ⊢ 3 knots flood ⊣ ⊢ 3.2 knots ebb ⟶ ⊢ 2.2 k

SAT JAN 21

dawn 6:21 sunrise 7:22 sunset 5:21 dark 6:21
moonrise 7:39 a.m. moonset 5:15 p.m.

New Moon 12:53 p.m.

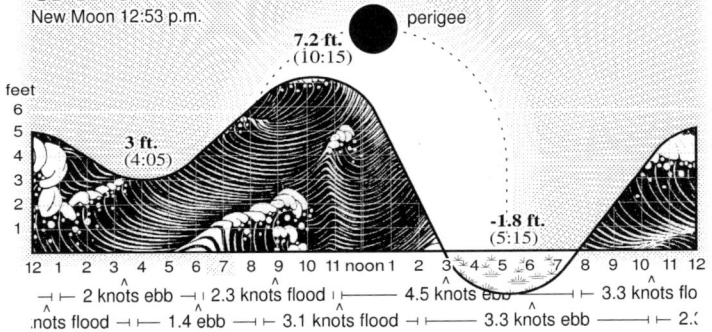

perigee

7.2 ft.
(10:15)

feet

3 ft.
(4:05)

-1.8 ft.
(5:15)

12 1 2 3 4 5 6 7 8 9 10 11 noon 1 2 3 4 5 6 7 8 9 10 11 12

⊣ ⊢ 2 knots ebb ⟶ ⊣ 2.3 knots flood ⊢ 4.5 knots ebb ⟶ ⊢ 3.3 knots flo
.nots flood ⊣ ⊢ 1.4 ebb ⊣ ⊢ 3.1 knots flood ⊣ ⊢ 3.3 knots ebb ⟶ ⊢ 2.:

SUN JAN 22

dawn 6:21 sunrise 7:21 sunset 5:22 dark 6:22
moonrise 8:26 a.m. moonset 6:35 p.m.

Venus South of Saturn .4 degrees

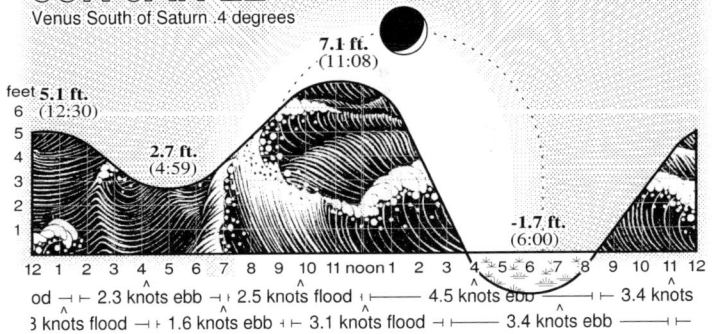

7.1 ft.
(11:08)

feet 5.1 ft.
(12:30)

2.7 ft.
(4:59)

-1.7 ft.
(6:00)

12 1 2 3 4 5 6 7 8 9 10 11 noon 1 2 3 4 5 6 7 8 9 10 11 12

od ⊣ ⊢ 2.3 knots ebb ⟶ ⊣ 2.5 knots flood ⊢ 4.5 knots ebb ⟶ ⊢ 3.4 knots
3 knots flood ⟶ ⊢ 1.6 knots ebb ⊣ ⊢ 3.1 knots flood ⊣ ⊢ 3.4 knots ebb ⟶ ⊢

Ⓥ Ⓙ
ⓜ Ⓜ

Moon at perigee On Jan 21st the Moon, in its new phase, will be at perigee, its closest point to the Earth at some 356,568 kilometers. On average the distance between the Moon in its orbit of the Earth is approximately 382,999 kilometers.

MON JAN 23
dawn 6:20 sunrise 7:20 sunset 5:23 dark 6:23
moonrise 9:04 a.m. moonset 7:53 p.m.

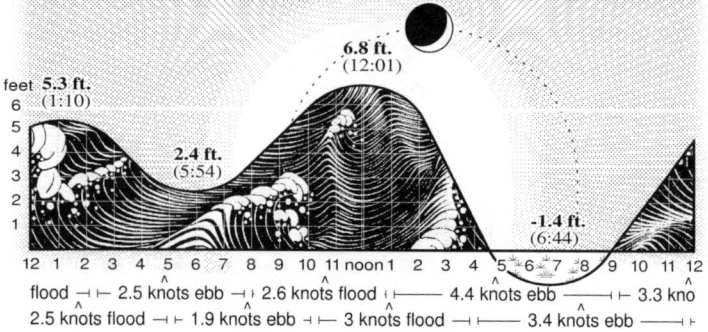

6.8 ft. (12:01)

feet **5.3 ft.** (1:10)

2.4 ft. (5:54)

-1.4 ft. (6:44)

12 1 2 3 4 5 6 7 8 9 10 11 noon 1 2 3 4 5 6 7 8 9 10 11 12

flood ⊣ ⊢ 2.5 knots ebb ⊣ ⊢ 2.6 knots flood ⊢⊣ 4.4 knots ebb ⊢ 3.3 kno
2.5 knots flood ⊣ ⊢ 1.9 knots ebb ⊣ ⊢ 3 knots flood ⊣ ⊢ 3.4 knots ebb ⊢

TUE JAN 24
dawn 6:20 sunrise 7:20 sunset 5:24 dark 6:24
moonrise 9:36 a.m. moonset 9:07 p.m.

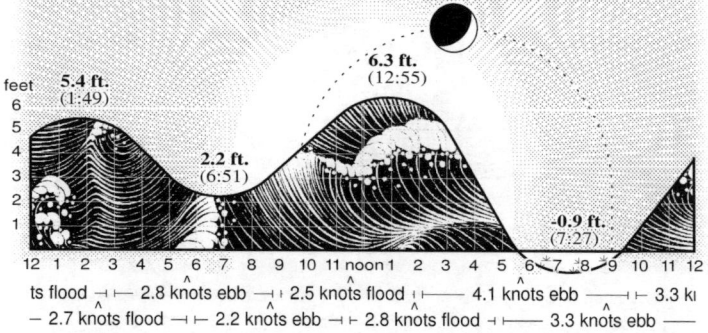

6.3 ft. (12:55)

feet **5.4 ft.** (1:49)

2.2 ft. (6:51)

-0.9 ft. (7:27)

12 1 2 3 4 5 6 7 8 9 10 11 noon 1 2 3 4 5 6 7 8 9 10 11 12

ts flood ⊣ ⊢ 2.8 knots ebb ⊣ ⊢ 2.5 knots flood ⊢⊣ 4.1 knots ebb ⊢ 3.3 k
⊢ 2.7 knots flood ⊣ ⊢ 2.2 knots ebb ⊢ 2.8 knots flood ⊣ ⊢ 3.3 knots ebb ⊢

WED JAN 25
dawn 6:19 sunrise 7:19 sunset 5:26 dark 6:25
moonrise 10:04 a.m. moonset 10:17 p.m.

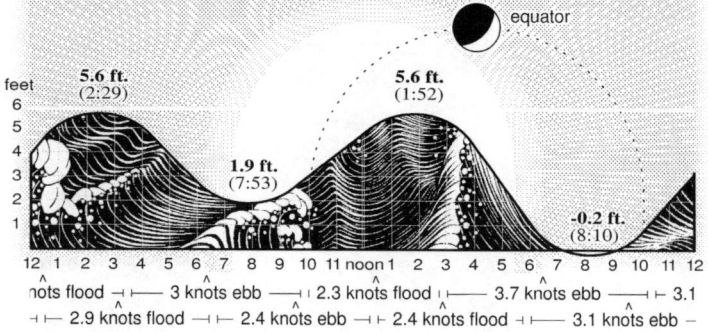

equator

feet **5.6 ft.** (2:29)

5.6 ft. (1:52)

1.9 ft. (7:53)

-0.2 ft. (8:10)

12 1 2 3 4 5 6 7 8 9 10 11 noon 1 2 3 4 5 6 7 8 9 10 11 12

nots flood ⊣ ⊢ 3 knots ebb ⊣ ⊢ 2.3 knots flood ⊢⊣ 3.7 knots ebb ⊢ 3.1
⊣ ⊢ 2.9 knots flood ⊣ ⊢ 2.4 knots ebb ⊣ ⊢ 2.4 knots flood ⊣ ⊢ 3.1 knots ebb ⊢

THU JAN 26
dawn 6:19 sunrise 7:19 sunset 5:27 dark 6:26
moonrise 10:31 a.m. moonset 11:25 p.m.

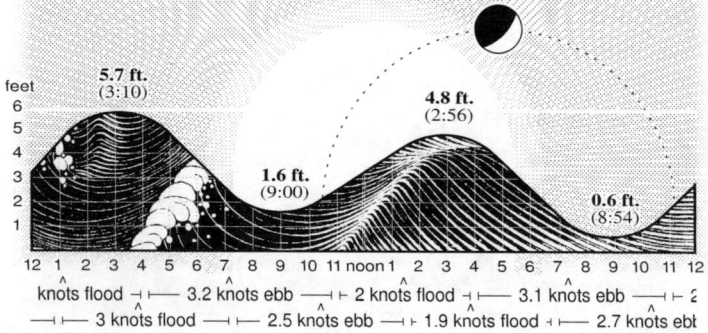

4.8 ft. (2:56)

feet **5.7 ft.** (3:10)

1.6 ft. (9:00)

0.6 ft. (8:54)

12 1 2 3 4 5 6 7 8 9 10 11 noon 1 2 3 4 5 6 7 8 9 10 11 12

knots flood ⊣ ⊢ 3.2 knots ebb ⊢ 2 knots flood ⊣ ⊢ 3.1 knots ebb ⊢ 2
⊣ ⊢ 3 knots flood ⊢ 2.5 knots ebb ⊢ 1.9 knots flood ⊣ ⊢ 2.7 knots ebb

FRI JAN 27

dawn 6:18 sunrise 7:18 sunset 5:28 dark 6:27
moonrise 10:56 a.m.

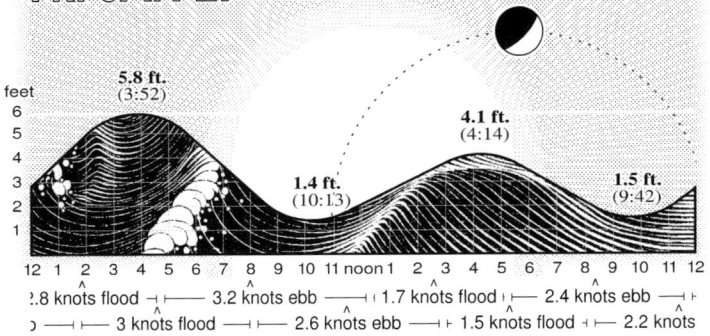

5.8 ft.
(3:52)

4.1 ft.
(4:14)

1.4 ft.
(10:13)

1.5 ft.
(9:42)

feet
6
5
4
3
2
1

12 1 2 3 4 5 6 7 8 9 10 11 noon 1 2 3 4 5 6 7 8 9 10 11 12

2.8 knots flood ⊣ ⊢— 3.2 knots ebb ——⊣ ⊢ 1.7 knots flood ⊢⊣ ⊢— 2.4 knots ebb —⊣ ⊢
⊃ —⊣ ⊢— 3 knots flood —⊣ ⊢— 2.6 knots ebb —⊣ ⊢ 1.5 knots flood ⊣ ⊢— 2.2 knots

SAT JAN 28

dawn 6:18 sunrise 7:17 sunset 5:29 dark 6:28
moonset 12:31 a.m. moonrise 11:24 a.m.

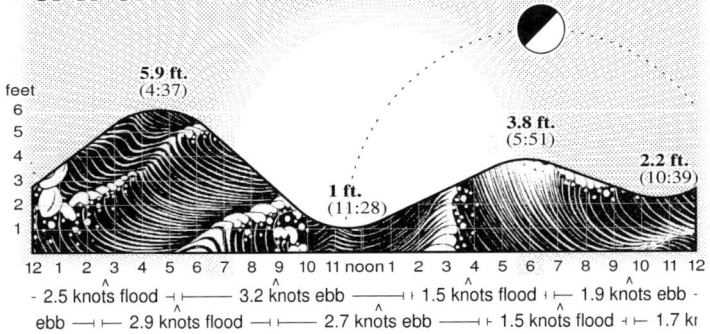

5.9 ft.
(4:37)

3.8 ft.
(5:51)

2.2 ft.
(10:39)

1 ft.
(11:28)

feet
6
5
4
3
2
1

12 1 2 3 4 5 6 7 8 9 10 11 noon 1 2 3 4 5 6 7 8 9 10 11 12

- 2.5 knots flood ⊣ ⊢— 3.2 knots ebb ——⊣ ⊢ 1.5 knots flood ⊢⊣ ⊢ 1.9 knots ebb -
ebb ⊣ ⊢— 2.9 knots flood —⊣ ⊢— 2.7 knots ebb ——⊣ ⊢ 1.5 knots flood ⊣ ⊢ 1.7 kt

SUN JAN 29

dawn 6:17 sunrise 7:16 sunset 5:30 dark 6:29
moonset 1:36 a.m. moonrise 11:53 a.m.

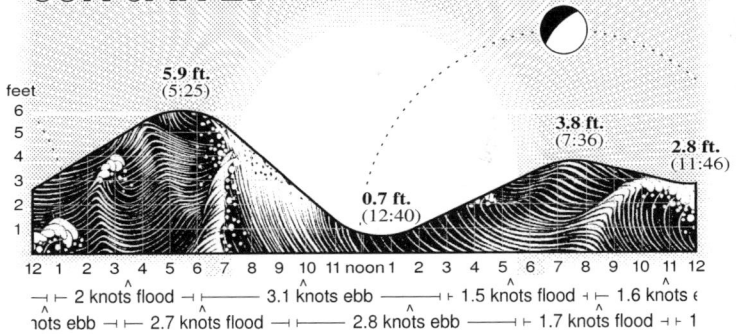

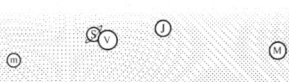

5.9 ft.
(5:25)

3.8 ft.
(7:36)

2.8 ft.
(11:46)

0.7 ft.
(12:40)

feet
6
5
4
3
2
1

12 1 2 3 4 5 6 7 8 9 10 11 noon 1 2 3 4 5 6 7 8 9 10 11 12

⊣ ⊢ 2 knots flood ⊣ ⊢—— 3.1 knots ebb ———⊣ ⊢ 1.5 knots flood ⊣ ⊢ 1.6 knots e
nots ebb ⊣ ⊢ 2.7 knots flood —⊣ ⊢— 2.8 knots ebb ——⊣ ⊢ 1.7 knots flood ⊣ ⊢ 1

Mercury's greatest elongations Mercury's orbit around the Sun at its
elongations allow the planet to be seen low in the east before sunrise
between Jan 13th to Mar 17th, May 11th to Jun 24th, Sep 14th to Oct 8th
and Dec 29th to Dec 31st. Mercury is visible in the western sky after
sunset Jan 1st & 2nd, Mar 26th to Apr 23rd, Jul 9th to Aug 30th and Nov 5th
to Dec 17th.

MON JAN 30
dawn 6:16 sunrise 7:16 sunset 5:31 dark 6:30
moonset 2:40 a.m. moonrise 12:27 p.m.
Comet 263P/Gibbs

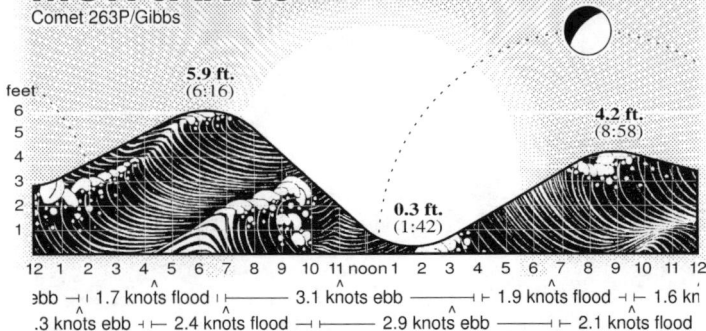

feet

5.9 ft.
(6:16)

4.2 ft.
(8:58)

0.3 ft.
(1:42)

12 1 2 3 4 5 6 7 8 9 10 11 noon 1 2 3 4 5 6 7 8 9 10 11 12

ebb ⊣⊢ 1.7 knots flood ⊢ ⊢— 3.1 knots ebb —⊣⊢ 1.9 knots flood ⊣⊢ 1.6 kn
.3 knots ebb ⊣⊢ 2.4 knots flood ⊣ ⊢— 2.9 knots ebb —⊢ 2.1 knots flood

TUE JAN 31
dawn 6:16 sunrise 7:15 sunset 5:32 dark 6:31
moonset 3:42 a.m. moonrise 1:06 p.m.
Comet 96P/Machholz

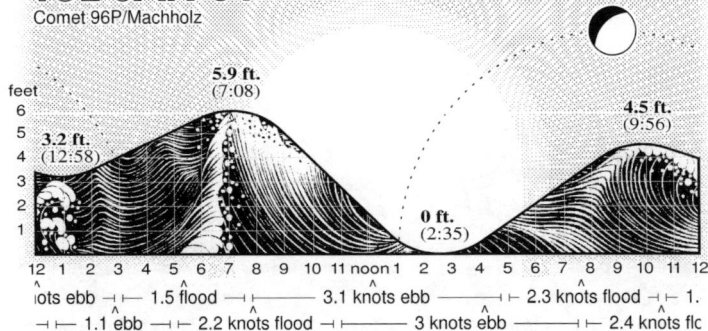

feet

5.9 ft.
(7:08)

4.5 ft.
(9:56)

3.2 ft.
(12:58)

0 ft.
(2:35)

12 1 2 3 4 5 6 7 8 9 10 11 noon 1 2 3 4 5 6 7 8 9 10 11 12

ots ebb ⊣⊢ 1.5 flood —⊣⊢— 3.1 knots ebb ——⊢ 2.3 knots flood ⊣⊢ 1.
⊣⊢ 1.1 ebb —⊣⊢ 2.2 knots flood ⊣ ⊢— 3 knots ebb ——⊢ 2.4 knots flo

WED FEB 1
dawn 6:15 sunrise 7:14 sunset 5:33 dark 6:32
moonset 4:40 a.m. moonrise 1:52 p.m.

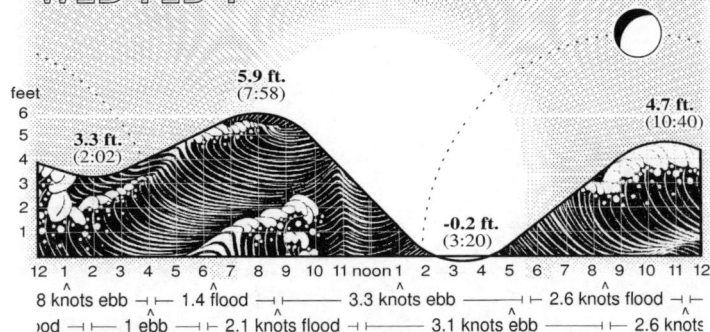

feet

5.9 ft.
(7:58)

4.7 ft.
(10:40)

3.3 ft.
(2:02)

-0.2 ft.
(3:20)

12 1 2 3 4 5 6 7 8 9 10 11 noon 1 2 3 4 5 6 7 8 9 10 11 12

8 knots ebb ⊣⊢ 1.4 flood —⊣⊢— 3.3 knots ebb —⊣⊢ 2.6 knots flood ⊣⊢
ood ⊣⊢ 1 ebb —⊢ 2.1 knots flood ⊣ ⊢— 3.1 knots ebb ——⊢ 2.6 knots

THU FEB 2
dawn 6:14 sunrise 7:13 sunset 5:34 dark 6:33
moonset 5:33 a.m. moonrise 2:44 p.m.

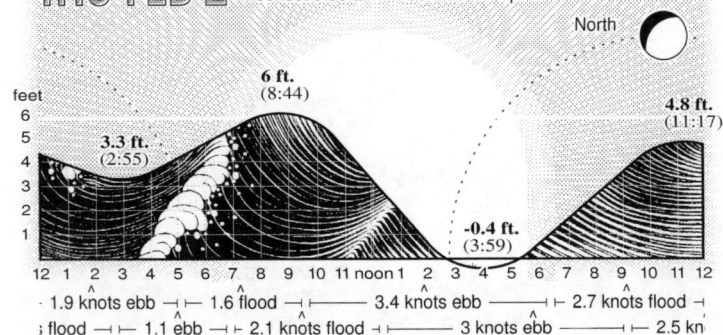

North

feet

6 ft.
(8:44)

4.8 ft.
(11:17)

3.3 ft.
(2:55)

-0.4 ft.
(3:59)

12 1 2 3 4 5 6 7 8 9 10 11 noon 1 2 3 4 5 6 7 8 9 10 11 12

· 1.9 knots ebb ⊣⊢ 1.6 flood —⊣⊢— 3.4 knots ebb —⊢ 2.7 knots flood ⊣
s flood ⊣⊢ 1.1 ebb ⊢ 2.1 knots flood ⊣ ⊢— 3 knots ebb ——⊢ 2.5 kn

FRI FEB 3

dawn 6:13 sunrise 7:12 sunset 5:36 dark 6:34
moonset 6:20 a.m. moonrise 3:40 p.m.

apogee

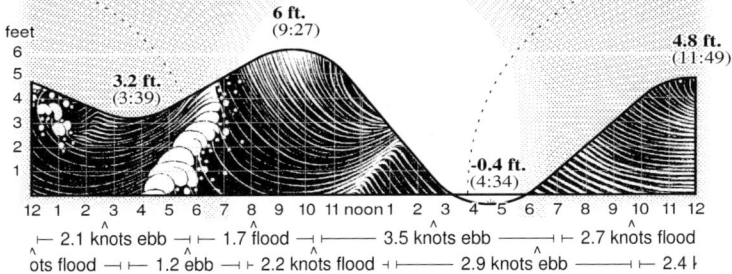

feet

6 ft.
(9:27)

4.8 ft.
(11:49)

3.2 ft.
(3:39)

-0.4 ft.
(4:34)

12 1 2 3 4 5 6 7 8 9 10 11 noon 1 2 3 4 5 6 7 8 9 10 11 12

⊢ 2.1 knots ebb ⊣ ⊢ 1.7 flood ⊣ ⊢——— 3.5 knots ebb ———⊣ ⊢ 2.7 knots flood

ots flood ⊣ ⊢ 1.2 ebb ⊣ ⊢ 2.2 knots flood ⊣ ⊢——— 2.9 knots ebb ———⊣ 2.4 k

SAT FEB 4

dawn 6:13 sunrise 7:11 sunset 5:37 dark 6:35
moonset 6:59 a.m. moonrise 4:40 p.m.

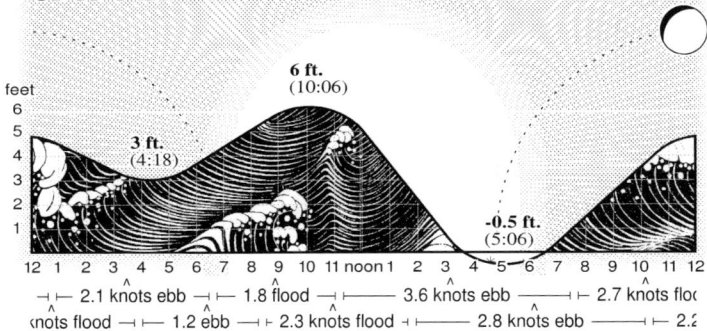

feet

6 ft.
(10:06)

3 ft.
(4:18)

-0.5 ft.
(5:06)

12 1 2 3 4 5 6 7 8 9 10 11 noon 1 2 3 4 5 6 7 8 9 10 11 12

⊣ ⊢ 2.1 knots ebb ⊣ ⊢ 1.8 flood ⊣ ⊢——— 3.6 knots ebb ———⊣ ⊢ 2.7 knots floo

knots flood ⊣ ⊢ 1.2 ebb ⊣ ⊢ 2.3 knots flood ⊣ ⊢——— 2.8 knots ebb ———⊣ ⊢ 2.2

SUN FEB 5

dawn 6:12 sunrise 7:10 sunset 5:38 dark 6:36
moonset 7:33 a.m. moonrise 5:40 p.m.

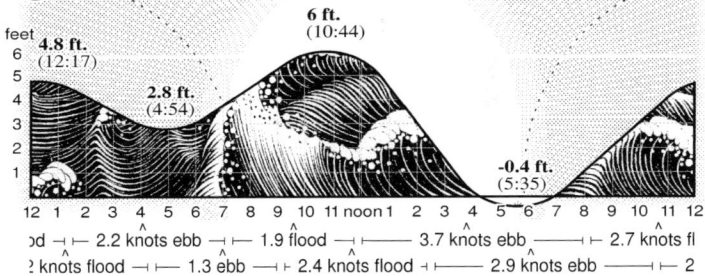

Full Moon 10:29 a.m.

feet

4.8 ft.
(12:17)

6 ft.
(10:44)

2.8 ft.
(4:54)

-0.4 ft.
(5:35)

12 1 2 3 4 5 6 7 8 9 10 11 noon 1 2 3 4 5 6 7 8 9 10 11 12

od ⊣ ⊢ 2.2 knots ebb ⊣ ⊢ 1.9 flood ⊣ ⊢——— 3.7 knots ebb ———⊣ ⊢ 2.7 knots fl

2 knots flood ⊣ ⊢ 1.3 ebb ⊣ ⊢ 2.4 knots flood ⊣ ⊢——— 2.9 knots ebb ———⊣ ⊢ 2

Comets Gibbs & Machholz On Jan 30th and Jan 31st, weather permitting, there will be two comets visible in the sky. Comet 263P/Gibbs on the 30th will pass within 1.24 astronomical units (or AU) of the Sun. On the 31st, Comet 96P/Machholz at its closest approach to the Sun will be a mere .12 AU - a distance of approximately 11,000,000 miles. In their perihelion passage around the Sun, the Comets should be fully illuminated and heated by the Sun causing their icy cores to evaporate forming their coma and tails.

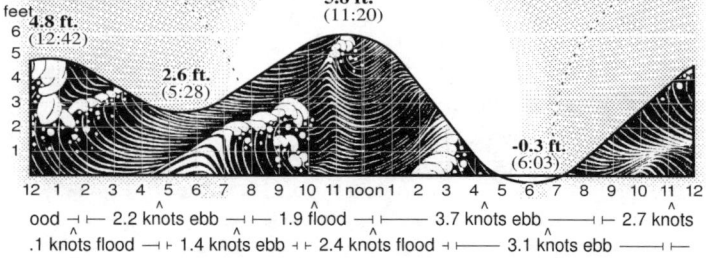

MON FEB 6
dawn 6:11 sunrise 7:09 sunset 5:39 dark 6:37
moonset 8:02 a.m. moonrise 6:41 p.m.

feet
4.8 ft.
(12:42)

2.6 ft.
(5:28)

5.8 ft.
(11:20)

-0.3 ft.
(6:03)

ood ⊣ ⊢ 2.2 knots ebb ⟶ ⊢ 1.9 flood ⊣ ⊢ 3.7 knots ebb ⟶ ⊢ 2.7 knots
.1 knots flood ⟶ ⊢ 1.4 knots ebb ⊣ ⊢ 2.4 knots flood ⊣ ⊢ 3.1 knots ebb ⟶ ⊢

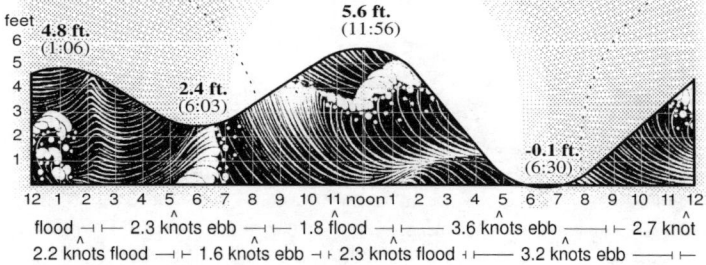

TUE FEB 7
dawn 6:10 sunrise 7:08 sunset 5:40 dark 6:38
moonset 8:28 a.m. moonrise 7:41 p.m.

feet
4.8 ft.
(1:06)

2.4 ft.
(6:03)

5.6 ft.
(11:56)

-0.1 ft.
(6:30)

flood ⊣ ⊢ 2.3 knots ebb ⟶ ⊢ 1.8 flood ⊣ ⊢ 3.6 knots ebb ⟶ ⊢ 2.7 knot
2.2 knots flood ⟶ ⊢ 1.6 knots ebb ⊣ ⊢ 2.3 knots flood ⊣ ⊢ 3.2 knots ebb ⟶ ⊢

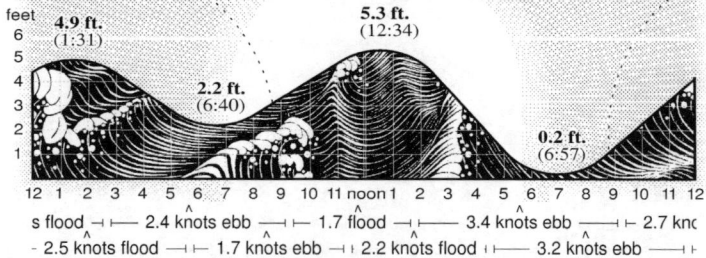

WED FEB 8
dawn 6:09 sunrise 7:07 sunset 5:41 dark 6:39
moonset 8:51 a.m. moonrise 8:40 p.m.

feet
4.9 ft.
(1:31)

2.2 ft.
(6:40)

5.3 ft.
(12:34)

0.2 ft.
(6:57)

s flood ⊣ ⊢ 2.4 knots ebb ⟶ ⊢ 1.7 flood ⊣ ⊢ 3.4 knots ebb ⟶ ⊢ 2.7 knc
- 2.5 knots flood ⟶ ⊢ 1.7 knots ebb ⊣ ⊢ 2.2 knots flood ⊢ ⊢ 3.2 knots ebb ⟶ ⊢

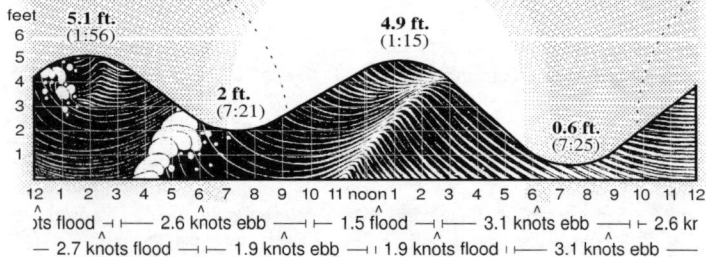

THU FEB 9
dawn 6:08 sunrise 7:06 sunset 5:42 dark 6:40
moonset 9:14 a.m. moonrise 9:40 p.m.

equator

feet
5.1 ft.
(1:56)

2 ft.
(7:21)

4.9 ft.
(1:15)

0.6 ft.
(7:25)

ots flood ⊣ ⊢ 2.6 knots ebb ⟶ ⊢ 1.5 flood ⊣ ⊢ 3.1 knots ebb ⟶ ⊢ 2.6 kr
- 2.7 knots flood ⟶ ⊢ 1.9 knots ebb ⊣ ⊢ 1.9 knots flood ⊢ ⊢ 3.1 knots ebb ⟶

FRI FEB 10
dawn 6:07 sunrise 7:05 sunset 5:43 dark 6:41
moonset 9:37 a.m. moonrise 10:42 p.m.

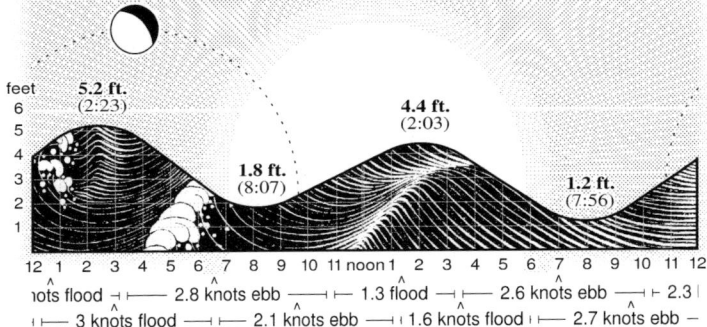

feet
6
5
4
3
2
1

5.2 ft.
(2:23)

1.8 ft.
(8:07)

4.4 ft.
(2:03)

1.2 ft.
(7:56)

12 1 2 3 4 5 6 7 8 9 10 11 noon 1 2 3 4 5 6 7 8 9 10 11 12

nots flood → ⊢— 2.8 knots ebb ——⊢ 1.3 flood →⊢— 2.6 knots ebb ——⊢ 2.3

⊢— 3 knots flood ——⊢— 2.1 knots ebb ——⊢ 1.6 knots flood ⊢— 2.7 knots ebb —

SAT FEB 11
dawn 6:06 sunrise 7:04 sunset 5:44 dark 6:42
moonset 10:01 a.m. moonrise 11:45 p.m.

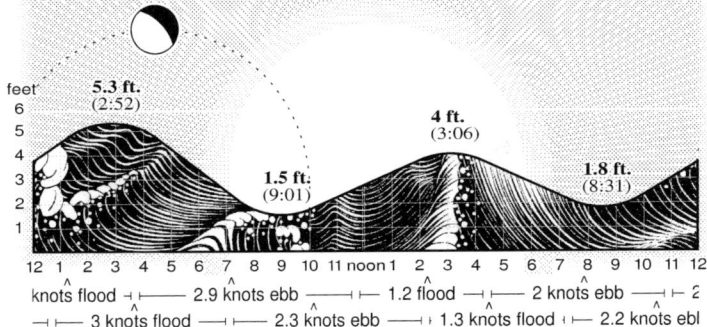

feet
6
5
4
3
2
1

5.3 ft.
(2:52)

1.5 ft.
(9:01)

4 ft.
(3:06)

1.8 ft.
(8:31)

12 1 2 3 4 5 6 7 8 9 10 11 noon 1 2 3 4 5 6 7 8 9 10 11 12

knots flood → ⊢— 2.9 knots ebb ——⊢— 1.2 flood →⊢— 2 knots ebb ——⊢ 2

→⊢— 3 knots flood ——⊢— 2.3 knots ebb ——⊢ 1.3 knots flood ⊢— 2.2 knots ebb

SUN FEB 12
dawn 6:05 sunrise 7:03 sunset 5:46 dark 6:43
moonset 10:28 a.m.

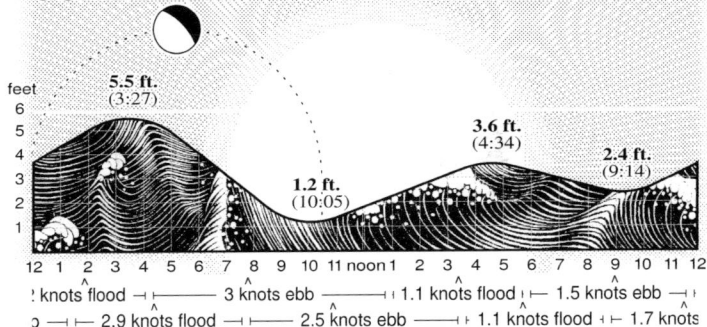

feet
6
5
4
3
2
1

5.5 ft.
(3:27)

1.2 ft.
(10:05)

3.6 ft.
(4:34)

2.4 ft.
(9:14)

12 1 2 3 4 5 6 7 8 9 10 11 noon 1 2 3 4 5 6 7 8 9 10 11 12

⊢ knots flood → ⊢— 3 knots ebb ——⊢ 1.1 knots flood ⊢— 1.5 knots ebb →⊢

⊃ —⊢⊢— 2.9 knots flood ——⊢— 2.5 knots ebb ——⊢ 1.1 knots flood ⊢— 1.7 knots

MON FEB 13

dawn 6:04 sunrise 7:02 sunset 5:47 dark 6:44
moonrise 12:53 a.m. moonset 11:01 a.m.

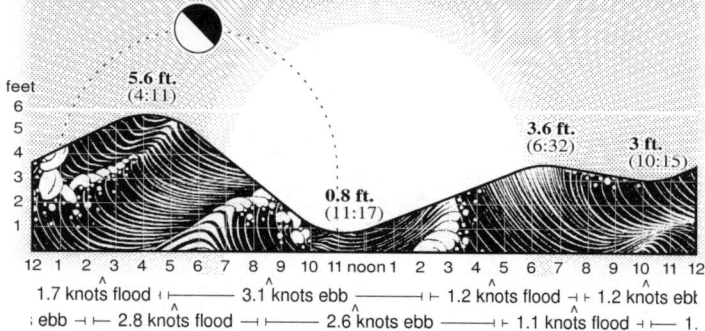

5.6 ft.
(4:11)

0.8 ft.
(11:17)

3.6 ft.
(6:32)

3 ft.
(10:15)

feet
6
5
4
3
2
1

12 1 2 3 4 5 6 7 8 9 10 11 noon 1 2 3 4 5 6 7 8 9 10 11 12

1.7 knots flood ⊢——— 3.1 knots ebb ———⊣ ⊢ 1.2 knots flood ⊣ ⊢ 1.2 knots ebb

⊢ ebb ⊢— 2.8 knots flood ——⊣ ⊢— 2.6 knots ebb ———⊣ ⊢ 1.1 knots flood ⊣ ⊢— 1.

TUE FEB 14

dawn 6:03 sunrise 7:01 sunset 5:48 dark 6:45
moonrise 2:03 a.m. moonset 11:41 a.m.

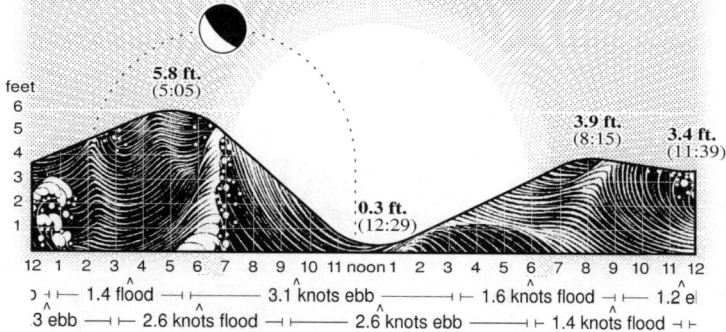

5.8 ft.
(5:05)

0.3 ft.
(12:29)

3.9 ft.
(8:15)

3.4 ft.
(11:39)

feet
6
5
4
3
2
1

12 1 2 3 4 5 6 7 8 9 10 11 noon 1 2 3 4 5 6 7 8 9 10 11 12

⊃ ⊣ ⊢ 1.4 flood ——⊣ ⊢ 3.1 knots ebb ———⊣ ⊢ 1.6 knots flood ⊣ ⊢ 1.2 el

3 ebb ⊢— 2.6 knots flood ⊣ ⊢ 2.6 knots ebb ———⊣ ⊢ 1.4 knots flood ⊣ ⊢

WED FEB 15

dawn 6:02 sunrise 7:00 sunset 5:49 dark 6:46
moonrise 3:14 a.m. moonset 12:31 p.m.

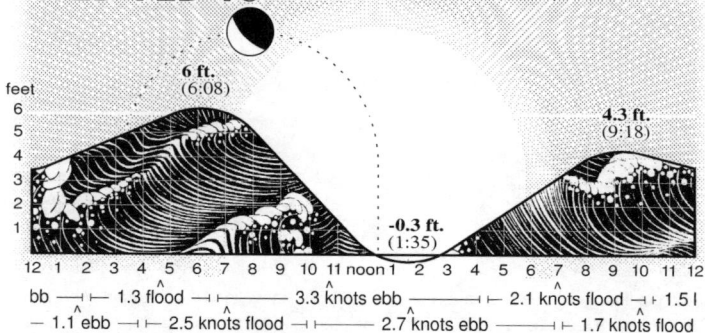

6 ft.
(6:08)

-0.3 ft.
(1:35)

4.3 ft.
(9:18)

feet
6
5
4
3
2
1

12 1 2 3 4 5 6 7 8 9 10 11 noon 1 2 3 4 5 6 7 8 9 10 11 12

bb ⊢— 1.3 flood ⊣ ⊢ 3.3 knots ebb ———⊣ ⊢ 2.1 knots flood ⊣ ⊢ 1.5 l

⊢ 1.1 ebb ⊣ ⊢ 2.5 knots flood ⊣ ⊢ 2.7 knots ebb ———⊣ ⊢ 1.7 knots flood

THU FEB 16

dawn 6:01 sunrise 6:58 sunset 5:50 dark 6:47
moonrise 4:22 a.m. moonset 1:32 p.m.

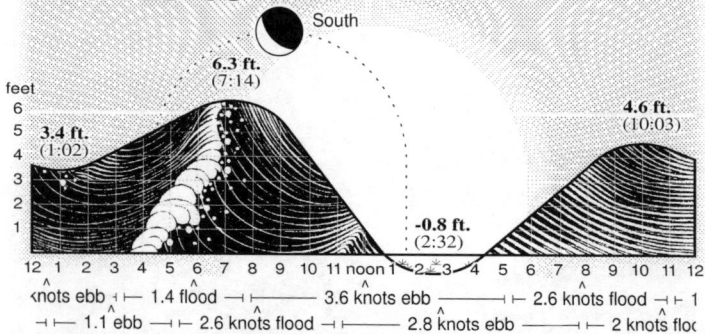

South

6.3 ft.
(7:14)

3.4 ft.
(1:02)

-0.8 ft.
(2:32)

4.6 ft.
(10:03)

feet
6
5
4
3
2
1

12 1 2 3 4 5 6 7 8 9 10 11 noon 1 2 3 4 5 6 7 8 9 10 11 12

knots ebb ⊢ 1.4 flood ⊣ ⊢ 3.6 knots ebb ———⊣ ⊢ 2.6 knots flood ⊣ ⊢ 1

⊣ ⊢ 1.1 ebb ⊣ ⊢ 2.6 knots flood ⊣ ⊢ 2.8 knots ebb ———⊣ ⊢ 2 knots flood

FRI FEB 17

dawn 6:00 sunrise 6:57 sunset 5:51 dark 6:48
moonrise 5:23 a.m. moonset 2:44 p.m.

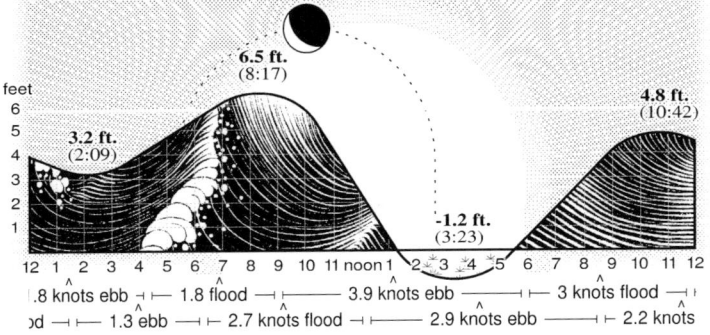

6.5 ft.
(8:17)

feet

4.8 ft.
(10:42)

3.2 ft.
(2:09)

-1.2 ft.
(3:23)

12 1 2 3 4 5 6 7 8 9 10 11 noon 1 2 3 4 5 6 7 8 9 10 11 12

.8 knots ebb ⊣ ⊢ 1.8 flood ⟶ ⊢ 3.9 knots ebb ⟶ ⊢ 3 knots flood ⟶ ⊢

od ⟶ ⊢ 1.3 ebb ⊢ 2.7 knots flood ⟶ ⊢ 2.9 knots ebb ⟶ ⊢ 2.2 knots

SAT FEB 18

dawn 5:59 sunrise 6:56 sunset 5:52 dark 6:49
moonrise 6:14 a.m. moonset 4:03 p.m.

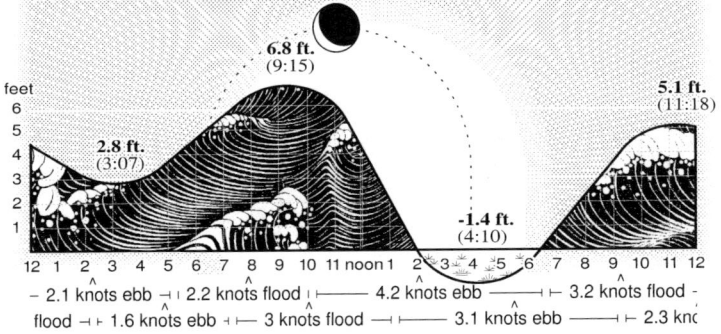

6.8 ft.
(9:15)

feet

5.1 ft.
(11:18)

2.8 ft.
(3:07)

-1.4 ft.
(4:10)

12 1 2 3 4 5 6 7 8 9 10 11 noon 1 2 3 4 5 6 7 8 9 10 11 12

– 2.1 knots ebb ⊣ ⊢ 2.2 knots flood ⊢ ⟶ 4.2 knots ebb ⟶ ⊢ 3.2 knots flood -

flood ⟶ ⊢ 1.6 knots ebb ⊣ ⊢ 3 knots flood ⟶ ⊢ 3.1 knots ebb ⟶ ⊢ 2.3 knc

SUN FEB 19

dawn 5:57 sunrise 6:55 sunset 5:53 dark 6:50
moonrise 6:56 a.m. moonset 5:22 p.m.

New Moon 11:06 p.m.   perigee

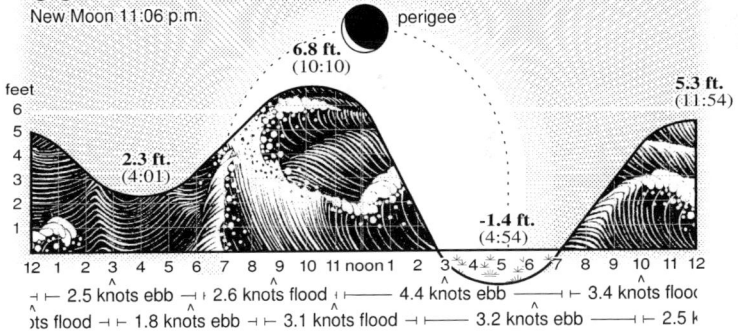

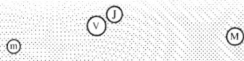

6.8 ft.
(10:10)

feet

5.3 ft.
(11:54)

2.3 ft.
(4:01)

-1.4 ft.
(4:54)

12 1 2 3 4 5 6 7 8 9 10 11 noon 1 2 3 4 5 6 7 8 9 10 11 12

⊣ ⊢ 2.5 knots ebb ⟶ ⊢ 2.6 knots flood ⊢ ⟶ 4.4 knots ebb ⟶ ⊢ 3.4 knots flood

ots flood ⊣ ⊢ 1.8 knots ebb ⊣ ⊢ 3.1 knots flood ⟶ ⊢ 3.2 knots ebb ⟶ ⊢ 2.5 k

MON FEB 20 dawn 5:56 sunrise 6:53 sunset 5:54 dark 6:51
moonrise 7:31 a.m. moonset 6:40 p.m.

Presidents' Day

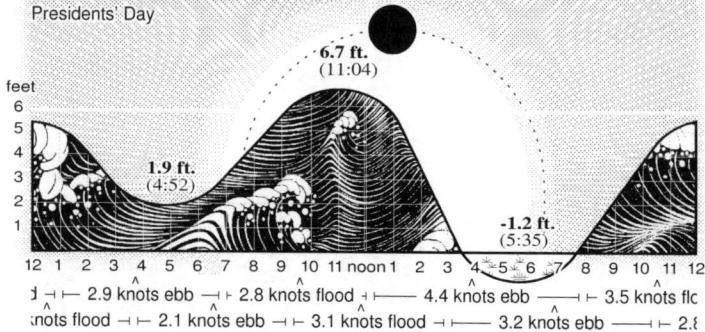

feet

6.7 ft.
(11:04)

1.9 ft.
(4:52)

-1.2 ft.
(5:35)

12 1 2 3 4 5 6 7 8 9 10 11 noon 1 2 3 4 5 6 7 8 9 10 11 12

d ⊣ ⊢ 2.9 knots ebb ⟶ ⊢ 2.8 knots flood ⊣ ⊢ 4.4 knots ebb ⟶ ⊢ 3.5 knots flo
knots flood ⊣ ⊢ 2.1 knots ebb ⊢ 3.1 knots flood ⊣ ⊢ 3.2 knots ebb ⟶ ⊢ 2.8

TUE FEB 21 dawn 5:55 sunrise 6:52 sunset 5:55 dark 6:52
moonrise 8:01 a.m. moonset 7:54 p.m.

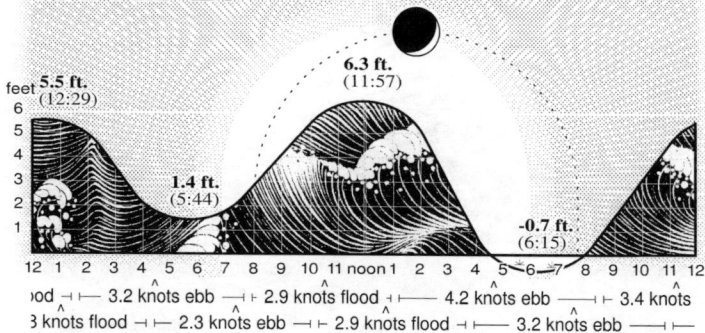

feet 5.5 ft.
(12:29)

6.3 ft.
(11:57)

1.4 ft.
(5:44)

-0.7 ft.
(6:15)

12 1 2 3 4 5 6 7 8 9 10 11 noon 1 2 3 4 5 6 7 8 9 10 11 12

ood ⊣ ⊢ 3.2 knots ebb ⟶ ⊢ 2.9 knots flood ⊣ ⊢ 4.2 knots ebb ⟶ ⊢ 3.4 knots
3 knots flood ⊣ ⊢ 2.3 knots ebb ⟶ ⊢ 2.9 knots flood ⊣ ⊢ 3.2 knots ebb ⟶ ⊢

WED FEB 22 dawn 5:54 sunrise 6:51 sunset 5:56 dark 6:53
moonrise 8:29 a.m. moonset 9:05 p.m.

Conjunction Venus Jupiter & Moon

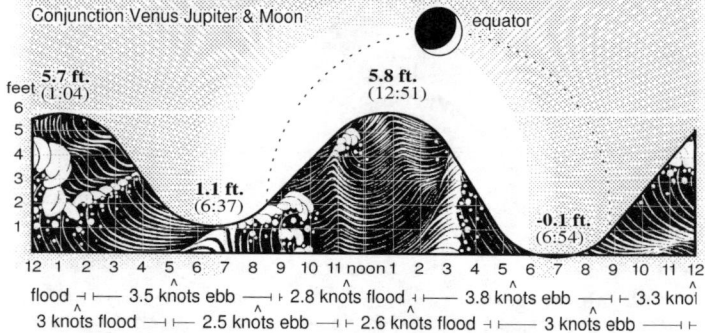

equator

5.7 ft.
(1:04)

feet

5.8 ft.
(12:51)

1.1 ft.
(6:37)

-0.1 ft.
(6:54)

12 1 2 3 4 5 6 7 8 9 10 11 noon 1 2 3 4 5 6 7 8 9 10 11 12

flood ⊣ ⊢ 3.5 knots ebb ⟶ ⊢ 2.8 knots flood ⊣ ⊢ 3.8 knots ebb ⟶ ⊢ 3.3 knot
3 knots flood ⊣ ⊢ 2.5 knots ebb ⟶ ⊢ 2.6 knots flood ⊣ ⊢ 3 knots ebb ⟶ ⊢

THU FEB 23 dawn 5:53 sunrise 6:50 sunset 5:57 dark 6:54
moonrise 8:55 a.m. moonset 10:14 p.m.

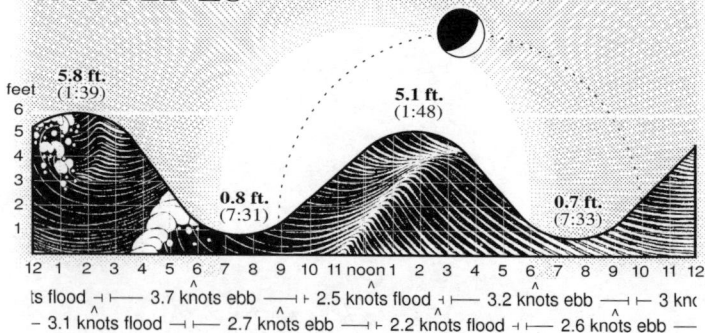

feet 5.8 ft.
(1:39)

5.1 ft.
(1:48)

0.8 ft.
(7:31)

0.7 ft.
(7:33)

12 1 2 3 4 5 6 7 8 9 10 11 noon 1 2 3 4 5 6 7 8 9 10 11 12

ts flood ⊣ ⊢ 3.7 knots ebb ⟶ ⊢ 2.5 knots flood ⊣ ⊢ 3.2 knots ebb ⟶ ⊢ 3 kn
⊢ 3.1 knots flood ⊣ ⊢ 2.7 knots ebb ⟶ ⊢ 2.2 knots flood ⊣ ⊢ 2.6 knots ebb ⟶

FRI FEB 24

dawn 5:51 sunrise 6:48 sunset 5:58 dark 6:55
moonrise 9:23 a.m. moonset 11:22 p.m.

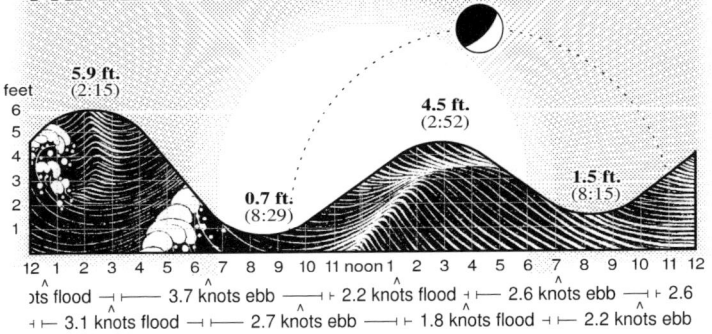

5.9 ft.
(2:15)

4.5 ft.
(2:52)

0.7 ft.
(8:29)

1.5 ft.
(8:15)

feet
6
5
4
3
2
1

12 1 2 3 4 5 6 7 8 9 10 11 noon 1 2 3 4 5 6 7 8 9 10 11 12

ɔts flood ⊣ ⊢ 3.7 knots ebb ——— ⊢ 2.2 knots flood ⊣ ⊢— 2.6 knots ebb —— ⊢ 2.6
⊣ ⊢— 3.1 knots flood ⊣ ⊢— 2.7 knots ebb ——— ⊢ 1.8 knots flood ⊣ ⊢ 2.2 knots ebb

SAT FEB 25

dawn 5:50 sunrise 6:47 sunset 5:59 dark 6:56
moonrise 9:52 a.m.

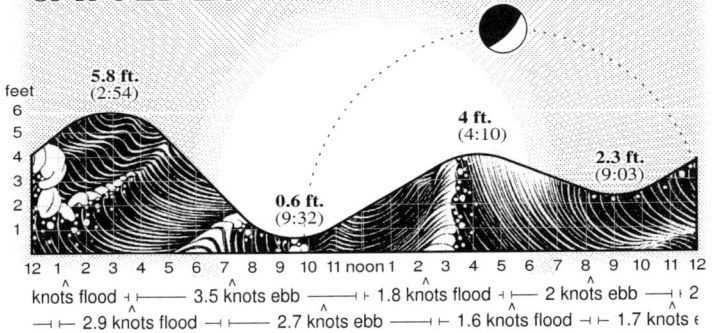

5.8 ft.
(2:54)

4 ft.
(4:10)

0.6 ft.
(9:32)

2.3 ft.
(9:03)

feet
6
5
4
3
2
1

12 1 2 3 4 5 6 7 8 9 10 11 noon 1 2 3 4 5 6 7 8 9 10 11 12

knots flood ⊣ ⊢—— 3.5 knots ebb ——— ⊢ 1.8 knots flood ⊣ ⊢— 2 knots ebb —— ⊢ 2
⊣ ⊢— 2.9 knots flood ⊣ ⊢— 2.7 knots ebb ——— ⊢ 1.6 knots flood ⊣ ⊢ 1.7 knots e

SUN FEB 26

dawn 5:49 sunrise 6:46 sunset 6:00 dark 6:57
moonset 12:28 a.m. moonrise 10:25 a.m.

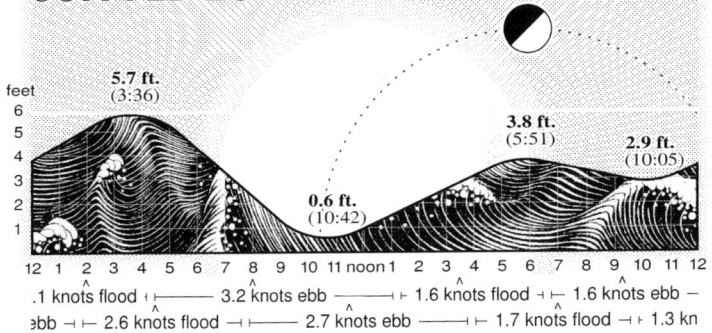

5.7 ft.
(3:36)

3.8 ft.
(5:51)

0.6 ft.
(10:42)

2.9 ft.
(10:05)

feet
6
5
4
3
2
1

12 1 2 3 4 5 6 7 8 9 10 11 noon 1 2 3 4 5 6 7 8 9 10 11 12

.1 knots flood ⊣ ⊢—— 3.2 knots ebb ——— ⊢ 1.6 knots flood ⊣ ⊢ 1.6 knots ebb —
ebb ⊣ ⊢ 2.6 knots flood ⊣ ⊢— 2.7 knots ebb ——— ⊢ 1.7 knots flood ⊣ ⊢ 1.3 kn

MON FEB 27
dawn 5:47 sunrise 6:44 sunset 6:01 dark 6:58
moonset 1:33 a.m. moonrise 11:03 a.m.

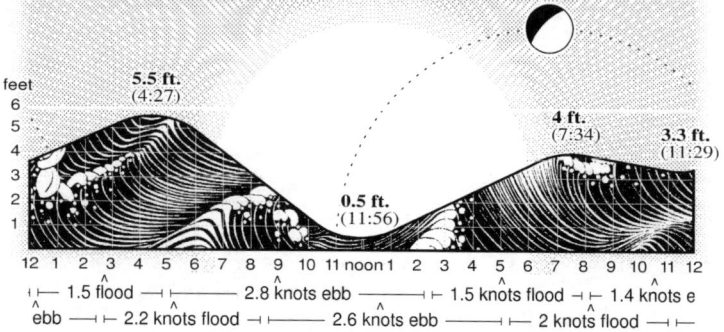

5.5 ft.
(4:27)

4 ft.
(7:34)

3.3 ft.
(11:29)

0.5 ft.
(11:56)

feet

├ 1.5 flood ─┤ ├── 2.8 knots ebb ──┤ ├ 1.5 knots flood ─┤ ├ 1.4 knots e
├ ebb ─┤ ├─ 2.2 knots flood ─┤ ├── 2.6 knots ebb ──┤ ├── 2 knots flood ──┤ ├─

TUE FEB 28
dawn 5:46 sunrise 6:43 sunset 6:02 dark 6:59
moonset 2:34 a.m. moonrise 11:47 a.m.

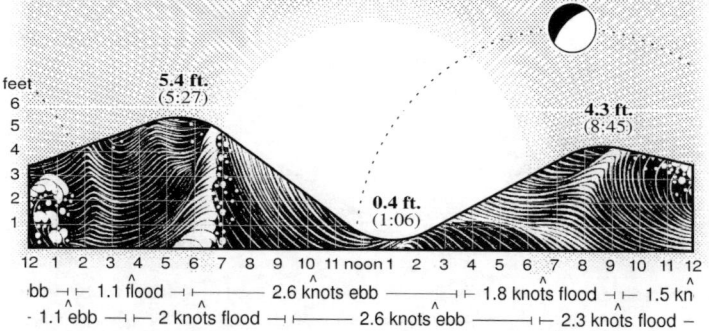

5.4 ft.
(5:27)

4.3 ft.
(8:45)

0.4 ft.
(1:06)

feet

ebb ─┤ ├ 1.1 flood ─┤ ├── 2.6 knots ebb ──┤ ├─ 1.8 knots flood ─┤ ├ 1.5 kn
├ 1.1 ebb ─┤ ├─ 2 knots flood ─┤ ├── 2.6 knots ebb ──┤ ├── 2.3 knots flood ─

WED MAR 1
dawn 5:45 sunrise 6:41 sunset 6:03 dark 7:00
moonset 3:29 a.m. moonrise 12:37 p.m.

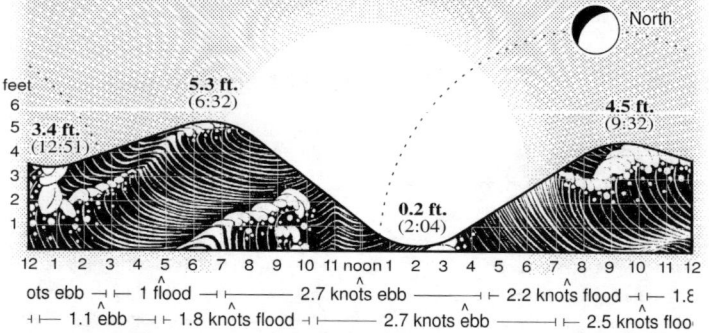

North

5.3 ft.
(6:32)

3.4 ft.
(12:51)

4.5 ft.
(9:32)

0.2 ft.
(2:04)

feet

ots ebb ─┤ ├─ 1 flood ─┤ ├── 2.7 knots ebb ──┤ ├─ 2.2 knots flood ─┤ ├─ 1.8
├── 1.1 ebb ──┤ ├ 1.8 knots flood ─┤ ├── 2.7 knots ebb ──┤ ├── 2.5 knots floo

THU MAR 2
dawn 5:43 sunrise 6:40 sunset 6:04 dark 7:01
moonset 4:18 a.m. moonrise 1:32 p.m.

Conjunction of Venus & Jupiter   Conjunction of Venus & Jupiter

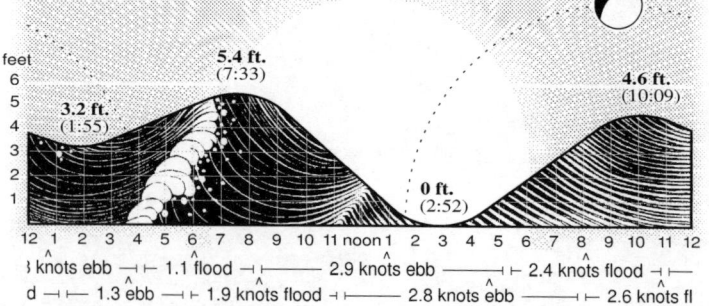

5.4 ft.
(7:33)

3.2 ft.
(1:55)

4.6 ft.
(10:09)

0 ft.
(2:52)

feet

3 knots ebb ─┤ ├ 1.1 flood ─┤ ├── 2.9 knots ebb ──┤ ├─ 2.4 knots flood ─┤ ├─
d ─┤ ├ 1.3 ebb ─┤ ├ 1.9 knots flood ─┤ ├── 2.8 knots ebb ──┤ ├── 2.6 knots fl

FRI MAR 3

dawn 5:42 sunrise 6:39 sunset 6:05 dark 7:02
moonset 5:00 a.m. moonrise 2:31 p.m.

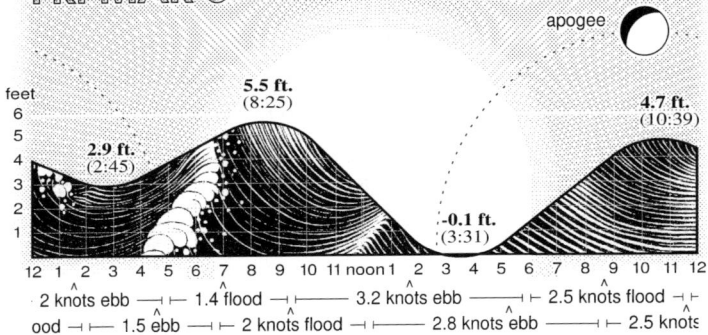

apogee

feet

6
5
4
3
2
1

2.9 ft.
(2:45)

5.5 ft.
(8:25)

4.7 ft.
(10:39)

-0.1 ft.
(3:31)

12 1 2 3 4 5 6 7 8 9 10 11 noon 1 2 3 4 5 6 7 8 9 10 11 12

2 knots ebb ⊢—⊣ 1.4 flood ⊣ ⊢— 3.2 knots ebb ——⊣ ⊢ 2.5 knots flood ⊣ ⊢
ood ⊣ ⊢— 1.5 ebb ——⊣ ⊢ 2 knots flood ⊣ ⊢—— 2.8 knots ebb ——⊣ ⊢ 2.5 knots

SAT MAR 4

dawn 5:41 sunrise 6:37 sunset 6:06 dark 7:03
moonset 5:35 a.m. moonrise 3:32 p.m.

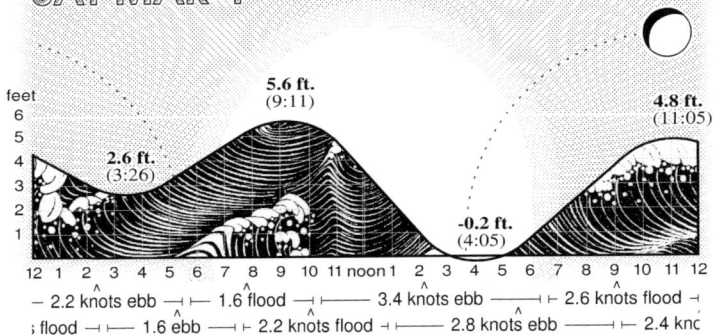

feet

6
5
4
3
2
1

2.6 ft.
(3:26)

5.6 ft.
(9:11)

4.8 ft.
(11:05)

-0.2 ft.
(4:05)

12 1 2 3 4 5 6 7 8 9 10 11 noon 1 2 3 4 5 6 7 8 9 10 11 12

⊢ 2.2 knots ebb ——⊣ ⊢ 1.6 flood ⊣ ⊢— 3.4 knots ebb ——⊣ ⊢ 2.6 knots flood ⊣
s flood ⊣ ⊢— 1.6 ebb ——⊣ ⊢ 2.2 knots flood ⊣ ⊢—— 2.8 knots ebb ——⊣ ⊢ 2.4 kno

SUN MAR 5

dawn 5:39 sunrise 6:36 sunset 6:07 dark 7:04
moonset 6:05 a.m. moonrise 4:33 p.m.

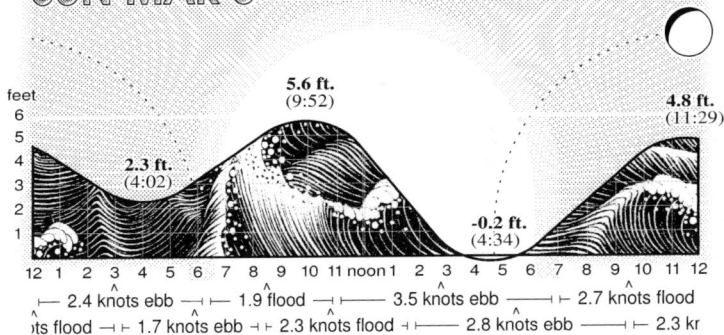

feet

6
5
4
3
2
1

2.3 ft.
(4:02)

5.6 ft.
(9:52)

4.8 ft.
(11:29)

-0.2 ft.
(4:34)

12 1 2 3 4 5 6 7 8 9 10 11 noon 1 2 3 4 5 6 7 8 9 10 11 12

⊢— 2.4 knots ebb —⊣ ⊢ 1.9 flood ⊣ ⊢— 3.5 knots ebb ——⊣ ⊢ 2.7 knots flood
ts flood ⊣ ⊢ 1.7 knots ebb ⊣ ⊢ 2.3 knots flood ⊣ ⊢—— 2.8 knots ebb ——⊣ ⊢ 2.3 kn

MON MAR 6

dawn 5:38 sunrise 6:34 sunset 6:08 dark 7:05
moonset 6:32 a.m. moonrise 5:33 p.m.

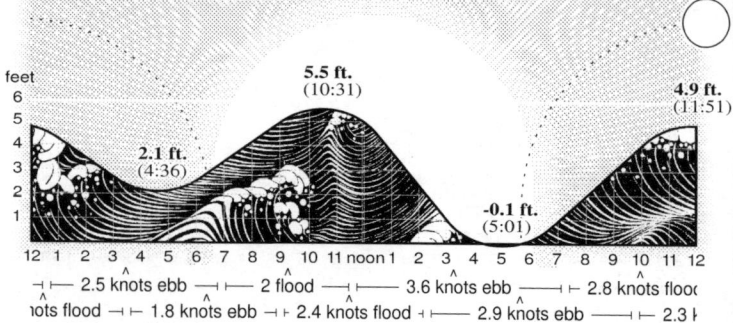

feet

5.5 ft.
(10:31)

4.9 ft.
(11:51)

2.1 ft.
(4:36)

-0.1 ft.
(5:01)

12 1 2 3 4 5 6 7 8 9 10 11 noon 1 2 3 4 5 6 7 8 9 10 11 12

⊣ ⊢ 2.5 knots ebb ⟶ ⊣ ⊢ 2 flood ⟶ ⊣ ⊢ 3.6 knots ebb ⟶ ⊢ 2.8 knots flood
nots flood ⊣ ⊢ 1.8 knots ebb ⊣ ⊢ 2.4 knots flood ⊣ ⟶ 2.9 knots ebb ⟶ ⊣ ⊢ 2.3 k

TUE MAR 7

dawn 5:36 sunrise 6:33 sunset 6:09 dark 7:06
moonset 6:56 a.m. moonrise 6:33 p.m.

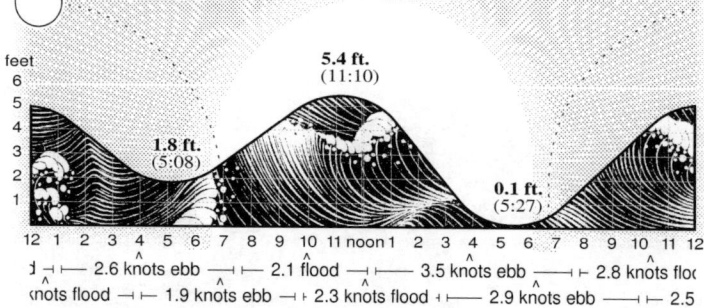

Full Moon 4:40 a.m.

feet

5.4 ft.
(11:10)

1.8 ft.
(5:08)

0.1 ft.
(5:27)

12 1 2 3 4 5 6 7 8 9 10 11 noon 1 2 3 4 5 6 7 8 9 10 11 12

d ⊣ ⊢ 2.6 knots ebb ⟶ ⊣ ⊢ 2.1 flood ⟶ ⊣ ⊢ 3.5 knots ebb ⟶ ⊢ 2.8 knots flood
knots flood ⊣ ⊢ 1.9 knots ebb ⊣ ⊢ 2.3 knots flood ⊣ ⟶ 2.9 knots ebb ⟶ ⊣ ⊢ 2.5

WED MAR 8

dawn 5:35 sunrise 6:31 sunset 6:10 dark 7:07
moonset 7:19 a.m. moonrise 7:34 p.m.

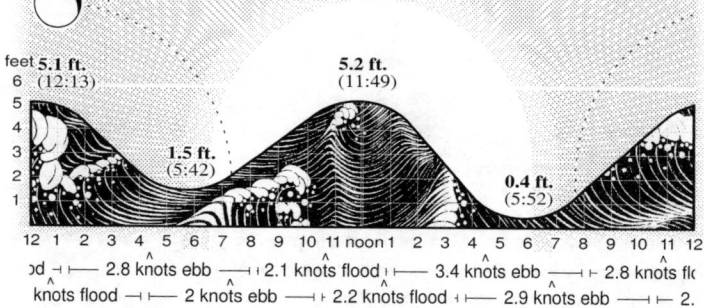

equator

feet **5.1 ft.**
(12:13)

5.2 ft.
(11:49)

1.5 ft.
(5:42)

0.4 ft.
(5:52)

12 1 2 3 4 5 6 7 8 9 10 11 noon 1 2 3 4 5 6 7 8 9 10 11 12

od ⊣ ⊢ 2.8 knots ebb ⟶ ⊢ 2.1 knots flood ⊢ 3.4 knots ebb ⟶ ⊢ 2.8 knots flo
knots flood ⊣ ⟶ 2 knots ebb ⟶ ⊢ 2.2 knots flood ⊣ ⟶ 2.9 knots ebb ⟶ ⊢ 2.

THU MAR 9

dawn 5:33 sunrise 6:30 sunset 6:11 dark 7:08
moonset 7:41 a.m. moonrise 8:35 p.m.

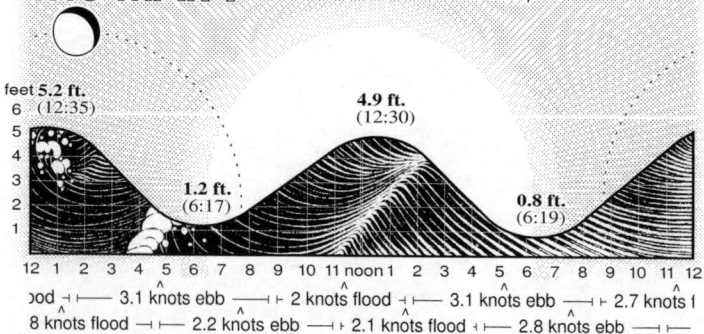

feet **5.2 ft.**
(12:35)

4.9 ft.
(12:30)

1.2 ft.
(6:17)

0.8 ft.
(6:19)

12 1 2 3 4 5 6 7 8 9 10 11 noon 1 2 3 4 5 6 7 8 9 10 11 12

ood ⊣ ⊢ 3.1 knots ebb ⟶ ⊢ 2 knots flood ⊣ ⊢ 3.1 knots ebb ⟶ ⊢ 2.7 knots f
8 knots flood ⊣ ⟶ 2.2 knots ebb ⟶ ⊢ 2.1 knots flood ⊣ ⟶ 2.8 knots ebb ⟶ ⊣ ⊢

FRI MAR 10

dawn 5:32 sunrise 6:29 sunset 6:12 dark 7:09
moonset 8:05 a.m. moonrise 9:39 p.m.

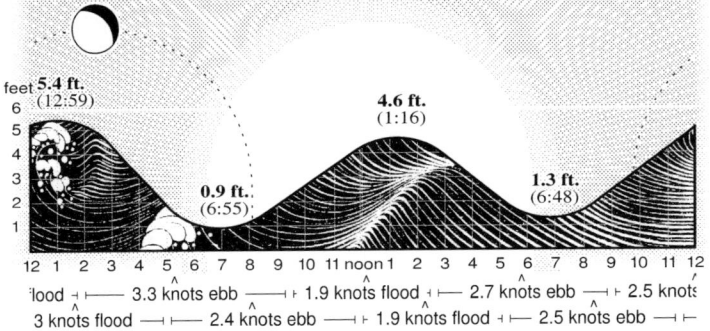

feet
5.4 ft.
(12:59)

4.6 ft.
(1:16)

0.9 ft.
(6:55)

1.3 ft.
(6:48)

12 1 2 3 4 5 6 7 8 9 10 11 noon 1 2 3 4 5 6 7 8 9 10 11 12

flood ⊣ ⊢— 3.3 knots ebb ——⊢ 1.9 knots flood ⊣⊢— 2.7 knots ebb ——⊢ 2.5 knots
3 knots flood —⊣ ⊢— 2.4 knots ebb ——⊢ 1.9 knots flood ⊣⊢— 2.5 knots ebb —⊣ ⊢

SAT MAR 11

dawn 5:31 sunrise 6:27 sunset 6:13 dark 7:10
moonset 8:31 a.m. moonrise 10:45 p.m.

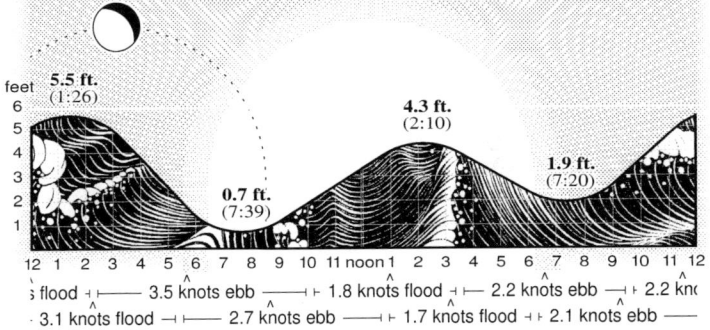

feet
5.5 ft.
(1:26)

4.3 ft.
(2:10)

0.7 ft.
(7:39)

1.9 ft.
(7:20)

12 1 2 3 4 5 6 7 8 9 10 11 noon 1 2 3 4 5 6 7 8 9 10 11 12

s flood ⊣⊢— 3.5 knots ebb ——⊢ 1.8 knots flood ⊣⊢— 2.2 knots ebb ⊢ 2.2 kn
3.1 knots flood ⊣⊢— 2.7 knots ebb ——⊢ 1.7 knots flood ⊣⊢ 2.1 knots ebb ——

SUN MAR 12

dawn 6:29 sunrise 7:26 sunset 7:14 dark 8:11
moonset 10:01 a.m.

Daylight Savings Time Begins

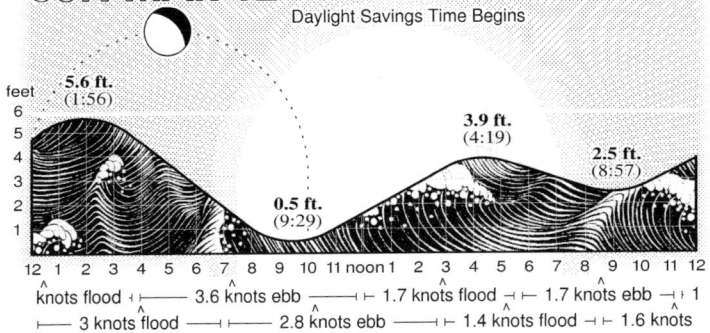

feet
5.6 ft.
(1:56)

3.9 ft.
(4:19)

2.5 ft.
(8:57)

0.5 ft.
(9:29)

12 1 2 3 4 5 6 7 8 9 10 11 noon 1 2 3 4 5 6 7 8 9 10 11 12

knots flood ⊣⊢— 3.6 knots ebb ——⊢ 1.7 knots flood ⊣⊢ 1.7 knots ebb ⊣⊢ 1
⊢— 3 knots flood —⊣ ⊢— 2.8 knots ebb ——⊢ 1.4 knots flood ⊣⊢ 1.6 knots

MON MAR 13
dawn 6:28 sunrise 7:24 sunset 7:15 dark 8:12
moonrise 12:53 a.m. moonset 10:38 a.m.

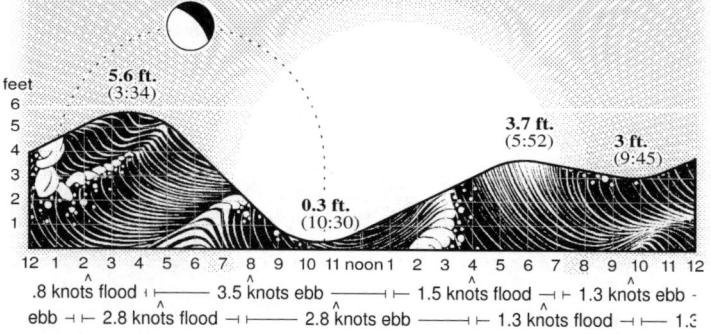

feet

5.6 ft.
(3:34)

3.7 ft.
(5:52)

3 ft.
(9:45)

0.3 ft.
(10:30)

12 1 2 3 4 5 6 7 8 9 10 11 noon 1 2 3 4 5 6 7 8 9 10 11 12

.8 knots flood ⊢ ⊢ —— 3.5 knots ebb —— ⊢ 1.5 knots flood ⊣ ⊢ 1.3 knots ebb -
ebb ⊣ ⊢ 2.8 knots flood ⊣ ⊢—— 2.8 knots ebb —— ⊢ 1.3 knots flood ⊣ ⊢ 1.3

TUE MAR 14
dawn 6:26 sunrise 7:23 sunset 7:16 dark 8:13
moonrise 2:03 a.m. moonset 11:23 a.m.

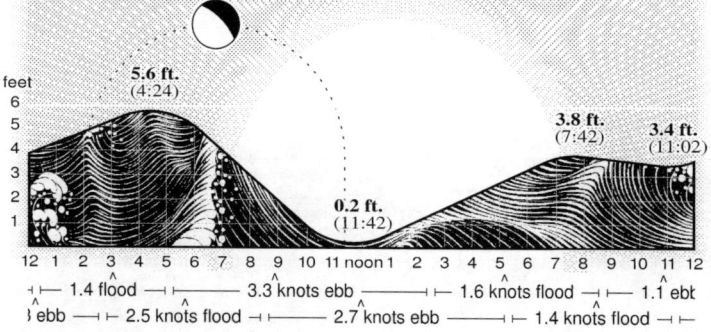

feet

5.6 ft.
(4:24)

3.8 ft.
(7:42)

3.4 ft.
(11:02)

0.2 ft.
(11:42)

12 1 2 3 4 5 6 7 8 9 10 11 noon 1 2 3 4 5 6 7 8 9 10 11 12

⊢ ⊢ 1.4 flood ⊣ ⊢ —— 3.3 knots ebb —— ⊢ 1.6 knots flood ⊣ ⊢ 1.1 ebt
3 ebb ⊢ ⊢ 2.5 knots flood ⊣ ⊢ —— 2.7 knots ebb —— ⊢ 1.4 knots flood ⊣ ⊢

WED MAR 15
dawn 6:25 sunrise 7:21 sunset 7:17 dark 8:14
moonrise 3:11 a.m. moonset 12:19 p.m.

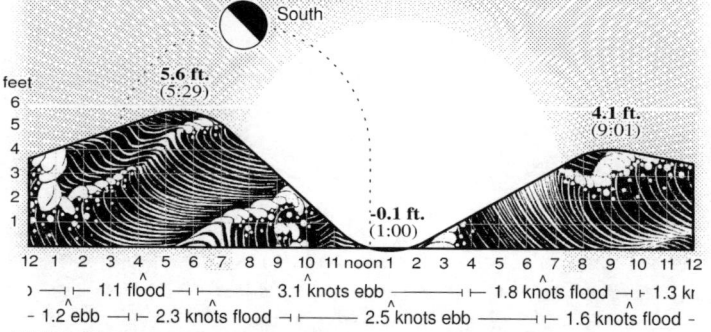

South

feet

5.6 ft.
(5:29)

4.1 ft.
(9:01)

-0.1 ft.
(1:00)

12 1 2 3 4 5 6 7 8 9 10 11 noon 1 2 3 4 5 6 7 8 9 10 11 12

) ⊢ ⊢ 1.1 flood ⊣ ⊢ —— 3.1 knots ebb —— ⊢ 1.8 knots flood ⊣ ⊢ 1.3 kr
- 1.2 ebb ⊣ ⊢ 2.3 knots flood ⊣ ⊢ —— 2.5 knots ebb —— ⊢ 1.6 knots flood -

THU MAR 16
dawn 6:23 sunrise 7:20 sunset 7:18 dark 8:15
moonrise 4:12 a.m. moonset 1:25 p.m.

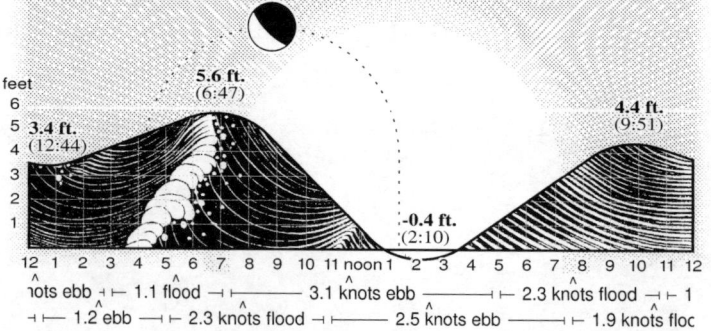

feet

5.6 ft.
(6:47)

3.4 ft.
(12:44)

4.4 ft.
(9:51)

-0.4 ft.
(2:10)

12 1 2 3 4 5 6 7 8 9 10 11 noon 1 2 3 4 5 6 7 8 9 10 11 12

nots ebb ⊣ ⊢ 1.1 flood ⊣ ⊢ —— 3.1 knots ebb —— ⊢ 2.3 knots flood ⊣ ⊢ 1
⊣ ⊢ 1.2 ebb ⊣ ⊢ 2.3 knots flood ⊣ ⊢ —— 2.5 knots ebb —— ⊢ 1.9 knots floc

FRI MAR 17

dawn 6:21 sunrise 7:18 sunset 7:19 dark 8:16
moonrise 5:05 a.m. moonset 2:39 p.m.

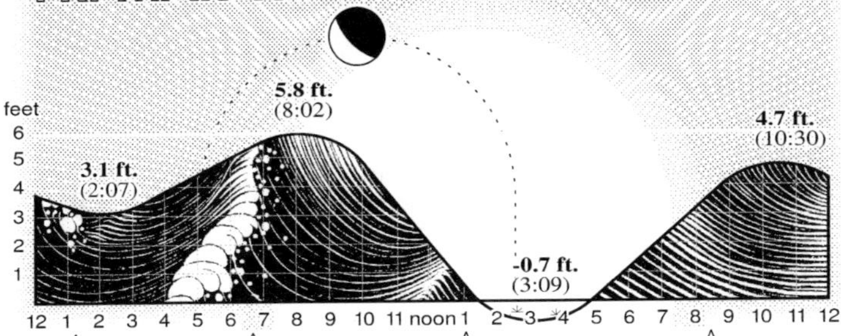

feet
6
5
4
3
2
1
5.8 ft.
(8:02)
3.1 ft.
(2:07)
4.7 ft.
(10:30)
-0.7 ft.
(3:09)
12 1 2 3 4 5 6 7 8 9 10 11 noon 1 2 3 4 5 6 7 8 9 10 11 12

.7 knots ebb ⊣ ⊢ 1.4 flood ⊣ ⊢ 3.4 knots ebb ⊣ ⊢ 2.7 knots flood ⊣ ⊢
od ⊣ ⊢ 1.5 ebb ⊣ ⊢ 2.4 knots flood ⊣ ⊢ 2.6 knots ebb ⊣ ⊢ 2.1 knots f

SAT MAR 18

dawn 6:20 sunrise 7:17 sunset 7:20 dark 8:17
moonrise 5:50 a.m. moonset 3:56 p.m.

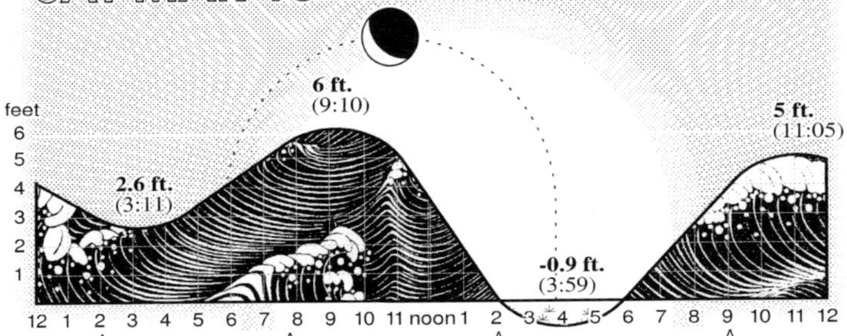

feet
6
5
4
3
2
1
6 ft.
(9:10)
2.6 ft.
(3:11)
5 ft.
(11:05)
-0.9 ft.
(3:59)
12 1 2 3 4 5 6 7 8 9 10 11 noon 1 2 3 4 5 6 7 8 9 10 11 12

- 2.1 knots ebb ⊣ ⊢ 1.9 knots flood ⊣ ⊢ 3.8 knots ebb ⊣ ⊢ 3 knots flood —
lood ⊣ ⊢ 1.8 knots ebb ⊣ ⊢ 2.6 knots flood ⊣ ⊢ 2.8 knots ebb ⊣ ⊢ 2.4 knot

SUN MAR 19

dawn 6:18 sunrise 7:15 sunset 7:21 dark 8:18
moonrise 6:26 a.m. moonset 5:12 p.m.

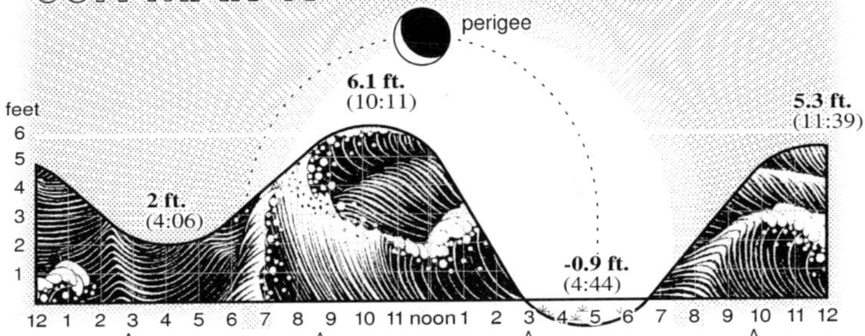

perigee
feet
6
5
4
3
2
1
6.1 ft.
(10:11)
2 ft.
(4:06)
5.3 ft.
(11:39)
-0.9 ft.
(4:44)
12 1 2 3 4 5 6 7 8 9 10 11 noon 1 2 3 4 5 6 7 8 9 10 11 12

⊢ 2.6 knots ebb ⊣ ⊢ 2.4 knots flood ⊣ ⊢ 4 knots ebb ⊣ ⊢ 3.3 knots flood
s flood ⊣ ⊢ 2.1 knots ebb ⊣ ⊢ 2.8 knots flood ⊣ ⊢ 2.9 knots ebb ⊣ ⊢ 2.6 kr

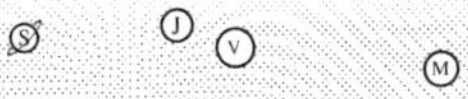

S
J
V
M

MON MAR 20

dawn 6:17 sunrise 7:14 sunset 7:22 dark 8:19
moonrise 6:58 a.m. moonset 6:27 p.m.

Vernal Equinox 2:24 p.m.

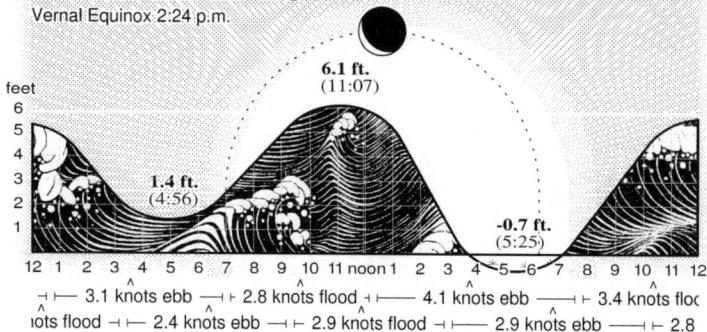

feet

6.1 ft.
(11:07)

1.4 ft.
(4:56)

-0.7 ft.
(5:25)

12 1 2 3 4 5 6 7 8 9 10 11 noon 1 2 3 4 5 6 7 8 9 10 11 12

⊣ ⊢ 3.1 knots ebb ——⊢ 2.8 knots flood ⊣ ⊢ 4.1 knots ebb ——⊢ 3.4 knots floc
ots flood ⊣ ⊢ 2.4 knots ebb ——⊢ 2.9 knots flood ⊣ ⊢ 2.9 knots ebb ——⊢ 2.8

TUE MAR 21

dawn 6:15 sunrise 7:12 sunset 7:23 dark 8:20
moonrise 7:26 a.m. moonset 7:40 p.m.

New Moon 10:23 a.m.

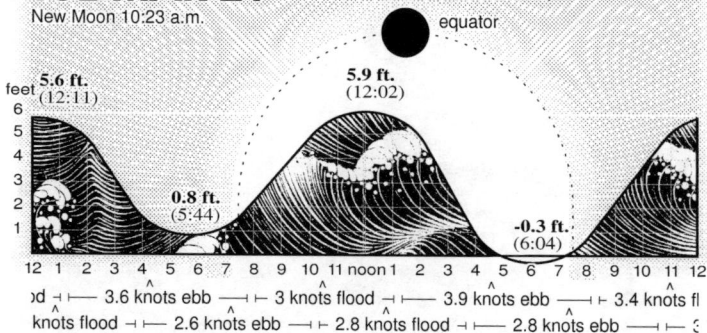

equator

feet
5.6 ft.
(12:11)

5.9 ft.
(12:02)

0.8 ft.
(5:44)

-0.3 ft.
(6:04)

12 1 2 3 4 5 6 7 8 9 10 11 noon 1 2 3 4 5 6 7 8 9 10 11 12

od ⊣ ⊢ 3.6 knots ebb ——⊢ 3 knots flood ⊣ ⊢ 3.9 knots ebb ——⊢ 3.4 knots fl
knots flood ⊣ ⊢ 2.6 knots ebb ——⊢ 2.8 knots flood ⊣ ⊢ 2.8 knots ebb ——⊢ 3

WED MAR 22

dawn 6:14 sunrise 7:10 sunset 7:24 dark 8:21
moonrise 7:53 a.m. moonset 8:51 p.m.

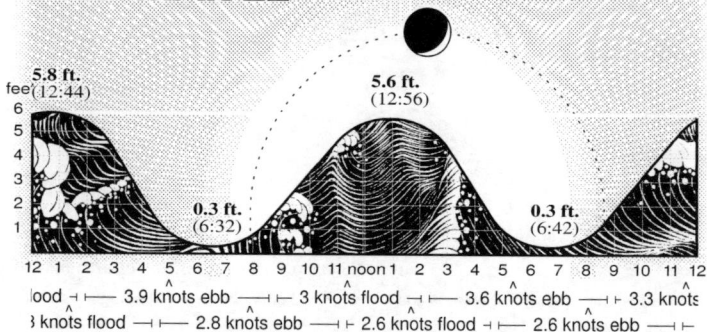

5.8 ft.
(12:44)

feet

5.6 ft.
(12:56)

0.3 ft.
(6:32)

0.3 ft.
(6:42)

12 1 2 3 4 5 6 7 8 9 10 11 noon 1 2 3 4 5 6 7 8 9 10 11 12

flood ⊣ ⊢ 3.9 knots ebb ——⊢ 3 knots flood ⊣ ⊢ 3.6 knots ebb ——⊢ 3.3 knots
8 knots flood ⊣ ⊢ 2.8 knots ebb ——⊢ 2.6 knots flood ⊣ ⊢ 2.6 knots ebb ——⊢

THU MAR 23

dawn 6:12 sunrise 7:09 sunset 7:24 dark 8:21
moonrise 8:20 a.m. moonset 10:01 p.m.

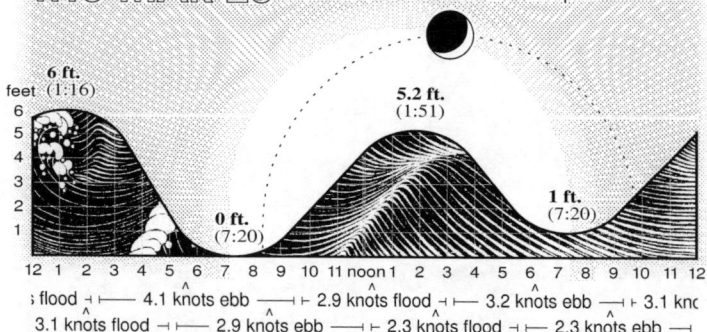

6 ft.
(1:16)

feet

5.2 ft.
(1:51)

0 ft.
(7:20)

1 ft.
(7:20)

12 1 2 3 4 5 6 7 8 9 10 11 noon 1 2 3 4 5 6 7 8 9 10 11 12

s flood ⊣ ⊢ 4.1 knots ebb ——⊢ 2.9 knots flood ⊣ ⊢ 3.2 knots ebb ——⊢ 3.1 knc
3.1 knots flood ⊣ ⊢ 2.9 knots ebb ——⊢ 2.3 knots flood ⊣ ⊢ 2.3 knots ebb ——⊣

FRI MAR 24

dawn 6:10 sunrise 7:07 sunset 7:25 dark 8:22
moonrise 8:49 a.m. moonset 11:10 p.m.

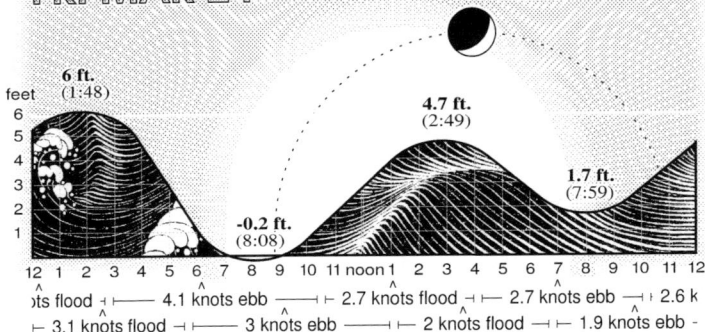

6 ft.
(1:48)

feet

4.7 ft.
(2:49)

1.7 ft.
(7:59)

-0.2 ft.
(8:08)

12 1 2 3 4 5 6 7 8 9 10 11 noon 1 2 3 4 5 6 7 8 9 10 11 12

ots flood ⊣ ⊢— 4.1 knots ebb ——⊣ ⊢ 2.7 knots flood ⊣ ⊢ 2.7 knots ebb —⊣ ⊢ 2.6 k
⊢ 3.1 knots flood ⊣ ⊢——— 3 knots ebb ———⊣ ⊢ 2 knots flood ⊣ ⊢ 1.9 knots ebb -

SAT MAR 25

dawn 6:09 sunrise 7:06 sunset 7:26 dark 8:23
moonrise 9:21 a.m.

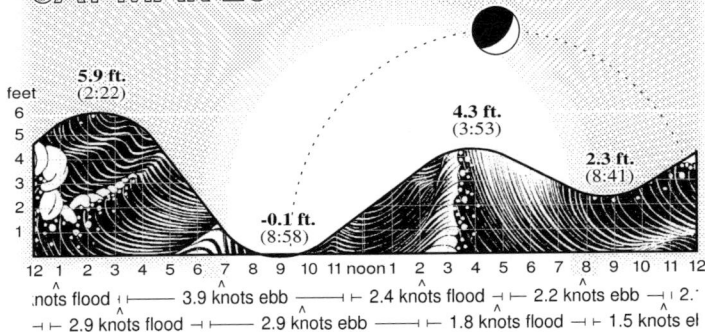

5.9 ft.
(2:22)

feet

4.3 ft.
(3:53)

2.3 ft.
(8:41)

-0.1 ft.
(8:58)

12 1 2 3 4 5 6 7 8 9 10 11 noon 1 2 3 4 5 6 7 8 9 10 11 12

.nots flood ⊣ ⊢——— 3.9 knots ebb ———⊣ ⊢ 2.4 knots flood ⊣ ⊢ 2.2 knots ebb ⊣ ⊢ 2.
⊣ ⊢ 2.9 knots flood ⊣ ⊢——— 2.9 knots ebb ———⊣ ⊢ 1.8 knots flood ⊣ ⊢ 1.5 knots el

SUN MAR 26

dawn 6:07 sunrise 7:04 sunset 7:27 dark 8:24
moonset 12:18 a.m. moonrise 9:57 a.m.

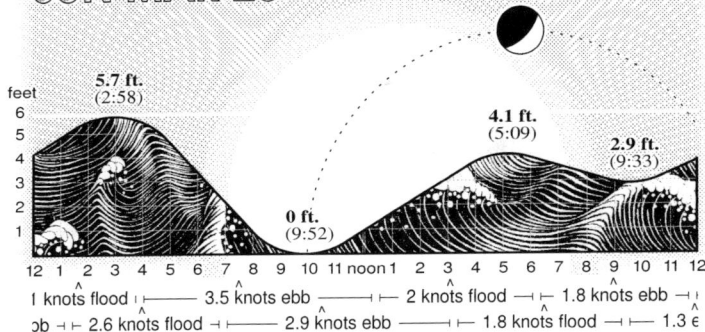

5.7 ft.
(2:58)

feet

4.1 ft.
(5:09)

2.9 ft.
(9:33)

0 ft.
(9:52)

12 1 2 3 4 5 6 7 8 9 10 11 noon 1 2 3 4 5 6 7 8 9 10 11 12

l knots flood ⊣ ⊢——— 3.5 knots ebb ———⊣ ⊢ 2 knots flood ⊣ ⊢ 1.8 knots ebb ⊣ ⊢
ob ⊣ ⊢ 2.6 knots flood ⊣ ⊢——— 2.9 knots ebb ———⊣ ⊢ 1.8 knots flood ⊣ ⊢ 1.3 ε

Ø   V   M

Vernal Equinox marks the first day of spring in the northern
hemisphere with nearly equal amounts of day and night throughout
the world. copyright 2022 Pacific Publishers, L.L.C. WWW.TIDELOG.COM

MON MAR 27

dawn 6:06 sunrise 7:03 sunset 7:28 dark 8:25
moonset 1:22 a.m. moonrise 10:40 a.m.

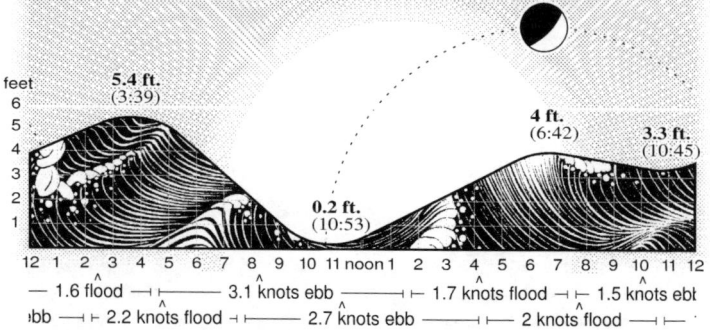

feet

5.4 ft.
(3:39)

4 ft.
(6:42)

3.3 ft.
(10:45)

0.2 ft.
(10:53)

12 1 2 3 4 5 6 7 8 9 10 11 noon 1 2 3 4 5 6 7 8 9 10 11 12

— 1.6 flood —| |— 3.1 knots ebb ——— |— 1.7 knots flood —| |— 1.5 knots ebb
ebb —| |— 2.2 knots flood —| |— 2.7 knots ebb ——— |— 2 knots flood —| |—

TUE MAR 28

dawn 6:04 sunrise 7:01 sunset 7:29 dark 8:26
moonset 2:21 a.m. moonrise 11:28 a.m.

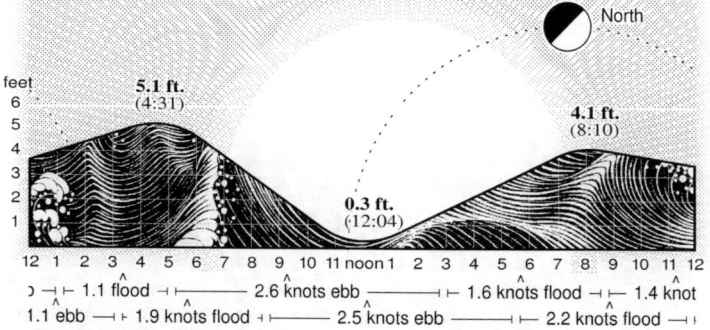

North

feet

5.1 ft.
(4:31)

4.1 ft.
(8:10)

0.3 ft.
(12:04)

12 1 2 3 4 5 6 7 8 9 10 11 noon 1 2 3 4 5 6 7 8 9 10 11 12

) —| |— 1.1 flood —| |— 2.6 knots ebb ——— |— 1.6 knots flood —| |— 1.4 knot
1.1 ebb —| |— 1.9 knots flood —| |— 2.5 knots ebb ——— |— 2.2 knots flood —| |—

WED MAR 29

dawn 6:03 sunrise 7:00 sunset 7:30 dark 8:27
moonset 3:13 a.m. moonrise 12:22 p.m.

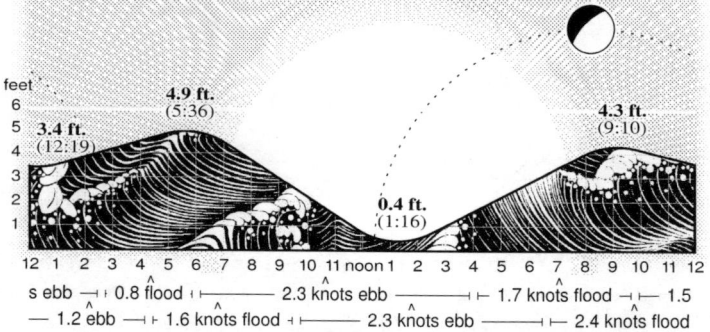

feet

3.4 ft.
(12:19)

4.9 ft.
(5:36)

4.3 ft.
(9:10)

0.4 ft.
(1:16)

12 1 2 3 4 5 6 7 8 9 10 11 noon 1 2 3 4 5 6 7 8 9 10 11 12

s ebb —| |— 0.8 flood |— 2.3 knots ebb ——— |— 1.7 knots flood —| |— 1.5
— 1.2 ebb —| |— 1.6 knots flood —| |— 2.3 knots ebb ——— |— 2.4 knots flood

THU MAR 30

dawn 6:01 sunrise 6:58 sunset 7:31 dark 8:28
moonset 3:58 a.m. moonrise 1:21 p.m.

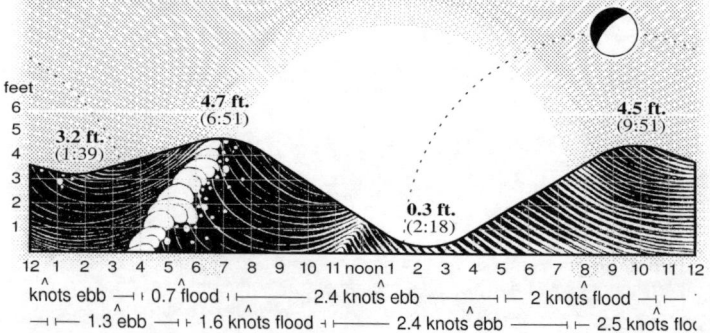

feet

3.2 ft.
(1:39)

4.7 ft.
(6:51)

4.5 ft.
(9:51)

0.3 ft.
(2:18)

12 1 2 3 4 5 6 7 8 9 10 11 noon 1 2 3 4 5 6 7 8 9 10 11 12

knots ebb —| |— 0.7 flood |— 2.4 knots ebb ——— |— 2 knots flood —| |—
—| |— 1.3 ebb —| |— 1.6 knots flood —| |— 2.4 knots ebb ——— |— 2.5 knots flood

FRI MAR 31

dawn 5:59 sunrise 6:57 sunset 7:32 dark 8:29
moonset 4:35 a.m. moonrise 2:21 p.m.

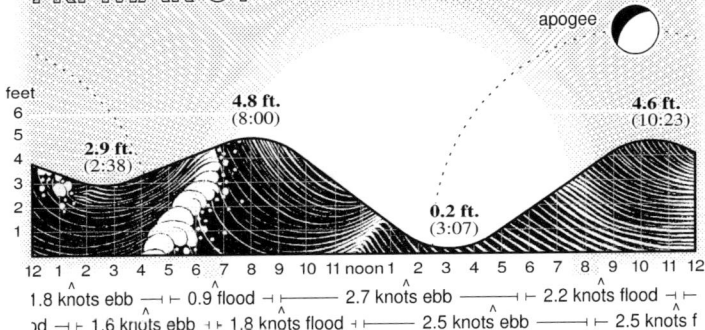

apogee

feet

4.8 ft.
(8:00)

4.6 ft.
(10:23)

2.9 ft.
(2:38)

0.2 ft.
(3:07)

12 1 2 3 4 5 6 7 8 9 10 11 noon 1 2 3 4 5 6 7 8 9 10 11 12

1.8 knots ebb ⊢ 0.9 flood ⊣ ⊢——— 2.7 knots ebb ——— ⊢ 2.2 knots flood ⊣ ⊢
od ⊣ ⊢ 1.6 knots ebb ⊣ ⊢ 1.8 knots flood ⊣ ⊢——— 2.5 knots ebb ——— ⊢ 2.5 knots f

SAT APR 1

dawn 5:58 sunrise 6:55 sunset 7:33 dark 8:30
moonset 5:07 a.m. moonrise 3:22 p.m.

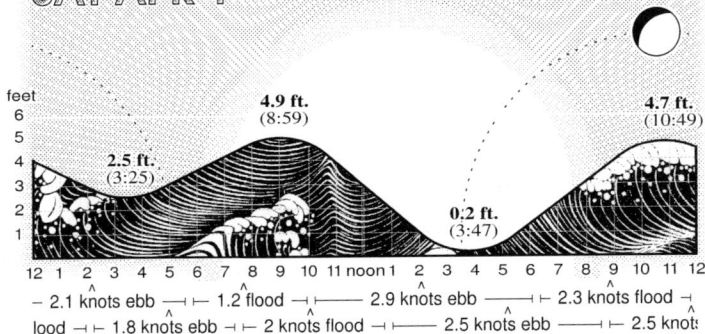

feet

4.9 ft.
(8:59)

4.7 ft.
(10:49)

2.5 ft.
(3:25)

0.2 ft.
(3:47)

12 1 2 3 4 5 6 7 8 9 10 11 noon 1 2 3 4 5 6 7 8 9 10 11 12

⊢ 2.1 knots ebb ⊣ ⊢ 1.2 flood ⊣ ⊢——— 2.9 knots ebb ——— ⊢ 2.3 knots flood ⊣
lood ⊣ ⊢ 1.8 knots ebb ⊣ ⊢ 2 knots flood ⊣ ⊢——— 2.5 knots ebb ——— ⊢ 2.5 knots

SUN APR 2

dawn 5:56 sunrise 6:54 sunset 7:34 dark 8:32
moonset 5:35 a.m. moonrise 4:22 p.m.

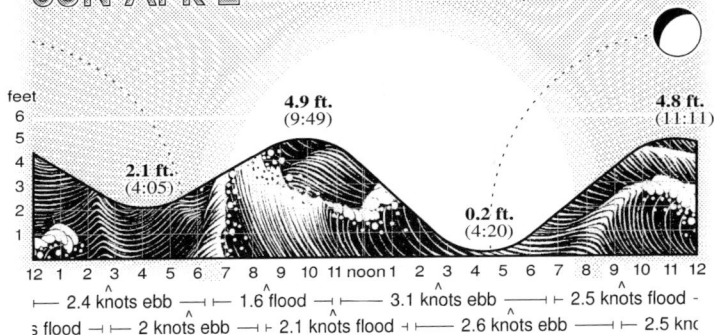

feet

4.9 ft.
(9:49)

4.8 ft.
(11:11)

2.1 ft.
(4:05)

0.2 ft.
(4:20)

12 1 2 3 4 5 6 7 8 9 10 11 noon 1 2 3 4 5 6 7 8 9 10 11 12

⊢——— 2.4 knots ebb ——⊣ ⊢ 1.6 flood ⊣ ⊢——— 3.1 knots ebb ——— ⊢ 2.5 knots flood ⊢
s flood ⊣ ⊢ 2 knots ebb ⊣ ⊢ 2.1 knots flood ⊣ ⊢——— 2.6 knots ebb ——— ⊢ 2.5 knc

Ⓢ   Ⓥ   Ⓜ

MON APR 3 dawn 5:55 sunrise 6:52 sunset 7:35 dark 8:33
moonset 6:00 a.m. moonrise 5:23 p.m.

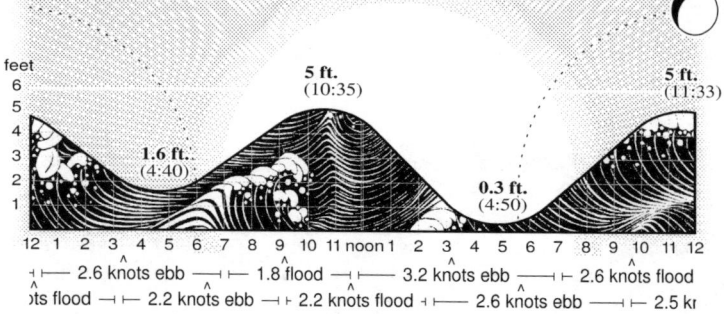

feet

5 ft.
(10:35)

5 ft.
(11:33)

1.6 ft.
(4:40)

0.3 ft.
(4:50)

12 1 2 3 4 5 6 7 8 9 10 11 noon 1 2 3 4 5 6 7 8 9 10 11 12

⊢— 2.6 knots ebb —⊣ ⊢ 1.8 flood —⊣ ⊢— 3.2 knots ebb —⊣ ⊢ 2.6 knots flood

ts flood ⊢ 2.2 knots ebb —⊣ ⊢ 2.2 knots flood ⊣ ⊢— 2.6 knots ebb —⊣ ⊢ 2.5 kr

TUE APR 4 dawn 5:53 sunrise 6:51 sunset 7:35 dark 8:34
moonset 6:23 a.m. moonrise 6:24 p.m.

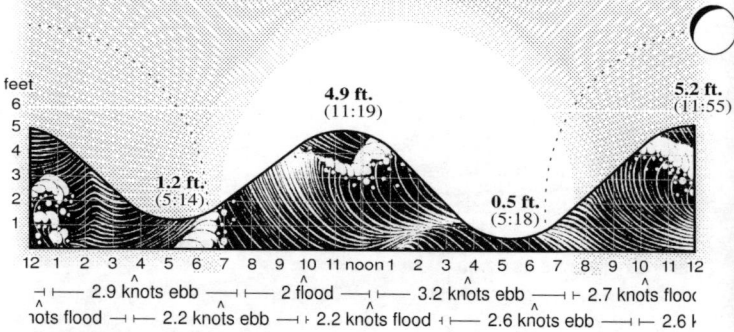

feet

4.9 ft.
(11:19)

5.2 ft.
(11:55)

1.2 ft.
(5:14)

0.5 ft.
(5:18)

12 1 2 3 4 5 6 7 8 9 10 11 noon 1 2 3 4 5 6 7 8 9 10 11 12

⊢ 2.9 knots ebb —⊣ ⊢ 2 flood —⊣ ⊢— 3.2 knots ebb —⊣ ⊢ 2.7 knots flood

ots flood ⊢ 2.2 knots ebb —⊣ ⊢ 2.2 knots flood ⊣ ⊢— 2.6 knots ebb —⊣ ⊢ 2.6 ⊦

WED APR 5 dawn 5:51 sunrise 6:49 sunset 7:36 dark 8:35
moonset 6:45 a.m. moonrise 7:25 p.m.

equator

Full Moon 9:34 p.m.

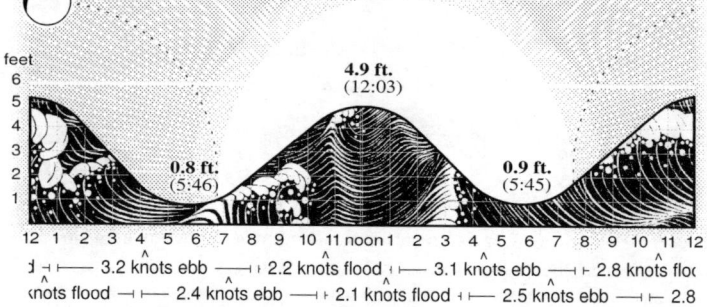

feet

4.9 ft.
(12:03)

0.8 ft.
(5:46)

0.9 ft.
(5:45)

12 1 2 3 4 5 6 7 8 9 10 11 noon 1 2 3 4 5 6 7 8 9 10 11 12

d ⊢— 3.2 knots ebb —⊣ ⊢ 2.2 knots flood ⊣ ⊢— 3.1 knots ebb —⊣ ⊢ 2.8 knots floo

knots flood ⊢— 2.4 knots ebb —⊣ ⊢ 2.1 knots flood ⊣ ⊢— 2.5 knots ebb —⊣ ⊢ 2.8

THU APR 6 dawn 5:50 sunrise 6:48 sunset 7:37 dark 8:36
moonset 7:09 a.m. moonrise 8:29 p.m.

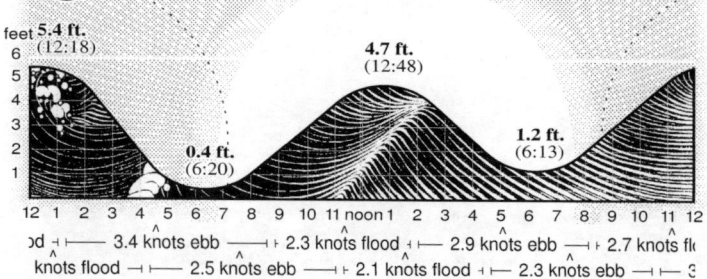

feet 5.4 ft.
(12:18)

4.7 ft.
(12:48)

0.4 ft.
(6:20)

1.2 ft.
(6:13)

12 1 2 3 4 5 6 7 8 9 10 11 noon 1 2 3 4 5 6 7 8 9 10 11 12

od ⊢— 3.4 knots ebb —⊣ ⊢ 2.3 knots flood ⊣ ⊢— 2.9 knots ebb —⊣ ⊢ 2.7 knots fl

knots flood ⊢— 2.5 knots ebb —⊣ ⊢ 2.1 knots flood ⊣ ⊢— 2.3 knots ebb —⊣ ⊢ 3

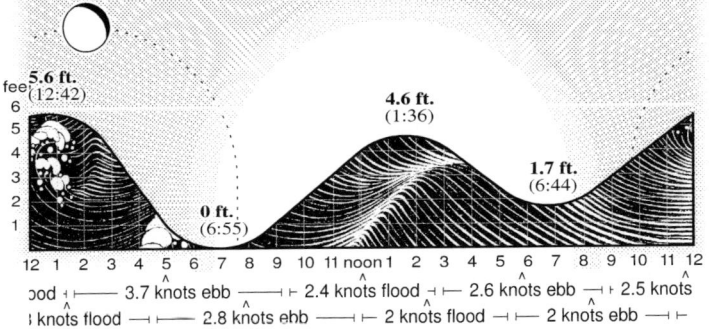

FRI APR 7

dawn 5:48 sunrise 6:46 sunset 7:38 dark 8:37
moonset 7:34 a.m. moonrise 9:36 p.m.

5.6 ft. (12:42)

4.6 ft. (1:36)

1.7 ft. (6:44)

0 ft. (6:55)

feet
6
5
4
3
2
1

12 1 2 3 4 5 6 7 8 9 10 11 noon 1 2 3 4 5 6 7 8 9 10 11 12

ood ⊣ ⊢—— 3.7 knots ebb —— ⊢ 2.4 knots flood ⊣ ⊢ 2.6 knots ebb —⊣ ⊢ 2.5 knots
3 knots flood —⊣ ⊢— 2.8 knots ebb —⊣ ⊢ 2 knots flood ⊣ ⊢ 2 knots ebb —⊣ ⊢

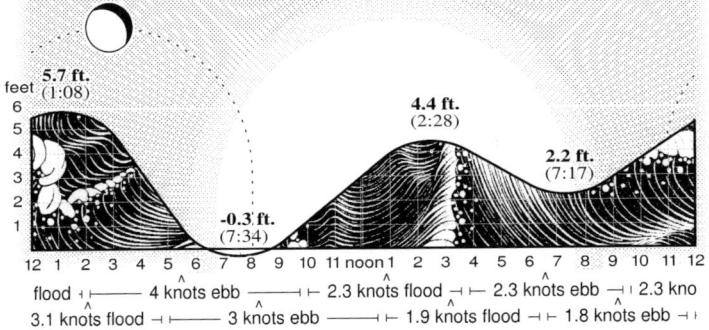

SAT APR 8

dawn 5:47 sunrise 6:45 sunset 7:39 dark 8:38
moonset 8:03 a.m. moonrise 10:45 p.m.

5.7 ft. (1:08)

4.4 ft. (2:28)

2.2 ft. (7:17)

-0.3 ft. (7:34)

feet
6
5
4
3
2
1

12 1 2 3 4 5 6 7 8 9 10 11 noon 1 2 3 4 5 6 7 8 9 10 11 12

flood ⊣ ⊢—— 4 knots ebb —— ⊣ ⊢ 2.3 knots flood ⊣ ⊢ 2.3 knots ebb —⊣ ⊢ 2.3 kno
3.1 knots flood ⊣ ⊢—— 3 knots ebb —— ⊢ 1.9 knots flood ⊢ 1.8 knots ebb ⊣ ⊢

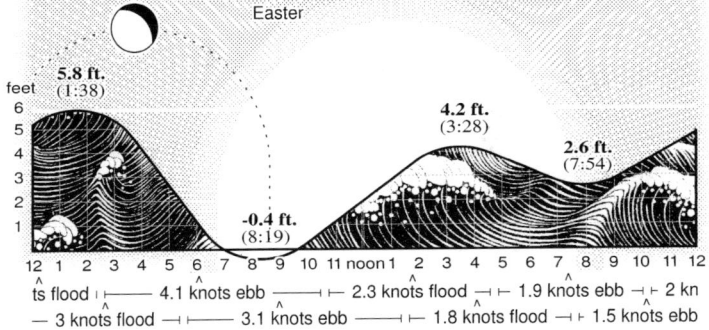

SUN APR 9

dawn 5:45 sunrise 6:43 sunset 7:40 dark 8:39
moonset 8:38 a.m. moonrise 11:55 p.m.

Easter

5.8 ft. (1:38)

4.2 ft. (3:28)

2.6 ft. (7:54)

-0.4 ft. (8:19)

feet
6
5
4
3
2
1

12 1 2 3 4 5 6 7 8 9 10 11 noon 1 2 3 4 5 6 7 8 9 10 11 12

ts flood ⊢—— 4.1 knots ebb —— ⊣ ⊢ 2.3 knots flood ⊣ ⊢ 1.9 knots ebb ⊢ 2 kn
— 3 knots flood ⊣ ⊢—— 3.1 knots ebb —— ⊢ 1.8 knots flood ⊢ 1.5 knots ebb

MON APR 10 dawn 5:43 sunrise 6:42 sunset 7:41 dark 8:40
moonset 9:21 a.m.

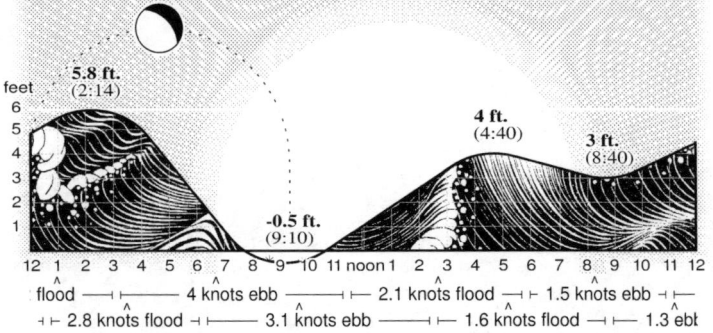

feet

5.8 ft.
(2:14)

4 ft.
(4:40)

3 ft.
(8:40)

-0.5 ft.
(9:10)

12 1 2 3 4 5 6 7 8 9 10 11 noon 1 2 3 4 5 6 7 8 9 10 11 12

flood — 4 knots ebb — 2.1 knots flood — 1.5 knots ebb —
2.8 knots flood — 3.1 knots ebb — 1.6 knots flood — 1.3 ebb

TUE APR 11 dawn 5:42 sunrise 6:41 sunset 7:42 dark 8:41
moonrise 1:04 a.m. moonset 10:13 a.m.

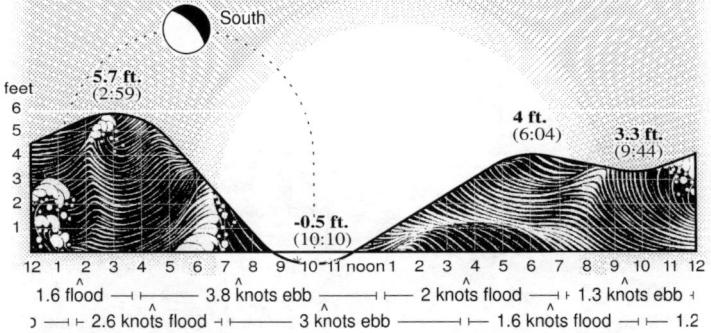

South

feet

5.7 ft.
(2:59)

4 ft.
(6:04)

3.3 ft.
(9:44)

-0.5 ft.
(10:10)

12 1 2 3 4 5 6 7 8 9 10 11 noon 1 2 3 4 5 6 7 8 9 10 11 12

1.6 flood — 3.8 knots ebb — 2 knots flood — 1.3 knots ebb —
2.6 knots flood — 3 knots ebb — 1.6 knots flood — 1.2

WED APR 12 dawn 5:40 sunrise 6:39 sunset 7:43 dark 8:42
moonrise 2:07 a.m. moonset 11:15 a.m.

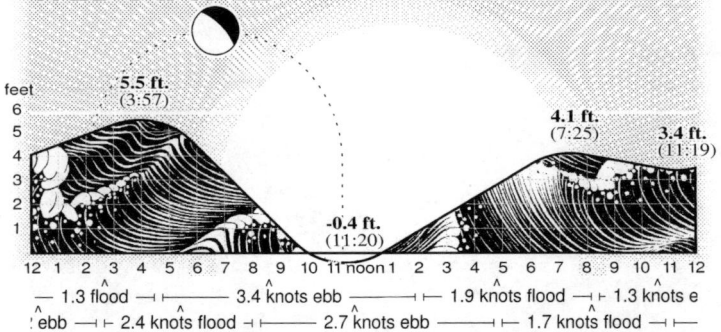

feet

5.5 ft.
(3:57)

4.1 ft.
(7:25)

3.4 ft.
(11:19)

-0.4 ft.
(11:20)

12 1 2 3 4 5 6 7 8 9 10 11 noon 1 2 3 4 5 6 7 8 9 10 11 12

1.3 flood — 3.4 knots ebb — 1.9 knots flood — 1.3 knots e
ebb — 2.4 knots flood — 2.7 knots ebb — 1.7 knots flood —

THU APR 13 dawn 5:39 sunrise 6:38 sunset 7:44 dark 8:43
moonrise 3:02 a.m. moonset 12:25 p.m.

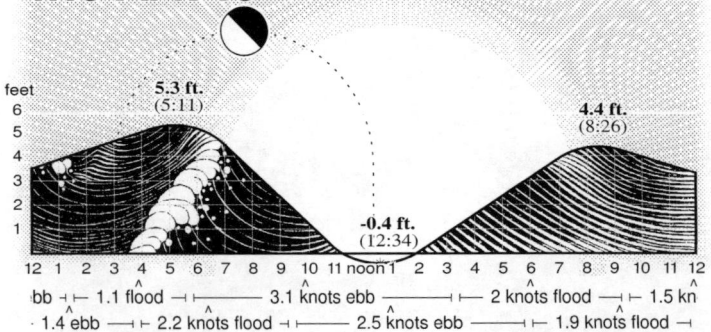

feet

5.3 ft.
(5:11)

4.4 ft.
(8:26)

-0.4 ft.
(12:34)

12 1 2 3 4 5 6 7 8 9 10 11 noon 1 2 3 4 5 6 7 8 9 10 11 12

bb — 1.1 flood — 3.1 knots ebb — 2 knots flood — 1.5 kn
1.4 ebb — 2.2 knots flood — 2.5 knots ebb — 1.9 knots flood —

FRI APR 14 dawn 5:37 sunrise 6:36 sunset 7:45 dark 8:44
moonrise 3:48 a.m. moonset 1:40 p.m.

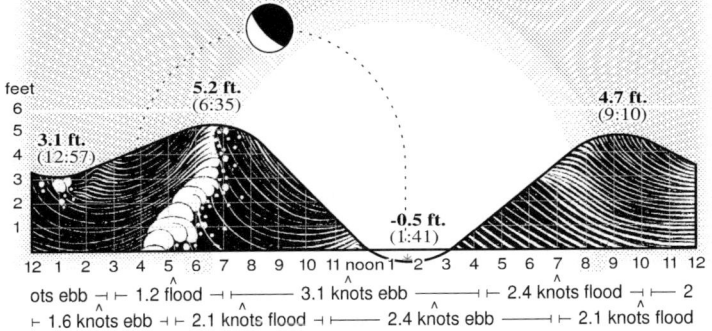

feet

6
5
4
3
2
1

5.2 ft.
(6:35)

4.7 ft.
(9:10)

3.1 ft.
(12:57)

-0.5 ft.
(1:41)

12 1 2 3 4 5 6 7 8 9 10 11 noon 1 2 3 4 5 6 7 8 9 10 11 12

ots ebb ⊣ ⊢ 1.2 flood ⊣ ⊢——— 3.1 knots ebb ——— ⊢ 2.4 knots flood ⊣ ⊢ 2
⊢ 1.6 knots ebb ⊣ ⊢ 2.1 knots flood ⊣ ⊢——— 2.4 knots ebb ——— ⊢ 2.1 knots flood

---

SAT APR 15 dawn 5:35 sunrise 6:35 sunset 7:46 dark 8:45
moonrise 4:26 a.m. moonset 2:54 p.m.

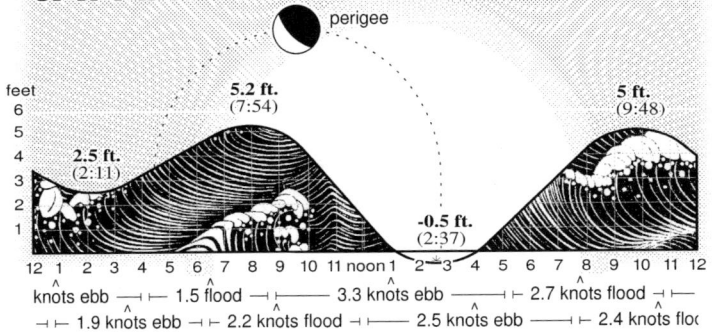

perigee

feet

6
5
4
3
2
1

5.2 ft.
(7:54)

5 ft.
(9:48)

2.5 ft.
(2:11)

-0.5 ft.
(2:37)

12 1 2 3 4 5 6 7 8 9 10 11 noon 1 2 3 4 5 6 7 8 9 10 11 12

knots ebb ——— ⊢ 1.5 flood ⊣ ⊢——— 3.3 knots ebb ——— ⊢ 2.7 knots flood ⊣ ⊢—
⊣ ⊢ 1.9 knots ebb ⊣ ⊢ 2.2 knots flood ⊣ ⊢——— 2.5 knots ebb ——— ⊢ 2.4 knots floo

---

SUN APR 16 dawn 5:34 sunrise 6:33 sunset 7:46 dark 8:46
moonrise 4:58 a.m. moonset 4:08 p.m.

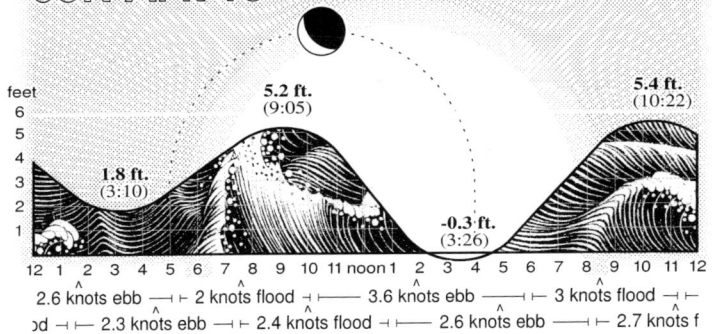

feet

6
5
4
3
2
1

5.2 ft.
(9:05)

5.4 ft.
(10:22)

1.8 ft.
(3:10)

-0.3 ft.
(3:26)

12 1 2 3 4 5 6 7 8 9 10 11 noon 1 2 3 4 5 6 7 8 9 10 11 12

2.6 knots ebb ——— ⊢ 2 knots flood ⊣ ⊢——— 3.6 knots ebb ——— ⊢ 3 knots flood ⊣ ⊢
od ⊣ ⊢ 2.3 knots ebb ——— ⊢ 2.4 knots flood ⊣ ⊢——— 2.6 knots ebb ——— ⊢ 2.7 knots f

MON APR 17
dawn 5:32 sunrise 6:32 sunset 7:47 dark 8:47
moonrise 5:26 a.m. moonset 5:19 p.m.

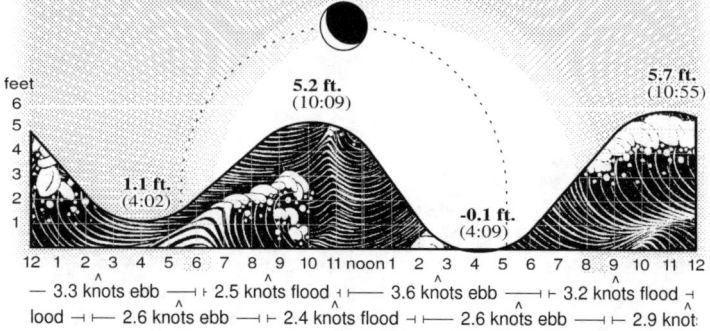

feet

5.2 ft.
(10:09)

5.7 ft.
(10:55)

1.1 ft.
(4:02)

-0.1 ft.
(4:09)

12 1 2 3 4 5 6 7 8 9 10 11 noon 1 2 3 4 5 6 7 8 9 10 11 12

— 3.3 knots ebb —— ⊢ 2.5 knots flood ⊣ ⊢ 3.6 knots ebb —— ⊢ 3.2 knots flood ⊣
flood ⊣ ⊢— 2.6 knots ebb —— ⊢ 2.4 knots flood ⊣ ⊢— 2.6 knots ebb —— ⊢ 2.9 knots

TUE APR 18
dawn 5:31 sunrise 6:31 sunset 7:48 dark 8:48
moonrise 5:53 a.m. moonset 6:29 p.m.

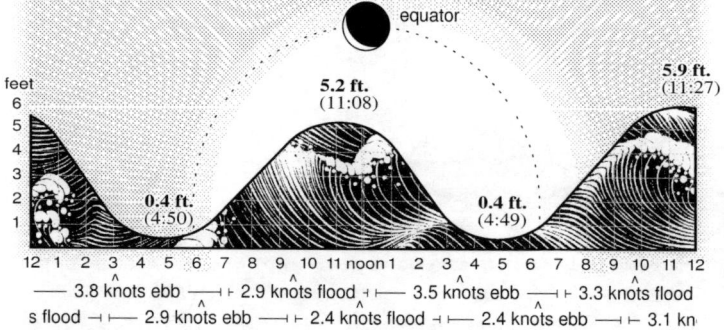

equator

feet

5.2 ft.
(11:08)

5.9 ft.
(11:27)

0.4 ft.
(4:50)

0.4 ft.
(4:49)

12 1 2 3 4 5 6 7 8 9 10 11 noon 1 2 3 4 5 6 7 8 9 10 11 12

— 3.8 knots ebb —— ⊢ 2.9 knots flood ⊣ ⊢ 3.5 knots ebb —— ⊢ 3.3 knots flood
s flood ⊣ ⊢— 2.9 knots ebb —— ⊢ 2.4 knots flood ⊣ ⊢— 2.4 knots ebb —— ⊢ 3.1 kn

WED APR 19
dawn 5:29 sunrise 6:29 sunset 7:49 dark 8:49
moonrise 6:19 a.m. moonset 7:39 p.m.

New Moon 9:12 p.m.

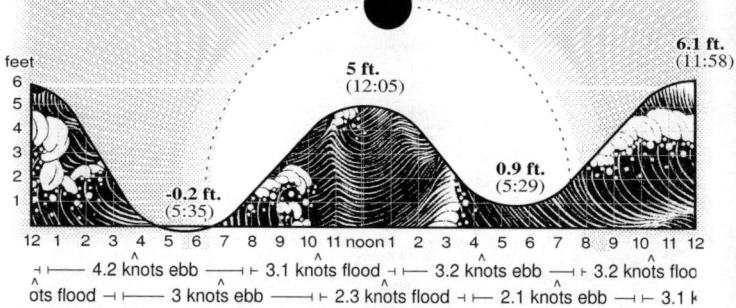

feet

5 ft.
(12:05)

6.1 ft.
(11:58)

-0.2 ft.
(5:35)

0.9 ft.
(5:29)

12 1 2 3 4 5 6 7 8 9 10 11 noon 1 2 3 4 5 6 7 8 9 10 11 12

⊣ ⊢— 4.2 knots ebb —— ⊢ 3.1 knots flood ⊣ ⊢— 3.2 knots ebb —— ⊢ 3.2 knots flood
ots flood ⊣ ⊢— 3 knots ebb —— ⊢ 2.3 knots flood ⊣ ⊢— 2.1 knots ebb —— ⊢ 3.1 k

THU APR 20
dawn 5:28 sunrise 6:28 sunset 7:50 dark 8:51
moonrise 6:47 a.m. moonset 8:49 p.m.

Annular total solar eclipse

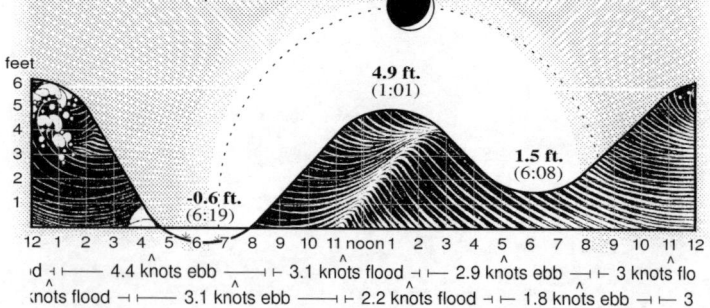

feet

4.9 ft.
(1:01)

1.5 ft.
(6:08)

-0.6 ft.
(6:19)

12 1 2 3 4 5 6 7 8 9 10 11 noon 1 2 3 4 5 6 7 8 9 10 11 12

d ⊣ ⊢— 4.4 knots ebb —— ⊢ 3.1 knots flood ⊣ ⊢— 2.9 knots ebb —— ⊢ 3 knots flo
knots flood ⊣ ⊢— 3.1 knots ebb —— ⊢ 2.2 knots flood ⊣ ⊢— 1.8 knots ebb —— ⊢ 3

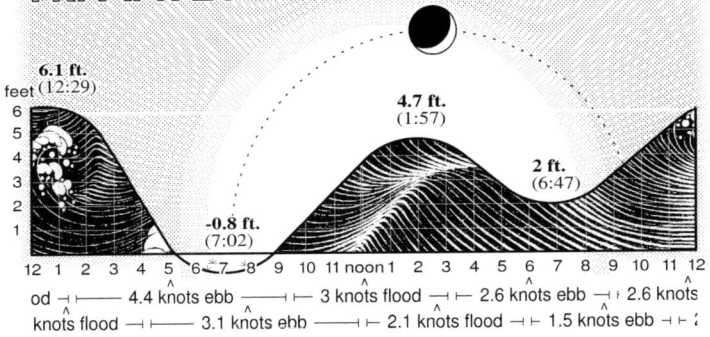

FRI APR 21

dawn 5:26 sunrise 6:27 sunset 7:51 dark 8:52
moonrise 7:17 a.m. moonset 9:58 p.m.

6.1 ft.
feet (12:29)

4.7 ft.
(1:57)

2 ft.
(6:47)

-0.8 ft.
(7:02)

12 1 2 3 4 5 6 7 8 9 10 11 noon 1 2 3 4 5 6 7 8 9 10 11 12

od ⊣ ⊢—— 4.4 knots ebb —— ⊢ 3 knots flood ⊣ ⊢ 2.6 knots ebb ⊣ ⊢ 2.6 knots

knots flood ⊣ ⊢—— 3.1 knots ebb ——⊣ ⊢ 2.1 knots flood ⊣ ⊢ 1.5 knots ebb ⊣ ⊢

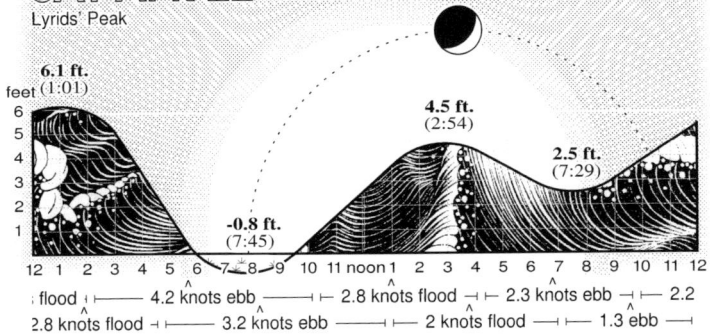

SAT APR 22

dawn 5:25 sunrise 6:25 sunset 7:52 dark 8:53
moonrise 7:51 a.m. moonset 11:05 p.m.

Lyrids' Peak

6.1 ft.
feet (1:01)

4.5 ft.
(2:54)

2.5 ft.
(7:29)

-0.8 ft.
(7:45)

12 1 2 3 4 5 6 7 8 9 10 11 noon 1 2 3 4 5 6 7 8 9 10 11 12

flood ⊣ ⊢—— 4.2 knots ebb —— ⊢ 2.8 knots flood ⊣ ⊢ 2.3 knots ebb ⊣ ⊢ 2.2

2.8 knots flood ⊣ ⊢—— 3.2 knots ebb ——⊣ ⊢ 2 knots flood ⊣ ⊢ 1.3 ebb ——

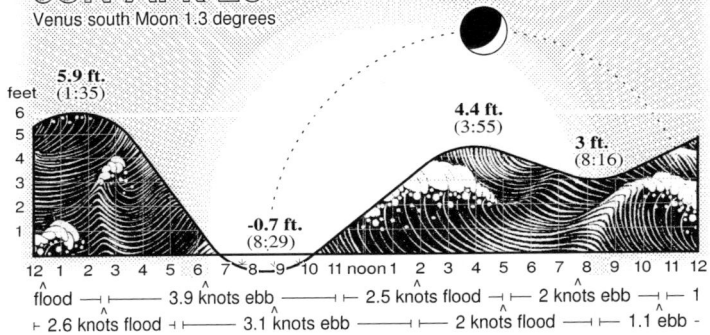

SUN APR 23

dawn 5:23 sunrise 6:24 sunset 7:53 dark 8:54
moonrise 8:32 a.m.

Venus south Moon 1.3 degrees

5.9 ft.
feet (1:35)

4.4 ft.
(3:55)

3 ft.
(8:16)

-0.7 ft.
(8:29)

12 1 2 3 4 5 6 7 8 9 10 11 noon 1 2 3 4 5 6 7 8 9 10 11 12

flood —⊣ ⊢—— 3.9 knots ebb ——⊣ ⊢ 2.5 knots flood ⊣ ⊢ 2 knots ebb ⊣ ⊢ 1

⊢ 2.6 knots flood ⊣ ⊢—— 3.1 knots ebb ——⊣ ⊢ 2 knots flood ⊣ ⊢ 1.1 ebb ⊢

Annular Total Eclipse The April 20th eclipse of the Sun will not be visible from the U.S. mainland. In this eclipse, the Moon will be very close to the Earth so the Earth's shadow will not be large enough to completely cover the Sun. Therefore, some locations will have a total eclipse and others will experience an annular eclipse. **Lyrids Meteor Shower** The Lyrids are active between Apr 16th - 25th with this year's peak on 22nd & 23rd. At peak, the Lyrids have produced 20 meteors per hour, some with bright dusty trails. The first phase moon will set around midnight leaving a dark sky for viewing. Look to the constellation Lyra, the harp, the Lyrids radiant point rising in the eastern horizon by 10:00 p.m.

MON APR 24
dawn 5:22 sunrise 6:23 sunset 7:54 dark 8:55
moonset 12:08 a.m. moonrise 9:18 a.m.

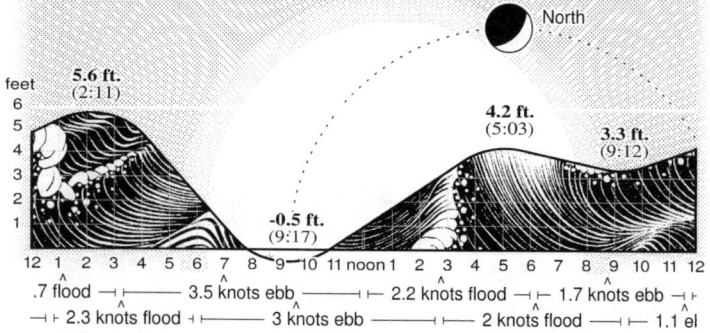

North

feet

5.6 ft.
(2:11)

4.2 ft.
(5:03)

3.3 ft.
(9:12)

-0.5 ft.
(9:17)

12 1 2 3 4 5 6 7 8 9 10 11 noon 1 2 3 4 5 6 7 8 9 10 11 12

.7 flood ⊢⊣ 3.5 knots ebb ⊢⊣ 2.2 knots flood ⊢⊣ 1.7 knots ebb ⊣⊢
⊣⊢ 2.3 knots flood ⊣⊢ 3 knots ebb ⊢⊣ 2 knots flood ⊢⊣ 1.1 el

TUE APR 25
dawn 5:20 sunrise 6:22 sunset 7:55 dark 8:56
moonset 1:04 a.m. moonrise 10:11 a.m.

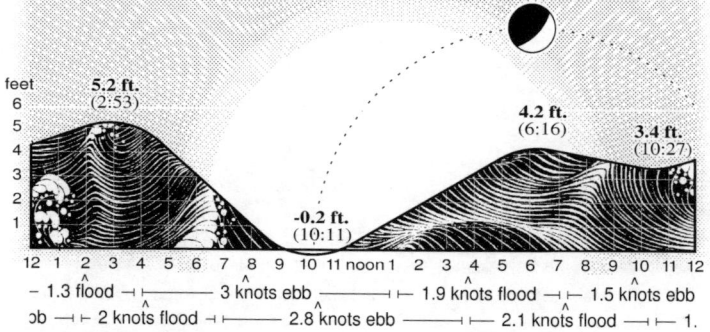

feet

5.2 ft.
(2:53)

4.2 ft.
(6:16)

3.4 ft.
(10:27)

-0.2 ft.
(10:11)

12 1 2 3 4 5 6 7 8 9 10 11 noon 1 2 3 4 5 6 7 8 9 10 11 12

⊢ 1.3 flood ⊣⊢ 3 knots ebb ⊢⊣ 1.9 knots flood ⊢⊣ 1.5 knots ebb
ɔb ⊢⊣ 2 knots flood ⊣⊢ 2.8 knots ebb ⊢⊣ 2.1 knots flood ⊢⊣ 1.

WED APR 26
dawn 5:19 sunrise 6:20 sunset 7:56 dark 8:57
moonset 1:53 a.m. moonrise 11:08 a.m.

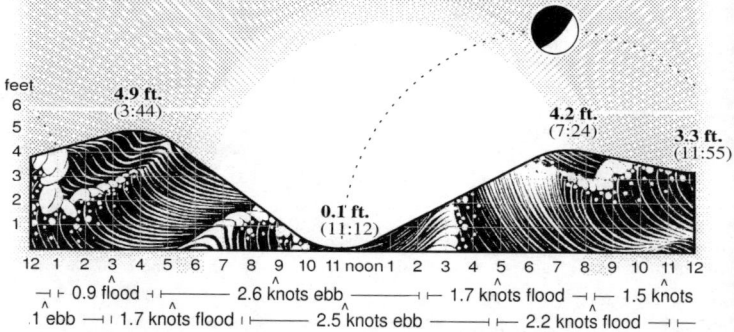

feet

4.9 ft.
(3:44)

4.2 ft.
(7:24)

3.3 ft.
(11:55)

0.1 ft.
(11:12)

12 1 2 3 4 5 6 7 8 9 10 11 noon 1 2 3 4 5 6 7 8 9 10 11 12

⊢⊣ 0.9 flood ⊣⊢ 2.6 knots ebb ⊢⊣ 1.7 knots flood ⊢⊣ 1.5 knots
.1 ebb ⊢⊣ 1.7 knots flood ⊢ 2.5 knots ebb ⊢⊣ 2.2 knots flood ⊢⊣

THU APR 27
dawn 5:17 sunrise 6:19 sunset 7:57 dark 8:58
moonset 2:33 a.m. moonrise 12:08 p.m.

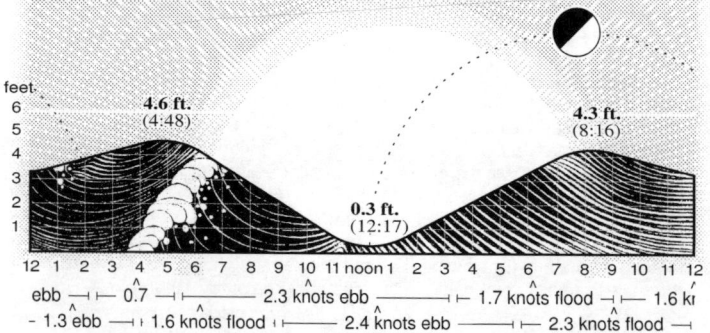

feet

4.6 ft.
(4:48)

4.3 ft.
(8:16)

0.3 ft.
(12:17)

12 1 2 3 4 5 6 7 8 9 10 11 noon 1 2 3 4 5 6 7 8 9 10 11 12

ebb ⊢⊣ 0.7 ⊣⊢ 2.3 knots ebb ⊢⊣ 1.7 knots flood ⊢⊣ 1.6 kr
⊢ 1.3 ebb ⊢⊣ 1.6 knots flood ⊢ 2.4 knots ebb ⊢⊣ 2.3 knots flood ⊣

FRI APR 28
dawn 5:16 sunrise 6:18 sunset 7:58 dark 9:00
moonset 3:07 a.m. moonrise 1:09 p.m.

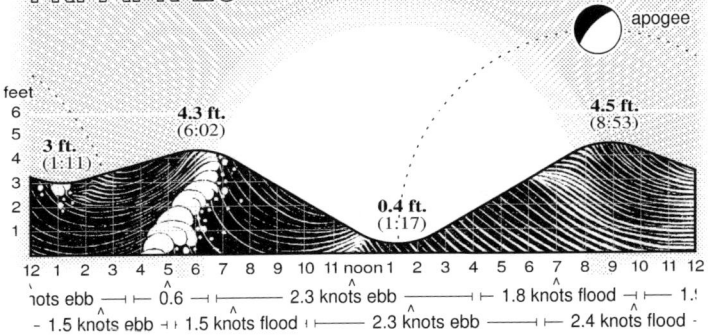

apogee

feet
6
5
4
3
2
1

3 ft.
(1:11)

4.3 ft.
(6:02)

4.5 ft.
(8:53)

0.4 ft.
(1:17)

12 1 2 3 4 5 6 7 8 9 10 11 noon 1 2 3 4 5 6 7 8 9 10 11 12

nots ebb ⊢— 0.6 —⊣ ⊢— 2.3 knots ebb ———⊣ ⊢— 1.8 knots flood —⊣ ⊢— 1.!
— 1.5 knots ebb —⊣⊢ 1.5 knots flood ⊢—— 2.3 knots ebb ——⊣ ⊢— 2.4 knots flood

SAT APR 29
dawn 5:15 sunrise 6:17 sunset 7:58 dark 9:01
moonset 3:37 a.m. moonrise 2:10 p.m.

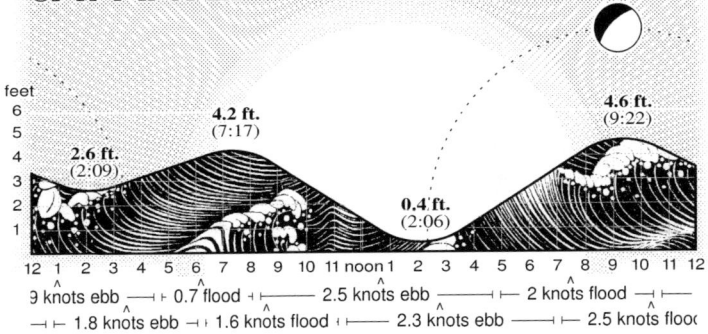

feet
6
5
4
3
2
1

2.6 ft.
(2:09)

4.2 ft.
(7:17)

4.6 ft.
(9:22)

0.4 ft.
(2:06)

12 1 2 3 4 5 6 7 8 9 10 11 noon 1 2 3 4 5 6 7 8 9 10 11 12

9 knots ebb ———⊢ 0.7 flood ⊣ ⊢—— 2.5 knots ebb ——⊣ ⊢— 2 knots flood —⊣ ⊢—
—⊣ ⊢ 1.8 knots ebb —⊣⊢ 1.6 knots flood ⊢—— 2.3 knots ebb ——⊣ ⊢— 2.5 knots flood

SUN APR 30
dawn 5:13 sunrise 6:15 sunset 7:59 dark 9:02
moonset 4:02 a.m. moonrise 3:10 p.m.

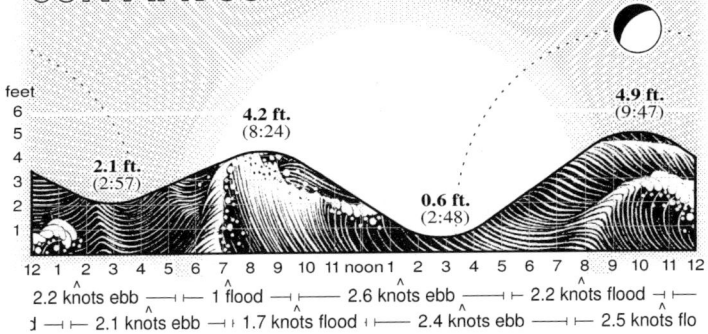

feet
6
5
4
3
2
1

2.1 ft.
(2:57)

4.2 ft.
(8:24)

4.9 ft.
(9:47)

0.6 ft.
(2:48)

12 1 2 3 4 5 6 7 8 9 10 11 noon 1 2 3 4 5 6 7 8 9 10 11 12

2.2 knots ebb ——⊣ ⊢— 1 flood —⊣ ⊢—— 2.6 knots ebb ——⊣ ⊢— 2.2 knots flood —⊣ ⊢—
d —⊣ ⊢— 2.1 knots ebb —⊣⊢ 1.7 knots flood ⊢—— 2.4 knots ebb ——⊣ ⊢— 2.5 knots flo

Ø   J   V   M

MON MAY 1
dawn 5:12 sunrise 6:14 sunset 8:00 dark 9:03
moonset 4:25 a.m. moonrise 4:10 p.m.

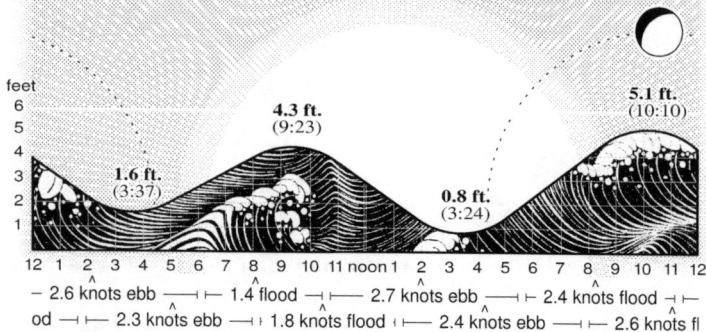

feet

4.3 ft.
(9:23)

5.1 ft.
(10:10)

1.6 ft.
(3:37)

0.8 ft.
(3:24)

12 1 2 3 4 5 6 7 8 9 10 11 noon 1 2 3 4 5 6 7 8 9 10 11 12

— 2.6 knots ebb —⊢ 1.4 flood —⊣⊢ 2.7 knots ebb —⊢ 2.4 knots flood ⊣⊢
od —⊢ 2.3 knots ebb —⊢ 1.8 knots flood ⊢ 2.4 knots ebb —⊢ 2.6 knots fl

TUE MAY 2
dawn 5:10 sunrise 6:13 sunset 8:01 dark 9:04
moonset 4:48 a.m. moonrise 5:11 p.m.

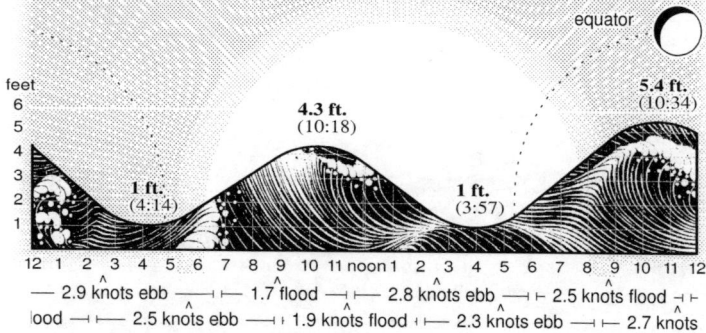

equator

feet

4.3 ft.
(10:18)

5.4 ft.
(10:34)

1 ft.
(4:14)

1 ft.
(3:57)

12 1 2 3 4 5 6 7 8 9 10 11 noon 1 2 3 4 5 6 7 8 9 10 11 12

— 2.9 knots ebb —⊢ 1.7 flood —⊣⊢ 2.8 knots ebb —⊢ 2.5 knots flood ⊣⊢
lood —⊢ 2.5 knots ebb —⊢ 1.9 knots flood ⊢ 2.3 knots ebb —⊢ 2.7 knots

WED MAY 3
dawn 5:09 sunrise 6:12 sunset 8:02 dark 9:05
moonset 5:11 a.m. moonrise 6:15 p.m.

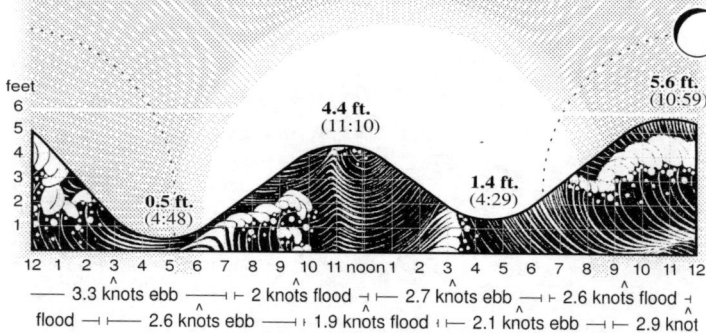

feet

4.4 ft.
(11:10)

5.6 ft.
(10:59)

0.5 ft.
(4:48)

1.4 ft.
(4:29)

12 1 2 3 4 5 6 7 8 9 10 11 noon 1 2 3 4 5 6 7 8 9 10 11 12

— 3.3 knots ebb —⊢ 2 knots flood ⊣⊢ 2.7 knots ebb —⊢ 2.6 knots flood ⊣
flood —⊢ 2.6 knots ebb —⊢ 1.9 knots flood ⊢ 2.1 knots ebb —⊢ 2.9 knot

THU MAY 4
dawn 5:08 sunrise 6:11 sunset 8:03 dark 9:06
moonset 5:36 a.m. moonrise 7:21 p.m.

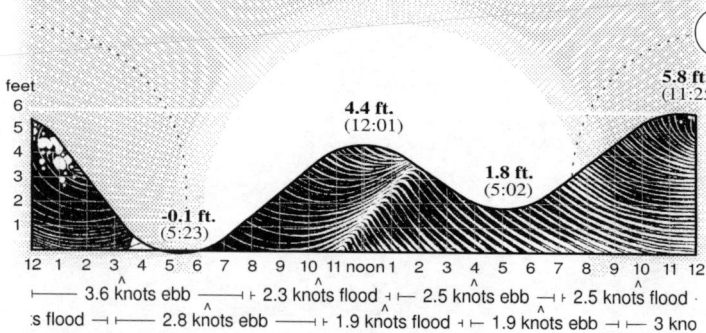

feet

4.4 ft.
(12:01)

5.8 ft.
(11:25)

-0.1 ft.
(5:23)

1.8 ft.
(5:02)

12 1 2 3 4 5 6 7 8 9 10 11 noon 1 2 3 4 5 6 7 8 9 10 11 12

⊢— 3.6 knots ebb —⊢ 2.3 knots flood ⊣⊢ 2.5 knots ebb —⊢ 2.5 knots flood ·
s flood —⊢ 2.8 knots ebb —⊢ 1.9 knots flood ⊣⊢ 1.9 knots ebb —⊢ 3 kno

FRI MAY 5

dawn 5:07 sunrise 6:10 sunset 8:04 dark 9:07
moonset 6:04 a.m. moonrise 8:30 p.m.

Full Moon 10:34 a.m.   Penumbral lunar eclipse

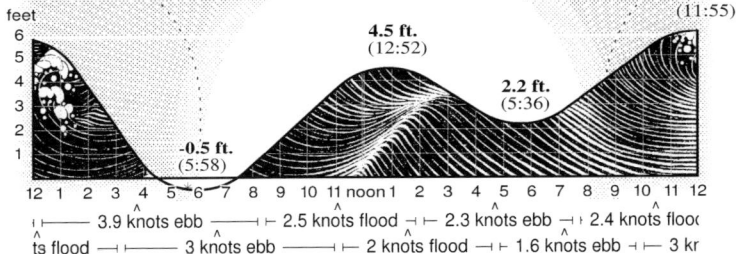

6 ft.
(11:55)

feet

4.5 ft.
(12:52)

2.2 ft.
(5:36)

-0.5 ft.
(5:58)

12 1 2 3 4 5 6 7 8 9 10 11 noon 1 2 3 4 5 6 7 8 9 10 11 12

⊢— 3.9 knots ebb ——⊣ ⊢ 2.5 knots flood ⊣ ⊢ 2.3 knots ebb ⊣ 2.4 knots flood
ts flood ⊣ ⊢— 3 knots ebb ———⊣ ⊢ 2 knots flood ⊣ ⊢ 1.6 knots ebb ⊣ ⊢ 3 kr

SAT MAY 6

dawn 5:05 sunrise 6:09 sunset 8:05 dark 9:09
moonset 6:37 a.m. moonrise 9:42 p.m.

Eta Aquarids' Peak

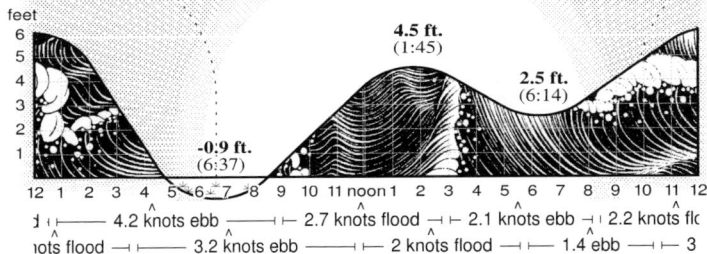

feet

4.5 ft.
(1:45)

2.5 ft.
(6:14)

-0.9 ft.
(6:37)

12 1 2 3 4 5 6 7 8 9 10 11 noon 1 2 3 4 5 6 7 8 9 10 11 12

d ⊢— 4.2 knots ebb ——⊣ ⊢ 2.7 knots flood ⊣ ⊢ 2.1 knots ebb ⊣ 2.2 knots flc
iots flood ⊣ ⊢— 3.2 knots ebb ——⊣ ⊢ 2 knots flood ⊣ ⊢ 1.4 ebb ⊣ ⊢ 3

SUN MAY 7

dawn 5:04 sunrise 6:08 sunset 8:06 dark 9:10
moonset 7:17 a.m. moonrise 10:53 p.m.

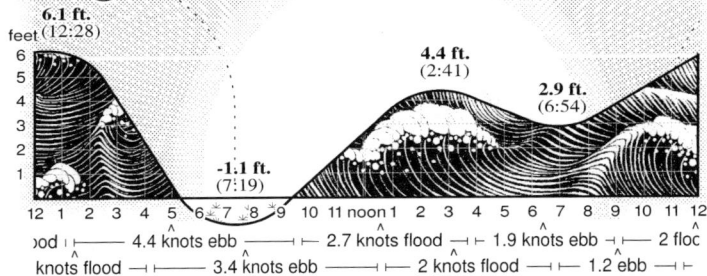

6.1 ft.
(12:28)

feet

4.4 ft.
(2:41)

2.9 ft.
(6:54)

-1.1 ft.
(7:19)

12 1 2 3 4 5 6 7 8 9 10 11 noon 1 2 3 4 5 6 7 8 9 10 11 12

od ⊢— 4.4 knots ebb ——⊣ ⊢ 2.7 knots flood ⊣ ⊢ 1.9 knots ebb ⊣ ⊢ 2 floc
knots flood ⊣ ⊢— 3.4 knots ebb ——⊣ ⊢ 2 knots flood ⊣ ⊢ 1.2 ebb ⊣ ⊢

Penumbral eclipse of the Moon The May 5th eclipse will not be visible from the U.S. mainland as its path takes it over Asia, Australia, parts of eastern Europe and Africa. During a penumbral eclipse, the Moon passes through the Earth's shadow, the penumbra, the Moon will partially darken but not completely. **Eta Aquarids Meteor Shower** the Eta Aquarids are active annually between Apr 19th to May 28th with this year's peak on May 6th & 7th. This shower is remnants of Comet Halley. This year's peak will be challenged by the just past full Moon. The shower's radiant point, the constellation Aquarius, will rise in the eastern horizon by 1:00 a.m. Despite the bright Moon the shower's peak production of 30 meteors per hours might make a respectable showing this year.

MON MAY 8
dawn 5:03 sunrise 6:07 sunset 8:07 dark 9:11
moonset 8:07 a.m. moonrise 12:00 midnight

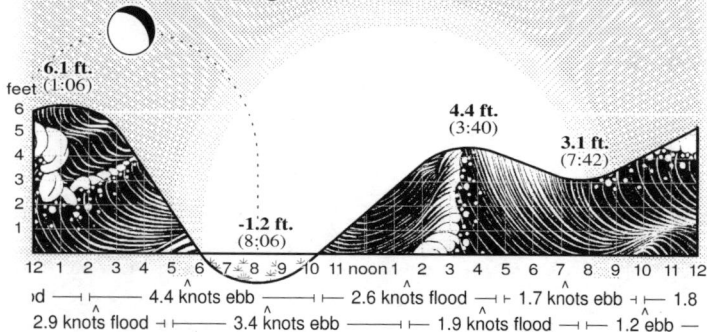

6.1 ft.
(1:06)

feet

4.4 ft.
(3:40)

3.1 ft.
(7:42)

-1.2 ft.
(8:06)

12 1 2 3 4 5 6 7 8 9 10 11 noon 1 2 3 4 5 6 7 8 9 10 11 12

ood ⊢— 4.4 knots ebb ——⊣⊢ 2.6 knots flood —⊢ 1.7 knots ebb ⊣⊢ 1.8

2.9 knots flood ⊣⊢— 3.4 knots ebb ——⊢ 1.9 knots flood —⊣⊢ 1.2 ebb —

TUE MAY 9
dawn 5:01 sunrise 6:06 sunset 8:08 dark 9:12
moonset 9:07 a.m.

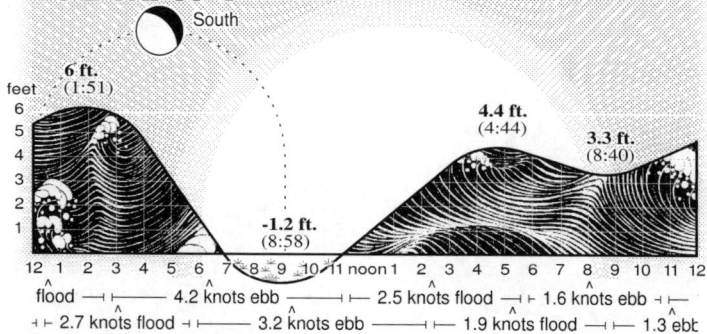

South

6 ft.
(1:51)

feet

4.4 ft.
(4:44)

3.3 ft.
(8:40)

-1.2 ft.
(8:58)

12 1 2 3 4 5 6 7 8 9 10 11 noon 1 2 3 4 5 6 7 8 9 10 11 12

flood —⊣⊢— 4.2 knots ebb ——⊢ 2.5 knots flood —⊢ 1.6 knots ebb ⊣⊢

⊣⊢ 2.7 knots flood ⊣⊢— 3.2 knots ebb ——⊢ 1.9 knots flood —⊣⊢ 1.3 ebb

WED MAY 10
dawn 5:00 sunrise 6:05 sunset 8:08 dark 9:13
moonrise 12:59 a.m. moonset 10:16 a.m.

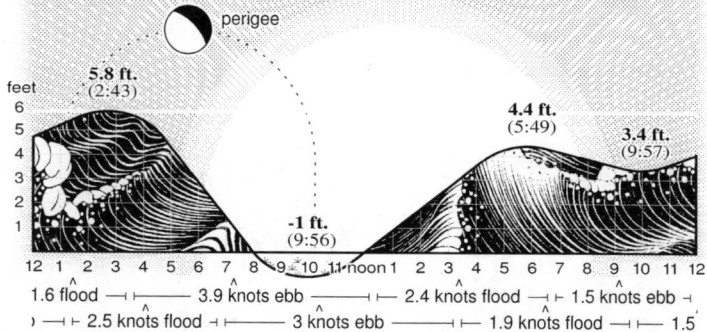

perigee

5.8 ft.
(2:43)

feet

4.4 ft.
(5:49)

3.4 ft.
(9:57)

-1 ft.
(9:56)

12 1 2 3 4 5 6 7 8 9 10 11 noon 1 2 3 4 5 6 7 8 9 10 11 12

1.6 flood —⊣⊢— 3.9 knots ebb ——⊢ 2.4 knots flood —⊢ 1.5 knots ebb ⊣

⊢ —⊢ 2.5 knots flood ⊣⊢— 3 knots ebb ——⊣⊢ 1.9 knots flood —⊣⊢ 1.5

THU MAY 11
dawn 4:59 sunrise 6:04 sunset 8:09 dark 9:14
moonrise 1:48 a.m. moonset 11:30 a.m.

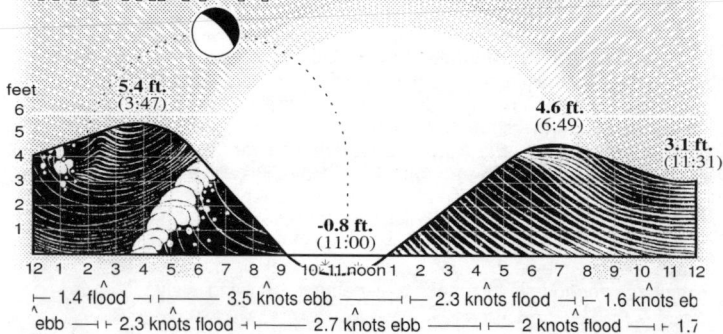

5.4 ft.
(3:47)

feet

4.6 ft.
(6:49)

3.1 ft.
(11:31)

-0.8 ft.
(11:00)

12 1 2 3 4 5 6 7 8 9 10 11 noon 1 2 3 4 5 6 7 8 9 10 11 12

⊢ 1.4 flood —⊣⊢— 3.5 knots ebb ——⊢ 2.3 knots flood —⊣⊢ 1.6 knots eb

ebb —⊢ 2.3 knots flood ⊣⊢— 2.7 knots ebb ——⊢ 2 knots flood —⊣⊢ 1.7

"Second Day of Creation"
~ M.C. Escher
Woodcut

Pacific Publishers, LLC
P.O. Box 2813
Tybee Island, GA 31328
(912) 472-4373
www.tidelog.com

TIDAL FACTORS

Earth's tides are primarily produced by the gravitational forces of the moon and sun. Even though the moon is millions of times smaller than the sun, its proximity to the Earth gives it a tidal influence more than twice that of the sun's.   Although the moon's gravitational pull is only one-ten millionith of the Earth's, when it is combined with the centrifugal force produced as the Earth spins on its axis, tractive force is created. Tractive force is responsible for creating a tidal bulge on the side of the Earth facing away from the moon twice a day, resulting in two high and low tides per day for most locations.

Twice a month, when the moon is full and when it is new, the moon, sun, and Earth are aligned. The resulting spring tides often have a greater range, with higher highs and lower lows than ordinarily. Conversely, when the moon is in quarter phase, the moon and sun's gravitational forces tend to counteract each other resulting neap tides, which are in turn much weaker.

Since the moon's orbit around the Earth is elliptical, its distance varies by about 11% during a month. At perigee, the moon is closest and its tidal influence is increased.   The opposite is true at apogee, the farthest point of its monthly orbit. The sun's influence is increased in January when the Earth is at perihelion and decreased in July when the Earth is at aphelion.   When a new or full moon coincides with perigee (augmented in winter by perihelion), the result is dramatically increased tidal ranges, called perigean spring tides.

The moon's declination also affects the tides.   Since its orbit is inclined relative to the earth's equator, the moon appears to cross over the equator twice a month, reaching maximum North declination and maximum South declination about two weeks apart. Either point of maximum declination tends to encourage inequality between day's two high (or low) tides. Note the difference in Tidelog's tide curves when the moon is at maximum declination compared with those when the moon is over the equator. (This effect is more pronounced on the Pacific coast than on the Atlantic.)

Planetary tidal influence is mostly negligible. Since a planet's tidal attraction varies directly with mass and inversely with distance squared, the planet having the greatest influence on Earth's tides (Venus, the closest) exerts a force only a few thousandths of one percent of that of the moon.   Tidelog's indications of planetary positions are intended as a guide to observation, not as a clue to tidal behavior.

Some geologists theorize that the same forces which cause the highest tides may also trigger earthquakes, with most major quakes occurring near times when a new or full moon closely coincides with perigee. In earthquake prone coastal areas, some suggest this theory has some basis, while others claim the relationship is hit or miss. Those who like to see for themselves will be able to identify several such periods in the year to come and form their own conclusions.

Imprinting is available should you wish to personalize your Tidelog. We can imprint one line of up to 22 characters (including spaces) on the cover. Imprinting is $10.00 per copy, per year (for subscriptions).

Please print clearly to ensure accurate imprinting.

#1:																						
#2:																						
#3:																						
#4:																						
#5:																						

Add up the total of your imprinting and include it on the reverse when totaling your order.

$10.00 per copy

QUANTITY ( )   AMOUNT ($)

Tidelogs make great gifts! We can design custom dies should you wish to imprint Tidelogs with your company logo or a phrase. Please call or email us for details and quantity pricing information.

Ground shipping is by USPS "Media Mail" (Special 4th Class). On average, media mail packages are received in 7 to 10 business days.

Air shipping is by USPS Priority or First Class Mail. It's more consistent than ground shipping, and is most advantageous to the West Coast, where it often cuts shipping time down to 3 or 4 days.

Order value:	$10 - $25	$26 - $40	$51 - $80	$81+
Ground	$5.00	$8.00	$11.00	$14.00
Air	10.00	$13.00	$16.00	$19.00

In a real hurry? Our Premium Shipping option is by FedEx or UPS Overnight, which starts at $41 but is not always "overnight" from our location. 2nd Day Air, at $20 to $26, is usually a better deal. Mark your choice on the order blank, or tell our order person.

Order value:	$10 - $25	$26 - $40	$51 - $80	$81+
2nd Day Air	$20.00	$22.00	$24.00	$26.00
Overnight	$41.00	$45.00	$49.00	$53.00

We consider your name, address, e-mail address and telephone number to be confidential. Your phone number is only used if there's a problem with your order. All that's mailed to your address is a reminder if we haven't received your renewal by a certain date. None of your information is ever shared with any third party.

We also safeguard your credit card information. Your card number is available only to our order personnel, whether your order is placed by phone, mail, fax or left on our voicemail. After processing, the number is not retained in our computer database.

WWW.TIDELOG.COM

TIDELOG ORDER FORM

East Coast Editions: *please specify below*

- [ ] **Eastport & Bar Harbor**
- [ ] **Northern New England**
- [ ] **Nantucket & Martha's Vineyard**
- [ ] **Southern New England**
- [ ] **Long Island Sound**
- [ ] **New York/New Jersey**
- [ ] **MidAtlantic**
- [ ] **Delaware Bay**
- [ ] **Chesapeake Tidewater**
- [ ] **Outer Banks**
- [ ] **Myrtle Beach & Wilmington**
- [ ] **Southeastern**
- [ ] **Savannah & Tybee Island**
- [ ] **Florida Atlantic**

		QUANTITY	AMOUNT
Tidelogs: $17.95* *Quantity discounts: 5 to 9 copies, subtract $2 each; 10 to 19 copies, subtract $3 each; 20 to 29 copies, subtract $4 each. Please call for quotes on larger quantities.*			$
2 Year Subscription:	$32.00*		$
3 Year Subscription:	$43.00*		$

START MY SUBSCRIPTION WITH THE 20___ TIDELOG.

		QUANTITY	AMOUNT
Angler's Log:	$14.00*		$
Captain's Log:	$14.00*		$
Lined Journal:	$12.00*		$
Blank Journal:	$10.00*		$

Lined & Blank Journals, please specify:
- [ ] Seahorse
- [ ] Shell Trio
- [ ] Starfish
- [ ] Compass
- [ ] Scatter
- [ ] Kayak
- [ ] Reindeer
- [ ] Fish on Line
- [ ] Turtles
- [ ] Sailboats
- [ ] Dolphin
- [ ] Octopus

⋆ *Plus Shipping, Please See Below* ⋆

Shipping:

Order value	$10 - $25	$26 - $40	$51 - $80	$81+	
Ground	$5.00	$8.00	$11.00	$14.00	$
Air	$10.00	$13.00	$16.00	$19.00	

GEORGIA Sales Tax: *GA residents only*, add 7% tax — $

- [ ] My check, payable to **Pacific Publishers**, is enclosed
- [ ] Charge my credit card

Total: $

NAME _____

ADDRESS _____

CITY, STATE, ZIP _____

EMAIL _____

CARD # _____

EXP DATE _____   CVC _____

Mail To: **Pacific Publishers LLC, P.O. Box 2813, Tybee Island, GA 31328**
Phone Orders: (912) 472-4373   *Fax:* (912) 786-7921
Order Online: www.tidelog.com

TIDELOG EAST COAST REGIONS COVERED

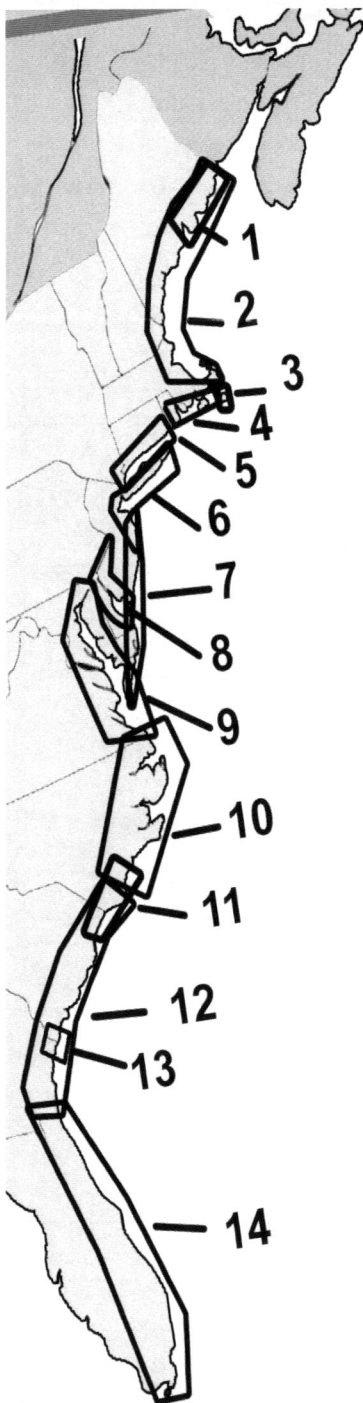

1. **EASTPORT & BAR HARBOR:** including Eastport south to Bar Harbor

2. **NORTHERN NEW ENGLAND:** including the coasts of ME, NH and MA

3. **NANTUCKET & MARTHA'S VINEYARD**

4. **SOUTHERN NEW ENGLAND:** including Rhode Island's Narragansett Bay, Buzzards Bay, Block Island Sound and Long Island's Peconic Bay

5. **LONG ISLAND SOUND:** including the north shore of Long Island from Willets Point to Orient, NY; the NY/CT shore from Throgs Neck to Old Saybrook

6. **NEW YORK/NEW JERSEY:** including New York Harbor

7. **MIDATLANTIC:** including coastal New Jersey, Delaware and Maryland

8. **DELAWARE BAY:** including Delaware Bay and River

9. **CHESAPEAKE TIDEWATER:** including Chesapeake Bay, Baltimore, Washington, DC and the Tidewater area of Virginia and south to Virginia Beach

10. **OUTER BANKS:** including the entire coast of North Carolina, including Cape Hatteras and south to Myrtle Beach, SC

11. **MYRTLE BEACH & WILMINGTON:** including Myrtle Beach and north to Wilmington

12. **SOUTHEASTERN:** including the entire coasts of South Carolina and Georgia

13. **SAVANNAH & TYBEE ISLAND**

14. **FLORIDA ATLANTIC:** including the entire Atlantic Coast of Florida, Miami and the Keys

TIDELOG ORDER FORM

West Coast Editions: *please specify below*

- [ ] **PUGET SOUND**
- [ ] **Pacific Northwest**
- [ ] **Coast of Northern CA**
- [ ] **Suisun Bay & Delta**

- [ ] **NORTHERN CALIFORNIA**
- [ ] **Monterey Bay**
- [ ] **Morro Bay**
- [ ] **SOUTHERN CALIFORNIA**
- [ ] **Gulf of Alaska**

		QUANTITY	AMOUNT
Tidelogs: $17.95* *Quantity discounts: 5 to 9 copies, subtract $2 each; 10 to 19 copies, subtract $3 each; 20 to 29 copies, subtract $4 each. Please call for quotes on larger quantities.*		( )	($)
2 Year Subscription: $32.00*		( )	($)
3 Year Subscription: $43.00*		( )	($)

START MY SUBSCRIPTION WITH THE 20___ TIDELOG.

		QUANTITY	AMOUNT
Angler's Log:	$14.00*	( )	($)
Captain's Log:	$14.00*	( )	($)
Lined Journal:	$12.00*	( )	($)
Blank Journal:	$10.00*	( )	($)

Lined & Blank Journals, please specify:
- [ ] Seahorse
- [ ] Shell Trio
- [ ] Starfish
- [ ] Compass
- [ ] Scatter
- [ ] Kayak
- [ ] Reindeer
- [ ] Fish on Line
- [ ] Turtles
- [ ] Sailboats
- [ ] Dolphin
- [ ] Octopus

⋆ *Plus Shipping, Please See Below* ⋆

Shipping:

Order value	$10 - $25	$26 - $40	$51 - $80	$81+	
Ground	$5.00	$8.00	$11.00	$14.00	($)
Air	$10.00	$13.00	$16.00	$19.00	

GEORGIA Sales Tax: *GA residents only*, add 7% tax ($)

- [ ] My check, payable to **Pacific Publishers**, is enclosed
- [ ] Charge my credit card

Total: ($)

NAME _____

ADDRESS _____

CITY, STATE, ZIP _____

EMAIL _____

CARD # _____

EXP DATE _____   CVC _____

Mail To: **Pacific Publishers LLC, P.O. Box 2813, Tybee Island, GA 31328**
Phone Orders: (912) 472-4373   *Fax:* (912) 786-7921
Order Online: www.tidelog.com

TIDELOG WEST COAST REGIONS COVERED

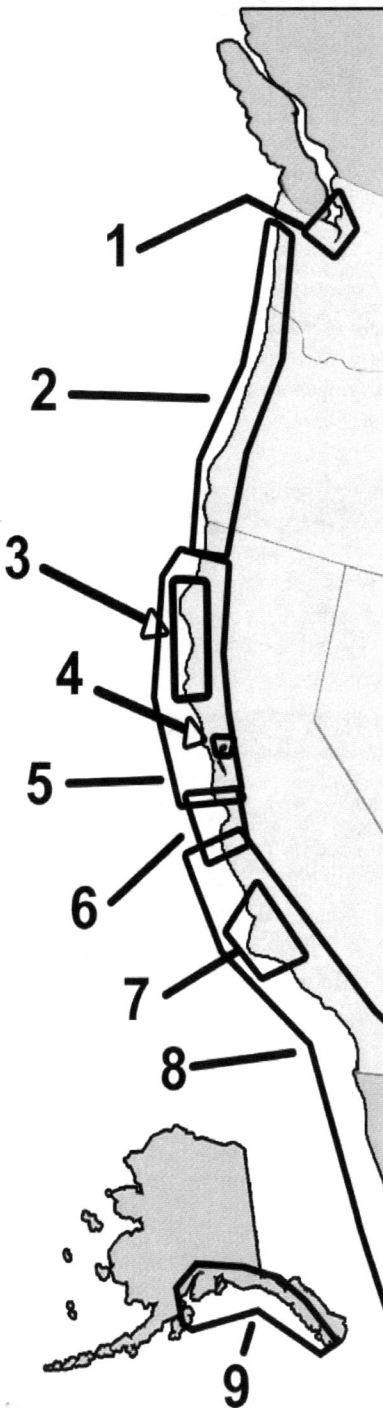

1. **PUGET SOUND:** including Seattle, Port Townsend, south to Tacoma and Olympia, and north to the San Juan Islands

2. **PACIFIC NORTHWEST:** including the Pacific Coast of Washington and Oregon, and south to Humboldt Bay, CA

3. **COAST OF NC:** including Arena Cove north to Humboldt Bay

4. **SUISUN BAY & DELTA:** including Suisun Bay and surrounding areas

5. **NORTHERN CALIFORNIA (SF BAY):** including San Francisco Bay and Delta, south to Monterey Bay and north to Shelter Cove

6. **MONTEREY BAY:** including Monterey Bay and Carmel

7. **MORRO BAY:** for the coast of Southern California near Morro Bay

8. **SOUTHERN CALIFORNIA:** including Los Angeles, San Diego, and the Gulf of California

9. **GULF OF ALASKA:** including tides for Ketchikan and Sika with Wrangell Narrows currents

SLACK WATER TIME DIFFERENCES FOR PLACES ALONG SAN FRANCISCO PIERS

Station or Locality	Latitude N	Longitude W	Beginning of Flood h. m.	Beginning of Ebb h. m.
		on San Francisco Bay Entrance		
St. Francis Yacht Club breakwater	37° 48.5'	122° 26.5'	-0 10	-1 50
Aquatic Park, 0.2 mile W of	37° 48.6'	122° 24.7'	-0 35	-2 05
Pier 37	37° 48.6'	122° 24.5'	-1 35	-2 20
Pier 29	37° 48.4'	122° 24.0'	-1 10	-2 20
Pier 7	37° 48.0'	122° 23.6'	-0 55	-2 05
Pier 14	37° 47.7'	122° 23.3'	-0 55	-3 00
Pier 26	37° 47.4'	122° 23.0'	-1 40	-1 50
Pier 38	37° 47.0'	122° 23.0'	-0 25	-2 25
Pier 50	37° 46.4'	122° 22.8'	-1 40	-2 20
Bethlehem Pier No. 8	37° 45.6'	122° 22.7'	-1 20	-1 55
Pier 90, 0.5 mile SE of	37° 44.5'	122° 22.4'	-1 50	-2 05
Point Avisadero	37° 43.7'	122° 21.3'	-1 25	-0 40
Point Avisadero, 0.8 mile S of	37° 43.0'	122° 21.5'	-1 30	-3 25

ROTARY TIDAL CURRENTS TABLE

HOURLY TIME INCREMENTS

STATION NAME	DEPTH	0	1	2	3	4	5	6	7	8	9	10	11	
						After Maximum Flood at San Francisco Bay								
Column Point, W of Cross Sound	74.4	0.42	0.23	0.32	0.52	0.56	0.47	0.34	0.19	0.33	0.42	0.51	0.59	knots
		91	132	187	204	208	215	232	292	353	28	62	80	degrees
Richardson Bay Entrance	4	0.19	0.35	0.45	0.49	0.41	0.25	0.32	0.27	0.12	0.16	0.34	0.39	knots
		313	250	236	228	221	175	120	113	97	27	16	11	degrees

ROTARY TIDAL CURRENTS EXPLANATION

Offshore and in some of the wider indentations of the coast, the tidal current is quite different from that found in the more protected bays and rivers. In these inside waters the tidal current is of the reversing type. The current sets in one direction for a period of 6 hours after which is ceases to flow momentarily and then sets in the opposite direction during the following 6 hours. The offshore tidal current, not being confined to a definite channel, changes its direction continually and never slows to a true slack water. Thus in a tidal cycle of 12 ½ hours it will have set in all directions of the compass. This type of current is referred to as a rotary current.

A characteristic feature of the rotary current is the absence of slack water. Although the current generally varies from hour to hour, this variation from greatest current to least current and back again to greatest does not give rise to a period of slack water. When the speed of the rotary tidal current is least, it is known as the minimum current, and when it is greatest it is known as the maximum current. The minimum and maximum speeds of the rotary current are related to each other in the same way as slack and strength of current. A minimum speed of the current follows a maximum speed by an interval of approximately 3 hours and followed in turn by another maximum after a further interval of 3 hours.

The following table provides the direction and speed of the rotary current for each hour at a number of offshore stations. The times and speeds are referred to predictions for a reference station in the daily graphics and corrections. All times are in local standard time for the secondary station.

The speeds given in the table are the average speeds for the station. The Moon when new, full, or at perigee tends to increase the speeds 15 to 20 percent above average. When perigee occurs at or near the time of new or full Moon, the current speeds will be 30 to 40 percent above average. The Moon when at first and third quarter or at apogee tend to decrease the current speeds below average by 15 to 20 percent. When apogee occurs at or near the first or third quarter Moon, the currents will be 30 to 40 percent below average. The speeds will be about average when apogee occurs at or near the time of the new or full Moon and also when perigee occurs at or near the first or third quarter Moon.

The direction of the current is given in degrees, true, reading clockwise from 0° at north, and is the direction toward which the water is flowing.

The speeds and directions are for tidal current only and do not include the effect of the wind. When a wind is blowing, a wind-driven current will be set up as is superimposed on the normal tidal current. The actual current encountered will thus be a combination of the wind-driven current and the tidal current.

As an example, in the following table the current at Richardson Bay Entrance is given for each hour after maximum flood at San Franciso Bay Entrance. Suppose it is desired to find the direction and speed of the current at Richardson Bay Entrance at 3:15 p.m. (15:15) on a day when the maximum flood at San Francisco Bay Entrance is predicted in the daily graphics to occur at 13:20. The desired time is therefore 2 hours after the maximum flood at San Francisco Bay Entrance. From the table the tidal current at Horse Head Island at 2 hours is setting 340° true with an average speed of 0.2 knots. If this day is near the time of new Moon and about half way between apogee and perigee, then the distance effect of the moon will be nil and the phase effect alone will increase the speed by about 15 percent.

Historic Current Corrections

Times with a minus sign occur *before* predictions; those with a plus sign occur *after*.
Maximum current speed = predicted current multiplied by speed ratio.

	POSITION		FLOOD			EBB		
	Latitude	Longitude	Slack before	Max flood	Speed ratio	Slack before	Max ebb	Speed ratio
	North	West	h. m.	h. m.		h. m.	h. m.	
SUISUN BAY, cont.			*(corrections apply to Benicia Bridge currents)*					
Benicia Bridge	38° 02.08'	122° 07.51'		daily predictions				
Avon Pier, 0.15 nm N of	38° 03.10'	122° 05.42'	+0 05	+0 21	0.7	+0 22	+0 11	0.7
Pt. Edith, 1.7 nm NNW of	38° 04.72'	122° 05.03'	+0 04	+0 03	0.6	+0 23	+0 07	0.5
Seal Island, S of	38° 03.20'	122° 02.97'	+0 14	-0 03	0.5	+0 54	+0 38	0.6
Roe Island Channel	38° 03.90'	122° 02.07'	+1 03	+0 40	0.7	+0 23	+0 52	1.2
Roe Island, Gilbert Pt., 0.15 nm NW of	38° 04.42'	122° 01.30'	+1 07	+0 43	0.5	+0 50	+1 02	0.8
Suisun Cutoff	38° 05.33'	122° 00.43'	+1 41	+1 42	0.5	+1 27	+1 05	0.5
Middle Point Lt., 0.18 nm NNW of	38° 03.45'	121° 59.58'	+1 06	+1 00	0.8	+0 56	+0 57	1.0
Stake Point, 0.9 nm NNW of	38° 03.88'	121° 57.33'	+0 13	+0 45	0.4	+0 33	+0 29	0.4
Simmons Point, 0.6 nm ESE of	38° 02.89'	121° 55.35'	+1 27	+1 21	0.9	+1 07	+1 12	1.4
Spoonbill Creek, near bridge	38° 03.53'	121° 54.28'	+0 11	+0 16	0.8	+1 02	+0 37	0.9
Montezuma Slough, east end, near bridge	38° 04.67'	121° 53.03'	+2 30	+2 10	0.5	+2 12	+2 22	0.8
New York Slough, 0.6 mile E of Pt. Emmet	38° 01.95'	121° 52.14'	+1 24	+1 13	0.8	+0 59	+1 22	1.1
New York Slough, Winter Island	38° 01.70'	121° 50.78'	+1 01	+0 34	0.6	+0 45	+1 11	0.8
SACRAMENTO RIVER[11]								
Entrance, 0.7 nm SW of Chain Island	38° 03.51'	121° 52.27'	+1 41	+1 20	0.7	+1 12	+1 37	1.1
Point Sacramento, 0.2 nm NE of	38° 03.86'	121° 50.02'	+1 36	+1 21	0.7	+1 16	+1 25	1.0
Sherman Island East, 0.2 mile N of	38° 03.52'	121° 48.25'	+1 21	+1 01	0.5	+1 08	+0 30	0.8
Sacramento River Light 14	38° 04.63'	121° 45.84'	+1 44	+1 40	0.6	+1 29	+1 26	0.8
SAN JOAQUIN RIVER[11]								
Pt. San Joaquin, 0.45 nm ENE of	38° 03.70'	121° 51.00'	+1 23	+1 26	0.8	+1 29	+1 14	0.7
Point Beenar, 0.7 nm N of	38° 02.53'	121° 50.28'	+2 35	+1 58	0.3	+1 39	+1 22	0.4
Point Beenar, 100 yards, NE of	38° 01.95'	121° 50.13'	+2 34	+1 58	0.5	+2 27	+2 25	0.9
Antioch Point	38° 01.44'	121° 49.35'	+1 48	+1 42	0.8	+1 39	+1 49	1.1
West Island Light, N of	38° 01.49'	121° 47.40'	+2 08	+1 50	0.6	+1 33	+1 55	1.1
Antioch, Route 160 bridge	38° 01.62'	121° 45.18'	+1 56	+1 51	0.7	+1 48	+1 56	0.9
Vulcan Island, 0.5 mile E of	37° 59.12'	121° 23.45'	+3 37	+3 23	0.4	+3 24	+3 30	0.3

END NOTES

1. The slough in this area goes dry at low water stages of the tide. The mean water high depth is about 5 feet.
2. Due to bottom configuration and depths at low water stages, a low water stand may occur at this station.
3. These data apply only during low river stages.
4. San Pedro Channel, 7 miles south of Los Angeles Harbor Breakwater. There are two periodic currents here both of which are rotary, turning clockwise, and rather weak. The tidal current has a speed at strength of about 0.2 knot. The other current, due apparently to daily land and sea breezes, has a period of 24 hours and an average speed of about 0.2 knot. The greatest speed during 5 months of observations was 1.5 knots. Currents greater than 1 knot occur infrequently.
5. In Los Angeles and Long Beach Harbors, the tidal current is weak. Currents can exceed 1 knot in the outer harbor at San Pedro, under strong wind conditions. Also it is reported that three minute surge waves are responsible for major ship movements and damage.
6. Observations indicate ebb is very weak.
7. Large current eddies which cause ships to steer off course are reported near the foundation piers of Golden Gate Bridge and San Francisco-Oakland Bay Bridge.
8. Current is somewhat rotary, turning clockwise.
9. See the Slack Water Time Differences Table on the following pages.
10. Current is somewhat rotary, turning counterclockwise. 4h 25m prior to computed maximum flood the current flows southward with a speed of 0.6 of the flood speed at the reference station.
11. Data do not apply during freshets.

Historic Current Corrections

Times with a minus sign occur *before* predictions; those with a plus sign occur *after*.
Maximum current speed = predicted current multiplied by speed ratio.

	POSITION		FLOOD			EBB		
	Latitude	Longitude	Slack before	Max flood	Speed ratio	Slack before	Max ebb	Speed ratio
	North	West	h. m.	h. m.		h. m.	h. m.	
SAN FRANCISCO BAY, North, cont.			*(corrections apply to Richmond currents)*					
Point Richmond, 0.8 nm NNW of	37° 55.25'	122° 23.80'	-0 48	-1 55	0.2	-1 14	-2 02	0.2
Richmond	37° 55.76'	122° 25.50'	daily predictions					
Red Rock, E of	37° 55.77'	122° 25.70'	+0 06	+0 03	0.8	+0 28	+0 07	0.8
Red Rock, 0.60 nm NNE of	37° 56.40'	122° 25.60'	-0 18	-0 37	1.1	+0 10	-0 33	0.9
Point San Quentin, 0.82 nm E of	37° 56.47'	122° 27.70'	-0 09	+0 02	0.4	+0 02	-0 46	0.5
Point San Quentin, 1.3 nm E of	37° 56.53'	122° 27.16'	+0 20	+0 19	0.8	+0 35	+0 23	0.9
Point San Quentin, 1.9 miles E of	37° 57.0'	122° 26.4'	+0 52	+0 26	0.9	+0 28	+0 37	1.3
SAN PABLO BAY								
Point San Pablo, midchannel	37° 58.13'	122° 26.35'	+0 43	+0 35	1.3	+0 16	+0 28	1.3
Point San Pedro, 0.55 nm SE of	37° 58.78'	122° 26.20'	+0 28	+0 23	1.3	+0 39	+0 30	1.5
Pinole Point, 1.18 nm W of	38° 00.48'	122° 23.38'	+0 07	-0 25	0.5	+0 07	+0 06	0.6
Pinole Point, 3.0 nm WNW of	38° 01.60'	122° 25.48'	+0 01	-0 19	0.5	+0 05	+0 03	0.5
Pinole Point, 1.27 nm NNW of	38° 01.85'	122° 22.63'	+1 21	+1 07	0.9	+1 00	+1 19	1.1
Pinole Point, 1.42 nm NNW of	38° 02.03'	122° 22.75'	+1 09	+0 51	0.7	+0 52	+1 11	0.8
Pinole Shoal	38° 02.85'	122° 20.05'	+1 59	+1 46	0.8	+1 26	+1 49	1.0
Petaluma River approach (Buoys 3 & 4)	38° 02.61'	122° 25.58'	-0 10	-0 11	0.6	+0 03	+0 12	0.6
Petaluma River approach	38° 04.2'	122° 25.2'	-0 01	-0 24	0.4	-0 15	-0 06	0.4
Petaluma River entrance	38° 06.63'	122° 29.58'	+0 10	+0 05	0.5	-0 19	-1 00	0.6
Wilson Point, 1.55 nm N of	38° 02.25'	122° 09.03'	+0 54	+0 57	0.5	+1 10	+1 08	0.5
Wilson Point 3.90 nm NNW of	38° 04.47'	122° 20.55'	-0 08	-0 44	0.3	+0 08	+0 22	0.3
			(corrections apply to Carquinez Strait currents)					
Davis Point, 1.0 nm NW of	38° 03.71'	122° 16.60'	-0 09	-0 16	0.6	-0 35	-0 21	0.8
Davis Point, (midchanel)	38° 03.80'	122° 15.5'	-0 13	-0 28	0.7	-0 17	-0 38	0.9
CARQUINEZ STRAIT								
Mare Island Strait NE of Pier 34	38° 04.63'	122° 14.74'	-1 46	-1 16	0.7	-1 14	-1 45	1.0
Mare Island Strait (Buoy "4")	38° 04.45'	122° 14.57'	-2 25	-1 05	0.3	-1 23	-3 07	0.2
Carquinez Bridge, I-80	38° 03.74'	122° 13.65'	+0 01	+0 04	0.7	-0 10	+0 05	0.9
Carquinez Strait (west end, bridge)	38° 03.68'	122° 13.09'	daily predictions					
Dillon Point	38° 03.53'	122° 11.58'	-0 14	-0 55	0.4	-0 50	+0 13	0.6
Martinez Marina, 0.65 nm NW of	38° 01.98'	122° 08.98'	-0 12	-0 03	0.7	+0 10	-0 02	0.6
Martinez Marina, 0.50 nm W of	38° 01.72'	122° 08.92'	-0 37	-0 43	0.7	+0 27	+0 11	0.7
Martinez Marina, 0.61 nm NNW of	38° 02.18'	122° 08.68'	-0 56	-0 35	0.5	-0 13	-1 00	0.6
Army Pt. Pier Lt. 0.2 nm SE of	38° 02.33'	122° 08.02'	-0 07	-0 13	0.7	-0 16	+0 08	1.0
SUISUN BAY			*(corrections apply to Benicia Bridge currents)*					
Grizzly Bay entrance	38° 06.19'	122° 03.15'	+0 00	+0 26	0.5	+0 05	-0 24	0.5
Montezuma Slough								
1 mile inside west entrance	38° 08.83'	122° 03.38'	-0 24	-0 50	0.4	-0 32	-1 42	0.5
West entrance	38° 07.92'	122° 03.48'	-0 10	-1 06	0.7	-0 09	-1 01	1.0
Suisun Slough								
1 mile inside entrance	38° 08.27'	122° 04.88'	-0 55	-1 03	0.3	-0 46	-1 41	0.3
Entrance	38° 07.27'	122° 04.05'	-0 30	-1 10	0.6	-0 39	-0 58	0.9
0.5 nm E of entrance	38° 07.13'	122° 03.20'	-0 21	-1 07	0.5	-0 06	+0 07	0.3

Historic Current Corrections

Times with a minus sign occur *before* predictions; those with a plus sign occur *after*.
Maximum current speed = predicted current multiplied by speed ratio.

	POSITION		FLOOD			EBB		
	Latitude	Longitude	Slack before	Max flood	Speed ratio	Slack before	Max ebb	Speed ratio
	North	West	h. m.	h. m.		h. m.	h. m.	
SAN FRANCISCO BAY, South, cont.[9]			*(corrections apply to San Mateo Bridge currents)*					
Sierra Point, 1.3 miles ENE of	37° 41.08'	122° 21.40'	-0 47	-0 34	0.8	-0 25	-0 40	0.7
Sierra Point, 1.2 nm E of	37° 40.68'	122° 19.05'	-0 42	-0 30	0.6	-0 26	-0 22	0.5
Oyster Point, 2.8 miles E of	37° 39.9'	122° 19.4'	-0 29	-0 20	0.7	-0 13	-0 16	0.8
Sierra Point, 4.4 miles E of	37° 40.4'	122° 17.7'	-0 48	-0 34	0.7	-0 09	-0 33	0.6
Point San Bruno, 0.51 nm E of	37° 39.25'	122° 21.83'	-1 16	-0 27	0.5	-0 21	-1 07	0.3
Mulford Gardens Channel Approach	37° 39.00'	122° 15.77'	-1 12	-0 58	0.7	-0 43	-1 07	0.6
Coyote Point, 2.3 nm NNE of	37° 37.53'	122° 17.76'	+0 07	-0 15	0.8	-0 17	+0 07	1.0
Little Coyote Pt., 3.4 nm NNE of	37° 37.43'	122° 13.88'	-1 06	-0 54	0.4	-0 50	-1 01	0.4
Little Coyote Pt., 3.1 nm ENE of	37° 35.88'	122° 12.33'	-1 52	-1 34	0.4	-0 58	-1 49	0.4
Little Coyote Pt., 1.2 nm NE of	37° 35.42'	122° 14.92'	-0 09	-0 26	1.1	-0 11	-0 11	1.1
San Mateo Bridge	37° 35.27'	122° 15.01'	*daily predictions*					
Redwood Pt., Blair I., 1.15 nm NNE of	37° 33.48'	122° 11.93'	-0 02	-0 21	1.0	-0 02	-0 06	1.1
Redwood Point, 1.7 nm E of	37° 31.84'	122° 09.61'	-0 04	-0 01	1.1	+0 00	+0 01	1.2
Redwood Creek	37° 31.55'	122° 11.95'	-0 36	+0 02	0.6	-0 22	-0 56	0.6
Dumbarton Highway Bridge	37° 30.11'	122° 06.96'	-0 01	+0 26	1.1	-0 07	-0 47	0.9
Dumbarton Hwy. Bridge, 0.28 nm SE of	37° 30.08'	122° 06.93'	-0 21	+0 06	1.0	+0 02	-0 37	1.2
Dumbarton Point, 1.15 nm SE of	37° 29.25'	122° 04.88'	-0 12	-0 20	0.8	+0 12	+0 54	0.6
Dumbarton Point, 2.25 miles SE of	37° 28.5'	122° 04.2'	+0 08	-0 06	0.9	+0 00	+0 56	0.8
Yellow Bluff, 0.81 nm NE of	37° 50.73'	122° 27.43'	-0 27	-0 28	1.2	-0 37	-0 59	1.1
SAN FRANCISCO BAY, North			*(corrections apply to Golden Gate Bridge currents)*					
Yellow Bluff, 0.8 mile E of	37° 50.1'	122° 27.3'	+0 24	+0 16	1.0	+0 22	+0 44	1.4
Point Cavallo, 1.3 miles E of	37° 49.9'	122° 26.6'	+0 31	+0 26	0.9	+0 42	+0 44	1.6
Point Blunt, Angel I., 0.5 nm SW of	37° 50.73'	122° 25.38'	+0 56	+0 09	0.4	+0 03	+0 33	1.0
Point Blunt, Angel I., 0.25 mile S of	37° 50.8'	122° 25.0'	+0 12	+0 11	0.6	+0 24	+1 08	1.3
Point Blunt, Angel I., 0.8 mile SE of[10]	37° 50.7'	122° 24.3'	-1 06	+0 02	0.4	+0 21	-0 12	0.8
Point Blunt, Angel I., 0.25 mile E of	37° 51.17'	122° 24.73'	+1 45	-0 06	0.4	+0 17	+2 23	1.0
Angel Island, off Quarry Point	37° 51.8'	122° 24.8'	+2 11	+0 22	0.2	+1 10	+1 47	1.2
Angel Island, 0.75 mile E of	37° 51.8'	122° 24.1'	+1 30	+1 10	0.4	+1 35	+1 59	0.6
Point Simpson, Angel I., 1.05 nm E of	37° 52.43'	122° 24.17'	+0 53	+1 08	0.5	+1 03	+0 33	0.5
Fleming Point, 1.72 nm SW of	37° 52.62'	122° 21.53	-1 04	-1 02	0.2	-0 24	-0 47	0.3
Richardson Bay Entrance	37° 51.40'	122° 28.19'	*see Rotary Tidal Currents Table on the following pages*					
Raccoon Strait, off Point Stuart	37° 51.67'	122° 27.12'	+0 11	+0 08	0.5	-0 02	+0 04	1.2
Raccoon Strait	37° 52.32'	122° 26.52'	+0 20	-0 22	0.5	-0 20	-0 10	0.9
Raccoon Strait, off Ayala Cove	37° 52.3'	122° 26.3'	- - -	-0 38	0.5	-0 06	+0 02	1.0
Bluff Point, 0.1 mile E of	37° 53.0'	122° 26.1'	+1 04	-0 26	0.6	+0 18	+0 50	1.2
Bluff Point, 1.15 nm E of	37° 53.23'	122° 24.78'	+0 55	+0 46	0.4	+0 58	+0 33	0.6
Southampton Shoal Light, 0.2 mile E of	37° 52.95'	122° 23.75'	+1 04	+0 55	0.3	+0 53	+0 25	0.7
			(corrections apply to Richmond currents)					
Point Chauncey, 1.3 miles E of	37° 53.45'	122° 25.13'	+0 08	+0 29	0.9	+0 13	+0 09	0.9
Point Chauncey, 0.75 nm NW of	37° 54.18'	122° 27.53'	+0 08	-0 46	0.7	+0 10	-0 09	0.6
Point Chauncey, 1.25 nm N of	37° 54.92'	122° 26.76'	+0 59	+0 36	0.8	+0 09	+0 33	1.1
Point Potrero Reach (Buoy "10")	37° 54.18'	122° 22.35'	*current weak and variable*					
Point Richmond, 0.5 mile W of	37° 54.3'	122° 24.0'	-0 16	+0 01	0.5	+0 10	-0 12	0.5

Historic Current Corrections

Times with a minus sign occur *before* predictions; those with a plus sign occur *after*.
Maximum current speed = predicted current multiplied by speed ratio.

	POSITION		FLOOD			EBB		
	Latitude	Longitude	Slack before	Max flood	Speed ratio	Slack before	Max ebb	Speed ratio
	North	West	h. m.	h. m.		h. m.	h. m.	
SAN FRANCISCO BAY, South, cont.[9]			*(corrections apply to Golden Gate Bridge currents)*					
North Point, Pier 35, N of	37° 48.85'	122° 24.42'	-0 24	-0 51	0.8	-0 57	-0 45	1.4
Emmeryville Marina	37° 50.60'	122° 19.52'	- - -	-1 02	0.1	- - -	- - -	- -
Treasure Island, 0.78 nm NW of	37° 50.24'	122° 23.23'	-0 58	-1 00	0.5	-0 38	-0 40	0.6
Treasure Island, 0.8 mile W of	37° 49.3'	122° 23.5'	-0 01	-0 37	0.4	-0 39	-0 01	1.5
Treasure Island, 0.2 mile W of	37° 49.3'	122° 22.7'	-0 54	-0 50	0.5	-0 32	-0 30	1.2
			(corrections apply to Oakland currents)					
Pier 23	37° 48.32'	122° 23.84'	+0 34	-1 00	0.9	-1 19	+0 06	1.5
Yerba Buena Island, W of (midchannel)	37° 48.60'	122° 22.98'	+0 49	-0 13	1.2	-0 16	+0 20	1.6
Oakland, Yerba Buena Island	37° 48.59'	122° 21.04'	daily predictions					
San Francisco-Oakland Bay Bridge[7]	- - -	- - -	- - -	- - -	- -	- - -	- - -	- -
Bay Bridge, Span B-C	37° 47.85'	122° 22.43'	+0 47	+0 05	1.4	+0 01	+0 33	1.6
Bay Bridge, Pier D	37° 48.06'	122° 22.43'	+0 56	+0 04	1.3	-0 01	+0 35	1.6
Treasure Island, 0.5 mile N of	37° 50.43'	122° 22.10'	+0 31	+0 02	0.8	+0 22	+0 42	0.9
Treasure Island, 0.85 nm E of	37° 49.50'	122° 20.78'	-0 13	+0 16	0.6	+0 24	-0 26	0.5
Treasure Island, 0.3 mile E of	37° 49.6'	122° 21.3'	+1 12	+0 13	1.0	+0 00	+1 02	1.2
Yerba Buena Island, 0.3 nm SE of	37° 48.25'	122° 21.43'	+0 31	+0 05	0.5	+0 07	+0 21	0.8
Oakland Outer Harbor entrance	37° 48.4'	122° 20.7'	-0 04	-0 07	1.1	+0 22	+0 09	1.3
Oakland Inner Harbor LB4	37° 48.06'	122° 20.87'	+0 05	+0 00	1.0	-0 04	-0 05	1.0
Oakland Inner Harbor entrance	37° 48.1'	122° 20.4'	-0 11	-0 12	0.7	-0 01	-0 09	1.2
Oakland Inner Harbor channel	37° 47.70'	122° 19.10'	+1 20	+0 15	0.3	-0 10	+0 36	0.5
Oakland Inner Harbor Reach	37° 47.57'	122° 17.13'	+0 38	-0 03	0.2	-0 28	+0 13	0.4
Oakland Harbor, Webster Street	37° 47.50'	122° 16.47'	+0 08	-0 32	0.6	-0 18	-0 03	0.8
Alameda Estuary, SE end	37° 45.69'	122° 13.42'	+0 01	-0 17	0.8	-0 33	-0 15	0.8
Oakland 7th St. Marine, 0.6 nm SSW of	37° 47.67'	122° 20.65'	-0 01	+0 27	0.8	-0 02	+0 03	0.6
Brooklyn Basin	37° 47.11'	122° 15.63'	+0 24	-0 26	0.1	-0 37	+0 34	0.3
			(corrections apply to Golden Gate Bridge currents)					
Rincon Point	37° 47.42'	122° 22.40'	-0 09	-0 32	0.7	-0 27	-0 20	1.3
Rincon Point, midbay	37° 47.00'	122° 21.23'	-0 22	-0 33	0.8	-0 38	-0 24	1.3
Mission Rock, 0.6 mile E of	37° 46.4'	122° 22.1'	-0 09	-0 21	0.9	-0 08	+0 06	1.4
Mission Rock, 1.3 mile E of	37° 46.5'	122° 21.2'	+0 01	-0 31	0.8	-0 02	+0 14	1.2
Mission Rock, 2.0 miles E of	37° 46.6'	122° 20.3'	-0 49	-0 51	0.6	-0 18	-0 20	1.4
Potrero Point, 1.08 nm E of	37° 45.45'	122° 21.47'	-0 08	-0 25	0.6	-0 06	-0 04	1.1
Potereo Point, 2 miles E of	37° 45'	122° 20'	-0 08	-0 44	0.6	+0 03	-0 02	1.0
Alameda Radar Tower, 0.9 nm SSW of	37° 44.73'	122° 16.98'	-0 55	-1 14	0.2	-1 18	-1 12	0.4
			(corrections apply to San Mateo Bridge currents)					
Point Avisadero, 0.3 mile E of	37° 43.8'	122° 20.9'	-0 30	-0 21	1.2	-0 13	-0 20	1.3
Point Avisadero, 1 mile E of	37° 43.8'	122° 20.2'	-0 32	+0 02	1.2	+0 25	-0 07	1.0
Point Avisadero, 2 miles E of	37° 43.9'	122° 18.8'	-0 32	-0 06	1.1	-0 10	-0 24	1.1
Point Avisadero, 0.6 nm ESE of	37° 43.38'	122° 19.43'	-0 32	-0 25	1.0	-0 14	-0 39	1.0
Point Avisadero Tower, 1.25 nm SSE of	37° 42.47'	122° 20.97'	-0 45	-0 15	0.9	-0 29	-0 52	0.8
Hunters Point, 1.6 nm SE of	37° 41.76'	122° 20.29'	-0 39	-0 37	0.9	-0 36	-0 40	0.9
Oakland Airport, SW of	37° 40.93'	122° 13.85'	-1 05	-0 46	0.5	-0 39	-1 18	0.5

Historic Current Corrections

Times with a minus sign occur *before* predictions; those with a plus sign occur *after*.
Maximum current speed = predicted current multiplied by speed ratio.

	POSITION		FLOOD			EBB		
	Latitude	Longitude	Slack before	Max flood	Speed ratio	Slack before	Max ebb	Speed ratio
	North	**West**	h. m.	h. m.		h. m.	h. m.	
CALIFORNIA COAST			*(corrections apply to San Francisco Bay Entrance currents)*					
San Pedro Channel[4]	33° 36'	118° 16'	- - -	- - -	- -	- - -	- - -	- -
Los Angeles and Long Beach Harbors[5]	- - -	- - -	- - -	- - -	- -	- - -	- - -	- -
El Segundo, Santa Monica Bay[6]	33° 54'	118° 26'	- - -	- - -	- -	- - -	- - -	- -
MONTEREY BAY								
Point Pinos	36° 38'	121° 57'	*current weak and variable*					
Point Santa Cruz, 2 miles S of	36° 55'	122° 01'	*current weak and variable*					
Ano Nuevo Island, 2 miles SW of	37° 05'	122° 22'	*current weak and variable*					
Point Montara, 2 miles W of	37° 32'	122° 34'	*current weak and variable*					
GOLDEN GATE and APPROACHES[7]								
San Fran. southern traffic lane, N end	37° 38.67'	122° 41.72'	-0 34	-0 32	0.1	-0 37	-0 40	0.1
San Fran. main traffic lane, E end	37° 41.29'	122° 47.99'	*current weak and variable*					
San Fran. traffic separation zone buoy	37° 45.03'	122° 41.98'	-2 14	-0 32	0.3	+0 02	-0 34	0.1
San Fran. northern traffic lane, SE end	37° 48.26'	122° 48.31'	*current weak and variable*					
Point Bonita Lt., 5.27 nm WSW of	37° 48.27'	122° 38.33'	-1 54	-1 35	0.2	-0 51	-1 01	0.2
San Francisco Bar, N of ship channel	37° 47.12'	122° 36.84'	-0 11	-0 08	0.4	+0 07	+0 03	0.4
Point Lobos, 3.73 nm W of	37° 47.25'	122° 35.32'	-2 16	-1 03	0.3	-0 20	-0 31	0.2
Point Lobos, 2.5 miles W of[8]	37° 46.37'	122° 34.90'	- - -	+0 32	0.4	- - -	-1 08	0.6
Point Lobos, 1.3 nm SW of	37° 46.30'	122° 32.13'	-1 26	-0 51	0.5	+0 27	-0 06	0.4
South Channel	37° 45'	122° 32'	-1 31	-1 21	0.5	-0 14	-0 52	0.5
Point Lobos, 5.47 nm SW of	37° 43.23'	122° 35.87'	-2 01	-2 02	0.3	-0 51	-1 10	0.3
Bonita Channel approach[8]	37° 50'	122° 37'	- - -	-0 10	0.2	- - -	-0 56	0.2
Bonita Channel, off Tennessee Cove[8]	37° 50.05'	122° 33.78'	- - -	-0 34	0.5	- - -	-0 56	0.3
Bonita Channel, off Point Bonita	37° 48.95'	122° 32.13'	- - -	-0 22	0.6	- - -	-1 56	0.1
Point Bonita, 0.8 nm NE of	37° 49.25'	122° 30.97'	-4 51	-3 38	0.4	-4 21	-4 01	0.3
Point Bonita Lt. 0.4 nm SSE of	37° 48.72'	122° 31.27'	-1 08	-1 04	0.3	-1 28	-1 25	0.5
Point Bonita, 0.95 nm SSE of	37° 48.07'	122° 31.10'	-0 26	-0 08	1.0	+0 13	-0 18	0.8
Mile Rock Lt., 0.2 nm NW of	37° 47.72'	122° 30.68'	-0 35	-0 25	1.1	+0 18	-0 33	0.9
Point Diablo, 0.2 mile SE of	37° 49.07'	122° 29.80'	-0 09	-0 53	0.8	-0 47	+0 08	1.0
Baker Beach (South Bay), 0.3 nm NW of	37° 47.87'	122° 29.31'	-5 06	-4 15	0.6	-1 59	-2 52	0.3
Fort Point, 0.3 nm W of	37° 48.55'	122° 28.97'	-2 10	-0 41	0.6	+1 02	+0 20	0.2
San Francisco Bay Entrance (Outside)	37° 48.64'	122° 30.12'	*daily predictions*					
			(corrections apply to Golden Gate Bridge currents)					
Golden Gate Bridge, 0.88 nm NE of	37° 49.75'	122° 27.72'	*daily predictions*					
Golden Gate Bridge, 0.46 nm E of	37° 49.20'	122° 28.38'	-0 02	-0 06	0.9	-0 06	-0 08	1.1
Golden Gate Bridge, 0.8 mile E of	37° 49.30'	122° 27.72'	+0 42	+0 15	0.9	+0 27	+0 43	1.4
Fort Point, 0.5 nm E of	37° 48.70'	122° 27.96'	-0 43	-2 47	0.2	-0 30	-1 12	0.8
SAN FRANCISCO BAY, South[9]								
Alcatraz Island, 0.2 mile W of	37° 49.67'	122° 25.82'	+0 15	+0 00	0.8	+0 24	+0 20	1.1
Alcatraz Island, SW of	37° 48.86'	122° 25.92'	-0 18	-0 44	0.5	-0 55	-0 43	1.0
Alcatraz Island, S of	37° 49.00'	122° 25.02'	+0 15	-0 03	0.5	+0 07	+0 02	1.2
Alcatraz Island, 0.5 mile N of	37° 50.11'	122° 25.21'	+0 24	+0 18	0.6	-0 04	-0 05	1.0

Historic Tide Corrections

Humboldt Bay, California to Nehalem River, Oregon

NOAA bases tide predictions for this area on the Humboldt Bay, rather than the Golden Gate. However the two are very similar:

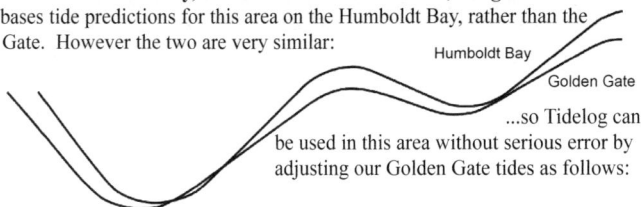

Humboldt Bay

Golden Gate

...so Tidelog can be used in this area without serious error by adjusting our Golden Gate tides as follows:

HIGH TIDE: +11 minutes, +1.0 ft.   **LOW TIDE:** +27 minutes, +0.1 ft.

The result approximates NOAA's Humboldt Bay tide predictions within 15 minutes and several inches. Appropriate corrections from the table below may then be applied

	DIFFERENCES			
	Time		Height	
	High Water	Low Water	High Water	Low Water
	h m	h m	ft	ft
NORTHERN CALIFORNIA				
Eel River Entrance	-0 31	-0.6	-0 16	0.0
Humboldt Bay:				
entrance	-0 09	-0.7	+0 07	0.9
North Spit	-----	-----	-----	-----
Fields Landing	-0 01	*0.99	+0 04	*0.99
Hookton Slough	+0 15	-0.2	+0 25	0.0
Elk River railroad bridge	+0 19	*0.71	+1 32	*0.31
Bucksport	+0 14	*1.01	+0 08	*1.03
Eureka	+0 26	*1.06	+0 13	*1.03
Eureka Slough bridge	+0 32	*1.09	+0 12	*1.02
Samoa	+0 19	+0.4	+0 07	0.0
Arcata Wharf	+0 48	+0.1	+0 54	+0.1
Trinidad Harbor	-0 25	-0.2	-0 13	0.0
Crescent City	-0 26	+0.1	-0 14	0.0
OREGON				
Brookings, Chetco Cove	-0 25	+0.1	-0 10	0.0
Wedderburn, Rogue River	-0 17	-0.2	+0 02	-0.1
Port Orford	-0 19	+0.4	-0 05	+0.1
Bandon, Coquille River	-0 03	+0.1	+0 14	-0.1
Coos Bay:				
Charleston	+0 04	+0.7	+0 16	0.0
Empire	+0 46	-0.2	+1 06	-0.1
Coos Bay	+1 35	+0.5	+1 44	-0.1
Umpqua River:				
entrance	+0 14	+0.1	+0 19	0.0
Gardiner	+1 05	-0.1	+1 25	-0.2
Reedsport	+1 20	-0.1	+1 40	-0.2
Siuslaw River:				
entrance	+0 03	+0.5	+0 19	0.0
Florence	+0 53	-0.2	+1 14	-0.2
Waldport, Alsea Bay	+0 30	+0.8	+0 47	0.0
Yaquina Bay and River:				
Bar at entrance	+0 08	+1.0	+0 25	+0.1
Newport	+0 18	+1.1	+0 28	+0.1
Southbeach	+0 07	+1.4	+0 17	+0.1
Yaquina	+0 29	+1.3	+0 41	+0.1
Winant	+0 37	+1.3	+1 02	0.0
Toledo	+1 03	+1.2	+1 25	-0.1
Taft, Siletz Bay	+0 22	-0.3	+0 59	-0.3
Kernville Bay entrance	+0 58	-0.8	+1 39	-0.4
Nestucca Bay entrance	+0 29	+0.7	+0 58	-0.1
Tillamook Bay:				
Barview	+0 16	+0.6	+0 42	-0.1
Garibaldi	+0 48	+0.9	+1 02	0.0
Miami Cove	+0 49	+0.5	+1 12	-0.1
Bay City	+1 07	+0.2	+1 46	-0.2
Tillamook, Hoquarten Slough	+1 26	-0.3	+3 01	-0.5
Nehalem River:				
Brighton	+0 25	+0.9	+0 40	0.0
Nehalem	+0 51	+0.3	+1 42	-0.3

Historic Tide Corrections

Times with a minus sign occur *before* predictions; those with a plus sign occur *after*.
*Heights preceded by an asterisk are ratios; multiply by predicted tidal height.

	POSITION		DIFFERENCES			
			Time		Height	
	Latitude	Longitude	High Water	Low Water	High Water	Low Water
	North	**West**	h m	h m	ft	ft
SAN JOAQUIN RIVER		*(corrections apply to Port Chicago tides)*				
Antioch	38° 01.2'	121° 48.9'	+1 12	+1 26	*0.77	*0.78
Threemile Slough entrance	38° 05.0'	121° 41.0'	+2 27	+2 52	*0.71	*0.68
Prisoners Point	38° 03.7'	121° 33.3'	+3 25	+3 29	*0.73	*0.69
Wards Island, Little Connection Slough	38° 03.0'	121° 29.8'	+3 45	+3 51	*0.68	*0.61
Blackslough Landing	37° 59.7'	121° 25.3'	+4 00	+4 15	*0.75	*0.62
Stockton	37° 57.5'	121° 17.4'	+4 06	+4 33	*0.81	*0.66
Mokelumne River						
Georgiana Slough entrance	38° 07.6'	121° 34.7'	+3 29	+3 41	*0.67	*0.59
Terminous, South Fork	38° 06.6'	121° 29.9'	+3 53	+4 11	*0.70	*0.59
New Hope Bridge[3]	38° 14.0'	121° 29.0'	+4 22	+4 56	*0.73	*0.68
Bishop Cut, Disappointment Slough	38° 02.6'	121° 25.1'	+4 12	+4 12	*0.79	*0.66
False River	38° 03.3'	121° 39.3'	+2 45	+2 45	*0.66	*0.64
Dutch Slough	38° 00.7'	121° 38.3'	+2 33	+2 46	*0.68	*0.72
Irish Landing, Sand Mound Slough	38° 02.0'	121° 35.0'	+3 29	+3 34	*0.73	*0.68
Orwood, Old River	37° 56.0'	121° 34.0'	+4 32	+4 33	*0.76	*0.68
Holt, Whiskey Slough	37° 56.0'	121° 26.0'	+4 18	+4 39	*0.80	*0.68
Borden Highway Bridge, Old River	37° 53.4'	121° 34.2'	+4 40	+4 35	*0.64	*0.61
Borden Highway Bridge, Middle River	37° 53.5'	121° 39.3'	+4 50	+4 54	*0.67	*0.62
Borden Highway Bridge, San Joaquin River	37° 56.2'	121° 20.0'	+4 28	+4 48	*0.78	*0.64
Grant Line Canal (drawbridge)	37° 49.0'	121° 27.0'	+6 14	+6 20	*0.76	*0.68
SACRAMENTO RIVER						
Collinsville	38° 04.4'	121° 50.9'	+1 11	+1 20	*0.80	*0.80
Threemile Slough	38° 06.4'	121° 42.0'	+1 49	+1 58	*0.82	*0.78
Rio Vista	38° 08.8'	121° 41.4'	+1 51	+2 02	*0.88	*0.78
Steamboat Slough, Snug Harbor Marina	38° 12.0'	121° 36.7'	+2 24	+2 48	*0.80	*0.65
Snodgrass Slough	38° 16.5'	121° 29.2'	+5 00	+5 36	*0.49	*0.39
Clarksburg[3]	38° 25.0'	121° 31.0'	+3 58	+5 02	*0.60	*0.41
Sacramento[3]	38° 35.0'	121° 30.0'	+5 07	+6 32	*0.60	*0.41
OUTER COAST		*(corrections apply to San Francisco tides)*				
Bolinas Lagoon	37° 54.4'	122° 40.7'	+0 01	+0 34	*0.74	*0.71
Point Reyes	37° 59.8'	122° 58.5'	-0 51	-0 31	*0.98	*1.04
Tomales Bay						
Tomales Bay entrance	38° 14'	122° 59'	-0 12	+0 20	*0.87	*0.91
Sand Point, Tomales Bay	38° 13.9'	122° 58.0'	-0 04	+0 17	*0.85	*0.86
Blakes Landing, Tomales Bay	38° 11.4'	122° 55.0'	+0 32	+1 15	*0.86	*0.79
Marshall, Tomales Bay	38° 10'	122° 54'	+0 38	+1 16	-0.6	-0.1
Reynolds, Tomales Bay	38° 08.8'	122° 53.0'	+0 26	+1 59	*0.89	*0.83
Inverness, Tomales Bay	38° 06.8'	122° 52.1'	+0 29	+1 08	*0.94	*0.91
Bodega Harbor entrance	38° 18'	123° 03'	-0 38	-0 16	-0.2	+0.1
Fort Ross	38° 31'	123° 15'	-0 51	-0 30	*0.96	*0.96
		(corrections apply to Arena Cove tides)				
Green Cove	38° 42.2'	123° 26.9'	+0 01	-0 01	*0.88	*0.81
Arena Cove	38° 54.8'	123° 42.5'		daily predictions		
Point Arena	38° 57'	123° 44'	+0 03	+0 01	*0.98	*0.95
Mendocino, Mendocino Bay	39° 18'	123° 48'	+0 07	+0 01	*0.98	*0.95
Noyo River	39° 25.5'	123° 48'.3	+0 03	+0 03	*1.04	*1.04
Westport	39° 38'	123° 47'	+0 14	+0 00	*0.98	*0.95
Shelter Cove	40° 01.5'	124° 03.5'	+0 12	+0 11	*1.05	*1.04

Historic Tide Corrections

Times with a minus sign occur *before* predictions; those with a plus sign occur *after*.
*Heights preceded by an asterisk are ratios; multiply by predicted tidal height.

	POSITION		DIFFERENCES			
			Time		Height	
	Latitude	Longitude	High Water	Low Water	High Water	Low Water
	North	**West**	h m	h m	ft	ft
SAN FRANCISCO BAY, cont.		*(corrections apply to San Francisco tides)*				
Angel Island (west side)	37° 52'	122° 27'	+0 13	+0 21	-0.2	0.0
Angel Island, East Garrison	37° 51.8'	122° 25.1'	+0 16	+0 20	*1.02	*1.04
Point Chauncey	37° 53.5'	122° 26.6'	+0 28	+0 32	*0.98	*0.96
Berkeley	37° 51.9'	122° 18.4'	+0 21	+0 26	*1.05	*1.00
Point Isabel	37° 54'	122° 19'	+0 23	+0 33	+0.1	0.0
Richmond Inner Harbor	37° 54.6'	122° 21.5'	+0 16	+0 30	*1.04	*0.98
Chevron Oil Company Pier, Richmond	37° 55.7'	122° 24.0'	+0 24	+0 38	*1.04	*0.98
Point Orient	37° 57.5'	122° 25.5'	+0 50	+0 52	*1.03	*0.96
Corte Madera Creek	37° 56.6'	122° 30.8'	+0 36	+0 51	*0.99	*0.95
Point San Quintin	37° 56.7'	122° 28.4'	+0 42	+0 50	*0.99	*0.93
SAN PABLO BAY						
Point San Pedro	37° 59.6'	122° 26.8'	+1 02	+1 07	*1.01	*0.92
Pinole Point	38° 00.9'	122° 21.7'	+1 16	+1 25	*1.03	*0.89
Hercules, Refugio Landing	38° 01.4'	122° 17.5'	+1 15	+1 39	*1.05	*0.85
Petaluma River entrance	38° 06.7'	122° 29.9'	+1 23	+2 08	*1.06	*0.86
Lakeville, Petaluma River	38° 12'	122° 34'	+1 59	+2 50	*1.11	*0.81
Upper drawbridge, Petaluma River	38° 13.7'	122° 36.8'	+2 11	+2 59	*1.15	*0.82
Gallinas, Gallinas Creek	38° 00.9'	122° 30.2'	+1 18	+1 25	*1.02	*0.89
Hog Island, San Antonio Creek	38° 09.4'	122° 33.0'	+1 47	+2 36	*1.07	*0.79
Sonoma Creek Entrance	38° 09.4'	122° 24.4'	+1 22	+2 46	*0.93	*0.59
Wingo, Sonoma Creek	38° 13'	122° 26'	+2 12	+3 11	+0.1	-0.3
CARQUINEZ STRAIT						
Mare Island	38° 04.2'	122° 15.0'	+1 34	+1 57	*0.99	*0.84
Vallejo, Mare Island Strait	38° 06.7'	122° 16.4'	+1 47	+2 12	*1.02	*0.84
Edgerly Island, Napa River	38° 11.6'	122° 18.8'	+2 02	+2 29	*1.06	*0.76
Brazos Drawbridge, Napa River	38° 12.5'	122° 18.2'	+2 02	+2 29	*1.14	*0.86
Napa, Napa River	38° 17.9'	122° 16.8'	+2 05	+2 37	*1.22	*0.90
Selby	38° 03'	122° 15'	+1 29	+2 04	+0.6	0.0
		(corrections apply to Port Chicago tides)				
Crockett	38° 03.5'	122° 13.4'	-0 58	-1 05	*1.22	*1.31
Benicia	38° 02.6'	122° 07.8'	-0 24	-0 33	*1.09	*1.18
Martinez - Amoroco Pier	38° 02.0'	122° 07.5'	-0 26	-0 30	*1.09	*1.18
SUISUN BAY						
Suisun Slough entrance	38° 07.3'	122° 04.4'	+0 13	+0 26	*0.97	*0.93
Pierce Harbor, Goodyear Slough	38° 07.6'	122° 06.0'	+0 27	+0 41	*1.00	*0.96
Joice Island, Suisun Slough	38° 10.8'	122° 02.7'	+0 21	+0 41	*1.07	*1.00
Suisun City, Suisun Slough	38° 14.2'	122° 01.8'	+0 36	+1 01	*1.11	*1.00
Port Chicago, Suisun Bay	38° 03.4'	122° 02.3'	daily predictions			
Montezuma Slough Bridge	38° 11.2'	121° 58.8'	+0 37	+0 46	*1.01	*0.95
Bradmoor Island, Nurse Slough	38° 11.0'	121° 55.4'	+0 59	+1 06	*1.07	*0.99
Meins Landing, Montezuma Slough	38° 08.2'	121° 54.4'	+0 57	+1 11	*1.11	*0.93
Montezuma Slough	38° 04.6'	121° 53.1'	+1 16	+1 27	*0.84	*0.82
Point Buckler	38° 06.0'	122° 01.0'	+0 13	+0 22	*1.12	*1.08
Mallard Island Ferry Wharf	38° 02.6'	121° 55.1'	+0 54	+0 57	*0.83	*0.81
Pittsburg, New York Slough	38° 02.1'	121° 52.8'	+0 59	+1 05	*0.83	*0.84

Historic Tide Corrections

Times with a minus sign occur *before* predictions; those with a plus sign occur *after*.
*Heights preceded by an asterisk are ratios; multiply by predicted tidal height.

	POSITION		DIFFERENCES			
			Time		Height	
	Latitude	Longitude	High Water	Low Water	High Water	Low Water
	North	West	h m	h m	ft	ft
SAN FRANCISCO BAY, cont.		*(corrections apply to San Francisco tides)*				
Oakland Harbor, Grove Street	37° 48'	122° 17'	+0 33	+0 42	+0.4	0.0
Oakland Harbor, Park Street Bridge	37° 46.3'	122° 14.1'	+0 24	+0 32	*1.13	*0.98
San Leandro Channel, San Leandro Bay	37° 44.9'	122° 14.1'	+0 42	+0 52	*1.16	*0.98
Oakland Airport	37° 43.9'	122° 12.5'	+0 40	+0 45	*1.15	*0.96
Potrero Point	37° 46'	122° 23'	+0 33	+0 46	+0.5	0.0
Hunters Point	37° 43.8'	122° 21.4'	+0 28	+0 43	*1.18	*1.00
San Leandro Marina	37° 41.7'	122° 11.5'	+0 54	+1 23	*1.28	*1.01
Roberts Landings, 1.3 miles west of	37° 40'	122° 12'	+0 52	+1 28	+1.4	+0.1
South San Francisco	37° 40'	122° 23'	+0 38	+0 56	+1.2	0.0
Oyster Point Marina	37° 39.9'	122° 22.6'	+0 41	+1 00	*1.23	*1.00
Point San Bruno	37° 39'	122° 23'	+0 38	+1 10	+1.1	+0.1
Seaplane Harbor	37° 38'	122° 23'	+0 42	+1 03	+1.4	0.0
Coyote Point Marina	37° 35.5'	122° 18.8'	+0 42	+1 08	*1.29	*1.01
San Mateo Bridge (west end)	37° 34.8'	122° 15.2'	+0 44	+1 11	*1.36	*1.04
San Mateo Bridge (east end)	37° 36'	122° 11'	+0 48	+1 19	+1.8	0.0
Alameda Creek	37° 35.7'	122° 08.7'	+0 57	+2 25	*1.05	*0.27
Coyote Hills Slough entrance	37° 33.8'	122° 07.7'	+0 52	+2 21	*1.17	*0.45
Bay Slough, west end	37° 33.1'	122° 14.6'	+0 48	+1 28	*1.35	*1.00
Bay Slough, east end	37° 32.7'	122° 13.3'	+0 49	+1 52	*1.27	*0.77
Redwood Creek Marker 8	37° 32'	122° 12'	+0 53	+1 28	*1.41	*1.05
South Bay Wreck	37° 33'	122° 10'	+1 02	+1 37	+2.2	+0.1
Corkscrew Slough	37° 30'	122° 13'	+1 03	+1 42	+2.2	+0.1
Redwood City, Wharf 5	37° 30.4'	122° 12.6'	+0 48	+1 15	*1.45	*1.05
West Point Slough	37° 30.3'	122° 11.5'	+0 56	+1 30	*1.44	*1.04
Smith Slough	37° 30'	122° 14'	+1 15	+1 58	+2.1	0.0
Newark Slough	37° 31'	122° 05'	+1 11	+1 58	+2.6	+0.1
Dumbarton Highway Bridge	37° 30.4'	122° 06.9'	+0 47	+1 14	*1.53	*1.10
Ravenswood Slough[1]	37° 29.8'	122° 10.3'	+0 58	- - -	- -	- -
Granite Rock, Redwood Creek	37° 29.7'	122° 12.8'	+0 55	+1 31	*1.43	*1.04
Palo Alto Marker 8[2]	37° 28.1'	122° 05.8'	+1 01	- - -	- -	- -
Palo Alto Yacht Harbor	37° 27.5'	122° 06.3'	+0 59	+2 14	*1.34	*0.68
Mowry Slough	37° 30'	122° 02'	+1 12	+2 07	+2.6	0.0
Calaveras Point, west of	37° 28'	122° 04'	+1 05	+1 49	+2.8	+0.1
Mud Slough railroad bridge[2]	37° 28.1'	121° 59.2'	+1 12	- - -	- -	- -
Guadalupe Slough	37° 27.2'	122° 02.0'	+1 06	- - -	- -	- -
Upper Guadalupe Slough	37° 26.1'	122° 00.4'	+1 14	+2 13	*1.66	*1.13
Coyote Creek, Alviso Slough	37° 27.8'	122° 01.4'	+0 59	+1 49	*1.61	*1.09
Gold Street Bridge, Alviso Slough	37° 25.4'	121° 58.5'	+1 03	+2 21	*1.67	*0.96
Coyote Creek, Tributary no. 1	37° 27'	121° 58'	+1 21	+2 45	+2.6	-0.3
Coyote Creek, Tributary no. 2[2]	37° 27.6'	121° 57.2'	+1 18	- - -	- -	- -
Coyote Creek, Tributary no. 3[2]	37° 27.7'	121° 57.1'	+1 15	- - -	- -	- -
Sausalito	37° 50.8'	122° 28.6'	+0 10	+0 14	*0.97	*1.00
Sausalito, Corps of Engineers Dock	37° 51.9'	122° 29.6'	+0 10	+0 21	*0.98	*1.00

HISTORIC NOAA TIDE & CURRENT CORRECTIONS

As of 2020 NOAA stopped supporting the correction tables on the following pages. The tables included in your Tidelog are historic and can provide only a reasonable approximation of the tide/current at the locations listed. NOAA does provide daily predictions for both harmonic and subordinate stations at:

tidesandcurrents.noaa.gov

The prudent mariner should always check the site above for the most accurate data and be aware of the other factors, including the weather, which may affect the tides and currents.

Historic Tide Corrections

Times with a minus sign occur *before* predictions; those with a plus sign occur *after*.
*Heights preceded by an asterisk are ratios; multiply by predicted tidal height.

	POSITION		DIFFERENCES			
			Time		Height	
	Latitude	Longitude	High Water	Low Water	High Water	Low Water
	North	**West**	h m	h m	ft	ft
OUTER COAST of CALIFORNIA		*(corrections apply to San Francisco tides)*				
Ano Nuevo Island	37° 06'	122° 20'	-1 24	-1 04	-0.7	-0.1
Pillar Point Harbor, Half Moon Bay	37° 30.1'	122° 28.9'	-1 04	-0 43	*0.95	*0.97
Southeast Farallon Island	37° 42'	123° 00'	-0 39	-0 19	-0.3	0.0
San Francisco Bar	37° 46'	122° 38'	-0 35	-0 31	-0.2	0.0
Ocean Beach, outer coast	37° 46'	122° 31'	-0 49	-0 35	+0.1	0.0
SAN FRANCISCO BAY						
Point Bonita, Bonita Cove	37° 49'	122° 32'	-0 17	-0 10	+0.3	0.0
San Francisco (Golden Gate)	37° 48.4'	122° 27.9'	daily predictions			
Alcatraz Island	37° 50'	122° 25'	+0 14	+0 18	0.0	0.0
San Francisco, North Point, Pier 41	37° 49'	122° 25'	+0 13	+0 11	+0.2	0.0
Rincon Point, Pier 22 1/2	37° 47'	122° 23'	+0 23	+0 25	+0.4	0.0
Yerba Buena Island	37° 48.6'	122° 21.6'	+0 25	+0 33	*1.06	*0.99
Oakland, Matson Wharf	37° 49'	122° 20'	+0 28	+0 36	+0.3	0.0
Oakland Middle Harbor	37° 48.3'	122° 20.3'	+0 21	+0 31	*1.07	*0.96
Oakland Pier	37° 48'	122° 20'	+0 33	+0 48	+0.2	0.0
Oakland Inner Harbor	37° 47.7'	122° 16.9'	+0 24	+0 31	*1.12	*0.99
Alameda Naval Air Station	37° 47.6'	122° 18.9'	+0 24	+0 33	*1.11	*1.00
Alameda	37° 46.3'	122° 17.9'	+0 29	+0 39	*1.11	*0.99

	GOLDEN GATE			BENICIA BRIDGE			RICHMOND			OAKLAND		
Day	Slack Time	Current Time	Knots	Slack Time	Current Time	Knots	Slack Time	Current Time	Knots	Slack Time	Current Time	Knots
Tue. 12/12	12:54a	2:48a	0.8e	4:18a	12:42a	1.7 f	1:54a	3:30a	0.5e	12:24a	2:18a	0.8e
	4:48a	8:48a	3.0 f	7:36a	6:00a	0.4e	5:30a	8:42a	1.7 f	5:06a	8:06a	1.2 f
	11:24a	2:18p	2.9e	1:54p	11:06a	2.2 f	11:42a	3:30p	2.7e	10:54a	1:42p	1.7e
	7:00p	10:06p	3.0 f	10:18p	5:12p	2.4e	7:42p	10:54p	1.7 f	5:18p	10:00p	1.6 f
Wed. 12/13	1:42a	3:42a	0.8e	5:18a	1:24a	1.7 f	2:48a	4:24a	0.5e	1:12a	3:06a	0.8e
	5:36a	9:36a	3.0 f	8:18a	6:48a	0.3e	6:12a	9:30a	1.7 f	5:54a	8:54a	1.2 f
	12:00p	2:54p	3.0e	2:36p	11:48a	2.2 f	12:24p	4:12p	2.8e	11:36a	2:24p	1.8e
	7:42p	10:54p	3.2 f	11:00p	5:54p	2.5e	8:24p	11:36p	1.7 f	6:00p	10:42p	1.6 f
Thu. 12/14	2:24a	4:30a	0.8e	6:12a	2:12a	1.8 f	3:36a	5:12a	0.5e	2:00a	3:54a	0.9e
	6:30a	10:24a	2.9 f	9:06a	7:42a	0.3e	7:06a	10:18a	1.7 f	6:42a	9:42a	1.3 f
	12:48p	3:42p	3.0e	3:24p	12:42p	2.1 f	1:12p	5:00p	2.9e	12:18p	3:12p	1.8e
	8:24p	11:36p	3.2 f	11:48p	6:48p	2.5e	9:12p			6:42p	11:24p	1.6 f
Fri. 12/15	3:06a	5:18a	0.9e	6:48a	2:54a	1.8 f	4:18a	12:18a	1.8 f	2:42a	4:42a	0.9e
	7:24a	11:12a	2.9 f	10:06a	8:30a	0.4e	8:00a	6:06a	0.6e	7:30a	10:30a	1.3 f
	1:36p	4:30p	2.8e	4:18p	1:30p	2.1 f	2:06p	11:12a	1.7 f	1:12p	4:06p	1.8e
	9:06p			7:42p	2:24p	2.8e	9:54p	5:48p	2.8e	7:30p		
Sat. 12/16	3:54a	12:24a	3.2 f	12:30a	3:36a	1.8 f	5:06a	1:06a	1.8 f	3:30a	12:06a	1.6 f
	8:18a	6:06a	0.9e	7:24a	9:24a	0.5e	9:06a	6:54a	0.7e	8:24a	5:30a	1.0e
	2:24p	12:00p	2.7 f	11:12a	2:24p	2.0 f	3:00p	12:12p	1.6 f	2:06p	11:24a	1.3 f
	9:48p	5:18p	2.6e	5:18p	8:36p	2.3e	10:42p	6:42p	2.7e	8:24p	5:00p	1.8e
Sun. 12/17	4:42a	1:12a	3.2 f	1:12a	4:18a	1.8 f	5:48a	1:54a	1.8 f	4:18a	12:48a	1.6 f
	9:18a	7:06a	1.0e	8:06a	10:24a	0.7e	10:18a	7:48a	0.9e	9:18a	6:24a	1.0e
	3:24p	12:54p	2.4 f	12:30p	3:30p	1.8 f	4:06p	1:12p	1.5 f	3:06p	12:18p	1.3 f
	10:36p	6:18p	2.3e	6:18p	9:42p	2.1e	11:30p	7:36p	2.5e	9:24p	5:54p	1.6e
Mon. 12/18	5:30a	2:06a	3.2 f	1:54a	5:00a	1.9 f	6:30a	2:42a	1.8 f	5:06a	1:36a	1.6 f
	10:30a	8:06a	1.1e	8:42a	11:24a	0.9e	11:42a	8:54a	1.1e	10:18a	7:18a	1.1e
	4:24p	2:00p	2.1 f	1:48p	4:36p	1.6 f	5:12p	2:18p	1.3 f	4:12p	1:18p	1.2 f
	11:24p	7:30p	1.9e	7:30p	10:48p	1.8e		8:36p	2.2e	10:24p	7:00p	1.5e
Tue. 12/19	6:24a	2:54a	3.2 f	2:36a	5:48a	1.9 f	7:18a	3:24a	1.8 f	5:54a	2:30a	1.6 f
	12:00p	9:06a	3.0e	9:24a	12:30p	1.2e		10:00a	1.3e	11:24a	8:12a	1.1e
	5:42p	3:06p	1.9 f	3:12p	5:54p	1.4 f	1:00p	3:30p	1.2 f	5:30p	2:24p	1.2 f
		8:54p	1.6e	8:42p	11:54p	1.6e	6:30p	9:42p	1.8e	11:30p	8:06p	1.3e
Wed. 12/20	12:12a	3:48a	3.3 f	3:18a	6:36a	2.1 f	1:06a	4:18a	1.9 f	6:48a	3:24a	1.6 f
	7:12a	10:12a	1.7e	10:18a	1:36p	1.5e	8:00a	11:06a	1.6e	12:30p	9:06a	1.2e
	1:36p	4:18p	1.9 f	4:36p	7:18p	1.3 f	2:24p	4:54p	1.1 f	6:48p	3:42p	1.1 f
	7:12p	10:12p	1.3e	10:06p			7:54p	10:48p	1.5e		9:12p	1.2e
Thu. 12/21	1:00a	4:42a	3.3 f	4:00a	1:00a	1.3e	1:54a	5:00a	1.9 f	12:30a	4:18a	1.6 f
	8:00a	11:06a	2.1e	10:54a	7:24a	2.2 f	8:48a	12:12p	2.0 f	7:36a	10:00a	1.3e
	3:00p	5:36p	2.1 f	6:00p	2:36p	1.8e	3:36p	6:30p	1.2 f	1:42p	5:12p	1.2 f
	8:42p	11:18p	1.2e	11:24p	8:42p	1.4 f	9:18p	11:54p	1.2e	8:06p	10:24p	1.1e
Fri. 12/22	1:48a	5:36a	3.4 f	4:42a	2:00a	1.1e	2:36a	5:48a	1.9 f	1:24a	5:06a	1.6 f
	8:42a	12:00p	2.5e	11:30a	8:12a	2.2 f	9:30a	1:06p	2.3e	8:18a	10:54a	1.4e
	4:00p	6:42p	2.4 f	7:06p	3:42p	2.0e	4:36p	7:48p	1.4 f	2:48p	6:36p	1.4 f
	10:00p			9:48p	6:42p	1.6 f	10:36p			9:18p	11:30p	1.6e
Sat. 12/23	2:36a	12:18a	1.0e	12:36a	3:00a	0.9e	3:24a	12:54a	1.0e	2:24a	5:54a	1.5 f
	9:24a	6:30a	3.4 f	5:24a	8:54a	2.3 f	10:06a	6:30a	1.7 f	9:06a	11:42a	1.5e
	5:00p	12:42p	2.8e	12:12p	4:36p	2.2e	5:36p	1:48p	2.5e	3:42p	7:42p	1.6 f
	11:06p	7:42p	2.8 f	8:06p	10:48p	1.8 f	11:48p	8:54p	1.6 f	10:24p		
Sun. 12/24	3:30a	1:12a	0.9e	1:48a	4:00a	0.8e	4:12a	1:54a	0.9e	3:18a	12:36a	1.0e
	10:06a	7:18a	3.4 f	6:12a	9:36a	2.2 f	10:48a	7:12a	1.8 f	9:42a	6:36a	1.5 f
	5:48p	1:18p	2.9e	12:48p	5:30p	2.3e	6:24p	2:36p	2.6e	4:36p	12:24p	1.6e
		8:36p	3.2 f	8:54p	11:42p	1.9 f		9:48p	1.8 f	11:24p	8:36p	1.7 f
Mon. 12/25	4:24a	2:06a	0.9e	2:54a	4:54a	0.7e	12:48a	2:48a	0.8e	4:12a	1:30a	1.0e
	10:48a	8:00a	3.2 f	6:54a	10:18a	2.1 f	5:00a	8:00a	1.7 f	10:24a	7:18a	1.4 f
	4:24p	2:00p	2.9e	1:24p	6:18p	2.2e	11:24a	3:12p	2.7e	5:18p	1:00p	1.6e
	6:36p	9:24p	3.4 f	9:42p			7:06p	10:36p	1.8 f		9:30p	1.8 f
Tue. 12/26	1:00a	3:00a	0.8e	3:54a	12:36a	2.0 f	1:42a	3:42a	0.8e	12:12a	2:24a	1.0e
	5:30a	8:54a	3.0 f	7:42a	5:54a	0.6e	6:48a	8:42a	1.7 f	5:06a	8:06a	1.3 f
	11:36a	2:42p	2.7e	2:00p	11:00a	2.2 f	12:00p	3:48p	2.6e	11:06a	1:42p	1.6e
	7:18p	10:12p	3.4 f	10:24p	7:00p	2.2e	7:48p	11:18p	1.9 f	5:54p	10:12p	1.8 f
Wed. 12/27	1:48a	4:00a	0.9e	4:54a	1:24a	2.1 f	2:30a	4:30a	0.8e	1:00a	3:12a	1.0e
	6:30a	9:42a	2.8 f	8:30a	6:48a	0.6e	6:36a	9:30a	1.6 f	5:54a	8:48a	1.3 f
	12:24p	3:36p	2.5e	2:42p	11:42a	1.9 f	12:42p	4:24p	2.6e	11:42a	2:24p	1.5e
	8:00p	10:54p	3.4 f	11:06p	7:24p	2.1e	8:24p			6:24p	10:48p	1.7 f
Thu. 12/28	2:36a	4:54a	0.9e	5:42a	2:12a	2.1 f	3:18a	12:00a	1.8 f	1:42a	3:54a	1.0e
	7:24a	10:30a	2.6 f	9:18a	7:36a	0.6e	7:24a	5:18a	0.8e	6:36a	9:30a	1.3 f
	1:06p	4:24p	2.3e	3:18p	12:24p	1.8 f	1:18p	10:12a	1.6 f	12:24p	3:06p	1.5e
	8:42p	11:36p	3.2 f	11:42p	7:12p	2.1e	9:00p	5:00p	2.5e	6:54p	11:24p	1.7 f
Fri. 12/29	3:24a	5:42a	0.9e	6:24a	2:54a	2.0 f	3:54a	12:30a	1.7 f	2:24a	4:36a	1.1e
	8:12a	11:18a	2.4 f	10:12a	8:18a	0.6e	8:12a	6:00a	0.8e	7:24a	10:12a	1.3 f
	1:54p	5:12p	2.1e	4:00p	1:12p	1.7 f	2:00p	11:00a	1.5 f	1:06p	3:42p	1.5e
	9:18p			7:42p	2:12p	2.1e	9:36p	5:36p	2.4e	7:24p	11:42p	1.5 f
Sat. 12/30	4:12a	12:18a	3.1 f	12:12a	3:30a	2.0 f	4:30a	12:54a	1.7 f	3:00a	5:12a	1.0e
	8:54a	6:24a	0.9e	7:00a	9:00a	0.6e	9:00a	6:36a	0.8e	8:06a	10:54a	1.3 f
	2:36p	12:00p	2.1 f	11:00a	1:54p	1.6 f	2:42p	11:42a	1.4 f	1:48p	4:30p	1.5e
	9:48p	5:54p	2.0e	4:48p	8:18p	2.0e	10:12p	6:12p	2.3e	7:54p		
Sun. 12/31	5:00a	1:00a	2.9 f	12:42a	4:00a	2.0 f	5:06a	1:12a	1.6 f	3:36a	12:00a	1.4 f
	9:36a	7:12a	0.9e	7:36a	9:42a	0.7e	9:54a	7:00a	0.9e	8:42a	5:48a	1.0e
	3:18p	12:48p	1.7 f	11:54a	2:42p	1.5 f	3:24p	12:30p	1.3 f	2:30p	11:36a	1.3 f
	10:18p	6:42p	1.8e	5:30p	9:00p	2.0e	10:42p	6:54p	2.1e	8:36p	5:18p	1.4e

	GOLDEN GATE			BENICIA BRIDGE			RICHMOND			OAKLAND		
	SLACK Time	CURRENT Time	Knots	SLACK Time	CURRENT Time	Knots	SLACK Time	CURRENT Time	Knots	SLACK Time	CURRENT Time	Knots
Sun. 11/19	6:18a	2:30a	2.8 f	2:36a	5:54a	1.6 f	12:00a	3:24a	1.6 f	5:42a	2:18a	1.4 f
	10:36a	8:36a	0.8 e	9:42a	11:54a	0.5 e	7:18a	9:24a	0.7 e	10:42a	7:48a	0.9 e
	4:30p	2:12p	1.9 f	1:48p	4:42p	1.6 f	11:42a	2:30p	1.2 f	4:24p	1:36p	1.1 f
	11:48p	7:24p	1.9 e	7:36p	10:54p	1.8 e	5:18p	9:00p	2.2 e	10:48p	7:12p	1.4 e
Mon. 11/20	7:12a	3:24a	2.9 f	3:24a	6:48a	1.7 f	1:00a	4:24a	1.7 f	6:36a	3:18a	1.5 f
	12:06p	9:42a	1.0 e	10:24a	1:00p	0.8 e	8:06a	10:30a	0.9 e	11:54a	8:48a	1.0 e
	5:48p	3:18p	1.8 f	3:12p	6:00p	1.4 f	1:12p	3:42p	1.2 f	5:42p	2:42p	1.2 f
		9:00p	1.6 e	8:54p			6:42p	10:06p	2.0 e		8:24p	1.4 e
Tue. 11/21	12:54a	4:24a	3.0 f	4:12a	12:18a	1.7 f	1:54a	5:18a	1.8 f	12:00a	4:18a	1.6 f
	8:00a	10:48a	1.4 e	11:00a	7:36a	1.9 f	8:54a	11:36a	1.3 e	7:30a	9:48a	1.2 e
	1:48p	4:36p	1.8 f	4:36p	2:00p	1.2 e	2:30p	5:00p	1.2 f	12:54p	3:54p	1.2 f
	7:18p	10:42p	1.5 e	10:12p	7:24p	1.4 f	8:06p	11:12p	1.9 e	7:00p	9:30p	1.3 e
Wed. 11/22	1:48a	5:24a	3.3 f	4:54a	1:30a	1.6 f	2:42a	6:00a	1.9 f	1:06a	5:06a	1.7 f
	8:42a	11:42a	1.9 e	11:36a	8:18a	2.1 f	9:30a	12:36p	1.8 e	8:18a	10:42a	1.3 e
	3:12p	5:48p	2.1 f	5:54p	2:54p	1.6 e	3:36p	6:18p	1.4 f	2:00p	5:12p	1.3 f
	8:48p	11:48p	1.4 e	11:24p	8:42p	1.6 f	9:18p			8:12p	10:36p	1.3 e
Thu. 11/23	2:36a	6:12a	3.5 f	5:36a	2:24a	1.5 f	3:24a	12:18a	1.8 f	2:00a	5:48a	1.7 f
	9:24a	12:30p	2.4 e	12:12p	8:54a	2.3 f	10:06a	6:36a	2.0 f	9:00a	11:30a	1.5 e
	4:18p	6:54p	2.5 f	7:00p	3:48p	1.9 e	4:36p	1:24p	2.1 e	2:54p	6:24p	1.4 f
	10:00p				9:48p	1.7 f	10:30p	7:30p	1.5 f	9:18p	11:42p	1.3 e
Fri. 11/24	3:24a	12:42a	1.4 e	12:30a	3:18a	1.3 f	4:06a	1:12a	1.6 f	2:48a	6:30a	1.7 f
	10:00a	7:00a	3.7 f	6:12a	9:30a	2.4 f	10:42a	7:12a	2.0 f	9:42a	12:12p	1.6 e
	5:12p	1:12p	2.8 e	12:42p	4:42p	2.1 e	5:36p	2:06p	2.4 e	3:48p	7:30p	1.5 f
	11:12p	7:54p	2.9 f	8:00p	10:48p	1.8 f	11:36p	8:36p	1.6 f	10:24p		
Sat. 11/25	4:06a	1:30a	1.2 e	1:36a	4:06a	1.2 e	4:42a	2:06a	1.4 e	3:36a	12:36a	1.3 e
	10:36a	7:48a	3.8 f	6:48a	10:06a	2.5 f	11:18a	7:48a	2.0 f	10:18a	7:12a	1.7 f
	6:06p	1:48p	3.1 e	1:18p	5:24p	2.2 e	6:24p	2:48p	2.6 e	4:42p	12:48p	1.7 e
		8:48p	3.2 f	8:54p	11:42p	1.9 f		9:36p	1.7 f	11:24p	8:30p	1.6 f
Sun. 11/26	12:12a	2:24a	1.1 e	2:36a	4:54a	1.0 e	12:36a	2:54a	1.1 e	4:24a	1:30a	1.2 e
	4:48a	8:30a	3.7 f	7:24a	10:42a	2.4 f	5:24a	8:24a	2.0 f	10:54a	7:48a	1.6 f
	11:18a	2:24p	3.2 e	1:54p	6:06p	2.3 e	11:48a	3:24p	2.7 e	5:24p	1:30p	1.7 e
	6:54p	9:36p	3.5 f	9:48p			7:12p	10:30p	1.8 f		9:30p	1.7 f
Mon. 11/27	1:12a	3:18a	0.9 e	3:42a	12:36a	1.9 f	1:42a	3:42a	0.9 e	12:18a	2:24a	1.1 e
	5:42a	9:18a	3.5 f	8:06a	5:54a	0.8 e	6:00a	9:00a	1.9 f	5:12a	8:24a	1.5 f
	11:54a	3:06p	3.2 e	2:24p	11:18a	2.3 f	12:24p	4:06p	2.7 e	11:30a	2:06p	1.7 e
	7:36p	10:24p	3.6 f	10:36p	6:30p	2.2 e	8:00p	11:24p	1.8 f	6:06p	10:24p	1.7 f
Tue. 11/28	2:12a	4:18a	0.9 e	4:48a	1:30a	1.9 f	2:36a	4:36a	0.8 e	1:12a	3:18a	1.0 e
	6:30a	10:00a	3.2 f	8:48a	6:48a	0.6 e	6:42a	9:42a	1.8 f	6:00a	9:06a	1.4 f
	12:36p	3:48p	3.0 e	3:00p	12:00p	2.1 f	12:54p	4:42p	2.6 e	12:06p	2:48p	1.6 e
	8:18p	11:12p	3.6 f	11:18p	6:42p	2.1 e	8:42p			6:42p	11:06p	1.6 f
Wed. 11/29	3:06a	5:12a	0.8 e	5:48a	2:24a	2.0 f	3:36a	12:12a	1.7 f	2:06a	4:12a	1.0 e
	7:24a	10:48a	2.8 f	9:30a	7:42a	0.5 e	7:30a	5:24a	0.7 e	6:54a	9:48a	1.3 f
	1:18p	4:24p	2.8 f	3:36p	12:42p	1.9 f	1:36p	10:30a	1.6 f	12:42p	3:24p	1.6 f
	9:00p				7:06p	2.1 e	9:24p	5:18p	2.5 e	7:12p	11:54p	1.5 f
Thu. 11/30	3:54a	12:00a	3.4 f	12:06a	3:18a	2.0 f	4:24a	12:00a	1.7 f	2:54a	5:00a	0.9 e
	8:18a	6:06a	0.8 e	6:48a	8:36a	0.5 e	8:24a	6:18a	0.7 e	7:42a	10:30a	1.2 f
	2:00p	11:36a	2.4 f	10:24a	1:30p	1.7 f	2:12p	11:12a	1.5 f	1:24p	4:06p	1.5 e
	9:36p	5:06p	2.4 e	4:18p	7:54p	2.0 e	10:06p	6:00p	2.4 e	7:48p		
Fri. 12/1	4:48a	12:42a	3.1 f	12:48a	4:06a	1.9 f	5:12a	1:42a	1.6 f	3:36a	12:30a	1.4 f
	9:12a	6:54a	0.8 e	7:42a	9:36a	0.5 e	9:18a	7:06a	0.6 e	8:36a	5:48a	0.9 e
	2:48p	12:24p	2.0 f	11:18a	2:18p	1.6 f	3:00p	12:06p	1.3 f	2:06p	11:18a	1.2 f
	10:12p	5:54p	2.0 e	5:06p	8:36p	1.9 e	10:48p	6:42p	2.2 e	8:24p	4:54p	1.4 e
Sat. 12/2	5:42a	1:30a	2.9 f	1:30a	4:54a	1.9 f	6:00a	2:30a	1.5 f	4:24a	1:06a	1.3 f
	10:06a	7:48a	0.7 e	8:36a	10:30a	0.5 e	10:18a	8:00a	0.7 e	9:24a	6:36a	0.9 e
	3:36p	1:12p	1.5 f	12:18p	3:06p	1.4 f	3:48p	1:00p	1.2 f	3:00p	12:06p	1.2 f
	10:48p	6:48p	1.6 e	5:54p	9:36p	1.8 e	11:36p	7:30p	2.0 e	9:12p	5:42p	1.3 e
Sun. 12/3	6:42a	2:24a	2.6 f	2:12a	5:42a	1.9 f	6:42a	3:06a	1.5 f	5:12a	1:36a	1.3 f
	11:12a	8:48a	0.7 e	9:18a	11:30a	0.6 e	11:30a	9:00a	0.7 e	10:18a	7:30a	0.9 e
	4:30p	2:12p	1.2 f	1:24p	4:06p	1.2 f	4:48p	2:00p	1.0 f	3:54p	1:00p	1.1 f
	11:30p	7:54p	1.4 e	6:54p	10:42p	1.7 e		8:18p	1.8 e	10:06p	6:36p	1.1 e
Mon. 12/4	7:36a	3:12a	2.5 f	2:54a	6:30a	1.9 f	12:18a	3:48a	1.4 f	6:00a	2:18a	1.2 f
	12:48p	9:42a	0.7 e	10:00a	12:24p	0.8 e	7:30a	10:00a	0.9 e	11:12a	8:18a	0.9 e
	5:30p	3:12p	0.9 f	2:42p	5:06p	1.0 f	12:42p	3:00p	0.9 f	5:00p	1:54p	1.1 f
		9:06p	1.2 e	8:00p	11:42p	1.6 e	5:54p	9:18p	1.6 e	11:06p	7:36p	1.1 e
Tue. 12/5	12:06a	4:00a	2.5 f	3:30a	7:06a	1.9 f	1:06a	4:18a	1.4 f	6:42a	3:00a	1.2 f
	8:18a	10:36a	0.8 e	10:36a	1:18p	1.0 e	8:06a	11:00a	1.1 e	12:06p	9:06a	0.9 e
	2:12p	4:18p	0.8 f	3:54p	6:24p	0.9 f	1:54p	4:06p	0.9 f	6:12p	2:54p	1.1 f
	6:54p	10:06p	1.1 e	9:18p			7:06p	10:12p	1.4 e		8:42p	1.0 e
Wed. 12/6	12:42a	4:48a	2.5 f	4:06a	12:42a	1.4 e	1:48a	4:48a	1.5 f	12:06a	3:48a	1.3 f
	8:48a	11:24a	1.1 e	11:06a	7:42a	2.0 f	8:42a	11:54a	1.3 e	7:24a	9:48a	1.0 e
	3:18p	5:30p	0.9 f	5:12p			3:00p	5:12p	0.9 f	1:06p	3:54p	1.1 f
	8:12p	11:00p	1.0 e	10:30p	7:54p	0.9 f	8:24p	11:18p	1.2 e	7:24p	9:42p	0.9 e
Thu. 12/7	1:18a	5:30a	2.6 f	4:42a	1:36a	1.3 e	2:24a	5:24a	1.5 f	1:00a	4:30a	1.3 f
	9:12a	12:00p	1.4 e	11:36a	8:12a	2.0 f	9:18a	12:30p	1.6 e	8:06a	10:30a	1.1 e
	4:06p	6:30p	1.2 f	6:18p	2:48p	1.5 e	3:54p	6:24p	1.0 f	1:54p	5:06p	1.1 f
	9:24p	11:48p	1.0 e	11:42p	9:06p	1.1 f	9:36p			8:30p	10:48p	0.9 e
Fri. 12/8	1:54a	6:06a	2.8 f	5:18a	2:30a	1.1 e	3:06a	12:12a	1.0 e	1:54a	5:12a	1.3 f
	9:30a	12:30p	1.8 e	12:00p	8:42a	2.1 f	9:42a	6:00a	1.5 f	8:36a	11:06a	1.2 e
	4:48p	7:18p	1.6 f	7:12p	3:24p	1.7 e	4:48p	1:06p	1.8 e	2:42p	6:18p	1.2 f
	10:24p			10:06p		1.3 f	10:48p	7:36p	1.1 f	9:36p	11:42p	0.9 e
Sat. 12/9	2:30a	12:30a	0.9 e	12:54a	3:18a	0.9 e	3:36a	1:00a	0.9 e	2:42a	5:54a	1.3 f
	9:48a	6:48a	2.9 f	5:48a	9:12a	2.1 f	10:12a	6:42a	1.6 f	9:12a	11:42a	1.3 e
	5:18p	12:54p	2.1 e	12:24p	3:48p	1.9 e	5:36p	1:36p	2.1 e	3:30p	7:24p	1.3 f
	11:18p	8:06p	2.0 f	8:06p	11:00p	1.4 f	11:54p	8:42p	1.3 f	10:36p		
Sun. 12/10	3:12a	1:18a	0.9 e	2:00a	4:12a	0.7 e	4:12a	1:54a	0.7 e	3:30a	12:36a	0.8 e
	10:18a	7:24a	2.9 f	6:24a	9:48a	2.2 f	10:36a	7:18a	1.6 f	9:42a	6:36a	1.2 f
	5:54p	1:12p	2.5 e	12:48p	4:12p	2.1 e	6:18p	2:12p	2.3 e	4:06p	12:24p	1.4 e
		8:48p	2.4 f	8:48p	11:48p	1.6 f		9:24p	1.4 f	11:30p	8:24p	1.4 f
Mon. 12/11	12:06a	2:00a	0.8 e	3:06a	5:06a	0.5 e	12:54a	2:42a	0.6 e	4:18a	1:30a	0.8 e
	3:54a	8:06a	2.9 f	6:54a	10:24a	2.2 f	4:48a	8:00a	1.6 f	10:12a	7:24a	1.2 f
	10:48a	1:42p	2.7 e	1:18p	4:36p	2.3 e	11:06a	2:48p	2.5 e	4:42p	1:00p	1.6 e
	6:24p	9:30p	2.8 f	9:36p			7:00p	10:12p	1.6 f		9:18p	1.5 f

		GOLDEN GATE			BENICIA BRIDGE			RICHMOND			OAKLAND		
		SLACK	CURRENT		SLACK	CURRENT		SLACK	CURRENT		SLACK	CURRENT	
Day	Date	Time	Time	Knots	Time	Time	Knots	Time	Time	Knots	Time	Time	Knots
Fri.	10/27	12:12a	2:54a	1.6e	2:36a	5:30a	1.6e	12:30a	3:24a	2.0e	5:12a	1:48a	1.6e
		6:00a	9:18a	3.8f	8:36a	11:48a	2.4f	6:30a	9:30a	2.1f	11:54a	8:54a	1.8f
		12:12p	3:18p	2.9e	2:54p	6:30p	2.1e	12:54p	4:06p	2.4e	5:48p	2:24p	1.6e
		7:12p	10:00p	3.3f	9:48p			7:30p	10:18p	1.9f		9:24p	1.6f
Sat.	10/28	1:12a	3:42a	1.5e	3:30a	12:36a	2.1f	1:30a	4:12a	1.7e	12:18a	2:42a	1.5e
		6:36a	10:00a	3.9f	9:12a	6:12a	1.5e	7:06a	10:00a	2.1f	5:54a	9:24a	1.8f
		12:48p	3:54p	3.1e	3:30p	12:18p	2.5f	1:24p	4:48p	2.5e	12:30p	3:00p	1.7e
		8:06p	10:54p	3.5f	10:42p	7:06p	2.2e	8:18p	11:12p	1.8f	6:36p	10:24p	1.6f
Sun.	10/29	2:12a	4:42a	1.3e	4:30a	1:30a	2.0f	2:30a	4:54a	1.5e	1:18a	3:30a	1.3e
		7:18a	10:42a	3.8f	9:42a	7:06a	1.3e	7:36a	10:36a	2.0f	6:36a	10:00a	1.7f
		1:24p	4:36p	3.3e	4:00p	12:54p	2.5f	2:00p	5:24p	2.6e	1:06p	3:36p	1.7e
		8:48p	11:42p	3.6f	11:36p	7:42p	2.2e	9:06p			7:24p	11:18p	1.6f
Mon.	10/30	3:12a	5:36a	1.1e	5:30a	2:30a	1.9f	3:30a	12:06a	1.8f	2:12a	4:24a	1.2e
		7:54a	11:24a	3.5f	10:18a	7:54a	1.0e	8:12a	5:42a	1.2e	7:18a	10:36a	1.6f
		2:00p	5:12p	3.3e	4:36p	1:30p	2.3f	2:30p	11:12a	1.9f	1:42p	4:18p	1.7e
		9:36p			8:06p	10:06p	2.2e	9:54p	6:42p	2.6e	8:00p		
Tue.	10/31	4:12a	12:30a	3.6f	12:30a	3:30a	1.9f	4:30a	1:00a	1.7f	3:12a	12:12a	1.5f
		8:24a	6:24a	1.0e	6:42a	8:48a	0.8e	8:54a	6:36a	0.9e	8:06a	5:18a	1.0e
		2:42p	12:12p	3.1f	11:00a	2:12p	2.1f	3:06p	11:54a	1.8f	2:12p	11:12a	1.4f
		10:12p	5:48p	3.1e	5:12p	8:36p	2.1e	10:48p	6:42p	2.5e	8:42p	4:54p	1.6e
Wed.	11/1	5:12a	1:18a	3.4f	1:24a	4:30a	1.8f	5:36a	2:06a	1.6f	4:12a	1:06a	1.4f
		9:30a	7:18a	0.8e	7:48a	9:48a	0.6e	9:42a	7:24a	0.7e	9:00a	6:12a	0.9e
		3:24p	12:54p	2.6f	11:48a	2:54p	1.9f	3:42p	12:36p	1.6f	2:54p	11:54a	1.3f
		10:54p	6:24p	2.7e	5:54p	9:12p	1.8e	11:36p	7:24p	2.3e	9:18p	5:36p	1.5e
Thu.	11/2	6:12a	2:06a	3.2f	2:18a	5:36a	1.8f	6:36a	3:06a	1.5f	5:06a	2:00a	1.4f
		10:18a	8:18a	0.7e	9:00a	10:54a	0.5e	10:36a	8:24a	0.6e	9:54a	7:12a	0.8e
		4:06p	1:42p	2.1f	12:42p	3:42p	1.7f	4:30p	1:30p	1.3f	3:36p	12:42p	1.2f
		11:36p	7:06p	2.2e	6:36p	10:06p	1.8e		8:12p	2.1e	10:00p	6:18p	1.3e
Fri.	11/3	7:18a	3:00a	2.9f	3:12a	6:36a	1.8f	12:30a	4:18a	1.5f	6:06a	3:00a	1.3f
		11:24a	9:18a	0.7e	10:12a	12:00p	0.5e	7:36a	9:36a	0.5e	10:54a	8:18a	0.8e
		4:54p	2:36p	1.6f	1:42p	4:36p	1.4f	11:42a	2:24p	1.1f	4:30p	1:36p	1.1f
			7:54p	1.7f	7:30p	11:18p	1.6e	5:24p	9:06p	1.9e	10:54p	7:12p	1.2e
Sat.	11/4	12:18a	4:00a	2.6f	4:06a	7:36a	1.9f	1:24a	5:18a	1.4f	7:00a	4:00a	1.3f
		8:18a	10:18a	0.6e	11:12a	12:06p	0.5e	8:36a	10:48a	0.6e	12:00p	9:24a	0.9e
		12:54p	3:36p	1.2f	2:54p	5:36p	1.1f	1:00p	3:30p	1.0f	5:36p	2:36p	1.0f
		5:54p	9:06p	1.2e	8:30p			6:30p	10:12p	1.7e	12:00p	8:12p	1.0e
Sun.	11/5	12:54a	4:00a	2.4f	4:00a	12:54a	1.5f	1:18a	5:12a	1.5f	12:00a	4:00a	1.3f
		8:18a	10:18a	0.7e	11:00a	7:30a	2.0f	8:24a	11:00a	0.8e	6:48a	9:18a	1.0e
		1:36p	3:48p	0.9f	3:12p	1:00p	0.7e	1:18p	3:42p	0.9f	12:00p	2:36p	1.0f
		6:18p	9:42p	1.0e	8:48p	5:48p	1.0f	6:42p	10:24p	1.6e	6:48p	8:12p	1.0e
Mon.	11/6	1:12a	5:00a	2.4f	4:48a	1:18a	1.5f	2:12a	6:00a	1.5f	12:06a	4:42a	1.3f
		9:00a	11:18a	0.9e	11:36a	8:18a	2.0f	9:12a	11:54a	1.0e	7:36a	10:12a	1.0e
		2:48p	5:00p	0.9f	4:30p	2:00p	0.9e	2:30p	4:48p	1.0f	12:54p	3:36p	1.1f
		7:48p	10:54p	1.0e	10:00p	7:06p	1.0f	8:00p	11:24p	1.6e	6:54p	9:24p	1.0e
Tue.	11/7	2:00a	5:48a	2.5f	5:24a	2:12a	1.6f	2:54a	6:36a	1.5f	1:06a	5:24a	1.4f
		9:36a	12:06p	1.1e	12:12p	8:54a	2.1f	9:48a	12:42p	1.1e	8:24a	11:00a	1.1e
		3:48p	6:12p	1.1f	5:36p	2:54p	1.2e	3:30p	6:00p	1.1f	1:48p	4:36p	1.2f
		9:00p	11:48p	1.0e	11:12p	8:24p	1.1f	9:06p			7:54p	10:24p	1.0e
Wed.	11/8	2:36a	6:30a	2.7f	6:00a	2:48a	1.5f	3:42a	12:18a	1.5f	1:54a	5:54a	1.4f
		10:06a	12:42p	1.4e	12:36p	9:24a	2.1f	10:18a	7:06a	1.6f	9:00a	11:36a	1.2e
		4:36p	7:06p	1.4f	6:36p	3:36p	1.4e	4:18p	1:24p	1.2e	2:36p	5:36p	1.3f
		9:54p			9:24p		1.3f	10:06p	7:00p	1.2f	8:54p	11:18p	1.1e
Thu.	11/9	3:12a	12:30a	1.2e	12:06a	3:24a	1.5f	4:12a	1:06a	1.5f	2:42a	6:24a	1.4f
		10:24a	7:00a	2.8f	6:30a	9:48a	2.2f	10:42a	7:18a	1.6f	9:36a	12:06p	1.2e
		5:18p	1:12p	1.4e	1:00p	4:12p	1.6e	5:06p	1:54p	1.7e	3:18p	6:30p	1.3f
		10:42p	7:48p	1.7f	7:30p	10:18p	1.4f	11:00p	7:54p	1.3f	9:48p		
Fri.	11/10	3:36a	1:06a	1.2e	1:00a	4:00a	1.3e	4:42a	1:42a	1.3e	3:24a	12:06a	1.1e
		10:48a	7:36a	3.0f	6:54a	10:12a	2.2f	11:06a	7:36a	1.6f	10:06a	6:48a	1.4f
		5:48p	1:42p	2.0e	1:18p	4:42p	1.8e	5:54p	2:24p	1.9e	4:00p	12:30p	1.3e
		11:30p	8:30p	2.0f	8:12p	11:00p	1.5f	11:54p	8:36p	1.4f	10:42p	7:24p	1.3f
Sat.	11/11	4:06a	1:48a	1.1e	1:54a	4:36a	1.1e	5:06a	2:18a	1.2e	4:00a	12:54a	1.1e
		11:06a	8:06a	3.1f	7:18a	10:30a	2.2f	11:30a	8:06a	1.7f	10:30a	7:18a	1.4f
		6:24p	2:06p	2.3e	1:42p	4:54p	1.9e	6:30p	2:48p	2.1e	4:36p	1:00p	1.4e
			9:12p	2.4f	9:00p	11:48p	1.5f		9:18p	1.5f	11:36p	8:12p	1.4f
Sun.	11/12	12:18a	2:30a	1.0e	2:54a	5:18a	0.9e	12:48a	3:00a	1.0e	4:36a	1:42a	1.0e
		4:42a	8:42a	3.1f	7:48a	11:00a	2.2f	5:36a	8:36a	1.7f	10:54a	7:54a	1.3f
		11:30a	2:24p	2.6e	2:00p	5:12p	2.1e	11:48a	3:18p	2.3e	5:06p	1:30p	1.5e
		6:48p	9:48p	2.7f	9:42p			7:12p	10:00p	1.5f		9:06p	1.4f
Mon.	11/13	1:06a	3:18a	0.9e	3:54a	12:36a	1.6f	1:42a	3:42a	0.8e	12:24a	2:30a	0.9e
		5:24a	9:18a	3.1f	8:12a	6:06a	0.7e	6:00a	9:12a	1.7f	5:18a	8:30a	1.3f
		11:54a	2:48p	2.9e	2:30p	11:30a	2.2f	12:12p	3:54p	2.5e	11:24a	2:06p	1.6e
		7:18p	10:30p	2.9f	10:24p	5:36p	2.3e	7:54p	10:42p	1.5f	5:36p	9:54p	1.4f
Tue.	11/14	2:00a	4:06a	0.9e	5:00a	1:24a	1.6f	2:42a	4:30a	0.7e	1:18a	3:12a	0.8e
		6:06a	10:00a	3.0f	8:42a	6:48a	0.5e	6:36a	9:48a	1.7f	5:54a	9:12a	1.2f
		12:30p	3:24p	3.1e	3:00p	12:12p	2.2f	12:42p	4:30p	2.6e	11:54a	2:48p	1.7e
		7:54p	11:12p	3.1f	11:12p	6:12p	2.4e	8:36p	11:30p	1.6f	6:06p	10:42p	1.4f
Wed.	11/15	2:48a	4:48a	0.8e	6:06a	2:18a	1.6f	3:36a	5:18a	0.6e	2:12a	4:06a	0.8e
		6:48a	10:42a	2.9f	9:18a	7:36a	0.3e	7:12a	10:36a	1.6f	6:42a	9:54a	1.2f
		1:06p	4:00p	3.1e	3:42p	12:54p	2.1f	1:18p	5:12p	2.7e	12:30p	3:30p	1.8e
		8:30p	11:54p	3.1f	11:54p	6:54p	2.5e	9:18p			6:42p	11:24p	1.4f
Thu.	11/16	3:36a	5:36a	0.6e	8:12a	3:06a	1.6f	4:36a	12:18a	1.6f	3:00a	4:54a	0.8e
		7:36a	11:24a	2.7f	10:06a	8:36a	0.3e	8:00a	6:12a	0.5e	7:36a	10:42a	1.2f
		1:48p	4:42p	3.0e	4:24p	1:42p	2.0f	2:06p	11:24a	2.7f	1:18p	4:18p	1.8e
		9:06p				7:42p	2.4e	10:12p	6:00p	2.7e	7:30p		
Fri.	11/17	4:24a	12:42a	3.1f	12:48a	4:00a	1.6f	5:36a	1:12a	1.6f	3:54a	12:12a	1.4f
		8:30a	6:30a	0.7e	8:12a	9:36a	0.2e	9:00a	7:06a	0.5e	8:36a	5:48a	0.8e
		2:36p	12:12p	2.5f	11:06a	2:36p	1.9f	3:00p	12:18p	1.4f	2:12p	11:36a	1.2f
		9:54p	5:24p	2.7e	5:18p	8:36p	2.2e	11:06p	6:54p	2.6e	8:24p	5:12p	1.7e
Sat.	11/18	5:18a	1:36a	2.9f	1:42a	5:00a	1.6f	6:30a	2:18a	1.5f	4:48a	1:12a	1.4f
		9:30a	7:30a	0.7e	9:00a	10:42a	0.3e	10:12a	8:12a	0.5e	9:36a	6:48a	0.8e
		3:30p	1:12p	2.2f	12:24p	3:36p	1.7f	4:06p	1:18p	1.3f	3:12p	12:30p	1.1f
		10:48p	6:18p	2.3e	6:24p	9:42p	2.0e		7:54p	2.4e	9:30p	6:06p	1.5e

GOLDEN GATE · BENICIA BRIDGE · RICHMOND · OAKLAND

	GOLDEN GATE SLACK Time	CURRENT Time	Knots	BENICIA BRIDGE SLACK Time	CURRENT Time	Knots	RICHMOND SLACK Time	CURRENT Time	Knots	OAKLAND SLACK Time	CURRENT Time	Knots
Wed. 10/4	6:12a	2:24a	3.1 f	2:42a	5:48a	1.6 f	12:06a	3:18a	1.4 f	5:24a	2:12a	1.3 f
	10:36a	8:30a	0.8e	8:54a	11:00a	0.7e	6:42a	8:42a	0.7e	10:12a	7:30a	0.9e
	4:36p	2:06p	2.4 f	1:12p	4:18p	1.8 f	11:00a	2:00p	1.5 f	4:18p	1:12p	1.3 f
	12:00p	7:36p	2.4e	7:24p	11:00p	1.7e	5:12p	8:48p	2.1e	10:48p	6:54p	1.3e
Thu. 10/5	7:30a	3:24a	2.8 f	3:48a	7:00a	1.6 f	1:06a	4:48a	1.3 f	6:30a	3:30a	1.2 f
	11:36a	9:36a	0.7e	10:18a	12:18p	0.5e	7:54a	9:54a	0.5e	11:18a	8:42a	0.8e
	5:24p	3:06p	1.9 f	2:06p	5:06p	1.5 f	12:00p	2:54p	1.2 f	5:06p	2:06p	1.1 f
		8:24p	1.9e	8:12p			6:06p	9:54p	1.9e	11:48p	7:48p	1.2e
Fri. 10/6	1:00a	4:24a	2.5 f	4:54a	1:24a	1.6e	2:12a	6:00a	1.4 f	7:36a	4:48a	1.3 f
	8:42a	10:36a	0.6e	11:42a	8:12a	1.7 f	9:12a	11:18a	0.5e	12:24p	9:54a	0.8e
	1:00p	4:06p	1.4 f	3:18p	1:36p	0.5e	1:24p	4:00p	1.1 f	6:12p	3:00p	1.0 f
	6:30p	9:36p	1.4e	9:18p	6:06p	1.3 f	7:12p	11:06p	1.7e		8:48p	1.0e
Sat. 10/7	2:06a	5:36a	2.4 f	6:00a	2:42a	1.6e	3:12a	7:06a	1.5 f	1:00a	5:48a	1.4 f
	9:42a	11:48a	0.7e	12:42p	9:18a	1.9 f	10:12a	12:36p	0.7e	8:30a	11:00a	0.9e
	2:48p	5:12p	1.2 f	4:36p	2:42p	0.6e	2:42p	5:12p	1.0 f	1:30p	4:06p	1.0 f
	7:54p	11:12p	1.1e	10:36p	7:24p	1.1 f	8:30p			7:24p	9:54p	0.9e
Sun. 10/8	3:12a	6:42a	2.4 f	6:54a	3:42a	1.7e	4:12a	12:30a	1.7e	2:06a	6:36a	1.5 f
	10:30a	12:42p	0.9e	1:24p	10:06a	2.1 f	11:00a	8:00a	1.6 f	9:24a	11:54a	1.1e
	4:06p	6:30p	1.2 f	5:48p	3:42p	0.8e	3:54p	1:30p	1.0e	2:30p	5:12p	1.1 f
	9:24p			11:42p	8:42p	1.2 f	9:42p	6:24p	1.1 f	8:30p	10:54p	1.0e
Mon. 10/9	4:12a	12:30a	1.0e	7:36a	4:24a	1.8e	4:54a	1:30a	1.8e	3:00a	7:24a	1.5 f
	11:12a	7:36a	2.5 f	2:00p	10:48a	2.2 f	11:36a	8:42a	1.7 f	10:06a	12:42p	1.2e
	5:06p	1:36p	1.1e	6:54p	4:30p	1.0e	4:48p	2:18p	1.2e	3:24p	6:12p	1.2 f
	10:36p	7:36p	1.5 f		9:54p	1.3 f	10:42p	7:36p	1.2 f	9:30p	12:00p	1.1e
Tue. 10/10	5:00a	1:24a	1.1e	12:42a	5:06a	1.8e	5:36a	2:12a	1.8e	3:48a	8:00a	1.6 f
	11:42a	8:18a	2.7 f	8:06a	11:24a	2.2 f	12:12p	9:18a	1.7 f	10:48a	1:24p	1.2e
	5:54p	2:12p	1.3e	2:30p	5:12p	1.2e	5:42p	3:00p	1.4e	4:12p	7:06p	1.3 f
	11:24p	8:30p	1.7 f	7:48p	10:42p	1.5 f	11:30p	8:24p	1.4 f	10:18p		
Wed. 10/11	5:30a	2:12a	1.3e	1:36a	5:30a	1.8e	6:12a	2:48a	1.8e	4:30a	12:48a	1.2e
	12:12p	8:48a	2.8 f	8:36a	11:48a	2.2 f	12:42p	9:42a	1.7 f	11:24a	8:30a	1.5 f
	6:36p	2:48p	1.5e	3:00p	5:54p	1.4e	6:24p	3:36p	1.6e	4:54p	1:54p	1.3e
		9:12p	2.0 f	8:36p	11:30p	1.6 f		9:12p	1.5 f	11:06p	7:54p	1.4 f
Thu. 10/12	12:06a	2:48a	1.4e	2:18a	5:48a	1.7e	12:18a	3:24a	1.8e	5:06a	1:36a	1.3e
	6:00a	9:24a	3.0 f	9:00a	12:12p	2.2 f	6:42a	9:48a	1.6 f	11:54a	8:54a	1.5 f
	12:36p	3:24p	1.7e	3:18p	6:24p	1.5e	1:06p	4:06p	1.7e	5:30p	2:24p	1.3e
	7:12p	9:54p	2.2 f	9:24p			7:06p	9:48p	1.5 f	11:54p	8:36p	1.4 f
Fri. 10/13	12:48a	3:30a	1.4e	3:06a	12:06a	1.6 f	1:06a	3:54a	1.6e	5:42a	2:18a	1.4e
	6:24a	9:54a	3.1 f	9:24a	6:18a	1.6e	7:06a	10:00a	1.6 f	12:24p	9:12a	1.4 f
	1:00p	3:54p	1.9e	3:36p	12:24p	2.2 f	1:24p	4:30p	1.8e	6:00p	2:42p	1.3e
	7:42p	10:30p	2.4 f	10:06p	6:48p	1.6e	7:48p	10:30p	1.5 f		9:24p	1.4 f
Sat. 10/14	1:30a	4:06a	1.4e	3:48a	12:48a	1.6 f	1:48a	4:30a	1.5e	12:36a	3:00a	1.2e
	6:48a	10:24a	3.2 f	9:42a	6:42a	1.4e	7:30a	10:18a	1.7 f	6:12a	9:36a	1.4 f
	1:18p	4:12p	2.2e	3:54p	12:48p	2.2 f	1:42p	4:54p	2.0e	12:48p	3:12p	1.3e
	8:12p	11:12p	2.6 f	10:48p	7:00p	1.8e	8:24p	11:06p	1.5 f	6:30p	10:06p	1.4 f
Sun. 10/15	2:18a	4:48a	1.3e	4:42a	1:30a	1.6 f	2:36a	5:00a	1.3e	1:24a	3:42a	1.1e
	7:18a	11:00a	3.2 f	10:06a	7:18a	1.2e	7:54a	10:48a	1.7 f	6:42a	10:06a	1.4 f
	1:42p	4:36p	2.5e	4:18p	1:12p	2.3 f	2:00p	5:24p	2.1e	1:06p	3:42p	1.5e
	8:42p	11:48p	2.8 f	11:30p	7:18p	2.0e	9:06p	11:48p	1.5 f	6:54p	10:48p	1.3 f
Mon. 10/16	3:06a	5:30a	1.2e	5:36a	2:18a	1.5 f	3:24a	5:42a	1.1e	2:12a	4:24a	1.0e
	7:48a	11:30a	3.1 f	10:30a	7:54a	1.0e	8:18a	11:18a	1.7 f	7:12a	10:36a	1.3 f
	2:06p	5:00p	2.8e	4:42p	1:48p	2.3 f	2:24p	5:54p	2.3e	1:30p	4:18p	1.6e
	9:12p				7:42p	2.1e	9:42p			7:24p	11:30p	1.3 f
Tue. 10/17	3:54a	12:30a	2.9 f	12:12a	3:06a	1.5 f	4:18a	12:30a	1.5 f	3:06a	5:12a	0.9e
	8:24a	6:12a	1.0e	6:36a	8:42a	0.7e	8:42a	6:24a	0.9e	7:48a	11:12a	1.3 f
	2:36p	12:06p	3.0 f	11:00a	2:24p	2.2 f	2:48p	12:00p	1.7 f	2:00p	4:54p	1.7e
	9:42p	5:30p	2.9e	5:12p	8:18p	2.3e	10:30p	6:30p	2.4e	7:54p		
Wed. 10/18	4:42a	1:12a	2.9 f	1:00a	4:00a	1.4 f	5:24a	1:18a	1.4 f	4:06a	12:12a	1.3 f
	9:06a	6:54a	0.9e	7:42a	9:30a	0.5e	9:18a	7:18a	0.7e	8:30a	6:00a	0.8e
	3:12p	12:48p	2.7 f	11:30a	3:06p	2.1 f	3:24p	12:42p	1.6 f	2:36p	11:54a	1.2 f
	10:18p	6:06p	2.9e	5:48p	9:00p	2.3e	11:18p	7:18p	2.4e	8:36p	5:36p	1.7e
Thu. 10/19	5:42a	2:00a	2.8 f	1:54a	5:00a	1.3 f	6:36a	2:12a	1.4 f	5:06a	1:00a	1.2 f
	9:48a	7:48a	0.7e	9:06a	10:30a	0.3e	10:00a	8:06a	0.5e	9:30a	7:00a	0.7e
	3:54p	1:30p	2.4 f	12:12p	3:54p	1.9 f	4:12p	1:30p	1.4 f	3:24p	12:48p	1.1 f
	11:00p	6:42p	2.7e	6:36p	9:48p	2.2e		8:06p	2.3e	9:30p	6:24p	1.6e
Fri. 10/20	6:42a	2:54a	2.7 f	2:54a	6:18a	1.3 f	12:18a	3:18a	1.3 f	6:12a	2:12a	1.2 f
	10:42a	8:48a	0.6e	10:30a	11:48a	0.2e	7:48a	9:12a	0.4e	10:42a	8:06a	0.6e
	4:42p	2:24p	2.1 f	1:12p	4:48p	1.7 f	11:00a	2:30p	1.3 f	4:18p	1:48p	1.1 f
	11:54p	7:30p	2.4e	7:30p	10:48p	2.0e	5:12p	9:06p	2.2e	10:30p	7:24p	1.5e
Sat. 10/21	7:54a	3:54a	2.5 f	4:06a	7:42a	1.3 f	1:30a	4:48a	1.3 f	7:18a	3:42a	1.2 f
	11:48a	10:06a	0.6e	11:36a	1:12p	0.3e	9:00a	10:30a	0.4e	12:00p	9:12a	0.7e
	5:42p	3:30p	1.8 f	2:36p	5:54p	1.6 f	12:36p	3:42p	1.2 f	5:30p	2:48p	1.0 f
		8:30p	1.9e	8:42p	12:00a	1.8e	6:24p	10:18p	2.1e	11:54p	8:30p	1.4e
Sun. 10/22	1:06a	4:54a	2.5 f	5:12a	8:48a	1.5 f	2:36a	6:24a	1.5 f	8:12a	5:06a	1.3 f
	8:54a	11:12a	0.8e	12:18p	2:18p	0.5e	9:54a	11:54a	0.6e	1:12p	10:18a	0.8e
	1:12p	4:36p	1.7 f	4:06p	7:06p	1.5 f	2:12p	4:54p	1.2 f	6:54p	4:00p	1.1 f
	7:00p	10:00p	1.6e	10:06p			7:48p	11:30p	2.1e		9:36p	1.3e
Mon. 10/23	2:24a	6:00a	2.7 f	6:06a	1:30a	1.7e	3:36a	7:12a	1.6 f	1:24a	6:06a	1.5 f
	9:42a	12:12p	1.1e	12:48p	9:30a	1.7 f	10:36a	1:00p	1.0e	9:06a	11:24a	1.0e
	2:48p	5:54p	1.8 f	5:30p	3:18p	0.8e	3:30p	6:06p	1.3 f	2:18p	5:12p	1.2 f
	8:36p	11:54p	1.5e	11:24p	8:24p	1.6 f	9:12p			8:12p	10:48p	1.4e
Tue. 10/24	3:30a	6:54a	3.0 f	6:54a	2:54a	1.7e	4:24a	12:42a	2.2e	2:36a	6:54a	1.7 f
	10:24a	1:06a	1.6e	1:18p	10:12a	1.9 f	11:12a	8:00a	1.8 f	9:54a	12:12p	1.2e
	4:12p	7:06p	2.1 f	6:48p	4:12p	1.2e	4:36p	1:54p	1.4e	3:18p	6:18p	1.4 f
	9:54p				9:42p	1.8 f	10:24p	7:18p	1.5 f	9:18p	11:54p	1.5e
Wed. 10/25	4:30a	1:12a	1.6e	12:36a	3:54a	1.8e	5:12a	1:42a	2.2e	3:36a	7:36a	1.8 f
	11:00a	7:48a	3.3 f	7:30a	10:42a	2.1 f	11:48a	8:30a	1.9 f	10:36a	1:00p	1.4e
	5:18p	1:54p	2.0e	1:54p	5:00p	1.6e	5:36p	2:42p	1.8e	4:12p	7:24p	1.5 f
	11:06p	8:06p	2.5 f	7:54p	10:42p	1.9 f	11:30p	8:24p	1.7 f	10:24p		
Thu. 10/26	5:18a	2:06a	1.6e	1:36a	4:48a	1.7e	5:48a	2:36a	2.1e	4:24a	12:54a	1.6e
	11:36a	8:36a	3.6 f	8:06a	11:12a	2.3 f	12:24p	9:00a	2.0 f	11:18a	8:18a	1.9 f
	6:24p	2:36p	2.5e	2:24p	5:48p	1.9e	6:36p	3:24p	2.1e	5:00p	1:42p	1.6e
		9:06p	2.9 f	8:54p	11:42p	2.0 f		9:24p	1.8 f	11:24p	8:24p	1.6 f

	GOLDEN GATE Slack Time	Current Time	Current Knots	BENICIA BRIDGE Slack Time	Current Time	Current Knots	RICHMOND Slack Time	Current Time	Current Knots	OAKLAND Slack Time	Current Time	Current Knots
Mon. 9/11	5:48a	1:54a	1.3e	1:12a	6:00a	2.0e	6:30a	2:54a	2.1e	4:36a	12:24a	1.1e
	12:18p	8:54a	2.7f	9:06a	12:06p	2.2f	1:00p	10:00a	1.8f	11:30a	8:48a	1.7f
	6:06p	2:36p	1.2e	3:24p	5:48p	0.9e	5:54p	3:30p	1.2e	4:42p	2:00p	1.2e
	11:42p	8:48p	2.0f	8:00p	11:00p	1.6f	11:54p	8:42p	1.4f	10:42p	7:30p	1.3f
Tue. 9/12	6:30a	2:42a	1.4e	1:54a	6:30a	2.0e	7:00a	3:30a	2.1e	5:12a	1:12a	1.2e
	12:54p	9:30a	2.8f	9:36a	12:36p	2.2f	1:30p	10:36a	1.8f	12:06p	9:24a	1.6f
	6:48p	3:18p	1.3e	3:54p	6:24p	1.1e	6:42p	4:12p	1.3e	5:24p	2:36p	1.2e
		9:30p	2.2f	8:42p	11:42p	1.7f		9:24p	1.5f	11:30p	8:18p	1.4f
Wed. 9/13	12:30a	3:24a	1.6e	2:36a	6:48a	1.9e	12:36a	4:00a	2.1e	5:48a	1:54a	1.3e
	7:06a	10:06a	2.9f	10:00a	1:06p	2.1f	7:36a	11:00a	1.7f	12:42p	9:54a	1.6f
	1:24p	4:00p	1.4e	4:18p	7:00p	1.2e	2:00p	4:42p	1.4e	6:00p	3:06p	1.2e
	7:24p	10:12p	2.3f	9:30p			7:24p	10:06p	1.6f		9:00p	1.4f
Thu. 9/14	1:06a	4:06a	1.7e	3:18a	12:18a	1.7f	1:18a	4:30a	2.0e	12:12a	2:36a	1.4e
	7:36a	10:36a	3.0f	10:24a	7:06a	1.9e	8:00a	11:00a	1.7f	6:24a	10:12a	1.5f
	1:54p	4:36p	1.5e	4:42p	1:24p	2.1f	2:24p	5:06p	1.5e	1:12p	3:30p	1.2e
	8:00p	10:54p	2.4f	10:12p	7:30p	1.3e	8:00p	10:42p	1.6f	6:36p	9:42p	1.4f
Fri. 9/15	1:48a	4:48a	1.7e	3:54a	1:00a	1.7f	1:54a	5:00a	1.9e	12:48a	3:18a	1.4e
	7:54a	11:06a	3.1f	10:42a	7:18a	1.8e	8:24a	11:12a	1.6f	6:48a	10:30a	1.5f
	2:18p	5:06p	1.7e	5:00p	1:42p	2.1f	2:48p	5:36p	1.6e	1:42p	3:54p	1.2e
	8:30p	11:30p	2.5f	10:54p	7:48p	1.4e	8:42p	11:18p	1.6f	7:06p	10:24p	1.4f
Sat. 9/16	2:24a	5:24a	1.7e	4:36a	1:36a	1.6f	2:36a	5:30a	1.8e	1:30a	4:00a	1.4e
	8:18a	11:42a	3.1f	11:00a	7:42a	1.7e	8:48a	11:30a	1.7f	7:18a	10:48a	1.5f
	2:36p	5:30p	1.9e	5:18p	2:00p	2.2f	3:00p	6:00p	1.7e	2:00p	4:24p	1.3e
	9:00p			11:36p	8:06p	1.5e	9:18p	12:00p	1.5f	7:30p	11:00p	1.4f
Sun. 9/17	3:06a	12:12a	2.5f	5:24a	2:18a	1.6f	3:18a	6:06a	1.8e	2:12a	4:42a	1.3e
	8:42a	6:00a	1.6e	11:24a	8:18a	1.5e	9:06a	12:00p	1.7f	7:42a	11:12a	1.5f
	3:00p	12:12p	3.1f	5:42p	2:30p	2.3f	3:18p	6:30p	1.8e	2:24p	4:54p	1.4e
	9:30p	5:48p	2.1e		8:24p	1.7e	10:00p			7:54p	11:36p	1.3f
Mon. 9/18	3:54a	12:48a	2.5f	12:18a	3:06a	1.5f	4:06a	12:36a	1.4f	3:00a	5:24a	1.1e
	9:06a	6:36a	1.4e	6:12a	8:54a	1.3e	9:30a	6:42a	1.4e	8:12a	11:42a	1.4f
	3:24p	12:42p	3.0f	11:48a	3:00p	2.3f	3:42p	12:36p	1.7f	2:42p	5:30p	1.4e
	10:00p	6:12p	2.3e	6:06p	8:54p	1.9e	10:42p	7:00p	2.0e	8:24p		
Tue. 9/19	4:42a	1:36a	2.5f	1:06a	3:54a	1.3f	5:00a	1:24a	1.3f	3:54a	12:12a	0.9f
	9:42a	7:12a	1.1e	7:12a	9:42a	1.0e	9:54a	7:30a	1.1e	8:48a	6:12a	0.9e
	3:54p	1:18p	2.8f	12:18p	3:36p	2.2f	4:06p	1:12p	1.7f	3:12p	12:24p	1.4f
	10:36p	6:42p	2.4e	6:36p	9:30p	2.0e	11:36p	7:42p	2.1e	9:06p	6:06p	1.5e
Wed. 9/20	5:42a	2:24a	2.4f	2:00a	4:54a	1.2f	6:12a	2:18a	1.2f	5:00a	1:00a	1.1f
	10:18a	8:06a	0.9e	8:24a	10:36a	0.6e	10:30a	8:18a	0.8e	9:36a	7:06a	0.7e
	4:30p	2:00p	2.5f	12:54p	4:18p	2.1f	4:48p	2:00p	1.5f	3:54p	1:06p	1.2f
	11:24p	7:18p	2.4e	7:12p	10:18p	2.0e		8:30p	2.1e	9:54p	6:54p	1.5e
Thu. 9/21	6:54a	3:18a	2.3f	3:12a	6:06a	1.0f	12:36a	3:24a	1.1f	6:18a	2:00a	1.0f
	11:06a	9:12a	0.6e	10:06a	11:42a	0.3e	7:36a	9:18a	0.5e	10:36a	8:12a	0.6e
	5:18p	2:48p	2.2f	1:30p	5:12p	1.9f	11:12a	2:48p	1.4f	4:42p	2:06p	1.1f
		8:06p	2.2e	8:00p	11:06p	1.9e	5:36p	9:24p	2.1e	10:48p	7:48p	1.4e
Fri. 9/22	12:12a	4:18a	2.2f	4:30a	8:06a	1.1f	1:48a	4:42a	1.1f	7:42a	3:42a	1.0f
	8:12a	10:24a	0.6e	11:48a	1:06p	0.2e	9:06a	10:30a	0.3e	12:00p	9:24a	0.5e
	12:06p	3:48p	1.9f	2:24p	6:06p	1.7f	12:18p	3:54p	1.3f	5:48p	3:06p	1.0f
	6:12p	9:00p	1.9e	9:00p			6:42p	10:36p	2.0e		8:48p	1.4e
Sat. 9/23	1:24a	5:18a	2.2f	5:48a	12:18a	1.8e	3:06a	6:48a	1.2f	12:06a	5:36a	1.1f
	9:24a	11:30a	0.7e	1:00p	9:30a	1.3f	10:24a	12:00p	0.4e	8:48a	10:42a	0.6e
	1:18p	5:00p	1.8f	3:54p	2:24p	0.2e	2:00p	5:06p	1.2f	1:18p	4:12p	1.0f
	7:24p	10:18p	1.6e	10:12p	7:18p	1.6f	8:00p	11:54p	2.1e	7:06p	9:54p	1.3e
Sun. 9/24	2:48a	6:30a	2.4f	6:54a	1:36a	1.7e	4:12a	8:00a	1.5f	1:42a	6:48a	1.4f
	10:12a	12:30p	0.9e	1:36p	10:18a	1.5f	11:18a	1:18p	0.6e	9:42a	11:48a	0.8e
	2:42p	6:12p	1.8f	5:18p	3:36p	0.5e	3:24p	6:18p	1.4f	2:30p	5:24p	1.2f
	8:48p	11:48p	1.6e	11:30p	8:30p	1.7f	9:24p			8:24p	11:00p	1.4e
Mon. 9/25	4:06a	7:30a	2.7f	7:42a	2:18a	1.8e	5:06a	1:00a	2.3e	3:00a	7:36a	1.6f
	10:54a	1:24p	1.3e	2:12p	10:54a	1.8f	11:54a	8:48a	1.7f	10:30a	12:42p	1.1e
	4:00p	7:18p	2.2f	6:36p	4:30p	0.8e	4:36p	2:12p	1.0e	3:30p	6:30p	1.3f
	10:06p				9:42p	1.9f	10:36p	7:24p	1.6f	9:30p		
Tue. 9/26	5:12a	1:24a	1.7e	12:42a	4:18a	2.0e	5:54a	2:06a	2.5e	4:06a	12:06a	1.5f
	11:36a	8:18a	3.0f	8:24a	11:30a	1.9f	12:30p	9:24a	1.8f	11:12a	8:18a	1.8f
	5:12p	2:12p	1.6e	2:36p	5:18p	1.1e	5:36p	3:00p	1.3e	4:30p	1:30p	1.3e
	11:12p	8:18p	2.6f	7:42p	10:48p	2.1f	11:36p	8:42p	1.8f	10:30p	7:30p	1.5f
Wed. 9/27	6:00a	2:24a	1.8e	1:42a	5:18a	2.0e	6:36a	3:00a	2.5e	4:54a	1:06a	1.7f
	12:12p	9:00a	3.4f	9:00a	12:00p	2.1f	1:06p	9:54a	2.0f	11:54a	9:00a	1.9f
	6:18p	2:54p	2.0e	3:06p	6:06p	1.4e	6:36p	3:48p	1.6e	5:18p	2:12p	1.4e
		9:18p	3.0f	8:48p	11:42p	2.2f		9:24p	2.0f	11:30p	8:30p	1.6f
Thu. 9/28	12:12a	3:18a	1.9e	2:42a	6:00a	2.1e	12:36a	3:48a	2.5e	5:42a	2:06a	1.7f
	6:48a	9:48a	3.7f	9:30a	12:30p	2.3f	7:12a	10:18a	2.0f	12:36p	9:36a	1.9f
	12:48p	3:42p	2.3e	3:36p	6:48p	1.7e	1:42p	4:30p	1.9e	6:06p	2:54p	1.5e
	7:12p	10:12p	3.3f	9:42p			7:30p	10:18p	2.0f		9:24p	1.7f
Fri. 9/29	1:12a	4:12a	1.9e	3:36a	12:36a	2.3f	1:30a	4:30a	2.3e	12:24a	2:54a	1.7e
	7:24a	10:30a	3.9f	10:06a	6:42a	2.0e	7:48a	10:42a	2.1f	6:24a	10:12a	1.9f
	1:24p	4:24p	2.7e	4:12p	1:06p	2.4f	2:12p	5:12p	2.2e	1:12p	3:36p	1.6e
	8:06p	11:00p	3.5f	10:42p	7:30p	1.9e	8:24p	11:12p	2.0f	6:54p	10:18p	1.6f
Sat. 9/30	2:06a	5:00a	1.8e	4:30a	1:30a	2.2f	2:30a	5:18a	2.1e	1:18a	3:48a	1.7e
	8:00a	11:12a	3.9f	10:36a	7:30a	1.8e	8:24a	11:18a	2.1f	7:06a	10:42a	1.9f
	2:00p	5:06p	2.9e	4:48p	1:36p	2.5f	2:42p	5:54p	2.3e	1:48p	4:12p	1.6e
	9:00p	11:54p	3.6f	11:36p	8:06p	2.0e	9:18p	12:00p	1.9f	7:42p	11:12p	1.6f
Sun. 10/1	3:06a	5:48a	1.6e	5:24a	2:30a	2.1f	3:24a	6:06a	1.8e	2:18a	4:36a	1.5e
	8:36a	11:54a	3.8f	11:06a	8:12a	1.6e	9:00a	11:48a	2.0f	7:48a	11:18a	1.8f
	2:36p	5:42p	3.1e	5:24p	2:12p	2.5f	3:18p	6:36p	2.4e	2:24p	4:54p	1.6e
	9:48p				8:42p	2.0e	10:12p			8:24p		
Mon. 10/2	4:06a	12:42a	3.5f	12:36a	3:30a	1.9f	4:24a	12:54a	1.7f	3:12a	12:06a	1.5f
	9:12a	6:42a	1.4e	6:30a	9:00a	1.3e	9:36a	6:48a	1.4e	8:30a	5:30a	1.3e
	3:18p	12:36p	3.5f	11:42a	2:48p	2.3f	3:54p	12:30p	1.9f	3:00p	11:48a	1.6f
	10:30p	6:18p	3.0e	6:00p	9:24p	2.0e	11:06p	7:18p	2.4e	9:12p	5:30p	1.6e
Tue. 10/3	5:06a	1:30a	3.3f	1:36a	4:30a	1.7f	5:30a	2:00a	1.5f	4:12a	1:00a	1.4f
	9:48a	7:30a	1.1e	7:36a	10:00a	1.0e	10:12a	7:42a	1.1e	9:18a	6:24a	1.0e
	3:54p	1:24p	3.0f	12:24p	3:30p	2.1f	4:30p	1:12p	1.7f	3:36p	12:30p	1.5f
	11:18p	6:54p	2.8e	6:42p	10:06p	1.9e		8:00p	2.3e	10:00p	6:12p	1.5e

GOLDEN GATE — BENICIA BRIDGE — RICHMOND — OAKLAND

Day	GG Slack Time	GG Current Time	GG Knots	BB Slack Time	BB Current Time	BB Knots	RICH Slack Time	RICH Current Time	RICH Knots	OAK Slack Time	OAK Current Time	OAK Knots
Sat 8/19	3:18a	12:30a	2.3 f	5:24a	2:30a	1.6 f	3:18a	12:18a	1.5 f	2:18a	5:00a	1.5e
	9:36a	6:24a	1.9e	12:18p	8:42a	2.0e	10:00a	6:30a	2.0e	8:18a	11:54a	1.5 f
	4:06p	12:54p	3.0 f	6:48p	3:18p	2.2 f	4:30p	12:48p	1.7 f	3:18p	5:36p	1.1e
	9:48p	6:42p	1.4e		9:24p	1.3e	10:18p	7:12p	1.4e	8:36p	12:00p	1.3 f
Sun 8/20	3:54a	1:12a	2.1 f	12:30a	3:18a	1.5 f	4:00a	1:00a	1.4 f	3:00a	5:42a	1.4e
	10:00a	7:00a	1.7e	6:06a	9:18a	1.8e	10:18a	7:12a	1.8e	8:48a	12:24p	1.5 f
	4:30p	1:30p	2.9 f	12:42p	3:48p	2.3 f	4:48p	1:18p	1.7 f	3:42p	6:12p	1.2e
	10:24p	7:06p	1.5e	7:12p	9:48p	1.4e	11:06p	7:42p	1.5e	9:12p		
Mon 8/21	4:42a	1:54a	2.0 f	1:24a	4:00a	1.3 f	4:48a	1:42a	1.3 f	3:48a	12:36a	1.2 f
	10:24a	7:42a	1.5e	7:00a	10:00a	1.5e	10:48a	7:48a	1.5e	9:24a	6:30a	1.2e
	4:54p	2:00p	2.8 f	1:12p	4:18p	2.3 f	5:12p	1:54p	1.7 f	4:12p	1:00p	1.5 f
	11:06p	7:30p	1.7 f	7:36p	10:24p	1.5e	12:00p	8:18p	1.6e	9:48p	6:48p	1.3e
Tue 8/22	5:42a	2:48a	1.9 f	2:24a	5:00a	1.1 f	5:48a	2:36a	1.1 f	4:54a	1:24a	1.1 f
	10:54a	8:30a	1.1e	8:00a	10:48a	1.1e	11:12a	8:36a	1.1e	10:00a	7:24a	0.9e
	5:30p	2:42p	2.6 f	1:42p	5:00p	2.2 f	5:42p	2:36p	1.6 f	4:42p	1:42p	1.4 f
	11:54p	8:12p	1.8e	8:12p	11:00p	1.6e		9:06p	1.7e	10:36p	7:30p	1.3e
Wed 8/23	7:00a	3:42a	1.8 f	3:30a	6:06a	0.9 f	1:06a	3:36a	1.0 f	6:12a	2:18a	1.0 f
	11:36a	9:36a	0.8e	9:30a	11:54a	0.7e	7:12a	9:30a	0.8e	10:54a	8:24a	0.7e
	6:06p	3:24p	2.4 f	2:12p	5:42p	2.0 f	11:48a	3:24p	1.5 f	5:24p	2:24p	1.3 f
		8:54p	1.8e	8:48p	11:48p	1.7e	6:24p	10:00p	1.8e	11:30p	8:24p	1.3e
Thu 8/24	12:54a	4:48a	1.8 f	4:54a	8:06a	0.8 f	2:18a	4:48a	0.9 f	7:48a	3:36a	0.9 f
	8:24a	10:42a	0.6e	11:24a	1:06p	0.4e	8:54a	10:36a	0.4e	12:00p	9:36a	0.6e
	12:24p	4:18p	2.2 f	2:54p	6:36p	1.9 f	12:36p	4:18p	1.4 f	6:18p	3:24p	1.2 f
	7:00p	9:48p	1.8e	9:42p			7:18p	11:00p	1.9e		9:18p	1.4e
Fri 8/25	2:06a	5:54a	1.9 f	6:18a	12:48a	1.8e	3:36a	6:36a	1.0 f	12:42a	5:48a	1.0 f
	9:42a	11:48a	0.6e	1:06p	9:48a	1.1 f	10:36a	12:00p	0.3e	9:06a	10:54a	0.5e
	1:30p	5:18p	2.1 f	3:48p	2:24p	0.2e	1:48p	5:18p	1.4 f	1:18p	4:30p	1.1 f
	8:00p	10:48p	1.8e	10:36p	7:36p	1.8 f	8:18p			7:24p	10:18p	1.4e
Sat 8/26	3:24a	7:00a	2.2 f	7:30a	1:54a	1.8e	4:42a	12:12a	2.1e	2:00a	7:12a	1.2 f
	10:42a	12:48p	0.8e	2:18p	10:48a	1.4 f	11:48a	8:30a	1.3 f	10:12a	12:06p	0.7e
	2:42p	6:24p	2.1 f	5:06p	3:42p	0.2e	3:12p	1:24p	0.4e	2:36p	5:36p	1.1 f
	9:06p			11:42p	8:42p	1.8 f	9:30p	6:24p	1.4 f	8:30p	11:18p	1.4e
Sun 8/27	4:42a	12:06a	1.8e	8:24a	3:06a	1.9e	5:36a	1:18a	2.3e	3:18a	8:12a	1.5 f
	11:24a	8:00a	2.5 f	3:00p	11:30a	1.6 f	12:36p	9:24a	1.5 f	11:00a	1:06p	0.9e
	3:48p	1:36p	1.0e	6:24p	4:48p	0.4e	4:30p	2:24p	0.6e	3:48p	6:42p	1.2 f
	10:12p	7:30p	2.4 f		9:48p	1.9 f	10:42p	7:30p	1.6 f	9:36p		
Mon 8/28	5:42a	1:18a	1.9e	12:48a	4:24a	2.1e	6:30a	2:24a	2.6e	4:24a	12:24a	1.6e
	12:06p	8:48a	2.8 f	9:06a	12:12p	1.8 f	1:18p	10:06a	1.8 f	11:48a	9:00a	1.7 f
	5:00p	2:30p	1.3e	3:30p	5:42p	0.6e	5:36p	3:18p	0.9e	4:42p	2:00p	1.0e
	11:18p	8:30p	2.7 f	7:36p	10:48p	2.1 f	11:42p	8:30p	1.8 f	10:42p	7:42p	1.4 f
Tue 8/29	6:36a	2:18a	2.0e	1:48a	5:36a	2.2e	7:12a	3:18a	2.8e	5:24a	1:24a	1.7e
	12:42p	9:36a	3.1 f	9:48a	12:48p	2.0 f	1:54p	10:36a	1.9 f	12:30p	9:42a	1.9 f
	6:06p	3:18p	1.5e	4:00p	6:30p	0.9e	6:30p	4:06p	1.1e	5:36p	2:42p	1.2e
		9:24p	3.0 f	8:36p	11:48p	2.3 f		9:30p	2.0 f	11:36p	8:42p	1.5 f
Wed 8/30	12:18a	3:24a	2.2e	2:48a	6:24a	2.3e	12:42a	4:06a	2.9e	6:12a	2:18a	1.8e
	7:24a	10:18a	3.4 f	10:24a	1:18p	2.1 f	7:54a	11:06a	2.0 f	1:12p	10:18a	2.0 f
	1:24p	4:06p	1.8e	4:30p	7:18p	1.2e	2:30p	4:54p	1.4e	6:30p	3:30p	1.3e
	7:06p	10:18p	3.3 f	9:42p			7:30p	10:24p	2.1 f		9:36p	1.6 f
Thu 8/31	1:12a	4:30a	2.2e	3:42a	12:42a	2.4 f	1:36a	4:54a	2.8e	12:30a	3:12a	1.9e
	8:06a	11:00a	3.7 f	10:54a	7:12a	2.4e	8:36a	11:36a	2.1 f	7:00a	10:54a	2.0 f
	2:00p	4:54p	2.0e	5:06p	1:48p	2.2 f	3:00p	5:36p	1.7e	1:54p	4:12p	1.4e
	8:06p	11:12p	3.5 f	10:42p	8:00p	1.4e	8:24p	11:18p	2.1 f	7:18p	10:30p	1.7 f
Fri 9/1	2:06a	5:18a	2.2e	4:36a	1:36a	2.4 f	2:30a	5:42a	2.6e	1:24a	4:00a	1.9e
	8:48a	11:42a	3.8 f	11:30a	7:54a	2.3e	9:12a	12:06p	2.1 f	7:42a	11:24a	2.0 f
	2:42p	5:36p	2.3e	5:36p	2:24p	2.4 f	3:36p	6:24p	1.9e	2:36p	4:48p	1.5e
	9:00p	12:00p	3.5 f	11:42p	8:42p	1.6e	9:24p			8:06p	11:18p	1.6 f
Sat 9/2	3:00a	6:06a	2.1e	5:30a	2:36a	2.2 f	3:24a	12:12a	2.0 f	2:18a	4:54a	1.8e
	9:18a	12:24p	3.8 f	12:00p	8:36a	2.1e	9:42a	6:24a	2.4e	8:24a	12:00p	1.9 f
	3:18p	6:18p	2.5e	6:12p	3:00p	2.4 f	4:12p	12:36p	2.1 f	3:12p	5:30p	1.5e
	9:54p				9:30p	1.8e	10:24p	7:06p	2.0e	8:54p		
Sun 9/3	3:54a	12:54a	3.3 f	12:42a	3:30a	2.0 f	4:24a	1:06a	1.8 f	3:12a	12:12a	1.5 f
	9:54a	6:54a	1.8e	6:30a	9:24a	1.8e	10:18a	7:12a	2.0e	9:00a	5:42a	1.6e
	4:00p	1:12p	3.7 f	12:30p	3:36p	2.4 f	4:48p	1:12p	2.0 f	3:48p	12:36p	1.8 f
	10:42p	6:54p	2.6e	6:54p	10:12p	1.8e	11:24p	7:54p	2.1e	9:42p	6:12p	1.5e
Mon 9/4	4:54a	1:48a	3.1 f	1:48a	4:36a	1.7 f	5:24a	2:00a	1.5 f	4:18a	1:06a	1.4 f
	10:24a	7:42a	1.5e	7:30a	10:18a	1.5e	10:54a	8:00a	1.5e	9:48a	6:36a	1.3e
	4:42p	1:54p	3.3 f	1:06p	4:12p	2.3 f	5:30p	1:54p	1.9 f	4:30p	1:12p	1.7 f
	11:36p	7:36p	2.5e	7:36p	11:12p	1.8e		8:42p	2.1e	10:36p	6:54p	1.4e
Tue 9/5	6:06a	2:42a	2.8 f	3:00a	5:48a	1.5 f	12:30a	3:18a	1.3 f	5:24a	2:12a	1.2 f
	11:06a	8:42a	1.1e	8:42a	11:18a	1.1e	6:36a	8:54a	1.1e	10:36a	7:42a	1.0e
	5:24p	2:42p	2.9 f	1:48p	5:00p	2.1 f	11:36a	2:36p	1.7 f	5:12p	1:48p	1.5 f
		8:24p	2.3e	8:18p			6:12p	9:36p	2.0e	11:36p	7:42p	1.3e
Wed 9/6	12:36a	3:48a	2.6 f	4:18a	12:30a	1.7 f	1:42a	4:54a	1.2 f	6:42a	3:42a	1.1 f
	7:30a	9:48a	0.8e	10:12a	7:12a	1.4 f	8:00a	10:06a	0.7e	11:30a	8:48a	0.8e
	11:48a	3:36p	2.4 f	2:36p	12:24p	0.7e	12:30p	3:30p	1.5 f	5:54p	2:36p	1.3 f
	6:12p	9:12p	2.0e	9:12p	5:48p	1.8 f	7:00p	10:42p	1.9e		8:30p	1.2e
Thu 9/7	1:42a	4:54a	2.4 f	5:36a	2:06a	1.7e	2:54a	6:30a	1.3 f	12:42a	5:12a	1.2 f
	8:54a	10:54a	0.7e	11:42a	8:36a	1.5 f	9:24a	11:30a	0.6e	8:00a	10:12a	0.8e
	1:00p	4:30p	1.9 f	3:36p	1:42p	0.6e	1:36p	4:30p	1.3 f	12:42p	3:36p	1.2 f
	7:12p	10:18p	1.7e	10:12p	6:42p	1.5 f	8:00p			6:54p	9:24p	1.1e
Fri 9/8	2:54a	6:06a	2.4 f	6:42a	3:24a	1.8e	4:00a	12:06a	1.9e	1:48a	6:24a	1.1 f
	10:06a	12:00p	0.7e	1:06p	9:42a	1.8 f	10:42a	7:36a	1.4 f	9:06a	11:24a	0.8e
	2:36p	5:36p	1.7 f	4:48p	3:00p	0.5e	2:54p	12:54p	0.6e	1:48p	4:36p	1.1 f
	8:24p	11:42p	1.4e	11:12p	7:48p	1.4 f	9:06p	5:36p	1.2 f	7:54p	10:24p	1.1e
Sat 9/9	4:00a	7:12a	2.5 f	7:42a	4:30a	1.9e	5:00a	1:18a	1.9e	2:54a	7:18a	1.5 f
	10:54a	1:06p	0.9e	2:00p	10:36a	2.0 f	11:36a	8:36a	1.6 f	10:00a	12:24p	1.0e
	4:06p	6:48p	1.6 f	6:00p	4:00p	0.6e	4:06p	2:00p	0.8e	2:54p	5:42p	1.1 f
	9:42p				9:06p	1.3 f	10:12p	6:48p	1.2 f	8:54p	11:30p	1.1e
Sun 9/10	5:00a	12:54a	1.3e	12:18a	5:18a	2.0e	5:48a	2:12a	2.0e	3:48a	8:06a	1.6 f
	11:42a	8:06a	2.6 f	8:24a	11:24a	2.2 f	12:24p	9:24a	1.7 f	10:48a	1:18p	1.1e
	5:12p	1:54p	1.1e	2:48p	5:00p	0.8e	5:06p	2:48p	1.0e	3:48p	6:42p	1.2 f
	10:48p	7:54p	1.8 f	7:00p	10:06p	1.4 f	11:06p	7:54p	1.3 f	9:54p		

	GOLDEN GATE Slack Time	Current Time	Current Knots	BENICIA BRIDGE Slack Time	Current Time	Current Knots	RICHMOND Slack Time	Current Time	Current Knots	OAKLAND Slack Time	Current Time	Current Knots
Thu. 7/27	3:12a	6:30a	1.6 f	6:48a	1:42a	1.7 e	4:06a	6:36a	0.9 f	1:36a	5:36a	0.9 f
	10:00a	12:06p	0.7 e	12:48p	10:00a	0.9 f	10:30a	12:12p	0.5 e	9:18a	11:06a	0.6 e
	1:54p	5:54p	2.4 f	4:24p	2:30p	0.4 e	2:12p	5:48p	1.5 f	1:30p	4:54p	1.2 f
	8:48p	11:48p	1.9 e	11:18p	8:12p	2.0 f	9:00p			8:00p	10:48p	1.4 e
Fri. 7/28	4:18a	7:30a	2.0 f	7:54a	2:30a	1.9 e	5:12a	12:42a	2.1 e	2:36a	7:24a	1.1 f
	11:00a	1:00p	0.7 e	2:24p	11:06a	1.3 f	11:54a	8:42a	1.1 f	10:30a	12:18p	0.6 e
	2:48p	6:54p	2.5 f	5:12p	3:42p	0.2 e	3:12p	1:24p	0.4 e	2:42p	5:54p	1.2 f
	9:36p				9:06p	2.0 f	9:54p	6:42p	1.6 f	8:48p	11:48p	1.5 e
Sat. 7/29	5:18a	12:36a	2.1 e	12:06a	3:24a	2.1 e	6:06a	1:42a	2.4 e	3:42a	8:30a	1.4 f
	11:54a	8:24a	2.4 f	8:48a	11:54a	1.5 f	1:00p	9:42a	1.4 f	11:30a	1:18p	0.7 e
	3:48p	1:54p	0.8 e	3:36p	4:54p	0.2 e	4:18p	2:36p	0.4 e	3:48p	6:54p	1.2 f
	10:30p	7:48p	2.6 f	6:12p	10:00p	2.0 f	10:48p	7:42p	1.6 f	9:48p		
Sun. 7/30	6:12a	1:24a	2.3 e	1:00a	4:24a	2.2 e	6:54a	2:42a	2.6 e	4:42a	12:42a	1.6 e
	12:36p	9:12a	2.7 f	9:36a	12:42p	1.7 f	1:54p	10:30a	1.7 f	12:18p	9:24a	1.6 f
	4:48p	2:42p	1.0 e	4:30p	6:00p	0.3 e	5:24p	3:36p	0.5 e	4:54p	2:18p	0.8 e
	11:24p	8:42p	2.8 f	7:18p	11:00p	2.2 f	11:48p	8:42p	1.7 f	10:48p	8:00p	1.2 f
Mon. 7/31	7:00a	2:12a	2.4 e	1:54a	5:30a	2.4 e	7:42a	3:30a	2.9 e	5:42a	1:36a	1.7 e
	1:18p	10:00a	3.0 f	10:18a	1:24p	1.9 f	2:36p	11:18a	1.8 f	1:06p	10:12a	1.8 f
	5:54p	3:30p	1.1 e	5:00p	6:54p	0.4 e	6:30p	4:30p	0.7 e	5:54p	3:12p	1.0 e
	9:36p	9:30p	3.0 f	8:30p	11:54p	2.3 f	9:36p			11:42p	8:54p	1.3 f
Tue. 8/1	12:18a	3:12a	2.5 e	2:48a	6:30a	2.5 e	12:42a	4:24a	3.0 e	6:30a	2:30a	1.8 e
	7:48a	10:48a	3.0 f	11:00a	2:00p	2.0 f	8:30a	11:48a	1.9 f	1:54p	10:54a	1.9 f
	2:00p	4:24p	1.3 e	5:30p	7:42p	0.7 e	3:12p	5:18p	0.9 e	6:48p	4:00p	1.2 e
	6:54p	10:30p	3.2 f	9:36p			7:30p	10:30p	2.0 f		9:54p	1.5 f
Wed. 8/2	1:12a	4:12a	2.5 e	3:48a	12:48a	2.4 f	1:42a	5:12a	3.0 e	12:42a	3:24a	1.9 e
	8:36a	11:30a	3.5 f	11:36a	7:24a	2.5 e	9:12a	12:24p	2.0 f	7:24a	11:30a	2.0 f
	2:42p	5:12p	1.5 e	6:00p	2:36p	2.1 f	3:54p	6:06p	1.2 e	2:36p	4:42p	1.2 e
	7:54p	11:30p	3.3 f	10:36p	8:30p	0.9 e	8:30p	11:24p	2.0 f	7:36p	10:48p	1.5 f
Thu. 8/3	2:00a	5:18a	2.5 e	4:42a	1:42a	2.4 f	2:36a	6:00a	3.0 e	1:36a	4:18a	1.9 e
	9:18a	12:12p	3.6 f	12:12p	8:18a	2.5 e	9:48a	12:54p	2.1 f	8:06a	12:06p	2.0 f
	3:24p	6:00p	1.7 e	6:36p	3:12p	2.2 f	4:30p	6:54p	1.4 e	3:12p	5:24p	1.3 e
	8:54p			11:42p	9:18p	1.2 e	9:30p			8:30p	11:36p	1.6 f
Fri. 8/4	2:54a	12:12a	3.1 f	5:36a	2:42a	2.3 f	3:30a	12:18a	2.0 f	2:24a	5:06a	1.9 e
	9:54a	6:06a	2.4 e	12:48p	9:00a	2.4 e	10:30a	6:48a	2.8 e	8:54a	12:42p	2.0 f
	4:06p	1:00p	3.7 f	7:12p	3:48p	2.3 f	5:06p	1:30p	2.1 f	3:54p	6:06p	1.3 e
	9:48p	6:48p	1.8 e		10:06p	1.4 e	10:30p	7:42p	1.6 f			
Sat. 8/5	3:48a	1:06a	3.1 f	12:48a	3:42a	2.1 f	4:24a	1:18a	1.8 f	3:24a	12:24a	1.5 f
	10:30a	6:54a	2.2 e	6:36a	9:48a	2.2 e	11:06a	7:36a	2.5 e	9:36a	6:00a	1.8 e
	4:48p	1:42p	3.6 f	1:24p	4:24p	2.4 f	5:42p	2:00p	2.0 f	4:36p	1:18p	1.9 f
	10:48p	7:36p	2.0 e	7:48p	11:00p	1.5 e	11:36p	8:30p	1.7 f	10:12p	6:54p	1.4 e
Sun. 8/6	4:48a	2:00a	2.8 f	2:00a	4:42a	1.8 f	5:24a	2:18a	1.5 f	4:18a	1:06a	1.4 f
	11:06a	7:54a	1.9 e	7:36a	10:36a	1.9 e	11:42a	8:24a	2.0 e	10:18a	6:54a	1.6 e
	5:30p	2:30p	3.5 f	1:54p	5:00p	2.4 f	6:24p	2:42p	2.0 f	5:18p	1:54p	1.8 f
	12:00p	8:24p	2.0 e	8:36p			9:24p			11:06p	7:42p	1.4 e
Mon. 8/7	6:00a	3:00a	2.5 f	3:12a	12:06a	1.6 e	12:54a	3:24a	1.3 f	5:30a	2:18a	1.2 f
	11:42a	8:54a	1.4 e	8:42a	7:24a	1.2 f	6:36a	9:18a	1.5 e	11:06a	7:54a	1.3 e
	6:18p	3:18p	3.2 f	2:30p	11:36a	1.5 e	12:24p	3:24p	1.9 f	6:00p	2:36p	1.7 f
		9:18p	2.1 e	9:18p	5:42p	2.3 f	7:12p	10:24p	1.9 e		8:30p	1.3 e
Tue. 8/8	1:12a	4:06a	2.3 f	4:36a	1:12a	1.7 e	2:06a	4:54a	1.1 f	12:12a	3:36a	1.1 f
	7:24a	10:00a	1.1 e	10:06a	7:24a	1.2 f	7:54a	10:18a	1.1 e	6:48a	9:00a	1.0 e
	12:24p	4:06p	2.9 f	3:12p	12:42p	1.1 e	1:06p	4:12p	1.7 f	11:54a	3:18p	1.1 f
	7:06p	10:12p	2.2 e	10:12p	6:30p	2.1 f	8:00p	11:36p	2.0 e	6:48p	9:18p	1.3 e
Wed. 8/9	2:30a	5:18a	2.2 f	5:42a	2:36a	1.8 e	3:24a	6:36a	1.1 f	1:18a	5:24a	1.1 f
	8:54a	11:06a	0.8 e	11:36a	8:48a	1.3 f	9:24a	11:36a	0.7 e	8:06a	10:18a	0.8 e
	1:18p	5:06p	2.6 f	4:00p	1:48p	0.7 e	2:00p	5:06p	1.6 f	12:54p	4:06p	1.4 f
	8:00p	11:18p	2.2 e	11:00p	7:24p	1.9 f	8:48p			7:36p	10:12p	1.3 e
Thu. 8/10	3:36a	6:18a	2.3 f	7:18a	3:48a	1.9 e	4:36a	12:48a	2.0 e	2:30a	6:42a	1.3 f
	10:18a	12:18p	0.7 e	1:06p	10:06a	1.6 f	10:54a	8:00a	1.3 f	9:24a	11:36a	0.8 e
	2:24p	6:06p	2.3 f	4:54p	3:06p	0.6 e	3:00p	1:00p	0.6 e	2:00p	5:06p	1.2 f
	9:00p			11:54p	8:24p	1.7 f	9:42p			8:24p	11:06p	1.2 e
Fri. 8/11	4:42a	12:18a	1.9 e	8:12a	4:54a	2.1 e	5:30a	1:48a	2.2 e	3:30a	7:42a	1.5 f
	11:18a	7:42a	2.5 f	2:24p	11:00a	1.8 f	12:00p	9:00a	1.5 f	10:24a	12:42p	0.8 e
	3:42p	1:18p	0.6 e	6:00p	4:18p	0.5 e	4:06p	2:12p	0.7 e	3:06p	6:00p	1.2 f
	10:00p	7:06p	2.2 f		9:24p	1.6 f	10:36p	7:06p	1.4 f	9:18p	11:54p	1.2 e
Sat. 8/12	5:36a	1:12a	1.9 e	12:42a	5:48a	2.2 e	6:24a	2:42a	2.3 e	4:24a	8:36a	1.6 f
	12:06p	8:30a	2.7 f	9:00a	11:54a	2.1 f	12:54p	9:54a	1.7 f	11:18a	1:36p	0.9 e
	5:00p	2:06p	0.9 e	3:24p	5:18p	0.5 e	5:06p	3:06p	0.8 e	4:06p	7:00p	1.2 f
	10:54p	8:06p	2.2 f	7:00p	10:18p	1.6 f	11:24p	8:00p	1.3 f	10:12p		
Sun. 8/13	6:24a	2:06a	1.8 e	1:24a	6:36a	2.2 e	7:06a	3:24a	2.3 e	5:12a	12:48a	1.2 e
	12:48p	9:18a	2.8 f	9:42a	12:36p	2.2 f	1:42p	10:36a	1.8 f	12:06p	9:24a	1.7 f
	6:06p	3:00p	1.0 e	4:06p	6:06p	0.6 e	6:06p	3:54p	0.9 e	5:00p	2:24p	1.0 e
	11:48p	9:00p	2.3 f	7:54p	11:06p	1.6 f		8:54p	1.4 f	11:00p	7:54p	1.2 f
Mon. 8/14	7:12a	3:00a	1.8 e	2:06a	7:06a	2.2 e	12:12a	4:00a	2.3 e	5:48a	1:30a	1.3 e
	1:30p	10:00a	2.9 f	10:18a	1:18p	2.2 f	7:42a	11:12a	1.8 f	12:48p	10:06a	1.7 f
	6:54p	3:48p	1.1 e	4:48p	6:54p	0.7 e	6:18p	4:36p	1.0 e	5:48p	3:12p	1.1 e
		9:48p	2.4 f	8:48p	11:48p	1.7 f	6:54p	9:36p	1.5 f	11:42p	8:42p	1.3 f
Tue. 8/15	12:36a	3:48a	1.8 e	2:48a	7:36a	2.1 e	12:54a	4:30a	2.3 e	6:24a	2:12a	1.3 e
	7:48a	10:42a	2.9 f	10:48a	1:54p	2.1 f	8:18a	11:48a	1.8 f	1:24p	10:42a	1.7 f
	2:06p	4:30p	1.1 e	5:18p	7:30p	0.8 e	2:48p	5:12p	1.1 e	6:30p	3:48p	1.1 e
	7:36p	10:30p	2.4 f	9:30p			7:36p	10:18p	1.6 f		9:24p	1.3 f
Wed. 8/16	1:24a	4:42a	1.8 e	3:24a	12:30a	1.7 f	1:30a	5:00a	2.3 e	12:24a	2:54a	1.4 e
	8:24a	11:18a	3.0 f	11:18a	7:48a	2.1 e	8:48a	12:06p	1.7 f	6:54a	11:06a	1.6 f
	2:42p	5:18p	1.2 e	5:42p	2:24p	2.1 f	3:18p	5:48p	1.1 e	2:00p	4:18p	1.1 e
	8:12p	11:12p	2.4 f	10:18p	8:06p	0.9 e	8:18p	11:00p	1.6 f	7:06p	10:06p	1.4 f
Thu. 8/17	2:00a	5:18a	1.9 e	4:06a	1:06a	1.7 f	2:06a	5:30a	2.2 e	1:06a	3:42a	1.4 e
	8:54a	11:48a	3.0 f	11:36a	8:48a	2.1 e	9:12a	12:12p	1.6 f	7:24a	11:18a	1.5 f
	3:12p	5:48p	1.3 e	6:06p	2:42p	2.1 f	3:48p	6:12p	1.2 e	2:30p	4:42p	1.1 e
	8:42p	11:54p	2.4 f	11:00p	8:30p	1.0 e	8:54p	11:36p	1.6 f	7:42p	10:42p	1.4 f
Fri. 8/18	2:36a	5:54a	2.0 e	4:42a	1:48a	1.7 f	2:42a	6:00a	2.1 e	1:42a	4:18a	1.5 e
	9:12a	12:24p	3.0 f	11:54a	8:06a	2.0 e	9:36a	12:24p	1.7 f	7:48a	11:36a	1.5 f
	3:42p	6:18p	1.3 e	6:24p	3:00p	2.1 f	4:06p	6:42p	1.3 e	3:00p	5:06p	1.1 e
	9:12p			11:42p	9:00p	1.1 e	9:36p			8:12p	11:18p	1.4 f

		GOLDEN GATE			BENICIA BRIDGE			RICHMOND			OAKLAND		
		Slack Time	Current Time	Knots	Slack Time	Current Time	Knots	Slack Time	Current Time	Knots	Slack Time	Current Time	Knots
Tue. 7/4		1:12a	4:06a	2.8e	3:48a	12:54a	2.3f	1:42a	5:30a	3.1e	12:42a	3:36a	1.9e
		8:48a	11:54a	3.4f	12:06p	7:18a	2.6e	9:36a	12:54p	1.9f	7:30a	12:00p	1.9f
		3:12p	5:36p	1.1e	7:06p	3:12p	2.0f	4:36p	6:24p	0.7e	3:06p	5:06p	1.0e
		7:48p	11:30p	3.1f	10:30p	8:54p	0.5e	8:30p	11:36p	1.9f	8:00p	10:54p	1.4f
Wed. 7/5		2:00a	5:00a	2.8e	4:42a	1:54a	2.3f	2:36a	6:18a	3.1e	1:36a	4:24a	1.9e
		9:36a	12:36p	3.4f	12:48p	8:18a	2.6e	10:18a	1:36p	2.0f	8:18a	12:36p	1.9f
		4:00p	6:24p	1.2e	7:36p	3:54p	2.1f	5:18p	7:18p	0.9e	3:48p	5:54p	1.1e
		8:48p			11:42p	9:48p	0.7e	9:30p			8:54p	11:48p	1.4f
Thu. 7/6		2:54a	12:24a	3.1f	5:42a	2:48a	2.2f	3:30a	12:30a	1.8f	2:36a	5:18a	1.9e
		10:18a	5:54a	2.6e	1:30p	9:12a	2.5e	11:00a	7:06a	2.9e	9:06a	1:18p	1.9f
		4:42p	1:24p	3.5f	8:06p	4:30p	2.2f	5:54p	2:12p	2.0f	4:36p	6:42p	1.2e
		9:48p	7:12p	1.3e		10:36p	0.9e	10:36p	8:06p	1.1e	9:42p		
Fri. 7/7		3:48a	1:12a	2.8f	12:54a	3:48a	2.0f	4:30a	1:30a	1.7f	3:30a	12:42a	1.4f
		11:00a	6:48a	2.4e	6:42a	10:06a	2.3e	11:42a	8:00a	2.7e	10:00a	6:18a	1.8e
		5:30p	2:12p	3.4f	2:06p	5:12p	2.2f	6:36p	2:54p	2.0f	5:18p	2:00p	1.9f
		10:54p	8:12p	1.4e	8:48p	11:36p	1.2e	11:54p	9:06p	1.3e	10:42p	7:36p	1.2e
Sat. 7/8		4:48a	2:12a	2.5f	2:06a	4:48a	1.8f	5:30a	2:30a	1.5f	4:30a	1:36a	1.3f
		11:42a	7:48a	2.1e	7:42a	11:00a	2.1e	12:24p	8:48a	2.3e	10:48a	7:12a	1.7e
		6:18p	3:00p	3.4f	2:42p	5:54p	2.3f	7:18p	3:36p	2.0f	6:06p	2:42p	1.9f
			9:12p	1.5e	9:30p				10:06p	1.5e	11:36p	8:24p	1.3e
Sun. 7/9		12:06a	3:12a	2.2f	3:24a	12:36a	1.4e	1:12a	3:36a	1.3f	5:36a	2:36a	1.2f
		5:54a	9:06a	1.7e	8:48a	6:00a	1.5f	6:42a	9:48a	1.9e	11:36a	8:12a	1.4e
		12:24p	3:54p	3.3f	3:18p	12:00p	1.7e	1:06p	4:18p	1.9f	6:48p	3:24p	1.8f
		7:12p	10:06p	1.7e	10:18p	6:36p	2.3f	8:06p	11:12p	1.7e		9:18p	1.3e
Mon. 7/10		1:36a	4:24a	2.0f	4:48a	1:48a	1.6e	2:30a	5:00a	1.1f	12:42a	3:48a	1.1f
		7:18a	10:18a	1.3e	10:06a	7:24a	1.2f	8:00a	10:48a	1.5e	6:54a	9:18a	1.2e
		1:06p	4:48p	3.2f	4:00p	1:00p	1.4e	1:54p	5:06p	1.9f	12:30p	4:06p	1.7f
		8:00p	11:06p	2.0e	11:00p	7:24p	2.3f	8:48p			7:36p	10:06p	1.3e
Tue. 7/11		3:00a	5:36a	2.0f	6:18a	2:54a	1.8e	3:48a	12:18a	1.9e	1:48a	5:18a	1.1f
		8:54a	11:30a	1.1e	11:30a	9:00a	1.2f	9:24a	6:42a	1.1f	8:12a	10:24a	1.0e
		1:54p	5:42p	3.1f	4:42p	2:06p	1.0e	2:36p	11:54a	1.1e	1:24p	4:54p	1.6f
		8:48p			11:48p	8:12p	2.2f	9:36p	5:48p	1.8f	8:18p	10:54p	1.4e
Wed. 7/12		4:12a	12:06a	2.2e	7:30a	4:06a	2.0e	4:54a	1:18a	2.2e	2:54a	6:48a	1.2f
		10:18a	6:54a	2.2f	12:54p	10:12a	1.4f	10:48a	8:06a	1.2f	9:30a	11:36a	0.9e
		2:42p	12:30p	0.9e	5:24p	3:12p	0.8e	3:30p	1:06p	0.9e	2:18p	5:42p	1.5f
		9:36p	6:36p	3.0f		9:00p	2.1f	10:18p	6:36p	1.7f	9:06p	11:42p	1.4e
Thu. 7/13		5:12a	12:54a	2.4e	12:30a	5:06a	2.2e	5:54a	2:12a	2.4e	3:54a	7:54a	1.4f
		11:30a	8:00a	2.5f	8:36a	11:12a	1.7f	12:06p	9:12a	1.5f	10:36a	12:48p	0.8e
		3:42p	1:30p	0.8e	2:18p	4:18p	0.6e	4:18p	2:12p	0.7e	3:12p	6:30p	1.3f
		10:24p	7:30p	2.9f	6:12p	9:48p	2.0f	11:00p	7:24p	1.6f	9:48p		
Fri. 7/14		6:06a	1:42a	2.5e	1:06a	6:00a	2.3e	6:48a	3:00a	2.5e	4:48a	12:30a	1.4e
		12:30p	8:54a	2.8f	9:24a	12:12p	1.9f	1:12p	10:06a	1.7f	11:42a	8:54a	1.6f
		4:42p	2:24p	0.8e	3:30p	5:24p	0.5e	5:12p	3:12p	0.7e	4:12p	1:48p	0.8e
		11:12p	8:24p	2.8f	7:00p	10:30p	1.9f	11:42p	8:12p	1.6f	10:30p	7:18p	1.3f
Sat. 7/15		6:54a	2:24a	2.4e	1:42a	6:54a	2.3e	7:30a	3:42a	2.5e	5:36a	1:06a	1.4e
		1:18p	9:42a	3.0f	10:12a	1:00p	2.0f	2:06p	11:00a	1.8f	12:36p	9:48a	1.7f
		5:48p	3:18p	0.8e	4:36p	6:18p	0.4e	6:06p	4:06p	0.7e	5:12p	2:42p	0.9e
		11:54p	9:12p	2.7f	7:54p	11:12p	1.8f		9:00p	1.5f	11:12p	8:06p	1.2f
Sun. 7/16		7:36a	3:06a	2.3e	2:18a	7:30a	2.2e	12:24a	4:18a	2.5e	6:18a	1:54a	1.4e
		2:00p	10:24a	3.1f	10:48a	1:48p	2.1f	8:12a	11:42a	1.8f	1:18p	10:30a	1.7f
		6:48p	4:12p	0.9e	5:24p	7:06p	0.4e	2:54p	4:54p	0.7e	6:06p	3:30p	0.9e
			10:00p	2.6f	8:42p	11:54p	1.8f	6:54p	9:42p	1.5f	11:54p	8:54p	1.2f
Mon. 7/17		12:42a	3:54a	2.2e	2:54a	8:00a	2.2e	1:00a	4:54a	2.4e	12:42a	2:30a	1.4e
		8:18a	11:12a	3.1f	11:24a	2:30p	2.1f	8:48a	12:18p	1.8f	2:00p	11:12a	1.7f
		2:48p	5:00p	0.9e	6:06p	7:54p	0.5e	3:30p	5:36p	0.8e	6:54a	4:18p	0.9e
		7:42p	10:48p	2.5f	9:30p			7:42p	10:30p	1.5f		9:42p	1.2f
Tue. 7/18		1:30a	4:48a	2.1e	3:36a	12:36a	1.7f	1:42a	5:18a	2.4e	12:36a	3:12a	1.4e
		8:54a	11:48a	3.0f	11:54a	8:12a	2.1e	9:18a	12:54p	1.7f	7:18a	11:48a	1.6f
		3:30p	5:48p	1.0e	6:42p	3:06p	2.1f	4:06p	6:18p	0.8e	2:42p	4:54p	1.0e
		8:24p	11:30p	2.4f	10:18p	8:36p	0.5e	8:30p	11:12p	1.5f	7:36p	10:24p	1.2f
Wed. 7/19		2:12a	5:30a	2.0e	4:12a	1:18a	1.7f	2:18a	5:54a	2.4e	1:18a	3:54a	1.4e
		9:30a	12:24p	3.0f	12:24p	8:12a	2.1e	9:48a	1:06p	1.6f	7:48a	12:06p	1.5f
		4:06p	6:30p	0.9e	7:06p	3:36p	2.1f	4:36p	6:48p	0.9e	3:12p	5:24p	1.0e
		9:00p			11:06p	9:12p	0.6e	9:12p	11:54p	1.5f	8:18p	11:06p	1.3f
Thu. 7/20		2:48a	12:12a	2.2f	4:54a	2:06a	1.7f	2:54a	6:24a	2.3e	2:00a	4:42a	1.5e
		10:00a	6:12a	2.0e	12:48p	8:30a	2.2e	10:18a	1:18p	1.6f	8:18a	12:24p	1.5f
		4:48p	1:00p	2.9f	7:36p	4:00p	2.1f	5:06p	7:18p	0.9e	3:48p	5:54p	1.0e
		9:30p	7:06p	0.9e	11:54p	9:48p	0.7e	9:54p			8:54p	11:48p	1.3f
Fri. 7/21		3:30a	12:54a	2.0f	5:36a	2:48a	1.6f	3:30a	12:36a	1.4f	2:36a	5:24a	1.5e
		10:24a	6:48a	2.0e	1:12p	9:06a	2.2e	10:42a	7:00a	2.2e	8:48a	12:36p	1.5f
		5:18p	1:36p	2.8f	8:00p	4:18p	2.1f	5:36p	1:36p	1.6f	4:18p	6:30p	1.0e
		10:06p	7:42p	0.9e		10:18p	0.9e	10:42p	7:54p	1.0e	9:30p		
Sat. 7/22		4:06a	1:36a	1.8f	12:48a	3:36a	1.5f	4:12a	1:18a	1.3f	3:18a	12:24a	1.3f
		10:42a	7:30a	1.8e	6:18a	9:42a	2.1e	11:12a	7:36a	2.0e	9:24a	6:06a	1.4e
		5:48p	2:12p	2.8f	1:36p	4:42p	2.2f	6:00p	2:06p	1.7f	4:48p	1:06p	1.5f
		10:48p	8:18p	0.9e	8:30p	10:54p	1.0e	11:36p	8:30p	1.1e	10:06p	7:00p	1.0e
Sun. 7/23		4:48a	2:18a	1.5f	1:48a	4:24a	1.3f	5:00a	2:12a	1.2f	4:06a	1:12a	1.2f
		11:12a	8:12a	1.6e	7:06a	10:30a	1.8e	11:42a	8:18a	1.8e	10:00a	7:00a	1.3e
		6:18p	2:54p	2.7f	2:06p	5:12p	2.2f	6:30p	2:42p	1.7f	5:18p	1:42p	1.5f
		11:42p	8:54p	1.0e	8:54p	11:30p	1.1e		9:12p	1.2e	10:48p	7:42p	1.1e
Mon. 7/24		5:42a	3:12a	1.3f	2:48a	5:18a	1.0f	12:36a	3:06a	1.0f	5:06a	1:54a	1.1f
		11:42a	9:00a	1.3e	8:00a	11:18a	1.5e	5:54a	9:06a	1.4e	10:42a	7:48a	1.1e
		6:48p	3:30p	2.6f	2:36p	5:48p	2.2f	12:12p	3:24p	1.7f	5:48p	2:24p	1.5f
			9:36p	1.2e	9:30p			7:00p	9:54p	1.4e	11:36p	8:24p	1.1e
Tue. 7/25		12:48a	4:12a	1.3f	4:06a	12:12a	1.3e	1:48a	4:06a	0.9f	6:18a	2:48a	1.0f
		10:00a	10:00a	1.0e	9:18a	6:24a	0.8f	7:06a	10:00a	1.1e	11:30a	8:48a	0.9e
		12:18p	4:12p	2.5f	3:06p	12:18p	1.1e	12:48p	4:06p	1.6f	6:24p	3:06p	1.4f
		7:24p	10:18p	1.4e	10:00p	6:30p	2.1f	7:30p	10:48p	1.6e		9:12p	1.2e
Wed. 7/26		2:00a	5:18a	1.3f	5:30a	12:54a	1.5e	3:00a	5:12a	0.8f	12:30a	3:54a	0.9f
		8:36a	11:00a	0.8e	11:06a	8:06a	0.7f	8:48a	11:00a	0.7e	7:48a	9:54a	0.7e
		1:00p	5:00p	2.5f	3:42p	1:24p	0.7e	1:24p	4:54p	1.6f	12:24p	3:54p	1.3f
		8:00p	11:00p	1.7e	10:36p	7:18p	2.0f	8:12p	11:42p	1.8e	7:12p	10:00p	1.3e

	GOLDEN GATE			BENICIA BRIDGE			RICHMOND			OAKLAND		
	SLACK	CURRENT		SLACK	CURRENT		SLACK	CURRENT		SLACK	CURRENT	
	Time	Time	Knots	Time	Time	Knots	Time	Time	Knots	Time	Time	Knots
Sun. 6/11	1:54a	4:42a	1.9 f	5:00a	2:12a	1.4 e	2:42a	5:12a	1.1 f	1:12a	4:00a	1.2 f
	7:24a	10:42a	1.5 e	10:18a	7:30a	1.3 f	8:06a	11:18a	1.8 e	7:06a	9:36a	1.3 e
	1:54p	5:24p	3.3 f	4:48p	1:30p	1.6 e	2:42p	6:06p	1.9 f	1:06p	5:06p	1.8 f
	8:48p	11:48p	1.8 e	11:48p	8:18p	2.2 f	9:42p			8:18p	10:54p	1.3 e
Mon. 6/12	3:24a	5:54a	1.9 f	6:18a	3:18a	1.7 e	4:00a	12:54a	1.8 e	2:12a	5:18a	1.2 f
	8:54a	11:54a	1.3 e	11:36a	9:00a	1.3 f	9:30a	6:36a	1.1 f	8:18a	10:48a	1.2 e
	2:42p	6:18p	3.4 f	5:30p	2:30p	1.3 e	3:24p	12:24p	1.5 e	2:00p	5:54p	1.7 f
	9:36p				9:00p	2.3 f	10:24p	6:42p	1.9 f	9:06p	11:42p	1.5 e
Tue. 6/13	4:36a	12:42a	2.2 e	12:30a	4:18a	2.0 e	5:06a	1:48a	2.1 e	3:18a	6:42a	1.3 f
	10:18a	7:12a	2.2 f	7:36a	10:12a	1.4 f	10:48a	8:06a	1.3 f	9:30a	11:48a	1.1 e
	3:24p	12:54p	2.1 e	12:54p	3:30p	1.1 e	4:12p	1:24p	1.3 e	2:48p	6:30p	1.7 f
	10:12p	7:06p	3.5 f	6:12p	9:42p	2.4 f	11:00p	7:24p	1.9 f	9:48p		
Wed. 6/14	5:36a	1:30a	2.6 e	1:06a	5:18a	2.2 e	6:06a	2:36a	2.4 e	4:12a	12:24a	1.5 e
	11:30a	8:12a	2.6 f	8:36a	11:18a	1.6 f	12:00p	9:18a	1.4 f	10:42a	7:54a	1.4 f
	4:12p	1:48p	1.0 e	2:06p	4:24p	0.9 e	4:48p	2:24p	1.1 e	3:36p	12:54p	1.0 e
	10:54p	8:00p	3.5 f	6:48p	10:24p	2.3 f	11:36p	8:00p	1.9 f	10:24p	7:12p	1.6 f
Thu. 6/15	6:30a	2:48a	2.9 e	1:36a	6:06a	2.3 e	6:54a	3:18a	2.6 e	5:06a	1:00a	1.6 e
	12:36p	9:06a	2.9 f	9:36a	12:12p	1.8 f	1:06p	10:12a	1.6 f	11:48a	9:00a	1.5 f
	5:00p	2:36p	0.9 e	3:18p	5:18p	0.7 e	5:30p	3:18p	0.9 e	4:30p	1:48p	0.9 e
	11:36p	8:42p	3.4 f	7:24p	10:54p	2.2 f		8:36p	1.8 f	11:00p	7:48p	1.4 f
Fri. 6/16	7:12a	2:48a	3.0 e	2:12a	6:54a	2.3 e	12:12a	3:54a	2.6 e	5:54a	1:42a	1.6 e
	1:36p	10:00a	3.2 f	10:24a	1:06p	1.9 f	7:42a	11:06a	1.7 f	12:42p	10:00a	1.6 f
	5:48p	3:36p	0.8 e	4:24p	6:18p	0.5 e	2:06p	4:12p	0.8 e	5:18p	2:48p	0.8 e
		9:30p	3.2 f	8:06p	11:36p	2.1 f	6:18p	9:18p	1.7 f	11:36p	8:30p	1.3 f
Sat. 6/17	12:12a	3:24a	2.9 e	2:42a	7:36a	2.3 e	12:42a	4:30a	2.6 e	6:30a	2:18a	1.6 e
	8:00a	10:48a	3.3 f	11:06a	2:00p	2.0 f	8:24a	11:54a	1.8 f	1:36p	10:48a	1.6 f
	2:30p	4:30p	0.8 e	5:36p	7:12p	0.4 e	3:06p	5:00p	0.7 e	6:12p	3:42p	0.8 e
	6:48p	10:18p	2.9 f	8:48p			7:00p	10:00p	1.6 f		9:12p	1.2 f
Sun. 6/18	12:54a	4:06a	2.7 e	3:12a	12:12a	2.0 f	1:12a	5:06a	2.6 e	12:12a	2:54a	1.5 e
	8:42a	11:30a	3.3 f	11:48a	8:06a	2.2 e	9:06a	12:36p	1.8 f	7:06a	11:36a	1.6 f
	3:18p	5:24p	0.8 e	6:30p	2:48p	2.0 f	3:54p	5:48p	0.6 e	6:24p	4:30p	0.8 e
	7:42p	11:00p	2.7 f	9:30p	8:06p	0.3 e	7:48p	10:42p	1.6 f	7:06p	10:00p	1.2 f
Mon. 6/19	1:36a	4:48a	2.5 e	3:48a	12:54a	1.8 f	1:48a	5:36a	2.5 e	12:48a	3:30a	1.5 e
	9:18a	12:12p	3.2 f	12:24p	7:48a	2.1 e	9:42a	1:18p	1.7 f	7:36a	12:12p	1.6 f
	4:06p	6:12p	0.8 e	7:18p	3:36p	2.0 f	4:36p	6:30p	0.6 e	3:12p	5:18p	0.9 e
	8:30p	11:48p	2.4 f	10:24p	8:54p	0.4 e	8:36p	11:24p	1.5 f	7:54p	10:42p	1.2 f
Tue. 6/20	2:18a	5:30a	2.3 e	4:24a	1:36a	1.7 f	2:24a	6:12a	2.4 e	1:30a	4:18a	1.5 e
	9:54a	12:54p	3.1 f	12:54p	8:06a	2.1 e	10:18a	1:48p	1.6 f	8:00a	12:42p	1.5 f
	4:54p	7:00p	0.8 e	8:00p	4:18p	2.0 f	5:18p	7:12p	0.7 e	3:48p	6:00p	0.9 e
	9:12p			11:12p	9:36p	0.4 e	9:24p			8:42p	11:24p	1.2 f
Wed. 6/21	3:00a	12:30a	2.1 f	5:06a	2:18a	1.6 f	3:06a	12:12a	1.4 f	2:12a	5:00a	1.5 e
	10:24a	6:12a	2.1 e	1:30p	8:42a	2.2 e	10:48a	6:48a	2.4 e	8:36a	1:06p	1.5 f
	5:42p	1:36p	2.9 f	8:36p	4:54p	2.0 f	6:00p	2:12p	1.6 f	4:30p	6:36p	0.9 e
	9:54p	7:48p	0.7 e		10:24p	0.5 e	10:12p	7:54p	0.7 e	9:30p		
Thu. 6/22	3:42a	1:12a	1.8 f	12:12a	3:06a	1.5 f	3:48a	1:00a	1.3 f	2:54a	12:12a	1.2 f
	10:54a	6:54a	1.9 e	5:48a	9:24a	2.1 e	11:24a	7:24a	2.2 e	9:12a	5:42a	1.4 e
	6:30p	2:18p	2.7 f	2:00p	5:24p	2.0 f	6:36p	2:30p	1.6 f	5:06p	1:24p	1.4 f
	10:30p	8:30p	0.6 e	9:06p	11:06p	0.6 e	11:06p	8:36p	0.7 e	10:12p	7:18p	0.9 e
Fri. 6/23	4:24a	2:00a	1.5 f	1:12a	3:54a	1.4 f	4:30a	1:48a	1.2 f	3:42a	1:00a	1.2 f
	11:24a	7:42a	1.7 e	6:36a	10:12a	2.0 e	12:00p	8:06a	2.1 e	9:54a	6:36a	1.4 e
	7:18p	3:00p	2.6 f	2:30p	5:54p	2.0 f	7:12p	3:00p	1.5 f	5:48p	2:00p	1.4 f
	11:18p	9:18p	0.6 e	9:42p	12:00a	0.7 e		9:24p	0.8 e	11:00p	8:00p	0.9 e
Sat. 6/24	5:06a	2:48a	1.2 f	2:12a	4:48a	1.2 f	12:12a	2:42a	1.0 f	4:36a	1:48a	1.1 f
	11:54a	8:42a	1.6 e	7:24a	11:06a	1.9 e	5:18a	8:54a	1.8 e	10:36a	7:24a	1.3 e
	8:00p	3:42p	2.5 f	3:00p	6:24p	2.0 f	12:36p	3:06p	1.5 f	6:24p	2:36p	1.4 f
		10:12p	0.6 e	10:18p			7:48p	10:12p	0.9 e	11:48p	8:42p	0.9 e
Sun. 6/25	12:30a	3:48a	1.0 f	3:24a	12:48a	0.9 e	1:18a	3:36a	0.9 f	5:36a	2:36a	1.1 f
	6:00a	9:42a	1.3 e	8:24a	5:48a	0.9 f	6:18a	9:42a	1.6 e	11:30a	8:24a	1.1 e
	12:30p	4:24p	2.5 f	3:36p	12:00p	1.6 e	1:06p	4:18p	1.6 f	7:00p	3:12p	1.4 f
	8:30p	11:00p	0.8 e	10:48p	6:54p	2.1 f	8:18p	11:06p	1.1 e		9:24p	1.0 e
Mon. 6/26	2:06a	4:48a	0.9 f	4:42a	1:30a	1.1 e	2:30a	4:42a	0.8 f	12:42a	3:30a	1.0 f
	7:18a	10:42a	1.1 e	9:42a	7:00a	0.8 f	7:30a	10:36a	1.3 e	6:48a	9:24a	1.0 e
	1:06p	5:06p	2.6 f	4:12p	12:54p	1.3 e	1:54p	5:00p	1.6 f	12:18p	3:54p	1.4 f
	8:54p	11:42p	1.2 e	11:18p	7:36p	2.1 f	8:54p	12:00a	1.1 e	7:42p	10:06p	1.1 e
Tue. 6/27	3:24a	6:00a	1.0 f	6:06a	2:18a	1.3 e	3:42a	5:48a	0.8 f	1:36a	4:36a	1.0 f
	8:54a	11:36a	1.0 e	11:12a	8:30a	0.7 f	9:00a	11:42a	1.2 e	8:06a	10:24a	0.9 e
	1:48p	5:54p	2.7 f	4:48p	1:54p	1.0 e	2:30p	5:42p	1.6 f	1:12p	4:42p	1.4 f
	9:18p			11:48p	8:12p	2.1 f	9:24p			8:18p	10:48p	1.2 e
Wed. 6/28	4:24a	12:18a	1.6 e	7:18a	2:54a	1.6 e	4:42a	12:42a	1.7 e	2:30a	5:54a	1.0 f
	10:12a	7:06a	1.4 f	12:42p	10:00a	0.9 f	10:30a	7:06a	0.9 f	9:24a	11:24a	0.7 e
	2:30p	12:30p	0.9 e	5:24p	2:54p	0.7 e	3:12p	12:42p	0.8 e	2:06p	5:36p	1.3 f
	9:42p	6:36p	2.7 f		8:54p	2.1 f	10:00p	6:30p	1.6 f	8:54p	11:36p	1.4 e
Thu. 6/29	5:12a	12:54a	2.0 e	12:18a	3:30a	1.8 e	5:36a	1:30a	2.0 e	3:24a	7:24a	1.1 f
	11:18a	8:00a	1.8 f	8:18a	11:12a	1.2 f	11:54a	8:36a	1.1 f	10:36a	12:30p	0.7 e
	3:12p	1:24p	0.8 e	2:12p	4:00p	0.5 e	3:54p	1:42p	0.6 e	3:00p	6:24p	1.3 f
	10:18p	7:24p	2.8 f	6:00p	9:42p	2.1 f	10:36p	7:18p	1.7 f	9:30p		
Fri. 6/30	5:54a	1:24a	2.3 e	12:48a	4:06a	2.1 e	6:30a	2:18a	2.3 e	4:12a	12:18a	1.5 e
	12:12p	8:48a	2.3 f	9:06a	12:12p	1.5 f	1:06p	9:42a	1.3 f	11:42a	8:36a	1.3 f
	4:00p	2:06p	0.8 e	3:36p	5:06p	0.3 e	4:42p	2:42p	0.5 e	4:00p	1:30p	0.7 e
	10:54p	8:12p	2.9 f	6:36p	10:24p	2.2 f	11:12p	8:06p	1.7 f	10:12p	7:18p	1.2 f
Sat. 7/1	6:36a	1:54a	2.6 e	1:24a	4:42a	2.3 e	7:18a	3:00a	2.6 e	5:00a	1:06a	1.6 e
	1:00p	9:36a	2.7 f	9:54a	1:00p	1.7 f	2:12p	10:42a	1.6 f	12:42p	9:42a	1.5 f
	4:54p	3:00p	0.8 e	4:54p	6:06p	0.2 e	5:30p	3:42p	0.5 e	5:00p	2:30p	0.7 e
	11:36p	9:00p	3.0 f	7:18p	11:12p	2.2 f	12:00a	8:54p	1.8 f	11:00p	8:12p	1.2 f
Sun. 7/2	7:18a	2:30a	2.8 e	2:06a	5:30a	2.5 e	8:00a	3:48a	2.8 e	5:48a	1:54a	1.8 e
	1:48p	10:24a	3.0 f	10:42a	1:48p	1.8 f	3:06p	11:30a	1.7 f	1:36p	10:30a	1.7 f
	5:54p	3:48p	0.9 e	5:54p	7:06p	0.2 e	6:30p	4:36p	0.5 e	6:06p	3:24p	0.7 e
		9:48p	3.0 f	8:18p	12:00a	2.2 f		9:48p	2.1 f	11:48p	9:06p	1.2 f
Mon. 7/3	12:24a	3:12a	2.9 e	2:54a	6:24a	2.6 e	12:48a	4:36a	3.0 e	6:42a	2:42a	1.8 e
	8:06a	11:06a	3.2 f	11:24a	2:36p	1.9 f	8:48a	12:12p	1.9 f	2:24p	11:18a	1.8 f
	2:30p	4:42p	0.9 e	6:30p	8:00p	0.3 e	3:54p	5:30p	0.6 e	7:00p	4:18p	0.9 e
	6:54p	10:42p	3.1 f	9:24p			7:24p	10:42p	1.9 f		10:06p	1.3 f

GOLDEN GATE · BENICIA BRIDGE · RICHMOND · OAKLAND

Date	GG Slack Time	GG Current Time	GG Knots	BB Slack Time	BB Current Time	BB Knots	Rich Slack Time	Rich Current Time	Rich Knots	Oak Slack Time	Oak Current Time	Oak Knots
Fri. 5/19	12:42a	3:54a	3.2e	3:12a	12:06a	2.3f	1:12a	4:48a	2.7e	12:12a	2:48a	1.7e
	8:18a	11:00a	3.5f	11:12a	7:30a	2.3e	8:36a	11:48a	1.7f	6:48a	10:48a	1.6f
	2:36p	4:48p	0.9e	5:12p	2:00p	1.9f	3:00p	5:06p	1.0e	1:42p	3:42p	1.0e
	7:06p	10:42p	3.4f	9:18p	7:18p	0.7e	7:24p	10:24p	1.9f	6:24p	9:42p	1.4f
Sat. 5/20	1:18a	4:30a	3.1e	3:42a	12:42a	2.2f	1:42a	5:24a	2.6e	12:42a	3:24a	1.7e
	9:00a	11:48a	3.5f	11:54a	7:42a	2.2e	9:18a	12:30p	1.7f	7:24a	11:36a	1.6f
	3:36p	5:42p	0.8e	6:18p	2:54p	1.9f	3:54p	5:54p	0.8e	2:36p	4:36p	0.9e
	7:54p	11:24p	3.0f	10:00p	8:06p	0.5e	8:00p	11:00p	1.7f	7:12p	10:18p	1.3f
Sun. 5/21	1:54a	5:06a	2.9e	4:12a	1:18a	2.0f	2:12a	5:54a	2.6e	1:12a	4:00a	1.6e
	9:36a	12:36p	3.4f	12:36p	7:48a	2.2e	10:00a	1:18p	1.7f	7:54a	12:24p	1.5f
	4:30p	6:36p	0.8e	7:24p	3:48p	1.9f	4:48p	6:42p	0.7e	3:30p	5:24p	0.8e
	8:42p			10:42p	9:00p	0.4e	8:42p	11:42p	1.6f	8:06p	11:00p	1.2f
Mon. 5/22	2:36a	12:06a	2.6f	4:48a	2:00a	1.9f	2:42a	6:30a	2.5e	1:48a	4:36a	1.6e
	10:12a	5:42a	2.6e	1:18p	8:18a	2.1e	10:36a	2:00p	1.6f	8:18a	1:06p	1.5f
	5:24p	1:18p	3.2f	8:24p	4:42p	2.0f	5:42p	7:30p	0.6e	4:18p	6:18p	0.8e
	9:30p	7:24p	0.7e	11:30p	9:54p	0.4e	9:30p			9:00p	11:48p	1.1f
Tue. 5/23	3:12a	12:54a	2.1f	5:24a	2:42a	1.7f	3:18a	12:30a	1.4f	2:30a	5:18a	1.5e
	10:48a	6:18a	2.3e	2:00p	8:54a	2.1e	11:18a	7:06a	2.3e	8:54a	1:42p	1.4f
	6:18p	2:06p	2.9f	9:18p	5:30p	1.9f	6:30p	2:48p	1.5f	5:06p	7:12p	0.8e
	10:18p	8:18p	0.6e		10:54p	0.4e	10:30p	8:18p	0.5e	10:00p		
Wed. 5/24	3:54a	1:36a	1.7f	12:24a	3:30a	1.5f	4:00a	1:18a	1.2f	3:12a	12:30a	1.1f
	11:18a	6:54a	1.9e	6:06a	9:42a	2.0e	12:06p	7:54a	2.1e	9:30a	6:06a	1.3e
	7:18p	2:54p	2.6f	2:42p	6:18p	1.9f	7:24p	3:30p	1.4f	5:48p	2:18p	1.3f
	11:06p	9:12p	0.5e	10:06p	11:48p	0.5e	11:30p	9:18p	0.5e	10:54p	8:12p	0.8e
Thu. 5/25	4:42a	2:30a	1.3f	1:30a	4:18a	1.3f	4:54a	2:12a	1.1f	4:06a	1:24a	1.0f
	11:54a	7:48a	1.5e	7:00a	10:36a	1.8e	12:48p	8:36a	1.9e	10:18a	7:00a	1.2e
	8:18p	3:42p	2.4f	3:24p	7:06p	1.9f	8:12p	4:24p	1.4f	6:36p	2:54p	1.3f
		10:06p	0.5e	10:48p				10:18p	0.6e	11:48p	9:00p	0.9e
Fri. 5/26	12:12a	3:24a	1.0f	2:48a	12:48a	0.6e	12:48a	3:12a	0.9f	5:06a	2:24a	1.0f
	5:30a	9:00a	1.2e	7:54a	5:18a	1.1f	5:54a	9:30a	1.7e	7:24p	3:42p	1.3f
	12:36p	4:36p	2.3f	4:06p	11:42a	1.7e	1:36p	5:06p	1.4f	9:48p		0.9e
	9:06p	11:00p	0.6e	11:24p	7:48p	1.9f	8:54p	11:30p	0.8e			
Sat. 5/27	2:00a	4:24a	0.8f	4:00a	1:42a	0.8e	2:06a	4:18a	0.8f	12:48a	3:18a	1.0f
	6:42a	10:24a	1.1e	9:06a	6:24a	0.9f	7:00a	10:30a	1.5e	6:18a	8:54a	1.0e
	1:24p	5:24p	2.3f	4:42p	12:48p	1.6e	2:24p	5:42p	1.4f	12:18p	4:24p	1.3f
	9:42p	11:54p	0.8e	12:00a	8:30p	2.0f	9:36p			8:06p	10:36p	1.0e
Sun. 5/28	3:24a	5:30a	0.8f	5:24a	2:36a	1.0e	3:18a	12:24a	1.0e	1:42a	4:18a	1.0f
	8:06a	11:24a	1.1e	10:24a	7:42a	0.8f	8:24a	5:24a	0.8f	7:30a	10:00a	1.0e
	2:06p	6:06p	2.5f	5:24p	1:54p	1.4e	3:06p	11:36a	1.4e	1:18p	5:06p	1.4f
	10:06p				9:00p	2.1f	10:06p	6:12p	1.5f	8:48p	11:18p	1.1e
Mon. 5/29	4:24a	12:42a	1.1e	12:30a	3:24a	1.3e	4:18a	1:12a	1.3e	2:30a	5:18a	1.1f
	9:24a	6:42a	1.0f	6:36a	9:06a	0.9f	9:42a	6:30a	0.9f	8:36a	11:00a	1.0e
	2:42p	12:18p	1.1e	11:42a	2:48p	1.3e	3:48p	12:30p	1.3e	2:06p	5:48p	1.4f
	10:24p	6:48p	2.7f	6:00p	9:30p	2.1f	10:36p	6:48p	1.5f	9:24p	11:54p	1.2e
Tue. 5/30	5:12a	1:18a	1.5e	12:54a	4:06a	1.5e	5:12a	1:54a	1.6e	3:18a	6:24a	1.1f
	10:30a	7:42a	1.4f	7:36a	10:18a	1.1f	10:54a	7:42a	1.0f	9:42a	12:00p	0.9e
	3:18p	1:06p	1.1e	12:54p	3:36p	1.1e	4:24p	1:30p	1.1e	2:54p	6:30p	1.4f
	10:42p	7:30p	2.9f	6:30p	10:00p	2.2f	11:06p	7:24p	1.6f	9:54p		
Wed. 5/31	5:54a	1:42a	1.9e	1:18a	4:42a	1.8e	6:00a	2:24a	1.9e	4:06a	12:24a	1.3e
	11:30a	8:30a	1.8f	8:30a	11:18a	1.3f	12:00p	8:42a	1.2f	10:48a	7:30a	1.2f
	4:00p	1:48p	1.1e	2:06p	4:30p	0.9e	4:54p	2:18p	1.0e	3:42p	12:54p	0.9e
	11:06p	8:06p	3.0f	7:06p	10:30p	2.2f	11:30p	8:00p	1.7f	10:24p	7:06p	1.4f
Thu. 6/1	6:30a	2:12a	2.3e	1:42a	5:00a	2.0e	6:48a	2:54a	2.2e	4:48a	1:00a	1.5e
	12:24p	9:18a	2.2f	9:18a	12:12p	1.4f	1:06p	9:42a	1.4f	11:48a	8:36a	1.3f
	4:36p	2:30p	1.0e	3:18p	5:24p	0.6e	5:30p	3:06p	0.8e	4:30p	1:48p	0.8e
	11:36p	8:48p	3.1f	7:36p	11:00p	2.2f	11:54p	8:42p	1.8f	10:54p	7:48p	1.3f
Fri. 6/2	7:06a	2:30a	2.6e	2:06a	5:24a	2.2e	7:30a	3:30a	2.5e	5:24a	1:42a	1.6e
	1:18p	10:00a	2.6f	10:06a	1:06p	1.6f	2:06p	10:36a	1.5f	12:48p	9:36a	1.4f
	5:24p	3:18p	0.9e	4:30p	6:18p	0.4e	6:06p	4:00p	0.7e	5:18p	2:36p	0.8e
		9:30p	3.2f	8:06p	11:42p	2.2f		9:18p	1.8f	11:30p	8:36p	1.3f
Sat. 6/3	12:06a	3:00a	2.9e	2:36a	5:54a	2.5e	12:24a	4:06a	2.7e	6:06a	2:18a	1.7e
	7:42a	10:42a	3.0f	10:54a	1:54p	1.7f	8:18a	11:24a	1.7f	1:48p	10:36a	1.5f
	2:06p	4:12p	0.8e	5:48p	7:18p	0.3e	3:06p	4:48p	0.6e	6:06p	3:30p	0.7e
	6:12p	10:12p	3.1f	8:42p			6:42p	10:06p	1.8f		9:24p	1.2f
Sun. 6/4	12:42a	3:36a	3.1e	3:12a	12:24a	2.2f	1:00a	4:48a	2.9e	12:06a	3:00a	1.8e
	8:18a	11:24a	3.2f	11:36a	6:36a	2.6e	9:00a	12:06p	1.7f	6:42a	11:24a	1.6f
	3:00p	5:00p	0.8e	6:54p	2:48p	1.8f	4:06p	5:42p	0.5e	2:36p	4:24p	0.8e
	7:00p	10:54p	3.1f	9:24p	8:12p	0.2e	7:30p	10:54p	1.8f	7:06p	10:12p	1.2f
Mon. 6/5	1:24a	4:18a	3.2e	3:54a	1:12a	2.2f	1:48a	5:36a	3.0e	12:48a	3:48a	1.9e
	9:00a	12:12p	3.3f	12:24p	7:18a	2.7e	9:48a	1:00p	1.8f	7:24a	12:12p	1.7f
	3:42p	5:48p	0.9e	7:48p	3:36p	1.9f	5:00p	6:30p	0.5e	3:30p	5:18p	0.8e
	7:54p	11:42p	3.0f	10:24p	9:06p	0.2e	8:24p	11:42p	1.8f	8:06p	11:06p	1.2f
Tue. 6/6	2:06a	5:00a	3.1e	4:48a	2:00a	2.2f	2:36a	6:24a	3.0e	1:42a	4:36a	1.9e
	9:42a	12:54p	3.3f	1:12p	8:12a	2.6e	10:36a	1:48p	1.8f	8:18a	1:00p	1.7f
	4:30p	6:42p	0.9e	8:24p	4:24p	1.9f	5:48p	7:30p	0.6e	4:18p	6:12p	0.9e
	8:48p			11:36p	10:06p	0.3e	9:24p			9:06p	12:00a	1.2f
Wed. 6/7	2:54a	12:36a	2.8f	5:42a	2:54a	2.1f	3:30a	12:36a	1.7f	2:36a	5:30a	1.8e
	10:24a	5:48a	2.9e	1:54p	9:06a	2.5e	11:24a	7:18a	2.9e	9:12a	1:48p	1.8f
	5:18p	1:48p	3.3f	9:06p	5:12p	1.9f	6:36p	2:42p	1.8f	5:06p	7:12p	0.9e
	9:48p	7:36p	0.9e	11:06p			10:36p	8:24p	0.7e	10:06p		
Thu. 6/8	3:48a	1:24a	2.6f	12:48a	3:54a	1.9f	4:30a	1:36a	1.5f	3:36a	12:54a	1.2f
	11:12a	6:42a	2.5e	6:42a	10:06a	2.3e	12:18p	8:12a	2.7e	10:06a	6:24a	1.7e
	6:12p	2:36p	3.2f	2:42p	5:54p	2.0f	7:24p	3:42p	1.8f	5:54p	2:36p	1.8f
	10:54p	8:36p	1.0e	9:42p			11:54p	9:30p	0.8e	11:06p	8:06p	1.0e
Fri. 6/9	4:48a	2:24a	2.3f	2:06a	12:06a	0.8e	5:36a	2:42a	1.4f	4:36a	1:54a	1.2f
	12:06p	7:42a	2.1e	7:48a	5:00a	1.7f	1:06p	9:12a	2.4e	11:06a	7:30a	1.6e
	7:06p	3:30p	3.1f	3:24p	11:12a	2.1e	8:12p	4:30p	1.8f	6:48p	3:24p	1.8f
		9:48p	1.1e	10:24p	6:42p	2.0f		10:36p	1.1e		9:00p	1.1e
Sat. 6/10	12:12a	3:30a	2.0f	3:30a	1:06a	1.0e	1:24a	3:54a	1.2f	12:06a	2:54a	1.2f
	6:00a	9:12a	1.7e	9:00a	6:06a	1.5f	6:48a	10:12a	2.1e	5:48a	8:30a	1.5e
	1:00p	4:30p	3.2f	4:06p	12:24p	1.8e	1:54p	5:18p	1.8f	12:06p	4:12p	1.8f
	8:00p	10:48p	1.4e	11:06p	7:30p	2.1f	9:00p	11:48p	1.4e	7:36p	10:00p	1.2e

GOLDEN GATE — BENICIA BRIDGE — RICHMOND — OAKLAND

Day/Date	GG Slack Time	GG Current Time	GG Knots	Benicia Slack Time	Benicia Current Time	Benicia Knots	Richmond Slack Time	Richmond Current Time	Richmond Knots	Oakland Slack Time	Oakland Current Time	Oakland Knots
Wed. 4/26	5:12a	3:00a	1.3 f	1:54a	12:18a	0.4e	5:24a	2:36a	1.0 f	4:36a	1:54a	0.9 f
	12:30p	8:06a	1.5e	7:30a	4:48a	1.3 f	1:42p	9:12a	1.8e	10:48a	7:24a	1.1e
	8:54p	4:18p	2.3 f	4:18p	11:06a	1.6e	9:06p	5:48p	1.3 f	7:24p	4:18p	1.2 f
		10:36p	0.5e	11:36p	8:00p	1.8 f		11:12p	0.5e		9:54p	0.8e
Thu. 4/27	1:06a	4:00a	1.0 f	3:12a	1:30a	0.5e	1:18a	3:42a	0.8 f	12:30a	2:54a	0.9 f
	6:12a	9:24a	1.1e	8:36a	5:48a	1.0 f	6:30a	10:18a	1.6e	5:42a	8:24a	1.0e
	1:24p	5:24p	2.2 f	5:12p	12:36p	1.5e	2:42p	6:42p	1.4 f	12:00p	5:18p	1.3 f
	9:48p	11:36p	0.6e		8:54p	1.9 f	10:00p			8:18p	10:48p	1.0e
Fri. 4/28	2:54a	5:06a	0.8 f	12:24a	2:30a	0.7e	2:42a	12:30a	0.7 f	1:30a	3:54a	0.9 f
	7:36a	11:00a	0.9e	4:36a	7:00a	0.9 f	7:54a	4:54a	0.9 f	7:00a	9:30a	0.9e
	2:30p	6:24p	2.3 f	9:54a	2:18p	1.4e	3:36p	11:36a	1.5e	1:12p	6:06p	1.4 f
	10:24p			6:00p	9:42p	2.0 f	10:36p	7:36p	1.5 f	9:00p	11:42p	1.1e
Sat. 4/29	4:06a	12:36a	0.8e	1:00a	3:24a	0.9e	3:54a	1:24a	1.0e	2:30a	5:00a	1.0 f
	9:06a	6:18a	1.0 f	5:54a	8:24a	0.9 f	9:18a	6:12a	0.9 f	8:12a	10:36a	0.9e
	3:18p	12:12p	1.0e	11:12a	3:18p	1.5e	4:18p	12:48p	1.5e	2:18p	6:42p	1.4 f
	11:00p	7:12p	2.4 f	6:42p	10:18p	2.1 f	11:12p	8:06p	1.5 f	9:42p		
Sun. 4/30	5:00a	1:18a	1.1e	1:30a	4:18a	1.2e	4:48a	2:06a	1.2e	3:18a	12:24a	1.2e
	10:12a	7:24a	1.2 f	7:00a	9:42a	1.1 f	10:24a	7:18a	1.0 f	9:18a	6:00a	1.1 f
	3:54p	1:00p	1.2e	12:24p	4:00p	1.5e	5:00p	1:36p	1.5e	3:12p	11:42a	1.0e
	11:18p	7:48p	2.6 f	7:18p	10:42p	2.2 f	11:42p	8:30p	1.6 f	10:18p	7:18p	1.4 f
Mon. 5/1	5:42a	1:54a	1.3e	1:54a	5:00a	1.4e	5:42a	2:42a	1.3e	4:00a	12:54a	1.2e
	11:00a	8:12a	1.5 f	7:54a	10:36a	1.3 f	11:24a	8:18a	1.2 f	10:12a	7:00a	1.3 f
	4:30p	1:42p	1.3e	1:24p	4:36p	1.4e	5:30p	2:18p	1.5e	3:54p	12:30p	1.1e
	11:42p	8:18p	2.8 f	7:42p	11:06p	2.2 f		8:42p	1.6 f	10:54p	7:36p	1.4 f
Tue. 5/2	6:18a	2:24a	1.7e	2:18a	5:30a	1.6e	12:06a	3:12a	1.3 f	4:42a	1:24a	1.3e
	11:48a	8:54a	1.8 f	8:42a	11:30a	1.4 f	6:24a	9:06a	1.3 f	11:06a	7:48a	1.3 f
	5:00p	2:24p	1.3e	2:18p	5:12p	1.3e	12:18p	3:00p	1.4e	4:36p	1:24p	1.1e
	12:00p	8:48p	3.0 f	8:12p	11:24p	2.2 f	6:00p	8:54p	1.7 f	11:18p	8:06p	1.4 f
Wed. 5/3	6:54a	2:54a	2.0e	2:36a	6:00a	1.8e	12:30a	3:42a	2.0e	5:18a	1:48a	1.4e
	12:36p	9:36a	2.2 f	9:30a	12:18p	1.5 f	7:06a	9:48a	1.5 f	12:00p	8:42a	1.4 f
	5:36p	3:06p	1.3e	3:12p	5:54p	1.1e	1:06p	3:36p	1.3e	5:12p	2:06p	1.1e
		9:24p	3.2 f	8:36p	11:48p	2.3 f	6:30p	9:24p	1.8 f	11:48p	8:36p	1.4 f
Thu. 5/4	12:18a	3:18a	2.4e	2:54a	6:12a	2.0e	12:48a	4:06a	2.2e	5:54a	2:18a	1.5e
	7:24a	10:18a	2.5 f	10:12a	1:00p	1.6 f	7:48a	10:30a	1.6 f	12:48p	9:30a	1.4 f
	1:30p	3:48p	1.2e	4:12p	6:36p	0.9e	2:00p	4:18p	1.1e	5:48p	2:54p	1.0e
	6:12p	10:00p	3.3 f	9:06p			6:54p	9:54p	1.8 f		9:12p	1.4 f
Fri. 5/5	12:48a	3:42a	2.7e	3:18a	12:18a	2.3 f	1:06a	4:36a	2.4e	12:12a	2:54a	1.6e
	8:00a	11:00a	2.9 f	10:54a	6:30a	2.2e	8:30a	11:12a	1.6 f	6:24a	10:24a	1.4 f
	2:18p	4:30p	1.1e	5:18p	1:48p	1.7 f	2:54p	5:00p	1.0e	1:42p	3:42p	0.9e
	6:48p	10:42p	3.3 f	9:30p	7:24p	0.7e	7:24p	10:30p	1.9 f	6:24p	9:48p	1.3 f
Sat. 5/6	1:12a	4:06a	3.0e	3:48a	12:54a	2.3 f	1:36a	5:12a	2.6e	12:36a	3:30a	1.8e
	8:30a	11:48a	3.1 f	11:42a	7:00a	2.5e	9:12a	12:00p	1.7 f	6:54a	11:12a	1.5 f
	3:12p	5:24p	1.0e	6:24p	2:42p	1.7 f	3:54p	5:48p	0.8e	2:36p	4:30p	0.8e
	7:30p	11:18p	3.2 f	10:00p	8:06p	0.5e	7:54p	11:12p	1.8 f	7:06p	10:30p	1.3 f
Sun. 5/7	1:48a	4:42a	3.2e	4:18a	1:36a	2.2 f	2:06a	5:54a	2.8e	1:12a	4:06a	1.9e
	9:06a	12:30p	3.2 f	12:30p	7:36a	2.6e	9:54a	12:48p	1.7 f	7:30a	12:00p	1.5 f
	4:00p	6:06p	0.9e	7:30p	3:36p	1.7 f	4:54p	6:36p	0.6e	3:36p	5:24p	0.8e
	8:12p	12:00p	3.0 f	10:36p	9:06p	0.3e	8:36p	11:54p	1.8 f	7:54p	11:12p	1.2 f
Mon. 5/8	2:24a	5:18a	3.2e	5:00a	2:18a	2.1 f	2:42a	6:36a	2.8e	1:48a	4:54a	1.9e
	9:48a	1:18p	3.2 f	1:18p	8:18a	2.6e	10:42a	1:42p	1.6 f	8:12a	12:54p	1.5 f
	4:54p	6:54p	0.8e	8:42p	4:30p	1.7 f	5:54p	7:30p	0.5e	4:30p	6:18p	0.7e
	9:06p			11:30p	10:00p	0.2e	9:18p			9:00p		
Tue. 5/9	3:12a	12:48a	2.7 f	5:48a	3:06a	2.0 f	3:30a	12:48a	1.6 f	2:36a	12:06a	1.2 f
	10:30a	6:00a	3.0e	2:12p	9:06a	2.5e	11:36a	7:24a	2.7e	9:00a	5:42a	1.8e
	5:48p	2:06p	3.1 f	9:42p	5:30p	1.7 f	7:00p	2:48p	1.6 f	5:30p	1:54p	1.5 f
	10:00p	7:54p	0.7e		11:12p	0.3e	10:24p	8:30p	0.4e	10:06p	7:24p	0.7e
Wed. 5/10	4:00a	1:42a	2.4 f	12:36a	4:00a	1.8 f	4:30a	1:42a	1.4 f	3:36a	1:00a	1.1 f
	11:18a	6:48a	2.7e	6:42a	10:00a	2.3e	12:36p	8:24a	2.6e	10:00a	6:36a	1.7e
	6:48p	3:00p	2.9 f	3:06p	6:36p	1.7 f	8:00p	4:00p	1.6 f	6:24p	3:00p	1.5 f
	11:00p	9:06p	0.7e	10:30p			11:48p	9:42p	0.5e	11:18p	8:30p	0.8e
Thu. 5/11	4:54a	2:36a	2.1 f	2:00a	12:24a	0.4e	5:36a	2:48a	1.3 f	4:42a	2:06a	1.1 f
	12:18p	7:42a	2.2e	7:48a	5:06a	1.4 f	1:36p	9:24a	2.3e	11:12a	7:36a	1.5e
	7:48p	4:00p	2.8 f	4:06p	11:12a	2.0e	9:00p	5:24p	1.6 f	7:24p	4:06p	1.6 f
		10:12p	0.8e	11:18p	7:30p	1.7 f	11:06p				9:36p	0.9e
Fri. 5/12	12:18a	3:42a	1.9 f	3:30a	1:30a	0.7e	1:24a	4:00a	1.2 f	12:30a	3:12a	1.1 f
	6:06a	9:00a	1.7e	9:06a	6:18a	1.4 f	6:54a	10:36a	2.1e	6:00a	8:48a	1.4e
	1:30p	5:00p	2.9 f	4:54p	12:30p	1.8e	2:36p	6:24p	1.7 f	12:30p	5:06p	1.7 f
	8:42p	11:18p	1.1e	11:54p	8:24p	1.9 f	9:48p			8:12p	10:36p	1.1e
Sat. 5/13	2:00a	4:54a	1.8 f	5:00a	2:36a	1.0e	2:54a	12:18a	1.0e	1:36a	4:24a	1.1 f
	7:30a	10:54a	1.5e	10:30a	7:36a	1.4 f	8:24a	5:18a	1.1 f	7:18a	9:54a	1.3e
	2:36p	6:00p	3.1 f	5:42p	2:00p	1.6e	3:30p	11:48a	2.0e	1:36p	6:00p	1.8 f
	9:30p				9:12p	2.1 f	10:30p	7:12p	1.9 f	9:00p	11:30p	1.3e
Sun. 5/14	3:30a	12:18a	1.5e	12:30a	3:36a	1.4e	4:06a	1:18a	1.4e	2:36a	5:36a	1.2 f
	9:06a	6:12a	1.9 f	6:18a	9:00a	1.4 f	9:42a	6:42a	1.2 f	8:36a	11:06a	1.3e
	3:30p	12:18p	1.5e	11:48a	3:06p	1.5e	4:18p	12:54p	1.9e	2:36p	6:42p	1.8 f
	10:12p	6:54p	3.3 f	6:24p	9:54p	2.2 f	11:06p	7:48p	1.9 f	9:48p		
Mon. 5/15	4:48a	1:12a	2.0e	1:06a	4:30a	1.8e	5:12a	2:12a	1.9e	3:36a	12:18a	1.5e
	10:24a	7:24a	2.3 f	7:30a	10:18a	1.6 f	10:54a	8:00a	1.4 f	9:42a	6:48a	1.4 f
	4:18p	1:24p	1.5e	1:00p	4:00p	1.4e	5:00p	1:54p	1.8e	3:30p	12:12p	1.3e
	10:54p	7:42p	3.6 f	7:06p	10:30p	2.4 f	11:42p	8:18p	2.0 f	10:24p	7:24p	1.8 f
Tue. 5/16	5:48a	1:54a	2.5e	1:42a	5:24a	2.0e	6:06a	2:54a	2.2e	4:30a	1:00a	1.6e
	11:36a	8:24a	2.6 f	8:36a	11:18a	1.7 f	12:00p	9:06a	1.6 f	10:48a	7:54a	1.5 f
	5:00p	2:12p	1.4e	2:00p	4:48p	1.3e	5:36p	2:42p	1.6e	4:12p	1:06p	1.3e
	11:30p	8:30p	3.8 f	7:36p	11:00p	2.4 f		8:48p	2.0 f	11:06p	8:00p	1.8 f
Wed. 5/17	6:42a	2:36a	2.9e	2:12a	6:12a	2.2e	12:12a	3:36a	2.5e	5:18a	1:36a	1.7e
	12:36p	9:18a	3.0 f	9:30a	12:12p	1.8 f	7:00a	10:06a	1.7 f	11:48a	8:54a	1.5 f
	5:42p	3:00p	1.2e	3:06p	5:36p	1.1e	1:00p	3:30p	1.4e	5:00p	2:00p	1.2e
		9:12p	3.8 f	8:12p	11:30p	2.4 f	6:12p	9:12p	2.0 f	11:42p	8:30p	1.6 f
Thu. 5/18	12:06a	3:18a	3.1e	2:42a	6:54a	2.3e	12:42a	4:12a	2.6e	6:06a	2:12a	1.7e
	7:30a	10:12a	3.3 f	10:24a	1:06p	1.9 f	7:48a	10:54a	1.7 f	12:42p	9:54a	1.6 f
	1:36p	3:54p	1.1e	4:06p	6:24p	0.9e	2:00p	4:18p	1.2e	5:42p	2:54p	1.1e
	6:24p	9:54p	3.6 f	8:48p			6:48p	9:48p	1.9 f		9:06p	1.5 f

	GOLDEN GATE			BENICIA BRIDGE			RICHMOND			OAKLAND		
	SLACK	CURRENT		SLACK	CURRENT		SLACK	CURRENT		SLACK	CURRENT	
Date	Time	Time	Knots	Time	Time	Knots	Time	Time	Knots	Time	Time	Knots
Mon. 4/3	12:30a	3:00a	1.4e	3:12a	12:06a	2.2f	1:06a	3:54a	1.5e	5:18a	2:18a	1.3e
	6:36a	9:18a	2.0f	8:54a	6:12a	1.4e	6:48a	9:30a	1.5f	11:30a	8:18a	1.4f
	12:12p	3:00p	1.5e	2:36p	11:42a	1.6f	12:36p	3:42p	1.8e	5:24p	1:54p	1.2e
	6:18p	9:36p	2.9f	9:18p	6:12p	1.7e	7:00p	10:06p	1.7f		9:12p	1.5f
Tue. 4/4	12:54a	3:36a	1.6e	3:36a	12:24a	2.2f	1:24a	4:24a	1.7e	12:12a	2:42a	1.3e
	7:12a	10:00a	2.2f	9:36a	6:42a	1.6e	7:24a	10:06a	1.6f	5:54a	9:00a	1.5f
	12:54p	3:42p	1.6e	3:24p	12:24p	1.7f	1:18p	4:12p	1.8e	12:12p	2:30p	1.3e
	6:42p	10:12p	3.1f	9:42p	6:36p	1.6e	7:24p	10:18p	1.7f	5:54p	9:30p	1.5f
Wed. 4/5	1:12a	4:06a	1.9e	3:54a	12:42a	2.2f	1:48a	4:42a	1.9e	12:36a	3:00a	1.4e
	7:42a	10:42a	2.5f	10:18a	7:00a	1.7e	8:00a	10:42a	1.6f	6:24a	9:42a	1.5f
	1:36p	4:24p	1.6e	4:06p	1:06p	1.7f	2:00p	4:42p	1.6e	12:54p	3:12p	1.3e
	7:12p	10:42p	3.2f	10:06p	7:00p	1.4e	7:48p	10:42p	1.8f	6:24p	9:54p	1.5f
Thu. 4/6	1:36a	4:30a	2.2e	4:12a	1:06a	2.2f	2:06a	5:12a	2.0e	1:00a	3:30a	1.5e
	8:12a	11:24a	2.7f	11:00a	7:18a	1.9e	8:42a	11:18a	1.7f	6:48a	10:24a	1.5f
	2:24p	5:06p	1.5e	5:00p	1:48p	1.7f	2:48p	5:18p	1.5e	1:42p	3:54p	1.2e
	7:42p	11:18p	3.3f	10:30p	7:36p	1.2e	8:12p	11:06p	1.9f	6:54p	10:18p	1.5f
Fri. 4/7	2:00a	4:48a	2.5e	4:36a	1:30a	2.3f	2:24a	5:42a	2.3e	1:18a	4:00a	1.6e
	8:48a	12:06p	2.9f	11:42a	7:36a	2.1e	9:18a	12:00p	1.7f	7:18a	11:00a	1.4f
	3:12p	5:42p	1.4e	5:54p	2:36p	1.7f	3:36p	6:00p	1.3e	2:30p	4:42p	1.1e
	8:12p	11:54p	3.2f	10:54p	8:18p	1.0e	8:36p	11:42p	1.9f	7:24p	10:54p	1.4f
Sat. 4/8	2:30a	5:18a	2.8e	5:00a	2:06a	2.3f	2:42a	6:12a	2.4e	1:42a	4:36a	1.7e
	9:24a	12:48p	3.0f	12:30p	8:00a	2.3e	10:00a	12:42p	1.6f	7:42a	11:42a	1.4f
	4:00p	6:24p	1.2e	6:54p	3:24p	1.6f	4:30p	6:42p	1.0e	3:24p	5:24p	0.9e
	8:48p			11:24p	9:00p	0.7e	9:06p			8:00p	11:30p	1.3f
Sun. 4/9	3:00a	12:30a	3.1f	5:30a	2:42a	2.2f	3:12a	12:18a	1.8f	2:12a	5:12a	1.8e
	10:00a	5:48a	2.9e	1:18p	8:42a	2.4e	10:48a	6:54a	2.5e	8:18a	12:24p	1.3f
	5:00p	1:30p	2.9f	8:06p	4:18p	1.5f	5:36p	1:36p	1.5f	4:24p	6:18p	0.8e
	9:30p	7:12p	0.9e	11:54p	9:54p	0.5e	9:36p	7:36p	0.7e	8:48p		
Mon. 4/10	3:36a	1:12a	2.8f	6:12a	3:24a	2.1f	3:48a	1:00a	1.7f	2:54a	12:12a	1.2f
	10:42a	6:24a	2.9e	2:18p	9:18a	2.4e	11:42a	7:42a	2.5e	9:06a	6:00a	1.7e
	6:00p	2:24p	2.8f	9:30p	5:24p	1.4f	6:54p	2:36p	1.4f	5:36p	1:30p	1.2f
	10:12p	8:12p	0.7e		11:00p	0.3e	10:18p	8:30p	0.5e	9:48p	7:24p	0.6e
Tue. 4/11	4:18a	2:00a	2.4f	12:36a	4:18a	1.9f	4:36a	1:54a	1.5f	3:42a	1:06a	1.1f
	11:24a	7:06a	2.7e	7:00a	10:12a	2.2e	12:48p	8:30a	2.4e	10:00a	6:48a	1.6e
	7:06p	3:18p	2.7f	3:24p	6:48p	1.3f	8:36p	3:48p	1.3f	6:48p	2:54p	1.2f
	11:12p	9:24p	0.6e	11:00p			11:24p	9:42p	0.3e	11:12p	8:36p	0.6e
Wed. 4/12	5:12a	2:54a	2.1f	1:42a	12:24a	0.2e	5:42a	2:54a	1.3f	4:48a	2:12a	1.0f
	12:24p	7:54a	2.2e	7:54a	5:12a	1.7f	2:06p	9:36a	2.2e	11:06a	7:48a	1.4e
	8:18p	4:24p	2.6f	4:30p	11:12a	2.0e	9:36p	5:54p	1.3f	7:54p	4:36p	1.3f
		10:30p	0.7e	12:00p	8:12p	1.4f		11:12p	0.3e		9:54p	0.7e
Thu. 4/13	12:24a	4:00a	1.8f	3:18a	1:42a	0.3e	1:06a	4:06a	1.1f	12:42a	3:24a	0.9f
	6:18a	9:12a	1.8e	9:12a	6:24a	1.5f	7:00a	10:54a	2.1e	6:06a	9:00a	1.3e
	1:42p	5:24p	2.6f	5:42p	12:30p	1.7e	3:12p	7:12p	1.5f	12:36p	5:48p	1.5f
	9:18p	11:42p	0.9e		9:18p	1.6f	10:30p			8:48p	11:06p	0.9e
Fri. 4/14	1:54a	5:12a	1.8f	12:42a	2:54a	0.6e	2:48a	12:42a	0.6e	1:54a	4:36a	1.0f
	7:42a	10:42a	1.5e	4:48a	7:42a	1.4f	8:30a	5:30a	1.2f	7:30a	10:12a	1.3e
	3:06p	6:30p	2.8f	10:36a	2:12p	1.6e	4:12p	12:12p	2.1e	2:06p	6:42p	1.7f
	10:06p			6:36p	10:00p	1.9f	11:12p	8:00p	1.8f	9:36p		
Sat. 4/15	3:24a	12:42a	1.3e	1:18a	3:54a	1.0e	4:12a	1:42a	1.1e	3:00a	12:06a	1.2e
	9:12a	6:30a	2.0f	6:12a	9:06a	1.6f	9:54a	6:48a	1.3f	8:48a	5:54a	1.2f
	4:12p	12:42p	1.5e	12:00p	3:42p	1.7e	5:06p	1:24p	2.2e	3:12p	11:24a	1.4e
	10:48p	7:30p	3.1f	7:24p	10:42p	2.1f	11:48p	8:42p	1.9f	10:24p	7:30p	1.8f
Sun. 4/16	4:42a	1:30a	1.7e	1:48a	4:48a	1.4e	5:12a	2:36a	1.5e	3:54a	12:54a	1.4e
	10:30a	7:36a	2.4f	7:24a	10:18a	1.8f	11:06a	8:00a	1.5f	9:54a	7:00a	1.4f
	5:06p	1:42p	1.7e	1:06p	4:36p	1.7e	5:48p	2:24p	2.2e	6:30p	12:30p	1.5e
	11:24p	8:18p	3.4f	8:00p	11:12p	2.2f	9:18p			11:06p	8:12p	1.9f
Mon. 4/17	5:48a	2:18a	2.1e	2:24a	5:36a	1.7e	12:24a	3:18a	1.9e	4:48a	1:36a	1.5e
	11:36a	8:36a	2.8f	8:30a	11:18a	2.0f	6:12a	9:00a	1.7f	10:54a	8:00a	1.6f
	5:54p	2:36p	1.7e	2:06p	5:24p	1.7e	12:06p	3:06p	2.2e	4:54p	1:24p	1.5e
		9:00p	3.7f	8:36p	11:42p	2.4f	6:24p	9:42p	2.1f	11:42p	8:48p	1.9f
Tue. 4/18	12:06a	3:00a	2.5e	2:54a	6:24a	2.0e	12:54a	4:00a	2.2e	5:36a	2:12a	1.6e
	6:48a	9:30a	3.1f	9:24a	12:12p	2.1f	7:00a	9:54a	1.9f	11:54a	8:54a	1.6f
	12:36p	3:30p	1.7e	3:06p	6:00p	1.6e	1:00p	3:54p	2.0e	5:36p	2:18p	1.5e
	6:36p	9:42p	3.9f	9:06p			7:00p	10:00p	2.1f		9:24p	1.9f
Wed. 4/19	12:42a	3:48a	2.8e	3:24a	12:18a	2.5f	1:24a	4:36a	2.4e	12:18a	2:48a	1.7e
	7:42a	10:24a	3.4f	10:18a	7:00a	2.1e	7:54a	10:48a	1.9f	6:18a	9:48a	1.6f
	1:36p	4:18p	1.5e	4:00p	1:06p	2.1f	1:54p	4:36p	1.8e	12:48p	3:06p	1.4e
	7:12p	10:30p	3.9f	9:36p	6:42p	1.4e	7:30p	10:30p	2.1f	6:12p	9:48p	1.8f
Thu. 4/20	1:18a	4:24a	3.1e	3:54a	12:48a	2.5f	1:54a	5:12a	2.5e	12:54a	3:24a	1.7e
	8:30a	11:18a	3.5f	11:06a	7:42a	2.2e	8:42a	11:36a	1.9f	7:00a	10:36a	1.6f
	2:36p	5:12p	1.3e	5:00p	2:00p	2.0f	2:48p	5:18p	1.5e	1:42p	3:54p	1.3e
	7:48p	11:06p	3.7f	10:12p	7:30p	1.2e	8:06p	11:00p	2.0f	6:54p	10:18p	1.6f
Fri. 4/21	1:54a	5:06a	3.2e	4:24a	1:18a	2.4f	2:24a	5:48a	2.6e	1:24a	4:00a	1.7e
	9:12a	12:06p	3.5f	12:00p	8:00a	2.2e	9:24a	12:18p	1.8f	7:36a	11:30a	1.5f
	3:36p	6:00p	1.1e	6:00p	2:54p	1.9f	3:48p	6:06p	1.2e	2:36p	4:42p	1.1e
	8:24p	11:48p	3.4f	10:42p	8:18p	1.0e	8:36p	11:30p	1.9f	7:36p	10:48p	1.5f
Sat. 4/22	2:30a	5:42a	3.1e	4:54a	1:54a	2.2f	2:48a	6:18a	2.5e	1:54a	4:36a	1.7e
	9:54a	12:48p	3.4f	12:48p	8:24a	2.2e	10:12a	1:06p	1.7f	8:12a	12:18p	1.5f
	4:36p	6:48p	1.0e	7:06p	3:48p	1.9f	4:42p	6:48p	1.0e	3:30p	5:36p	1.0e
	9:00p			11:18p	9:06p	0.8e	9:12p			8:18p	11:24p	1.4f
Sun. 4/23	3:06a	12:30a	3.0f	5:30a	2:30a	2.0f	3:18a	12:12a	1.8f	2:24a	5:06a	1.6e
	10:36a	6:06a	2.9e	1:36p	8:48a	2.1e	11:00a	6:54a	2.4e	8:48a	1:06p	1.4f
	5:36p	1:36p	3.2f	8:12p	4:54p	1.8f	5:42p	2:00p	1.5f	4:30p	6:30p	0.8e
	9:48p	7:42p	0.8e	12:00p	10:06p	0.6e	9:54p	7:36p	0.7e	9:12p		
Mon. 4/24	3:42a	1:18a	2.4f	6:00a	3:12a	1.8f	3:54a	12:54a	1.5f	3:00a	12:06a	1.2f
	11:12a	6:42a	2.5e	2:30p	9:24a	2.0e	11:48a	7:36a	2.3e	9:18a	5:48a	1.5e
	6:42p	2:30p	2.9f	9:30p	5:54p	1.8f	6:48p	3:00p	1.4f	5:30p	2:00p	1.3f
	10:36p	8:36p	0.6e		11:06p	0.4e	10:42p	8:36p	0.5e	10:12p	7:30p	0.7e
Tue. 4/25	4:24a	2:06a	1.8f	12:54a	3:54a	1.5f	4:30a	1:42a	1.3f	3:42a	12:54a	1.1f
	11:48a	7:18a	2.0e	6:42a	10:06a	1.8e	12:42p	8:18a	2.0e	10:00a	6:36a	1.3e
	7:48p	3:24p	2.6f	3:24p	7:00p	1.8f	8:00p	4:30p	1.3f	6:30p	3:06p	1.2f
	11:36p	9:36p	0.5e	10:36p			11:54p	9:42p	0.4e	11:18p	8:42p	0.8e

	GOLDEN GATE			BENICIA BRIDGE			RICHMOND			OAKLAND		
	SLACK	CURRENT		SLACK	CURRENT		SLACK	CURRENT		SLACK	CURRENT	
	Time	Time	Knots	Time	Time	Knots	Time	Time	Knots	Time	Time	Knots
Sat. 3/11	2:48a	12:06a	3.1 f	5:24a	2:24a	2.3 f	3:00a	6:18a	2.1 e	1:54a	4:48a	1.6 e
	9:18a	5:30a	2.3 e	12:24p	8:18a	1.9 e	10:00a	12:42p	1.4 f	7:42a	11:24a	1.3 f
	3:54p	12:48p	2.5 f	6:36p	3:12p	1.4 f	4:06p	6:42p	1.2 e	3:06p	5:30p	1.0 e
	9:06p	6:30p	1.2 e	11:42p	9:00p	1.0 e	9:12p			8:00p	11:36p	1.4 f
Sun. 3/12	4:18a	12:42a	2.9 f	6:54a	4:00a	2.2 f	4:30a	12:30a	1.8 f	3:30a	6:30a	1.6 e
	11:00a	7:00a	2.4 e	2:24p	9:54a	2.0 e	11:54a	8:00a	2.1 e	9:24a	1:12p	1.1 f
	6:00p	2:42p	2.4 f	8:54p	5:12p	1.2 f	6:24p	2:36p	1.2 f	5:24p	7:30p	0.7 e
	10:42p	8:30p	0.9 e		10:54p	0.6 e	10:42p	8:36p	0.8 e	9:48p		
Mon. 3/13	5:00a	2:30a	2.6 f	1:12a	4:42a	2.0 f	5:12a	2:18a	1.6 f	4:12a	1:24a	1.2 f
	11:48a	7:42a	2.3 e	7:30a	10:36a	2.4 e	1:06p	8:54a	2.2 e	10:12a	7:18a	1.5 e
	7:18p	3:42p	2.3 f	3:30p	6:36p	1.1 f	8:00p	3:42p	1.1 f	6:54p	2:30p	1.0 f
	11:30p	9:36p	0.7 e	10:36p			11:30p	9:36p	0.5 e	11:00p	8:36p	0.5 e
Tue. 3/14	5:48a	3:18a	2.3 f	1:54a	12:12a	0.3 e	6:00a	3:12a	1.4 f	5:06a	2:24a	1.0 f
	12:54p	8:30a	2.2 e	8:24a	5:36a	1.8 f	2:24p	9:54a	2.1 e	11:18a	8:12a	1.4 e
	8:42p	4:48p	2.2 f	4:54p	11:36a	1.9 e	9:48p	5:24p	1.0 f	8:12p	4:54p	1.0 f
		10:48p	0.6 e		8:36p	1.1 f		11:06p	0.2 e		10:00p	0.5 e
Wed. 3/15	12:36a	4:18a	2.0 f	12:18a	1:42a	0.2 e	12:42a	4:18a	1.2 f	12:36a	3:36a	0.9 f
	6:48a	9:36a	1.9 e	3:00a	6:36a	1.6 f	7:12a	11:12a	2.0 e	6:18a	9:18a	1.3 e
	2:06p	5:54p	2.3 f	9:30a	12:42p	1.8 e	3:42p	7:42p	1.3 f	12:48p	6:24p	1.3 f
	9:42p	12:00p	0.8 e	6:18p	9:48p	1.4 f	11:06p			9:18p	11:24p	0.7 e
Thu. 3/16	1:54a	5:30a	2.0 f	1:24a	3:00a	0.3 e	2:36a	12:48a	0.3 e	2:06a	4:48a	1.0 f
	8:00a	10:54a	1.7 e	4:36a	7:48a	1.5 f	8:36a	5:36a	1.2 f	7:42a	10:24a	1.3 e
	3:36p	7:00p	2.5 f	10:48a	2:06p	1.7 e	4:48p	12:30p	2.2 e	2:24p	7:18p	1.6 f
	10:36p			7:18p	10:42p	1.7 f	11:54p	8:42p	1.6 f	10:12p		
Fri. 3/17	3:18a	12:54a	1.1 e	6:00a	4:12a	0.6 e	4:00a	2:00a	0.7 e	3:18a	12:30a	1.0 e
	9:24a	6:42a	2.1 f	12:06p	9:06a	1.7 f	10:00a	6:48a	1.4 f	9:00a	6:06a	1.1 f
	4:48p	12:36p	1.7 e	8:12p	3:48p	1.8 e	5:42p	1:12p	1.7 e	3:42p	11:36a	1.4 e
	11:18p	7:54p	2.9 f	11:18p	11:18p	1.9 f	9:24p	9:24p	1.9 f	11:00p	8:12p	1.8 f
Sat. 3/18	4:36a	1:48a	1.4 e	2:30a	5:06a	0.9 e	12:30a	2:54a	1.0 e	4:12a	1:18a	1.2 e
	10:36a	7:48a	2.5 f	7:18a	10:18a	1.9 f	5:12a	8:00a	1.6 f	10:06a	7:12a	1.4 f
	5:48p	1:54p	1.8 e	1:12p	5:12p	1.9 e	11:12a	2:42p	2.5 e	4:42p	12:42p	1.5 e
	12:00p	8:48p	3.2 f	8:54p	11:54p	2.1 f	6:30p	10:00p	2.0 f	11:42p	8:48p	2.0 f
Sun. 3/19	5:42a	2:36a	1.7 e	3:06a	5:54a	1.3 e	1:06a	3:36a	1.4 e	5:06a	2:06a	1.4 e
	11:42a	8:48a	2.9 f	8:18a	11:18a	2.1 f	6:12a	9:00a	1.8 f	11:06a	8:12a	1.6 f
	6:36p	2:54p	1.9 e	2:12p	6:00p	2.0 e	12:12p	3:30p	2.6 e	5:30p	1:42p	1.7 e
	9:30p	9:30p	3.5 f	9:24p			7:06p	10:30p	2.1 f	9:30p	9:30p	2.0 f
Mon. 3/20	12:36a	3:24a	2.0 e	3:36a	12:30a	2.2 f	1:36a	4:18a	1.7 e	12:24a	2:48a	1.6 e
	6:42a	9:42a	3.2 f	9:18a	6:42a	1.6 e	7:06a	9:54a	2.0 f	5:54a	9:06a	1.7 f
	12:42p	3:54p	2.0 e	3:12p	12:12p	2.3 f	1:06p	4:18p	2.6 e	12:00p	2:30p	1.8 e
	7:18p	10:18p	3.7 f	10:00p	6:36p	2.0 e	7:48p	10:54p	2.1 f	6:12p	10:06p	2.0 f
Tue. 3/21	1:18a	4:12a	2.3 e	4:06a	1:30a	2.3 f	2:12a	5:00a	2.0 e	1:00a	3:24a	1.6 e
	7:42a	10:36a	3.4 f	10:12a	7:24a	1.8 e	7:54a	10:48a	2.1 f	6:36a	9:54a	1.7 f
	1:36p	4:42p	2.0 e	4:06p	1:06p	2.3 f	2:00p	5:06p	2.4 e	12:54p	3:24p	1.8 e
	8:00p	11:00p	3.9 f	10:30p	7:18p	2.0 e	8:18p	11:18p	2.1 f	6:54p	10:36p	2.0 f
Wed. 3/22	1:54a	5:00a	2.6 e	4:42a	1:30a	2.4 f	2:42a	5:42a	2.2 e	1:36a	4:00a	1.7 e
	8:30a	11:24a	3.5 f	11:06a	8:00a	1.9 e	8:48a	11:36a	2.0 f	7:18a	10:42a	1.7 f
	2:30p	5:30p	2.2 e	5:00p	2:00p	2.2 f	2:48p	5:42p	2.2 e	1:42p	4:06p	1.7 e
	8:36p	11:42p	3.9 f	11:00p	7:54p	1.8 e	8:48p	11:42p	2.1 f	7:30p	11:00p	1.9 f
Thu. 3/23	2:30a	5:48a	2.8 e	5:12a	2:00a	2.4 f	3:12a	6:18a	2.3 e	2:12a	4:36a	1.7 e
	9:24a	12:12p	3.5 f	12:00p	8:36a	2.0 e	9:36a	12:18p	1.9 f	8:00a	11:24a	1.6 f
	3:30p	6:18p	1.6 e	5:54p	2:54p	2.1 f	3:42p	6:24p	1.8 e	2:36p	4:54p	1.5 e
	9:06p			11:36p	8:36p	1.6 e	9:18p			8:06p	11:30p	1.7 f
Fri. 3/24	3:06a	12:18a	3.7 f	5:48a	2:36a	2.4 f	3:42a	12:12a	2.1 f	2:42a	5:12a	1.6 e
	10:12a	6:12a	2.9 e	1:00p	9:06a	2.0 e	10:24a	6:54a	2.3 e	8:42a	12:12p	1.5 f
	4:24p	1:06p	3.3 f	6:54p	3:48p	1.9 f	4:36p	1:12p	1.7 f	3:30p	5:48p	1.2 e
	9:42p	7:00p	1.3 e		9:24p	1.4 e	9:54p	7:06p	1.5 e	8:42p	12:00p	1.6 f
Sat. 3/25	3:48a	1:00a	3.3 f	12:06a	3:12a	2.2 f	11:18a	7:30a	2.3 e	3:12a	5:48a	1.6 e
	10:54a	6:48a	2.8 e	6:18a	9:36a	1.9 e	5:42p	2:06p	1.5 f	9:18a	1:00p	1.3 f
	5:30p	1:54p	3.1 f	1:54p	4:54p	1.7 f	10:30p	7:54p	1.1 e	4:30p	6:42p	1.0 e
	10:12p	7:54p	1.0 e	8:00p	10:18p	1.0 e				9:30p		
Sun. 3/26	4:24a	1:48a	2.8 f	12:48a	3:48a	2.0 f	4:42a	1:24a	1.7 f	3:48a	12:42a	1.4 f
	11:42a	7:24a	2.5 e	6:54a	10:12a	1.8 e	12:18p	8:12a	2.1 e	10:00a	6:24a	1.4 e
	6:42p	2:54p	2.8 f	3:00p	6:06p	1.6 f	6:54p	3:12p	1.3 f	5:42p	2:12p	1.2 f
	10:54p	8:54p	0.9 e	9:18p	11:24p	0.6 e	11:12p	8:48p	0.7 e	10:24p	7:48p	0.8 e
Mon. 3/27	5:06a	2:36a	2.2 f	1:30a	4:30a	1.7 f	5:24a	2:12a	1.4 f	4:24a	1:24a	1.2 f
	12:30p	8:06a	2.1 e	7:36a	11:00a	1.6 e	1:24p	9:00a	1.9 e	10:48a	7:12a	1.3 e
	8:06p	3:54p	2.5 f	4:06p	7:24p	1.6 f	8:18p	4:54p	1.2 f	6:54p	3:48p	1.1 f
	11:54p	10:00p	0.6 e	10:48p				10:00p	0.7 e	11:36p	9:00p	0.7 e
Tue. 3/28	5:54a	3:24a	1.7 f	2:24a	12:36a	0.5 e	12:12a	3:12a	1.1 f	5:18a	2:18a	1.0 f
	1:24p	8:54a	1.6 e	8:24a	5:24a	1.4 f	6:12a	10:00a	1.6 e	11:48a	8:00a	1.1 e
	9:18p	5:00p	2.3 f	5:12p	12:12p	1.4 e	2:30p	6:30p	1.2 f	8:00p	5:12p	1.2 f
		11:00p	0.6 e		8:42p	1.7 f	9:42p	11:42p	0.4 e		10:24p	0.7 e
Wed. 3/29	1:18a	4:30a	1.3 f	12:06a	1:54a	0.4 e	1:42a	4:12a	0.9 f	12:54a	3:24a	0.9 f
	7:00a	10:00a	1.2 e	3:36a	6:24a	1.1 f	7:24a	11:30a	1.6 e	6:24a	9:00a	0.9 e
	2:30p	6:06p	2.2 f	9:30a	2:54p	1.5 e	3:36p	7:30p	1.4 f	1:00p	6:18p	1.3 f
	10:12p			6:18p	9:36p	1.9 f	10:48p			9:00p	11:30p	0.9 e
Thu. 3/30	3:06a	12:06a	0.7 e	1:06a	3:00a	0.6 e	3:06a	1:06a	0.6 e	2:06a	4:36a	0.9 f
	8:24a	5:36a	1.1 f	4:54a	7:36a	1.0 f	8:48a	5:30a	0.8 f	7:42a	10:06a	0.8 e
	3:36p	11:30a	1.0 e	10:42a	4:00p	1.6 e	4:36p	1:00p	1.6 e	2:18p	7:06p	1.5 f
	10:54p	7:12p	2.3 f	7:12p	10:24p	2.1 f	11:30p	8:24p	1.6 f	9:48p		
Fri. 3/31	4:24a	1:00a	0.8 e	1:48a	4:00a	0.8 e	4:18a	2:00a	0.9 e	3:06a	12:24a	1.1 f
	9:42a	6:48a	1.2 f	6:12a	9:00a	1.1 f	10:00a	6:48a	0.9 f	8:54a	5:42a	1.0 f
	4:36p	12:48p	1.0 e	12:00p	4:48p	1.7 e	5:24p	1:54p	1.7 e	3:18p	11:18a	0.9 e
	11:30p	8:00p	2.4 f	7:54p	11:06p	2.2 f	9:06p	9:06p	1.7 f	10:30p	7:48p	1.6 f
Sat. 4/1	5:18a	1:48a	1.0 e	2:24a	4:48a	1.0 e	12:06a	2:48a	1.2 e	3:54a	1:12a	1.2 e
	10:48a	7:48a	1.5 f	7:18a	10:06a	1.2 f	5:12a	7:54a	1.1 f	9:54a	6:42a	1.2 f
	5:18p	1:42p	1.2 e	1:00p	5:24p	1.7 e	11:00a	2:36p	1.8 e	4:06p	12:18p	1.0 e
	12:00p	8:36p	2.6 f	8:24p	11:42p	2.2 f	6:00p	9:42p	1.7 f	11:06p	8:18p	1.6 f
Sun. 4/2	6:00a	2:24a	1.2 e	2:48a	5:36a	1.2 e	12:36a	3:24a	1.4 e	4:42a	1:48a	1.3 e
	11:30a	8:36a	1.4 f	8:06a	10:54a	1.4 f	6:00a	8:48a	1.3 f	10:42a	7:30a	1.3 f
	5:54p	2:24p	1.4 e	1:48p	5:48p	1.7 e	11:54a	3:12p	1.8 e	4:48p	1:06p	1.1 e
		9:06p	2.7 f	8:54p			6:36p	10:00p	1.7 f	11:42p	8:48p	1.6 f

	GOLDEN GATE			BENICIA BRIDGE			RICHMOND			OAKLAND		
	SLACK	CURRENT		SLACK	CURRENT		SLACK	CURRENT		SLACK	CURRENT	
Day/Date	Time	Time	Knots	Time	Time	Knots	Time	Time	Knots	Time	Time	Knots
Thu. 2/16	2:06a	12:06a	0.9e	1:36a	3:12a	0.3e	2:48a	1:00a	0.4e	2:24a	5:18a	1.1f
	8:36a	5:54a	2.4f	4:48a	8:12a	1.8f	9:06a	5:54a	1.5f	8:12a	10:54a	1.4e
	4:18p	11:36a	2.0e	11:12a	2:36p	1.9e	5:12p	1:00p	2.5e	3:00p	7:36p	1.7f
	10:48p	7:24p	2.7f	7:42p	10:54p	1.8f		8:54p	1.7f	10:30p		
Fri. 2/17	3:18a	1:00a	1.1e	2:12a	4:18a	0.5e	12:06a	2:00a	0.7e	3:30a	12:42a	1.0e
	9:42a	7:00a	2.6f	6:06a	9:18a	2.0f	4:06a	7:00a	1.6f	9:18a	6:24a	1.3f
	5:12p	12:42p	2.1e	12:18p	4:00p	2.1e	10:12a	2:00p	2.7e	4:00p	11:54a	1.6e
	11:30p	8:12p	3.0f	8:30p	11:30p	1.9f	6:00p	9:36p	2.0f	11:12p	8:24p	1.9f
Sat. 2/18	4:30a	1:48a	1.3e	2:48a	5:12a	0.8e	12:42a	2:54a	1.0e	4:24a	1:30a	1.2e
	10:42a	7:54a	2.9f	7:12a	10:18a	2.2f	5:06a	8:06a	1.9f	10:18a	7:24a	1.5f
	6:06p	1:42p	2.2e	1:18p	5:06p	2.2e	11:12a	2:48p	2.9e	4:54p	12:54p	1.7e
		9:00p	3.3f	9:12p			6:42p	10:12p	2.1f	11:54p	9:06p	2.1f
Sun. 2/19	12:06a	2:42a	1.5e	3:24a	12:06a	2.1f	1:18a	3:42a	1.2e	5:12a	2:18a	1.4e
	5:30a	8:48a	3.2f	8:12a	6:00a	1.1e	6:06a	9:00a	2.0f	11:12a	8:18a	1.6f
	11:36a	2:48p	2.3e	2:12p	11:12a	2.4f	12:12p	3:36p	3.0e	5:42p	1:48p	1.9e
	6:54p	9:48p	3.5f	9:48p	6:00p	2.3e	7:24p	10:42p	2.1f		9:42p	2.1f
Mon. 2/20	12:48a	3:30a	1.8e	3:54a	12:42a	2.2f	1:54a	4:24a	1.5e	12:36a	2:54a	1.5e
	6:30a	9:42a	3.4f	9:12a	6:42a	1.3e	7:00a	9:54a	2.1f	5:54a	9:06a	1.7f
	12:36p	3:54p	2.3e	3:12p	12:06p	2.4f	1:06p	4:24p	2.9e	12:00p	2:36p	1.9e
	7:36p	10:30p	3.7f	10:18p	6:42p	2.3e	8:00p	11:06p	2.1f	6:24p	10:18p	2.1f
Tue. 2/21	1:30a	4:24a	2.0e	4:30a	1:18a	2.3f	2:30a	5:06a	1.7e	1:18a	3:36a	1.6e
	7:30a	10:36a	3.4f	10:06a	7:30a	1.5e	7:54a	10:42a	2.1f	6:42a	9:54a	1.8f
	1:30p	4:48p	2.3e	4:06p	1:06p	2.4f	1:54p	5:06p	2.7e	12:48p	3:24p	1.9e
	8:12p	11:12p	3.8f	10:54p	7:24p	2.3e	8:36p	11:30p	2.1f	7:00p	10:48p	2.0f
Wed. 2/22	2:12a	5:06a	2.2e	5:06a	1:48a	2.4f	3:00a	5:48a	1.9e	1:54a	4:12a	1.6e
	8:24a	11:24a	3.4f	11:06a	8:12a	1.7e	8:48a	11:30a	2.0f	7:24a	10:36a	1.7f
	2:24p	5:36p	2.1e	5:00p	2:00p	2.2f	2:48p	5:48p	2.4e	1:42p	4:12p	1.8e
	8:48p	11:54p	3.8f	11:24p	8:06p	2.1e	9:06p			7:42p	11:18p	1.9f
Thu. 2/23	2:54a	5:48a	2.3e	5:42a	2:24a	2.4f	3:36a	12:00a	2.1f	2:30a	4:48a	1.5e
	9:18a	12:18p	3.1f	12:06p	8:54a	1.7e	9:42a	6:30a	2.0e	8:06a	11:24a	1.5f
	3:18p	6:18p	1.8e	5:54p	2:54p	1.9f	3:42p	12:24p	1.7f	2:36p	5:06p	1.5e
	9:18p			8:48p		1.8e	9:42p	6:30p	2.0e	8:18p	11:48p	1.7f
Fri. 2/24	3:30a	12:36a	3.6f	12:00a	3:00a	2.3f	4:12a	12:36a	2.0f	3:06a	5:30a	1.4e
	10:12a	6:30a	2.4e	6:18a	9:48a	1.7e	10:42a	7:12a	2.0e	8:54a	12:12p	1.3f
	4:24p	1:12p	2.8f	1:12p	4:00p	1.7f	4:42p	1:18p	1.5f	3:36p	5:54p	1.2e
	9:54p	7:12p	1.4e	6:54p	9:42p	1.4e	10:12p	7:18p	1.5e	9:00p		
Sat. 2/25	4:12a	1:24a	3.2f	12:36a	3:42a	2.2f	4:48a	1:12a	1.8f	3:42a	12:24a	1.5f
	11:12a	7:18a	2.3e	7:00a	10:36a	1.6e	11:48a	8:00a	1.9e	9:42a	6:12a	1.3e
	5:36p	2:12p	2.5f	2:24p	5:18p	1.4f	5:54p	2:30p	1.2f	4:48p	1:18p	1.1f
	10:30p	8:12p	1.0e	8:12p	10:42p	1.0e	10:54p	8:12p	1.0e	9:54p	7:00p	0.9e
Sun. 2/26	5:00a	2:06a	2.8f	1:12a	4:18a	1.9f	5:30a	1:54a	1.6f	4:24a	1:00a	1.3e
	12:18p	8:06a	2.1e	7:42a	11:54a	1.6e	1:06p	9:00a	1.8e	10:42a	7:00a	1.2e
	7:06p	3:18p	2.3f	3:42p	6:48p	1.4f	7:18p	4:18p	1.0f	6:06p	3:06p	1.0f
	11:18p	9:12p	0.7e	9:42p	11:54p	0.7e	11:48p	9:18p	0.6e	10:54p	8:12p	0.7e
Mon. 2/27	5:48a	3:00a	2.3f	2:00a	5:06a	1.6f	6:18a	2:48a	1.3f	5:18a	1:54a	1.1f
	1:24p	9:00a	1.8e	8:36a	1:30p	1.6e	2:18p	10:12a	1.7e	11:54a	7:48a	1.1e
	8:30p	4:30p	2.2f	5:00p	8:06p	1.5f	9:00p	5:54p	1.1f	7:30p	4:42p	1.1f
		10:18p	0.6e	11:18p				11:00p	0.4e		9:42p	0.7e
Tue. 2/28	12:24a	4:00a	1.9f	3:00a	1:12a	0.5e	1:00a	3:48a	1.1f	12:12a	2:54a	1.0e
	6:48a	9:54a	1.5e	9:30a	6:06a	1.4f	7:24a	11:36a	1.7e	6:18a	8:48a	1.0e
	2:30p	5:42p	2.2f	6:06p	2:48p	1.7e	3:24p	7:06p	1.4f	1:06p	5:48p	1.4f
	9:36p	11:24p	0.7e		9:06p	1.8f	10:18p			8:36p	10:54p	0.8e
Wed. 3/1	1:54a	5:06a	1.7f	12:30a	2:24a	0.5e	2:18a	12:24a	0.5e	1:24a	4:00a	0.9f
	7:54a	11:12a	1.4e	4:12a	7:12a	1.2f	8:30a	4:54a	1.0f	7:18a	9:48a	0.9e
	3:30p	6:42p	2.4f	10:30a	3:48p	1.8e	4:24p	12:48p	1.9e	2:12p	6:42p	1.5f
	10:24p			7:00p	10:00p	2.0f	11:12p	8:00p	1.6f	9:24p	11:54p	1.0e
Thu. 3/2	3:18a	12:18a	0.8e	1:24a	3:24a	0.6e	3:30a	1:24a	0.8e	2:30a	5:12a	1.0f
	9:06a	6:12a	1.7f	5:24a	8:24a	1.3f	9:30a	6:12a	1.1f	8:24a	10:48a	0.9e
	4:24p	12:12p	1.3e	11:30a	4:36p	1.9e	5:12p	1:36p	2.0e	3:06p	7:24p	1.7f
	11:00p	7:30p	2.5f	7:42p	10:48p	2.2f	11:48p	8:48p	1.8f	10:12p		
Fri. 3/3	4:18a	1:06a	0.9e	2:06a	4:18a	0.8e	4:30a	2:12a	1.0e	3:24a	12:42a	1.2e
	10:00a	7:06a	1.8f	6:24a	9:24a	1.4f	10:24a	7:12a	1.2f	9:18a	6:12a	1.1f
	5:12p	1:06p	1.4e	12:24p	5:12p	1.9e	5:48p	2:18p	2.1e	3:54p	11:48a	1.0e
	11:36p	8:12p	2.6f	8:18p	11:24p	2.2f		9:24p	1.8f	10:48p	8:06p	1.7f
Sat. 3/4	5:06a	1:48a	1.1e	2:42a	5:06a	0.9e	12:24a	2:54a	1.1e	4:12a	1:24a	1.3e
	10:54a	7:54a	2.0f	7:18a	10:12a	1.5f	5:18a	8:06a	1.4f	10:06a	7:00a	1.3f
	5:48p	1:48p	1.5e	1:12p	5:42p	1.9e	11:12a	2:54p	2.1e	4:30p	12:30p	1.2e
		8:48p	2.7f	8:48p	11:54p	2.2f	6:24p	9:54p	1.8f	11:24p	8:42p	1.7f
Sun. 3/5	12:12a	2:36a	1.1e	3:06a	5:42a	1.1e	12:54a	3:30a	1.3e	4:48a	2:00a	1.3e
	5:48a	8:42a	2.2f	8:00a	10:54a	1.7f	6:00a	8:48a	1.5f	10:48a	7:42a	1.4f
	11:36a	2:36p	1.6e	1:54p	6:00p	1.9e	11:54a	3:18p	2.1e	5:06p	1:12p	1.3e
	6:24p	9:24p	2.8f	9:18p			6:54p	10:18p	1.7f		9:06p	1.6f
Mon. 3/6	12:42a	3:12a	1.2e	3:36a	12:24a	2.1f	1:18a	4:00a	1.4e	12:00a	2:24a	1.3e
	6:18a	9:24a	2.3f	8:42a	6:12a	1.2e	6:42a	9:24a	1.6f	5:24a	8:24a	1.5f
	12:12p	3:18p	1.8e	2:30p	11:30a	1.8f	12:30p	3:42p	2.1e	11:30a	1:54p	1.4e
	6:48p	9:54p	2.9f	9:36p	6:12p	1.9e	7:18p	10:18p	1.7f	5:30p	9:24p	1.6f
Tue. 3/7	1:06a	3:48a	1.4e	3:54a	12:42a	2.1f	1:42a	4:24a	1.5e	12:30a	2:48a	1.3e
	6:54a	10:00a	2.4f	9:24a	6:42a	1.3e	7:18a	10:00a	1.7f	5:54a	9:00a	1.5f
	12:48p	4:00p	1.9e	3:12p	12:12p	1.8f	1:06p	4:12p	2.1e	12:06p	2:36p	1.4e
	7:12p	10:24p	3.1f	10:00p	6:30p	1.8e	7:42p	10:30p	1.8f	6:00p	9:36p	1.5f
Wed. 3/8	1:30a	4:18a	1.6e	4:12a	1:00a	2.1f	2:06a	4:48a	1.6e	12:48a	3:12a	1.3e
	7:24a	10:42a	2.5f	10:06a	7:00a	1.4e	7:54a	10:36a	1.7f	6:18a	9:36a	1.5f
	1:30p	4:36p	1.9e	3:54p	12:54p	1.8f	1:48p	4:48p	1.9e	12:42p	3:12p	1.4e
	7:36p	10:54p	3.2f	10:24p	7:00p	1.8e	8:00p	10:54p	1.8f	6:24p	10:00p	1.5f
Thu. 3/9	1:54a	4:42a	1.8e	4:36a	1:18a	2.2f	2:18a	5:18a	1.8e	1:12a	3:36a	1.4e
	8:00a	11:18a	2.6f	10:48a	7:24a	1.6e	8:30a	11:12a	1.6f	6:42a	10:12a	1.5f
	2:12p	5:12p	1.8e	4:42p	1:36p	1.7f	2:24p	5:24p	1.8e	1:24p	3:54p	1.4e
	8:00p	11:30p	3.2f	10:48p	7:36p	1.6e	8:24p	11:18p	1.9f	6:54p	10:24p	1.5f
Fri. 3/10	2:18a	5:00a	2.0e	4:54a	1:48a	2.3f	2:36a	5:48a	1.9e	1:30a	4:12a	1.5e
	8:36a	12:06p	2.6f	11:36a	7:42a	1.8e	9:12a	11:54a	1.5f	7:12a	10:48a	1.4f
	3:00p	5:48p	1.5e	5:30p	2:18p	1.6f	3:12p	6:00p	1.5e	2:12p	4:36p	1.2e
	8:30p			11:12p	8:12p	1.3e	8:48p	11:54p	1.9f	7:24p	10:54p	1.5f

		GOLDEN GATE			BENICIA BRIDGE			RICHMOND			OAKLAND		
		SLACK Time	CURRENT Time	CURRENT Knots	SLACK Time	CURRENT Time	CURRENT Knots	SLACK Time	CURRENT Time	CURRENT Knots	SLACK Time	CURRENT Time	CURRENT Knots
Tue.	1/24	2:54a	5:30a	1.6e	6:00a	2:36a	2.2f	3:54a	12:24a	2.1f	2:36a	4:48a	1.4e
		8:18a	11:36a	3.2f	11:12a	8:42a	1.2e	8:54a	6:18a	1.4e	7:48a	10:54a	1.6f
		2:18p	5:36p	2.4e	5:06p	2:06p	2.2f	2:54p	11:48a	1.9f	1:54p	4:30p	1.9e
		9:24p				8:30p	2.3e	9:54p	6:12p	2.7e	8:12p		
Wed.	1/25	3:36a	12:24a	3.6f	12:12a	3:18a	2.3f	4:30a	12:54a	2.0f	3:18a	12:00a	1.9f
		9:18a	6:18a	1.7e	6:36a	9:36a	1.4e	10:00a	7:06a	1.5e	8:36a	5:30a	1.4e
		3:18p	12:30p	2.9f	12:18p	3:06p	2.0f	3:48p	12:42p	1.7f	2:42p	11:42a	1.5f
		10:00p	6:30p	2.1e	6:00p	9:12p	2.1e	10:30p	7:00p	2.4e	8:54p	5:24p	1.7e
Thu.	1/26	4:18a	1:12a	3.6f	12:48a	3:54a	2.3f	5:12a	1:30a	2.0f	4:00a	12:36a	1.8f
		10:24a	7:12a	1.8e	7:24a	10:30a	1.5e	11:06a	7:54a	1.6e	9:30a	6:12a	1.3e
		4:18p	1:24p	2.6f	1:24p	4:12p	1.7f	4:48p	1:42p	1.4f	3:42p	12:36p	1.3f
		10:36p	7:24p	1.8e	7:06p	10:12p	1.8e	11:06p	7:48p	1.9e	9:42p	6:18p	1.4e
Fri.	1/27	5:06a	2:00a	3.4f	1:24a	4:36a	2.2f	5:54a	2:06a	1.9f	4:42a	1:18a	1.6f
		11:36a	8:06a	1.9e	8:06a	11:36a	1.5e	12:18p	8:54a	1.7e	10:24a	7:00a	1.2e
		5:30p	2:30p	2.2f	2:42p	5:30p	1.4f	6:00p	2:48p	1.2f	4:54p	1:36p	1.2f
		11:12p	8:30p	1.8e	8:18p	11:12p	1.4e	11:48p	8:42p	1.4e	10:30p	7:18p	1.1e
Sat.	1/28	5:54a	2:48a	3.2f	2:06a	5:18a	2.1f	6:36a	2:48a	1.7f	5:30a	2:00a	1.5f
		1:00p	9:00a	1.9e	8:54a	12:48p	1.6e	1:36p	10:00a	1.7e	11:30a	7:54a	1.2e
		7:00p	3:36p	2.0f	4:06p	7:00p	1.3f	7:24p	4:30p	1.0f	6:18p	3:06p	1.0f
		11:54p	9:30p	1.0e	9:36p			9:48p			11:24p	8:30p	0.9e
Sun.	1/29	6:48a	3:36a	2.9f	2:48a	12:12a	1.0e	12:36a	3:36a	1.6f	6:18a	2:42a	1.3f
		2:12p	10:00a	2.0e	9:42a	6:06a	1.9f	7:24a	11:12a	1.9e	12:42p	8:42a	1.1e
		8:30p	4:54p	2.0f	5:30p	2:06p	1.7e	2:54p	6:12p	1.1f	7:36p	5:00p	1.1f
		10:36p			11:06p	8:18p	1.4f	8:54p	11:12p	0.7e		9:48p	0.8e
Mon.	1/30	12:42a	4:36a	2.6f	3:36a	1:24a	0.7e	1:30a	4:30a	1.4f	12:30a	3:42a	1.2f
		7:36a	10:54a	2.0e	10:30a	7:00a	1.7f	8:18a	12:18p	2.0e	7:06a	9:42a	1.1e
		3:18p	6:06p	2.2f	6:36p	3:18p	1.9e	4:00p	7:24p	1.3f	1:54p	6:12p	1.3f
		9:48p	11:42p	0.7e		9:30p	1.6f	10:24p			8:54p	11:12p	0.8e
Tue.	1/31	1:48a	3:36a	2.4f	12:36a	2:36a	0.6e	2:30a	12:30a	0.6e	1:36a	4:36a	1.1f
		8:30a	11:48a	2.0e	4:30a	7:54a	1.6f	9:06a	5:30a	1.3f	8:00a	10:36a	1.1e
		4:12p	7:06p	2.5f	11:18a	4:18p	2.0e	4:54p	1:12p	2.1e	2:54p	7:06p	1.5f
		10:42p			7:30p	10:24p	1.9f	11:30p	8:24p	1.6f	9:54p		
Wed.	2/1	3:00a	12:36a	0.7e	1:42a	3:36a	0.5e	3:36a	1:36a	0.7e	2:42a	12:12a	0.9e
		9:24a	6:30a	2.3f	5:30a	8:48a	1.6f	10:00a	6:30a	1.3f	8:48a	5:36a	1.5f
		5:00p	12:36p	1.9e	12:00p	5:06p	2.1e	5:42p	2:06p	2.2e	3:42p	11:24a	1.1e
		11:30p	8:00p	2.7f	8:18p	11:12p	2.1f		9:12p	1.8f	10:42p	7:54p	1.7f
Thu.	2/2	4:06a	1:24a	0.8e	2:36a	4:36a	0.6e	12:18a	2:30a	0.8e	3:42a	1:06a	1.0e
		10:12a	7:24a	2.2f	6:24a	9:30a	1.6f	4:36a	7:24a	1.3f	9:36a	6:30a	1.1f
		5:48p	1:18p	1.8e	12:42p	5:48p	2.1e	10:42a	2:42p	2.3e	4:24p	12:06p	1.2e
			8:42p	2.8f	9:00p	11:54p	2.1f	6:24p	9:54p	1.8f	11:24p	8:42p	1.7f
Fri.	2/3	12:12a	2:12a	0.9e	3:24a	5:24a	0.6e	1:00a	3:18a	0.9e	4:30a	1:48a	1.1e
		5:06a	8:12a	2.2f	7:12a	10:18a	1.6f	5:24a	8:12a	1.4f	10:24a	7:18a	1.2f
		11:00a	2:06p	1.8e	1:18p	6:24p	2.1e	11:24a	3:18p	2.3e	5:00p	12:48p	1.2e
		6:30p	9:18p	2.8f	9:36p			7:00p	10:30p	1.8f		9:18p	1.7f
Sat.	2/4	12:48a	3:00a	0.9e	4:00a	12:36a	2.1f	1:36a	3:54a	1.0e	12:00a	2:30a	1.2e
		5:54a	9:00a	2.3f	8:00a	6:06a	0.7e	6:12a	8:54a	1.5f	5:12a	8:00a	1.3f
		11:42a	3:00p	1.8e	2:00p	11:00a	1.7f	12:06p	3:42p	2.3e	11:06a	1:30p	1.3e
		7:06p	10:00p	2.8f	10:00p	6:42p	2.0e	7:30p	11:00p	1.8f	5:30p	9:48p	1.7f
Sun.	2/5	1:30a	3:48a	1.0e	4:30a	1:06a	2.1f	2:06a	4:30a	1.0e	12:36a	3:00a	1.2e
		6:30a	9:42a	2.3f	8:48a	6:42a	0.8e	6:54a	9:36a	1.5f	5:54a	8:42a	1.4f
		12:24p	3:42p	1.9e	2:42p	11:42a	1.8f	12:42p	4:12p	2.3e	11:42a	2:12p	1.4e
		7:36p	10:30p	2.8f	10:30p	6:42p	2.0e	8:00p	11:12p	1.7f	6:00p	10:12p	1.6f
Mon.	2/6	2:00a	4:24a	1.0e	4:54a	1:36a	2.0f	2:36a	5:00a	1.1e	1:12a	3:30a	1.2e
		7:06a	10:18a	2.4f	9:30a	7:12a	0.9e	7:30a	10:12a	1.6f	6:24a	9:18a	1.5f
		1:06p	4:24p	2.0e	3:18p	12:24p	1.8f	1:18p	4:42p	2.3e	12:18p	2:54p	1.5e
		8:06p	11:06p	2.9f	10:48p	6:54p	2.0e	8:24p	11:18p	1.7f	6:24p	10:24p	1.5f
Tue.	2/7	2:30a	5:00a	1.1e	5:18a	1:54a	2.0f	3:00a	5:24a	1.2e	1:36a	3:54a	1.2e
		7:36a	11:00a	2.3f	10:12a	7:48a	1.0e	8:06a	10:48a	1.6f	6:54a	9:54a	1.5f
		1:42p	5:00p	2.1e	4:00p	1:06p	1.8f	1:54p	5:12p	2.2e	12:54p	3:30p	1.5e
		8:24p	11:36p	3.0f	11:12p	7:24p	2.0e	8:48p	11:36p	1.7f	6:54p	10:36p	1.5f
Wed.	2/8	3:00a	5:30a	1.1e	5:42a	2:12a	2.1f	3:24a	5:54a	1.3e	2:06a	4:18a	1.2e
		8:06a	11:42a	2.3f	10:54a	8:12a	1.1e	8:48a	11:30a	1.5f	7:18a	10:36a	1.5f
		2:18p	5:36p	2.0e	4:42p	1:48p	1.7f	2:30p	5:42p	2.1e	1:30p	4:12p	1.5e
		8:48p			11:36p	7:54p	2.0e	9:12p			7:24p	11:00p	1.5f
Thu.	2/9	3:24a	12:12a	3.0f	6:06a	2:36a	2.1f	3:42a	12:00a	1.8f	2:24a	4:48a	1.2e
		8:48a	5:54a	1.3e	11:42a	8:36a	1.3e	9:30a	6:24a	1.4e	7:48a	11:06a	1.4f
		3:00p	12:24p	2.1f	5:24p	2:30p	1.6f	3:12p	12:12p	1.4f	2:12p	4:54p	1.4e
		9:18p	6:12p	1.8e		8:36p	1.8e	9:36p	6:24p	1.9e	7:54p	11:30p	1.5f
Fri.	2/10	3:48a	12:48a	3.0f	12:06a	3:06a	2.2f	4:06a	12:36a	1.8f	2:48a	5:24a	1.3e
		9:36a	6:24a	1.4e	6:30a	9:06a	1.4e	10:18a	7:00a	1.5e	8:18a	11:48a	1.2f
		3:54p	1:12p	2.0f	12:36p	3:24p	1.4f	4:00p	1:00p	1.3f	3:00p	5:48p	1.2e
		9:48p	6:54p	1.5e	6:18p	9:24p	1.5f	10:00p	7:06p	1.6e	8:30p		
Sat.	2/11	4:18a	1:24a	2.9f	12:30a	3:42a	2.2f	4:30a	1:12a	1.8f	3:18a	12:12a	1.4f
		10:30a	6:54a	1.6e	6:54a	9:42a	1.5e	11:18a	7:42a	1.7e	9:00a	6:06a	1.3e
		4:54p	2:06p	1.8f	1:36p	4:18p	1.1f	5:00p	1:54p	1.1f	4:12p	12:36p	1.1f
		10:24p	7:48p	1.2e	7:30p	10:12p	1.1e	10:30p	7:54p	1.2e	9:12p	6:42p	0.9e
Sun.	2/12	4:54a	2:06a	2.7f	1:06a	4:24a	2.1f	5:06a	1:54a	1.7f	4:00a	12:54a	1.3f
		11:30a	7:36a	1.7e	7:30a	10:24a	1.6e	12:30p	8:30a	1.8e	9:48a	6:54a	1.3e
		6:18p	3:06p	1.8f	2:54p	5:36p	0.9f	6:36p	3:00p	0.9f	5:42p	1:36p	0.9f
		11:06p	8:54p	0.9e	9:06p	11:18p	0.7e	11:12p	8:54p	0.9e	10:12p	7:48p	0.6e
Mon.	2/13	5:42a	2:54a	2.5f	1:42a	5:06a	1.9f	5:48a	2:48a	1.5f	4:48a	1:48a	1.2f
		12:36p	8:30a	1.8e	8:12a	11:12a	1.6e	1:54p	9:30a	1.8e	10:54a	7:48a	1.3e
		7:48p	4:12p	1.8f	4:18p	7:42p	0.9f	8:30p	4:24p	0.9f	7:24p	3:18p	0.9f
		11:54p	10:06p	0.7e	10:54p				10:06p	0.9e	11:30p	9:06p	0.5e
Tue.	2/14	6:30a	3:48a	2.4f	2:24a	12:36a	0.4e	12:00a	3:42a	1.4f	5:48a	2:54a	1.1f
		1:54p	9:24a	1.9e	9:06a	6:06a	1.8f	6:48a	10:36a	2.0e	12:18p	8:48a	1.3e
		9:06p	5:24p	2.0f	5:42p	12:12p	1.8e	3:06p	6:54p	1.1f	8:42p	5:42p	1.1f
			11:12p	0.7e		9:12p	1.2f	10:12p	11:36p	0.3e		10:30p	0.6e
Wed.	2/15	1:00a	4:54a	2.3f	12:30a	1:54a	0.6e	1:18a	4:48a	1.4f	1:00a	4:06a	1.0f
		7:30a	10:30a	2.0e	3:30a	7:06a	1.7f	7:54a	11:48a	2.2e	7:00a	9:48a	1.3e
		3:06p	6:24p	2.4f	10:06a	1:24p	1.8e	4:12p	8:00p	1.1f	1:48p	6:48p	1.4f
		10:00p			6:48p	10:06p	1.5f	11:18p			9:42p	11:42p	0.8e

GOLDEN GATE · BENICIA BRIDGE · RICHMOND · OAKLAND

	GOLDEN GATE			BENICIA BRIDGE			RICHMOND			OAKLAND		
	SLACK	CURRENT		SLACK	CURRENT		SLACK	CURRENT		SLACK	CURRENT	
Day	Time	Time	Knots	Time	Time	Knots	Time	Time	Knots	Time	Time	Knots
Sun. 1/1	1:24a	5:12a	3.2 f	4:24a	1:48a	1.1e	2:12a	5:24a	1.7 f	1:00a	4:36a	1.4 f
	8:24a	11:42a	2.3e	11:18a	7:54a	2.1 f	9:06a	12:48p	2.2e	7:54a	10:30a	1.3e
	3:48p	6:30p	2.2 f	6:54p	3:30p	2.0e	4:18p	7:30p	1.3 f	2:24p	6:18p	1.3 f
	9:48p				9:36p	1.6 f	10:18p			9:00p	11:18p	0.9e
Mon. 1/2	2:12a	12:00a	0.9e	12:24a	2:48a	0.9e	3:00a	12:42a	0.9e	2:00a	5:24a	1.4 f
	9:06a	6:06a	3.1 f	5:06a	8:36a	2.0 f	9:48a	6:06a	1.6 f	8:36a	11:12a	1.3e
	4:42p	12:24p	2.5e	12:00p	4:30p	2.1e	5:12p	1:36p	2.3e	3:18p	7:18p	1.5 f
	11:00p	7:24p	2.6 f	7:48p	10:36p	1.8 f	11:30p	8:36p	1.5 f	10:00p		
Tue. 1/3	3:00a	12:48a	0.8e	1:36a	3:48a	0.7e	3:48a	1:42a	0.8e	2:54a	12:18a	0.9e
	9:48a	6:54a	3.0 f	5:48a	9:12a	2.0 f	10:24a	6:54a	1.6 f	9:18a	6:06a	1.3e
	5:30p	1:06p	2.5e	12:30p	5:18p	2.2e	6:00p	2:18p	2.4e	4:06p	11:54a	1.3e
	11:54p	8:18p	2.8 f	8:42p	11:24p	1.9 f		9:24p	1.7 f	11:00p	8:12p	1.6 f
Wed. 1/4	4:00a	1:42a	0.7e	2:42a	4:42a	0.6e	12:30a	2:36a	0.7e	3:48a	1:12a	0.9e
	10:30a	7:42a	2.8 f	6:30a	9:54a	1.9 f	4:36a	7:36a	1.5 f	10:00a	6:48a	1.2 f
	6:18p	1:42p	2.5e	1:00p	6:06p	2.2e	11:00a	2:54p	2.4e	4:48p	12:30p	1.4e
		9:06p	3.0 f	9:24p			6:42p	10:12p	1.8 f	11:48p	9:00p	1.7 f
Thu. 1/5	12:42a	2:36a	0.7e	3:42a	12:18a	2.0 f	1:24a	3:24a	0.7e	4:42a	2:00a	1.0e
	5:00a	8:30a	2.6 f	7:12a	5:30a	0.5e	5:30a	8:18a	1.5 f	10:36a	7:30a	1.2 f
	11:12a	2:18p	2.3e	1:36p	10:30a	1.8 f	11:36a	3:30p	2.4e	5:18p	1:12p	1.4e
	6:54p	9:48p	3.0 f	10:00p	6:36p	2.1e	7:24p	10:54p	1.8 f		9:42p	1.7 f
Fri. 1/6	1:30a	3:30a	0.7e	4:30a	1:00a	2.0 f	2:06a	4:12a	0.7e	12:30a	2:48a	1.0e
	5:54a	9:18a	2.5 f	8:00a	6:18a	0.5e	6:12a	9:00a	1.5 f	5:30a	8:18a	1.2 f
	11:54a	3:06p	2.2e	2:06p	11:06a	1.8 f	12:12p	4:00p	2.4e	11:12a	1:48p	1.4e
	7:36p	10:24p	3.0 f	10:36p	6:54p	2.0e	7:54p	11:30p	1.7 f	5:48p	10:18p	1.6 f
Sat. 1/7	2:12a	4:18a	0.8e	5:12a	1:42a	2.0 f	2:48a	4:48a	0.8e	1:12a	3:24a	1.1e
	6:36a	10:00a	2.4 f	8:42a	7:00a	0.5e	7:00a	9:42a	1.5 f	6:12a	9:00a	1.3 f
	12:36p	3:48p	2.1e	2:48p	11:48a	1.8 f	12:48p	4:30p	2.3e	11:54a	2:30p	1.4e
	8:06p	11:06p	2.9 f	11:06p	6:36p	2.0e	8:30p			6:12p	10:42p	1.5 f
Sun. 1/8	2:54a	5:00a	0.8e	5:48a	2:18a	1.9 f	3:18a	12:00a	1.7 f	1:48a	4:00a	1.1e
	7:18a	10:42a	2.2 f	9:30a	7:42a	0.6e	7:42a	5:24a	0.8e	6:54a	9:42a	1.3 f
	1:12p	4:30p	2.1e	3:24p	12:36p	1.8 f	1:24p	10:24a	1.5 f	12:30p	3:06p	1.5e
	8:36p	11:42p	2.8 f	11:30p	7:00p	2.1e	9:00p	5:00p	2.3e	6:42p	11:00p	1.5 f
Mon. 1/9	3:30a	5:42a	0.8e	6:18a	2:48a	1.9 f	3:54a	12:06a	1.6 f	2:18a	4:30a	1.0e
	7:48a	11:18a	2.1 f	10:18a	8:18a	0.7e	8:24a	6:00a	0.8e	7:24a	10:18a	1.3 f
	1:54p	5:12p	2.0e	4:06p	1:18p	1.7 f	2:00p	11:06a	1.4 f	1:06p	3:54p	1.5e
	9:06p				7:36p	2.1e	9:30p	5:36p	2.3e	7:12p	11:18p	1.4 f
Tue. 1/10	4:06a	12:18a	2.8 f	12:00a	3:12a	1.9 f	4:24a	12:24a	1.6 f	2:54a	5:00a	1.0e
	8:24a	6:18a	0.7e	6:48a	8:54a	0.7e	9:06a	6:30a	0.9e	8:00a	11:00a	1.3 f
	2:30p	12:00p	1.9 f	11:06a	2:06p	1.6 f	2:42p	11:54a	1.4 f	1:48p	4:36p	1.5e
	9:30p	5:48p	2.0e	4:48p	8:18p	2.1e	9:54p	6:12p	2.2e	7:48p	11:42p	1.4 f
Wed. 1/11	4:42a	12:54a	2.7 f	12:24a	3:36a	2.0 f	4:54a	12:48a	1.6 f	3:24a	5:36a	1.0e
	9:06a	7:00a	0.7e	7:18a	9:30a	0.8e	9:54a	7:06a	1.0e	8:36a	11:42a	1.3 f
	3:12p	12:42p	1.7 f	12:00p	2:48p	1.5 f	3:24p	12:36p	1.3 f	2:30p	5:18p	1.4e
	10:00p	6:36p	1.9e	5:36p	9:00p	2.0e	10:24p	6:48p	2.0e	8:24p		
Thu. 1/12	5:12a	1:30a	2.7 f	12:54a	4:00a	2.0 f	5:18a	1:24a	1.6 f	3:54a	12:12a	1.4 f
	9:54a	7:36a	0.8e	7:48a	10:12a	0.9e	10:48a	7:48a	1.1e	9:12a	6:12a	1.0e
	3:54p	1:36p	1.5 f	1:00p	3:42p	1.3 f	4:06p	1:24p	1.1 f	3:18p	12:24p	1.2 f
	10:30p	7:24p	1.6e	6:24p	9:48p	1.7e	10:54p	7:36p	1.8e	9:06p	6:12p	1.2e
Fri. 1/13	5:42a	2:12a	2.7 f	1:30a	4:36a	2.0 f	5:48a	2:00a	1.7 f	4:30a	12:54a	1.3 f
	11:00a	8:24a	0.9e	8:18a	10:48a	1.1e	11:54a	8:24a	1.2e	9:54a	6:54a	1.0e
	4:54p	2:30p	1.3 f	2:06p	4:36p	1.1 f	5:06p	2:24p	1.0 f	4:24p	1:12p	1.1 f
	11:06p	8:18p	1.4e	7:30p	10:48p	1.4e	11:30p	8:24p	1.4e	9:54p	7:06p	1.0e
Sat. 1/14	6:18a	2:54a	2.7 f	2:00a	5:12a	2.0 f	6:24a	2:42a	1.6 f	5:06a	1:36a	1.3 f
	12:18p	9:06a	1.2e	8:48a	11:30a	1.2e	1:06p	9:18a	1.4e	10:48a	7:42a	1.1e
	6:06p	3:36p	1.3 f	3:24p	5:48p	0.9 f	6:30p	3:24p	0.9 f	5:48p	2:12p	0.9 f
	11:42p	9:24p	1.1e	8:54p	11:42p	1.1e		9:24p	1.1e	10:48p	8:12p	0.8e
Sun. 1/15	6:54a	3:42a	2.7 f	2:42a	6:00a	2.0 f	12:12a	3:30a	1.6 f	5:54a	2:30a	1.2 f
	1:36p	9:48a	1.5e	9:24a	12:18p	1.5e	7:00a	10:18a	1.6e	11:54a	8:30a	1.1e
	7:54p	4:42p	1.4 f	4:48p	7:36p	0.9 f	2:24p	4:42p	0.8 f	7:24p	3:30p	0.9 f
		10:30p	0.9e	10:36p			8:18p	10:30p	0.7e	11:54p	9:24p	0.7e
Mon. 1/16	12:30a	4:30a	2.7 f	3:18a	12:48a	0.7e	12:54a	4:24a	1.6 f	6:42a	3:24a	1.2 f
	7:30a	10:36a	1.8e	10:00a	6:48a	1.9 f	7:42a	11:18a	1.9e	1:06p	9:24a	1.3e
	2:48p	5:54p	1.8 f	6:06p	1:06p	1.7e	3:30p	6:18p	1.0 f	8:48p	5:30p	1.0 f
	9:18p	11:30p	0.8e		9:12p	1.1 f	10:00p	11:42p	0.5e		10:36p	0.6e
Tue. 1/17	1:18a	5:24a	2.7 f	12:12a	2:00a	0.5e	1:48a	5:18a	1.6 f	1:12a	4:30a	1.2 f
	8:12a	11:18a	2.2e	4:00a	7:36a	1.9 f	8:30a	12:18p	2.2e	7:36a	10:24a	1.4e
	3:48p	6:54p	2.1 f	10:48a	1:54p	1.9e	4:36p	8:06p	1.3 f	2:12p	6:54p	1.3 f
	10:18p			7:06p	10:18p	1.4 f	11:18p			9:54p	11:48p	0.7e
Wed. 1/18	2:12a	12:24a	0.8e	1:36a	3:12a	0.3e	2:48a	1:00a	0.5e	2:24a	5:30a	1.2 f
	9:00a	6:18a	2.7 f	4:54a	8:36a	2.0 f	9:24a	6:12a	1.6 f	8:30a	11:18a	1.5e
	4:42p	12:00p	2.4e	11:30a	2:48p	2.1e	5:30p	1:12p	2.5e	3:18p	7:54p	1.6 f
	11:12p	7:48p	2.6 f	8:06p	11:12p	1.7 f	9:06p		1.6 f	10:48p		
Thu. 1/19	3:12a	1:12a	0.9e	2:42a	4:18a	0.3e	12:24a	2:06a	0.5e	3:30a	12:48a	0.8e
	9:54a	7:12a	2.8 f	5:54a	9:30a	2.1 f	3:54a	7:12a	1.7 f	9:24a	6:36a	1.3 f
	5:36p	12:48p	2.5e	12:24p	3:48p	2.3e	10:18a	2:06p	2.8e	4:12p	12:12p	1.7e
		8:36p	3.0 f	8:54p	11:54p	1.8 f	6:18p	9:54p	1.8 f	11:42p	8:48p	1.8 f
Fri. 1/20	12:00a	2:06a	1.0e	3:30a	5:18a	0.4e	1:12a	3:00a	0.7e	4:30a	1:48a	1.0e
	4:18a	8:06a	3.0 f	7:00a	10:24a	2.3 f	5:00a	8:06a	1.8 f	10:24a	7:30a	1.4 f
	10:42a	1:36p	2.6e	1:18p	4:48p	2.4e	11:18a	3:00p	3.0e	5:06p	1:06p	1.8e
	6:24p	9:24p	3.2 f	9:36p			7:06p	10:36p	2.0 f		9:30p	2.0 f
Sat. 1/21	12:42a	3:00a	1.1e	4:12a	12:42a	2.0 f	2:00a	3:54a	0.8e	12:24a	2:36a	1.2e
	5:24a	9:00a	3.1 f	8:00a	6:12a	0.6e	6:00a	9:06a	2.0 f	5:24a	8:24a	1.5 f
	11:36a	2:30p	2.6e	2:18p	11:18a	2.4 f	12:12p	3:54p	3.1e	11:18a	2:00p	1.9e
	7:18p	10:06p	3.4 f	10:18p	5:54p	2.5e	7:54p	11:18p	2.1 f	5:54p	10:12p	2.0 f
Sun. 1/22	1:24a	3:48a	1.3e	4:42a	1:18a	2.0 f	2:36a	4:42a	1.0e	1:12a	3:24a	1.3e
	6:24a	9:54a	3.3 f	9:06a	7:00a	0.8e	7:00a	10:00a	2.0 f	6:18a	9:18a	1.6 f
	12:30p	3:36p	2.6e	3:12p	12:12p	2.4 f	1:06p	4:42p	3.1e	12:06p	2:48p	2.0e
	8:00p	10:54p	3.6 f	11:00p	6:54p	2.5e	8:36p	11:54p	2.1 f	6:42p	10:48p	2.1 f
Mon. 1/23	2:06a	4:42a	1.5e	5:18a	2:00a	2.1 f	3:18a	5:30a	1.2e	1:54a	4:06a	1.4e
	7:24a	10:42a	3.3 f	10:06a	7:54a	1.0e	7:54a	10:54a	2.0 f	7:06a	10:06a	1.7 f
	1:24p	4:42p	2.5e	4:12p	1:12p	2.4 f	2:00p	5:24p	3.0e	1:00p	3:42p	2.0e
	8:42p	11:36p	3.6 f	11:36p	7:42p	2.5e	9:12p			7:30p	11:24p	2.0 f

<table>
<thead>
<tr><th rowspan="3"></th><th colspan="3">SAN MATEO CURRENTS</th><th colspan="2">PORT CHICAGO</th><th colspan="2">ARENA COVE</th><th colspan="2">HUMBOLDT BAY</th></tr>
<tr><th>SLACK</th><th colspan="2">CURRENT</th><th colspan="2">TIDE</th><th colspan="2">TIDE</th><th colspan="2">TIDE</th></tr>
<tr><th>Time</th><th>Time</th><th>Knots</th><th>Time</th><th>Feet</th><th>Time</th><th>Feet</th><th>Time</th><th>Feet</th></tr>
</thead>
<tbody>
<tr><td>Tue. 12/12</td><td>1:06a</td><td>3:42a</td><td>1.1e</td><td>2:06a</td><td>3.7</td><td>3:20a</td><td>3.2</td><td>4:15a</td><td>3.5</td></tr>
<tr><td></td><td>6:24a</td><td>8:54a</td><td>1.2 f</td><td>6:18a</td><td>2.3</td><td>9:26a</td><td>6.9</td><td>10:20a</td><td>8.0</td></tr>
<tr><td></td><td>11:30a</td><td>3:24p</td><td>1.9e</td><td>12:05p</td><td>5.6</td><td>4:55p</td><td>-1.0</td><td>5:35p</td><td>-1.2</td></tr>
<tr><td></td><td>7:00p</td><td>10:00p</td><td>1.7 f</td><td>8:34p</td><td>-0.3</td><td>11:52p</td><td>4.6</td><td></td><td></td></tr>
<tr><td>Wed. 12/13</td><td>1:54a</td><td>4:36a</td><td>1.1e</td><td>2:57a</td><td>3.8</td><td>4:04a</td><td>3.3</td><td>12:31a</td><td>5.6</td></tr>
<tr><td></td><td>7:12a</td><td>9:36a</td><td>1.2 f</td><td>7:09a</td><td>2.4</td><td>10:06a</td><td>7.0</td><td>4:59a</td><td>3.6</td></tr>
<tr><td></td><td>12:12p</td><td>4:12p</td><td>2.0e</td><td>12:48p</td><td>5.8</td><td>5:38p</td><td>-1.3</td><td>11:00a</td><td>8.1</td></tr>
<tr><td></td><td>7:48p</td><td>10:42p</td><td>1.8 f</td><td>9:17p</td><td>-0.4</td><td></td><td></td><td>6:17p</td><td>-1.4</td></tr>
<tr><td>Thu. 12/14</td><td>2:48a</td><td>5:24a</td><td>1.1e</td><td>3:47a</td><td>3.9</td><td>12:40a</td><td>4.7</td><td>1:17a</td><td>5.7</td></tr>
<tr><td></td><td>8:00a</td><td>10:24a</td><td>1.3 f</td><td>8:03a</td><td>2.4</td><td>4:51a</td><td>3.4</td><td>5:45a</td><td>3.7</td></tr>
<tr><td></td><td>1:00p</td><td>5:00p</td><td>2.1e</td><td>1:36p</td><td>5.7</td><td>10:49a</td><td>7.0</td><td>11:43a</td><td>8.1</td></tr>
<tr><td></td><td>8:30p</td><td>11:24p</td><td>1.8 f</td><td>10:01p</td><td>-0.4</td><td>6:24p</td><td>-1.3</td><td>7:01p</td><td>-1.5</td></tr>
<tr><td>Fri. 12/15</td><td>3:36a</td><td>6:12a</td><td>1.2e</td><td>4:35a</td><td>3.9</td><td>1:28a</td><td>4.7</td><td>2:05a</td><td>5.7</td></tr>
<tr><td></td><td>8:48a</td><td>11:12a</td><td>1.3 f</td><td>9:01a</td><td>2.3</td><td>5:43a</td><td>3.4</td><td>6:34a</td><td>3.7</td></tr>
<tr><td></td><td>1:48p</td><td>5:48p</td><td>2.1e</td><td>2:28p</td><td>5.5</td><td>11:37a</td><td>6.8</td><td>12:30p</td><td>8.0</td></tr>
<tr><td></td><td>9:18p</td><td></td><td></td><td>10:44p</td><td>-0.4</td><td>7:10p</td><td>-1.2</td><td>7:47p</td><td>-1.4</td></tr>
<tr><td>Sat. 12/16</td><td>4:24a</td><td>12:12a</td><td>1.8 f</td><td>5:22a</td><td>3.9</td><td>2:17a</td><td>4.8</td><td>2:52a</td><td>5.8</td></tr>
<tr><td></td><td>9:42a</td><td>7:06a</td><td>1.2e</td><td>10:02a</td><td>2.1</td><td>6:41a</td><td>3.4</td><td>7:30a</td><td>3.6</td></tr>
<tr><td></td><td>2:42p</td><td>12:06p</td><td>1.2 f</td><td>3:24p</td><td>5.2</td><td>12:29p</td><td>6.5</td><td>1:21p</td><td>7.6</td></tr>
<tr><td></td><td>10:06p</td><td>6:42p</td><td>2.0e</td><td>11:29p</td><td>-0.4</td><td>7:58p</td><td>-0.9</td><td>8:34p</td><td>-1.1</td></tr>
<tr><td>Sun. 12/17</td><td>5:12a</td><td>1:00a</td><td>1.7 f</td><td>6:09a</td><td>3.9</td><td>3:06a</td><td>5.0</td><td>3:41a</td><td>6.0</td></tr>
<tr><td></td><td>10:42a</td><td>7:54a</td><td>1.2e</td><td>11:08a</td><td>1.9</td><td>7:50a</td><td>3.3</td><td>8:34a</td><td>3.5</td></tr>
<tr><td></td><td>3:48p</td><td>1:06p</td><td>1.2 f</td><td>4:27p</td><td>4.7</td><td>1:28p</td><td>6.0</td><td>2:19p</td><td>7.0</td></tr>
<tr><td></td><td>10:54p</td><td>7:30p</td><td>1.8e</td><td></td><td></td><td>8:47p</td><td>-0.5</td><td>9:23p</td><td>-0.6</td></tr>
<tr><td>Mon. 12/18</td><td>5:54a</td><td>1:54a</td><td>1.7 f</td><td>12:14a</td><td>-0.3</td><td>3:54a</td><td>5.3</td><td>4:30a</td><td>6.2</td></tr>
<tr><td></td><td>11:48a</td><td>8:48a</td><td>1.3e</td><td>6:56a</td><td>4.0</td><td>9:11a</td><td>3.1</td><td>9:47a</td><td>3.2</td></tr>
<tr><td></td><td>5:00p</td><td>2:06p</td><td>1.1 f</td><td>12:22p</td><td>1.6</td><td>2:37p</td><td>5.3</td><td>3:26p</td><td>6.3</td></tr>
<tr><td></td><td>11:48p</td><td>8:30p</td><td>1.6e</td><td>5:41p</td><td>4.2</td><td>9:37p</td><td>0.1</td><td>10:13p</td><td>0.0</td></tr>
<tr><td>Tue. 12/19</td><td>6:36a</td><td>2:42a</td><td>1.6 f</td><td>1:01a</td><td>-0.1</td><td>4:39a</td><td>5.6</td><td>5:18a</td><td>6.5</td></tr>
<tr><td></td><td>12:54p</td><td>9:48a</td><td>1.4e</td><td>7:42a</td><td>4.2</td><td>10:37a</td><td>2.6</td><td>11:06a</td><td>2.8</td></tr>
<tr><td></td><td>6:24p</td><td>3:18p</td><td>1.1 f</td><td>1:41p</td><td>1.3</td><td>3:58p</td><td>4.7</td><td>4:42p</td><td>5.6</td></tr>
<tr><td></td><td></td><td>9:36p</td><td>1.3e</td><td>7:08p</td><td>3.7</td><td>10:28p</td><td>0.7</td><td>11:05p</td><td>0.7</td></tr>
<tr><td>Wed. 12/20</td><td>12:42a</td><td>3:36a</td><td>1.5 f</td><td>1:49a</td><td>0.1</td><td>5:23a</td><td>5.9</td><td>6:04a</td><td>6.9</td></tr>
<tr><td></td><td>7:18a</td><td>10:48a</td><td>1.6e</td><td>8:28a</td><td>4.4</td><td>11:57a</td><td>1.8</td><td>12:24a</td><td>2.0</td></tr>
<tr><td></td><td>2:00p</td><td>4:30p</td><td>1.1 f</td><td>2:59p</td><td>0.8</td><td>5:29p</td><td>4.2</td><td>6:07p</td><td>5.1</td></tr>
<tr><td></td><td>7:48p</td><td>10:48p</td><td>1.1e</td><td>8:37p</td><td>3.4</td><td>11:19p</td><td>1.4</td><td>11:58p</td><td>1.5</td></tr>
<tr><td>Thu. 12/21</td><td>1:42a</td><td>4:30a</td><td>1.4 f</td><td>2:38a</td><td>0.5</td><td>6:05a</td><td>6.3</td><td>6:50a</td><td>7.3</td></tr>
<tr><td></td><td>8:06a</td><td>11:48a</td><td>1.6e</td><td>9:12a</td><td>4.7</td><td>1:05p</td><td>1.0</td><td>1:34p</td><td>1.2</td></tr>
<tr><td></td><td>3:06p</td><td>5:42p</td><td>1.2 f</td><td>4:10p</td><td>0.4</td><td>7:02p</td><td>4.1</td><td>7:35p</td><td>4.9</td></tr>
<tr><td></td><td>9:12p</td><td></td><td></td><td>9:57p</td><td>3.4</td><td></td><td></td><td></td><td></td></tr>
<tr><td>Fri. 12/22</td><td>2:42a</td><td>12:00a</td><td>1.0e</td><td>3:26a</td><td>0.9</td><td>12:11a</td><td>2.0</td><td>12:53a</td><td>2.2</td></tr>
<tr><td></td><td>8:48a</td><td>5:24a</td><td>1.3 f</td><td>9:53a</td><td>5.0</td><td>6:47a</td><td>6.6</td><td>7:35a</td><td>7.7</td></tr>
<tr><td></td><td>4:00p</td><td>12:42p</td><td>1.8e</td><td>5:13p</td><td>-0.3</td><td>2:03p</td><td>0.2</td><td>2:34p</td><td>0.4</td></tr>
<tr><td></td><td>10:24p</td><td>6:48p</td><td>1.4 f</td><td>11:07p</td><td>3.5</td><td>8:25p</td><td>4.1</td><td>8:58p</td><td>5.0</td></tr>
<tr><td>Sat. 12/23</td><td>3:48a</td><td>1:12a</td><td>1.0e</td><td>4:14a</td><td>1.3</td><td>1:03a</td><td>2.5</td><td>1:49a</td><td>2.8</td></tr>
<tr><td></td><td>9:30a</td><td>6:18a</td><td>1.2 f</td><td>10:33a</td><td>5.2</td><td>7:29a</td><td>6.4</td><td>8:18a</td><td>7.9</td></tr>
<tr><td></td><td>4:54p</td><td>1:36p</td><td>1.8e</td><td>6:10p</td><td>-0.3</td><td>2:54p</td><td>-0.4</td><td>3:26p</td><td>-0.3</td></tr>
<tr><td></td><td>11:30p</td><td>7:54p</td><td>1.5 f</td><td></td><td></td><td>9:34p</td><td>4.3</td><td>10:10p</td><td>5.2</td></tr>
<tr><td>Sun. 12/24</td><td>4:48a</td><td>2:18a</td><td>1.0e</td><td>12:09a</td><td>3.7</td><td>1:55a</td><td>2.9</td><td>2:43a</td><td>3.2</td></tr>
<tr><td></td><td>10:12a</td><td>7:12a</td><td>1.2 f</td><td>5:03a</td><td>1.7</td><td>8:10a</td><td>6.9</td><td>9:01a</td><td>8.1</td></tr>
<tr><td></td><td>5:48p</td><td>2:24p</td><td>1.9e</td><td>11:10a</td><td>5.4</td><td>3:40p</td><td>-0.8</td><td>4:13p</td><td>-0.8</td></tr>
<tr><td></td><td></td><td>8:48p</td><td>1.6 f</td><td>7:02p</td><td>-0.4</td><td>10:32p</td><td>4.5</td><td>11:09p</td><td>5.5</td></tr>
<tr><td>Mon. 12/25</td><td>12:30a</td><td>3:18a</td><td>1.0e</td><td>1:07a</td><td>3.9</td><td>2:30a</td><td>3.2</td><td>3:36a</td><td>3.5</td></tr>
<tr><td></td><td>5:42a</td><td>8:00a</td><td>1.2 f</td><td>5:53a</td><td>2.1</td><td>8:51a</td><td>6.9</td><td>9:44a</td><td>8.1</td></tr>
<tr><td></td><td>10:54a</td><td>3:06p</td><td>1.9e</td><td>11:45a</td><td>5.5</td><td>4:23p</td><td>-1.0</td><td>4:57p</td><td>-1.1</td></tr>
<tr><td></td><td>6:30p</td><td>9:36p</td><td>1.7 f</td><td>7:51p</td><td>-0.4</td><td>11:21p</td><td>4.6</td><td>11:59p</td><td>5.7</td></tr>
<tr><td>Tue. 12/26</td><td>1:24a</td><td>4:06a</td><td>1.0e</td><td>2:01a</td><td>4.0</td><td>3:35a</td><td>3.4</td><td>4:25a</td><td>3.6</td></tr>
<tr><td></td><td>6:30a</td><td>8:48a</td><td>1.1 f</td><td>6:43a</td><td>2.3</td><td>9:32a</td><td>6.9</td><td>10:26a</td><td>8.0</td></tr>
<tr><td></td><td>11:36a</td><td>3:48p</td><td>1.8e</td><td>12:21p</td><td>5.5</td><td>5:05p</td><td>-1.1</td><td>5:38p</td><td>-1.1</td></tr>
<tr><td></td><td>7:18p</td><td>10:18p</td><td>1.7 f</td><td>8:36p</td><td>-0.4</td><td></td><td></td><td></td><td></td></tr>
<tr><td>Wed. 12/27</td><td>2:12a</td><td>4:54a</td><td>1.0e</td><td>2:51a</td><td>4.1</td><td>12:06a</td><td>4.7</td><td>12:42a</td><td>5.8</td></tr>
<tr><td></td><td>7:18a</td><td>9:30a</td><td>1.1 f</td><td>7:33a</td><td>2.5</td><td>4:21a</td><td>3.4</td><td>5:11a</td><td>3.7</td></tr>
<tr><td></td><td>12:12p</td><td>4:24p</td><td>1.8e</td><td>12:57p</td><td>5.4</td><td>10:13a</td><td>6.7</td><td>11:06a</td><td>7.9</td></tr>
<tr><td></td><td>7:54p</td><td>11:00p</td><td>1.7 f</td><td>9:16p</td><td>-0.3</td><td>5:44p</td><td>-1.0</td><td>6:17p</td><td>-1.1</td></tr>
<tr><td>Thu. 12/28</td><td>3:00a</td><td>5:36a</td><td>1.0e</td><td>3:37a</td><td>4.2</td><td>12:47a</td><td>4.8</td><td>1:22a</td><td>5.8</td></tr>
<tr><td></td><td>8:06a</td><td>10:18a</td><td>1.1 f</td><td>8:22a</td><td>2.5</td><td>5:06a</td><td>3.4</td><td>5:55a</td><td>3.7</td></tr>
<tr><td></td><td>12:54p</td><td>4:54p</td><td>1.8e</td><td>1:36p</td><td>5.3</td><td>10:53a</td><td>6.5</td><td>11:46a</td><td>7.6</td></tr>
<tr><td></td><td>8:36p</td><td>11:30p</td><td>1.6 f</td><td>9:53p</td><td>-0.3</td><td>6:23p</td><td>-0.8</td><td>6:57p</td><td>-0.9</td></tr>
<tr><td>Fri. 12/29</td><td>3:36a</td><td>6:18a</td><td>1.0e</td><td>4:21a</td><td>4.2</td><td>1:26a</td><td>4.8</td><td>2:00a</td><td>5.8</td></tr>
<tr><td></td><td>8:48a</td><td>11:00a</td><td>1.0 f</td><td>9:09a</td><td>2.3</td><td>5:50a</td><td>3.4</td><td>6:39a</td><td>3.7</td></tr>
<tr><td></td><td>1:36p</td><td>5:24p</td><td>1.7e</td><td>2:17p</td><td>5.0</td><td>11:33a</td><td>6.2</td><td>12:26p</td><td>7.3</td></tr>
<tr><td></td><td>9:06p</td><td></td><td></td><td>10:25p</td><td>-0.2</td><td>7:00p</td><td>-0.5</td><td>7:34p</td><td>-0.6</td></tr>
<tr><td>Sat. 12/30</td><td>4:12a</td><td>12:06a</td><td>1.6 f</td><td>5:02a</td><td>4.1</td><td>2:04a</td><td>4.8</td><td>2:37a</td><td>5.7</td></tr>
<tr><td></td><td>9:36a</td><td>6:54a</td><td>1.0e</td><td>9:57a</td><td>2.2</td><td>6:37a</td><td>3.4</td><td>7:23a</td><td>3.7</td></tr>
<tr><td></td><td>2:18p</td><td>11:48a</td><td>1.0 f</td><td>3:01p</td><td>4.7</td><td>12:13p</td><td>5.9</td><td>1:05p</td><td>6.9</td></tr>
<tr><td></td><td>9:36p</td><td>6:00p</td><td>1.6e</td><td>10:53p</td><td>-0.1</td><td>7:36p</td><td>-0.1</td><td>8:11p</td><td>-0.2</td></tr>
<tr><td>Sun. 12/31</td><td>4:42a</td><td>12:36a</td><td>1.5 f</td><td>5:41a</td><td>4.0</td><td>2:42a</td><td>4.8</td><td>3:13a</td><td>5.7</td></tr>
<tr><td></td><td>10:30a</td><td>7:30a</td><td>1.1e</td><td>10:46a</td><td>2.0</td><td>7:27a</td><td>3.4</td><td>8:12a</td><td>3.6</td></tr>
<tr><td></td><td>3:06p</td><td>12:36p</td><td>0.9 f</td><td>3:48p</td><td>4.3</td><td>12:56p</td><td>5.4</td><td>1:47p</td><td>6.4</td></tr>
<tr><td></td><td>10:00p</td><td>6:36p</td><td>1.4e</td><td>11:18p</td><td>-0.1</td><td>8:12p</td><td>0.3</td><td>8:47p</td><td>0.2</td></tr>
</tbody>
</table>

SAN MATEO CURRENTS · PORT CHICAGO · ARENA COVE · HUMBOLDT BAY

	SAN MATEO CURRENTS			PORT CHICAGO		ARENA COVE		HUMBOLDT BAY	
	SLACK	CURRENT		TIDE		TIDE		TIDE	
	Time	Time	Knots	Time	Feet	Time	Feet	Time	Feet
Sun. 11/19	6:36a	2:18a	1.4 f	12:49a	-0.2	4:42a	4.7	5:08a	5.5
	12:00p	9:12a	1.0e	7:38a	3.7	9:13a	3.6	9:49a	3.8
	5:00p	2:18p	1.0 f	12:25p	2.0	2:43p	5.5	3:30p	6.4
		8:48p	1.6e	5:39p	4.4	10:15p	-0.1	10:47p	-0.2
Mon. 11/20	12:18a	3:18a	1.4 f	1:46a	-0.2	5:31a	5.0	6:03a	5.8
	7:24a	10:18a	1.1e	8:28a	3.9	10:47a	3.2	11:17a	3.5
	1:12p	3:30p	1.0 f	1:49p	1.7	4:06p	5.1	4:52p	5.9
	6:24p	9:54p	1.4e	7:08p	4.0	11:12p	0.2	11:46p	0.2
Tue. 11/21	1:18a	4:18a	1.4 f	2:40a	-0.1	6:14a	5.4	6:52a	6.2
	8:12a	11:18a	1.4e	9:15a	4.1	12:08p	2.5	12:39p	2.7
	2:24p	4:42p	1.1 f	3:07p	1.2	5:33p	4.8	6:17p	5.6
	7:54p	11:06p	1.3e	8:41p	3.8				
Wed. 11/22	2:18a	5:12a	1.4 f	3:29a	0.0	12:05a	0.6	12:42a	0.6
	8:54a	12:18p	1.6e	9:57a	4.4	6:52a	5.8	7:36a	6.7
	3:24p	5:54p	1.3 f	4:16p	0.7	1:14p	1.7	1:48p	1.8
	9:12p			10:00p	3.7	6:55p	4.7	7:38p	5.4
Thu. 11/23	3:18a	12:18a	1.3e	4:13a	0.3	12:54a	1.1	1:35a	1.1
	9:30a	6:00a	1.5 f	10:35a	4.7	7:28a	6.3	8:16a	7.2
	4:18p	1:06p	1.8e	5:17p	0.2	2:10p	0.8	2:46p	0.8
	10:24p	7:00p	1.4 f	11:07p	3.7	8:10p	4.6	8:52p	5.5
Fri. 11/24	4:12a	1:18a	1.3e	4:55a	0.6	1:40a	1.6	2:25a	1.6
	10:12a	6:48a	1.5 f	11:10a	5.0	8:04a	6.6	8:54a	7.7
	5:12p	1:54p	1.9e	6:14p	-0.1	3:00p	0.0	3:37p	-0.1
	11:24p	7:54p	1.6 f			9:17p	4.7	9:59p	5.6
Sat. 11/25	5:00a	2:18a	1.2e	12:08a	3.8	2:24a	2.0	3:12a	2.1
	10:48a	7:36a	1.5 f	5:35a	1.0	8:39a	6.9	9:32a	8.0
	6:00p	2:42p	2.0e	11:42a	5.2	3:47p	-0.6	4:24p	-0.8
		8:42p	1.7 f	7:07p	-0.4	10:17p	4.7	10:59p	5.7
Sun. 11/26	12:24a	3:18a	1.2e	1:06a	3.8	3:08a	2.5	3:57a	2.6
	5:54a	8:24a	1.4 f	6:15a	1.4	9:15a	7.0	10:09a	8.2
	11:24a	3:24p	2.0e	12:13p	5.4	4:32p	-1.0	5:08p	-1.2
	6:42p	9:30p	1.8 f	7:58p	-0.4	11:14p	4.8	11:53p	5.8
Mon. 11/27	1:18a	4:12a	1.2e	2:03a	3.9	3:52a	2.9	4:42a	3.0
	6:42a	9:06a	1.3 f	6:58a	1.8	9:52a	7.0	10:46a	8.2
	12:00p	4:06p	1.9e	12:44p	5.5	5:15p	-1.2	5:51p	-1.4
	7:30p	10:18p	1.7 f	8:46p	-0.4				
Tue. 11/28	2:12a	5:00a	1.1e	2:59a	4.0	12:07a	4.8	12:44a	5.8
	7:30a	9:48a	1.3 f	7:43a	2.1	4:35a	3.1	5:26a	3.3
	12:36p	4:42p	1.8e	1:16p	5.5	10:30a	6.8	11:24a	8.0
	8:12p	11:00p	1.7 f	9:32p	-0.3	5:58p	-1.1	6:33p	-1.3
Wed. 11/29	3:06a	5:48a	1.0e	3:53a	4.0	1:00a	4.7	1:33a	5.8
	8:18a	10:36a	1.2 f	8:31a	2.3	5:20a	3.4	6:09a	3.6
	1:12p	5:18p	1.8e	1:52p	5.3	11:09a	6.6	12:02p	7.7
	8:54p	11:48p	1.6 f	10:16p	-0.3	6:42p	-0.9	7:16p	-1.1
Thu. 11/30	4:00a	6:36a	1.0e	4:46a	4.0	1:52a	4.7	2:21a	5.7
	9:06a	11:18a	1.1 f	9:21a	2.4	6:06a	3.5	6:54a	3.8
	1:54p	5:48p	1.7e	2:32p	5.1	11:50a	6.2	12:42p	7.3
	9:36p			10:59p	-0.2	7:26p	-0.6	7:58p	-0.7
Fri. 12/1	4:48a	12:36a	1.5 f	5:38a	4.0	2:44a	4.6	3:10a	5.5
	10:00a	7:24a	0.9e	10:15a	2.4	6:57a	3.6	7:43a	3.9
	2:36p	12:06p	0.9 f	3:17p	4.8	12:34p	5.8	1:24p	6.8
	10:18p	6:30p	1.6e	11:40p	-0.1	8:12p	-0.2	8:43p	-0.3
Sat. 12/2	5:30a	1:18a	1.4 f	6:28a	3.9	3:36a	4.6	3:59a	5.5
	10:54a	8:12a	0.9e	11:13a	2.3	7:56a	3.7	8:37a	4.0
	3:24p	1:00p	0.8 f	4:08p	4.4	1:22p	5.4	2:10p	6.3
	10:54p	7:06p	1.4e			8:59p	0.2	9:28p	0.2
Sun. 12/3	6:12a	2:06a	1.3 f	12:21a	0.0	4:25a	4.7	4:48a	5.5
	12:00p	9:00a	0.9e	7:15a	3.9	9:09a	3.6	9:42a	4.0
	4:24p	2:00p	0.7 f	12:17p	2.0	2:18p	4.9	3:04p	5.8
	11:36p	7:54p	1.2e	5:08p	3.9	9:46p	0.6	10:15p	0.6
Mon. 12/4	6:54a	2:48a	1.2 f	1:02a	0.1	5:09a	4.8	5:34a	5.6
	1:06p	9:54a	1.0e	8:01a	3.9	10:32a	3.4	10:57a	3.8
	5:36p	3:06p	0.6 f	1:26p	1.8	3:25p	4.5	4:08p	5.2
		8:48p	1.1e	6:22p	3.5	10:33p	1.0	11:02p	1.1
Tue. 12/5	12:18a	3:36a	1.2 f	1:41a	0.2	5:47a	5.0	6:16a	5.8
	7:24a	10:42a	1.1e	8:42a	3.9	11:47a	3.0	12:12p	3.3
	2:06p	4:12p	0.7 f	2:35p	1.4	4:43p	4.1	5:21p	4.8
	6:54p	9:48p	0.9e	7:47p	3.2	11:17p	1.4	11:49p	1.5
Wed. 12/6	1:00a	4:18a	1.2 f	2:20a	0.3	6:19a	5.3	6:53a	6.1
	8:00a	11:24a	1.3e	9:19a	4.0	12:47p	2.4	1:17p	2.7
	3:00p	5:18p	0.8 f	3:39p	1.0	6:04p	3.9	6:39p	4.6
	8:12p	10:48p	0.8e	9:07p	3.1	11:59p	1.8		
Thu. 12/7	1:54a	5:00a	1.1 f	2:57a	0.6	6:48a	5.5	12:36a	1.9
	8:36a	12:06p	1.4e	9:50a	4.2	1:35p	1.7	7:28a	6.4
	3:48p	6:18p	0.9 f	4:37p	0.6	7:19p	3.9	2:10p	2.0
	9:24p	11:48p	0.8e	10:17p	3.1			7:53p	4.6
Fri. 12/8	2:48a	5:48a	1.1 f	3:33a	0.9	12:38a	2.1	1:21a	2.3
	9:06a	12:48p	1.5e	10:14a	4.5	7:16a	5.8	8:01a	6.8
	4:30p	7:06p	1.1 f	5:29p	0.3	2:17p	1.1	2:54p	1.2
	10:24p			11:19p	3.2	8:25p	4.0	9:01p	4.7
Sat. 12/9	3:42a	12:54a	0.8e	4:10a	1.3	1:17a	2.5	2:06a	2.7
	9:42a	6:36a	1.1 f	10:34a	4.8	7:44a	6.1	8:34a	7.1
	5:06p	1:24p	1.6e	6:18p	0.1	2:56p	0.4	3:35p	0.5
	11:18p	7:54p	1.3 f			9:23p	4.1	10:01p	5.0
Sun. 12/10	4:42a	1:54a	0.9e	12:18a	3.4	1:57a	2.8	2:49a	3.1
	10:18a	7:18a	1.1 f	4:49a	1.7	8:15a	6.4	9:07a	7.5
	5:42p	2:00p	1.7e	10:57a	5.1	3:34p	-0.2	4:14p	-0.2
		8:36p	1.5 f	7:04p	-0.1	10:15p	4.3	10:54p	5.2
Mon. 12/11	12:12a	2:48a	1.0e	1:13a	3.5	2:38a	3.0	3:32a	3.3
	5:36a	8:06a	1.2 f	5:31a	2.0	8:49a	6.6	9:42a	7.8
	10:54a	2:42p	1.8e	11:28a	5.4	4:14p	-0.7	4:54p	-0.8
	6:24p	9:18p	1.6 f	7:50p	-0.2	11:04p	4.5	11:44p	5.5

		SAN MATEO CURRENTS		PORT CHICAGO		ARENA COVE		HUMBOLDT BAY	
	SLACK	CURRENT		TIDE		TIDE		TIDE	
	Time	Time	Knots	Time	Feet	Time	Feet	Time	Feet
Fri. 10/27	12:24a	3:30a	1.6e	1:08a	4.2	4:02a	0.9	4:47a	0.8
	6:30a	9:12a	1.7 f	7:19a	0.4	10:17a	6.5	11:09a	7.5
	12:30p	4:06p	2.0e	1:23p	4.9	4:53p	0.0	5:34p	-0.3
	7:12p	9:54p	1.8 f	8:10p	0.0	11:05p	5.3	11:53p	6.3
Sat. 10/28	1:18a	4:24a	1.5e	2:05a	4.2	4:42a	1.4	5:28a	1.3
	7:12a	9:48a	1.7 f	7:55a	0.7	10:50a	6.7	11:44a	7.9
	1:06p	4:48p	2.1e	1:53p	5.1	5:40p	-0.6	6:20p	-0.9
	8:00p	10:42p	1.9 f	9:02p	-0.2				
Sun. 10/29	2:18a	5:12a	1.4e	3:01a	4.1	12:02a	5.2	12:48a	6.2
	8:00a	10:30a	1.6 f	8:31a	1.1	5:22a	1.9	6:09a	1.8
	1:36p	5:24p	2.0e	2:22p	5.3	11:24a	6.8	12:19p	8.0
	8:42p	11:24p	1.8 f	9:53p	-0.3	6:26p	-0.9	7:05p	-1.2
Mon. 10/30	3:12a	6:06a	1.3e	3:58a	4.0	1:00a	5.0	1:41a	6.1
	8:48a	11:12a	1.5 f	9:09a	1.5	6:02a	2.4	6:50a	2.4
	2:12p	6:06p	1.9e	2:52p	5.3	12:00p	6.8	12:54p	7.9
	9:30p			10:43p	-0.2	7:13p	-0.9	7:50p	-1.2
Tue. 10/31	4:06a	12:12a	1.7 f	4:58a	3.9	1:58a	4.8	2:35a	5.8
	9:30a	6:54a	1.2e	9:51a	1.9	6:43a	2.9	7:31a	2.9
	2:48p	12:00p	1.3 f	3:25p	5.3	12:37p	6.6	1:31p	7.7
	10:12p	6:42p	1.8e	11:34p	-0.2	8:00p	-0.8	8:35p	-1.0
Wed. 11/1	5:00a	1:00a	1.6 f	5:58a	3.9	3:00a	4.6	3:30a	5.6
	10:18a	7:42a	1.0e	10:38a	2.1	7:27a	3.2	8:15a	3.4
	3:24p	12:42p	1.2 f	4:02p	5.1	1:18p	6.2	2:10p	7.3
	11:00p	7:18p	1.6e			8:51p	-0.5	9:23p	-0.7
Thu. 11/2	6:00a	1:54a	1.4 f	12:26a	0.0	4:07a	4.5	4:29a	5.4
	11:12a	8:42a	0.9e	7:00a	3.8	8:18a	3.5	9:03a	3.8
	4:06p	1:30p	1.0 f	11:32a	2.3	2:03p	5.8	2:52p	6.8
	11:54p	8:00p	1.5e	4:45p	4.8	9:46p	-0.1	10:14p	-0.2
Fri. 11/3	7:06a	2:54a	1.2 f	1:21a	0.1	5:16a	4.5	5:33a	5.2
	12:18p	9:36a	0.8e	8:01a	3.8	9:24a	3.7	10:01a	4.0
	4:54p	2:30p	0.9 f	12:35p	2.3	2:57p	5.3	3:43p	6.2
		8:48p	1.3e	5:36p	4.5	10:46p	0.3	11:09p	0.3
Sat. 11/4	12:48a	4:06a	1.2 f	2:17a	0.1	6:23a	4.5	6:40a	5.2
	8:06a	10:42a	0.8e	8:58a	3.9	10:50a	3.7	11:16a	4.1
	1:30p	3:30p	0.7 f	1:47p	2.3	4:04p	4.9	4:45p	5.7
	6:00p	9:42p	1.2e	6:42p	4.0	11:47p	0.5		
Sun. 11/5	1:00a	4:12a	1.1 f	2:12a	0.1	6:16a	4.6	12:08a	.6
	8:00a	10:48a	0.8e	8:51a	3.9	11:20a	3.5	6:40a	5.3
	1:42p	3:42p	0.6 f	2:02p	2.0	4:21p	4.7	11:42a	3.9
	6:12p	9:42p	1.2e	7:07p	3.7	11:44p	0.8	4:58p	5.3
Mon. 11/6	1:36a	5:12a	1.2 f	3:02a	0.1	6:56a	4.8	12:07a	0.9
	8:42a	11:48a	1.0e	9:38a	4.0	12:29p	3.1	7:27a	5.5
	2:42p	4:48p	0.7 f	3:10p	1.6	5:38p	4.5	12:59p	3.4
	7:30p	10:42p	1.0e	8:33p	3.5			6:14p	5.1
Tue. 11/7	2:30a	5:48a	1.2 f	3:45a	0.2	12:32a	1.0	1:01a	1.1
	9:18a	12:36p	1.2e	10:18a	4.1	7:26a	5.0	8:03a	5.7
	3:42p	5:54p	0.8 f	4:10p	1.2	1:22p	2.5	1:58p	2.8
	8:48p	11:42p	1.0e	9:43p	3.4	6:47p	4.5	7:24p	5.1
Wed. 11/8	3:12a	6:24a	1.2 f	4:21a	0.3	1:12a	1.2	1:47a	1.3
	9:48a	1:18p	1.4e	10:53a	4.2	7:52a	5.3	8:33a	6.0
	4:24p	6:54p	1.0 f	5:03p	0.8	2:05p	2.0	2:44p	2.2
	9:48p			10:42p	3.4	7:46p	4.5	8:26p	5.1
Thu. 11/9	3:54a	12:36a	1.0e	4:52a	0.5	1:47a	1.5	2:27a	1.5
	10:18a	6:54a	1.3 f	11:21a	4.3	8:15a	5.5	9:01a	6.4
	5:06p	1:48p	1.6e	5:51p	0.4	2:43p	1.4	3:24p	1.5
	10:42p	7:42p	1.2 f	11:35p	3.5	8:39p	4.5	9:21p	5.2
Fri. 11/10	4:30a	1:30a	1.0e	5:18a	0.7	2:19a	1.7	3:04a	1.8
	10:42a	7:24a	1.3 f	11:41a	4.5	8:39a	5.8	9:28a	6.7
	5:42p	2:18p	1.6e	6:36p	0.2	3:19p	0.8	4:01p	0.8
	11:36p	8:18p	1.3 f			9:28p	4.5	10:12p	5.4
Sat. 11/11	5:12a	2:18a	1.1e	12:26a	3.5	2:50a	2.0	3:38a	2.1
	11:06a	8:00a	1.3 f	5:44a	1.1	9:03a	6.0	9:55a	7.1
	6:18p	2:48p	1.7e	11:56a	4.7	3:55p	0.3	4:37p	0.2
		8:54p	1.5 f	7:19p	0.0	10:15p	4.5	11:00p	5.5
Sun. 11/12	12:24a	3:00a	1.1e	1:16a	3.5	3:22a	2.3	4:12a	2.5
	6:00a	8:36a	1.3 f	6:13a	1.4	9:29a	6.3	10:22a	7.3
	11:36a	3:18p	1.7e	12:12p	5.0	4:31p	-0.2	5:13p	-0.3
	6:48p	9:36p	1.6 f	8:01p	-0.1	11:03p	4.6	11:46p	5.6
Mon. 11/13	1:12a	3:54a	1.1e	2:07a	3.6	3:55a	2.6	4:46a	2.8
	6:42a	9:12a	1.3 f	6:47a	1.7	9:57a	6.4	10:51a	7.5
	12:00p	3:48p	1.8e	12:37p	5.3	5:10p	-0.5	5:51p	-0.7
	7:24p	10:12p	1.6 f	8:42p	-0.1	11:52p	4.6		
Tue. 11/14	2:00a	4:42a	1.1e	2:59a	3.6	4:29a	2.9	12:34a	5.6
	7:24a	9:54a	1.3 f	7:26a	2.0	10:29a	6.5	5:21a	3.1
	12:36p	4:24p	1.8e	1:10p	5.6	5:51p	-0.8	11:22a	7.7
	8:00p	10:54p	1.6 f	9:24p	-0.1			6:31p	-1.0
Wed. 11/15	2:48a	5:30a	1.1e	3:53a	3.7	12:44a	4.5	1:22a	5.5
	8:06a	10:36a	1.2 f	8:12a	2.2	5:07a	3.2	5:59a	3.4
	1:12p	5:06p	1.8e	1:49p	5.6	11:05a	6.5	11:57a	7.7
	8:42p	11:36p	1.6 f	10:08p	-0.2	6:36p	-0.8	7:14p	-1.1
Thu. 11/16	3:42a	6:18a	1.0e	4:49a	3.7	1:40a	4.5	2:14a	5.5
	8:54a	11:24a	1.2 f	9:03a	2.3	5:49a	3.4	6:40a	3.7
	1:54p	5:54p	1.8e	2:35p	5.5	11:46a	6.5	12:36p	7.6
	9:30p			10:57p	-0.2	7:25p	-0.8	8:01p	-1.0
Fri. 11/17	4:42a	12:24a	1.6 f	5:46a	3.6	2:41a	4.5	3:10a	5.4
	9:48a	7:12a	1.0e	10:01a	2.3	6:39a	3.6	7:29a	3.8
	2:42p	12:18p	1.1 f	3:27p	5.2	12:34p	6.3	1:23p	7.3
	10:24p	6:48p	1.8e	11:51p	-0.2	8:19p	-0.7	8:52p	-0.8
Sat. 11/18	5:42a	1:18a	1.5 f	6:43a	3.7	3:43a	4.5	4:09a	5.4
	10:48a	8:12a	0.9e	11:07a	2.2	7:46a	3.7	8:31a	3.9
	3:42p	1:12p	1.0 f	4:27p	4.8	1:32p	5.9	2:20p	6.9
	11:18p	7:42p	1.7e			9:16p	-0.4	9:48p	-0.6

SAN MATEO CURRENTS — PORT CHICAGO — ARENA COVE — HUMBOLDT BAY

	SAN MATEO CURRENTS			PORT CHICAGO		ARENA COVE		HUMBOLDT BAY	
	SLACK	CURRENT		TIDE		TIDE		TIDE	
	Time	Time	Knots	Time	Feet	Time	Feet	Time	Feet
Wed. 10/4	6:06a	2:12a	1.4 f	12:49a	0.2	4:13a	4.4	4:38a	5.3
	11:30a	8:48a	0.9 e	7:10a	3.8	8:44a	3.1	9:28a	3.3
	4:48p	2:00p	1.1 f	11:54a	2.0	2:45p	5.8	3:33p	6.9
		8:36p	1.5 e	5:28p	4.9	10:21p	0.1	10:47p	0.0
Thu. 10/5	12:30a	3:18a	1.2 f	1:55a	0.3	5:38a	4.2	5:52a	5.0
	7:24a	9:54a	0.7 e	8:21a	3.7	9:46a	3.5	10:24a	3.8
	12:36p	2:54p	0.8 f	12:54p	2.2	3:41p	5.5	4:25p	6.4
	5:36p	9:30p	1.3 e	6:19p	4.6	11:31p	0.3	11:50p	0.4
Fri. 10/6	1:36a	4:48a	1.1 f	3:03a	0.3	7:03a	4.3	7:17a	4.9
	8:42a	11:18a	0.7 e	9:28a	3.8	11:14a	3.6	11:40a	4.0
	1:48p	4:00p	0.7 f	2:08p	2.3	4:51p	5.1	5:30p	6.0
	6:36p	10:36p	1.2 e	7:26p	4.3				
Sat. 10/7	2:42a	6:24a	1.1 f	4:06a	0.3	12:41a	0.5	12:59a	0.6
	9:48a	12:36p	0.7 e	10:28a	3.9	8:08a	4.4	8:35a	5.0
	3:06p	5:06p	0.6 f	3:26p	2.2	12:46p	3.5	1:09p	3.9
	7:48p	11:48p	1.2 e	8:52p	4.1	6:10p	5.0	6:45p	5.7
Sun. 10/8	3:42a	7:24a	1.2 f	5:01a	0.1	1:43a	0.5	2:05a	0.7
	10:42a	1:36p	0.9 e	11:20a	4.1	8:52a	4.6	9:28a	5.2
	4:12p	6:18p	0.7 f	4:35p	1.9	1:54p	3.2	2:27p	3.6
	9:06p			10:12p	4.0	7:22p	5.0	7:58p	5.6
Mon. 10/9	4:36a	12:54a	1.2 e	5:48a	0.1	2:32a	0.6	3:01a	0.7
	11:24a	8:06a	1.3 f	12:04p	4.2	9:24a	4.7	10:04a	5.4
	5:06p	2:24p	1.1 e	5:34p	1.6	2:45p	2.8	3:24p	3.1
	10:12p	7:24p	0.8 f	11:14p	4.0	8:22p	5.1	9:02p	5.7
Tue. 10/10	5:18a	1:48a	1.3 e	6:27a	0.1	3:13a	0.7	3:46a	0.7
	11:54a	8:42a	1.4 f	12:42p	4.2	9:50a	4.9	10:33a	5.7
	5:54p	3:06p	1.3 e	6:26p	1.2	3:26p	2.3	4:09p	2.5
	11:12p	8:18p	1.0 f			9:12p	5.1	9:55p	5.8
Wed. 10/11	5:54a	2:30a	1.3 e	12:06a	4.0	3:46a	0.8	4:23a	0.8
	12:24p	9:00a	1.4 f	6:59a	0.2	10:13a	5.1	10:58a	5.9
	6:36p	3:42p	1.5 e	1:15p	4.3	4:03p	1.9	4:48p	1.9
	12:00p	9:06p	1.2 f	7:12p	0.9	9:56p	5.2	10:42p	5.9
Thu. 10/12	6:24a	3:06a	1.3 e	12:53a	4.0	4:16a	1.0	4:56a	0.9
	12:48p	9:18a	1.5 f	7:26a	0.3	10:34a	5.3	11:22a	6.2
	7:18p	4:06p	1.6 e	1:41p	4.3	4:39p	1.4	5:24p	1.4
		9:42p	1.3 f	7:55p	0.7	10:38p	5.1	11:26p	5.9
Fri. 10/13	12:48a	3:48a	1.3 e	1:36a	3.9	4:44a	1.2	5:26a	1.1
	6:54a	9:42a	1.5 f	7:47a	0.6	10:56a	5.5	11:46a	6.5
	1:06p	4:36p	1.7 e	2:00p	4.4	5:14p	1.0	5:59p	0.9
	7:48p	10:24p	1.4 f	8:36p	0.5	11:20p	5.0		
Sat. 10/14	1:36a	4:24a	1.3 e	2:19a	3.9	5:11a	1.5	12:08a	5.9
	7:30a	10:12a	1.5 f	8:07a	0.8	11:18a	5.7	5:56a	1.5
	1:30p	5:00p	1.7 e	2:11p	4.5	5:50p	0.6	12:10p	6.8
	8:18p	10:54p	1.5 f	9:14p	0.4			6:34p	0.4
Sun. 10/15	2:18a	5:06a	1.3 e	3:04a	3.8	12:02a	4.9	12:51a	5.9
	8:00a	10:42a	1.4 f	8:29a	1.1	5:38a	1.9	6:25a	1.9
	1:48p	5:24p	1.7 e	2:24p	4.8	11:41a	5.9	12:35p	7.0
	8:48p	11:30p	1.5 f	9:51p	0.3	6:26p	0.3	7:10p	0.1
Mon. 10/16	3:00a	5:48a	1.2 e	3:51a	3.7	12:47a	4.8	1:34a	5.7
	8:36a	11:18a	1.4 f	8:59a	1.4	6:06a	2.2	6:54a	2.3
	2:12p	5:54p	1.7 e	2:47p	5.1	12:07p	6.0	1:00p	7.1
	9:18p			10:28p	0.2	7:05p	0.0	7:48p	-0.2
Tue. 10/17	3:42a	12:06a	1.5 f	4:43a	3.6	1:37a	4.6	2:21a	5.5
	9:18a	6:36a	1.2 e	9:35a	1.6	6:36a	2.6	7:24a	2.7
	2:36p	11:54a	1.3 f	3:19p	5.3	12:36p	6.1	1:27p	7.2
	9:54p	6:24p	1.7 e	11:08p	0.2	7:49p	-0.1	8:28p	-0.3
Wed. 10/18	4:36a	12:48a	1.5 f	5:42a	3.5	2:33a	4.4	3:12a	5.3
	10:00a	7:18a	1.0 e	10:17a	1.9	7:08a	3.0	7:57a	3.2
	3:12p	12:42p	1.2 f	3:57p	5.4	1:10p	6.0	1:59p	7.1
	10:36p	7:06p	1.7 e	11:57p	0.2	8:38p	-0.1	9:14p	-0.3
Thu. 10/19	5:36a	1:36a	1.4 f	6:49a	3.5	3:40a	4.2	4:10a	5.1
	10:48a	8:12a	0.9 e	11:06a	2.1	7:47a	3.3	8:36a	3.5
	3:54p	1:30p	1.1 f	4:43p	5.3	1:52p	5.9	2:37p	7.0
	11:30p	7:54p	1.6 e			9:35p	-0.1	10:07p	-0.2
Fri. 10/20	6:48a	2:30a	1.3 f	1:00a	0.3	4:58a	4.1	5:18a	4.9
	11:48a	9:18a	0.8 e	8:00a	3.4	8:39a	3.6	9:26a	3.8
	4:48p	2:24p	1.0 f	12:06p	2.3	2:45p	5.8	3:28p	6.8
		8:54p	1.6 e	5:37p	5.0	10:40p	0.0	11:09p	-0.1
Sat. 10/21	12:36a	3:36a	1.2 f	2:15a	0.2	6:16a	4.2	6:32a	4.9
	8:00a	10:24a	0.7 e	9:07a	3.5	10:00a	3.7	10:40a	4.0
	1:00p	3:30p	0.9 f	1:19p	2.3	3:55p	5.6	4:38p	6.5
	6:00p	10:00p	1.5 e	6:44p	4.7	11:49p	0.0		
Sun. 10/22	1:48a	4:48a	1.2 f	3:26a	0.1	7:17a	4.5	12:16a	0.0
	9:06a	11:42a	0.8 e	10:05a	3.7	11:41a	3.6	7:41a	5.1
	2:18p	4:42p	0.9 f	2:46p	2.1	5:18p	5.4	12:15p	3.9
	7:24p	11:18p	1.5 e	8:07p	4.4			6:03p	6.2
Mon. 10/23	3:00a	6:00a	1.3 f	4:26a	0.0	12:52a	0.0	1:23a	0.0
	10:00a	12:48p	1.1 e	10:55a	3.9	8:01a	4.8	8:36a	5.5
	3:36p	5:54p	1.0 f	4:09p	1.7	1:08p	3.1	1:44p	3.3
	8:54p			9:42p	4.3	6:42p	5.4	7:28p	6.1
Tue. 10/24	4:00a	12:30a	1.5 e	5:17a	-0.1	1:48a	0.0	2:23a	0.0
	10:42a	7:00a	1.4 f	11:38a	4.1	8:38a	5.2	9:20a	6.0
	4:36p	1:48p	1.4 e	5:19p	1.2	2:15p	2.4	2:55p	2.5
	10:12p	7:06p	1.2 f	11:02p	4.3	7:58p	5.4	8:45p	6.2
Wed. 10/25	4:54a	1:36a	1.6 e	6:02a	-0.1	2:36a	0.2	3:16a	0.1
	11:24a	7:42a	1.6 f	12:16p	4.4	9:11a	5.6	9:58a	6.5
	5:36p	2:36p	1.7 e	6:20p	0.7	3:12p	1.5	3:54p	1.5
	11:42p	8:06p	1.5 f			9:05p	5.4	9:53p	6.3
Thu. 10/26	5:42a	2:36a	1.6 e	12:09a	4.3	3:20a	0.5	4:03a	0.4
	11:54a	8:30a	1.7 f	6:42a	0.1	9:44a	6.1	10:34a	7.1
	6:24p	3:24p	1.9 e	12:51p	4.6	4:04p	0.7	4:46p	0.6
		9:00p	1.7 f	7:17p	0.3	10:07p	5.4	10:55p	6.3

SAN MATEO CURRENTS   PORT CHICAGO   ARENA COVE   HUMBOLDT BAY

		SLACK	CURRENT		PORT CHICAGO TIDE		ARENA COVE TIDE		HUMBOLDT BAY TIDE	
		Time	Time	Knots	Time	Feet	Time	Feet	Time	Feet
Mon.	9/11	6:06a	2:42a	1.5e	7:16a	0.0	3:59a	0.2	4:30a	0.3
		12:48p	9:30a	1.5 f	1:24p	4.3	10:42a	4.6	11:24a	5.4
		6:18p	3:48p	1.2e	6:43p	1.9	3:41p	2.8	4:26p	3.0
		11:24p	8:36p	1.0 f			9:32p	5.7	10:17p	6.5
Tue.	9/12	6:42a	3:24a	1.5e	12:25a	4.7	4:34a	0.2	5:07a	0.2
		1:18p	10:00a	1.6 f	7:52a	0.0	11:07a	4.7	11:51a	5.6
		7:00p	4:24p	1.3e	2:01p	4.3	4:20p	2.5	5:06p	2.6
			9:24p	1.1 f	7:30p	1.6	10:13p	5.8	11:01p	6.5
Wed.	9/13	12:12a	3:48a	1.5e	1:07a	4.6	5:05a	0.3	5:40a	0.2
		7:12a	10:18a	1.6 f	8:22a	0.1	11:30a	4.9	12:15p	5.8
		1:48p	4:54p	1.3e	2:33p	4.3	4:56p	2.2	5:44p	2.2
		7:42p	10:06p	1.2 f	8:13p	1.4	10:51p	5.7	11:41p	6.5
Thu.	9/14	1:00a	4:18a	1.5e	1:47a	4.5	5:32a	0.5	6:10a	0.3
		7:36a	10:30a	1.6 f	8:46a	0.3	11:52a	5.1	12:39p	6.0
		2:06p	5:18p	1.5e	3:00p	4.3	5:31p	1.8	6:20p	1.8
		8:18p	10:42p	1.3 f	8:53p	1.2	11:29p	5.6		
Fri.	9/15	1:42a	4:48a	1.5e	2:25a	4.4	5:58a	0.7	12:20a	6.4
		8:06a	10:54a	1.6 f	9:05a	0.4	12:14p	5.2	6:38a	0.5
		2:24p	5:42p	1.6e	3:18p	4.3	6:08p	1.6	1:02p	6.2
		8:54p	11:18p	1.4 f	9:31p	1.0			6:55p	1.4
Sat.	9/16	2:24a	5:24a	1.4e	3:04a	4.2	12:07a	5.4	12:58a	6.3
		8:30a	11:18a	1.6 f	9:21a	0.6	6:23a	1.0	7:06a	0.9
		2:42p	6:06p	1.6e	3:29p	4.4	12:36p	5.4	1:26p	6.4
		9:24p	11:54a	1.4 f	10:06p	0.9	6:45p	1.3	7:31p	1.1
Sun.	9/17	3:00a	6:00a	1.4e	3:46a	4.1	12:47a	5.1	1:38a	6.0
		9:00a	11:48a	1.5 f	9:42a	0.8	6:49a	1.4	7:32a	1.3
		3:00p	6:30p	1.6e	3:41p	4.6	1:00p	5.5	1:50p	6.5
		9:54p			10:41p	0.8	7:24p	1.1	8:09p	0.9
Mon.	9/18	3:42a	12:30a	1.3 f	4:32a	3.9	1:31a	4.8	2:21a	5.7
		9:30a	6:42a	1.3e	10:10a	1.0	7:15a	1.8	7:59a	1.8
		3:18p	12:24p	1.4 f	4:03p	4.9	1:25p	5.6	2:15p	6.6
		10:24p	7:00p	1.6e	11:19p	0.7	8:07p	0.9	8:49p	0.7
Tue.	9/19	4:30a	1:06a	1.3 f	5:26a	3.6	2:23a	4.4	3:09a	5.4
		10:06a	7:30a	1.1e	10:45a	1.3	7:42a	2.3	8:28a	2.4
		3:48p	1:00p	1.3 f	4:35p	5.1	1:55p	5.6	2:42p	6.7
		11:00p	7:30p	1.5e			8:57p	0.7	9:35p	0.6
Wed.	9/20	5:24a	1:54a	1.2 f	12:04a	0.7	3:25a	4.1	4:05a	5.0
		10:54a	8:18a	1.0e	6:35a	3.4	8:13a	2.8	8:59a	2.9
		4:24p	1:48p	1.2 f	11:26a	1.7	2:31p	5.7	3:15p	6.7
		11:48p	8:18p	1.5e	5:15p	5.2	9:55p	0.7	10:28p	0.6
Thu.	9/21	6:36a	2:42a	1.1 f	1:07a	0.7	4:46a	3.9	5:13a	4.7
		11:48a	9:18a	0.8e	7:58a	3.3	8:51a	3.1	9:37a	3.4
		5:12p	2:42p	1.0 f	12:16p	2.0	3:17p	5.6	3:58p	6.7
			9:06p	1.4e	6:03p	5.2	11:05p	0.5	11:32p	0.5
Fri.	9/22	12:54a	3:54a	1.0 f	2:35a	0.7	6:24a	3.8	6:37a	4.5
		8:06a	10:30a	0.6e	9:21a	3.4	9:51a	3.5	10:33a	3.8
		1:00p	3:42p	0.9 f	1:19p	2.3	4:20p	5.6	5:00p	6.6
		6:12p	10:12p	1.4e	7:02p	5.0				
Sat.	9/23	2:12a	5:12a	1.0 f	3:58a	0.5	12:19a	0.3	12:44a	0.4
		9:30a	11:54a	0.6e	10:31a	3.5	7:48a	4.0	8:04a	4.6
		2:24p	4:54p	0.9 f	2:36p	2.4	11:25a	3.6	12:04p	3.9
		7:30p	11:36p	1.5e	8:14p	4.9	5:36p	5.7	6:19p	6.5
Sun.	9/24	3:30a	6:30a	1.2 f	5:05a	0.3	1:26a	0.0	1:55a	0.1
		10:36a	1:06p	0.8e	11:28a	3.7	8:41a	4.3	9:11a	5.0
		3:42p	6:06p	1.0 f	4:01p	2.2	12:57p	3.4	1:39p	3.7
		8:54p			9:40p	4.9	6:54p	5.9	7:40p	6.7
Mon.	9/25	4:36a	12:48a	1.6e	5:59a	0.0	2:24a	-0.3	2:58a	-0.2
		11:24a	7:42a	1.4 f	12:15p	4.0	9:20a	4.6	9:59a	5.4
		4:48p	2:12p	1.1e	5:16p	1.9	2:10p	2.9	2:56p	3.2
		10:12p	7:18p	1.2 f	11:01p	4.9	8:05p	6.1	8:53p	6.9
Tue.	9/26	5:24a	1:54a	1.8e	6:46a	-0.1	3:14a	-0.4	3:52a	-0.5
		12:06p	8:24a	1.6 f	12:56p	4.2	9:54a	5.0	10:39a	5.8
		5:48p	3:06p	1.4e	6:21p	1.5	3:10p	2.3	3:58p	2.4
		11:24p	8:18p	1.4 f			9:08p	6.3	9:58p	7.1
Wed.	9/27	6:12a	2:54a	1.9e	12:09a	5.0	3:58a	-0.4	4:39a	-0.6
		12:42p	9:06a	1.8 f	7:27a	-0.2	10:26a	5.4	11:15a	6.3
		6:42p	3:54p	1.7e	1:33p	4.4	4:05p	1.6	4:52p	1.5
			9:12p	1.6 f	7:19p	1.0	10:06p	6.3	10:57p	7.2
Thu.	9/28	12:24a	3:48a	1.9e	1:09a	5.0	4:40a	-0.2	5:22a	-0.4
		7:00a	9:42a	1.9 f	8:05a	-0.1	10:59a	5.8	11:50a	6.8
		1:18p	4:36p	1.9e	2:08p	4.6	4:57p	0.9	5:43p	0.7
		7:30p	10:06p	1.8 f	8:14p	0.7	11:02p	6.2	11:53p	7.2
Fri.	9/29	1:18a	4:36a	1.9e	2:05a	4.8	5:20a	0.2	6:03a	-0.1
		7:42a	10:24a	1.9 f	8:41a	0.2	11:32a	6.2	12:25p	7.3
		1:54p	5:18p	2.0e	2:40p	4.8	5:48p	0.3	6:32p	0.0
		8:18p	10:54p	1.9 f	9:08p	0.4	11:57p	5.9		
Sat.	9/30	2:12a	5:24a	1.8e	3:00a	4.6	5:58a	0.7	12:47a	6.9
		8:24a	11:00a	1.9 f	9:15a	0.5	12:06p	6.4	6:42a	0.5
		2:24p	6:00p	2.1e	3:10p	5.0	6:38p	-0.1	1:00p	7.6
		9:06p	11:42p	1.9 f	10:01p	0.2			7:20p	-0.4
Sun.	10/1	3:12a	6:12a	1.6e	3:57a	4.4	12:53a	5.5	1:41a	6.6
		9:06a	11:42a	1.8 f	9:49a	0.8	6:36a	1.4	7:21a	1.0
		2:54p	6:36p	2.0e	3:41p	5.1	12:42p	6.5	1:35p	7.7
		9:48p			10:54p	0.1	7:29p	-0.3	8:09p	-0.6
Mon.	10/2	4:06a	12:30a	1.8 f	4:57a	4.1	1:53a	5.1	2:36a	6.1
		9:48a	7:00a	1.4e	10:25a	1.2	7:15a	2.0	8:01a	1.9
		3:30p	12:24p	1.6 f	4:12p	5.2	1:19p	6.4	2:12p	7.6
		10:36p	7:12p	1.8e	11:50p	0.1	8:22p	-0.3	8:58p	-0.6
Tue.	10/3	5:06a	1:18a	1.6 f	6:01a	3.9	2:58a	4.7	3:34a	5.7
		10:36a	7:54a	1.2e	11:06a	1.6	7:57a	2.6	8:42a	2.6
		4:06p	1:06p	1.3 f	4:48p	5.1	1:59p	6.2	2:50p	7.3
		11:30p	7:54p	1.7e			9:18p	-0.2	9:50p	-0.3

	SAN MATEO CURRENTS			PORT CHICAGO		ARENA COVE		HUMBOLDT BAY	
	SLACK	CURRENT		TIDE		TIDE		TIDE	
	Time	Time	Knots	Time	Feet	Time	Feet	Time	Feet
Sat. 8/19	3:06a	12:18a	1.2 f	3:48a	4.5	12:54a	5.4	1:47a	6.3
	9:24a	6:24a	1.5e	10:30a	0.3	7:34a	0.6	8:13a	0.5
	4:00p	12:24p	1.6 f	4:54p	4.3	2:02p	5.1	2:47p	6.0
	10:30p	7:18p	1.5e	11:04p	1.4	7:47p	2.1	8:33p	2.0
Sun. 8/20	3:48a	1:00a	1.1 f	4:32a	4.2	1:35a	5.0	2:28a	5.9
	9:54a	7:00a	1.3e	10:52a	0.5	7:59a	1.0	8:40a	1.0
	4:18p	12:54p	1.5 f	5:08p	4.5	2:29p	5.2	3:13p	6.2
	11:06p	7:42p	1.5e	11:45p	1.2	8:33p	1.9	9:16p	1.8
Mon. 8/21	4:36a	1:36a	1.1 f	5:22a	3.9	2:22a	4.6	3:12a	5.5
	10:24a	7:42a	1.2e	11:22a	0.7	8:26a	1.5	9:08a	1.5
	4:36p	1:30p	1.4 f	5:30p	4.7	2:57p	5.3	3:41p	6.3
	11:42p	8:12p	1.4e			9:26p	1.7	10:05p	1.6
Tue. 8/22	5:24a	2:24a	1.0 f	12:33a	1.2	3:19a	4.1	4:06a	5.0
	11:06a	8:30a	1.0e	6:24a	3.5	8:55a	2.0	9:37a	2.1
	5:06p	2:12p	1.3 f	11:59a	1.1	3:30p	5.4	4:13p	6.4
		8:54p	1.4e	6:03p	4.9	10:28p	1.4	11:00p	1.4
Wed. 8/23	12:30a	3:12a	0.9 f	1:35a	1.1	4:34a	3.7	5:13a	4.6
	6:36a	9:24a	0.8e	7:48a	3.3	9:28a	2.5	10:11a	2.7
	12:00p	3:06p	1.1 f	12:42p	1.5	4:10p	5.5	4:51p	6.5
	5:48p	9:36p	1.3e	6:45p	5.1	11:39p	1.1		
Thu. 8/24	1:30a	4:18a	0.9 f	3:01a	1.0	6:12a	3.6	12:05a	1.1
	8:06a	10:36a	0.7e	9:23a	3.2	10:14a	3.0	6:36a	4.3
	1:06p	4:06p	0.9 f	1:35p	2.0	5:02p	5.7	10:56a	3.3
	6:42p	10:42p	1.3e	7:36p	5.2			5:42p	6.6
Fri. 8/25	2:42a	5:36a	0.9 f	4:26a	0.8	12:51a	0.7	1:16a	0.8
	9:36a	11:54a	0.6e	10:46a	3.4	7:56a	3.7	8:10a	4.3
	2:30p	5:12p	0.9 f	2:39p	2.3	11:23a	3.3	12:06p	3.7
	7:48p	11:54p	1.4e	8:37p	5.3	6:04p	5.9	6:46p	6.8
Sat. 8/26	3:54a	6:54a	1.1 f	5:35a	0.5	1:56a	0.2	2:25a	0.3
	10:54a	1:18p	0.7e	11:53a	3.6	9:07a	3.9	9:33a	4.6
	3:48p	6:24p	0.9 f	3:52p	2.5	12:47p	3.4	1:35p	3.8
	9:06p			9:47p	5.4	7:10p	6.2	7:56p	7.0
Sun. 8/27	5:00a	1:06a	1.6e	6:32a	0.2	2:53a	-0.3	3:26a	-0.3
	11:54a	8:00a	1.3 f	12:47p	3.9	9:55a	4.2	10:31a	5.0
	5:00p	2:30p	0.9e	5:08p	2.4	2:03p	3.2	2:54p	3.6
	10:18p	7:30p	1.1 f	10:59p	5.5	8:14p	6.5	9:03p	7.4
Mon. 8/28	5:54a	2:12a	1.8e	7:22a	-0.1	3:44a	-0.7	4:20a	-0.8
	12:48p	9:00a	1.6 f	1:33p	4.1	10:33a	4.5	11:15a	5.4
	6:00p	3:24p	1.2e	6:17p	2.2	3:07p	2.9	4:00p	3.1
	11:24p	8:30p	1.3 f			9:14p	6.8	10:05p	7.7
Tue. 8/29	6:42a	3:12a	2.0e	12:07a	5.6	4:30a	-1.0	5:09a	-1.2
	1:30p	9:42a	1.8 f	8:06a	-0.2	11:08a	4.9	11:54a	5.8
	6:54p	4:18p	1.4e	2:14p	4.2	4:05p	2.4	4:57p	2.4
		9:24p	1.6 f	7:20p	1.9	10:10p	7.0	11:03p	7.9
Wed. 8/30	12:24a	4:06a	2.2e	1:08a	5.6	5:14a	-1.0	5:53a	-1.3
	7:24a	10:18a	2.0 f	8:47a	-0.3	11:43a	5.2	12:32p	6.2
	2:06p	5:06p	1.7e	2:53p	4.4	5:01p	1.9	5:51p	1.8
	7:48p	10:18p	1.7 f	8:19p	1.5	11:04p	7.0	11:57p	7.9
Thu. 8/31	1:18a	4:54a	2.2e	2:05a	5.5	5:55a	-0.8	6:35a	-1.1
	8:06a	10:54a	2.1 f	9:24a	-0.2	12:18p	5.6	1:08p	6.6
	2:42p	5:48p	1.9e	3:29p	4.5	5:55p	1.4	6:43p	1.2
	8:36p	11:06p	1.8 f	9:16p	1.2	11:57p	6.7		
Fri. 9/1	2:18a	5:42a	2.1e	3:01a	5.3	6:35a	-0.4	12:50a	7.7
	8:48a	11:36a	2.1 f	10:00a	-0.1	12:54p	5.9	7:16a	-0.7
	3:12p	6:30p	2.0e	4:03p	4.7	6:50p	1.0	1:45p	6.9
	9:24p	12:00p	1.8 f	10:11p	0.9			7:35p	0.7
Sat. 9/2	3:12a	6:30a	1.9e	3:57a	4.9	12:52a	6.2	1:44a	7.2
	9:30a	12:12p	2.0 f	10:33a	0.2	7:14a	0.2	7:55a	-0.1
	3:48p	7:12p	2.0e	4:37p	4.8	1:31p	6.1	2:21p	7.2
	10:18p			11:08p	0.7	7:46p	0.7	8:28p	0.4
Sun. 9/3	4:06a	12:48a	1.7 f	4:56a	4.5	1:51a	5.5	2:39a	6.6
	10:12a	7:18a	1.7e	11:07a	0.6	7:53a	0.9	8:35a	0.7
	4:18p	12:54p	1.8 f	5:11p	5.0	2:10p	6.2	3:00p	7.3
	11:06p	7:54p	1.9e			8:44p	0.5	9:22p	0.3
Mon. 9/4	5:06a	1:36a	1.5 f	12:07a	0.6	2:55a	4.9	3:38a	5.9
	11:00a	8:06a	1.4e	6:01a	4.1	8:33a	1.7	9:16a	1.6
	4:54p	1:42p	1.6 f	11:44a	1.0	2:51p	6.2	3:40p	7.2
	12:00p	8:30p	1.7e	5:47p	5.0	9:47p	0.5	10:20p	0.3
Tue. 9/5	6:18a	2:36a	1.3 f	1:12a	0.6	4:10a	4.3	4:44a	5.3
	11:48a	9:00a	1.1e	7:14a	3.8	9:17a	2.4	9:59a	2.4
	5:36p	2:30p	1.3 f	12:26p	1.4	3:37p	6.0	4:23p	7.0
		9:18p	1.5e	6:28p	5.0	10:58p	0.5	11:22p	0.4
Wed. 9/6	1:00a	3:42a	1.1 f	2:23a	0.6	5:41a	4.0	6:01a	4.9
	7:36a	10:12a	0.8e	8:31a	3.6	10:11a	3.0	10:51a	3.2
	12:54p	3:24p	1.0 f	1:18p	1.8	4:31p	5.8	5:14p	6.8
	6:18p	10:18p	1.3e	7:18p	4.9				
Thu. 9/7	2:12a	5:12a	1.0 f	3:37a	0.5	12:13a	0.5	12:31a	0.5
	9:00a	11:36a	0.7e	9:47a	3.7	7:21a	4.0	7:34a	4.7
	2:06p	4:24p	0.8 f	2:23p	2.2	11:24a	3.4	11:58a	3.7
	7:18p	11:36p	1.3e	8:19p	4.8	5:35p	5.6	6:14p	6.5
Fri. 9/8	3:24a	6:54a	1.1 f	4:45a	0.4	1:24a	0.4	1:42a	0.6
	10:24a	1:00p	0.7e	10:55a	3.8	8:42a	4.2	9:07a	4.8
	3:24p	5:36p	0.7 f	3:38p	2.3	12:51p	3.5	1:20p	3.9
	8:24p			9:30p	4.7	6:45p	5.5	7:21p	6.3
Sat. 9/9	4:30a	1:00a	1.3e	5:44a	0.2	2:26a	0.3	2:49a	0.5
	11:24a	8:00a	1.3 f	11:52a	4.1	9:35a	4.4	10:11a	5.0
	4:30p	2:06p	0.8e	4:49p	2.3	2:03p	3.3	2:38p	3.7
	9:30p	6:42p	0.7 f	10:39p	4.7	7:50p	5.5	8:29p	6.3
Sun. 9/10	5:18a	2:00a	1.4e	6:33a	0.1	3:17a	0.2	3:44a	0.4
	12:12p	8:48a	1.4 f	12:41p	4.2	10:12a	4.5	10:53a	5.2
	5:30p	3:00p	1.0e	5:50p	2.1	2:58p	3.1	3:38p	3.4
	10:30p	7:42p	0.9 f	11:36p	4.7	8:46p	5.6	9:27p	6.3

| | **SAN MATEO CURRENTS** | | | **PORT CHICAGO** | | **ARENA COVE** | | **HUMBOLDT BAY** | |
| | SLACK | CURRENT | | TIDE | | TIDE | | TIDE | |
	Time	Time	Knots	Time	Feet	Time	Feet	Time	Feet
Thu.	3:24a	6:06a	0.9 f	4:53a	0.9	1:28a	1.0	1:55a	1.1
7/27	9:48a	12:12p	0.7e	10:55a	3.2	7:53a	3.4	8:18a	4.1
	2:48p	5:42p	1.0 f	3:02p	1.9	11:56a	2.8	12:41p	3.1
	8:30p			9:17p	5.3	6:44p	5.9	7:28p	6.9
Fri.	4:24a	12:24a	1.4e	5:58a	0.6	2:25a	0.3	2:56a	0.4
7/28	11:06a	7:18a	1.1 f	12:08p	3.4	9:16a	3.6	9:43a	4.4
	4:06p	1:30p	0.7e	4:02p	2.3	1:00p	3.0	1:51p	3.5
	9:30p	6:42p	1.0 f	10:10p	5.6	7:36p	6.3	8:22p	7.2
Sat.	5:18a	1:30a	1.6e	6:56a	0.3	3:18a	-0.4	3:51a	-0.3
7/29	12:12p	8:18a	1.3 f	1:09p	3.7	10:16a	3.9	10:50a	4.7
	5:12p	2:36p	0.8e	5:06p	2.6	2:05p	3.1	3:01p	3.5
	10:30p	7:48p	1.1 f	11:08p	5.8	8:29p	6.7	9:18p	7.6
Sun.	6:12a	2:30a	1.8e	7:48a	0.0	4:07a	-0.9	4:43a	-1.0
7/30	1:06p	9:18a	1.6 f	2:02p	3.9	11:03a	4.2	11:42a	5.1
	6:18p	3:42p	1.0e	6:12p	2.6	3:08p	3.1	4:05p	3.4
	11:30p	8:42p	1.1 f			9:23p	7.0	10:15p	7.9
Mon.	7:06a	3:24a	2.0e	12:06a	6.0	4:55a	-1.3	5:32a	-1.5
7/31	2:00p	10:06a	1.8 f	8:35a	-0.2	11:44a	4.5	12:27p	5.4
	7:12p	4:36p	1.2e	2:50p	4.1	4:07p	2.9	5:03p	3.1
		9:36p	1.4 f	7:18p	2.5	10:16p	7.2	11:09p	8.2
Tue.	12:24a	4:18a	2.2e	1:05a	6.0	5:40a	-1.6	6:18a	-1.8
8/1	7:48a	10:48a	2.0 f	9:20a	-0.4	12:24p	4.7	1:08p	5.7
	2:42p	5:24p	1.4e	3:33p	4.2	5:04p	2.6	5:58p	2.7
	8:06p	10:30p	1.6 f	8:22p	2.3	11:08p	7.3		
Wed.	1:24a	5:12a	2.3e	2:03a	6.0	6:24a	-1.6	12:03a	8.3
8/2	8:36a	11:30a	2.1 f	10:01a	-0.4	1:03p	5.0	7:03a	-1.8
	3:24p	6:12p	1.6e	4:14p	4.4	6:01p	2.3	1:48p	6.0
	8:54p	11:24p	1.6 f	9:22p	1.9			6:52p	2.3
Thu.	2:18a	6:00a	2.3e	3:00a	5.8	12:01a	7.1	12:56a	8.1
8/3	9:18a	12:06p	2.1 f	10:39a	-0.4	7:07a	-1.3	7:46a	-1.6
	4:00p	7:00p	1.7e	4:53p	4.5	1:42p	5.3	2:28p	6.3
	9:48p			10:21p	1.6	6:59p	2.0	7:47p	1.9
Fri.	3:12a	12:12a	1.6 f	3:58a	5.4	12:55a	6.6	1:49a	7.6
8/4	10:00a	6:48a	2.1e	11:15a	-0.3	7:49a	-0.8	8:28a	-1.1
	4:36p	12:48p	2.1 f	5:32p	4.6	2:22p	5.5	3:08p	6.6
	10:42p	7:42p	1.8e	11:21p	1.3	8:00p	1.8	8:44p	1.6
Sat.	4:12a	1:06a	1.6 f	4:57a	4.9	1:52a	6.0	2:45a	7.0
8/5	10:42a	7:36a	1.9e	11:51a	0.0	8:30a	-0.2	9:10a	-0.4
	5:12p	1:30p	1.9 f	6:10p	4.7	3:03p	5.8	3:49p	6.8
	11:36p	8:30p	1.8e			9:05p	1.5	9:44p	1.3
Sun.	5:12a	2:00a	1.4 f	12:24a	1.1	2:56a	5.2	3:44a	6.2
8/6	11:24a	8:24a	1.6e	6:03a	4.4	9:11a	0.6	9:52a	0.5
	5:48p	2:12p	1.7 f	12:27p	0.3	3:46p	5.9	4:31p	7.0
		9:18p	1.7e	6:51p	4.9	10:16p	1.2	10:48p	1.1
Mon.	12:36a	3:00a	1.3 f	1:32a	1.0	4:09a	4.5	4:50a	5.4
8/7	6:24a	9:24a	1.2e	7:16a	3.9	9:55a	1.4	10:36a	1.4
	12:18p	3:00p	1.4 f	1:07p	0.8	4:32p	6.0	5:16p	7.0
	6:30p	10:06p	1.6e	7:34p	5.0	11:32p	0.9	11:56p	0.9
Tue.	1:36a	4:12a	1.1 f	2:47a	0.8	5:37a	3.9	6:07a	4.8
8/8	7:42a	10:30a	0.9e	8:37a	3.6	10:44a	2.2	11:24a	2.3
	1:12p	3:54p	1.2 f	1:52p	1.3	5:21p	6.0	6:04p	7.0
	7:12p	11:06p	1.5e	8:21p	5.1				
Wed.	2:42a	5:30a	1.1 f	4:02a	0.6	12:48a	0.6	1:08a	0.7
8/9	9:12a	11:48a	0.7e	9:57a	3.5	7:19a	3.8	7:38a	4.5
	2:24p	4:54p	1.0 f	2:47p	1.7	11:43a	2.8	12:22p	3.0
	8:06p			9:12p	5.1	6:16p	6.0	6:56p	6.9
Thu.	3:54a	12:18a	1.4e	5:11a	0.4	1:57a	0.3	2:17a	0.4
8/10	10:36a	7:06a	1.1 f	11:11a	3.6	8:53a	3.9	9:15a	4.6
	3:42p	1:18p	0.7e	3:50p	2.1	12:52p	3.2	1:30p	3.5
	9:00p	6:00p	0.8 f	10:06p	5.2	7:12p	6.0	7:53p	6.9
Fri.	4:54a	1:24a	1.5e	6:12a	0.2	2:56a	0.0	3:20a	0.2
8/11	11:48a	8:18a	1.3 f	12:14p	3.9	10:01a	4.1	10:33a	4.8
	4:48p	2:30p	0.8e	4:56p	2.4	2:02p	3.3	2:41p	3.7
	9:54p	7:00p	1.0 f	11:00p	5.2	8:08p	6.0	8:50p	6.8
Sat.	5:48a	2:30a	1.5e	7:04a	0.1	3:46a	-0.2	4:14a	0.0
8/12	12:48p	9:18a	1.5 f	1:09p	4.1	10:48a	4.3	11:25a	5.1
	5:48p	3:24p	0.9e	5:57p	2.5	3:01p	3.3	3:44p	3.6
	10:48p	8:00p	0.9 f	11:49p	5.2	9:00p	6.1	9:44p	6.9
Sun.	6:36a	3:12a	1.6e	7:50a	0.0	4:30a	-0.3	4:59a	-0.2
8/13	1:30p	10:00a	1.6 f	1:57a	4.3	11:24a	4.4	12:04p	5.2
	6:36p	4:12p	1.0e	6:53p	2.4	3:49p	3.1	4:36p	3.4
	11:36p	8:54p	1.0 f			9:45p	6.1	10:32p	6.9
Mon.	7:18a	3:48a	1.7e	12:34a	5.2	5:08a	-0.3	5:39a	-0.3
8/14	2:06p	10:36a	1.6 f	8:31a	0.0	11:54a	4.5	12:35p	5.4
	7:24p	4:54p	1.1e	2:40p	4.4	4:31p	3.0	5:20p	3.1
		9:36p	1.1 f	7:42p	2.3	10:26p	6.2	11:16p	7.0
Tue.	12:24a	4:18a	1.7e	1:14a	5.1	5:42a	-0.3	6:14a	-0.4
8/15	7:48a	11:00a	1.6 f	9:05a	0.0	12:21p	4.6	1:03p	5.5
	2:36p	5:30p	1.2e	3:18p	4.4	5:09p	2.8	6:00p	2.9
	8:06p	10:18p	1.1 f	8:28p	2.2	11:04p	6.1	11:55p	7.0
Wed.	1:06a	4:48a	1.7e	1:53a	5.0	6:12a	-0.2	6:47a	-0.3
8/16	8:18a	11:18a	1.6 f	9:34a	0.1	12:47p	4.7	1:29p	5.6
	3:06p	6:00p	1.3e	3:51p	4.3	5:47p	2.6	6:37p	2.6
	8:42p	11:00p	1.2 f	9:09p	2.0	11:40p	6.0		
Thu.	1:48a	5:12a	1.6e	2:30a	4.9	6:41a	0.0	12:33a	6.8
8/17	8:42a	11:36a	1.6 f	9:57a	0.2	1:12p	4.8	7:17a	-0.2
	3:24p	6:30p	1.4e	4:19p	4.2	6:25p	2.4	1:55p	5.7
	9:24p	11:42p	1.2 f	9:49p	1.8			7:15p	2.4
Fri.	2:30a	5:48a	1.6e	3:08a	4.7	12:16a	5.8	1:10a	6.6
8/18	9:06a	12:00p	1.6 f	10:13a	0.2	7:07a	0.3	7:46a	0.1
	3:42p	6:48p	1.4e	4:40p	4.2	1:37p	4.9	2:21p	5.9
	10:00p			10:26p	1.6	7:05p	2.2	7:53p	2.2

	SAN MATEO CURRENTS			PORT CHICAGO		ARENA COVE		HUMBOLDT BAY	
	SLACK	CURRENT		TIDE		TIDE		TIDE	
	Time	Time	Knots	Time	Feet	Time	Feet	Time	Feet
Tue. 7/4	1:24a	5:24a	2.2e	2:01a	6.1	6:46a	-1.9	12:09a	8.2
	8:54a	11:48a	2.0 f	10:26a	-0.5	1:40p	4.6	7:23a	-2.1
	3:54p	6:36p	1.3e	4:51p	4.2	6:05p	2.9	2:20p	5.6
	9:06p	11:36p	1.5 f	9:25p	2.5			7:00p	3.0
Wed. 7/5	2:18a	6:12a	2.3e	2:57a	5.9	12:06a	7.1	1:01a	8.1
	9:42a	12:36p	2.0 f	11:09a	-0.5	7:32a	-1.8	8:09a	-2.1
	4:36p	7:24p	1.4e	5:35p	4.2	2:25p	4.7	3:05p	5.8
	10:00p			10:28p	2.2	7:05p	2.8	7:56p	2.8
Thu. 7/6	3:12a	12:24a	1.5 f	3:55a	5.6	12:59a	6.7	1:54a	7.7
	10:24a	7:06a	2.2e	11:50a	-0.5	8:18a	-1.5	8:55a	-1.7
	5:18p	1:18p	2.0 f	6:19p	4.3	3:11p	5.0	3:50p	5.9
	11:00p	8:12p	1.5e	11:31p	1.9	8:09p	2.6	8:56p	2.5
Fri. 7/7	4:12a	1:18a	1.4 f	4:56a	5.1	1:56a	6.2	2:50a	7.1
	11:12a	7:54a	2.0e	12:30p	-0.4	9:04a	-1.0	9:41a	-1.2
	6:00p	2:06p	1.9 f	7:03p	4.4	3:56p	5.2	4:35p	6.2
	12:00p	9:00p	1.6e			9:20p	2.4	10:01p	2.3
Sat. 7/8	5:18a	2:18a	1.3 f	12:38a	1.6	2:59a	5.5	3:51a	6.4
	11:54a	8:48a	1.7e	6:03a	4.6	9:50a	-0.3	10:27a	-0.5
	6:42p	2:48p	1.7 f	1:11p	-0.1	4:41p	5.5	5:20p	6.4
		9:54p	1.6e	7:47p	4.6	10:39p	2.0	11:11p	2.0
Sun. 7/9	1:06a	3:24a	1.2 f	1:50a	1.3	4:11a	4.7	4:58a	5.6
	6:30a	9:42a	1.4e	7:20a	4.0	10:36a	0.5	11:14a	0.4
	12:48p	3:42p	1.6 f	1:53p	0.2	5:26p	5.7	6:06p	6.7
	7:24p	10:48p	1.6e	8:31p	4.8	12:00p	1.5		
Mon. 7/10	2:12a	4:36a	1.1 f	3:06a	1.0	5:35a	4.0	12:25a	1.5
	7:54a	10:48a	1.1e	8:43a	3.6	11:25a	1.2	6:15a	4.9
	1:42p	4:30p	1.4 f	2:37p	0.6	6:12p	6.0	12:03p	1.2
	8:06p	11:48p	1.6e	9:17p	5.0			6:53p	6.9
Tue. 7/11	3:12a	5:48a	1.1 f	4:20a	0.7	1:15a	0.9	1:38a	1.0
	9:18a	12:06p	0.9e	10:04a	3.4	7:10a	3.7	7:40a	4.5
	2:48p	5:30p	1.2 f	3:25p	1.1	12:16p	1.9	12:56p	2.0
	8:54p			10:01p	5.2	6:58p	6.2	7:40p	7.1
Wed. 7/12	4:18a	12:54a	1.6e	5:29a	0.3	2:20a	0.3	2:44a	0.4
	10:42a	7:12a	1.2 f	11:19a	3.4	8:44a	3.7	9:10a	4.4
	3:54p	1:24p	0.8e	4:16p	1.6	1:11p	2.5	1:54p	2.7
	9:36p	6:30p	1.1 f	10:45p	5.3	7:43p	6.3	8:27p	7.2
Thu. 7/13	5:12a	1:54a	1.6e	6:29a	0.1	3:16a	-0.2	3:42a	-0.1
	11:54a	8:24a	1.3 f	12:26p	3.6	10:01a	3.8	10:32a	4.6
	5:00p	2:36p	0.8e	5:09p	2.0	2:08p	2.9	2:54p	3.2
	10:24p	7:18p	1.0 f	11:26p	5.4	8:29p	6.3	9:14p	7.3
Fri. 7/14	6:06a	2:42a	1.7e	7:24a	-0.1	4:05a	-0.5	4:33a	-0.5
	1:00p	9:18a	1.5 f	1:25p	3.9	11:01a	4.0	11:36a	4.9
	6:00p	3:36p	0.9e	6:03p	2.3	3:03p	3.1	3:51p	3.4
	11:06p	8:18p	1.0 f			9:13p	6.3	10:01p	7.3
Sat. 7/15	6:54a	3:30a	1.7e	12:04a	5.5	4:49a	-0.7	5:18a	-0.7
	1:48p	10:12a	1.6 f	8:12a	-0.1	11:48a	4.2	12:25p	5.1
	6:48p	4:30p	0.9e	2:19p	4.1	3:53p	3.2	4:43p	3.5
	11:54p	9:06p	1.0 f	6:56p	2.6	9:55p	6.3	10:45p	7.3
Sun. 7/16	7:36a	4:12a	1.7e	12:41a	5.5	5:29a	-0.8	6:00a	-0.8
	2:36p	10:54a	1.6 f	8:56a	-0.1	12:27p	4.3	1:05p	5.2
	7:36p	5:18p	1.0e	3:08p	4.2	4:38p	3.2	5:30p	3.4
		9:54p	1.0 f	7:48p	2.7	10:36p	6.3	11:27p	7.2
Mon. 7/17	12:30a	4:42a	1.8e	1:18a	5.4	6:07a	-0.8	6:38a	-0.9
	8:18a	11:30a	1.6 f	9:36a	-0.1	1:02p	4.3	1:39p	5.3
	3:18p	5:54p	1.0e	3:52p	4.3	5:20p	3.1	6:13p	3.3
	8:18p	10:36p	1.1 f	8:36p	2.7	11:15p	6.2		
Tue. 7/18	1:12a	5:12a	1.7e	1:55a	5.3	6:42a	-0.7	12:07a	7.1
	8:48a	11:54a	1.6 f	10:10a	0.0	1:34p	4.4	7:14a	-0.8
	3:48p	6:36p	1.1e	4:33p	4.3	6:01p	3.0	2:11p	5.3
	9:06p	11:18p	1.1 f	9:22p	2.5	11:52p	6.1	6:53p	3.2
Wed. 7/19	1:54a	5:42a	1.7e	2:34a	5.2	7:15a	-0.5	12:45a	7.0
	9:18a	12:18p	1.6 f	10:39a	0.0	2:06p	4.5	7:48a	-0.7
	4:18p	7:06p	1.1e	5:09p	4.2	6:41p	3.0	2:41p	5.4
	9:48p	12:00p	1.1 f	10:06p	2.3			7:33p	3.1
Thu. 7/20	2:36a	6:12a	1.6e	3:14a	5.0	12:29a	5.9	1:23a	6.7
	9:42a	12:42p	1.6 f	11:01a	0.0	7:46a	-0.3	8:21a	-0.5
	4:42p	7:36p	1.2e	5:41p	4.2	2:37p	4.5	3:12p	5.4
	10:30p			10:48p	2.1	7:24p	2.9	8:15p	3.0
Fri. 7/21	3:18a	12:42a	1.0 f	3:56a	4.7	1:07a	5.6	2:01a	6.4
	10:06a	6:42a	1.5e	11:20a	0.0	8:17a	0.0	8:53a	-0.1
	5:00p	1:06p	1.5 f	6:09p	4.1	3:07p	4.7	3:43p	5.5
	11:12p	8:00p	1.2e	11:32p	1.9	8:12p	2.8	8:59p	2.8
Sat. 7/22	4:00a	1:24a	0.9 f	4:42a	4.4	1:47a	5.2	2:41a	6.0
	10:30a	7:18a	1.4e	11:40a	0.1	8:46a	0.4	9:23a	0.3
	5:24p	1:36p	1.5 f	6:32p	4.1	3:38p	4.8	4:14p	5.7
	11:54p	8:30p	1.3e			9:05p	2.7	9:48p	2.7
Sun. 7/23	4:48a	2:12a	0.9 f	12:20a	1.7	2:33a	4.7	3:26a	5.5
	10:54a	8:06a	1.2e	5:33a	4.0	9:16a	0.8	9:54a	0.8
	5:42p	2:12p	1.4 f	12:08p	0.3	4:09p	5.0	4:46p	5.9
		9:06p	1.3e	6:52p	4.3	10:06p	2.4	10:43p	2.5
Mon. 7/24	12:42a	3:00a	0.8 f	1:15a	1.5	3:29a	4.2	4:19a	5.0
	5:42a	8:54a	1.0e	6:33a	3.6	9:47a	1.3	10:26a	1.4
	11:36a	2:54p	1.3 f	12:42p	0.6	4:41p	5.1	5:20p	6.1
	6:12p	9:42p	1.3e	7:16p	4.5	11:14p	2.1	11:44p	2.1
Tue. 7/25	1:30a	3:54a	0.8 f	2:22a	1.4	4:41a	3.7	5:26a	4.5
	5:54a	9:48a	0.9e	7:51a	3.2	10:22a	1.9	11:01a	2.0
	12:24p	3:42p	1.2 f	1:22p	1.0	5:17p	5.4	5:57p	6.3
	6:48p	10:30p	1.3e	7:48p	4.7				
Wed. 7/26	2:24a	5:00a	0.8 f	3:39a	1.2	12:23a	1.6	12:49a	1.7
	8:18a	10:54a	0.7e	9:27a	3.1	6:13a	3.4	6:48a	4.2
	1:30p	4:36p	1.0 f	2:09p	1.5	11:03a	2.3	11:44a	2.6
	7:36p	11:24p	1.3e	8:29p	5.0	5:58p	5.6	6:39p	6.6

	SAN MATEO CURRENTS			PORT CHICAGO		ARENA COVE		HUMBOLDT BAY	
	SLACK	CURRENT		TIDE		TIDE		TIDE	
	Time	Time	Knots	Time	Feet	Time	Feet	Time	Feet
Sun. 6/11	2:36a	4:54a	1.0 f	3:21a	1.3	12:18a	2.1	12:45a	2.2
	8:00a	11:18a	1.3e	8:49a	3.7	5:39a	4.3	6:24a	5.2
	2:24p	5:18p	1.4 f	3:28p	0.1	12:08p	0.3	12:44p	0.3
	9:00p			10:05p	4.7	7:01p	5.6	7:40p	6.4
Mon. 6/12	3:42a	12:30a	1.6e	4:34a	0.8	1:33a	1.4	1:59a	1.5
	9:24a	6:06a	1.1 f	10:12a	3.5	7:07a	3.9	7:46a	4.8
	3:18p	12:24p	1.1e	4:14p	0.4	12:59p	0.9	1:37p	1.0
	9:42p	6:06p	1.4 f	10:47p	4.9	7:42p	5.9	8:24p	6.8
Tue. 6/13	4:36a	1:24a	1.7e	5:40a	0.4	2:36a	0.6	3:04a	0.7
	10:42a	7:18a	1.3 f	11:25a	3.4	8:32a	3.8	9:08a	4.6
	4:18p	1:36p	1.0e	4:58p	0.8	1:47p	1.5	2:30p	1.6
	10:24p	7:00p	1.3 f	11:25p	5.2	8:20p	6.2	9:06p	7.1
Wed. 6/14	5:30a	2:18a	1.8e	6:40a	0.0	3:30a	-0.1	4:00a	-0.1
	11:54a	8:18a	1.4 f	12:30p	3.5	9:47a	3.8	10:24a	4.7
	5:18p	2:42p	1.0e	5:41p	1.3	2:34p	2.0	3:21p	2.2
	11:00p	7:48p	1.2 f	12:00p	5.3	8:58p	6.3	9:46p	7.3
Thu. 6/15	6:18a	3:06a	1.8e	7:34a	-0.2	4:18a	-0.6	4:49a	-0.7
	12:54p	9:18a	1.5 f	1:31p	3.6	10:52a	3.9	11:29a	4.8
	6:12p	3:42p	1.0e	6:24p	1.7	3:21p	2.4	4:10p	2.7
	11:36p	8:36p	1.2 f			9:35p	6.4	10:26p	7.4
Fri. 6/16	7:06a	3:48a	1.8e	12:32a	5.5	5:02a	-1.0	5:33a	-1.0
	1:54p	10:06a	1.6 f	8:25a	-0.3	11:49a	4.0	12:26p	5.0
	7:00p	4:36p	1.0e	2:28p	3.8	4:06p	2.7	4:58p	3.0
		9:24p	1.1 f	7:08p	2.2	10:12p	6.4	11:04p	7.4
Sat. 6/17	12:12a	4:24a	1.8e	1:02a	5.5	5:43a	-1.2	6:15a	-1.2
	7:48a	10:48a	1.6 f	9:11a	-0.3	12:38p	4.1	1:14p	5.1
	2:42p	5:24p	1.0e	3:22p	4.0	4:50p	2.9	5:43p	3.2
	7:48p	10:06p	1.1 f	7:54p	2.5	10:50p	6.3	11:43p	7.3
Sun. 6/18	12:48a	5:00a	1.8e	1:32a	5.5	6:23a	-1.2	6:55a	-1.3
	8:30a	11:36a	1.6 f	9:55a	-0.2	1:23p	4.2	1:57p	5.2
	3:30p	6:06p	1.0e	4:13p	4.1	5:33p	3.1	6:27p	3.3
	8:36p	10:48p	1.1 f	8:42p	2.6	11:27p	6.2		
Mon. 6/19	1:24a	5:30a	1.7e	2:05a	5.4	7:02a	-1.1	12:21a	7.2
	9:12a	12:12p	1.6 f	10:34a	-0.2	2:06p	4.2	7:33a	-1.2
	4:12p	6:48p	0.9e	5:01p	4.1	6:15p	3.1	2:38p	5.2
	9:18p	11:30p	1.0 f	9:31p	2.7			7:09p	3.4
Tue. 6/20	2:06a	6:00a	1.7e	2:42a	5.3	12:06a	6.0	12:59a	6.9
	9:48a	12:42p	1.5 f	11:10a	-0.1	7:40a	-0.9	8:12a	-1.0
	4:54p	7:30p	0.9e	5:46p	4.1	2:48p	4.2	3:16p	5.2
	10:06p			10:19p	2.6	6:58p	3.2	7:51p	3.4
Wed. 6/21	2:48a	12:18a	1.0 f	3:23a	5.1	12:44a	5.8	1:38a	6.7
	10:18a	6:30a	1.6e	11:41a	-0.1	8:18a	-0.7	8:50a	-0.7
	5:30p	1:18p	1.4 f	6:28p	4.1	3:28p	4.2	3:55p	5.1
	10:54p	8:06p	0.9e	11:09p	2.4	7:45p	3.2	8:36p	3.4
Thu. 6/22	3:30a	1:00a	0.9 f	4:08a	4.8	1:25a	5.5	2:18a	6.3
	10:48a	7:12a	1.5e	12:09p	-0.1	8:56a	-0.4	9:28a	-0.4
	6:00p	1:54p	1.4 f	7:08p	4.0	4:09p	4.3	4:34p	5.1
	11:42p	8:48p	1.0e			8:38p	3.2	9:25p	3.4
Fri. 6/23	4:18a	1:54a	0.8 f	12:01a	2.2	2:08a	5.1	3:01a	5.9
	11:12a	7:48a	1.4e	4:57a	4.4	9:33a	0.0	10:06a	-0.1
	6:30p	2:24p	1.4 f	12:35p	-0.1	4:47p	4.4	5:12p	5.2
		9:24p	1.1e	7:45p	4.0	9:41p	3.1	10:22p	3.2
Sat. 6/24	12:42a	2:48a	0.7 f	12:58a	2.0	2:57a	4.6	3:49a	5.4
	5:12a	8:30a	1.2e	5:52a	4.0	10:11a	0.4	10:44a	0.4
	11:42a	3:00p	1.3 f	1:05p	0.0	5:23p	4.6	5:50p	5.4
	7:00p	10:06p	1.1e	8:20p	4.0	10:54p	2.9	11:26p	3.0
Sun. 6/25	1:42a	3:42a	0.7 f	2:01a	1.8	3:56a	4.1	4:47a	4.9
	6:18a	9:24a	1.0e	6:57a	3.5	10:48a	0.8	11:23a	0.8
	12:24p	3:48p	1.3 f	1:39p	0.2	5:57p	4.8	6:28p	5.6
	7:30p	10:48p	1.2e	8:52p	4.1				
Mon. 6/26	2:36a	4:42a	0.7 f	3:11a	1.5	12:07a	2.4	12:34a	2.6
	7:30a	10:12a	0.9e	8:17a	3.2	5:10a	3.7	5:56a	4.5
	1:12p	4:36p	1.2 f	2:18p	0.5	11:27a	1.2	12:04p	1.4
	8:06p	11:36p	1.3e	9:20p	4.3	6:29p	5.1	7:05p	5.9
Tue. 6/27	3:30a	5:48a	0.8 f	4:19a	1.1	1:12a	1.8	1:39a	2.0
	8:54a	11:24a	0.8e	9:46a	3.0	6:35a	3.4	7:15a	4.2
	2:12p	5:24p	1.1 f	3:00p	0.9	12:08p	1.7	12:49p	1.9
	8:42p			9:47p	4.6	7:02p	5.4	7:42p	6.3
Wed. 6/28	4:12a	12:18a	1.4e	5:23a	0.8	2:07a	1.2	2:37a	1.3
	10:06a	6:48a	0.9 f	11:07a	3.1	8:02a	3.4	8:36a	4.1
	3:18p	12:36p	0.8e	3:46p	1.4	12:53p	2.1	1:38p	2.4
	9:24p	6:18p	1.1 f	10:17p	5.0	7:36p	5.8	8:21p	6.7
Thu. 6/29	5:00a	1:06a	1.5e	6:21a	0.5	2:55a	0.4	3:29a	0.5
	11:18a	7:42a	1.1 f	12:18p	3.3	9:19a	3.5	9:53a	4.3
	4:30p	1:42p	0.8e	4:34p	1.8	1:40p	2.5	2:32p	2.8
	10:06p	7:12p	1.1 f	10:52p	5.4	8:14p	6.1	9:02p	7.1
Fri. 6/30	5:48a	2:00a	1.6e	7:15a	0.2	3:42a	-0.3	4:17a	-0.3
	12:18p	8:36a	1.4 f	1:22p	3.5	10:23a	3.8	11:00a	4.6
	5:36p	2:48p	0.9e	5:25p	2.2	2:31p	2.7	3:27p	3.1
	10:54p	8:12p	1.1 f	11:33p	5.7	8:55p	6.5	9:45p	7.5
Sat. 7/1	6:30a	2:48a	1.8e	8:06a	-0.1	4:27a	-0.9	5:04a	-1.0
	1:18p	9:30a	1.6 f	2:20p	3.7	11:18a	4.0	11:57a	4.9
	6:30p	3:54p	1.0e	6:20p	2.5	3:23p	2.9	4:21p	3.2
	11:42p	9:00p	1.2 f			9:39p	6.8	10:31p	7.8
Sun. 7/2	7:18a	3:42a	1.9e	12:19a	6.0	5:13a	-1.4	5:50a	-1.6
	2:12p	10:18a	1.8 f	8:55a	-0.2	12:07p	4.2	12:47p	5.2
	7:24p	4:54p	1.1e	3:14p	3.9	4:16p	3.0	5:14p	3.2
		9:54p	1.3 f	7:19p	2.7	10:26p	7.0	11:20p	8.0
Mon. 7/3	12:36a	4:30a	2.1e	1:09a	6.1	5:59a	-1.8	6:37a	-1.9
	8:06a	11:06a	1.9 f	9:41a	-0.4	12:54p	4.4	1:34p	5.4
	3:06p	5:42p	1.2e	4:04p	4.1	5:10p	2.9	6:06p	3.1
	8:18p	10:42p	1.4 f	8:22p	2.6	11:15p	7.1		

		SAN MATEO CURRENTS			PORT CHICAGO TIDE		ARENA COVE TIDE		HUMBOLDT BAY TIDE	
		SLACK	CURRENT							
Day	Date	Time	Time	Knots	Time	Feet	Time	Feet	Time	Feet
Fri.	5/19	12:48a	4:48a	1.9e	1:37a	5.3	5:54a	-1.2	6:29a	-1.3
		8:06a	10:48a	1.7 f	9:19a	-0.4	12:31p	4.2	1:11p	5.3
		2:36p	5:30p	1.1e	3:24p	3.8	5:14p	2.3	6:06p	2.5
		8:06p	10:24p	1.3 f	8:17p	1.8	11:15p	6.3		
Sat.	5/20	1:18a	5:18a	1.8e	2:03a	5.4	6:36a	-1.3	12:10a	7.4
		8:48a	11:36a	1.7 f	10:05a	-0.3	1:24p	4.2	7:10a	-1.4
		3:30p	6:18p	1.0e	4:19p	3.9	5:54p	2.6	2:01p	5.3
		8:48p	11:06p	1.2 f	8:58p	2.2	11:50p	6.1	6:47p	2.8
Sun.	5/21	1:48a	5:48a	1.8e	2:31a	5.4	7:18a	-1.2	12:45a	7.2
		9:30a	12:18p	1.6 f	10:49a	-0.3	2:17p	4.1	7:51a	-1.3
		4:24p	7:00p	0.9e	5:14p	3.9	6:35p	2.9	2:48p	5.2
		9:30p	11:54p	1.1 f	9:42p	2.4			7:28p	3.1
Mon.	5/22	2:24a	6:24a	1.7e	3:04a	5.3	12:27a	5.9	1:21a	6.9
		10:12a	1:00p	1.4 f	11:32a	-0.2	8:00a	-1.0	8:33a	-1.1
		5:12p	7:48p	0.8e	6:08p	3.9	3:10p	4.0	3:36p	5.1
		10:18p			10:31p	2.5	7:17p	3.1	8:10p	3.3
Tue.	5/23	3:06a	12:36a	1.0 f	3:42a	5.1	1:05a	5.6	1:59a	6.6
		10:48a	7:00a	1.6e	12:13p	-0.1	8:45a	-0.8	9:15a	-0.8
		6:00p	1:48p	1.3e	7:00p	3.9	4:05p	4.0	4:24p	4.9
		11:12p	8:36p	0.8e	11:25p	2.5	8:05p	3.2	8:56p	3.5
Wed.	5/24	3:48a	1:24a	0.9 f	4:26a	4.8	1:48a	5.3	2:40a	6.2
		11:30a	7:36a	1.5e	12:54a	-0.1	9:31a	-0.4	10:00a	-0.4
		6:48p	2:36p	1.2 f	7:51p	3.9	5:00p	4.0	5:15p	4.8
			9:24p	0.8e			9:04p	3.3	9:50p	3.6
Thu.	5/25	12:12a	2:18a	0.7 f	12:25a	2.4	2:36a	4.9	3:27a	5.8
		4:42a	8:24a	1.3e	5:17a	4.4	10:20a	-0.1	10:47a	-0.1
		12:12p	3:24p	1.2 f	1:36p	0.0	5:52p	4.1	6:06p	4.8
		7:30p	10:18p	0.8e	8:40p	3.9	10:19p	3.3	10:55p	3.5
Fri.	5/26	1:18a	3:18a	0.6 f	1:33a	2.2	3:33a	4.5	4:22a	5.3
		5:42a	9:12a	1.2e	6:17a	3.9	11:10a	0.2	11:36a	0.3
		12:54p	4:12p	1.1 f	2:19p	0.1	6:35p	4.2	6:53p	4.9
		8:12p	11:12p	0.9e	9:26p	3.9	11:43p	3.0		
Sat.	5/27	2:24a	4:24a	0.6 f	2:44a	1.9	4:41a	4.1	12:10a	3.3
		6:54a	10:06a	1.0e	7:31a	3.5	11:57a	0.5	5:27a	4.9
		1:36p	4:54p	1.1 f	3:00p	0.1	7:11p	4.5	12:25p	0.6
		8:54p			10:07p	4.0			7:36p	5.2
Sun.	5/28	3:30a	12:06a	1.1e	3:54a	1.5	12:57a	2.6	1:23a	2.9
		8:12a	5:30a	0.6 f	8:57a	3.2	5:57a	3.8	6:40a	4.6
		2:24p	11:06a	0.9e	3:39p	0.3	12:41p	0.8	1:14p	1.0
		9:24p	5:42p	1.2 f	10:42p	4.1	7:41p	4.7	8:13p	5.5
Mon.	5/29	4:18a	12:48a	1.3e	4:56a	1.1	1:55a	2.0	2:26a	2.3
		9:30a	6:36a	0.8 f	10:18a	3.1	7:13a	3.7	7:54a	4.4
		3:18p	12:06p	0.9e	4:16p	0.5	1:21p	1.1	2:00p	1.3
		10:00p	6:24p	1.2 f	11:10p	4.3	8:08p	5.0	8:47p	5.8
Tue.	5/30	5:00a	1:30a	1.4e	5:52a	0.7	2:43a	1.4	3:18a	1.6
		10:36a	7:30a	1.0 f	11:28a	3.1	8:24a	3.6	9:04a	4.4
		4:12p	1:12p	0.9e	4:51p	0.8	2:00p	1.4	2:44p	1.7
		10:30p	7:12p	1.2 f	11:32p	4.6	8:35p	5.4	9:20p	6.3
Wed.	5/31	5:42a	2:06a	1.5e	6:44a	0.4	3:25a	0.7	4:03a	0.8
		11:36a	8:18a	1.2 f	12:30p	3.2	9:28a	3.7	10:09a	4.5
		5:06p	2:12p	1.0e	5:27p	1.2	2:38p	1.7	3:27p	2.0
		11:06p	7:54p	1.2 f	11:52p	4.9	9:03p	5.7	9:52p	6.7
Thu.	6/1	6:18a	2:42a	1.6e	7:32a	0.1	4:06a	0.0	4:45a	0.0
		12:30p	9:00a	1.4 f	1:29p	3.4	10:26a	3.8	11:09a	4.8
		6:00p	3:06p	1.1e	6:05p	1.6	3:16p	2.1	4:10p	2.4
		11:36p	8:42p	1.3 f			9:34p	6.1	10:26p	7.1
Fri.	6/2	6:54a	3:18a	1.8e	12:16a	5.3	4:47a	-0.7	5:26a	-0.7
		1:24p	9:48a	1.6 f	8:20a	-0.1	11:21a	4.0	12:04p	5.0
		6:54p	4:06p	1.1e	2:26p	3.5	3:57p	2.4	4:52p	2.6
			9:24p	1.3 f	6:47p	2.0	10:08p	6.4	11:01p	7.4
Sat.	6/3	12:12a	4:00a	1.9e	12:48a	5.6	5:29a	-1.2	6:08a	-1.3
		7:36a	10:30a	1.7 f	9:06a	-0.3	12:14p	4.1	12:56p	5.2
		2:18p	5:00p	1.2e	3:22p	3.7	4:39p	2.6	5:36p	2.9
		7:42p	10:12p	1.3 f	7:35p	2.3	10:46p	6.6	11:40p	7.7
Sun.	6/4	12:48a	4:48a	2.0e	1:26a	5.9	6:14a	-1.6	6:52a	-1.8
		8:18a	11:12a	1.8 f	9:53a	-0.4	1:07p	4.2	1:46p	5.3
		3:12p	5:54p	1.2e	4:18p	3.8	5:24p	2.8	6:21p	3.0
		8:30p	11:00p	1.3 f	8:28p	2.5	11:28p	6.7		
Mon.	6/5	1:36a	5:36a	2.0e	2:10a	5.9	7:00a	-1.8	12:22a	7.8
		9:06a	12:00p	1.8 f	10:40a	-0.4	2:00p	4.2	7:38a	-2.0
		4:06p	6:48p	1.2e	5:11p	3.9	6:13p	2.9	2:37p	5.3
		9:18p	11:48p	1.3 f	9:25p	2.5			7:09p	3.1
Tue.	6/6	2:24a	6:24a	2.1e	2:59a	5.9	12:14a	6.7	1:08a	7.7
		9:54a	12:48p	1.8 f	11:27a	-0.5	7:49a	-1.8	8:25a	-2.0
		5:00p	7:36p	1.2e	6:04p	3.9	2:55p	4.3	3:28p	5.3
		10:12p			10:27p	2.4	7:07p	3.0	8:01p	3.2
Wed.	6/7	3:18a	12:36a	1.3 f	3:52a	5.6	1:04a	6.5	1:58a	7.5
		10:42a	7:12a	2.0e	12:15p	-0.5	8:39a	-1.6	9:15a	-1.8
		5:54p	1:42p	1.8 f	6:55p	4.0	3:49p	4.4	4:20p	5.4
		11:12p	8:36p	1.2e	11:33p	2.3	8:11p	3.0	9:01p	3.1
Thu.	6/8	4:12a	1:30a	1.2 f	4:52a	5.2	2:00a	6.1	2:54a	7.1
		11:36a	8:06a	1.9e	1:03p	-0.4	9:31a	-1.3	10:06a	-1.5
		6:42p	2:36p	1.7 f	7:45p	4.1	4:42p	4.6	5:13p	5.5
			9:30p	1.2e			9:26p	3.0	10:09p	3.0
Fri.	6/9	12:18a	2:36a	1.1 f	12:45a	2.0	3:03a	5.5	3:56a	6.5
		5:24a	9:06a	1.7e	6:00a	4.7	10:24a	-0.9	10:58a	-1.0
		12:30p	3:30p	1.6 f	1:52p	-0.3	5:32p	4.9	6:04p	5.7
		7:30p	10:30p	1.3e	8:33p	4.2	10:52p	2.7	11:25p	2.7
Sat.	6/10	1:24a	3:42a	1.1 f	2:03a	1.7	4:16a	4.9	5:06a	5.8
		6:36a	10:06a	1.5e	7:20a	4.1	11:17a	-0.3	11:51a	-0.4
		1:24p	4:24p	1.5 f	2:41p	-0.2	6:18p	5.2	6:53p	6.1
		8:18p	11:30p	1.5e	9:21p	4.4				

SAN MATEO CURRENTS · PORT CHICAGO · ARENA COVE · HUMBOLDT BAY

Day	Date	SLACK Time	CURRENT Time	Knots	PORT CHICAGO Time	Feet	ARENA COVE Time	Feet	HUMBOLDT BAY Time	Feet
Wed.	4/26	12:30a	2:42a	0.7 f	12:45a	2.4	3:13a	4.8	4:01a	5.8
		5:12a	9:00a	1.3e	5:45a	4.4	11:08a	0.0	11:29a	0.2
		1:12p	4:30p	1.0 f	2:35p	0.2	6:49p	3.8	6:53p	4.6
		8:24p	11:00p	0.6e	9:22p	3.7	10:52p	3.3	11:22p	3.7
Thu.	4/27	1:48a	3:48a	0.6 f	2:01a	2.3	4:18a	4.5	5:02a	5.4
		6:18a	9:54a	1.1e	6:48a	4.0	12:11p	0.2	12:30p	0.5
		2:12p	5:48p	1.0 f	3:33p	0.1	7:43p	4.0	7:58p	4.7
		9:18p			10:15p	3.8				
Fri.	4/28	3:00a	12:12a	0.8e	3:19a	2.1	12:25a	3.1	12:47a	3.6
		7:36a	5:00a	0.6 f	8:12a	3.6	5:34a	4.3	6:15a	5.1
		3:06p	11:00a	1.1e	4:23p	0.1	1:07p	0.3	1:30p	0.6
		10:06p	6:36p	1.1 f	11:02p	3.9	8:21p	4.2	8:46p	4.8
Sat.	4/29	4:06a	1:12a	1.0e	4:29a	1.7	1:36a	2.7	2:04a	3.2
		8:54a	6:12a	0.7 f	9:43a	3.5	6:50a	4.2	7:28a	5.0
		3:48p	12:06p	1.0e	5:06p	0.1	1:53p	0.4	2:23p	0.7
		10:42p	7:12p	1.2 f	11:41p	4.0	8:49p	4.4	9:22p	5.1
Sun.	4/30	5:00a	1:54a	1.2e	5:28a	1.3	2:29a	2.3	3:03a	2.6
		10:00a	7:12a	0.8 f	10:55a	3.4	7:55a	4.2	8:36a	4.9
		4:30p	1:00p	1.1e	5:41p	0.2	2:32p	0.6	3:09p	0.8
		11:12p	7:42p	1.3 f			9:14p	4.6	9:53p	5.4
Mon.	5/1	5:42a	2:30a	1.4e	12:14a	4.1	3:13a	1.7	3:51a	2.0
		11:00a	8:06a	1.0 f	6:20a	0.8	8:53a	4.2	9:36a	5.0
		5:12p	1:54p	1.1e	11:54a	3.5	3:07p	0.7	3:48p	0.9
		11:36p	8:12p	1.3 f	6:11p	0.4	9:36p	4.9	10:21p	5.8
Tue.	5/2	6:18a	3:06a	1.6e	12:41a	4.3	3:52a	1.1	4:33a	1.3
		11:54a	8:48a	1.2 f	7:07a	0.5	9:45a	4.2	10:31a	5.1
		5:48p	2:42p	1.2e	12:47p	3.5	3:39p	1.0	4:24p	1.2
			8:42p	1.4 f	6:37p	0.6	9:59p	5.3	10:48p	6.2
Wed.	5/3	12:06a	3:36a	1.7e	1:00a	4.5	4:30a	0.5	5:12a	0.6
		6:54a	9:30a	1.4 f	7:51a	0.3	10:34a	4.2	11:21a	5.2
		12:42p	3:30p	1.2e	1:37p	3.5	4:10p	1.3	4:59p	1.4
		6:30p	9:18p	1.4 f	7:03p	0.9	10:24p	5.6	11:16p	6.6
Thu.	5/4	12:30a	4:00a	1.7e	1:15a	4.7	5:08a	-0.1	5:33a	-0.1
		7:24a	10:06a	1.6 f	8:34a	0.0	11:23a	4.3	12:10p	5.3
		1:30p	4:18p	1.3e	2:28p	3.6	4:42p	1.6	5:33p	1.8
		7:18p	9:54p	1.4 f	7:32p	1.3	10:50p	5.8	11:44p	6.9
Fri.	5/5	12:54a	4:36a	1.8e	1:32a	5.0	5:47a	-0.6	6:28a	-0.7
		8:00a	10:48a	1.7 f	9:16a	-0.1	12:13p	4.2	12:59p	5.4
		2:18p	5:06p	1.3e	3:20p	3.6	5:15p	1.9	6:08p	2.2
		8:00p	10:36p	1.4 f	8:07p	1.6	11:20p	6.0		
Sat.	5/6	1:24a	5:06a	1.8e	1:59a	5.4	6:28a	-1.0	12:14a	7.2
		8:36a	11:24a	1.7 f	9:58a	-0.2	1:05p	4.2	7:09a	-1.1
		3:12p	6:00p	1.3e	4:14p	3.6	5:51p	2.3	1:48p	5.3
		8:42p	11:18p	1.4 f	8:47p	1.9	11:53p	6.2	6:44p	2.5
Sun.	5/7	1:54a	5:48a	1.9e	2:33a	5.6	7:12a	-1.3	12:47a	7.3
		9:18a	12:12p	1.7 f	10:43a	-0.3	2:00p	4.1	7:51a	-1.4
		4:06p	6:48p	1.2e	5:12p	3.6	6:29p	2.6	2:40p	5.2
		9:30p	12:00p	1.3 f	9:34p	2.1			7:24p	2.8
Mon.	5/8	2:36a	6:30a	1.9e	3:14a	5.6	12:31a	6.2	1:24a	7.4
		10:06a	1:00p	1.6 f	11:31a	-0.3	8:00a	-1.4	8:37a	-1.5
		5:06p	7:42p	1.1e	6:12p	3.6	3:02p	4.0	3:34p	5.1
		10:18p			10:26p	2.3	7:13p	2.9	8:07p	3.1
Tue.	5/9	3:18a	12:48a	1.2 f	4:00a	5.5	1:14a	6.1	2:07a	7.2
		10:54a	7:24a	1.8e	12:25p	-0.3	8:53a	-1.3	9:28a	-1.4
		6:06p	1:54p	1.5 f	7:14p	3.6	4:08p	4.0	4:34p	5.0
		11:12p	8:42p	1.0e	11:27p	2.3	8:06p	3.1	9:00p	3.3
Wed.	5/10	4:18a	1:42a	1.1 f	4:54a	5.2	2:06a	5.9	2:58a	7.0
		11:54a	8:18a	1.8e	1:25p	-0.2	9:51a	-1.2	10:23a	-1.2
		7:12p	2:48p	1.4 f	8:15p	3.7	5:16p	4.0	5:37p	4.9
		9:42p		0.9e			9:18p	3.2	10:05p	3.4
Thu.	5/11	12:18a	2:42a	1.0 f	12:40a	2.3	3:08a	5.5	4:00a	6.5
		5:24a	9:18a	1.7e	5:57a	4.8	10:53a	-0.9	11:23a	-0.9
		1:00p	4:00p	1.4 f	2:27p	-0.2	6:17p	4.2	6:39p	5.1
		8:12p	10:48p	1.0e	9:11p	3.8	10:50p	3.1	11:26p	3.3
Fri.	5/12	1:36a	3:54a	1.0 f	2:04a	2.1	4:23a	5.1	5:13a	6.1
		6:42a	10:30a	1.5e	7:16a	4.3	11:54a	-0.7	12:24p	-0.6
		2:00p	5:06p	1.4 f	3:26p	-0.2	7:08p	4.5	7:36p	5.3
		9:06p	12:00p	1.2e	10:03p	4.0				
Sat.	5/13	2:48a	5:06a	1.0 f	3:29a	1.7	12:23a	2.7	12:52a	2.9
		8:06a	11:42a	1.4e	8:52a	3.9	5:47a	4.7	6:34a	5.6
		3:06p	6:00p	1.4 f	4:18p	-0.2	12:51p	-0.3	1:24p	-0.2
		9:48p			10:49p	4.3	7:50p	4.9	8:25p	5.8
Sun.	5/14	4:00a	1:00a	1.4e	4:44a	1.1	1:41a	2.0	2:11a	2.2
		9:30a	6:18a	1.1 f	10:19a	3.8	7:10a	4.5	7:55a	5.4
		4:00p	12:48p	1.4e	5:05p	-0.1	1:43p	0.0	2:20p	0.1
		10:30p	6:54p	1.5 f	11:30p	4.5	8:27p	5.3	9:09p	6.2
Mon.	5/15	4:54a	1:54a	1.4e	5:48a	0.6	2:44a	1.2	3:16a	1.3
		10:48a	7:30a	1.3 f	11:31a	3.7	8:27a	4.4	9:10a	5.2
		4:54p	1:54p	1.3e	5:47p	0.2	2:30p	0.5	3:11p	0.6
		11:06p	7:36p	1.5 f			9:02p	5.7	9:48p	6.7
Tue.	5/16	11:48a	2:42a	1.9e	12:07a	4.8	3:38a	0.4	4:12a	0.4
		5:42p	8:24a	1.5 f	6:47a	0.2	9:36a	4.3	10:20a	5.2
		11:42p	2:54p	1.3e	12:34p	3.7	3:13p	1.0	3:58p	1.0
			8:24p	1.5 f	6:26p	0.5	9:35p	6.1	10:25p	7.1
Wed.	5/17	6:36a	3:24a	1.9e	12:40a	5.0	4:26a	-0.3	5:01a	-0.4
			9:18a	1.6 f	7:40a	-0.1	10:39a	4.3	11:22a	5.3
		6:30p	3:48p	1.3e	1:32p	3.7	3:54p	1.4	4:42p	1.5
		9:06p		1.5 f	7:03p	1.0	10:08p	6.3	11:00p	7.3
Thu.	5/18	12:18a	4:06a	2.0e	1:10a	5.2	5:11a	-0.9	5:47a	-1.0
		7:24a	10:06a	1.7 f	8:31a	-0.3	11:37a	4.2	12:19p	5.3
		1:48p	4:36p	1.2e	2:28p	3.8	4:34p	1.9	5:24p	2.0
		7:18p	9:48p	1.4 f	7:39p	1.4	10:42p	6.3	11:35p	7.4

SAN MATEO CURRENTS · PORT CHICAGO · ARENA COVE · HUMBOLDT BAY

Day/Date	Slack Time	Current Time	Knots	Port Chicago Time	Feet	Arena Cove Time	Feet	Humboldt Bay Time	Feet
Mon. 4/3	12:42a	3:54a	1.5e	1:37a	4.2	4:14a	1.8	4:58a	2.0
	6:54a	9:18a	1.2 f	7:29a	1.0	10:05a	5.0	10:53a	5.9
	12:12p	3:18p	1.4e	1:04p	4.0	4:35p	0.3	5:17p	0.5
	6:42p	9:36p	1.5 f	7:45p	0.2	10:58p	4.9	11:45p	5.9
Tue. 4/4	1:06a	4:24a	1.6e	2:02a	4.2	4:51a	1.3	5:36a	1.4
	7:30a	9:54a	1.3 f	8:11a	0.7	10:46a	4.9	11:37a	6.0
	12:54p	4:00p	1.4e	1:48p	4.0	5:03p	0.5	5:47p	0.6
	7:12p	10:00p	1.6 f	8:06p	0.4	11:19p	5.1		
Wed. 4/5	1:30a	4:48a	1.6e	2:19a	4.3	5:28a	0.8	12:10a	6.2
	8:00a	10:30a	1.4 f	8:50a	0.5	11:28a	4.8	6:13a	0.9
	1:42p	4:36p	1.4e	2:31p	3.9	5:30p	0.8	12:19p	5.9
	7:42p	10:30p	1.6 f	8:26p	0.6	11:42p	5.4	6:17p	0.9
Thu. 4/6	1:48a	5:18a	1.7e	2:31a	4.5	6:05a	0.4	12:35a	6.5
	8:30a	11:06a	1.5 f	9:28a	0.3	12:12p	4.7	6:50a	0.4
	2:24p	5:18p	1.4e	3:15p	3.8	5:58p	1.1	1:03p	5.8
	8:18p	11:00p	1.5 f	8:49p	0.9			6:46p	1.3
Fri. 4/7	2:06a	5:42a	1.7e	2:46a	4.8	12:06a	5.6	1:00a	6.7
	9:00a	11:48a	1.6 f	10:05a	0.2	6:44a	0.0	7:27a	0.0
	3:12p	6:06p	1.4e	4:03p	3.7	12:58p	4.5	1:48p	5.7
	8:54p	11:36p	1.5 f	9:19p	1.1	6:27p	1.6	7:16p	1.7
Sat. 4/8	2:30a	6:12a	1.7e	3:10a	5.1	12:33a	5.7	1:27a	6.9
	9:36a	12:24p	1.6 f	10:44a	0.1	7:26a	-0.3	8:07a	-0.3
	4:00p	6:54p	1.3e	4:57p	3.6	1:50p	4.2	2:36p	5.4
	9:36p			9:56p	1.4	6:57p	2.0	7:48p	2.2
Sun. 4/9	3:00a	12:18a	1.4 f	3:43a	5.3	1:03a	5.8	1:56a	7.0
	10:18a	6:48a	1.7e	11:28a	0.1	8:12a	-0.5	8:51a	-0.5
	4:54p	1:06p	1.5 f	6:00p	3.4	2:50p	3.9	3:29p	5.1
	10:24p	7:42p	1.1e	10:38p	1.7	7:30p	2.4	8:23p	2.7
Mon. 4/10	3:36a	1:06a	1.2 f	4:22a	5.4	1:39a	5.8	2:30a	7.0
	11:06a	7:36a	1.7e	12:23p	0.1	9:05a	-0.6	9:41a	-0.5
	6:00p	2:00p	1.4 f	7:13p	3.4	4:01p	3.7	4:30p	4.8
	11:12p	8:42p	0.9e	11:29p	2.0	8:09p	2.8	9:03p	3.1
Tue. 4/11	4:24a	1:54a	1.1 f	5:09a	5.2	2:23a	5.7	3:13a	6.9
	12:06p	8:24a	1.6e	1:35p	0.2	10:07a	-0.6	10:38a	-0.5
	7:18p	3:00p	1.2 f	8:29p	3.4	5:25p	3.6	5:41p	4.6
		9:48p	0.8e			9:03p	3.1	9:56p	3.4
Wed. 4/12	12:18a	2:54a	1.0 f	12:31a	2.2	3:20a	5.5	4:08a	6.7
	5:24a	9:30a	1.5e	6:05a	5.0	11:16a	-0.5	11:43a	-0.4
	1:18p	4:12p	1.2 f	2:54p	0.1	6:50p	3.8	7:00p	4.6
	8:36p	11:00p	0.7e	9:38p	3.5	10:29p	3.3	11:12p	3.6
Thu. 4/13	1:36a	4:06a	0.9 f	1:52a	2.3	4:32a	5.3	5:20a	6.4
	6:42a	10:42a	1.5e	7:16a	4.6	12:26p	-0.6	12:53p	-0.3
	2:36p	5:36p	1.2 f	4:05p	0.0	7:52p	4.0	8:12p	4.8
	9:42p			10:37p	3.7				
Fri. 4/14	3:00a	12:18a	0.9e	3:25a	2.1	12:13a	3.1	12:46a	3.5
	8:12a	5:18a	0.9 f	8:48a	4.3	5:56a	5.2	6:43a	6.2
	3:42p	12:00p	1.5e	5:03p	-0.2	1:29p	-0.6	2:00p	-0.4
	10:36p	6:48p	1.3 f	11:27p	4.0	8:36p	4.4	9:08p	5.2
Sat. 4/15	4:06a	1:24a	1.1e	4:46a	1.7	1:38a	2.6	2:12a	2.9
	9:36a	6:30a	1.1 f	10:22a	4.3	7:17a	5.2	8:04a	6.1
	4:36p	1:12p	1.6e	5:53p	-0.3	2:23p	-0.6	2:59p	-0.4
	11:18p	7:42p	1.5 f			9:12p	4.8	9:53p	5.6
Sun. 4/16	5:12a	2:24a	1.4e	12:10a	4.2	2:44a	1.9	3:22a	2.1
	10:48a	7:36a	1.3 f	5:53a	1.1	8:29a	5.2	9:17a	6.2
	5:24p	2:12p	1.7e	11:37a	4.3	3:11p	-0.4	3:51p	-0.3
	11:54p	8:18p	1.6 f	6:36p	-0.2	9:45p	5.2	10:31p	6.1
Mon. 4/17	6:06a	3:12a	1.7e	12:48a	4.4	3:40a	1.2	4:20a	1.3
	11:48a	8:36a	1.5 f	6:52a	0.6	9:33a	5.2	10:22a	6.2
	6:12p	3:06p	1.7e	12:38p	4.3	3:53p	-0.1	4:36p	-0.1
		9:00p	1.7 f	7:14p	-0.1	10:17p	5.6	11:07p	6.6
Tue. 4/18	12:30a	3:54a	1.9e	1:22a	4.7	4:31a	0.4	5:11a	0.4
	6:54a	9:30a	1.7 f	7:46a	0.2	10:32a	5.1	11:21a	6.2
	12:48p	4:00p	1.6e	1:34p	4.2	4:33p	0.3	5:18p	0.3
	6:54p	9:36p	1.7 f	7:49p	0.2	10:49p	5.9	11:41p	7.0
Wed. 4/19	1:00a	4:36a	2.0e	1:53a	4.9	5:19a	-0.2	5:59a	-0.3
	7:42a	10:18a	1.8 f	8:37a	0.0	11:28a	4.9	12:16p	6.1
	1:42p	4:48p	1.5e	2:28p	4.1	5:11p	0.8	5:58p	0.8
	7:36p	10:12p	1.7 f	8:23p	0.6	11:21p	6.1		
Thu. 4/20	1:30a	5:18a	2.0e	2:21a	5.0	6:05a	-0.7	12:15a	7.3
	8:24a	11:00a	1.8 f	9:26a	-0.2	12:22p	4.7	6:44a	-0.8
	2:36p	5:36p	1.4e	3:22p	4.0	5:48p	1.3	1:08p	5.9
	8:24p	10:54p	1.6 f	8:55p	1.0	11:53p	6.2	6:36p	1.4
Fri. 4/21	2:00a	5:48a	1.9e	2:47a	5.1	6:50a	-1.0	12:48a	7.4
	9:06a	11:48a	1.7 f	10:14a	-0.3	1:18p	4.4	7:28a	-1.1
	3:30p	6:24p	1.3e	4:18p	3.9	6:25p	1.8	1:59p	5.7
	9:06p	11:36p	1.4 f	9:29p	1.4			7:15p	2.0
Sat. 4/22	2:30a	6:24a	1.8e	3:13a	5.2	12:26a	6.1	1:21a	7.3
	9:48a	12:30p	1.6 f	11:01a	-0.2	7:35a	-1.0	8:11a	-1.1
	4:18p	7:06p	1.1e	5:16p	3.8	2:15p	4.2	2:51p	5.4
	9:48p			10:07p	1.8	7:03p	2.3	7:53p	2.5
Sun. 4/23	3:00a	12:18a	1.3 f	3:42a	5.1	1:01a	5.9	1:55a	7.1
	10:30a	6:54a	1.7e	11:49a	-0.1	8:21a	-0.9	8:55a	-0.9
	5:18p	1:18p	1.4 f	6:17p	3.7	3:16p	4.0	3:44p	5.1
	10:36p	7:54p	0.9e	10:50p	2.1	7:42p	2.7	8:33p	3.0
Mon. 4/24	3:36a	1:00a	1.1 f	4:15a	5.0	1:39a	5.6	2:31a	6.7
	11:18a	7:30a	1.5e	12:40p	0.0	9:11a	-0.6	9:42a	-0.5
	6:18p	2:12p	1.2 f	7:20p	3.7	4:24p	3.8	4:41p	4.9
	11:24p	8:48p	0.7e	11:42p	2.3	8:27p	3.0	9:18p	3.4
Tue. 4/25	4:18a	1:48a	0.9 f	4:56a	4.7	2:21a	5.2	3:12a	6.3
	12:12p	8:06a	1.4e	1:36p	0.1	10:07a	-0.3	10:32a	-0.2
	7:24p	3:12p	1.1 f	8:23p	3.7	5:38p	3.8	5:44p	4.7
		9:48p	0.6e			9:26p	3.2	10:11p	3.6

		SAN MATEO CURRENTS			PORT CHICAGO		ARENA COVE		HUMBOLDT BAY	
		SLACK	CURRENT		TIDE		TIDE		TIDE	
		Time	Time	Knots	Time	Feet	Time	Feet	Time	Feet
Sat. 3/11		2:42a	6:24a	1.6e	3:25a	4.8	12:51a	5.5	1:42a	6.7
		9:42a	12:30p	1.3 f	10:35a	0.6	7:30a	0.7	8:10a	0.8
		3:48p	6:48p	1.2e	4:40p	3.5	1:36p	4.2	2:22p	5.4
		9:30p			10:04p	1.1	7:01p	1.8	7:49p	2.0
Sun. 3/12		4:12a	12:24a	1.3 f	4:59a	5.0	1:22a	5.6	3:11a	6.8
		11:24a	8:00a	1.5e	12:26p	0.5	9:23a	0.5	10:00a	0.7
		5:48p	2:18p	1.2 f	6:54p	3.3	3:42p	3.7	4:21p	4.9
		11:18p	8:42p	1.0e	11:46p	1.5	8:32p	2.3	9:22p	2.6
Mon. 3/13		4:48a	2:12a	1.2 f	5:40a	5.1	2:59a	5.6	3:47a	6.9
		12:24p	8:42a	1.5e	1:39p	0.6	10:26a	0.3	10:57a	0.5
		7:06p	3:18p	1.1 f	8:25p	3.2	5:10p	3.5	5:34p	4.5
			9:42p	0.8e			9:10p	2.8	10:02p	3.1
Tue. 3/14		12:18a	3:12a	1.0 f	12:38a	1.9	3:48a	5.6	4:34a	6.9
		5:42a	9:42a	1.4e	6:30a	5.1	11:40a	0.1	12:05p	0.4
		1:36p	4:30p	1.0 f	3:14p	0.5	6:57p	3.5	7:03p	4.4
		8:42p	11:00p	0.6e	9:52p	3.3	10:11p	3.2	11:00p	3.6
Wed. 3/15		1:30a	4:18a	0.9 f	1:45a	2.2	4:52a	5.6	5:37a	6.8
		6:48a	10:54a	1.4e	7:32a	4.9	12:54p	-0.2	1:19p	0.2
		2:54p	5:54p	1.1 f	4:35p	0.4	8:25p	3.7	8:35p	4.5
		10:06p			11:02p	3.5	11:50p	3.3		
Thu. 3/16		3:00a	12:30a	0.7e	3:10a	2.4	6:08a	5.7	12:32a	3.8
		8:12a	5:30a	0.9 f	8:49a	4.8	2:00p	-0.5	6:54a	6.8
		4:06p	12:18p	1.5e	5:39p	0.0	9:16p	4.0	2:30p	-0.2
		11:06p	7:18p	1.2 f	11:59p	3.8			9:44p	4.8
Fri. 3/17		4:12a	1:42a	0.9e	4:38a	2.2	1:25a	3.1	2:06a	3.6
		9:36a	6:42a	1.1 f	10:18a	4.8	7:25a	5.9	8:13a	6.9
		5:06p	1:30p	1.7e	6:31p	-0.2	2:57p	-0.8	3:32p	-0.5
		12:00p	8:18p	1.5 f			9:54p	4.4	10:33p	5.3
Sat. 3/18		5:18a	2:42a	1.2e	12:45a	4.0	2:38a	2.7	3:22a	3.0
		10:48a	7:48a	1.3 f	5:52a	1.8	8:33a	6.1	9:24a	7.1
		6:00p	2:30p	1.9e	11:36a	4.9	3:46p	-1.0	4:24p	-0.8
			9:00p	1.7 f	7:17p	-0.4	10:28p	4.8	11:12p	5.7
Sun. 3/19		12:36a	3:36a	1.5e	1:26a	4.2	3:39a	2.1	4:24a	2.3
		6:18a	8:42a	1.5 f	6:54a	1.4	9:35a	6.2	10:26a	7.3
		11:48a	3:30p	2.0e	12:40p	5.0	4:30p	-0.9	5:11p	-0.9
		6:42p	9:36p	1.9 f	7:58p	-0.4	11:00p	5.2	11:49p	6.2
Mon. 3/20		1:18a	4:24a	1.7e	2:03a	4.4	4:34a	1.4	5:18a	1.5
		7:12a	9:36a	1.6 f	7:50a	0.9	10:31a	6.1	11:24a	7.3
		12:48p	4:18p	2.0e	1:37p	4.9	5:10p	-0.7	5:53p	-0.7
		7:24p	10:12p	1.9 f	8:34p	-0.3	11:33p	5.5		
Tue. 3/21		1:48a	5:06a	1.9e	2:37a	4.6	5:25a	0.8	12:24a	6.7
		8:00a	10:30a	1.8 f	8:43a	0.6	11:25a	5.9	6:09a	0.8
		1:42p	5:00p	1.9e	2:30p	4.7	5:49p	-0.3	12:17p	7.2
		8:06p	10:48p	2.0 f	9:08p	0.0			6:32p	-0.4
Wed. 3/22		2:24a	5:48a	2.0e	3:09a	4.7	12:05a	5.8	12:58a	7.0
		8:42a	11:18a	1.8 f	9:34a	0.3	6:15a	0.3	6:58a	0.2
		2:36p	5:48p	1.8e	3:23p	4.5	12:19p	5.6	1:09p	6.8
		8:48p	11:24p	1.9 f	9:40p	0.3	6:25p	0.2	7:10p	0.2
Thu. 3/23		2:54a	6:24a	2.0e	3:38a	4.8	12:38a	6.0	1:31a	7.3
		9:30a	12:00p	1.7 f	10:24a	0.1	7:05a	-0.1	7:45a	-0.1
		3:30p	6:36p	1.6e	4:17p	4.2	1:13p	5.1	2:01p	6.4
		9:24p			10:11p	0.6	7:01p	0.9	7:48p	0.9
Fri. 3/24		3:24a	12:06a	1.7 f	4:06a	4.9	1:12a	6.1	2:05a	7.3
		10:12a	7:00a	1.9e	11:15a	0.1	7:54a	-0.2	8:33a	-0.3
		4:24p	12:48p	1.6 f	5:15p	3.9	2:11p	4.6	2:53p	5.9
		10:06p	7:18p	1.3e	10:44p	1.0	7:37p	1.5	8:25p	1.6
Sat. 3/25		3:54a	12:42a	1.5 f	4:35a	5.0	1:47a	6.0	2:40a	7.2
		11:00a	7:36a	1.7e	12:08p	0.1	8:46a	-0.2	9:21a	-0.2
		5:24p	1:36p	1.4 f	6:19p	3.7	3:15p	4.1	3:49p	5.4
		10:54p	8:06p	1.1e	11:21p	1.5	8:15p	2.2	9:03p	2.4
Sun. 3/26		4:24a	1:30a	1.3 f	5:06a	4.9	2:25a	5.7	3:16a	7.0
		11:54a	8:06a	1.5e	1:07p	0.2	9:42a	-0.1	10:12a	0.0
		6:30p	2:36p	1.2 f	7:30p	3.5	4:29p	3.8	4:51p	4.9
		11:48p	9:06p	0.8e			8:56p	2.7	9:44p	3.0
Mon. 3/27		5:00a	2:18a	1.0 f	12:07a	1.9	3:08a	5.4	3:57a	6.6
		12:54p	8:54a	1.4e	5:43a	4.7	10:46a	0.1	11:09a	0.3
		7:48p	3:48p	1.0 f	2:14p	0.3	6:00p	3.6	6:04p	4.6
			10:12p	0.6e	8:44p	3.5	9:49p	3.1	10:34p	3.5
Tue. 3/28		12:54a	3:12a	0.8 f	1:05a	2.2	4:00a	5.1	4:46a	6.2
		5:48a	9:42a	1.2e	6:30a	4.5	11:58a	0.2	12:13p	0.6
		2:00p	5:24p	1.0 f	3:25p	0.3	7:35p	3.7	7:33p	4.5
		9:06p	11:42p	0.6e	9:53p	3.6	11:13p	3.3	11:44p	3.8
Wed. 3/29		2:06a	4:18a	0.6 f	2:21a	2.4	5:07a	4.8	5:47a	5.8
		6:54a	10:48a	1.1e	7:33a	4.2	1:08p	0.3	1:23p	0.7
		3:12p	6:54p	1.1 f	4:30p	0.2	8:42p	3.9	9:00p	4.6
		10:12p			10:54p	3.8				
Thu. 3/30		3:24a	12:54a	0.7e	3:44a	2.3	12:51a	3.3	1:12a	3.8
		8:12a	5:30a	0.6 f	9:00a	4.0	6:24a	4.7	7:00a	5.6
		4:12p	12:06p	1.1e	5:24p	0.1	2:07p	0.2	2:29p	0.7
		11:06p	7:48p	1.2 f	11:45p	4.0	9:22p	4.0	9:54p	4.8
Fri. 3/31		4:30a	1:54a	0.9e	4:55a	2.0	2:02a	3.0	2:32a	3.6
		9:24a	6:42a	0.7 f	10:24a	3.9	7:34a	4.7	8:12a	5.6
		4:54p	1:12p	1.2e	6:10p	0.0	2:55p	0.2	3:24p	0.6
		11:42p	8:30p	1.3 f			9:51p	4.2	10:29p	5.0
Sat. 4/1		5:24a	2:42a	1.1e	12:28a	4.1	2:54a	2.6	3:31a	3.1
		10:30a	7:42a	0.9 f	5:53a	1.7	8:32a	4.8	9:14a	5.7
		5:36p	2:00p	1.3e	11:27a	4.0	3:33p	0.2	4:08p	0.5
			9:00p	1.4 f	6:48p	0.0	10:15p	4.4	10:56p	5.2
Sun. 4/2		12:12a	3:18a	1.3e	1:05a	4.2	3:36a	2.2	4:18a	2.6
		6:12a	8:30a	1.0 f	6:44a	1.3	9:21a	4.9	10:06a	5.8
		11:24a	2:42p	1.3e	12:19p	4.0	4:06p	0.2	4:44p	0.4
		6:06p	9:18p	1.5 f	7:19p	0.1	10:36p	4.6	11:21p	5.5

SAN MATEO CURRENTS   PORT CHICAGO   ARENA COVE   HUMBOLDT BAY

	SLACK	CURRENT		TIDE		TIDE		TIDE	
	Time	Time	Knots	Time	Feet	Time	Feet	Time	Feet
Thu. **2/16**	3:18a	12:48a	0.8e	3:27a	2.4	12:14a	3.3	1:03a	3.9
	8:42a	5:54a	1.1 f	9:20a	5.3	6:37a	6.4	7:26a	7.5
	4:30p	12:42p	1.7e	5:59p	-0.1	2:21p	-0.8	2:57p	-0.5
	11:24p	7:36p	1.5 f			9:26p	4.2	10:02p	5.1
Fri. **2/17**	4:30a	1:54a	1.0e	12:13a	3.9	1:31a	3.2	2:21a	3.7
	9:48a	6:54a	1.2 f	4:43a	2.3	7:40a	6.7	8:31a	7.9
	5:24p	1:48p	2.0e	10:32a	5.5	3:12p	-1.2	3:50p	-1.1
		8:24p	1.7 f	6:48p	-0.4	10:04p	4.6	10:46p	5.6
Sat. **2/18**	12:12a	2:54a	1.2e	12:59a	4.1	2:36a	2.8	3:26a	3.2
	5:30a	7:54a	1.4 f	5:51a	2.1	8:39a	7.0	9:32a	8.1
	10:54a	2:42p	2.1e	11:37a	5.6	3:58p	-1.4	4:37p	-1.4
	6:12p	9:06p	1.9 f	7:32p	-0.5	10:40p	4.9	11:26p	6.0
Sun. **2/19**	12:54a	3:42a	1.5e	1:41a	4.3	3:34a	2.4	4:23a	2.6
	6:24a	8:48a	1.6 f	6:52a	1.7	9:34a	7.0	10:28a	8.3
	11:48a	3:36p	2.2e	12:36p	5.6	4:41p	-1.4	5:21p	-1.5
	6:54p	9:48p	2.0 f	8:13p	-0.5	11:15p	5.2		
Mon. **2/20**	1:36a	4:30a	1.7e	2:19a	4.4	4:29a	1.9	12:03a	6.4
	7:12a	9:42a	1.7 f	7:48a	1.4	10:28a	6.9	5:17a	2.0
	12:42p	4:24p	2.2e	1:31p	5.4	5:22p	-1.2	11:22a	8.1
	7:36p	10:24p	2.1 f	8:50p	-0.5	11:50p	5.5	6:03p	-1.3
Tue. **2/21**	2:12a	5:18a	1.8e	2:56a	4.5	5:24a	1.5	12:40a	6.7
	8:06a	10:30a	1.7 f	8:42a	1.0	11:20a	6.5	6:09a	1.5
	1:36p	5:06p	2.1e	2:25p	5.1	6:01p	-0.7	12:14p	7.8
	8:12p	11:00p	2.1 f	9:24p	-0.3			6:43p	-0.8
Wed. **2/22**	2:42a	6:00a	1.9e	3:31a	4.6	12:26a	5.8	1:16a	7.0
	8:54a	11:18a	1.7 f	9:36a	0.8	6:18a	1.1	7:01a	1.1
	2:30p	5:54p	1.8e	3:19p	4.7	12:14p	5.9	1:05p	7.2
	8:54p	11:42p	1.9 f	9:57p	0.0	6:39p	-0.1	7:22p	-0.2
Thu. **2/23**	3:18a	6:36a	1.9e	4:04a	4.7	1:03a	5.9	1:53a	7.2
	9:42a	12:12p	1.5 f	10:31a	0.6	7:14a	0.9	7:54a	0.9
	3:30p	6:36p	1.6e	4:17p	4.3	1:11p	5.2	1:59p	6.5
	9:36p			10:29p	0.4	7:16p	0.7	8:00p	0.7
Fri. **2/24**	3:48a	12:18a	1.7 f	4:38a	4.8	1:40a	6.0	2:30a	7.3
	10:36a	7:18a	1.8e	11:29a	0.5	8:13a	0.7	8:49a	0.8
	4:30p	1:06p	1.4 f	5:22p	3.8	2:15p	4.5	2:56p	5.8
	10:18p	7:30p	1.3e	11:03p	0.8	7:53p	1.5	8:38p	1.5
Sat. **2/25**	4:24a	1:06a	1.5 f	5:12a	4.8	2:20a	5.9	3:09a	7.2
	11:30a	8:00a	1.6e	12:35p	0.5	9:18a	0.7	9:47a	0.8
	5:36p	2:00p	1.2 f	6:37p	3.5	3:31p	3.9	4:01p	5.1
	11:12p	8:24p	0.9e	11:44p	1.3	8:34p	2.2	9:19p	2.4
Sun. **2/26**	5:00a	1:54a	1.2 f	5:51a	4.7	3:04a	5.8	3:51a	7.0
	12:30p	8:42a	1.4e	1:48p	0.5	10:30a	0.6	10:50a	0.9
	7:00p	3:12p	1.0 f	7:57p	3.3	5:07p	3.6	5:19p	4.6
		9:30p	0.7e			9:22p	2.8	10:06p	3.2
Mon. **2/27**	12:18a	2:48a	0.9 f	12:36a	1.8	3:55a	5.6	4:39a	6.7
	5:42a	9:42a	1.3e	6:38a	4.6	11:45a	0.5	12:00p	0.9
	1:42p	4:48p	1.0 f	3:03p	0.4	6:58p	3.6	6:58p	4.4
	8:30p	11:00p	0.6e	9:14p	3.4	10:32p	3.2	11:08p	3.7
Tue. **2/28**	1:30a	3:48a	0.7 f	1:43a	2.2	4:56a	5.4	5:36a	6.5
	6:42a	10:54a	1.2e	7:37a	4.5	12:54p	0.3	1:12p	0.8
	2:54p	6:18p	1.1 f	4:10p	0.3	8:21p	3.9	8:41p	4.6
	9:48p			10:22p	3.7				
Wed. **3/1**	2:48a	12:24a	0.6e	3:00a	2.3	12:01a	3.4	12:29a	4.0
	7:48a	5:00a	0.7 f	8:47a	4.5	6:02a	5.3	6:40a	6.4
	3:54p	12:12p	1.3e	5:07p	0.1	1:52p	0.1	2:16p	0.7
	10:48p	7:24p	1.3 f	11:18p	3.9	9:08p	4.1	9:44p	4.9
Thu. **3/2**	3:48a	1:30a	0.8e	4:11a	2.3	1:15a	3.3	1:48a	3.9
	8:48a	6:00a	0.7 f	9:54a	4.5	7:05a	5.4	7:44a	6.4
	4:42p	1:12p	1.4e	5:55p	-0.1	2:40p	0.0	3:09p	0.4
	11:36p	8:12p	1.4 f			9:41p	4.2	10:22p	5.1
Fri. **3/3**	4:48a	2:18a	0.9e	12:06a	4.1	2:10a	3.1	2:49a	3.6
	9:48a	7:00a	0.9 f	5:11a	2.1	7:58a	5.5	8:41a	6.5
	5:24p	1:54p	1.5e	10:49a	4.5	3:19p	-0.1	3:52p	0.2
		8:48p	1.5 f	6:36p	-0.1	10:08p	4.3	10:50p	5.3
Sat. **3/4**	12:12a	3:00a	1.1e	12:47a	4.2	2:53a	2.8	3:37a	3.3
	5:36a	7:54a	1.0 f	6:02a	1.9	8:43a	5.6	9:30a	6.6
	10:36a	2:24p	1.5e	11:36a	4.5	3:52p	-0.2	4:28p	0.0
	5:54p	9:12p	1.6 f	7:10p	-0.1	10:31p	4.5	11:15p	5.5
Sun. **3/5**	12:36a	3:36a	1.3e	1:23a	4.2	3:32a	2.5	4:18a	2.8
	6:18a	8:36a	1.1 f	6:47a	1.6	9:23a	5.7	10:13a	6.7
	11:24a	2:54p	1.6e	12:18p	4.5	4:22p	-0.1	5:00p	0.0
	6:24p	9:30p	1.6 f	7:39p	0.0	10:53p	4.7	11:39p	5.7
Mon. **3/6**	1:06a	4:06a	1.4e	1:54a	4.2	4:09a	2.2	4:56a	2.4
	7:00a	9:18a	1.2 f	7:28a	1.4	10:01a	5.6	10:52a	6.7
	12:06p	3:30p	1.6e	12:56p	4.5	4:50p	0.0	5:30p	0.0
	6:54p	9:48p	1.6 f	8:02p	0.1	11:15p	4.8		
Tue. **3/7**	1:30a	4:36a	1.5e	2:18a	4.2	4:45a	1.9	12:03a	5.9
	7:36a	9:54a	1.3 f	8:07a	1.2	10:38a	5.5	5:33a	2.1
	12:48p	4:00p	1.6e	1:35p	4.4	5:16p	0.2	11:31a	6.6
	7:18p	10:12p	1.6 f	8:20p	0.2	11:38p	5.0	5:58p	0.2
Wed. **3/8**	1:48a	5:00a	1.5e	2:36a	4.2	5:23a	1.5	12:27a	6.1
	8:06a	10:30a	1.3 f	8:43a	0.9	11:16a	5.3	6:10a	1.7
	1:30p	4:36p	1.5e	2:14p	4.2	5:41p	0.5	12:09p	6.4
	7:42p	10:36p	1.6 f	8:37p	0.3			6:25p	0.5
Thu. **3/9**	2:06a	5:24a	1.6e	2:47a	4.3	12:01a	5.2	12:52a	6.4
	8:36a	11:06a	1.4 f	9:18a	0.8	6:02a	1.2	6:47a	1.4
	2:12p	5:18p	1.5e	2:56p	4.0	11:57a	5.0	12:50p	6.1
	8:12p	11:06p	1.6 f	8:59p	0.5	6:07p	0.9	6:52p	0.9
Fri. **3/10**	2:24a	5:54a	1.6e	3:01a	4.6	12:25a	5.4	1:16a	6.5
	9:06a	11:48a	1.4 f	9:54a	0.6	6:43a	1.0	7:27a	1.1
	2:54p	6:00p	1.4e	3:44p	3.8	12:43p	4.6	1:33p	5.8
	8:48p	11:42p	1.5 f	9:28p	0.7	6:33p	1.3	7:20p	1.5

SAN MATEO CURRENTS | PORT CHICAGO | ARENA COVE | HUMBOLDT BAY

	SLACK	CURRENT		TIDE		TIDE		TIDE	
	Time	Time	Knots	Time	Feet	Time	Feet	Time	Feet
Tue. **1/24**	3:30a	6:30a	1.7e	4:19a	4.4	1:13a	5.5	1:58a	6.6
	9:18a	11:36a	1.5 f	9:48a	1.4	6:29a	2.3	7:14a	2.4
	2:36p	6:12p	2.0 e	3:22p	5.1	12:18p	6.6	1:11p	7.8
	9:24p			10:39p	-0.4	7:13p	-0.8	7:53p	-1.0
Wed. **1/25**	4:06a	12:18a	2.0 f	4:59a	4.5	1:54a	5.7	2:39a	6.8
	10:12a	7:12a	1.7e	10:47a	1.2	7:31a	2.1	8:12a	2.1
	3:36p	12:30p	1.4 f	4:22p	4.6	1:16p	5.8	2:07p	7.0
	10:06p	7:00p	1.8e	11:16p	-0.1	7:55p	-0.1	8:35p	-0.2
Thu. **1/26**	4:42a	1:00a	1.8 f	5:39a	4.5	2:36a	5.9	3:20a	7.0
	11:06a	8:00a	1.7e	11:51a	1.0	8:39a	1.8	9:14a	1.9
	4:42p	1:30p	1.3 f	5:29p	4.0	2:20p	5.0	3:06p	6.1
	10:54p	7:48p	1.4e	11:53p	0.3	8:36p	0.7	9:17p	0.7
Fri. **1/27**	5:24a	1:42a	1.6 f	6:21a	4.6	3:19a	6.0	4:03a	7.1
	12:06p	8:48a	1.6e	1:02p	0.8	9:53a	1.5	10:21a	1.7
	5:54p	2:30p	1.1 f	6:46p	3.6	3:36p	4.2	4:13p	5.3
	11:42p	8:48p	1.1e			9:19p	1.6	10:00p	1.6
Sat. **1/28**	6:00a	2:30a	1.4 f	12:34a	0.7	4:04a	6.0	4:47a	7.2
	1:12p	9:42a	1.5e	7:05a	4.7	11:11a	1.2	11:32a	1.4
	7:12p	3:42p	1.1 f	2:17p	0.6	5:10p	3.7	5:33p	4.7
		9:54p	0.8e	8:08p	3.3	10:07p	2.3	10:48p	2.5
Sun. **1/29**	12:42a	3:24a	1.1 f	1:21a	1.2	4:52a	6.0	5:34a	7.2
	6:42a	10:42a	1.4e	7:52a	4.7	12:25p	0.7	12:44p	1.1
	2:18p	5:12p	1.1 f	3:31p	0.4	6:58p	3.7	7:10p	4.5
	8:42p	11:18p	0.7e	9:28p	3.3	11:05p	2.9	11:44p	3.3
Mon. **1/30**	1:54a	4:24a	0.9 f	2:16a	1.7	5:43a	6.0	6:25a	7.1
	7:30a	11:48a	1.4e	8:41a	4.8	1:29p	0.3	1:51p	0.8
	3:18p	6:36p	1.2 f	4:38p	0.2	8:30p	3.8	8:52p	4.6
	10:06p			10:39p	3.5				
Tue. **1/31**	3:06a	12:42a	0.7e	3:19a	2.0	12:13a	3.3	12:51a	3.8
	8:24a	5:24a	0.8 f	9:31a	4.9	6:35a	6.0	7:18a	7.1
	4:18p	12:54p	1.5e	5:35p	0.0	2:23p	0.0	2:49p	0.4
	11:12p	7:42p	1.3 f	11:40p	3.8	9:32p	4.1	10:05p	4.9
Wed. **2/1**	4:06a	1:48a	0.7e	4:21a	2.3	1:20a	3.4	2:00a	4.0
	9:12a	6:24a	0.8 f	10:19a	4.9	7:27a	6.0	8:11a	7.1
	5:06p	1:42p	1.5e	6:25p	-0.1	3:08p	-0.2	3:38p	0.2
		8:30p	1.5 f			10:15p	4.3	10:53p	5.2
Thu. **2/2**	12:06a	2:42a	0.8e	12:32a	4.0	2:17a	3.4	3:00a	3.9
	5:06a	7:18a	1.0 f	5:19a	2.4	8:14a	6.1	9:00a	7.1
	10:06a	2:24p	1.6e	11:04a	5.0	3:48p	-0.3	4:20p	-0.1
	5:54p	9:18p	1.6 f	7:08p	-0.2	10:48p	4.4	11:28p	5.4
Fri. **2/3**	12:48a	3:30a	0.9e	1:18a	4.2	3:04a	3.3	3:49a	3.8
	5:54a	8:06a	1.0 f	6:12a	2.4	8:57a	6.1	9:46a	7.2
	10:54a	3:00p	1.7e	11:44a	5.0	4:24p	-0.4	4:57p	-0.2
	6:30p	9:48p	1.6 f	7:47p	-0.2	11:16p	4.5	11:57p	5.5
Sat. **2/4**	1:24a	4:12a	1.0e	1:59a	4.3	3:44a	3.1	4:32a	3.5
	6:36a	8:54a	1.0 f	6:59a	2.3	9:36a	6.2	10:27a	7.3
	11:36a	3:24p	1.7e	12:23p	5.0	4:56p	-0.4	5:31p	-0.3
	7:06p	10:12p	1.6 f	8:20p	-0.1	11:42p	4.6		
Sun. **2/5**	1:54a	4:42a	1.1e	2:36a	4.2	4:22a	2.9	12:23a	5.6
	7:18a	9:30a	1.1 f	7:42a	2.1	10:13a	6.1	5:12a	3.3
	12:18p	3:54p	1.7e	1:00p	4.9	5:26p	-0.4	11:06a	7.2
	7:30p	10:30p	1.6 f	8:47p	-0.1			6:03p	-0.4
Mon. **2/6**	2:18a	5:12a	1.2e	3:08a	4.2	12:08a	4.7	12:50a	5.7
	8:00a	10:12a	1.1 f	8:22a	1.9	5:00a	2.8	5:50a	3.1
	12:54p	4:24p	1.7e	1:38p	4.8	10:49a	6.0	11:42a	7.1
	7:54p	10:48p	1.6 f	9:08p	-0.1	5:54p	-0.2	6:33p	-0.3
Tue. **2/7**	2:42a	5:42a	1.3e	3:35a	4.1	12:33a	4.8	1:16a	5.9
	8:36a	10:54a	1.1 f	8:59a	1.6	5:39a	2.6	6:28a	2.9
	1:36p	5:00p	1.6e	2:17p	4.6	11:25a	5.8	12:19p	6.9
	8:18p	11:12p	1.6 f	9:24p	0.0	6:21p	0.0	7:02p	0.0
Wed. **2/8**	3:06a	6:06a	1.4e	3:55a	4.1	12:59a	5.0	1:43a	6.0
	9:12a	11:36a	1.1 f	9:37a	1.4	6:20a	2.4	7:07a	2.6
	2:18p	5:36p	1.5e	2:58p	4.4	12:02p	5.5	12:56p	6.6
	8:42p	11:42p	1.6 f	9:42p	0.0	6:48p	0.3	7:29p	0.3
Thu. **2/9**	3:24a	6:36a	1.4e	4:09a	4.1	1:25a	5.1	2:10a	6.2
	9:48a	12:12p	1.1 f	10:15a	1.2	7:04a	2.2	7:49a	2.4
	3:00p	6:18p	1.4e	3:43p	4.1	12:44p	5.0	1:36p	6.1
	9:12p			10:07p	0.2	7:14p	0.8	7:57p	0.8
Fri. **2/10**	3:42a	12:18a	1.6 f	4:25a	4.3	1:51a	5.2	2:38a	6.4
	10:24a	7:06a	1.4e	10:59a	1.1	7:54a	2.0	8:35a	2.2
	3:48p	1:00p	1.1 f	4:35p	3.7	1:32p	4.5	2:23p	5.6
	9:48p	7:00p	1.2e	10:39p	0.5	7:41p	1.3	8:25p	1.4
Sat. **2/11**	4:00a	12:54a	1.4 f	4:51a	4.5	2:21a	5.4	3:07a	6.6
	11:06a	7:36a	1.4e	11:51a	1.0	8:51a	1.7	9:27a	1.9
	4:48p	1:48p	1.0 f	5:41p	3.3	2:34p	4.0	3:19p	5.1
	10:36p	7:54p	1.0e	11:18p	0.9	8:11p	1.8	8:56p	2.0
Sun. **2/12**	4:36a	1:36a	1.3 f	5:27a	4.8	2:55a	5.5	3:40a	6.7
	12:00p	8:18a	1.4e	1:03p	0.9	9:57a	1.3	10:28a	1.6
	6:06p	2:42p	1.0 f	7:13p	3.1	3:56p	3.6	4:31p	4.6
	11:30p	8:54p	0.8e			8:46p	2.4	9:32p	2.7
Mon. **2/13**	5:18a	2:30a	1.1 f	12:04a	1.4	3:37a	5.7	4:21a	6.9
	1:06p	9:12a	1.4e	6:11a	4.9	11:11a	0.9	11:37a	1.2
	7:42p	3:48p	1.0 f	2:35p	0.8	5:44p	3.4	6:02p	4.3
		10:06p	0.7e	8:54p	3.1	9:33p	2.9	10:20p	3.3
Tue. **2/14**	12:42a	3:36a	1.0 f	1:00a	1.9	4:29a	5.9	5:13a	7.1
	6:18a	10:18a	1.4e	7:05a	5.1	12:22p	0.3	12:49p	0.7
	2:18p	5:06p	1.0 f	3:58p	0.5	7:31p	3.6	7:42p	4.4
	9:12p	11:30p	0.7e	10:16p	3.3	10:47p	3.2	11:33p	3.7
Wed. **2/15**	2:00a	4:42a	1.0 f	2:09a	2.3	5:31a	6.1	6:17a	7.3
	7:24a	11:30a	1.5e	8:09a	5.2	1:26p	-0.3	1:57p	0.1
	3:30p	6:24p	1.2 f	5:04p	0.2	8:40p	3.9	9:05p	4.7
	10:24p			11:20p	3.6				

	SAN MATEO CURRENTS			PORT CHICAGO		ARENA COVE		HUMBOLDT BAY	
	SLACK	CURRENT		TIDE		TIDE		TIDE	
	Time	Time	Knots	Time	Feet	Time	Feet	Time	Feet
Sun. 1/1	2:24a	5:00a	1.2 f	3:03a	1.0	6:29a	6.3	12:29a	2.5
	8:24a	12:24p	1.6e	9:34a	4.9	1:52p	0.5	7:13a	7.4
	3:42p	6:42p	1.2 f	4:55p	0.1	8:19p	3.9	2:20p	.7
	10:12p			10:48p	3.4			8:47p	4.7
Mon. 1/2	3:24a	12:54a	0.8e	3:51a	1.4	12:43a	2.8	1:25a	3.1
	9:06a	5:54a	1.0 f	10:13a	5.1	7:10a	6.4	7:56a	7.5
	4:36p	1:18p	1.7e	5:51p	-0.1	2:42p	0.0	3:12p	0.2
	11:18p	7:42p	1.4 f	11:50p	3.6	9:29p	4.1	10:02p	4.9
Tue. 1/3	4:24a	2:00a	0.8e	4:40a	1.8	1:35a	3.1	2:20a	3.5
	9:42a	6:48a	1.0 f	10:49a	5.2	7:51a	6.5	8:39a	7.6
	5:24p	2:06p	1.7e	6:42p	-0.3	3:26p	-0.3	3:57p	-0.2
		8:42p	1.5 f			10:24p	4.3	10:59p	5.2
Wed. 1/4	12:18a	2:54a	0.9e	12:46a	3.8	2:25a	3.4	3:12a	3.8
	5:18p	7:36a	1.0 f	5:28a	2.2	8:30a	6.5	9:20a	7.6
	10:24a	2:42p	1.7e	11:22a	5.2	4:06p	-0.5	4:38p	-0.4
	6:12p	9:24p	1.6 f	7:28p	-0.3	11:07p	4.4	11:44p	5.4
Thu. 1/5	1:06a	3:48a	0.9e	1:37a	4.0	3:11a	3.4	4:00a	3.8
	6:06a	8:18a	1.0 f	6:17a	2.4	9:09a	6.5	10:00a	7.6
	11:06a	3:18p	1.7e	11:54a	5.2	4:43p	-0.6	5:15p	-0.5
	6:54p	10:06p	1.6 f	8:10p	-0.2	11:44p	4.5		
Fri. 1/6	1:54a	4:30a	0.9e	2:24a	4.1	3:53a	3.5	12:21a	5.5
	6:54a	9:06a	1.0 f	7:03a	2.5	9:46a	6.4	4:43a	3.8
	11:42a	3:48p	1.7e	12:27p	5.2	5:18p	-0.6	10:38a	7.5
	7:30p	10:36p	1.6 f	8:47p	-0.2			5:52p	-0.6
Sat. 1/7	2:30a	5:06a	0.9e	3:08a	4.1	12:18a	4.6	12:54a	5.6
	7:36a	9:48a	1.0 f	7:49a	2.5	4:33a	3.4	5:24a	3.8
	12:24p	4:18p	1.7e	1:02p	5.2	10:23a	6.3	11:16a	7.5
	8:00p	11:06p	1.5 f	9:20p	-0.1	5:52p	-0.5	6:26p	-0.6
Sun. 1/8	3:06a	5:42a	1.0e	3:47a	4.1	12:51a	4.6	1:26a	5.6
	8:18a	10:30a	1.0 f	8:32a	2.4	5:12a	3.4	6:03a	3.7
	1:06p	4:48p	1.7e	1:40p	5.0	10:59a	6.2	11:53a	7.3
	8:30p	11:30p	1.5 f	9:47p	-0.1	6:25p	-0.4	7:00p	-0.5
Mon. 1/9	3:30a	6:18a	1.0e	4:23a	4.0	1:23a	4.7	1:58a	5.7
	9:00a	11:12a	1.0 f	9:14a	2.2	5:53a	3.3	6:43a	3.6
	1:42p	5:18p	1.6e	2:22p	4.8	11:36a	6.0	12:29p	7.0
	8:54p	11:54p	1.5 f	10:08p	-0.1	6:57p	-0.2	7:33p	-0.3
Tue. 1/10	4:00a	6:48a	1.1e	4:55a	3.9	1:55a	4.7	2:30a	5.7
	9:42a	11:54a	0.9 f	9:57a	2.0	6:37a	3.2	7:25a	3.5
	2:24p	6:00p	1.5e	3:05p	4.6	12:13p	5.7	1:06p	6.7
	9:12p			10:28p	-0.1	7:28p	0.1	8:05p	0.0
Wed. 1/11	4:24a	12:24a	1.5 f	5:24a	3.9	2:27a	4.8	3:03a	5.8
	10:30a	7:18a	1.2e	10:42a	1.8	7:26a	3.1	8:11a	3.4
	3:06p	12:42p	0.9 f	3:53p	4.2	12:54p	5.3	1:46p	6.3
	9:42p	6:36p	1.4e	10:52p	-0.1	7:59p	0.5	8:37p	0.4
Thu. 1/12	4:48a	12:54a	1.5 f	5:48a	3.9	2:59a	5.0	3:36a	6.0
	11:12a	7:54a	1.2e	11:33a	1.6	8:24a	3.0	9:03a	3.3
	4:00p	1:30p	0.8 f	4:46p	3.8	1:42p	4.8	2:33p	5.7
	10:18p	7:24p	1.3e	11:24p	0.1	8:30p	0.9	9:09p	0.9
Fri. 1/13	5:12a	1:30a	1.4 f	6:11a	4.0	3:31a	5.2	4:10a	6.2
	12:00p	8:30a	1.3e	12:33p	1.4	9:30a	2.7	10:04a	3.0
	5:00p	2:24p	0.8 f	5:51p	3.4	2:43p	4.2	3:30p	5.2
	11:00p	8:12p	1.1e			9:04p	1.4	9:43p	1.5
Sat. 1/14	5:42a	2:18a	1.3 f	12:02a	0.4	4:04a	5.4	4:45a	6.4
	12:54p	9:12a	1.3e	6:39a	4.2	10:42a	2.2	11:10a	2.5
	6:18p	3:18p	0.8 f	1:46p	1.2	4:03p	3.8	4:45p	4.7
	11:54p	9:18p	0.9e	7:17p	3.1	9:41p	2.0	10:22p	2.2
Sun. 1/15	6:18a	3:12a	1.2 f	12:46a	0.9	4:40a	5.7	12:19p	1.9
	1:48p	10:00a	1.3e	7:15a	4.5	11:51a	1.6	6:14a	4.4
	7:48p	4:24p	0.9 f	3:05p	0.9	5:43p	3.5	11:10p	2.8
		10:24p	0.8e	8:56p	3.0	10:27p	2.5		
Mon. 1/16	1:06a	4:06a	1.1 f	1:36a	1.4	5:22a	6.0	6:07a	7.1
	7:06a	10:54a	1.4e	7:58a	4.9	12:53p	0.8	1:24p	1.1
	2:48p	5:30p	1.1 f	4:18p	0.6	7:23p	3.6	7:48p	4.4
	9:12p	11:42p	0.8e	10:21p	3.1	11:24p	2.9		
Tue. 1/17	2:18a	5:12a	1.1 f	2:33a	1.8	6:08a	6.3	12:11a	3.3
	8:00a	11:54a	1.6e	8:47a	5.2	1:49p	0.0	6:56a	7.5
	3:48p	6:36p	1.3 f	5:21p	0.2	8:42p	3.9	2:23p	0.3
	10:30p			11:31p	3.4			9:11p	4.7
Wed. 1/18	3:36a	12:54a	0.8e	3:35a	2.2	12:29a	3.2	1:21a	3.7
	9:00a	6:12a	1.1 f	9:41a	5.5	6:59a	6.7	7:49a	7.9
	4:42p	12:54p	1.7e	6:17p	-0.1	2:40p	-0.7	3:17p	-0.5
	11:36p	7:42p	1.5 f			9:40p	4.2	10:16p	5.1
Thu. 1/19	4:42a	2:06a	0.9e	12:31a	3.7	1:34a	3.3	2:29a	3.8
	10:00a	7:12a	1.2 f	4:40a	2.4	7:52a	7.0	8:44a	8.2
	5:36p	1:54p	2.0e	10:37a	5.8	3:30p	-1.2	4:08p	-1.2
		8:36p	1.7 f	7:09p	-0.3	10:28p	4.5	11:08p	5.5
Fri. 1/20	12:30a	3:06a	1.1e	1:24a	4.0	2:36a	3.2	3:31a	3.6
	5:36a	8:06a	1.4 f	5:46a	2.4	8:46a	7.3	9:39a	8.5
	10:54a	2:54p	2.1e	11:34a	5.9	4:17p	-1.6	4:56p	-1.6
	6:30p	9:24p	1.9 f	7:57p	-0.5	11:11p	4.8	11:53p	5.8
Sat. 1/21	1:24a	4:00a	1.3e	2:11a	4.1	3:35a	3.1	4:28a	3.4
	6:36a	9:00a	1.5 f	6:50a	2.3	9:39a	7.5	10:33a	8.7
	11:54a	3:48p	2.3e	12:32p	5.9	5:03p	-1.8	5:43p	-1.9
	7:18p	10:12p	2.0 f	8:41p	-0.6	11:52p	5.0		
Sun. 1/22	2:06a	4:54a	1.5e	2:56a	4.2	4:32a	2.8	12:35a	6.1
	7:30a	9:54a	1.6 f	7:51a	2.0	10:31a	7.4	5:23a	3.0
	12:48p	4:36p	2.3e	1:28p	5.8	5:48p	-1.7	11:26a	8.7
	8:00p	10:54p	2.1 f	9:23p	-0.6			6:27p	-1.9
Mon. 1/23	2:48a	5:42a	1.6e	3:38a	4.3	12:32a	5.2	1:17a	6.4
	8:24a	10:48a	1.6 f	8:50a	1.7	5:30a	2.6	6:18a	2.7
	1:42p	5:24p	2.2e	2:24p	5.6	11:24a	7.1	12:18p	8.4
	8:42p	11:36p	2.1 f	10:02p	-0.6	6:31p	-1.4	7:11p	-1.5

S.F. BAY CURRENTS

3 Hours After Maximum Ebb At S.F. Bay Entrance

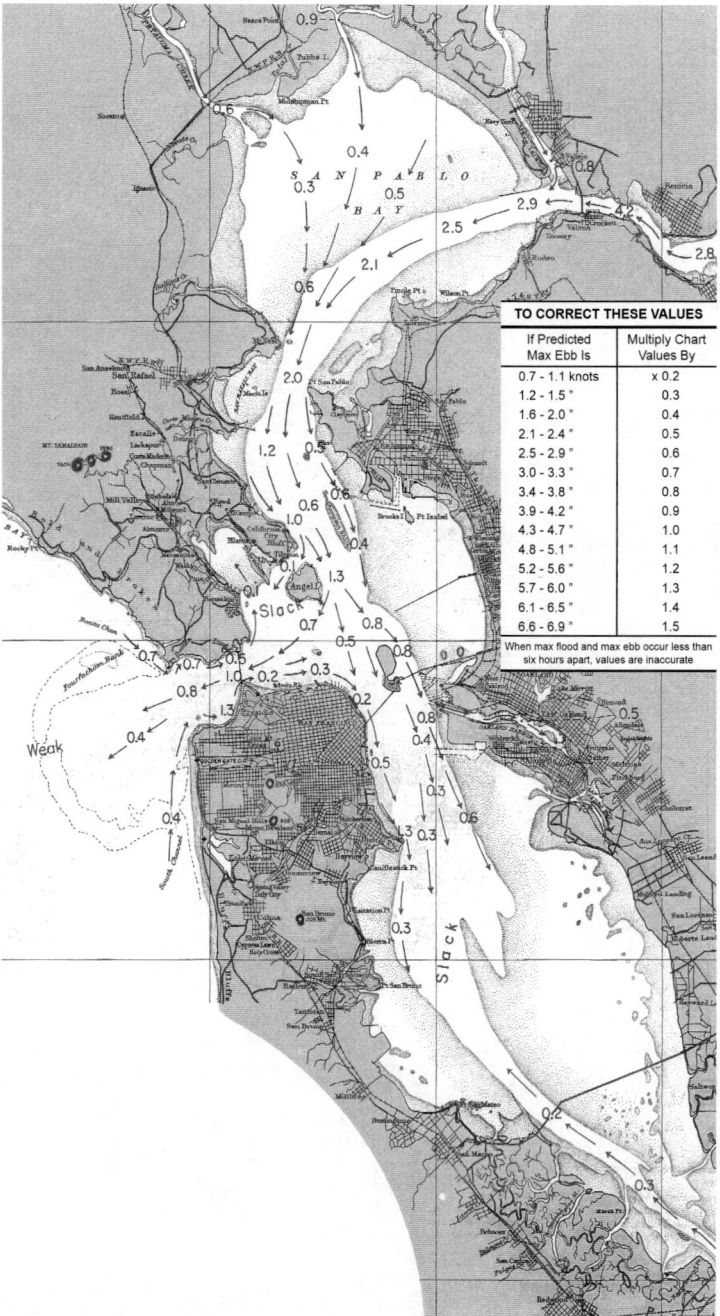

TO CORRECT THESE VALUES

If Predicted Max Ebb Is	Multiply Chart Values By
0.7 - 1.1 knots	x 0.2
1.2 - 1.5 "	0.3
1.6 - 2.0 "	0.4
2.1 - 2.4 "	0.5
2.5 - 2.9 "	0.6
3.0 - 3.3 "	0.7
3.4 - 3.8 "	0.8
3.9 - 4.2 "	0.9
4.3 - 4.7 "	1.0
4.8 - 5.1 "	1.1
5.2 - 5.6 "	1.2
5.7 - 6.0 "	1.3
6.1 - 6.5 "	1.4
6.6 - 6.9 "	1.5

When max flood and max ebb occur less than six hours apart, values are inaccurate

S.F. BAY CURRENTS

2 Hours After Maximum Ebb At S.F. Bay Entrance

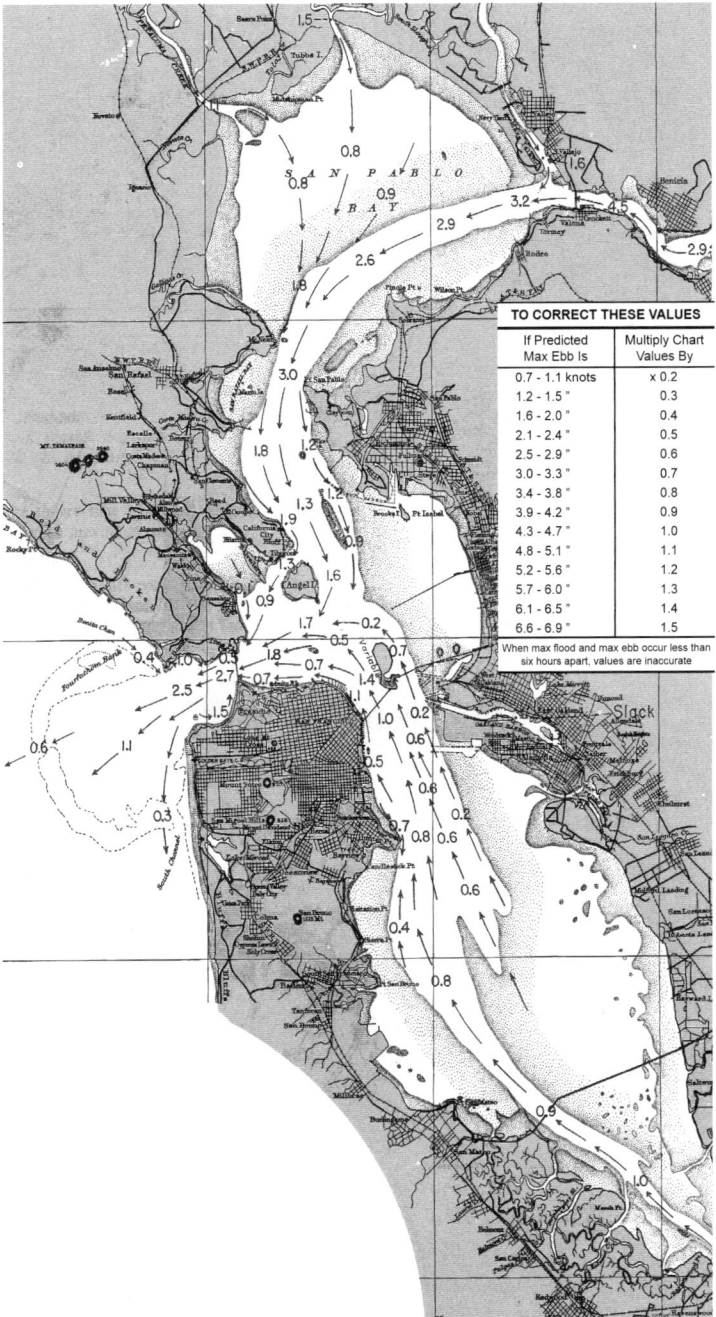

TO CORRECT THESE VALUES

If Predicted Max Ebb Is	Multiply Chart Values By
0.7 - 1.1 knots	x 0.2
1.2 - 1.5 "	0.3
1.6 - 2.0 "	0.4
2.1 - 2.4 "	0.5
2.5 - 2.9 "	0.6
3.0 - 3.3 "	0.7
3.4 - 3.8 "	0.8
3.9 - 4.2 "	0.9
4.3 - 4.7 "	1.0
4.8 - 5.1 "	1.1
5.2 - 5.6 "	1.2
5.7 - 6.0 "	1.3
6.1 - 6.5 "	1.4
6.6 - 6.9 "	1.5

When max flood and max ebb occur less than six hours apart, values are inaccurate

S.F. BAY CURRENTS

1 HOUR AFTER MAXIMUM EBB AT S.F. BAY ENTRANCE

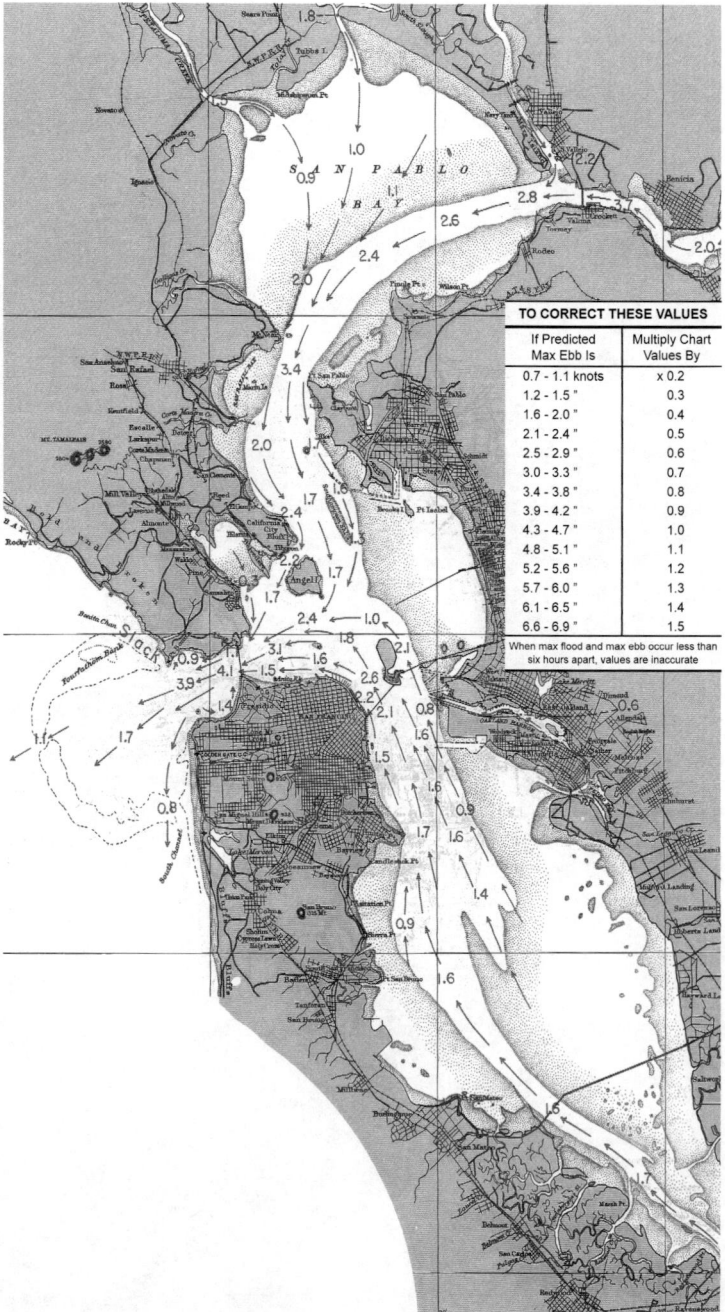

TO CORRECT THESE VALUES

If Predicted Max Ebb Is	Multiply Chart Values By
0.7 - 1.1 knots	x 0.2
1.2 - 1.5 "	0.3
1.6 - 2.0 "	0.4
2.1 - 2.4 "	0.5
2.5 - 2.9 "	0.6
3.0 - 3.3 "	0.7
3.4 - 3.8 "	0.8
3.9 - 4.2 "	0.9
4.3 - 4.7 "	1.0
4.8 - 5.1 "	1.1
5.2 - 5.6 "	1.2
5.7 - 6.0 "	1.3
6.1 - 6.5 "	1.4
6.6 - 6.9 "	1.5

When max flood and max ebb occur less than six hours apart, values are inaccurate

S.F. BAY CURRENTS

Maximum Ebb At S.F. Bay Entrance

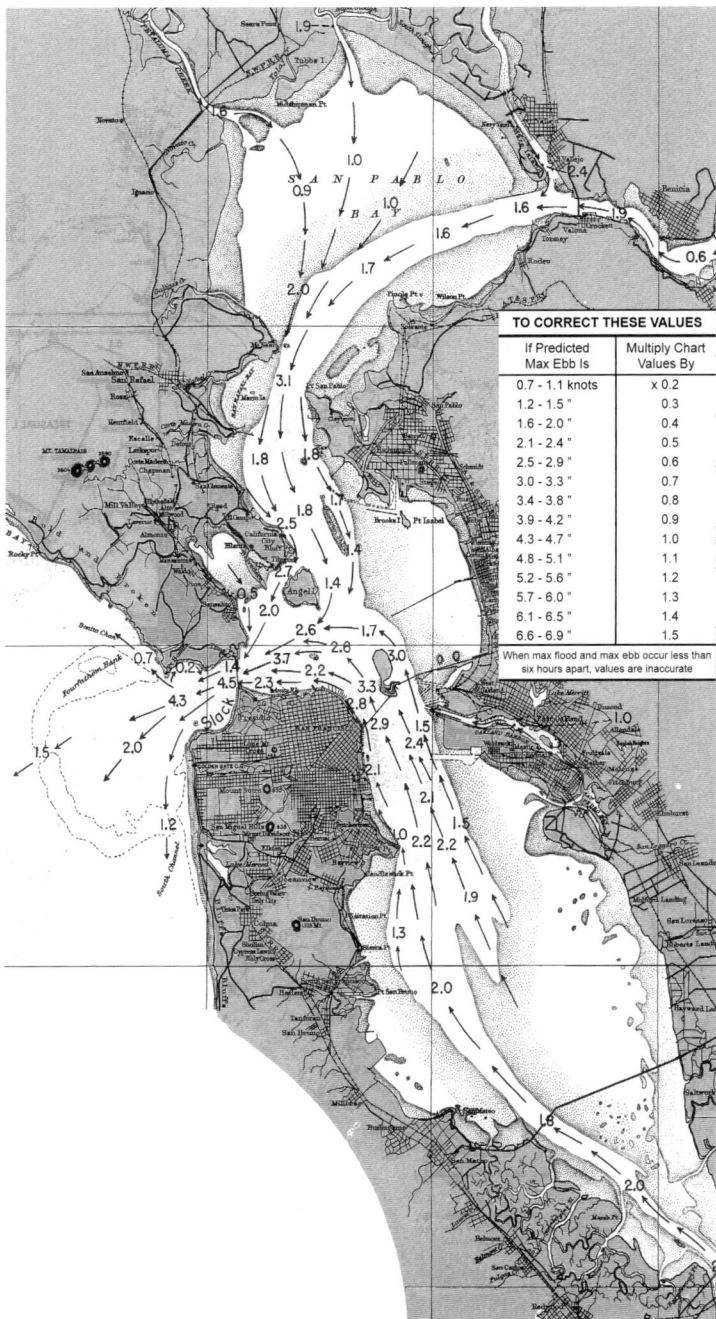

TO CORRECT THESE VALUES

If Predicted Max Ebb Is	Multiply Chart Values By
0.7 - 1.1 knots	x 0.2
1.2 - 1.5 "	0.3
1.6 - 2.0 "	0.4
2.1 - 2.4 "	0.5
2.5 - 2.9 "	0.6
3.0 - 3.3 "	0.7
3.4 - 3.8 "	0.8
3.9 - 4.2 "	0.9
4.3 - 4.7 "	1.0
4.8 - 5.1 "	1.1
5.2 - 5.6 "	1.2
5.7 - 6.0 "	1.3
6.1 - 6.5 "	1.4
6.6 - 6.9 "	1.5

When max flood and max ebb occur less than six hours apart, values are inaccurate

S.F. BAY CURRENTS

1 Hour Before Maximum Ebb At S.F. Bay Entrance

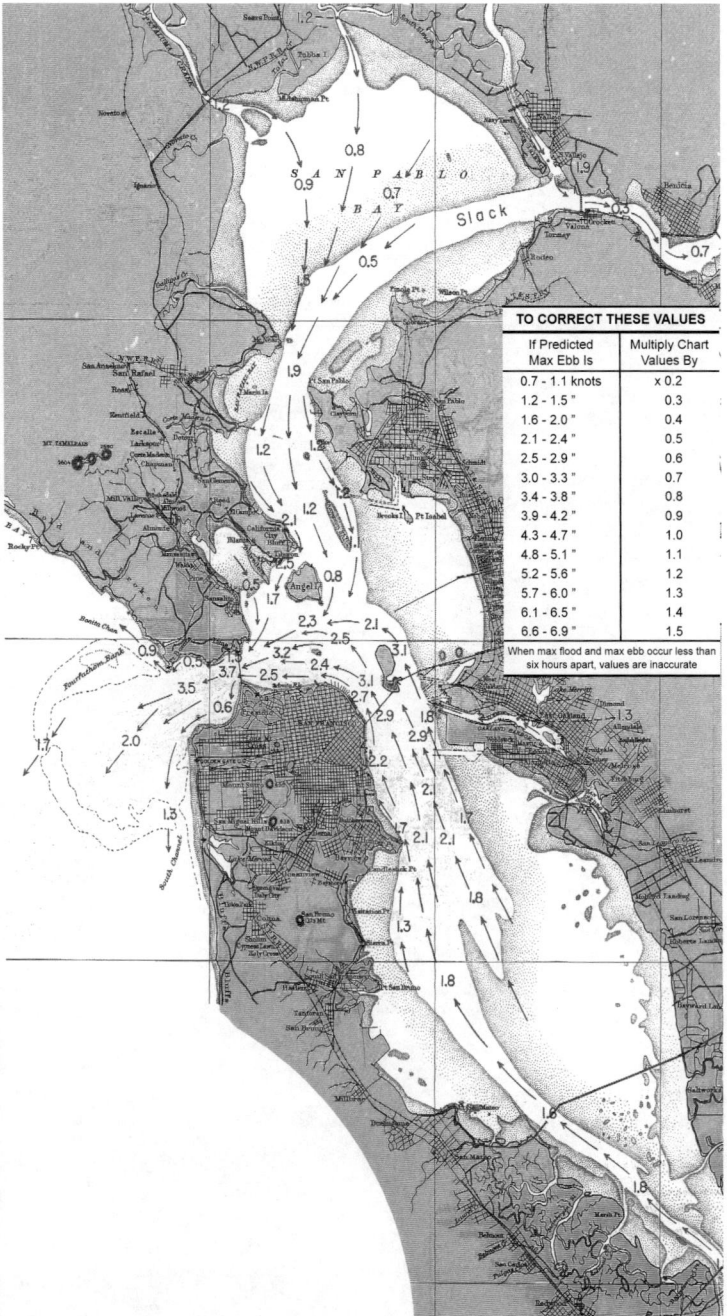

TO CORRECT THESE VALUES

If Predicted Max Ebb Is	Multiply Chart Values By
0.7 - 1.1 knots	x 0.2
1.2 - 1.5 "	0.3
1.6 - 2.0 "	0.4
2.1 - 2.4 "	0.5
2.5 - 2.9 "	0.6
3.0 - 3.3 "	0.7
3.4 - 3.8 "	0.8
3.9 - 4.2 "	0.9
4.3 - 4.7 "	1.0
4.8 - 5.1 "	1.1
5.2 - 5.6 "	1.2
5.7 - 6.0 "	1.3
6.1 - 6.5 "	1.4
6.6 - 6.9 "	1.5

When max flood and max ebb occur less than six hours apart, values are inaccurate

S.F. BAY CURRENTS

2 Hours Before Maximum Ebb At S.F. Bay Entrance

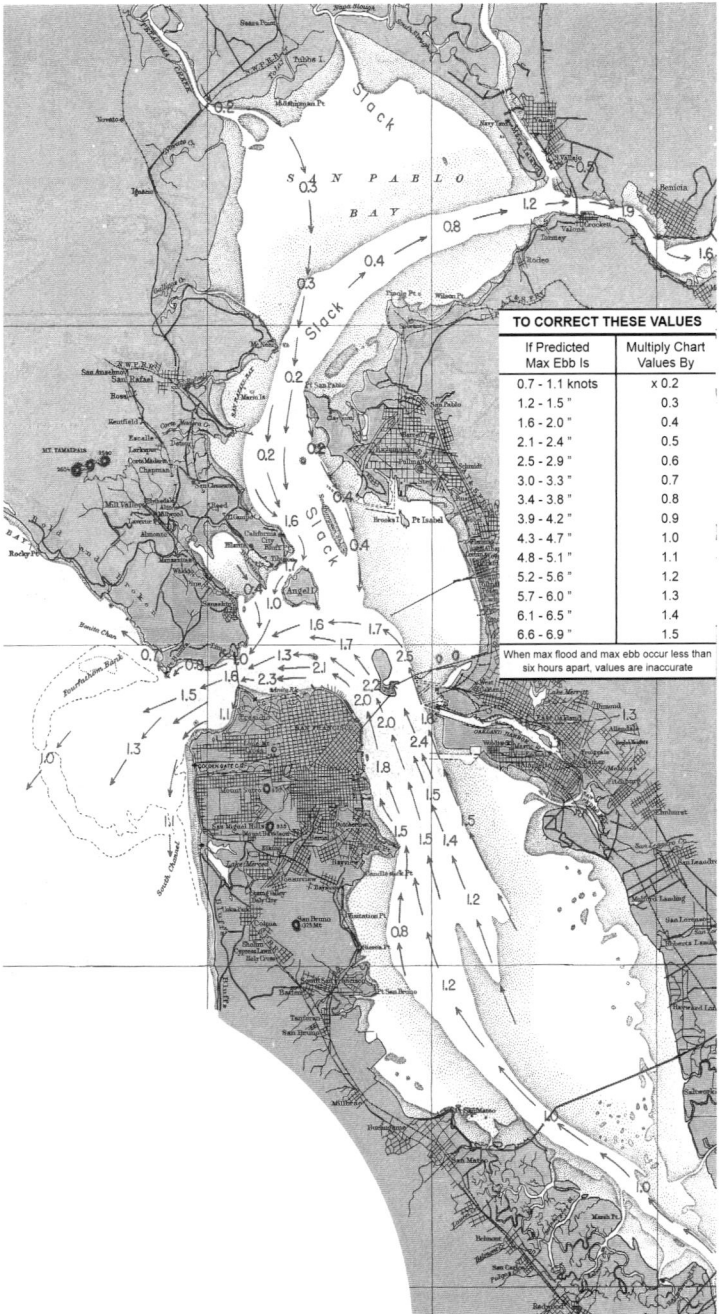

TO CORRECT THESE VALUES	
If Predicted Max Ebb Is	Multiply Chart Values By
0.7 - 1.1 knots	x 0.2
1.2 - 1.5 "	0.3
1.6 - 2.0 "	0.4
2.1 - 2.4 "	0.5
2.5 - 2.9 "	0.6
3.0 - 3.3 "	0.7
3.4 - 3.8 "	0.8
3.9 - 4.2 "	0.9
4.3 - 4.7 "	1.0
4.8 - 5.1 "	1.1
5.2 - 5.6 "	1.2
5.7 - 6.0 "	1.3
6.1 - 6.5 "	1.4
6.6 - 6.9 "	1.5

When max flood and max ebb occur less than
six hours apart, values are inaccurate

S.F. BAY CURRENTS

3 Hours After Maximum Flood At S.F. Bay Entrance

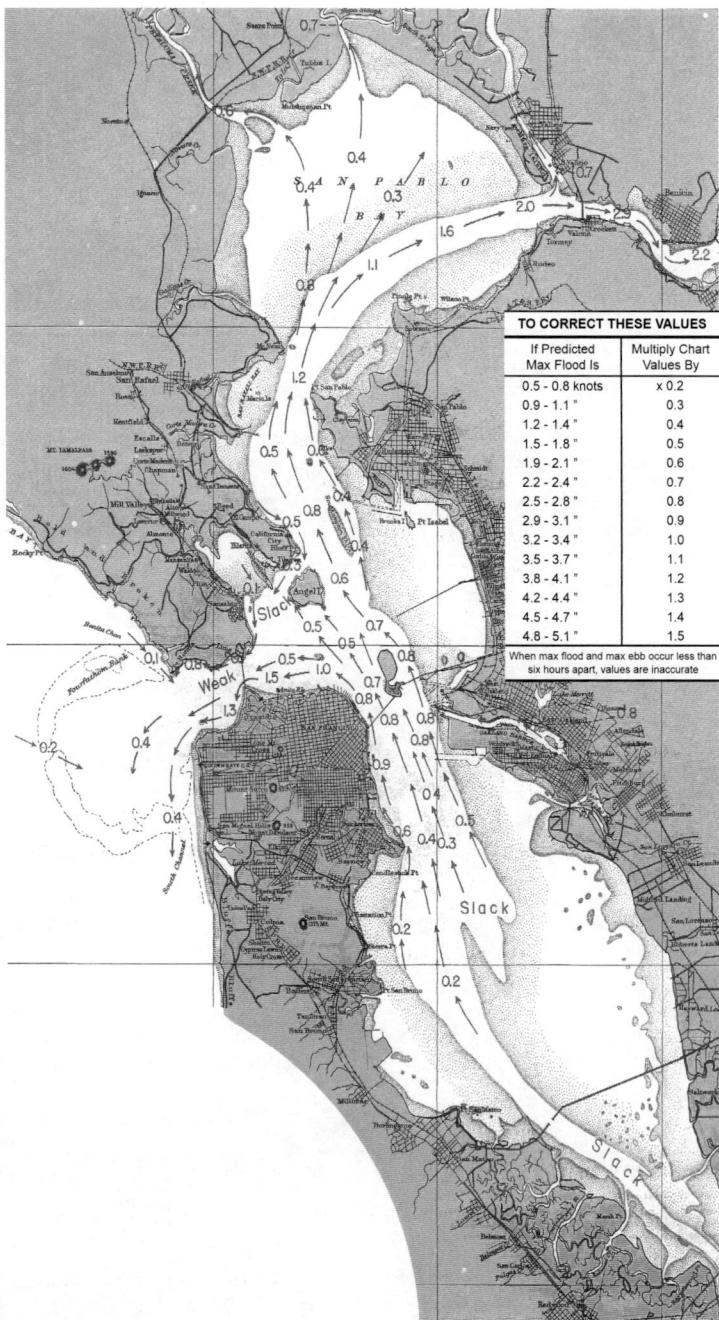

TO CORRECT THESE VALUES

If Predicted Max Flood Is	Multiply Chart Values By
0.5 - 0.8 knots	x 0.2
0.9 - 1.1 "	0.3
1.2 - 1.4 "	0.4
1.5 - 1.8 "	0.5
1.9 - 2.1 "	0.6
2.2 - 2.4 "	0.7
2.5 - 2.8 "	0.8
2.9 - 3.1 "	0.9
3.2 - 3.4 "	1.0
3.5 - 3.7 "	1.1
3.8 - 4.1 "	1.2
4.2 - 4.4 "	1.3
4.5 - 4.7 "	1.4
4.8 - 5.1 "	1.5

When max flood and max ebb occur less than six hours apart, values are inaccurate

S.F. BAY CURRENTS

2 Hours After Maximum Flood At S.F. Bay Entrance

TO CORRECT THESE VALUES

If Predicted Max Flood Is	Multiply Chart Values By
0.5 - 0.8 knots	x 0.2
0.9 - 1.1 "	0.3
1.2 - 1.4 "	0.4
1.5 - 1.8 "	0.5
1.9 - 2.1 "	0.6
2.2 - 2.4 "	0.7
2.5 - 2.8 "	0.8
2.9 - 3.1 "	0.9
3.2 - 3.4 "	1.0
3.5 - 3.7 "	1.1
3.8 - 4.1 "	1.2
4.2 - 4.4 "	1.3
4.5 - 4.7 "	1.4
4.8 - 5.1 "	1.5

When max flood and max ebb occur less than six hours apart, values are inaccurate

S.F. BAY CURRENTS

1 Hour After Maximum Flood At S.F. Bay Entrance

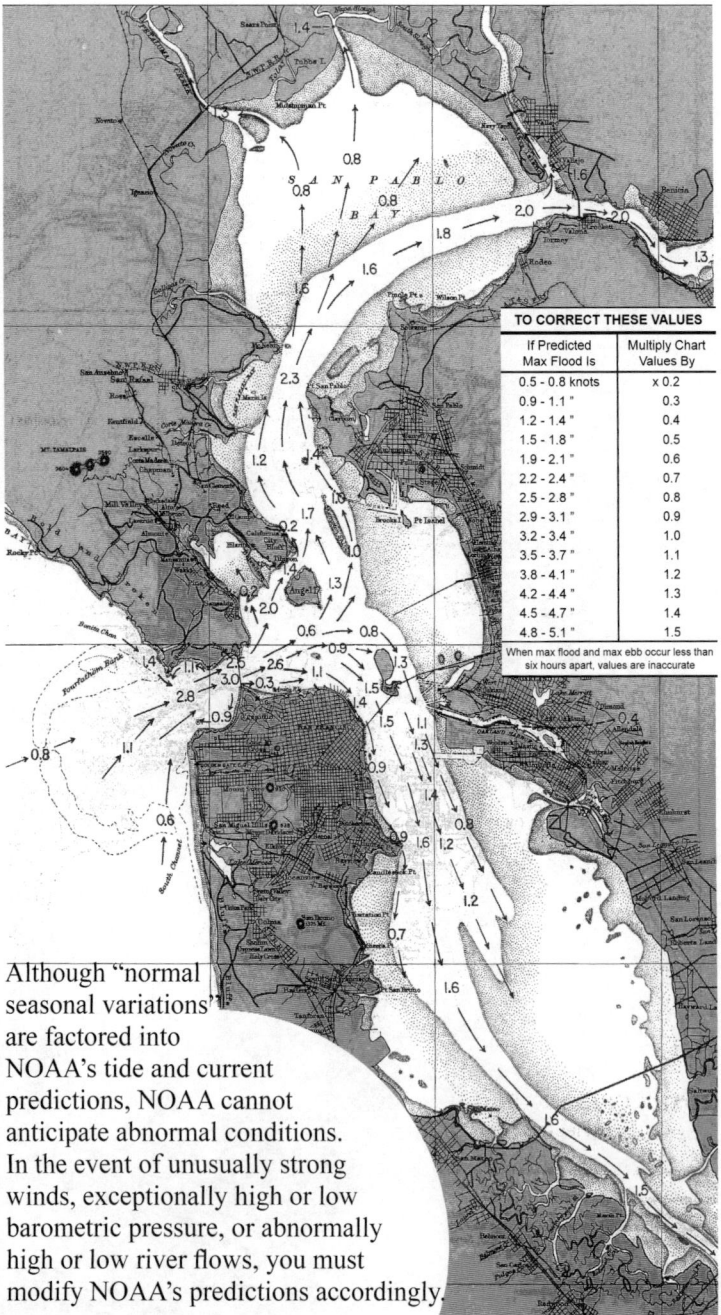

TO CORRECT THESE VALUES

If Predicted Max Flood Is	Multiply Chart Values By
0.5 - 0.8 knots	x 0.2
0.9 - 1.1 "	0.3
1.2 - 1.4 "	0.4
1.5 - 1.8 "	0.5
1.9 - 2.1 "	0.6
2.2 - 2.4 "	0.7
2.5 - 2.8 "	0.8
2.9 - 3.1 "	0.9
3.2 - 3.4 "	1.0
3.5 - 3.7 "	1.1
3.8 - 4.1 "	1.2
4.2 - 4.4 "	1.3
4.5 - 4.7 "	1.4
4.8 - 5.1 "	1.5

When max flood and max ebb occur less than six hours apart, values are inaccurate

Although "normal seasonal variations" are factored into NOAA's tide and current predictions, NOAA cannot anticipate abnormal conditions. In the event of unusually strong winds, exceptionally high or low barometric pressure, or abnormally high or low river flows, you must modify NOAA's predictions accordingly.

S.F. BAY CURRENTS

Maximum Flood At S.F. Bay Entrance

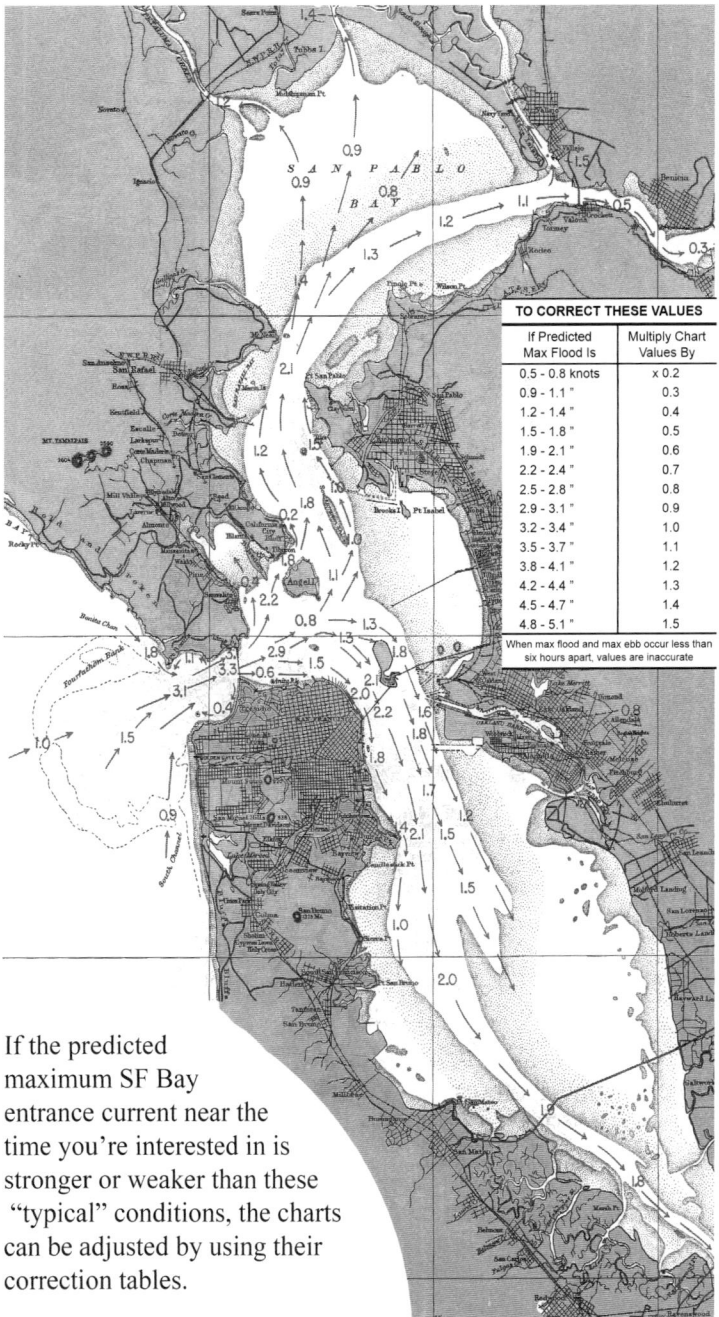

TO CORRECT THESE VALUES

If Predicted Max Flood Is	Multiply Chart Values By
0.5 - 0.8 knots	x 0.2
0.9 - 1.1 "	0.3
1.2 - 1.4 "	0.4
1.5 - 1.8 "	0.5
1.9 - 2.1 "	0.6
2.2 - 2.4 "	0.7
2.5 - 2.8 "	0.8
2.9 - 3.1 "	0.9
3.2 - 3.4 "	1.0
3.5 - 3.7 "	1.1
3.8 - 4.1 "	1.2
4.2 - 4.4 "	1.3
4.5 - 4.7 "	1.4
4.8 - 5.1 "	1.5

When max flood and max ebb occur less than six hours apart, values are inaccurate

If the predicted maximum SF Bay entrance current near the time you're interested in is stronger or weaker than these "typical" conditions, the charts can be adjusted by using their correction tables.

S.F. BAY CURRENTS

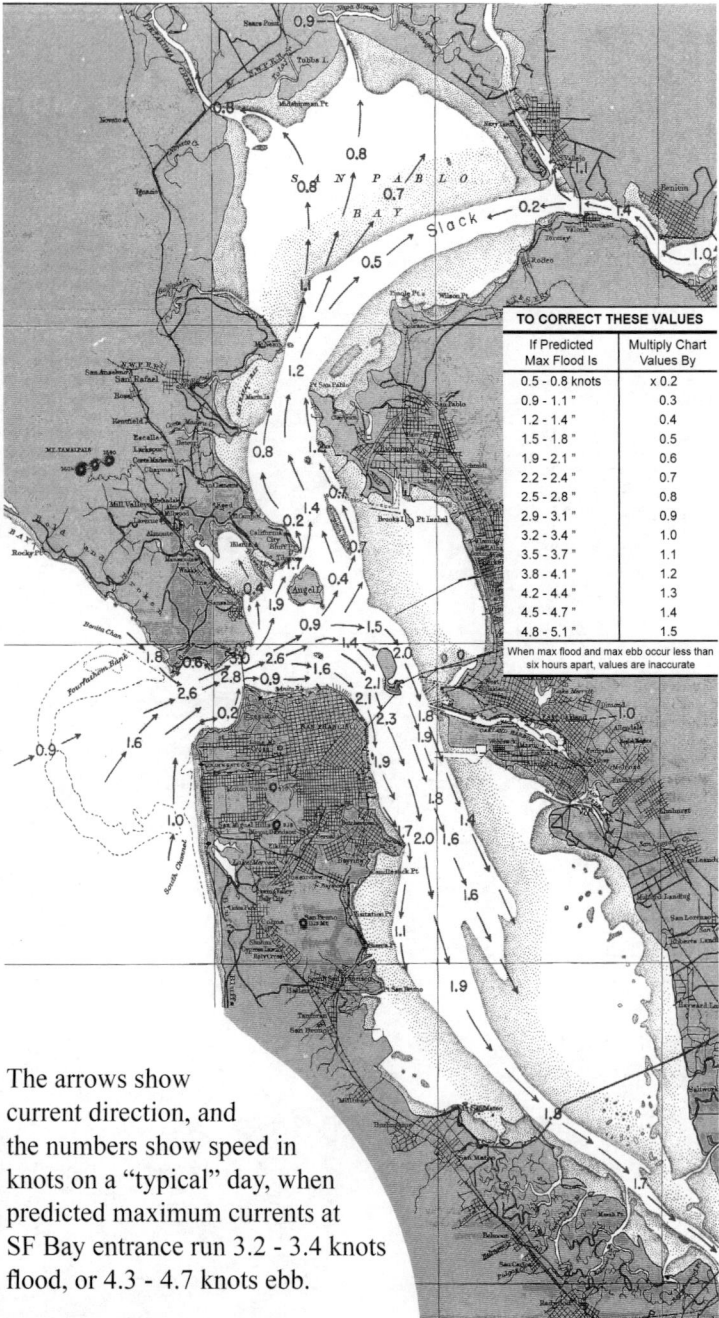

TO CORRECT THESE VALUES	
If Predicted Max Flood Is	Multiply Chart Values By
0.5 - 0.8 knots	x 0.2
0.9 - 1.1 "	0.3
1.2 - 1.4 "	0.4
1.5 - 1.8 "	0.5
1.9 - 2.1 "	0.6
2.2 - 2.4 "	0.7
2.5 - 2.8 "	0.8
2.9 - 3.1 "	0.9
3.2 - 3.4 "	1.0
3.5 - 3.7 "	1.1
3.8 - 4.1 "	1.2
4.2 - 4.4 "	1.3
4.5 - 4.7 "	1.4
4.8 - 5.1 "	1.5

When max flood and max ebb occur less than six hours apart, values are inaccurate

The arrows show current direction, and the numbers show speed in knots on a "typical" day, when predicted maximum currents at SF Bay entrance run 3.2 - 3.4 knots flood, or 4.3 - 4.7 knots ebb.

S.F. BAY CURRENTS

2 HOURS BEFORE MAXIMUM FLOOD AT S.F. BAY ENTRANCE

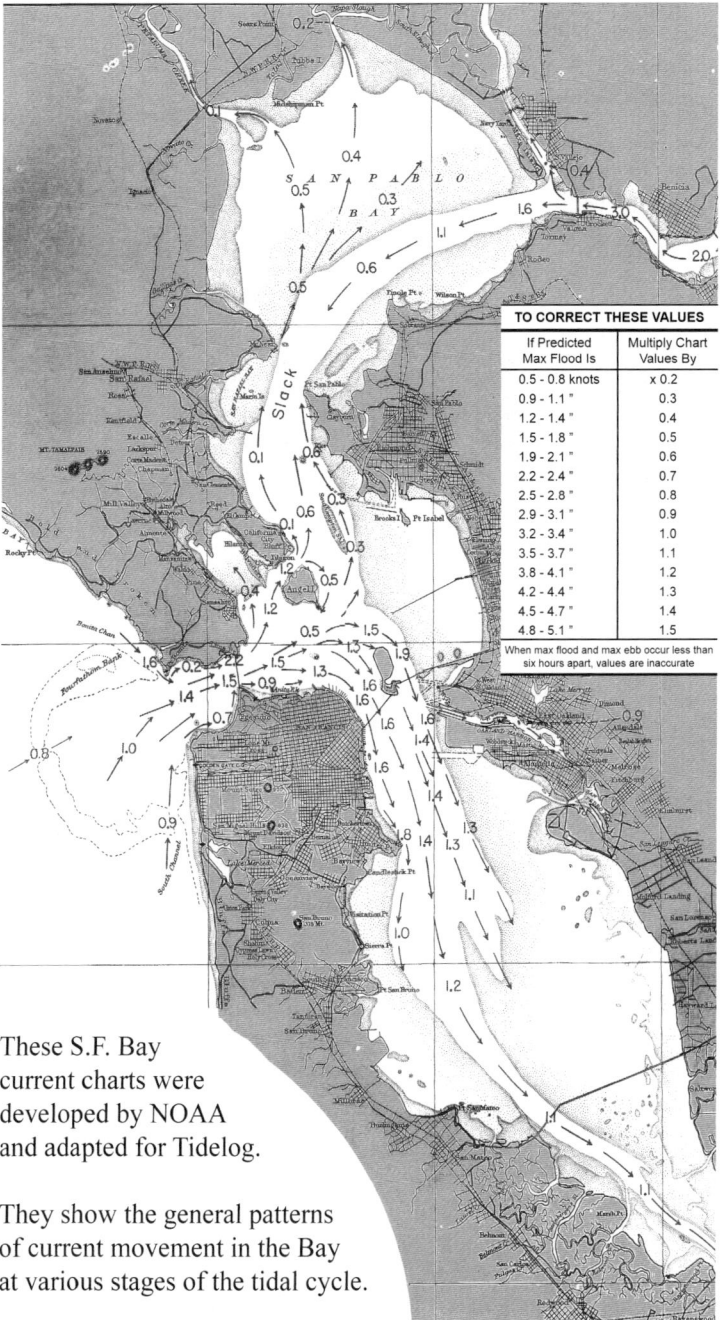

TO CORRECT THESE VALUES	
If Predicted Max Flood Is	Multiply Chart Values By
0.5 - 0.8 knots	x 0.2
0.9 - 1.1 "	0.3
1.2 - 1.4 "	0.4
1.5 - 1.8 "	0.5
1.9 - 2.1 "	0.6
2.2 - 2.4 "	0.7
2.5 - 2.8 "	0.8
2.9 - 3.1 "	0.9
3.2 - 3.4 "	1.0
3.5 - 3.7 "	1.1
3.8 - 4.1 "	1.2
4.2 - 4.4 "	1.3
4.5 - 4.7 "	1.4
4.8 - 5.1 "	1.5

When max flood and max ebb occur less than six hours apart, values are inaccurate

These S.F. Bay current charts were developed by NOAA and adapted for Tidelog.

They show the general patterns of current movement in the Bay at various stages of the tidal cycle.

FRI DEC 29

dawn 6:22 sunrise 7:25 sunset 4:59 dark 6:01
moonset 9:43 a.m. moonrise 7:38 p.m.

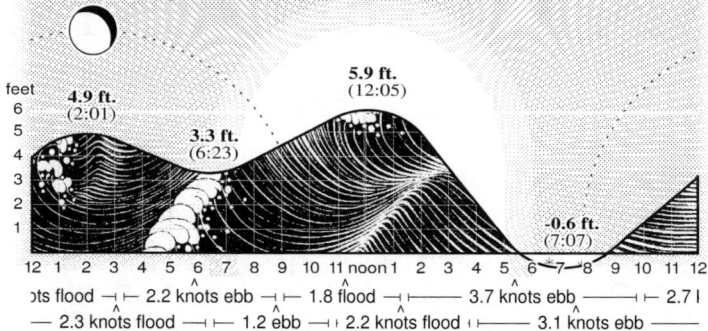

feet

4.9 ft.
(2:01)

3.3 ft.
(6:23)

5.9 ft.
(12:05)

-0.6 ft.
(7:07)

12 1 2 3 4 5 6 7 8 9 10 11 noon 1 2 3 4 5 6 7 8 9 10 11 12

ots flood →⊢ 2.2 knots ebb →⊢ 1.8 flood →⊣ 3.7 knots ebb ——⊢ 2.7 l
— 2.3 knots flood —⊣⊢ 1.2 ebb —⊣ 2.2 knots flood ⊢— 3.1 knots ebb —

SAT DEC 30

dawn 6:23 sunrise 7:25 sunset 5:00 dark 6:02
moonset 10:14 a.m. moonrise 8:40 p.m.

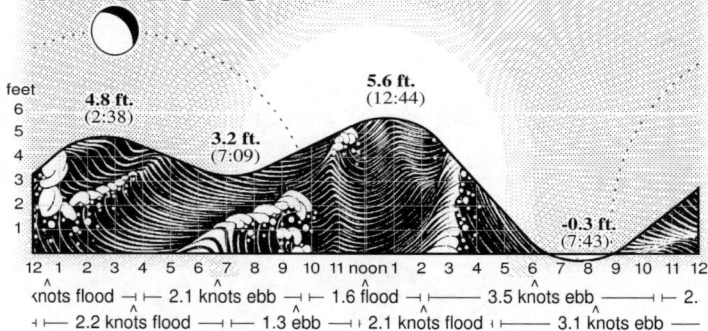

feet

4.8 ft.
(2:38)

3.2 ft.
(7:09)

5.6 ft.
(12:44)

-0.3 ft.
(7:43)

12 1 2 3 4 5 6 7 8 9 10 11 noon 1 2 3 4 5 6 7 8 9 10 11 12

knots flood →⊣ 2.1 knots ebb →⊣ 1.6 flood →⊣ 3.5 knots ebb ——⊢ 2.
⊣⊢ 2.2 knots flood —⊣⊢ 1.3 ebb —⊣ 2.1 knots flood ⊢— 3.1 knots ebb —

SUN DEC 31

dawn 6:23 sunrise 7:25 sunset 5:01 dark 6:03
moonset 10:40 a.m.

New Year's Eve

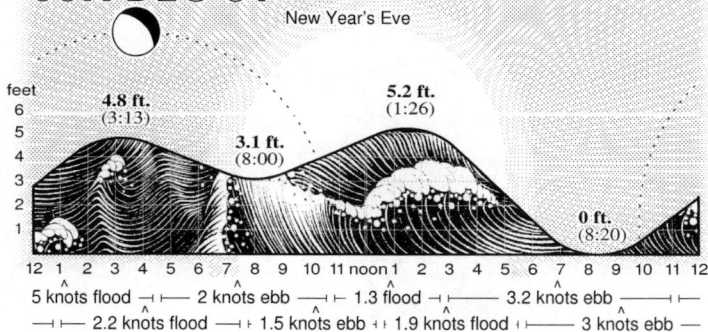

feet

4.8 ft.
(3:13)

3.1 ft.
(8:00)

5.2 ft.
(1:26)

0 ft.
(8:20)

12 1 2 3 4 5 6 7 8 9 10 11 noon 1 2 3 4 5 6 7 8 9 10 11 12

5 knots flood →⊣ ⊢ 2 knots ebb —⊣ ⊢ 1.3 flood →⊣ ⊢— 3.2 knots ebb ——⊢ ⊢—
—⊣ ⊢ 2.2 knots flood —⊣ ⊢ 1.5 knots ebb ⊣⊢ 1.9 knots flood ⊣ ⊢— 3 knots ebb —

Ⓥ　Ⓜ　Ⓢ　Ⓙ

MON DEC 25

dawn 6:21 sunrise 7:23 sunset 4:57 dark 5:59
moonset 6:26 a.m. moonrise 3:41 p.m.

Christmas Day

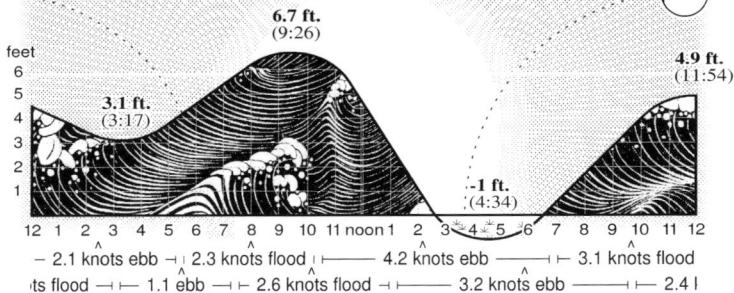

6.7 ft.
(9:26)

4.9 ft.
(11:54)

feet

3.1 ft.
(3:17)

-1 ft.
(4:34)

12 1 2 3 4 5 6 7 8 9 10 11 noon 1 2 3 4 5 6 7 8 9 10 11 12

— 2.1 knots ebb ⊣⊢ 2.3 knots flood ⊢ 4.2 knots ebb ⊣⊢ 3.1 knots flood

ts flood ⊣⊢ 1.1 ebb ⊣⊢ 2.6 knots flood ⊣⊢ 3.2 knots ebb ⊢ 2.4 l

TUE DEC 26

dawn 6:21 sunrise 7:24 sunset 4:57 dark 6:00
moonset 7:28 a.m. moonrise 4:34 p.m.

Full Moon 4:43 p.m.

North

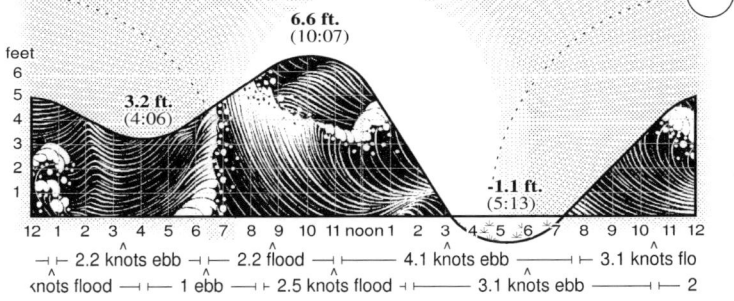

6.6 ft.
(10:07)

feet

3.2 ft.
(4:06)

-1.1 ft.
(5:13)

12 1 2 3 4 5 6 7 8 9 10 11 noon 1 2 3 4 5 6 7 8 9 10 11 12

⊣⊢ 2.2 knots ebb ⊣⊢ 2.2 flood ⊣⊢ 4.1 knots ebb ⊢ 3.1 knots flo

knots flood ⊣⊢ 1 ebb ⊣⊢ 2.5 knots flood ⊣⊢ 3.1 knots ebb ⊢ 2

WED DEC 27

dawn 6:22 sunrise 7:24 sunset 4:58 dark 6:00
moonset 8:22 a.m. moonrise 5:33 p.m.

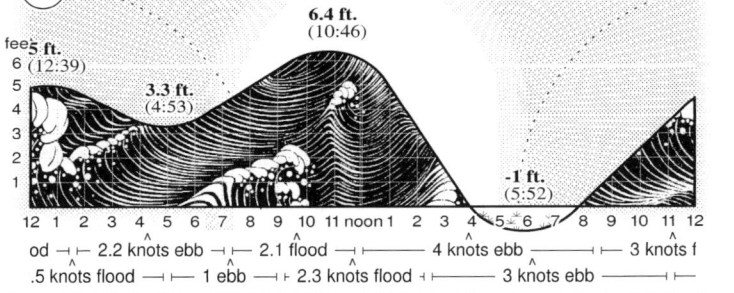

6.4 ft.
(10:46)

feet
5 ft.
(12:39)

3.3 ft.
(4:53)

-1 ft.
(5:52)

12 1 2 3 4 5 6 7 8 9 10 11 noon 1 2 3 4 5 6 7 8 9 10 11 12

od ⊣⊢ 2.2 knots ebb ⊣⊢ 2.1 flood ⊣⊢ 4 knots ebb ⊢ 3 knots f

.5 knots flood ⊣⊢ 1 ebb ⊣⊢ 2.3 knots flood ⊣⊢ 3 knots ebb ⊢

THU DEC 28

dawn 6:22 sunrise 7:24 sunset 4:59 dark 6:01
moonset 9:06 a.m. moonrise 6:35 p.m.

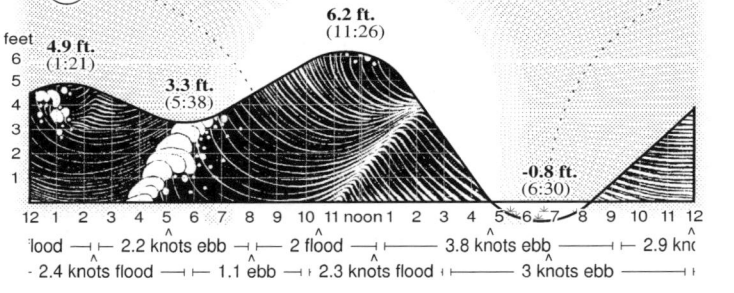

6.2 ft.
(11:26)

feet
4.9 ft.
(1:21)

3.3 ft.
(5:38)

-0.8 ft.
(6:30)

12 1 2 3 4 5 6 7 8 9 10 11 noon 1 2 3 4 5 6 7 8 9 10 11 12

flood ⊣⊢ 2.2 knots ebb ⊣⊢ 2 flood ⊣⊢ 3.8 knots ebb ⊣⊢ 2.9 kn

· 2.4 knots flood ⊣⊢ 1.1 ebb ⊣⊢ 2.3 knots flood ⊢ 3 knots ebb ⊣

FRI DEC 22

dawn 6:20 sunrise 7:22 sunset 4:55 dark 5:57
moonset 2:59 a.m. moonrise 1:44 p.m.

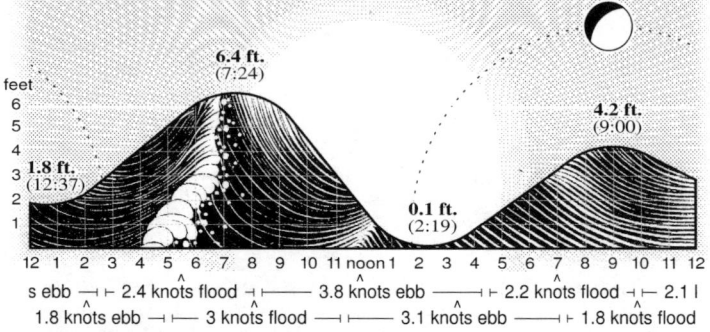

6.4 ft.
(7:24)

4.2 ft.
(9:00)

feet
6
5
4
3
2
1

1.8 ft.
(12:37)

0.1 ft.
(2:19)

12 1 2 3 4 5 6 7 8 9 10 11 noon 1 2 3 4 5 6 7 8 9 10 11 12

s ebb ⊣ ⊢ 2.4 knots flood ⊣ ⊢— 3.8 knots ebb ——⊢ 2.2 knots flood ⊣⊣ 2.1 l
1.8 knots ebb ⊣ ⊢— 3 knots flood —⊣ ⊢— 3.1 knots ebb ——⊢ 1.8 knots flood

SAT DEC 23

dawn 6:20 sunrise 7:23 sunset 4:55 dark 5:58
moonset 4:09 a.m. moonrise 2:17 p.m.

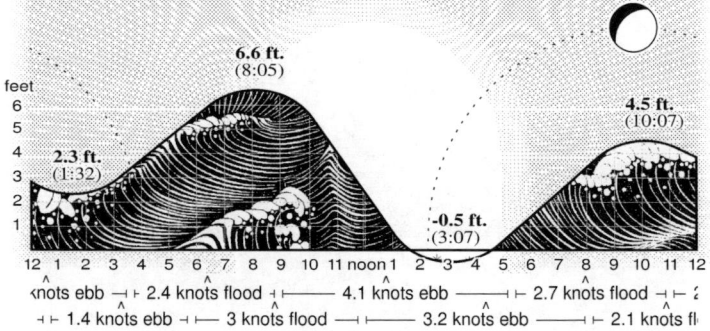

6.6 ft.
(8:05)

4.5 ft.
(10:07)

feet
6
5
4
3
2
1

2.3 ft.
(1:32)

-0.5 ft.
(3:07)

12 1 2 3 4 5 6 7 8 9 10 11 noon 1 2 3 4 5 6 7 8 9 10 11 12

knots ebb ⊣ ⊢ 2.4 knots flood ⊣⊢— 4.1 knots ebb ——⊢ 2.7 knots flood ⊣⊣
⊣ ⊢ 1.4 knots ebb ⊣ ⊢— 3 knots flood ——⊣ ⊢— 3.2 knots ebb ——⊢ 2.1 knots fl

SUN DEC 24

dawn 6:21 sunrise 7:23 sunset 4:56 dark 5:58
moonset 5:19 a.m. moonrise 2:55 p.m.

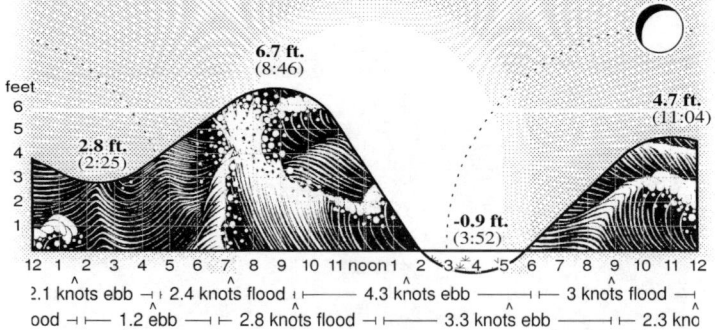

6.7 ft.
(8:46)

4.7 ft.
(11:04)

feet
6
5
4
3
2
1

2.8 ft.
(2:25)

-0.9 ft.
(3:52)

12 1 2 3 4 5 6 7 8 9 10 11 noon 1 2 3 4 5 6 7 8 9 10 11 12

2.1 knots ebb ⊣ ⊢ 2.4 knots flood ⊣ ⊢— 4.3 knots ebb ——⊢ 3 knots flood —⊣
ood ⊣ ⊢— 1.2 ebb —⊣ ⊢— 2.8 knots flood ⊣ ⊢— 3.3 knots ebb ——⊢ 2.3 kno

ⓥ   Ⓜ   Ⓢ   Ⓙ

Winter Solstice On Dec 21st the Earth's north pole tilts the farthest away from the Sun providing the shortest day of the year. The Solstice marks the first day of winter in the northern hemisphere.

 Ursids Meteor Shower The Ursids, active Dec 17th - 25th, is a minor shower producing 5 to 10 meteors per hour at peak. The evening of the 21st and the following morning is the shower's peak. The radiant point is the constellation Ursa Minor, the little dipper, find it high in the sky with Polaris. The waxing gibbous Moon will overwhelm all but the brightest meteors until it sets at approximately 2:00 a.m. leaving a dark sky for early morning viewing.

MON DEC 18

dawn 6:18 sunrise 7:20 sunset 4:53 dark 5:55
moonrise 11:57 a.m. moonset 11:31 p.m.

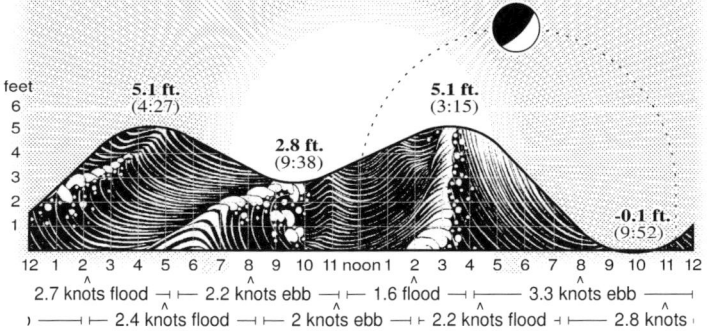

5.1 ft.
(4:27)

2.8 ft.
(9:38)

5.1 ft.
(3:15)

-0.1 ft.
(9:52)

feet
6
5
4
3
2
1

12 1 2 3 4 5 6 7 8 9 10 11 noon 1 2 3 4 5 6 7 8 9 10 11 12

2.7 knots flood → ← 2.2 knots ebb → ← 1.6 flood → ← 3.3 knots ebb →

) → ← 2.4 knots flood → ← 2 knots ebb → ← 2.2 knots flood → ← 2.8 knots

TUE DEC 19

dawn 6:18 sunrise 7:21 sunset 4:53 dark 5:56
moonrise 12:24 p.m.

equator

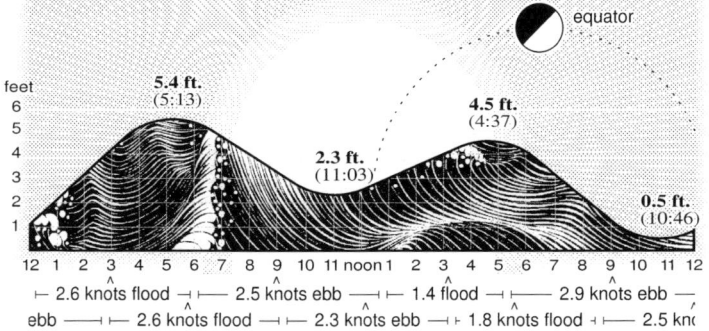

5.4 ft.
(5:13)

2.3 ft.
(11:03)

4.5 ft.
(4:37)

0.5 ft.
(10:46)

feet
6
5
4
3
2
1

12 1 2 3 4 5 6 7 8 9 10 11 noon 1 2 3 4 5 6 7 8 9 10 11 12

← 2.6 knots flood → ← 2.5 knots ebb → ← 1.4 flood → ← 2.9 knots ebb →

ebb → ← 2.6 knots flood → ← 2.3 knots ebb → ← 1.8 knots flood → ← 2.5 kno

WED DEC 20

dawn 6:19 sunrise 7:21 sunset 4:54 dark 5:56
moonset 12:41 a.m. moonrise 12:49 p.m.

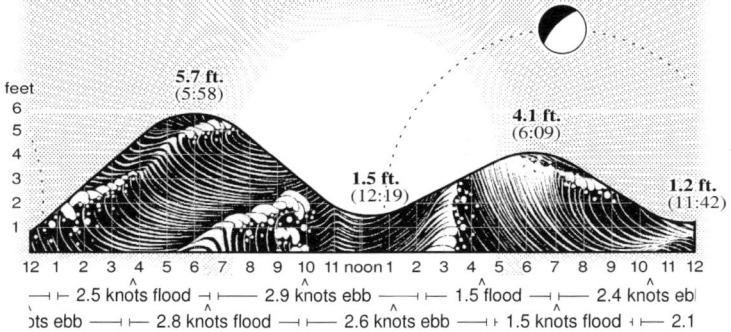

5.7 ft.
(5:58)

1.5 ft.
(12:19)

4.1 ft.
(6:09)

1.2 ft.
(11:42)

feet
6
5
4
3
2
1

12 1 2 3 4 5 6 7 8 9 10 11 noon 1 2 3 4 5 6 7 8 9 10 11 12

→ ← 2.5 knots flood → ← 2.9 knots ebb → ← 1.5 flood → ← 2.4 knots ebb

ots ebb → ← 2.8 knots flood → ← 2.6 knots ebb → ← 1.5 knots flood → ← 2.1

THU DEC 21

dawn 6:19 sunrise 7:22 sunset 4:54 dark 5:57
moonset 1:50 a.m. moonrise 1:15 p.m.

Winter Solstice 7:27 p.m.   Ursids' peak

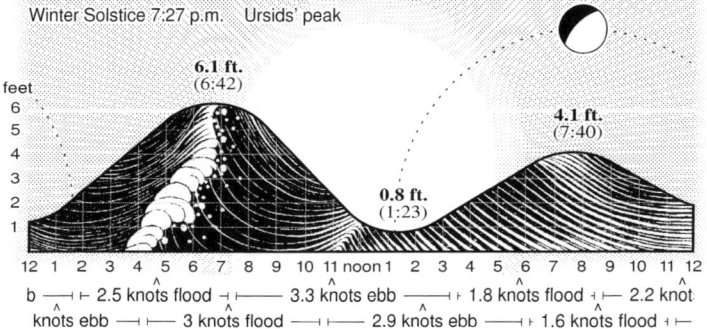

6.1 ft.
(6:42)

0.8 ft.
(1:23)

4.1 ft.
(7:40)

feet
6
5
4
3
2
1

12 1 2 3 4 5 6 7 8 9 10 11 noon 1 2 3 4 5 6 7 8 9 10 11 12

b → ← 2.5 knots flood → ← 3.3 knots ebb → ← 1.8 knots flood → ← 2.2 knot

knots ebb → ← 3 knots flood → ← 2.9 knots ebb → ← 1.6 knots flood → ←

FRI DEC 15

dawn 6:16 sunrise 7:18 sunset 4:52 dark 5:54
moonrise 10:13 a.m. moonset 7:50 p.m.

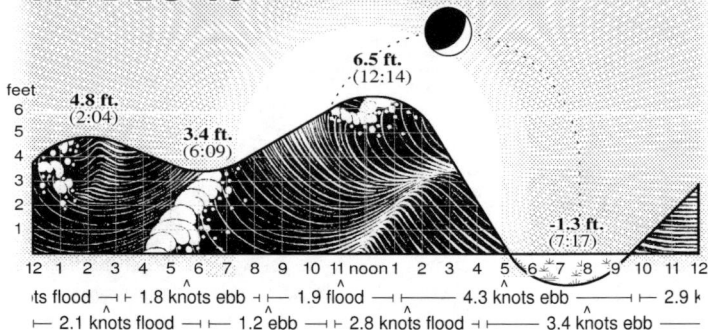

feet
6.5 ft.
(12:14)
4.8 ft.
(2:04)
3.4 ft.
(6:09)
-1.3 ft.
(7:17)

12 1 2 3 4 5 6 7 8 9 10 11 noon 1 2 3 4 5 6 7 8 9 10 11 12

ts flood —┤ ├ 1.8 knots ebb ┤ ├ 1.9 flood —┤ ├— 4.3 knots ebb ——┤ ├ 2.9 k
├— 2.1 knots flood —┤ ├ 1.2 ebb —┤ ├ 2.8 knots flood ┤ ├—— 3.4 knots ebb ——

SAT DEC 16

dawn 6:16 sunrise 7:19 sunset 4:52 dark 5:55
moonrise 10:54 a.m. moonset 9:05 p.m.

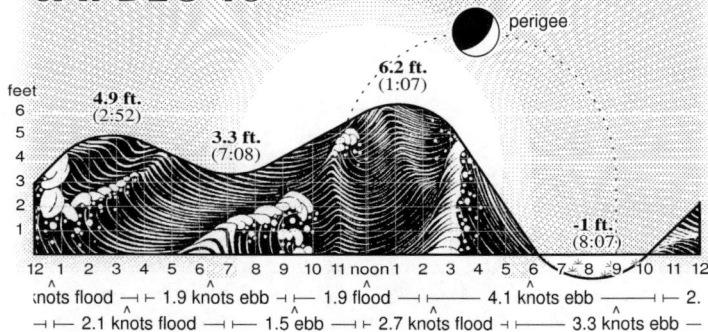

perigee

feet
6.2 ft.
(1:07)
4.9 ft.
(2:52)
3.3 ft.
(7:08)
-1 ft.
(8:07)

12 1 2 3 4 5 6 7 8 9 10 11 noon 1 2 3 4 5 6 7 8 9 10 11 12

knots flood —┤ ├ 1.9 knots ebb ┤ ├ 1.9 flood —┤ ├— 4.1 knots ebb ——┤ ├ 2.
┤ ├ 2.1 knots flood —┤ ├— 1.5 ebb —┤ ├ 2.7 knots flood ┤ ├—— 3.3 knots ebb —

SUN DEC 17

dawn 6:17 sunrise 7:19 sunset 4:53 dark 5:55
moonrise 11:28 a.m. moonset 10:19 p.m.

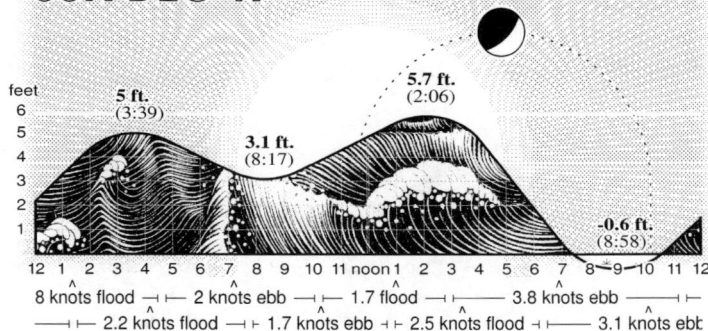

feet
5.7 ft.
(2:06)
5 ft.
(3:39)
3.1 ft.
(8:17)
-0.6 ft.
(8:58)

12 1 2 3 4 5 6 7 8 9 10 11 noon 1 2 3 4 5 6 7 8 9 10 11 12

8 knots flood —┤ ├— 2 knots ebb —┤ ├— 1.7 flood —┤ ├—— 3.8 knots ebb ——┤ ├—
——┤ ├ 2.2 knots flood —┤ ├ 1.7 knots ebb ┤ ├ 2.5 knots flood ┤ ├—— 3.1 knots ebb

(V)   (M)   (S)   (J)

Geminids Meteor Shower the Geminids, active Dec 17th - 25th,
have delivered memorable showers producing up to 120 multicolored
meteors per hour at peak. This year's peak, Dec 13th - 14th, will benefit
from an early setting moon. The constellation Gemini, the shower's
radiant point, will be rising above the eastern horizon at twilight.
Saturn, on the 17th, will be 2 degrees north of the moon.

MON DEC 11
dawn 6:13 sunrise 7:15 sunset 4:51 dark 5:53
moonrise 6:05 a.m. moonset 3:42 p.m.

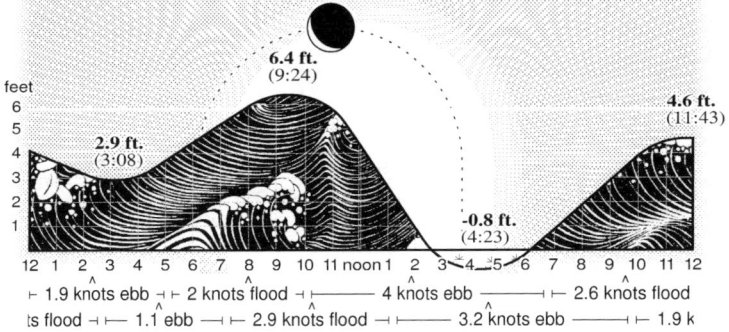

6.4 ft. (9:24)

feet

2.9 ft. (3:08)

4.6 ft. (11:43)

-0.8 ft. (4:23)

12 1 2 3 4 5 6 7 8 9 10 11 noon 1 2 3 4 5 6 7 8 9 10 11 12

⊢ 1.9 knots ebb ⊣ ⊢ 2 knots flood ⊣ ⊢ 4 knots ebb ⊣ ⊢ 2.6 knots flood
ts flood ⊣ ⊢ 1.1 ebb ⊢ 2.9 knots flood ⊣ ⊢ 3.2 knots ebb ⊣ ⊢ 1.9 k

TUE DEC 12
dawn 6:14 sunrise 7:16 sunset 4:51 dark 5:53
moonrise 7:16 a.m. moonset 4:29 p.m.

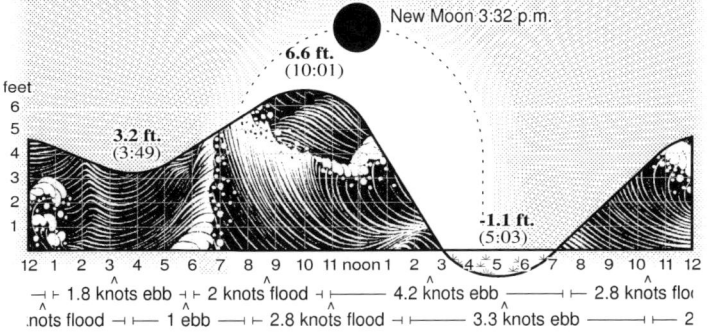

New Moon 3:32 p.m.

6.6 ft. (10:01)

feet

3.2 ft. (3:49)

-1.1 ft. (5:03)

12 1 2 3 4 5 6 7 8 9 10 11 noon 1 2 3 4 5 6 7 8 9 10 11 12

⊣ ⊢ 1.8 knots ebb ⊣ ⊢ 2 knots flood ⊣ ⊢ 4.2 knots ebb ⊣ ⊢ 2.8 knots floo
nots flood ⊣ ⊢ 1 ebb ⊣ ⊢ 2.8 knots flood ⊣ ⊢ 3.3 knots ebb ⊣ ⊢ 2

WED DEC 13
dawn 6:14 sunrise 7:17 sunset 4:51 dark 5:54
moonrise 8:23 a.m. moonset 5:28 p.m.

Geminids' peak   South

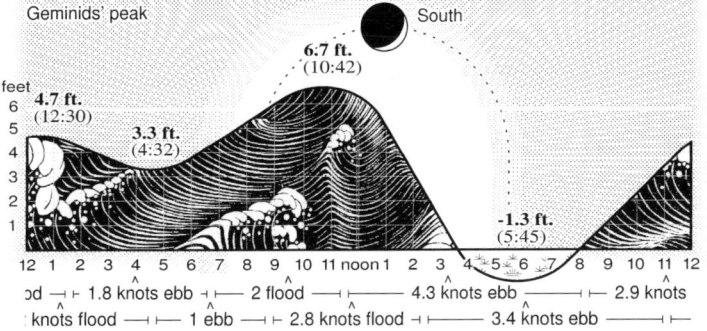

6:7 ft. (10:42)

4.7 ft. (12:30)

feet

3.3 ft. (4:32)

-1.3 ft. (5:45)

12 1 2 3 4 5 6 7 8 9 10 11 noon 1 2 3 4 5 6 7 8 9 10 11 12

od ⊢ 1.8 knots ebb ⊣ ⊢ 2 knots flood ⊣ ⊢ 4.3 knots ebb ⊣ ⊢ 2.9 knots
knots flood ⊣ ⊢ 1 ebb ⊢ 2.8 knots flood ⊣ ⊢ 3.4 knots ebb ⊣ ⊢

THU DEC 14
dawn 6:15 sunrise 7:17 sunset 4:52 dark 5:54
moonrise 9:23 a.m. moonset 6:36 p.m.

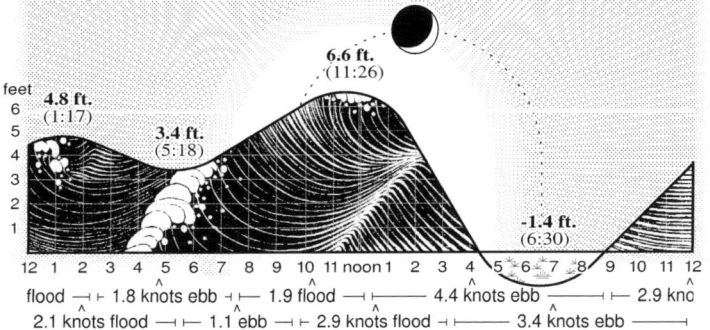

6.6 ft. (11:26)

4.8 ft. (1:17)

feet

3.4 ft. (5:18)

-1.4 ft. (6:30)

12 1 2 3 4 5 6 7 8 9 10 11 noon 1 2 3 4 5 6 7 8 9 10 11 12

flood ⊣ ⊢ 1.8 knots ebb ⊣ ⊢ 1.9 flood ⊣ ⊢ 4.4 knots ebb ⊣ ⊢ 2.9 kno
2.1 knots flood ⊣ ⊢ 1.1 ebb ⊣ ⊢ 2.9 knots flood ⊣ ⊢ 3.4 knots ebb

FRI DEC 8
dawn 6:11 sunrise 7:13 sunset 4:51 dark 5:53
moonrise 2:47 a.m. moonset 2:06 p.m.

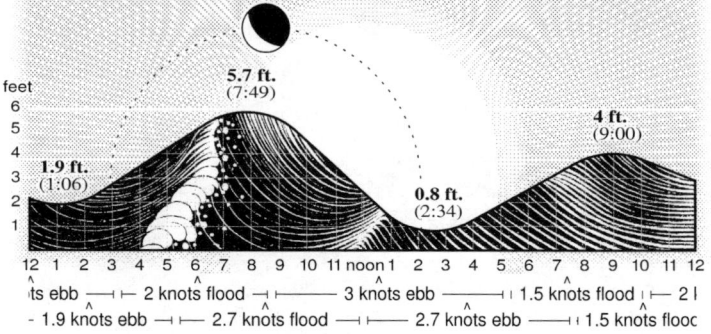

feet
6
5
4
3
2
1

5.7 ft.
(7:49)

1.9 ft.
(1:06)

0.8 ft.
(2:34)

4 ft.
(9:00)

12 1 2 3 4 5 6 7 8 9 10 11 noon 1 2 3 4 5 6 7 8 9 10 11 12

ts ebb ⊢ 2 knots flood ⊣ ⊢ 3 knots ebb ⊣ 1.5 knots flood ⊢ 2 l

- 1.9 knots ebb ⊣ ⊢ 2.7 knots flood ⊣ ⊢ 2.7 knots ebb ⊣ 1.5 knots flood

SAT DEC 9
dawn 6:12 sunrise 7:14 sunset 4:51 dark 5:53
moonrise 3:50 a.m. moonset 2:32 p.m.

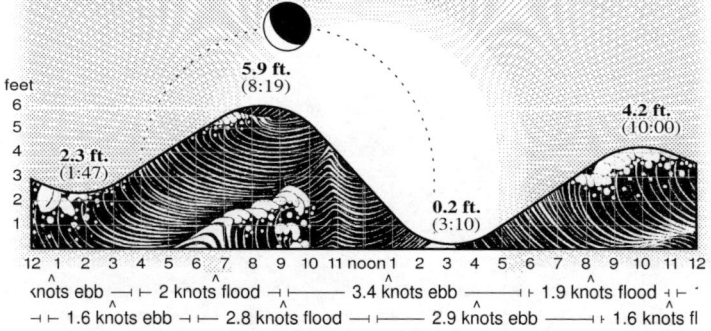

feet
6
5
4
3
2
1

5.9 ft.
(8:19)

2.3 ft.
(1:47)

0.2 ft.
(3:10)

4.2 ft.
(10:00)

12 1 2 3 4 5 6 7 8 9 10 11 noon 1 2 3 4 5 6 7 8 9 10 11 12

knots ebb ⊣ ⊢ 2 knots flood ⊣ ⊢ 3.4 knots ebb ⊣ 1.9 knots flood ⊢

⊣ 1.6 knots ebb ⊣ ⊢ 2.8 knots flood ⊣ ⊢ 2.9 knots ebb ⊣ 1.6 knots fl

SUN DEC 10
dawn 6:12 sunrise 7:14 sunset 4:51 dark 5:53
moonrise 4:56 a.m. moonset 3:03 p.m.

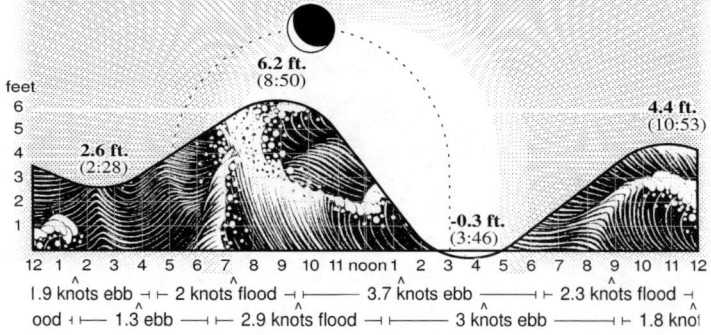

feet
6
5
4
3
2
1

6.2 ft.
(8:50)

2.6 ft.
(2:28)

-0.3 ft.
(3:46)

4.4 ft.
(10:53)

12 1 2 3 4 5 6 7 8 9 10 11 noon 1 2 3 4 5 6 7 8 9 10 11 12

1.9 knots ebb ⊣ ⊢ 2 knots flood ⊣ ⊢ 3.7 knots ebb ⊣ 2.3 knots flood ⊣

ood ⊣ ⊢ 1.3 ebb ⊣ ⊢ 2.9 knots flood ⊣ ⊢ 3 knots ebb ⊣ ⊢ 1.8 knot

MON DEC 4

dawn 6:08 sunrise 7:09 sunset 4:51 dark 5:52
moonset 12:38 p.m. moonrise 11:51 p.m.

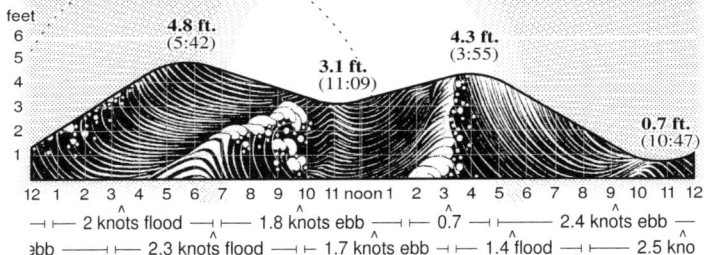

apogee

feet
6
5
4
3
2
1

4.8 ft.
(5:42)

3.1 ft.
(11:09)

4.3 ft.
(3:55)

0.7 ft.
(10:47)

12 1 2 3 4 5 6 7 8 9 10 11 noon 1 2 3 4 5 6 7 8 9 10 11 12

2 knots flood — 1.8 knots ebb — 0.7 — 2.4 knots ebb
ebb — 2.3 knots flood — 1.7 knots ebb — 1.4 flood — 2.5 kno

TUE DEC 5

dawn 6:08 sunrise 7:10 sunset 4:51 dark 5:52
moonset 1:01 p.m.

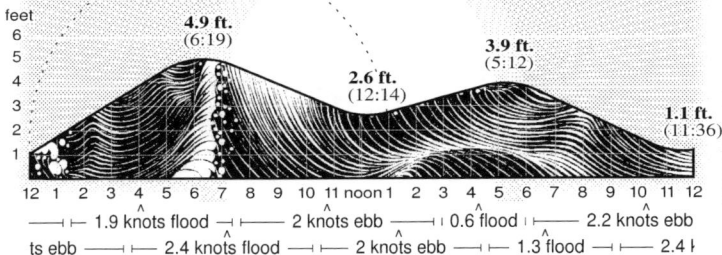

feet
6
5
4
3
2
1

4.9 ft.
(6:19)

2.6 ft.
(12:14)

3.9 ft.
(5:12)

1.1 ft.
(11:36)

12 1 2 3 4 5 6 7 8 9 10 11 noon 1 2 3 4 5 6 7 8 9 10 11 12

1.9 knots flood — 2 knots ebb — 0.6 flood — 2.2 knots ebb
ts ebb — 2.4 knots flood — 2 knots ebb — 1.3 flood — 2.4 h

WED DEC 6

dawn 6:09 sunrise 7:11 sunset 4:51 dark 5:52
moonrise 12:49 a.m. moonset 1:22 p.m.

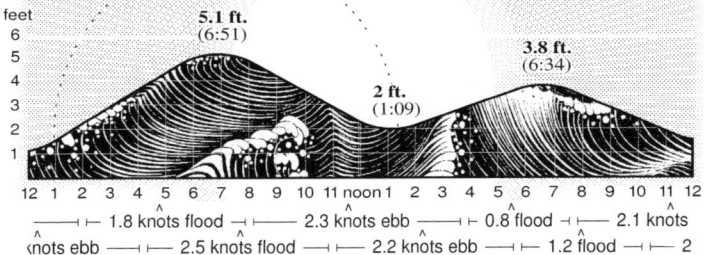

equator

feet
6
5
4
3
2
1

5.1 ft.
(6:51)

2 ft.
(1:09)

3.8 ft.
(6:34)

12 1 2 3 4 5 6 7 8 9 10 11 noon 1 2 3 4 5 6 7 8 9 10 11 12

1.8 knots flood — 2.3 knots ebb — 0.8 flood — 2.1 knots
knots ebb — 2.5 knots flood — 2.2 knots ebb — 1.2 flood — 2

THU DEC 7

dawn 6:10 sunrise 7:12 sunset 4:51 dark 5:53
moonrise 1:47 a.m. moonset 1:43 p.m.

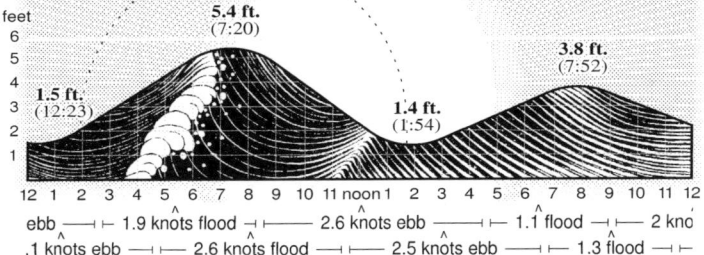

feet
6
5
4
3
2
1

5.4 ft.
(7:20)

3.8 ft.
(7:52)

1.5 ft.
(12:23)

1.4 ft.
(1:54)

12 1 2 3 4 5 6 7 8 9 10 11 noon 1 2 3 4 5 6 7 8 9 10 11 12

ebb — 1.9 knots flood — 2.6 knots ebb — 1.1 flood — 2 kno
.1 knots ebb — 2.6 knots flood — 2.5 knots ebb — 1.3 flood — h

FRI DEC 1

dawn 6:05 sunrise 7:06 sunset 4:51 dark 5:53
moonset 11:12 a.m. moonrise 8:49 p.m.

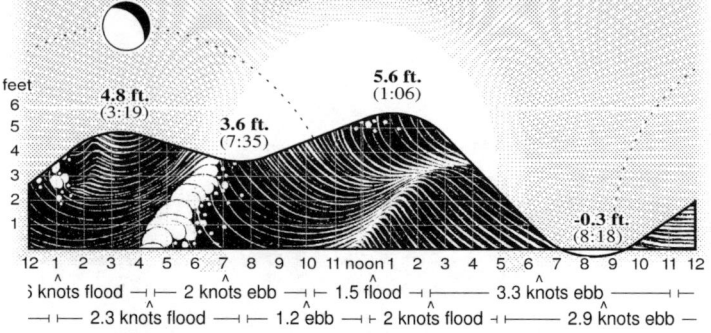

feet

5.6 ft.
(1:06)

4.8 ft.
(3:19)

3.6 ft.
(7:35)

6
5
4
3
2
1

-0.3 ft.
(8:18)

12 1 2 3 4 5 6 7 8 9 10 11 noon 1 2 3 4 5 6 7 8 9 10 11 12

5 knots flood —| |— 2 knots ebb —| |— 1.5 flood —| |— 3.3 knots ebb —— |—
|— 2.3 knots flood —| |— 1.2 ebb —| |— 2 knots flood —| |— 2.9 knots ebb —

SAT DEC 2

dawn 6:06 sunrise 7:07 sunset 4:51 dark 5:52
moonset 11:45 a.m. moonrise 9:51 p.m.

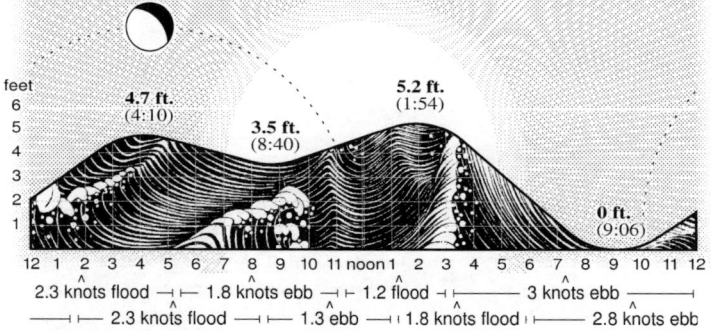

feet

5.2 ft.
(1:54)

4.7 ft.
(4:10)

3.5 ft.
(8:40)

6
5
4
3
2
1

0 ft.
(9:06)

12 1 2 3 4 5 6 7 8 9 10 11 noon 1 2 3 4 5 6 7 8 9 10 11 12

2.3 knots flood —| |— 1.8 knots ebb —| |— 1.2 flood —| |— 3 knots ebb ——
—| |— 2.3 knots flood —| |— 1.3 ebb —| |— 1.8 knots flood |— 2.8 knots ebb

SUN DEC 3

dawn 6:07 sunrise 7:08 sunset 4:51 dark 5:52
moonset 12:14 p.m. moonrise 10:52 p.m.

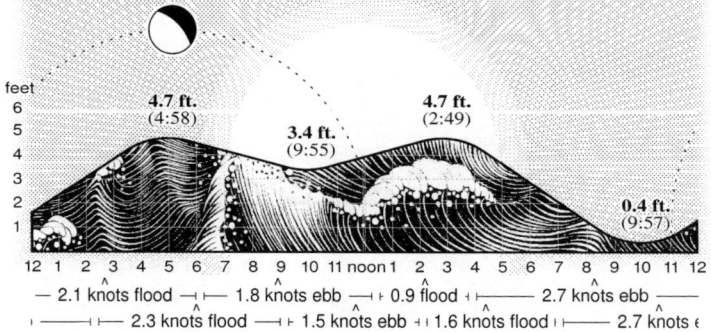

feet

4.7 ft.
(4:58)

4.7 ft.
(2:49)

3.4 ft.
(9:55)

6
5
4
3
2
1

0.4 ft.
(9:57)

12 1 2 3 4 5 6 7 8 9 10 11 noon 1 2 3 4 5 6 7 8 9 10 11 12

— 2.1 knots flood —| |— 1.8 knots ebb —| |— 0.9 flood —| |— 2.7 knots ebb ——
|— |— 2.3 knots flood —| |— 1.5 knots ebb —| |— 1.6 knots flood |— 2.7 knots e

Ⓥ   ⓢ   Ⓙ
       ⓜ

MON NOV 27
dawn 6:02 sunrise 7:03 sunset 4:52 dark 5:53
moonset 7:34 a.m. moonrise 5:01 p.m.

Full Moon 1:16 a.m.

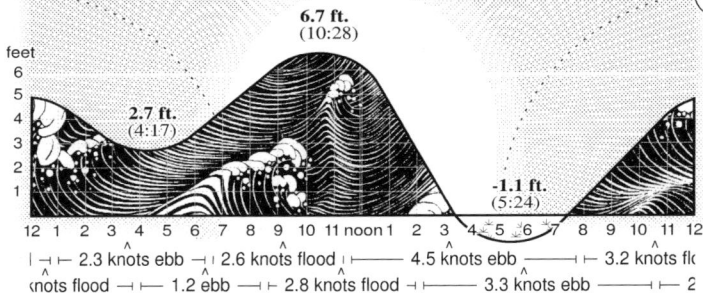

feet

6.7 ft.
(10:28)

2.7 ft.
(4:17)

-1.1 ft.
(5:24)

12 1 2 3 4 5 6 7 8 9 10 11 noon 1 2 3 4 5 6 7 8 9 10 11 12

⊢ ⊣ ⊢ 2.3 knots ebb ⊣ ⊢ 2.6 knots flood ⊢ ⊢ 4.5 knots ebb ⊢ ⊢ 3.2 knots flo
knots flood ⊣ ⊢ 1.2 ebb ⊢ ⊢ 2.8 knots flood ⊣ ⊢ 3.3 knots ebb ⊢ 2

TUE NOV 28
dawn 6:02 sunrise 7:04 sunset 4:52 dark 5:53
moonset 8:41 a.m. moonrise 5:50 p.m.

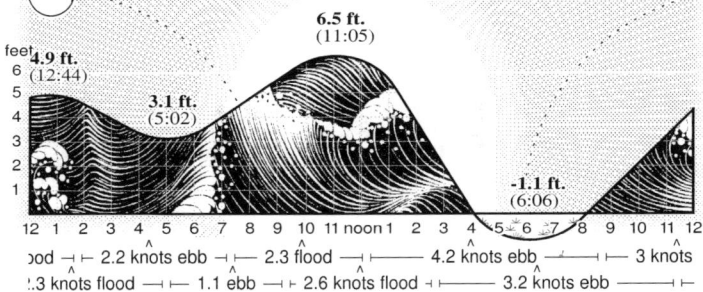

feet
4.9 ft.
(12:44)

6.5 ft.
(11:05)

3.1 ft.
(5:02)

-1.1 ft.
(6:06)

12 1 2 3 4 5 6 7 8 9 10 11 noon 1 2 3 4 5 6 7 8 9 10 11 12

ood ⊣ ⊢ 2.2 knots ebb ⊣ ⊢ 2.3 flood ⊣ ⊢ 4.2 knots ebb ⊢ ⊢ 3 knots
.3 knots flood ⊣ ⊢ 1.1 ebb ⊣ ⊢ 2.6 knots flood ⊣ ⊢ 3.2 knots ebb ⊢ ⊢

WED NOV 29
dawn 6:03 sunrise 7:05 sunset 4:52 dark 5:53
moonset 9:40 a.m. moonrise 6:46 p.m.

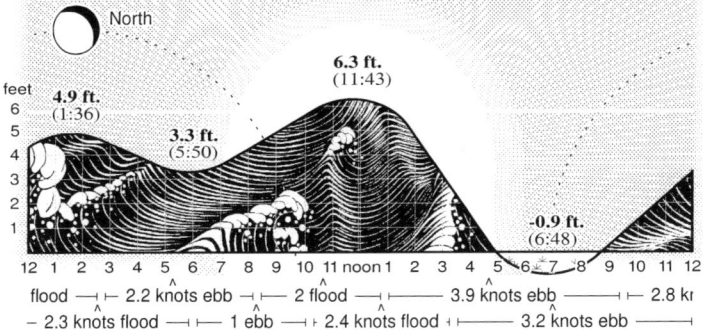

North

feet
4.9 ft.
(1:36)

6.3 ft.
(11:43)

3.3 ft.
(5:50)

-0.9 ft.
(6:48)

12 1 2 3 4 5 6 7 8 9 10 11 noon 1 2 3 4 5 6 7 8 9 10 11 12

flood ⊢ ⊢ 2.2 knots ebb ⊣ ⊢ 2 flood ⊣ ⊢ 3.9 knots ebb ⊢ ⊢ 2.8 kr
⊢ 2.3 knots flood ⊣ ⊢ 1 ebb ⊣ ⊢ 2.4 knots flood ⊣ ⊢ 3.2 knots ebb ⊢

THU NOV 30
dawn 6:04 sunrise 7:05 sunset 4:51 dark 5:53
moonset 10:30 a.m. moonrise 7:47 p.m.

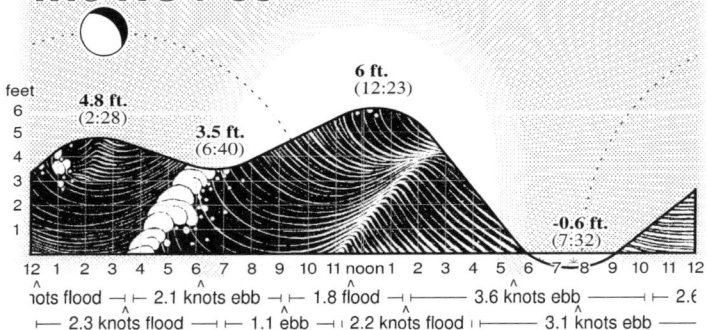

feet
4.8 ft.
(2:28)

6 ft.
(12:23)

3.5 ft.
(6:40)

-0.6 ft.
(7:32)

12 1 2 3 4 5 6 7 8 9 10 11 noon 1 2 3 4 5 6 7 8 9 10 11 12

nots flood ⊣ ⊢ 2.1 knots ebb ⊣ ⊢ 1.8 flood ⊣ ⊢ 3.6 knots ebb ⊢ ⊢ 2.6
⊢ 2.3 knots flood ⊣ ⊢ 1.1 ebb ⊣ ⊢ 2.2 knots flood ⊢ ⊢ 3.1 knots ebb ⊢

FRI NOV 24

dawn 5:59 sunrise 7:00 sunset 4:53 dark 5:54
moonset 4:00 a.m. moonrise 3:13 p.m.

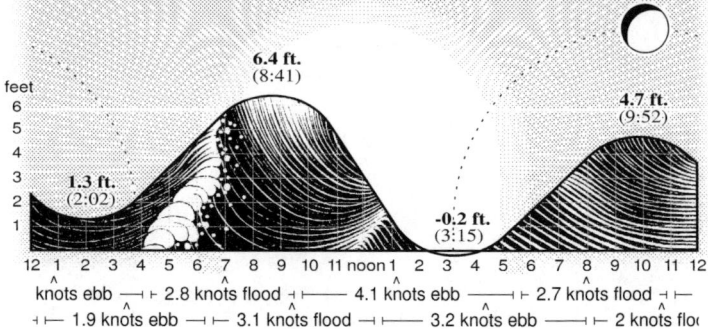

6.4 ft.
(8:41)

4.7 ft.
(9:52)

feet
6
5
4
3
2
1

1.3 ft.
(2:02)

-0.2 ft.
(3:15)

12 1 2 3 4 5 6 7 8 9 10 11 noon 1 2 3 4 5 6 7 8 9 10 11 12

knots ebb ⟶ ⊢ 2.8 knots flood ⊣ ⊢ 4.1 knots ebb ⟶ ⊢ 2.7 knots flood ⊣ ⊢
⊣ ⊢ 1.9 knots ebb ⟶ ⊢ 3.1 knots flood ⟶ ⊢ 3.2 knots ebb ⟶ ⊢ 2 knots floo

SAT NOV 25

dawn 6:00 sunrise 7:01 sunset 4:53 dark 5:54
moonset 5:11 a.m. moonrise 3:44 p.m.

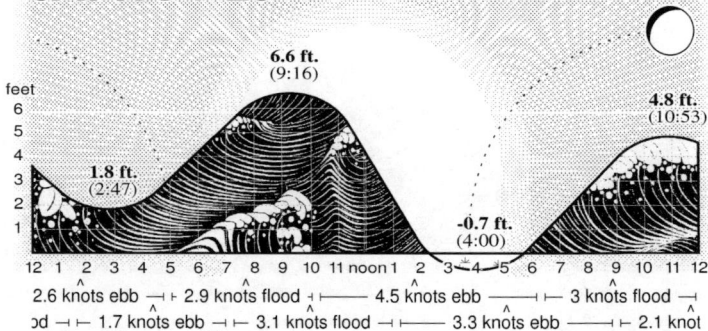

6.6 ft.
(9:16)

4.8 ft.
(10:53)

feet
6
5
4
3
2
1

1.8 ft.
(2:47)

-0.7 ft.
(4:00)

12 1 2 3 4 5 6 7 8 9 10 11 noon 1 2 3 4 5 6 7 8 9 10 11 12

2.6 knots ebb ⟶ ⊢ 2.9 knots flood ⊣ ⊢ 4.5 knots ebb ⟶ ⊢ 3 knots flood ⟶
od ⟶ ⊢ 1.7 knots ebb ⟶ ⊢ 3.1 knots flood ⟶ ⊢ 3.3 knots ebb ⟶ ⊢ 2.1 knot

SUN NOV 26

dawn 6:01 sunrise 7:02 sunset 4:53 dark 5:53
moonset 6:23 a.m. moonrise 4:19 p.m.

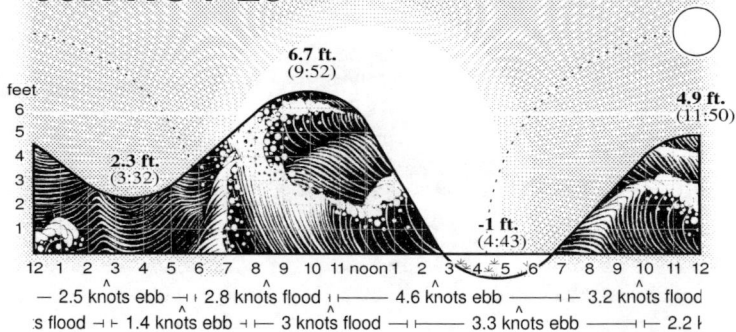

6.7 ft.
(9:52)

4.9 ft.
(11:50)

feet
6
5
4
3
2
1

2.3 ft.
(3:32)

-1 ft.
(4:43)

12 1 2 3 4 5 6 7 8 9 10 11 noon 1 2 3 4 5 6 7 8 9 10 11 12

— 2.5 knots ebb ⟶ ⊢ 2.8 knots flood ⊣ ⊢ 4.6 knots ebb ⟶ ⊢ 3.2 knots flood
s flood ⟶ ⊢ 1.4 knots ebb ⟶ ⊢ 3 knots flood ⟶ ⊢ 3.3 knots ebb ⟶ ⊢ 2.2 k

ⓥ   Ⓢ   Ⓙ
    ⓜ

MON NOV 20

dawn 5:55 sunrise 6:55 sunset 4:55 dark 5:56
moonrise 1:26 p.m.

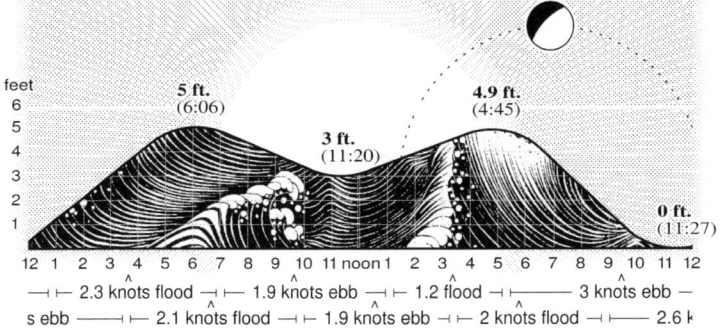

feet
6
5
4
3
2
1

5 ft.
(6:06)

3 ft.
(11:20)

4.9 ft.
(4:45)

0 ft.
(11:27)

12 1 2 3 4 5 6 7 8 9 10 11 noon 1 2 3 4 5 6 7 8 9 10 11 12

⊢ 2.3 knots flood ⊣ ⊢ 1.9 knots ebb ⊣ ⊢ 1.2 flood ⊣ ⊢ 3 knots ebb ⊣

s ebb ⊣ ⊢ 2.1 knots flood ⊣ ⊢ 1.9 knots ebb ⊣ ⊢ 2 knots flood ⊣ ⊢ 2.6 k

TUE NOV 21

dawn 5:56 sunrise 6:56 sunset 4:55 dark 5:55
moonset 12:28 a.m. moonrise 1:54 p.m.

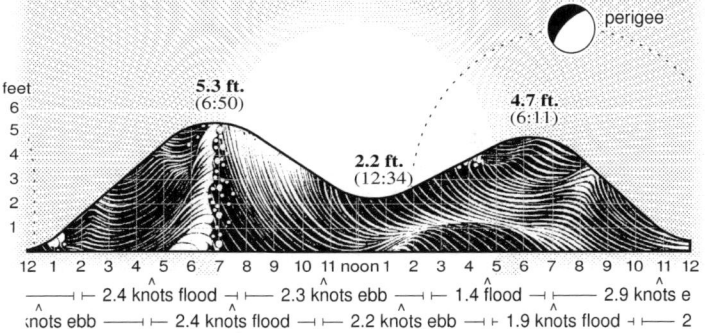

perigee

feet
6
5
4
3
2
1

5.3 ft.
(6:50)

2.2 ft.
(12:34)

4.7 ft.
(6:11)

12 1 2 3 4 5 6 7 8 9 10 11 noon 1 2 3 4 5 6 7 8 9 10 11 12

⊢ 2.4 knots flood ⊣ ⊢ 2.3 knots ebb ⊣ ⊢ 1.4 flood ⊣ ⊢ 2.9 knots e

knots ebb ⊣ ⊢ 2.4 knots flood ⊣ ⊢ 2.2 knots ebb ⊣ ⊢ 1.9 knots flood ⊣ ⊢ 2

WED NOV 22

dawn 5:57 sunrise 6:57 sunset 4:54 dark 5:55
moonset 1:39 a.m. moonrise 2:20 p.m.

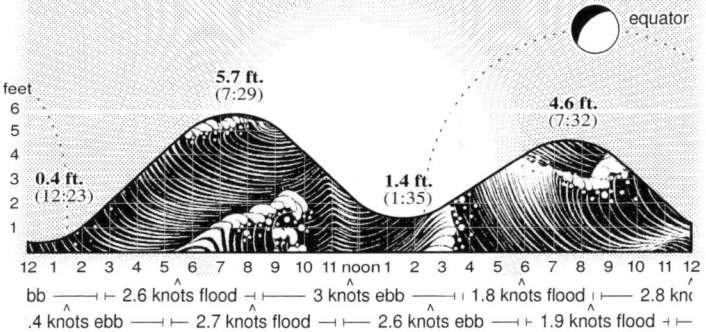

equator

feet
6
5
4
3
2
1

0.4 ft.
(12:23)

5.7 ft.
(7:29)

1.4 ft.
(1:35)

4.6 ft.
(7:32)

12 1 2 3 4 5 6 7 8 9 10 11 noon 1 2 3 4 5 6 7 8 9 10 11 12

bb ⊣ ⊢ 2.6 knots flood ⊣ ⊢ 3 knots ebb ⊣ ⊢ 1.8 knots flood ⊣ ⊢ 2.8 kn

.4 knots ebb ⊣ ⊢ 2.7 knots flood ⊣ ⊢ 2.6 knots ebb ⊣ ⊢ 1.9 knots flood ⊣ ⊢

THU NOV 23

dawn 5:58 sunrise 6:58 sunset 4:54 dark 5:54
moonset 2:49 a.m. moonrise 2:46 p.m.

Thanksgiving Day

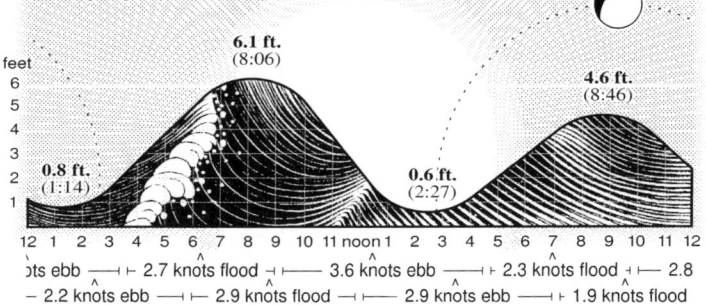

feet
6
5
4
3
2
1

0.8 ft.
(1:14)

6.1 ft.
(8:06)

0.6 ft.
(2:27)

4.6 ft.
(8:46)

12 1 2 3 4 5 6 7 8 9 10 11 noon 1 2 3 4 5 6 7 8 9 10 11 12

ots ebb ⊣ ⊢ 2.7 knots flood ⊣ ⊢ 3.6 knots ebb ⊣ ⊢ 2.3 knots flood ⊣ ⊢ 2.8

⊢ 2.2 knots ebb ⊣ ⊢ 2.9 knots flood ⊣ ⊢ 2.9 knots ebb ⊣ ⊢ 1.9 knots flood

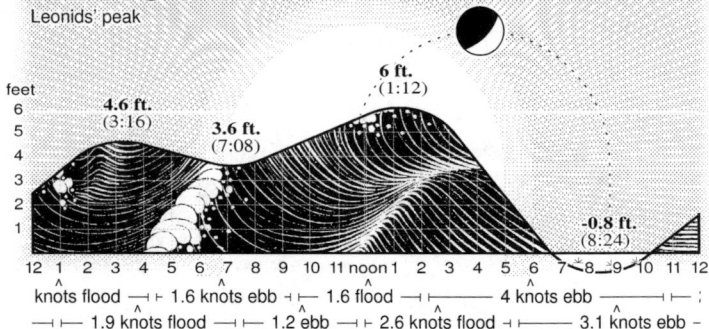

FRI NOV 17
Leonids' peak

dawn 5:52 sunrise 6:52 sunset 4:57 dark 5:57
moonrise 11:30 a.m. moonset 8:48 p.m.

6 ft.
(1:12)

4.6 ft.
(3:16)

3.6 ft.
(7:08)

-0.8 ft.
(8:24)

feet
6
5
4
3
2
1

12 1 2 3 4 5 6 7 8 9 10 11 noon 1 2 3 4 5 6 7 8 9 10 11 12

knots flood —ᴧ— ⊢ 1.6 knots ebb ⊣ ⊢ 1.6 flood —ᴧ— ⊢——— 4 knots ebb ——— ⊢— :

—⊣ ⊢— 1.9 knots flood —ᴧ—⊣ ⊢— 1.2 ebb —ᴧ—⊣ ⊢ 2.6 knots flood ⊣ ⊢——— 3.1 knots ebb –

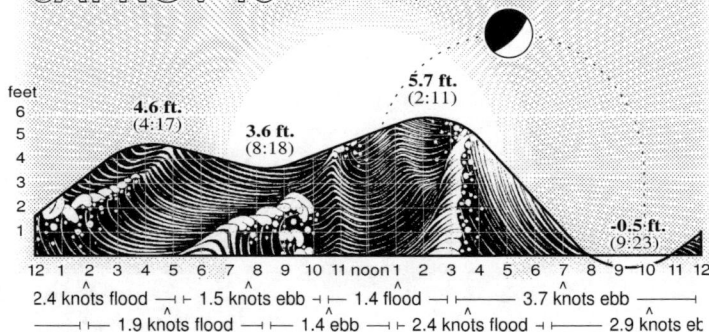

SAT NOV 18
dawn 5:53 sunrise 6:53 sunset 4:56 dark 5:57
moonrise 12:16 p.m. moonset 10:02 p.m.

5.7 ft.
(2:11)

4.6 ft.
(4:17)

3.6 ft.
(8:18)

-0.5 ft.
(9:23)

feet
6
5
4
3
2
1

12 1 2 3 4 5 6 7 8 9 10 11 noon 1 2 3 4 5 6 7 8 9 10 11 12

2.4 knots flood —ᴧ— ⊢ 1.5 knots ebb ⊣ ⊢ 1.4 flood —ᴧ— ⊢——— 3.7 knots ebb ———

——⊣ ⊢— 1.9 knots flood —ᴧ— ⊢— 1.4 ebb —ᴧ—⊣ ⊢ 2.4 knots flood ⊣ ⊢——— 2.9 knots eb:

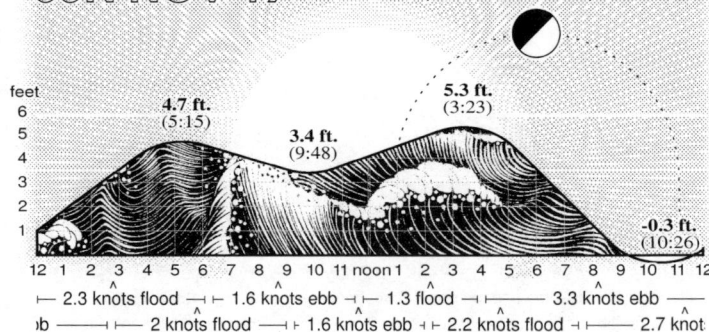

SUN NOV 19
dawn 5:54 sunrise 6:54 sunset 4:56 dark 5:56
moonrise 12:54 p.m. moonset 11:15 p.m.

5.3 ft.
(3:23)

4.7 ft.
(5:15)

3.4 ft.
(9:48)

-0.3 ft.
(10:26)

feet
6
5
4
3
2
1

12 1 2 3 4 5 6 7 8 9 10 11 noon 1 2 3 4 5 6 7 8 9 10 11 12

⊢— 2.3 knots flood —ᴧ— ⊢ 1.6 knots ebb ⊣ ⊢ 1.3 flood —ᴧ— ⊢——— 3.3 knots ebb ———

ᴧb ——⊣ ⊢— 2 knots flood ——ᴧ—⊢ 1.6 knots ebb ⊣ ⊢ 2.2 knots flood ⊣ ⊢——— 2.7 knot:

Uranus at opposition Uranus the seventh planet from the Sun is a gas giant made up of layers of hydrogen, helium and methane that surrounds a rock and ice core. At opposition, its closest approach to Earth, a telescope is essential to view Uranus, and even then Uranus appears as a blue point of light. **Leonids Meteor Shower** the Leonids, active between Nov 6th to the 30th, can produce 15 meteors per hour at peak. This year the peak falls on Nov 17th. The early moonset provides a dark sky as the shower's radiant point, the Constellation Leo, begins its ascent above the eastern horizon at approximately 11:00 p.m.

MON NOV 13
dawn 5:48 sunrise 6:48 sunset 5:00 dark 5:59
moonrise 7:15 a.m. moonset 5:07 p.m.
Uranus opposition   New Moon 1:27 a.m.

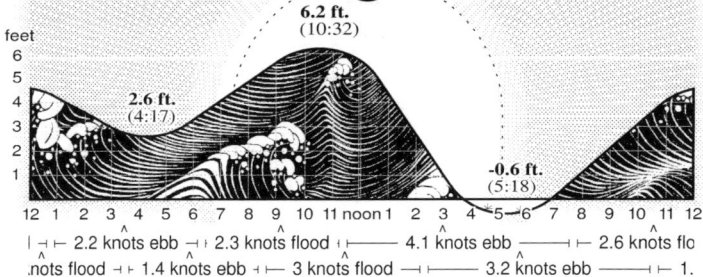

6.2 ft.
(10:32)

2.6 ft.
(4:17)

-0.6 ft.
(5:18)

feet

⊢ ⊣ ⊢ 2.2 knots ebb ⊣ ⊢ 2.3 knots flood ⊢ ⊢ 4.1 knots ebb ⊢ ⊢ 2.6 knots flo
knots flood ⊣ ⊢ 1.4 knots ebb ⊣ ⊢ 3 knots flood ⊣ ⊢ 3.2 knots ebb ⊢ 1.

TUE NOV 14
dawn 5:49 sunrise 6:49 sunset 4:59 dark 5:59
moonrise 8:24 a.m. moonset 5:48 p.m.

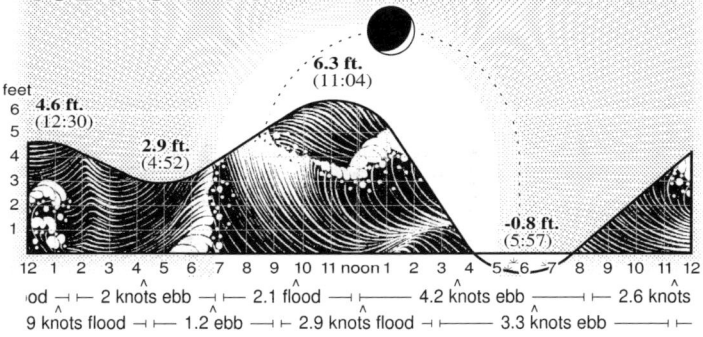

6.3 ft.
(11:04)

4.6 ft.
(12:30)

2.9 ft.
(4:52)

-0.8 ft.
(5:57)

feet

od ⊣ ⊢ 2 knots ebb ⊣ ⊢ 2.1 flood ⊣ ⊢ 4.2 knots ebb ⊢ ⊢ 2.6 knots
9 knots flood ⊣ ⊢ 1.2 ebb ⊣ ⊢ 2.9 knots flood ⊣ ⊢ 3.3 knots ebb ⊢ ⊢

WED NOV 15
dawn 5:50 sunrise 6:50 sunset 4:59 dark 5:58
moonrise 9:32 a.m. moonset 6:39 p.m.

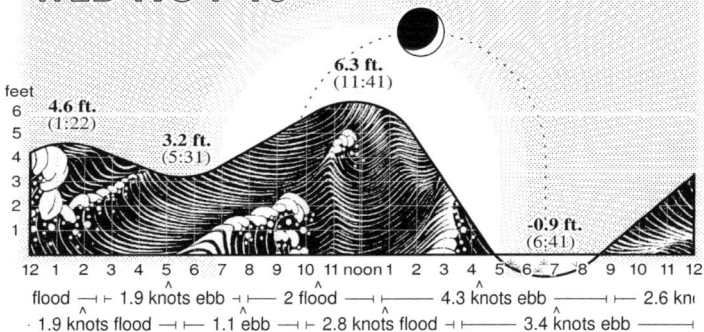

6.3 ft.
(11:41)

4.6 ft.
(1:22)

3.2 ft.
(5:31)

-0.9 ft.
(6:41)

feet

flood ⊣ ⊢ 1.9 knots ebb ⊣ ⊢ 2 flood ⊣ ⊢ 4.3 knots ebb ⊢ ⊢ 2.6 kn
⊢ 1.9 knots flood ⊣ ⊢ 1.1 ebb ⊣ ⊢ 2.8 knots flood ⊣ ⊢ 3.4 knots ebb ⊢

THU NOV 16
dawn 5:51 sunrise 6:51 sunset 4:58 dark 5:58
moonrise 10:35 a.m. moonset 7:40 p.m.

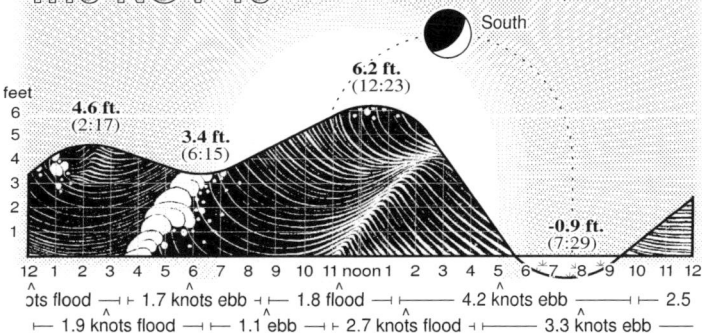

South

6.2 ft.
(12:23)

4.6 ft.
(2:17)

3.4 ft.
(6:15)

-0.9 ft.
(7:29)

feet

ots flood ⊣ ⊢ 1.7 knots ebb ⊣ ⊢ 1.8 flood ⊣ ⊢ 4.2 knots ebb ⊢ ⊢ 2.5
⊢ 1.9 knots flood ⊣ ⊢ 1.1 ebb ⊣ ⊢ 2.7 knots flood ⊣ ⊢ 3.3 knots ebb ⊢

FRI NOV 10

dawn 5:46 sunrise 6:45 sunset 5:02 dark 6:02
moonrise 4:01 a.m. moonset 3:42 p.m.

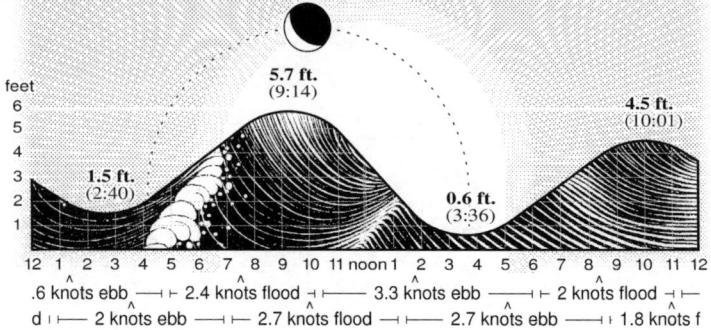

5.7 ft.
(9:14)

4.5 ft.
(10:01)

feet
6
5
4
3
2
1

1.5 ft.
(2:40)

0.6 ft.
(3:36)

12 1 2 3 4 5 6 7 8 9 10 11 noon 1 2 3 4 5 6 7 8 9 10 11 12

.6 knots ebb ⊢ 2.4 knots flood ⊣ ⊢ 3.3 knots ebb ⊢ 2 knots flood ⊣ ⊢
d ⊢ 2 knots ebb ⊢ 2.7 knots flood ⊣ ⊢ 2.7 knots ebb ⊣ 1.8 knots f

SAT NOV 11

dawn 5:47 sunrise 6:46 sunset 5:02 dark 6:01
moonrise 5:03 a.m. moonset 4:06 p.m.

Veterans' Day

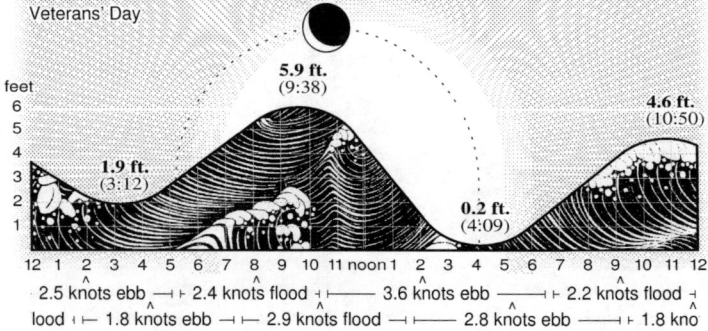

5.9 ft.
(9:38)

4.6 ft.
(10:50)

feet
6
5
4
3
2
1

1.9 ft.
(3:12)

0.2 ft.
(4:09)

12 1 2 3 4 5 6 7 8 9 10 11 noon 1 2 3 4 5 6 7 8 9 10 11 12

2.5 knots ebb ⊢ 2.4 knots flood ⊣ ⊢ 3.6 knots ebb ⊢ 2.2 knots flood ⊣
lood ⊢ 1.8 knots ebb ⊢ 2.9 knots flood ⊣ ⊢ 2.8 knots ebb ⊢ 1.8 kno

SUN NOV 12

dawn 5:47 sunrise 6:47 sunset 5:01 dark 6:00
moonrise 6:07 a.m. moonset 4:34 p.m.

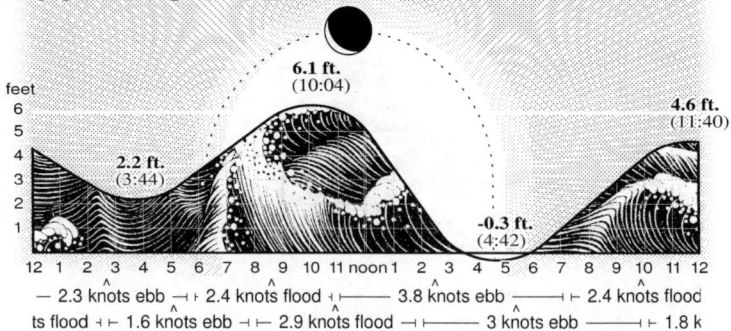

6.1 ft.
(10:04)

4.6 ft.
(11:40)

feet
6
5
4
3
2
1

2.2 ft.
(3:44)

-0.3 ft.
(4:42)

12 1 2 3 4 5 6 7 8 9 10 11 noon 1 2 3 4 5 6 7 8 9 10 11 12

— 2.3 knots ebb ⊢ 2.4 knots flood ⊣ ⊢ 3.8 knots ebb ⊢ 2.4 knots flood
ts flood ⊢ 1.6 knots ebb ⊢ 2.9 knots flood ⊣ ⊢ 3 knots ebb ⊢ 1.8 k

Ⓥ   Ⓢ   Ⓙ

MON NOV 6 dawn 5:42 sunrise 6:40 sunset 5:06 dark 6:05
moonrise 12:04 a.m. moonset 2:13 p.m.

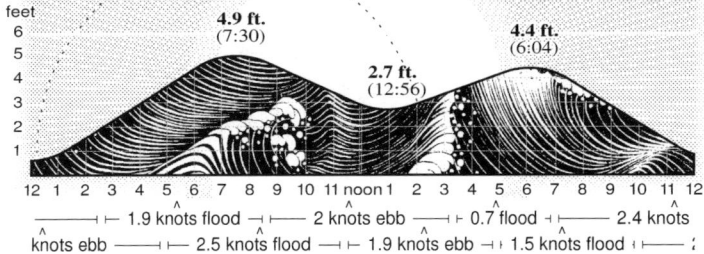

apogee

feet
6
5
4
3
2
1

4.9 ft.
(7:30)

2.7 ft.
(12:56)

4.4 ft.
(6:04)

12 1 2 3 4 5 6 7 8 9 10 11 noon 1 2 3 4 5 6 7 8 9 10 11 12

├─ 1.9 knots flood ─┤ ├─ 2 knots ebb ──┤ ├─ 0.7 flood ─┤ ├─ 2.4 knots
knots ebb ─┤ ├─ 2.5 knots flood ─┤ ├─ 1.9 knots ebb ─┤ ├─ 1.5 knots flood ─┤ ├─ 2

TUE NOV 7 dawn 5:43 sunrise 6:42 sunset 5:05 dark 6:04
moonrise 1:04 a.m. moonset 2:36 p.m.

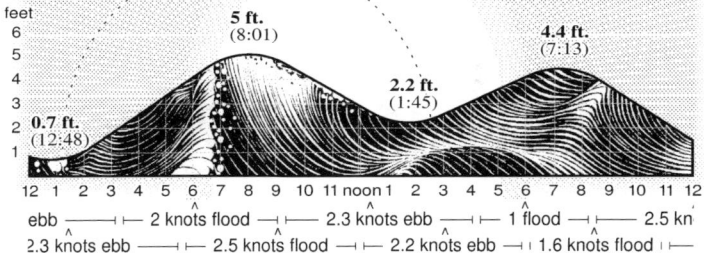

feet
6
5
4
3
2
1

5 ft.
(8:01)

2.2 ft.
(1:45)

4.4 ft.
(7:13)

0.7 ft.
(12:48)

12 1 2 3 4 5 6 7 8 9 10 11 noon 1 2 3 4 5 6 7 8 9 10 11 12

ebb ─┤ ├─ 2 knots flood ─┤ ├─ 2.3 knots ebb ──┤ ├─ 1 flood ─┤ ├─ 2.5 kn
2.3 knots ebb ──┤ ├─ 2.5 knots flood ─┤ ├─ 2.2 knots ebb ─┤ ├─ 1.6 knots flood ─┤ ├─

WED NOV 8 dawn 5:44 sunrise 6:43 sunset 5:04 dark 6:03
moonrise 2:03 a.m. moonset 2:58 p.m.

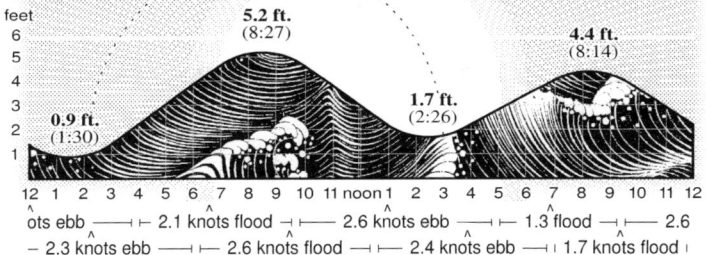

feet
6
5
4
3
2
1

5.2 ft.
(8:27)

1.7 ft.
(2:26)

4.4 ft.
(8:14)

0.9 ft.
(1:30)

12 1 2 3 4 5 6 7 8 9 10 11 noon 1 2 3 4 5 6 7 8 9 10 11 12

ots ebb ─┤ ├─ 2.1 knots flood ─┤ ├─ 2.6 knots ebb ──┤ ├─ 1.3 flood ─┤ ├─ 2.6
├─ 2.3 knots ebb ──┤ ├─ 2.6 knots flood ─┤ ├─ 2.4 knots ebb ─┤ ├─ 1.7 knots flood ─┤

THU NOV 9 dawn 5:45 sunrise 6:44 sunset 5:03 dark 6:02
moonrise 3:02 a.m. moonset 3:20 p.m.

equator   Venus south Moon 1 degree

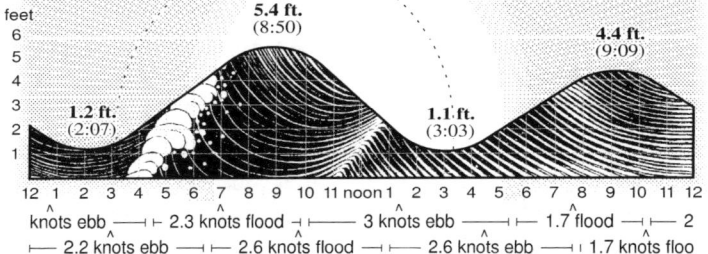

feet
6
5
4
3
2
1

5.4 ft.
(8:50)

4.4 ft.
(9:09)

1.2 ft.
(2:07)

1.1 ft.
(3:03)

12 1 2 3 4 5 6 7 8 9 10 11 noon 1 2 3 4 5 6 7 8 9 10 11 12

knots ebb ──┤ ├─ 2.3 knots flood ─┤ ├─ 3 knots ebb ───┤ ├─ 1.7 flood ─┤ ├─ 2
├─ 2.2 knots ebb ──┤ ├─ 2.6 knots flood ─┤ ├─ 2.6 knots ebb ──┤ ├─ 1.7 knots floo

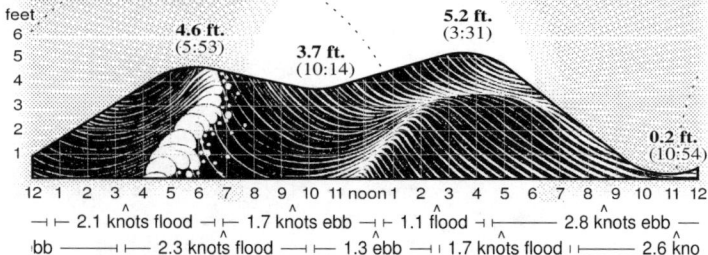

FRI NOV 3

dawn 6:39 sunrise 7:37 sunset 6:09 dark 7:07
moonset 1:38 p.m. moonrise 11:01 p.m.

Jupiter opposition

5.2 ft. (3:31)
4.6 ft. (5:53)
3.7 ft. (10:14)
0.2 ft. (10:54)

feet
6
5
4
3
2
1

12 1 2 3 4 5 6 7 8 9 10 11 noon 1 2 3 4 5 6 7 8 9 10 11 12

⊣ ⊢ 2.1 knots flood ⊣ ⊢ 1.7 knots ebb ⊣ ⊢ 1.1 flood ⊣ ⊢ 2.8 knots ebb ⊢
bb ⊢ 2.3 knots flood ⊣ ⊢ 1.3 ebb ⊣ 1.7 knots flood ⊢ 2.6 kno

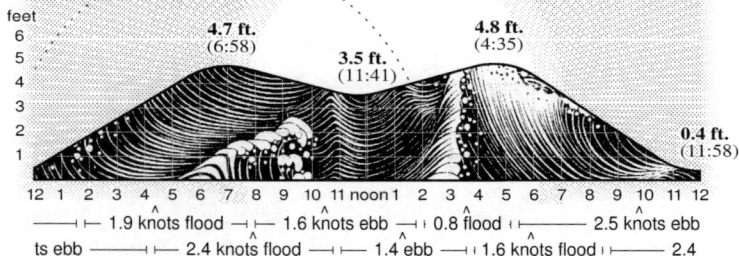

SAT NOV 4

dawn 6:40 sunrise 7:38 sunset 6:08 dark 7:07
moonset 2:15 p.m.

Taurids' Peak

4.7 ft. (6:58)
4.8 ft. (4:35)
3.5 ft. (11:41)
0.4 ft. (11:58)

feet
6
5
4
3
2
1

12 1 2 3 4 5 6 7 8 9 10 11 noon 1 2 3 4 5 6 7 8 9 10 11 12

⊣ ⊢ 1.9 knots flood ⊣ ⊢ 1.6 knots ebb ⊣ ⊢ 0.8 flood ⊣ ⊢ 2.5 knots ebb ⊢
ts ebb ⊢ 2.4 knots flood ⊣ ⊢ 1.4 ebb ⊣ 1.6 knots flood ⊢ 2.4

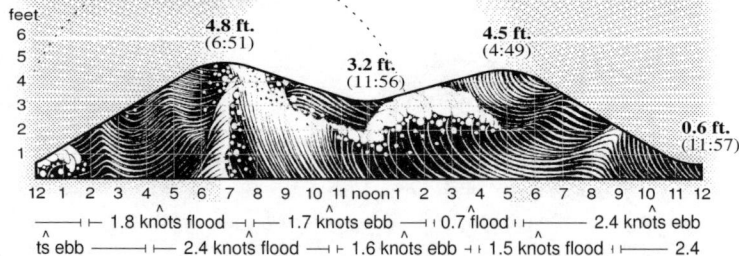

SUN NOV 5

dawn 5:41 sunrise 6:39 sunset 5:07 dark 6:06
moonset 1:46 p.m.

Daylight Savings Time Ends

4.8 ft. (6:51)
4.5 ft. (4:49)
3.2 ft. (11:56)
0.6 ft. (11:57)

feet
6
5
4
3
2
1

12 1 2 3 4 5 6 7 8 9 10 11 noon 1 2 3 4 5 6 7 8 9 10 11 12

⊣ ⊢ 1.8 knots flood ⊣ ⊢ 1.7 knots ebb ⊣ 0.7 flood ⊢ 2.4 knots ebb ⊢
ts ebb ⊢ 2.4 knots flood ⊣ ⊢ 1.6 knots ebb ⊣ 1.5 knots flood ⊢ 2.4

ⓥ   Ⓢ   Ⓙ

Jupiter at opposition On Nov 3rd, Jupiter will be at its closest approach to Earth. The planet will be shining brightly and visible all night. With a clear dark sky and a good pair of binoculars you should be able to identify Jupiter's four largest moons. **Taurids Meteor Shower** The Taurids run annually between Sep 7th to Dec 10th with this year's peak on Nov 4th. The Taurids are a minor shower producing at peak 5 to 10 meteors per hour. The constellation Taurus, the shower's radiant point, will rise above the eastern horizon by 8:00 p.m. into a dark sky provided by an early setting second quarter moon.

MON OCT 30
dawn 6:35 sunrise 7:33 sunset 6:13 dark 7:11
moonset 9:45 a.m. moonrise 7:26 p.m.

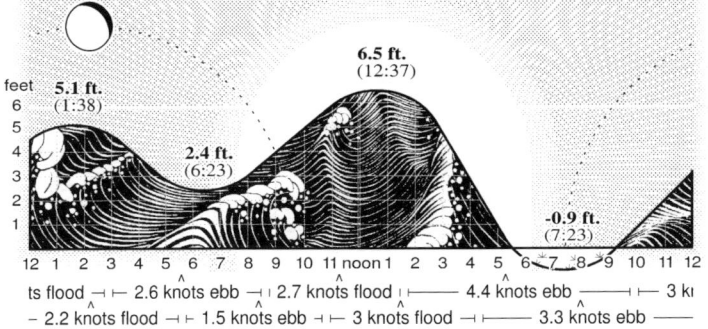

feet

6.5 ft.
(12:37)

5.1 ft.
(1:38)

2.4 ft.
(6:23)

-0.9 ft.
(7:23)

6
5
4
3
2
1

12 1 2 3 4 5 6 7 8 9 10 11 noon 1 2 3 4 5 6 7 8 9 10 11 12

ts flood ⊣ ⊢ 2.6 knots ebb ⊣ ⊢ 2.7 knots flood ⊢—— 4.4 knots ebb ——⊢ 3 kı
– 2.2 knots flood ⊣ ⊢ 1.5 knots ebb ⊣ ⊢ 3 knots flood ⊣ ⊢—— 3.3 knots ebb ——

TUE OCT 31
dawn 6:36 sunrise 7:34 sunset 6:12 dark 7:10
moonset 10:54 a.m. moonrise 8:11 p.m.

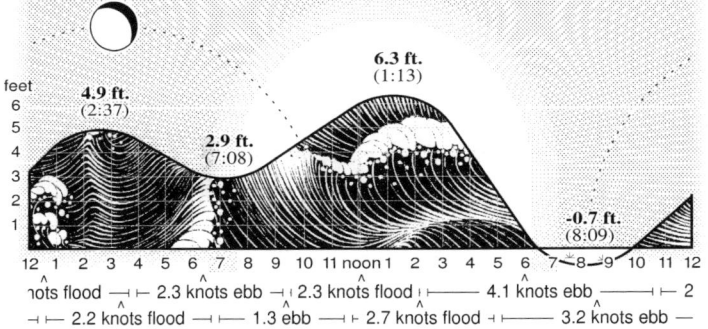

feet

6.3 ft.
(1:13)

4.9 ft.
(2:37)

2.9 ft.
(7:08)

-0.7 ft.
(8:09)

6
5
4
3
2
1

12 1 2 3 4 5 6 7 8 9 10 11 noon 1 2 3 4 5 6 7 8 9 10 11 12

nots flood ⊣ ⊢ 2.3 knots ebb ⊣ ⊢ 2.3 knots flood ⊢—— 4.1 knots ebb ——⊢ 2
⊣ ⊢ 2.2 knots flood ⊣ ⊢ 1.3 ebb —— ⊢ 2.7 knots flood ⊣ ⊢—— 3.2 knots ebb —

WED NOV 1
dawn 6:37 sunrise 7:35 sunset 6:11 dark 7:09
moonset 11:58 a.m. moonrise 9:03 p.m.

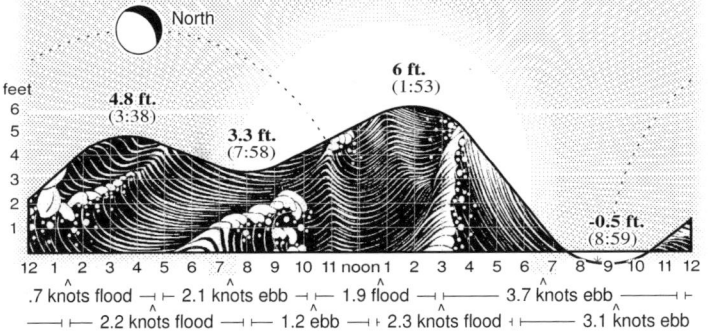

North

feet

6 ft.
(1:53)

4.8 ft.
(3:38)

3.3 ft.
(7:58)

-0.5 ft.
(8:59)

6
5
4
3
2
1

12 1 2 3 4 5 6 7 8 9 10 11 noon 1 2 3 4 5 6 7 8 9 10 11 12

.7 knots flood ⊣ ⊢ 2.1 knots ebb ⊢— 1.9 flood ⊣ ⊢—— 3.7 knots ebb ——— ⊢
—— ⊢ 2.2 knots flood ⊣ ⊢ 1.2 ebb —— ⊢ 2.3 knots flood ⊣ ⊢—— 3.1 knots ebb

THU NOV 2
dawn 6:38 sunrise 7:36 sunset 6:10 dark 7:08
moonset 12:52 p.m. moonrise 10:00 p.m.

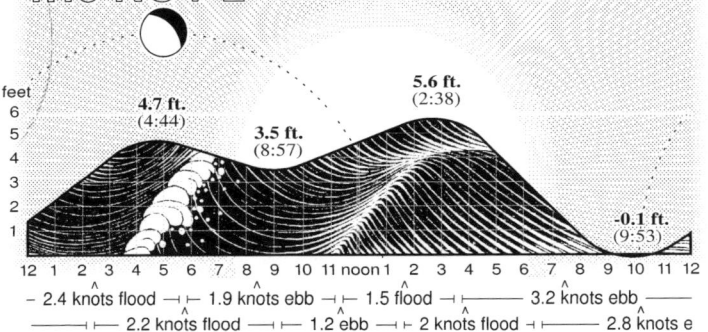

feet

5.6 ft.
(2:38)

4.7 ft.
(4:44)

3.5 ft.
(8:57)

-0.1 ft.
(9:53)

6
5
4
3
2
1

12 1 2 3 4 5 6 7 8 9 10 11 noon 1 2 3 4 5 6 7 8 9 10 11 12

– 2.4 knots flood ⊣ ⊢ 1.9 knots ebb ⊣ ⊢ 1.5 flood ⊣ ⊢—— 3.2 knots ebb ——
—— ⊣ ⊢ 2.2 knots flood ⊣ ⊢ 1.2 ebb — ⊢ 2 knots flood ⊣ ⊢—— 2.8 knots e

FRI OCT 27

dawn 6:32 sunrise 7:30 sunset 6:17 dark 7:15
moonset 6:06 a.m. moonrise 5:45 p.m.

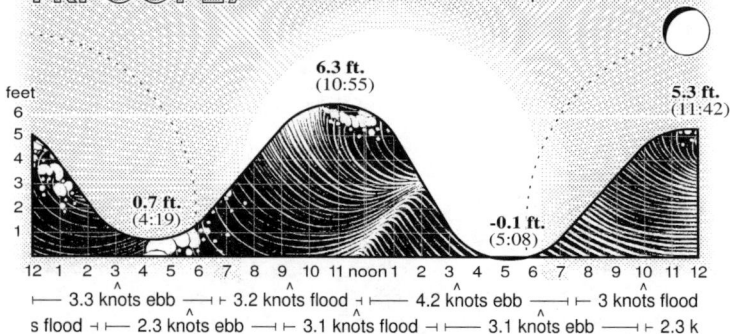

6.3 ft.
(10:55)

5.3 ft.
(11:42)

feet
6
5
4
3
2
1

0.7 ft.
(4:19)

-0.1 ft.
(5:08)

12 1 2 3 4 5 6 7 8 9 10 11 noon 1 2 3 4 5 6 7 8 9 10 11 12

⊢— 3.3 knots ebb —⊣ ⊢ 3.2 knots flood ⊣⊢— 4.2 knots ebb —⊣ ⊢ 3 knots flood
s flood ⊣ ⊢— 2.3 knots ebb —⊣ ⊢ 3.1 knots flood ⊣ ⊢— 3.1 knots ebb —⊣ ⊢ 2.3 k

SAT OCT 28

dawn 6:33 sunrise 7:31 sunset 6:16 dark 7:14
moonset 7:19 a.m. moonrise 6:14 p.m.

Full Moon 1:24 p.m.   Partial Lunar eclipse

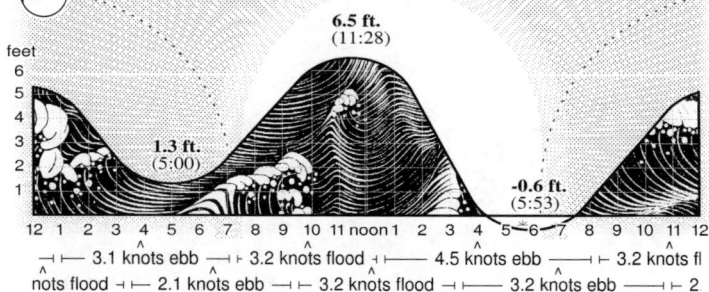

6.5 ft.
(11:28)

feet
6
5
4
3
2
1

1.3 ft.
(5:00)

-0.6 ft.
(5:53)

12 1 2 3 4 5 6 7 8 9 10 11 noon 1 2 3 4 5 6 7 8 9 10 11 12

⊣ ⊢— 3.1 knots ebb —⊣ ⊢ 3.2 knots flood ⊣ ⊢— 4.5 knots ebb —⊣ ⊢ 3.2 knots fl
nots flood ⊣ ⊢— 2.1 knots ebb —⊣ ⊢ 3.2 knots flood ⊣ ⊢— 3.2 knots ebb —⊣ ⊢ 2

SUN OCT 29

dawn 6:34 sunrise 7:32 sunset 6:15 dark 7:12
moonset 8:32 a.m. moonrise 6:47 p.m.

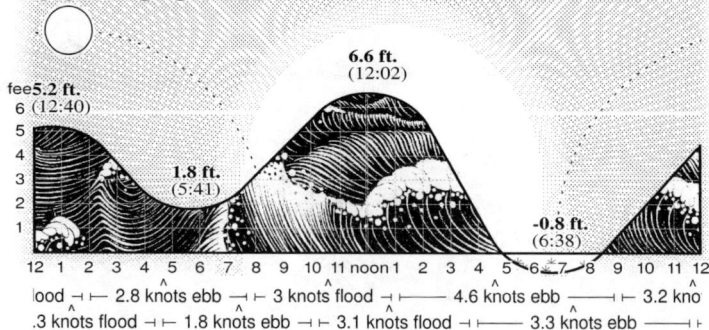

6.6 ft.
(12:02)

fee**5.2 ft.**
6 (12:40)
5
4
3
2
1

1.8 ft.
(5:41)

-0.8 ft.
(6:38)

12 1 2 3 4 5 6 7 8 9 10 11 noon 1 2 3 4 5 6 7 8 9 10 11 12

lood ⊣ ⊢— 2.8 knots ebb —⊣ ⊢ 3 knots flood ⊣ ⊢— 4.6 knots ebb —⊣ ⊢ 3.2 kno
.3 knots flood ⊣ ⊢ 1.8 knots ebb ⊣ ⊢ 3.1 knots flood ⊣ ⊢— 3.3 knots ebb —⊣ ⊢

Ⓙ   Ⓥ   Ⓢ

Partial Lunar Eclipse a partial lunar eclipse occurs when the Moon
passes through the Earth's shadow. The Oct 28 partial lunar eclipse will
principally be visible in Europe and Africa - hopefully the experience will
be shared on social media. In the U.S. as the moon rises in late afternoon
over the mid Atlantic and northern New England regions, the eclipse enters
its final phase with the moon moving out of the Earth's penumbral shadow.

MON OCT 23

dawn 6:29 sunrise 7:26 sunset 6:22 dark 7:19
moonset 1:11 a.m. moonrise 3:52 p.m.

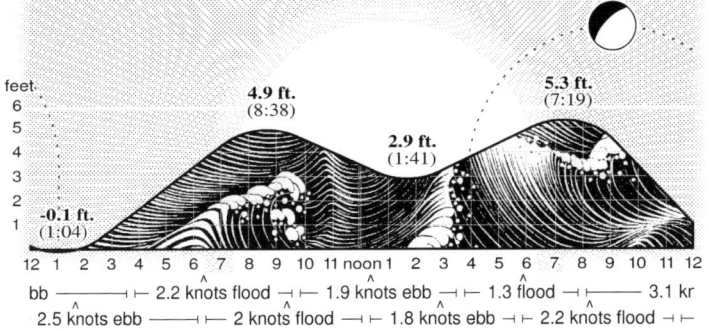

feet

4.9 ft.
(8:38)

2.9 ft.
(1:41)

5.3 ft.
(7:19)

-0.1 ft.
(1:04)

12 1 2 3 4 5 6 7 8 9 10 11 noon 1 2 3 4 5 6 7 8 9 10 11 12

bb ⊢— 2.2 knots flood —⊢ ⊢ 1.9 knots ebb —⊢ ⊢ 1.3 flood —⊢ ⊢—— 3.1 kr
2.5 knots ebb ——⊢ ⊢— 2 knots flood —⊢ ⊢ 1.8 knots ebb —⊢ ⊢ 2.2 knots flood —⊢ ⊢

TUE OCT 24

dawn 6:30 sunrise 7:27 sunset 6:21 dark 7:18
moonset 2:26 a.m. moonrise 4:23 p.m.

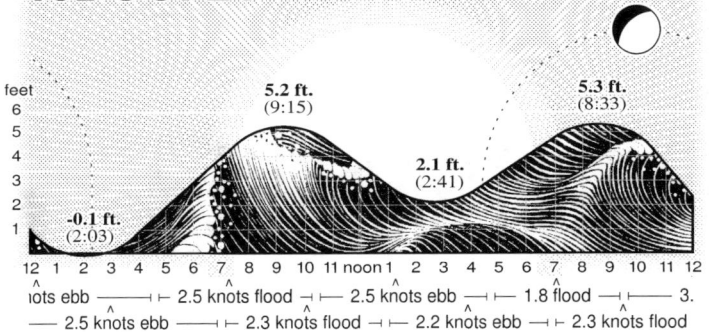

feet

5.2 ft.
(9:15)

5.3 ft.
(8:33)

2.1 ft.
(2:41)

-0.1 ft.
(2:03)

12 1 2 3 4 5 6 7 8 9 10 11 noon 1 2 3 4 5 6 7 8 9 10 11 12

ιots ebb —— ⊢ ⊢ 2.5 knots flood —⊢ ⊢— 2.5 knots ebb —⊢ ⊢— 1.8 flood —⊢ ⊢—— 3.
⊢— 2.5 knots ebb ——⊢ ⊢— 2.3 knots flood —⊢ ⊢— 2.2 knots ebb —⊢ ⊢ 2.3 knots flood

WED OCT 25

dawn 6:30 sunrise 7:28 sunset 6:19 dark 7:17
moonset 3:40 a.m. moonrise 4:51 p.m.

perigee

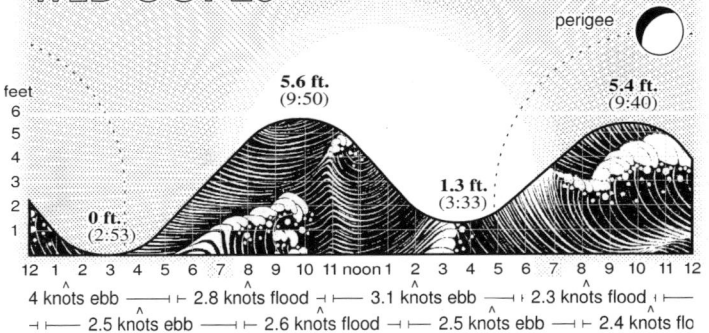

feet

5.6 ft.
(9:50)

5.4 ft.
(9:40)

0 ft.
(2:53)

1.3 ft.
(3:33)

12 1 2 3 4 5 6 7 8 9 10 11 noon 1 2 3 4 5 6 7 8 9 10 11 12

4 knots ebb ——⊢ ⊢ 2.8 knots flood —⊢ ⊢— 3.1 knots ebb —⊢ ⊢ 2.3 knots flood —⊢ ⊢—
⊢—— 2.5 knots ebb ——⊢ ⊢— 2.6 knots flood —⊢ ⊢— 2.5 knots ebb —⊢ ⊢ 2.4 knots flo

THU OCT 26

dawn 6:31 sunrise 7:29 sunset 6:18 dark 7:16
moonset 4:53 a.m. moonrise 5:18 p.m.

equator

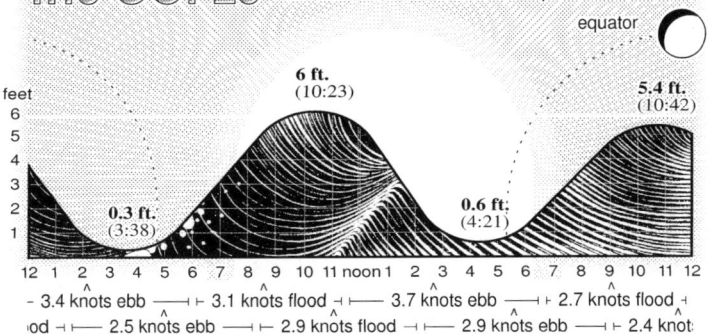

feet

6 ft.
(10:23)

5.4 ft.
(10:42)

0.3 ft.
(3:38)

0.6 ft.
(4:21)

12 1 2 3 4 5 6 7 8 9 10 11 noon 1 2 3 4 5 6 7 8 9 10 11 12

⊢ 3.4 knots ebb ——⊢ ⊢ 3.1 knots flood —⊢ ⊢— 3.7 knots ebb ——⊢ ⊢ 2.7 knots flood —⊢
ιod —⊢ ⊢— 2.5 knots ebb ——⊢ ⊢ 2.9 knots flood —⊢ ⊢— 2.9 knots ebb ——⊢ ⊢ 2.4 knot:

FRI OCT 20

dawn 6:26 sunrise 7:23 sunset 6:26 dark 7:23
moonrise 1:41 p.m. moonset 10:47 p.m.

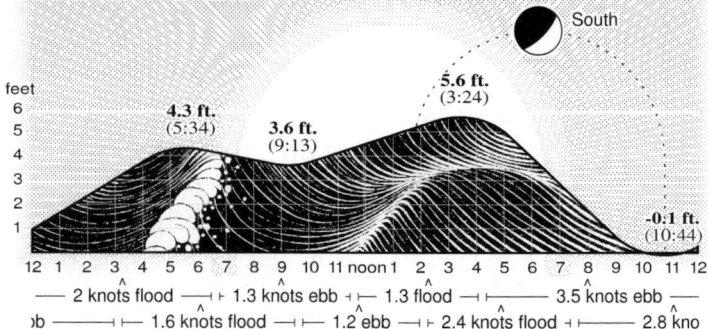

South

feet

4.3 ft.
(5:34)

3.6 ft.
(9:13)

5.6 ft.
(3:24)

-0.1 ft.
(10:44)

12 1 2 3 4 5 6 7 8 9 10 11 noon 1 2 3 4 5 6 7 8 9 10 11 12

— 2 knots flood —| |— 1.3 knots ebb —| |— 1.3 flood —| |— 3.5 knots ebb —

)b ———| |— 1.6 knots flood —| |— 1.2 ebb —| |— 2.4 knots flood —| |— 2.8 kno

SAT OCT 21

dawn 6:27 sunrise 7:24 sunset 6:24 dark 7:22
moonrise 2:33 p.m. moonset 11:57 p.m.

Orionids' Peak

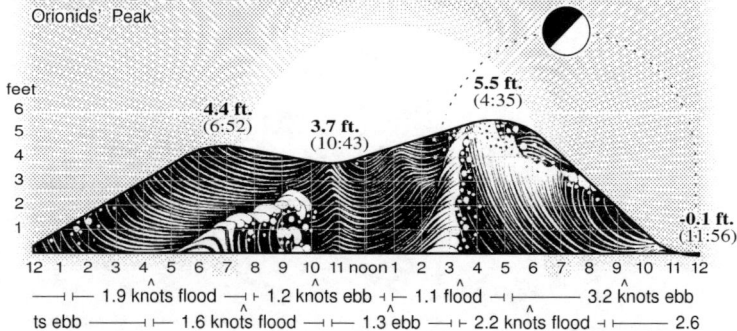

feet

4.4 ft.
(6:52)

3.7 ft.
(10:43)

5.5 ft.
(4:35)

-0.1 ft.
(11:56)

12 1 2 3 4 5 6 7 8 9 10 11 noon 1 2 3 4 5 6 7 8 9 10 11 12

—| |— 1.9 knots flood —| |— 1.2 knots ebb —| |— 1.1 flood —| |— 3.2 knots ebb —

ts ebb ———| |— 1.6 knots flood —| |— 1.3 ebb —| |— 2.2 knots flood —| |— 2.6

SUN OCT 22

dawn 6:28 sunrise 7:25 sunset 6:23 dark 7:20
moonrise 3:16 p.m.

Comet 2P/Encke Perihelion

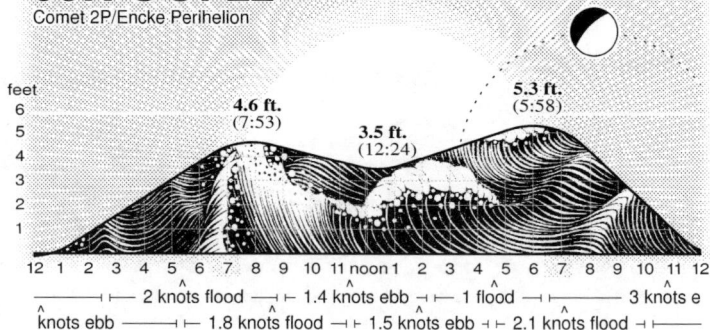

feet

4.6 ft.
(7:53)

3.5 ft.
(12:24)

5.3 ft.
(5:58)

12 1 2 3 4 5 6 7 8 9 10 11 noon 1 2 3 4 5 6 7 8 9 10 11 12

—| |— 2 knots flood —| |— 1.4 knots ebb —| |— 1 flood —| |— 3 knots e

knots ebb ———| |— 1.8 knots flood —| |— 1.5 knots ebb —| |— 2.1 knots flood —| |—

ⓙ   ⓥ   Ⓢ

Orionids Meteor Shower The Orionids run annually from Oct 2nd to Nov 7th and are thought to be Comet Halley remnants. This year's peak, Oct 21st & 22nd, could produce 20 meteors per hour from its radiant point, the constellation Orion. The moon sets near midnight with Orion high above the eastern horizon. **Comet 2P/Encke** on the 22nd will be at perihelion with the Sun at a distance of .34 AU, or little more than 1/3 of the mean distance between the Sun and the Earth. At this distance, Comet Encke's coma and tail will be fully illuminated by the solar winds and glowing brightly.

MON OCT 16

dawn 6:22 sunrise 7:19 sunset 6:31 dark 7:28
moonrise 9:20 a.m. moonset 7:33 p.m.

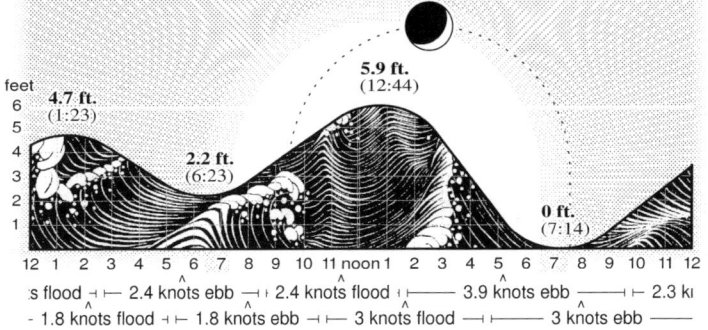

feet

4.7 ft.
(1:23)

5.9 ft.
(12:44)

2.2 ft.
(6:23)

0 ft.
(7:14)

s flood ⊣ ⊢ 2.4 knots ebb ⊣ ⊢ 2.4 knots flood ⊢ ⊢ 3.9 knots ebb ⊣ ⊢ 2.3 kı

- 1.8 knots flood ⊣ ⊢ 1.8 knots ebb ⊣ ⊢ 3 knots flood ⊢ ⊣ ⊢ 3 knots ebb ⸺

TUE OCT 17

dawn 6:23 sunrise 7:20 sunset 6:30 dark 7:27
moonrise 10:27 a.m. moonset 8:08 p.m.

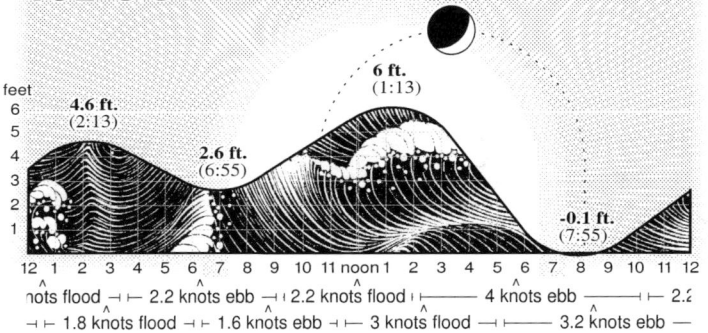

feet

4.6 ft.
(2:13)

6 ft.
(1:13)

2.6 ft.
(6:55)

-0.1 ft.
(7:55)

ınots flood ⊣ ⊢ 2.2 knots ebb ⊣ ⊢ 2.2 knots flood ⊢ ⊢ 4 knots ebb ⸺ ⊢ 2.2

⊣ ⊢ 1.8 knots flood ⊣ ⊢ 1.6 knots ebb ⊣ ⊢ 3 knots flood ⊣ ⊢ 3.2 knots ebb ⸺

WED OCT 18

dawn 6:24 sunrise 7:21 sunset 6:28 dark 7:25
moonrise 11:35 a.m. moonset 8:51 p.m.

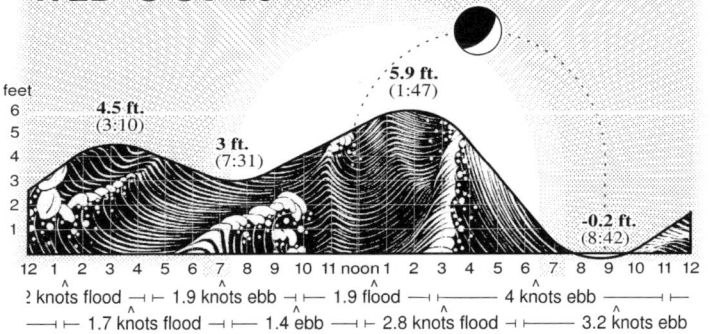

feet

4.5 ft.
(3:10)

5.9 ft.
(1:47)

3 ft.
(7:31)

-0.2 ft.
(8:42)

2 knots flood ⸺ ⊢ 1.9 knots ebb ⊣ ⊢ 1.9 flood ⸺ ⊢ ⊢ 4 knots ebb ⸺ ⊢

⸺ ⊢ 1.7 knots flood ⊣ ⊢ 1.4 ebb ⸺ ⊢ 2.8 knots flood ⊣ ⊢ 3.2 knots ebb

THU OCT 19

dawn 6:25 sunrise 7:22 sunset 6:27 dark 7:24
moonrise 12:41 p.m. moonset 9:44 p.m.

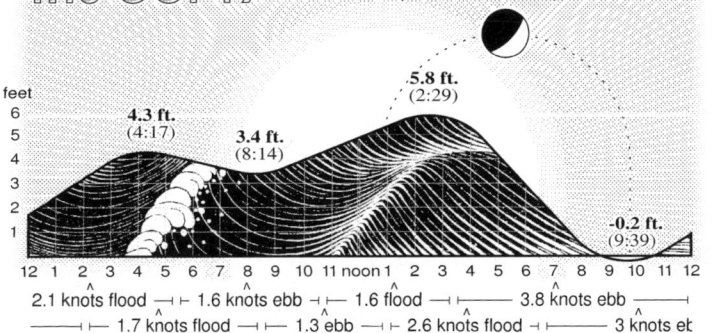

feet

4.3 ft.
(4:17)

5.8 ft.
(2:29)

3.4 ft.
(8:14)

-0.2 ft.
(9:39)

2.1 knots flood ⸺ ⊣ ⊢ 1.6 knots ebb ⊣ ⊢ 1.6 flood ⸺ ⊢ ⊢ 3.8 knots ebb ⸺

⸺ ⊣ ⊢ 1.7 knots flood ⸺ ⊢ 1.3 ebb ⸺ ⊢ 2.6 knots flood ⊣ ⊢ 3 knots et

12 1 2 3 4 5 6 7 8 9 10 11 noon 1 2 3 4 5 6 7 8 9 10 11 12

FRI OCT 13

dawn 6:19 sunrise 7:16 sunset 6:35 dark 7:32
moonrise 6:13 a.m. moonset 6:16 p.m.

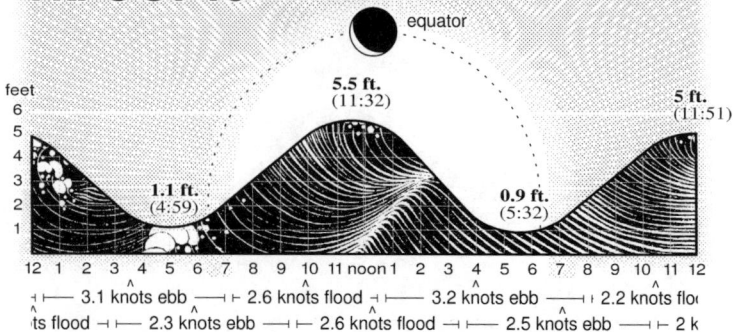

equator

5.5 ft.
(11:32)

5 ft.
(11:51)

feet

1.1 ft.
(4:59)

0.9 ft.
(5:32)

12 1 2 3 4 5 6 7 8 9 10 11 noon 1 2 3 4 5 6 7 8 9 10 11 12

⊢—— 3.1 knots ebb ——⌐ ⊢ 2.6 knots flood ⊣ ⊢—— 3.2 knots ebb ——— ⊢ 2.2 knots floo

ts flood ⊣ ⊢— 2.3 knots ebb —⊢ ⊢— 2.6 knots flood ⊣ ⊢— 2.5 knots ebb ——⊢ 2 k

SAT OCT 14

dawn 6:20 sunrise 7:17 sunset 6:34 dark 7:31
moonrise 7:13 a.m. moonset 6:39 p.m.

Annular solar eclipse

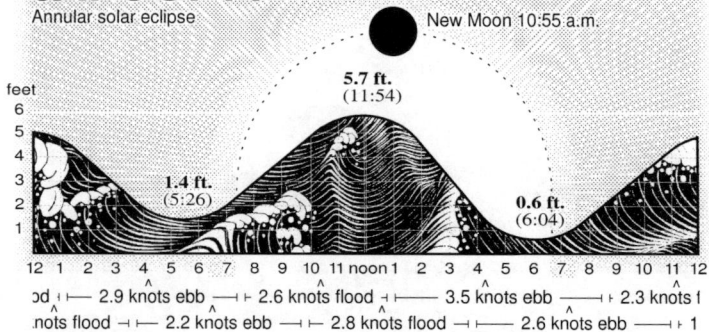

New Moon 10:55 a.m.

5.7 ft.
(11:54)

feet

1.4 ft.
(5:26)

0.6 ft.
(6:04)

12 1 2 3 4 5 6 7 8 9 10 11 noon 1 2 3 4 5 6 7 8 9 10 11 12

od ⌐ ⊢— 2.9 knots ebb —⌐ ⊢ 2.6 knots flood ⌐ ⊢——— 3.5 knots ebb ——— ⊢ 2.3 knots f

knots flood ⊣ ⊢— 2.2 knots ebb —⊣ ⊢— 2.8 knots flood ⌐ ⊢—— 2.6 knots ebb ——⊢ 1

SUN OCT 15

dawn 6:21 sunrise 7:18 sunset 6:33 dark 7:29
moonrise 8:15 a.m. moonset 7:04 p.m.

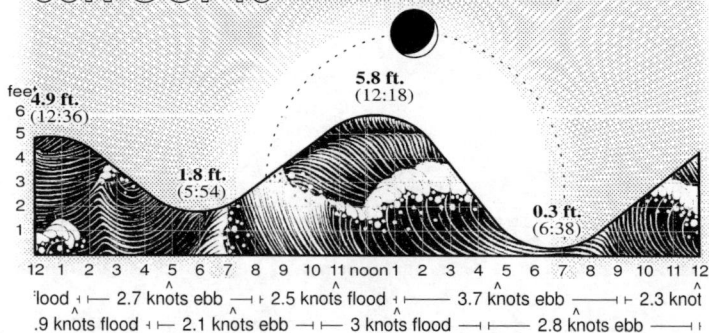

5.8 ft.
(12:18)

feet
4.9 ft.
(12:36)

1.8 ft.
(5:54)

0.3 ft.
(6:38)

12 1 2 3 4 5 6 7 8 9 10 11 noon 1 2 3 4 5 6 7 8 9 10 11 12

flood ⌐ ⊢— 2.7 knots ebb —⌐ ⊢ 2.5 knots flood ⌐ ⊢——— 3.7 knots ebb ——— ⊢ 2.3 knot

.9 knots flood ⌐ ⊢— 2.1 knots ebb —⌐ ⊢ 3 knots flood ⌐ ⊢—— 2.8 knots ebb ——⊣

Ⓙ   Ⓥ   Ⓢ

Annular Solar Eclipse The Oct 14th eclipse's path will begin
in the Pacific Ocean and come ashore in Oregon at approximately 8:05 a.m.
passing by Eugene, Florence, Reedsport, North Bend and Coos Bay with
the eclipse's path heading southwesterly towards Albuquerque, then
Texas, Central and South America.

MON OCT 9

dawn 6:16 sunrise 7:13 sunset 6:41 dark 7:38
moonrise 2:15 a.m. moonset 4:45 p.m.

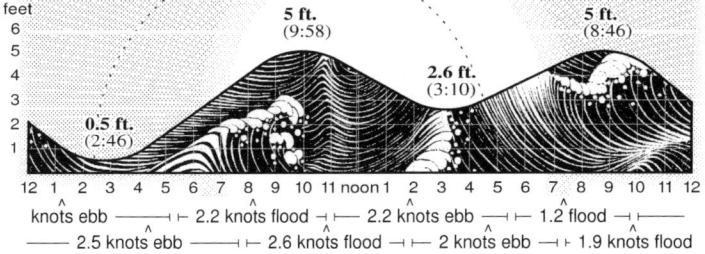

Columbus Day

apogee

feet

5 ft.
(9:58)

5 ft.
(8:46)

2.6 ft.
(3:10)

0.5 ft.
(2:46)

12 1 2 3 4 5 6 7 8 9 10 11 noon 1 2 3 4 5 6 7 8 9 10 11 12

knots ebb ⊢ 2.2 knots flood ⊣ ⊢ 2.2 knots ebb ⊢ 1.2 flood ⊣ ⊢

2.5 knots ebb ⊢ 2.6 knots flood ⊣ ⊢ 2 knots ebb ⊢ 1.9 knots flood

TUE OCT 10

dawn 6:17 sunrise 7:14 sunset 6:40 dark 7:36
moonrise 3:16 a.m. moonset 5:10 p.m.

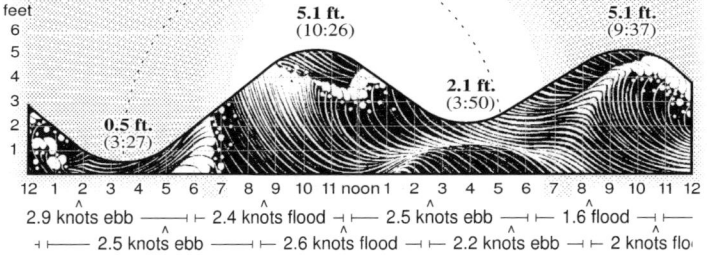

feet

5.1 ft.
(10:26)

5.1 ft.
(9:37)

2.1 ft.
(3:50)

0.5 ft.
(3:27)

12 1 2 3 4 5 6 7 8 9 10 11 noon 1 2 3 4 5 6 7 8 9 10 11 12

2.9 knots ebb ⊢ 2.4 knots flood ⊣ ⊢ 2.5 knots ebb ⊢ 1.6 flood ⊣ ⊢

⊣ ⊢ 2.5 knots ebb ⊢ 2.6 knots flood ⊣ ⊢ 2.2 knots ebb ⊢ 2 knots flo

WED OCT 11

dawn 6:18 sunrise 7:14 sunset 6:38 dark 7:35
moonrise 4:15 a.m. moonset 5:33 p.m.

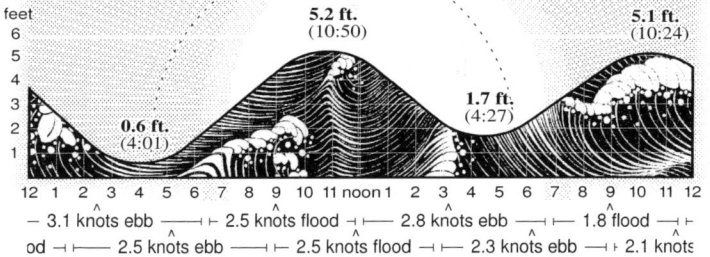

feet

5.2 ft.
(10:50)

5.1 ft.
(10:24)

1.7 ft.
(4:27)

0.6 ft.
(4:01)

12 1 2 3 4 5 6 7 8 9 10 11 noon 1 2 3 4 5 6 7 8 9 10 11 12

⊢ 3.1 knots ebb ⊢ 2.5 knots flood ⊣ ⊢ 2.8 knots ebb ⊢ 1.8 flood ⊣ ⊢

od ⊣ ⊢ 2.5 knots ebb ⊢ 2.5 knots flood ⊣ ⊢ 2.3 knots ebb ⊢ 2.1 knots

THU OCT 12

dawn 6:19 sunrise 7:15 sunset 6:37 dark 7:33
moonrise 5:14 a.m. moonset 5:54 p.m.

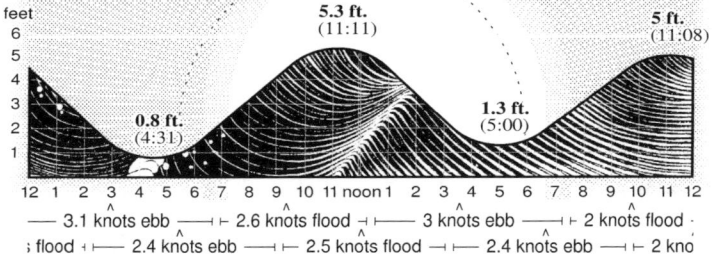

feet

5.3 ft.
(11:11)

5 ft.
(11:08)

1.3 ft.
(5:00)

0.8 ft.
(4:31)

12 1 2 3 4 5 6 7 8 9 10 11 noon 1 2 3 4 5 6 7 8 9 10 11 12

⊢ 3.1 knots ebb ⊢ 2.6 knots flood ⊣ ⊢ 3 knots ebb ⊢ 2 knots flood

s flood ⊣ ⊢ 2.4 knots ebb ⊢ 2.5 knots flood ⊣ ⊢ 2.4 knots ebb ⊢ 2 kno

FRI OCT 6
dawn 6:13 sunrise 7:10 sunset 6:45 dark 7:42
moonset 3:01 p.m.

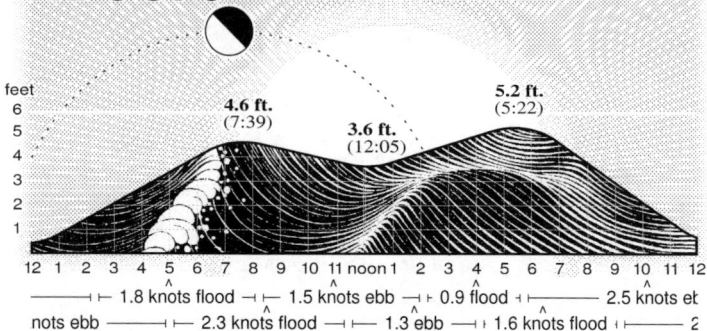

feet

4.6 ft.
(7:39)

3.6 ft.
(12:05)

5.2 ft.
(5:22)

6
5
4
3
2
1

12 1 2 3 4 5 6 7 8 9 10 11 noon 1 2 3 4 5 6 7 8 9 10 11 12

├─┤ ├ 1.8 knots flood → ├ 1.5 knots ebb → ├ 0.9 flood ┤ ├──── 2.5 knots et

nots ebb ────┤ ├ 2.3 knots flood → ├ 1.3 ebb → ├ 1.6 knots flood ┤ ├──── 2

SAT OCT 7
dawn 6:14 sunrise 7:11 sunset 6:44 dark 7:41
moonrise 12:13 a.m. moonset 3:42 p.m.

Draconids' Peak

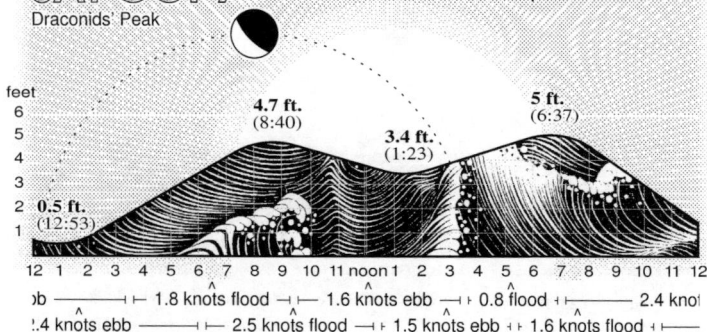

feet

4.7 ft.
(8:40)

3.4 ft.
(1:23)

5 ft.
(6:37)

6
5
4
3
2
1

0.5 ft.
(12:53)

12 1 2 3 4 5 6 7 8 9 10 11 noon 1 2 3 4 5 6 7 8 9 10 11 12

)b ──── ├ 1.8 knots flood → ├ 1.6 knots ebb → ├ 0.8 flood ┤ ├──── 2.4 knot

.4 knots ebb ──── ├ 2.5 knots flood → ├ 1.5 knots ebb ┤ ├ 1.6 knots flood ┤ ├──

SUN OCT 8
dawn 6:15 sunrise 7:12 sunset 6:43 dark 7:39
moonrise 1:14 a.m. moonset 4:16 p.m.

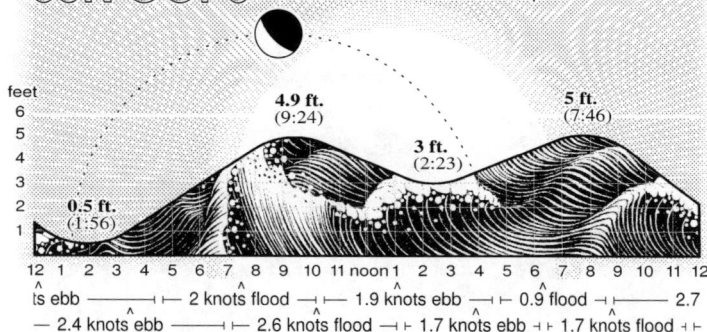

feet

4.9 ft.
(9:24)

3 ft.
(2:23)

5 ft.
(7:46)

6
5
4
3
2
1

0.5 ft.
(1:56)

12 1 2 3 4 5 6 7 8 9 10 11 noon 1 2 3 4 5 6 7 8 9 10 11 12

ts ebb ──── ├ 2 knots flood → ├ 1.9 knots ebb → ├ 0.9 flood → ├──── 2.7

── 2.4 knots ebb ──── ├ 2.6 knots flood → ├ 1.7 knots ebb ┤ ├ 1.7 knots flood ┤ ├

ⓙ   ⓥ   Ⓢ

Draconids Meteor Shower The Dracoinds are a minor shower active
between Oct 6th to the 10th. At peak the hourly rate can reach 10 per hour.
On Oct 7th, the early setting Moon will leave a dark sky for early evening
viewing. The shower's radiant, the constellation Draco, will be high
in the night sky not far from the little dipper.

MON OCT 2 — dawn 6:10 sunrise 7:06 sunset 6:51 dark 7:48
moonset 10:57 a.m. moonrise 8:54 p.m.

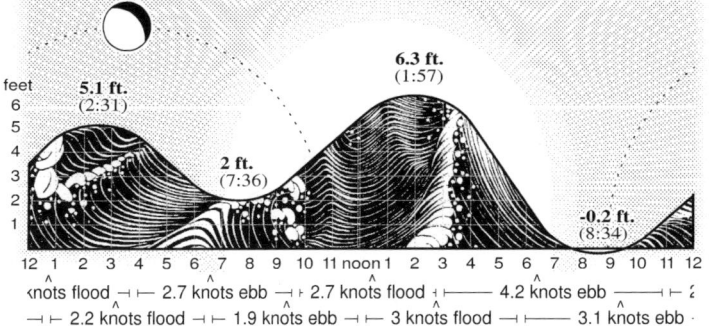

feet

5.1 ft.
(2:31)

6.3 ft.
(1:57)

2 ft.
(7:36)

-0.2 ft.
(8:34)

12 1 2 3 4 5 6 7 8 9 10 11 noon 1 2 3 4 5 6 7 8 9 10 11 12

knots flood —| |— 2.7 knots ebb —| |— 2.7 knots flood |— 4.2 knots ebb ——| |— 2
—| |— 2.2 knots flood —| |— 1.9 knots ebb —| |— 3 knots flood —| |—— 3.1 knots ebb

TUE OCT 3 — dawn 6:11 sunrise 7:07 sunset 6:50 dark 7:47
moonset 12:07 p.m. moonrise 9:34 p.m.

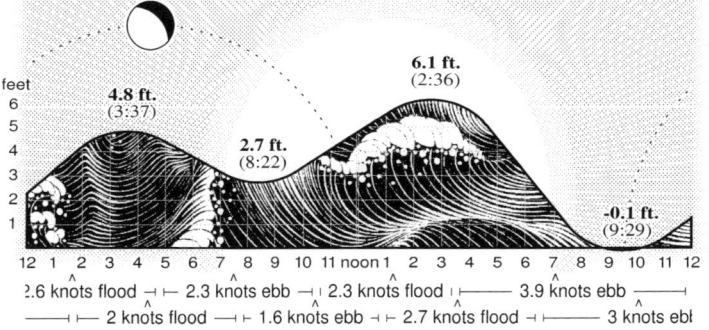

feet

4.8 ft.
(3:37)

6.1 ft.
(2:36)

2.7 ft.
(8:22)

-0.1 ft.
(9:29)

12 1 2 3 4 5 6 7 8 9 10 11 noon 1 2 3 4 5 6 7 8 9 10 11 12

2.6 knots flood —| |— 2.3 knots ebb —| |— 2.3 knots flood |— 3.9 knots ebb ——
—— |— 2 knots flood —| |— 1.6 knots ebb —| |— 2.7 knots flood —| |—— 3 knots ebb

WED OCT 4 — dawn 6:11 sunrise 7:08 sunset 6:48 dark 7:45
moonset 1:13 p.m. moonrise 10:21 p.m.

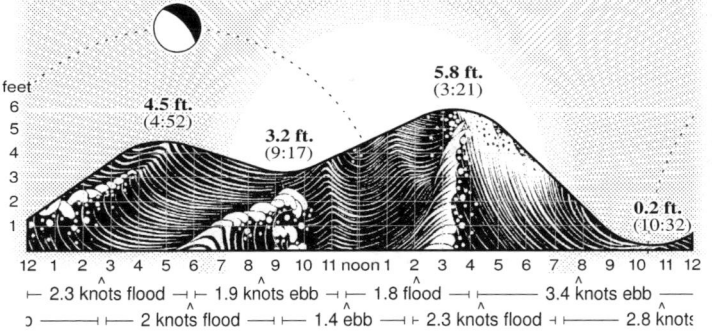

feet

4.5 ft.
(4:52)

5.8 ft.
(3:21)

3.2 ft.
(9:17)

0.2 ft.
(10:32)

12 1 2 3 4 5 6 7 8 9 10 11 noon 1 2 3 4 5 6 7 8 9 10 11 12

|— 2.3 knots flood —| |— 1.9 knots ebb —| |— 1.8 flood —| |—— 3.4 knots ebb ——
|——— |— 2 knots flood —| |— 1.4 ebb —| |— 2.3 knots flood —| |—— 2.8 knots

THU OCT 5 — dawn 6:12 sunrise 7:09 sunset 6:47 dark 7:44
moonset 2:11 p.m. moonrise 11:15 p.m.

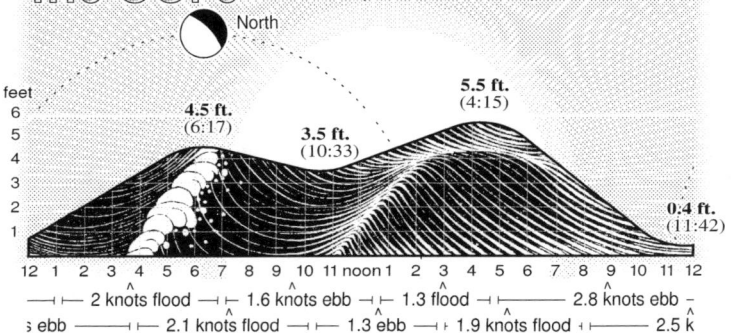

North

feet

4.5 ft.
(6:17)

5.5 ft.
(4:15)

3.5 ft.
(10:33)

0.4 ft.
(11:42)

12 1 2 3 4 5 6 7 8 9 10 11 noon 1 2 3 4 5 6 7 8 9 10 11 12

—| |— 2 knots flood —| |— 1.6 knots ebb —| |— 1.3 flood —| |—— 2.8 knots ebb —
s ebb ——— |— 2.1 knots flood —| |— 1.3 ebb —| |— 1.9 knots flood —| |—— 2.5 k

FRI SEP 29

dawn 6:07 sunrise 7:04 sunset 6:56 dark 7:53
moonset 7:17 a.m. moonrise 7:20 p.m.

Full Moon 2:57 a.m.

equator

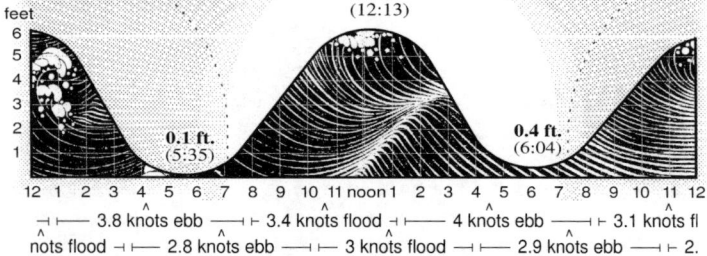

feet

6.1 ft.
(12:13)

0.1 ft.
(5:35)

0.4 ft.
(6:04)

12 1 2 3 4 5 6 7 8 9 10 11 noon 1 2 3 4 5 6 7 8 9 10 11 12

⊢ 3.8 knots ebb ⟶ ⊢ 3.4 knots flood ⊣ ⊢ 4 knots ebb ⟶ ⊢ 3.1 knots fl

nots flood ⊣ ⊢ 2.8 knots ebb ⟶ ⊢ 3 knots flood ⊣ ⊢ 2.9 knots ebb ⟶ ⊢ 2.

SAT SEP 30

dawn 6:08 sunrise 7:05 sunset 6:55 dark 7:51
moonset 8:31 a.m. moonrise 7:48 p.m.

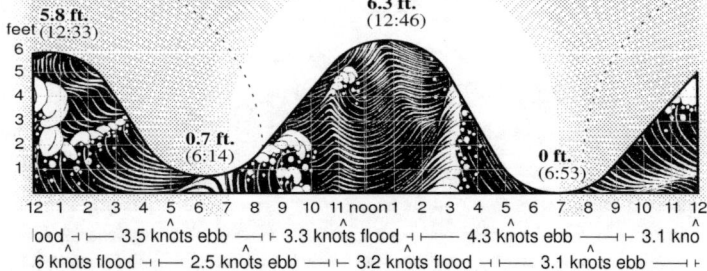

5.8 ft.
(12:33)

feet

6.3 ft.
(12:46)

0.7 ft.
(6:14)

0 ft.
(6:53)

12 1 2 3 4 5 6 7 8 9 10 11 noon 1 2 3 4 5 6 7 8 9 10 11 12

lood ⊣ ⊢ 3.5 knots ebb ⟶ ⊢ 3.3 knots flood ⊣ ⊢ 4.3 knots ebb ⟶ ⊢ 3.1 kno

6 knots flood ⊣ ⊢ 2.5 knots ebb ⟶ ⊢ 3.2 knots flood ⊣ ⊢ 3.1 knots ebb ⟶ ⊢

SUN OCT 1

dawn 6:09 sunrise 7:05 sunset 6:53 dark 7:50
moonset 9:44 a.m. moonrise 8:19 p.m.

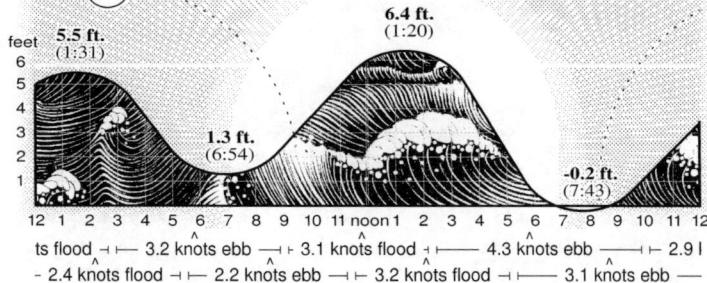

5.5 ft.
(1:31)

feet

6.4 ft.
(1:20)

1.3 ft.
(6:54)

-0.2 ft.
(7:43)

12 1 2 3 4 5 6 7 8 9 10 11 noon 1 2 3 4 5 6 7 8 9 10 11 12

ts flood ⊣ ⊢ 3.2 knots ebb ⟶ ⊢ 3.1 knots flood ⊣ ⊢ 4.3 knots ebb ⟶ ⊢ 2.9 l

- 2.4 knots flood ⊣ ⊢ 2.2 knots ebb ⟶ ⊢ 3.2 knots flood ⊣ ⊢ 3.1 knots ebb ⟶

Ⓙ   Ⓥ   Ⓜ   Ⓢ
        ⓜ   Ⓜ

MON SEP 25
dawn 6:03 sunrise 7:00 sunset 7:02 dark 7:59
moonset 2:11 a.m. moonrise 5:18 p.m.

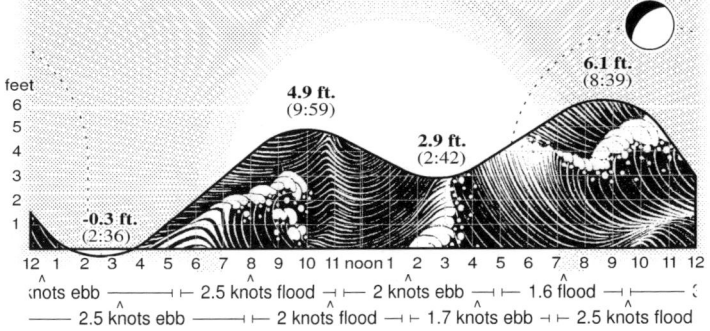

feet
6
5
4
3
2
1

-0.3 ft.
(2:36)

4.9 ft.
(9:59)

2.9 ft.
(2:42)

6.1 ft.
(8:39)

12 1 2 3 4 5 6 7 8 9 10 11 noon 1 2 3 4 5 6 7 8 9 10 11 12

knots ebb ——⊣ ⊢ 2.5 knots flood ⊣ ⊢ 2 knots ebb —⊣ ⊢ 1.6 flood ⊣ ⊢ ⊂
—— 2.5 knots ebb ——⊣ ⊢ 2 knots flood ⊣ ⊢ 1.7 knots ebb ⊣ ⊢ 2.5 knots flood

TUE SEP 26
dawn 6:04 sunrise 7:01 sunset 7:01 dark 7:57
moonset 3:29 a.m. moonrise 5:53 p.m.

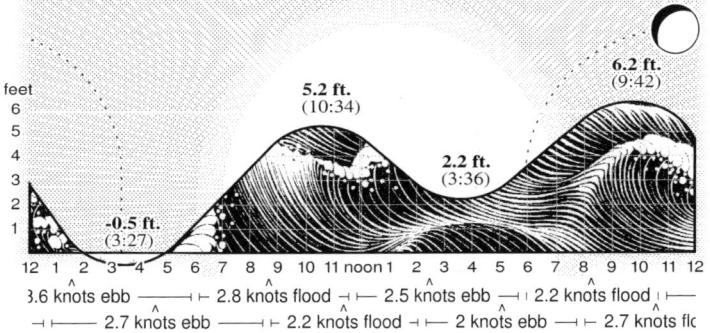

feet
6
5
4
3
2
1

-0.5 ft.
(3:27)

5.2 ft.
(10:34)

2.2 ft.
(3:36)

6.2 ft.
(9:42)

12 1 2 3 4 5 6 7 8 9 10 11 noon 1 2 3 4 5 6 7 8 9 10 11 12

3.6 knots ebb ——⊣ ⊢ 2.8 knots flood ⊣ ⊢ 2.5 knots ebb —⊣ 2.2 knots flood ⊣ ⊢
⊣ —— 2.7 knots ebb ——⊣ ⊢ 2.2 knots flood ⊣ ⊢ 2 knots ebb —⊣ ⊢ 2.7 knots fl

WED SEP 27
dawn 6:05 sunrise 7:02 sunset 6:59 dark 7:56
moonset 4:46 a.m. moonrise 6:24 p.m.

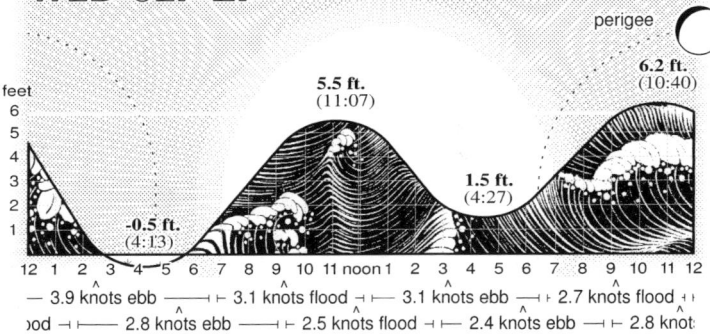

perigee

feet
6
5
4
3
2
1

-0.5 ft.
(4:13)

5.5 ft.
(11:07)

1.5 ft.
(4:27)

6.2 ft.
(10:40)

12 1 2 3 4 5 6 7 8 9 10 11 noon 1 2 3 4 5 6 7 8 9 10 11 12

— 3.9 knots ebb ——⊣ ⊢ 3.1 knots flood ⊣ ⊢ 3.1 knots ebb —⊣ ⊢ 2.7 knots flood ⊣⊢
ood ⊣ —— 2.8 knots ebb ——⊣ ⊢ 2.5 knots flood ⊣ ⊢ 2.4 knots ebb —⊣ ⊢ 2.8 knot

THU SEP 28
dawn 6:06 sunrise 7:03 sunset 6:58 dark 7:54
moonset 6:02 a.m. moonrise 6:52 p.m.

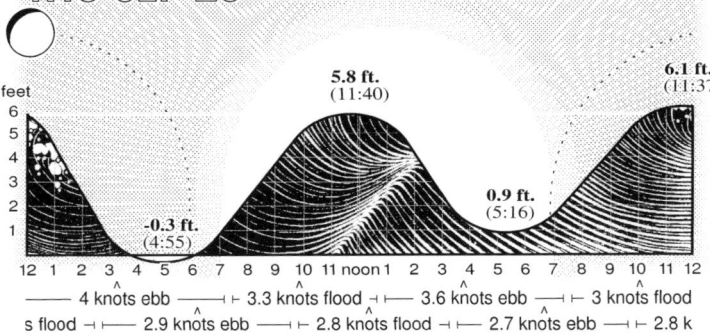

feet
6
5
4
3
2
1

-0.3 ft.
(4:55)

5.8 ft.
(11:40)

0.9 ft.
(5:16)

6.1 ft.
(11:37)

12 1 2 3 4 5 6 7 8 9 10 11 noon 1 2 3 4 5 6 7 8 9 10 11 12

—— 4 knots ebb ——⊣ ⊢ 3.3 knots flood ⊣ ⊢ 3.6 knots ebb —⊣ ⊢ 3 knots flood
s flood ⊣ ⊢ 2.9 knots ebb ——⊣ ⊢ 2.8 knots flood ⊣ ⊢ 2.7 knots ebb —⊣ ⊢ 2.8 k

FRI SEP 22
dawn 6:01 sunrise 6:58 sunset 7:07 dark 8:04
moonrise 2:47 p.m. moonset 11:50 p.m.

Autumnal Equinox 11:50 p.m.

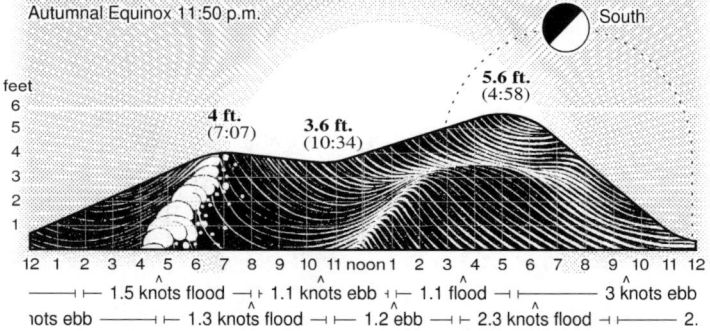

South

feet

5.6 ft.
(4:58)

4 ft.
(7:07)

3.6 ft.
(10:34)

12 1 2 3 4 5 6 7 8 9 10 11 noon 1 2 3 4 5 6 7 8 9 10 11 12

⊢— 1.5 knots flood —⊣ ⊢ 1.1 knots ebb ⊣⊢ 1.1 flood ⊣ ⊢—— 3 knots ebb ——⊣

ots ebb ————⊣ ⊢ 1.3 knots flood ⊣ ⊢ 1.2 ebb ⊣⊢ 2.3 knots flood ⊣ ⊢— 2.

SAT SEP 23
dawn 6:02 sunrise 6:58 sunset 7:05 dark 8:02
moonrise 3:46 p.m.

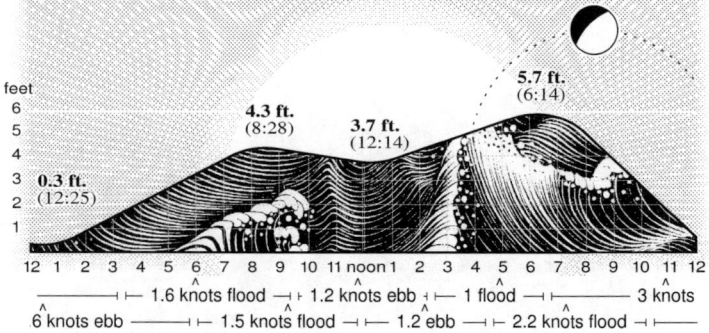

feet

5.7 ft.
(6:14)

4.3 ft.
(8:28)

3.7 ft.
(12:14)

0.3 ft.
(12:25)

12 1 2 3 4 5 6 7 8 9 10 11 noon 1 2 3 4 5 6 7 8 9 10 11 12

⊢— 1.6 knots flood —⊣ ⊢ 1.2 knots ebb ⊣⊢— 1 flood —⊣ ⊢—— 3 knots

6 knots ebb ————⊣ ⊢ 1.5 knots flood ⊣ ⊢ 1.2 ebb ⊣⊢ 2.2 knots flood ⊣ ⊢

SUN SEP 24
dawn 6:03 sunrise 6:59 sunset 7:04 dark 8:00
moonset 12:57 a.m. moonrise 4:36 p.m.

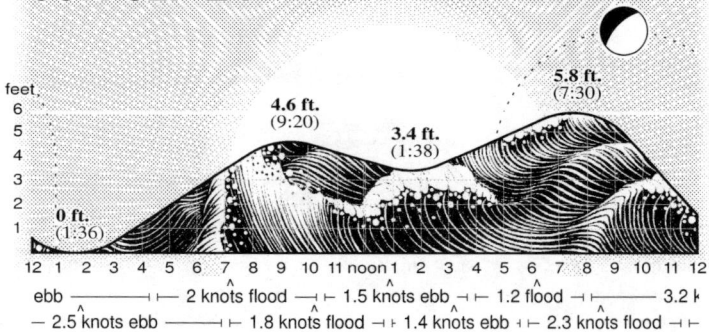

feet

5.8 ft.
(7:30)

4.6 ft.
(9:20)

3.4 ft.
(1:38)

0 ft.
(1:36)

12 1 2 3 4 5 6 7 8 9 10 11 noon 1 2 3 4 5 6 7 8 9 10 11 12

ebb ————⊣ ⊢— 2 knots flood —⊣ ⊢ 1.5 knots ebb ⊣ ⊢ 1.2 flood ⊣ ⊢—— 3.2 k

— 2.5 knots ebb ————⊣ ⊢ 1.8 knots flood ⊣⊢ 1.4 knots ebb ⊣⊢ 2.3 knots flood ⊣ ⊢

Ⓙ   Ⓥ   Ⓜ   Ⓢ
Ⓜ   Ⓜ

Autumnal Equinox The autumnal equinox on Sep 22nd marks the first
day of fall in the northern hemisphere. At equinox the sun shines directly
on the equator and the Earth will be bathed in nearly equal amounts of day
and night.

MON SEP 18

dawn 5:57 sunrise 6:54 sunset 7:13 dark 8:10
moonrise 10:23 a.m. moonset 9:00 p.m.

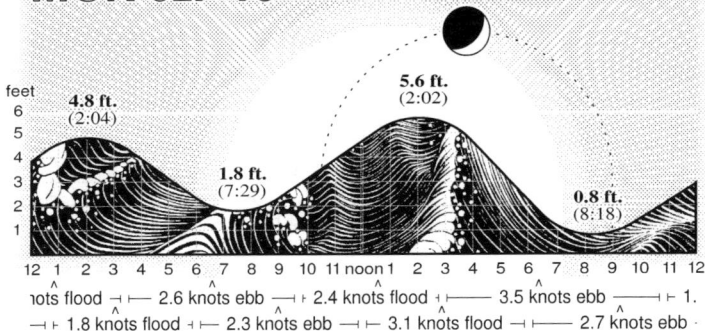

feet

4.8 ft.
(2:04)

1.8 ft.
(7:29)

5.6 ft.
(2:02)

0.8 ft.
(8:18)

ots flood ⊣ ⊢ 2.6 knots ebb ⊢ 2.4 knots flood ⊣ ⊢ 3.5 knots ebb ⊢ 1.
⊣ ⊢ 1.8 knots flood ⊣ ⊢ 2.3 knots ebb ⊣ ⊢ 3.1 knots flood ⊣ ⊢ 2.7 knots ebb

TUE SEP 19

dawn 5:58 sunrise 6:55 sunset 7:12 dark 8:09
moonrise 11:28 a.m. moonset 9:31 p.m.

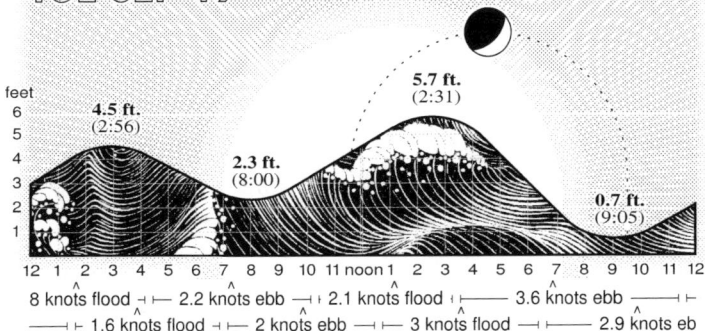

feet

4.5 ft.
(2:56)

2.3 ft.
(8:00)

5.7 ft.
(2:31)

0.7 ft.
(9:05)

8 knots flood ⊣ ⊢ 2.2 knots ebb ⊣ ⊢ 2.1 knots flood ⊣ ⊢ 3.6 knots ebb ⊢
⊣ ⊢ 1.6 knots flood ⊣ ⊢ 2 knots ebb ⊣ ⊢ 3 knots flood ⊣ ⊢ 2.9 knots eb

WED SEP 20

dawn 5:59 sunrise 6:56 sunset 7:10 dark 8:07
moonrise 12:35 p.m. moonset 10:08 p.m.

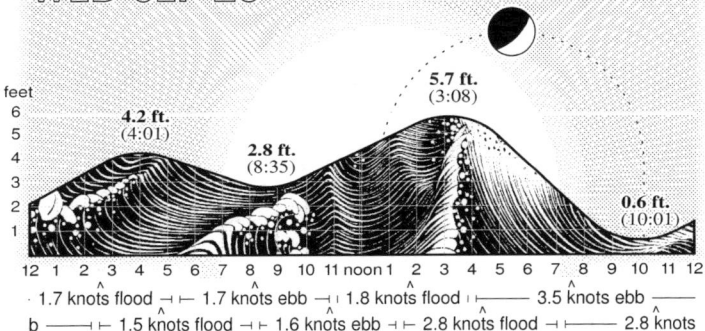

feet

4.2 ft.
(4:01)

2.8 ft.
(8:35)

5.7 ft.
(3:08)

0.6 ft.
(10:01)

1.7 knots flood ⊣ ⊢ 1.7 knots ebb ⊣ 1.8 knots flood ⊣ ⊢ 3.5 knots ebb
b ⊢ 1.5 knots flood ⊣ ⊢ 1.6 knots ebb ⊣ ⊢ 2.8 knots flood ⊣ ⊢ 2.8 knots

THU SEP 21

dawn 6:00 sunrise 6:57 sunset 7:08 dark 8:05
moonrise 1:42 p.m. moonset 10:54 p.m.

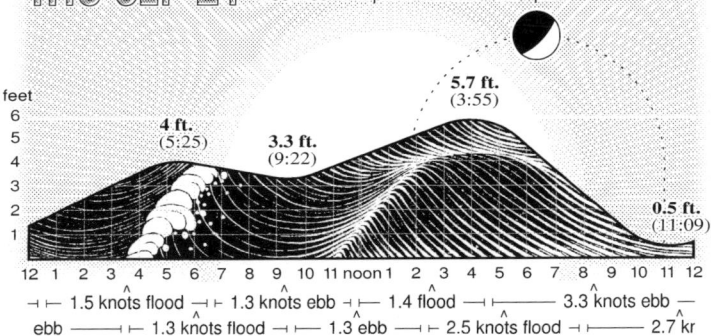

feet

4 ft.
(5:25)

3.3 ft.
(9:22)

5.7 ft.
(3:55)

0.5 ft.
(11:09)

⊣ ⊢ 1.5 knots flood ⊣ ⊢ 1.3 knots ebb ⊣ ⊢ 1.4 flood ⊣ ⊢ 3.3 knots ebb
ebb ⊢ 1.3 knots flood ⊣ ⊢ 1.3 ebb ⊣ ⊢ 2.5 knots flood ⊣ ⊢ 2.7 kr

FRI SEP 15

dawn 5:54 sunrise 6:52 sunset 7:18 dark 8:15
moonrise 7:22 a.m. moonset 7:49 p.m.

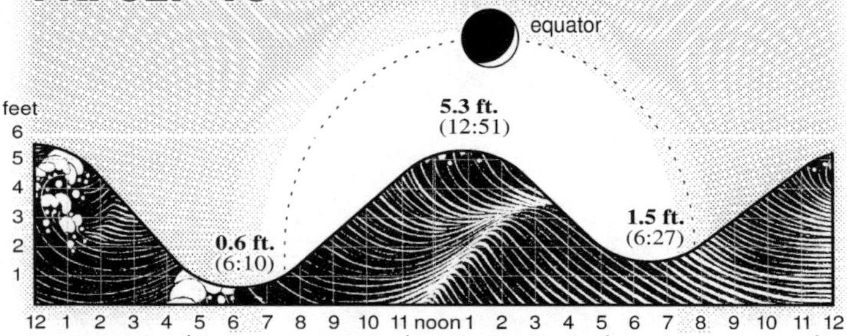
equator
feet
6
5
4
3
2
1
5.3 ft.
(12:51)
0.6 ft.
(6:10)
1.5 ft.
(6:27)
12 1 2 3 4 5 6 7 8 9 10 11 noon 1 2 3 4 5 6 7 8 9 10 11 12

3.4 knots ebb — 2.8 knots flood — 3 knots ebb — 2.1 knots
knots flood — 2.7 knots ebb — 2.5 knots flood — 2.2 knots ebb — 2

SAT SEP 16

dawn 5:55 sunrise 6:53 sunset 7:16 dark 8:13
moonrise 8:21 a.m. moonset 8:11 p.m.

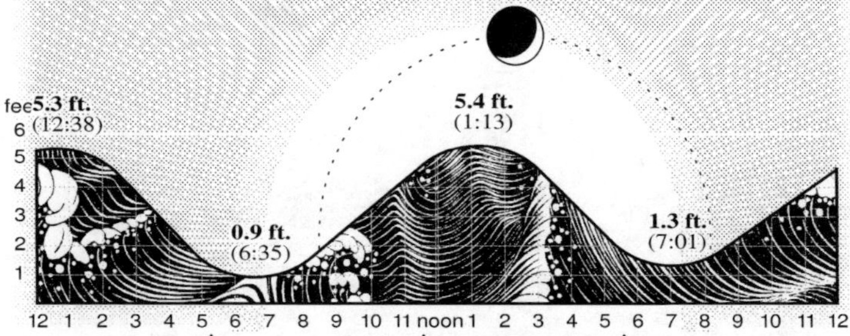
feet
5.3 ft.
(12:38)
6
5
4
3
2
1
5.4 ft.
(1:13)
0.9 ft.
(6:35)
1.3 ft.
(7:01)
12 1 2 3 4 5 6 7 8 9 10 11 noon 1 2 3 4 5 6 7 8 9 10 11 12

od — 3.2 knots ebb — 2.7 knots flood — 3.2 knots ebb — 2.1 knc
2.1 knots flood — 2.7 knots ebb — 2.8 knots flood — 2.3 knots ebb —

SUN SEP 17

dawn 5:56 sunrise 6:53 sunset 7:15 dark 8:12
moonrise 9:21 a.m. moonset 8:34 p.m.

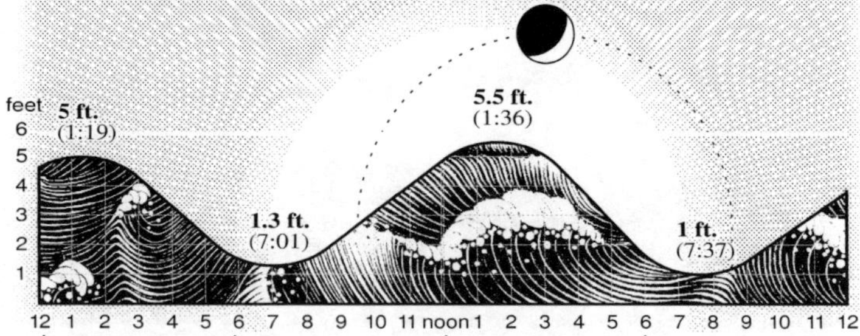
feet
5 ft.
(1:19)
6
5
4
3
2
1
5.5 ft.
(1:36)
1.3 ft.
(7:01)
1 ft.
(7:37)
12 1 2 3 4 5 6 7 8 9 10 11 noon 1 2 3 4 5 6 7 8 9 10 11 12

ts flood — 3 knots ebb — 2.6 knots flood — 3.4 knots ebb — 2 kn
1.9 knots flood — 2.5 knots ebb — 3 knots flood — 2.5 knots ebb —

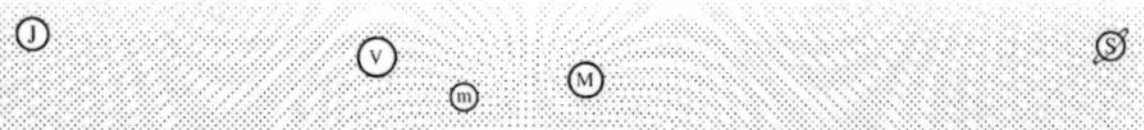

MON SEP 11
dawn 5:51 sunrise 6:48 sunset 7:24 dark 8:22
moonrise 3:24 a.m. moonset 6:14 p.m.

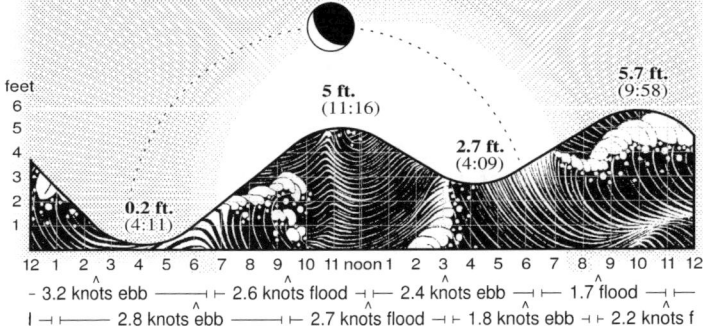

feet
6
5
4
3
2
1

5.7 ft.
(9:58)

5 ft.
(11:16)

2.7 ft.
(4:09)

0.2 ft.
(4:11)

12 1 2 3 4 5 6 7 8 9 10 11 noon 1 2 3 4 5 6 7 8 9 10 11 12

- 3.2 knots ebb ——— ⊢ 2.6 knots flood ⊣ ⊢ 2.4 knots ebb ——— ⊣ 1.7 flood ——— ⊢ ⊢
l ⊣ ⊢——— 2.8 knots ebb ———⊣ ⊢ 2.7 knots flood ⊣ ⊢ 1.8 knots ebb ⊣ ⊢ 2.2 knots f

TUE SEP 12
dawn 5:52 sunrise 6:49 sunset 7:22 dark 8:20
moonrise 4:24 a.m. moonset 6:42 p.m.

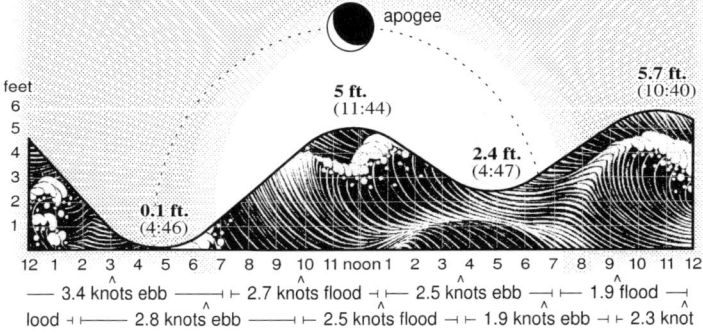

apogee

feet
6
5
4
3
2
1

5.7 ft.
(10:40)

5 ft.
(11:44)

2.4 ft.
(4:47)

0.1 ft.
(4:46)

12 1 2 3 4 5 6 7 8 9 10 11 noon 1 2 3 4 5 6 7 8 9 10 11 12

——— 3.4 knots ebb ——— ⊢ 2.7 knots flood ⊣ ⊢— 2.5 knots ebb ——— ⊣ 1.9 flood ———⊣
lood ⊣ ⊢——— 2.8 knots ebb ———⊣ ⊢ 2.5 knots flood ⊣ ⊢ 1.9 knots ebb ⊣ ⊢ 2.3 knot

WED SEP 13
dawn 5:52 sunrise 6:50 sunset 7:21 dark 8:18
moonrise 5:24 a.m. moonset 7:06 p.m.

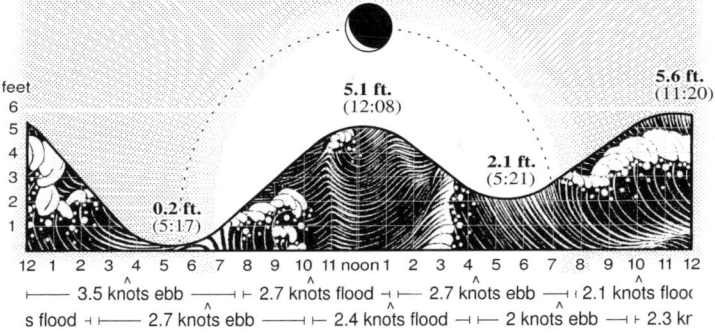

feet
6
5
4
3
2
1

5.6 ft.
(11:20)

5.1 ft.
(12:08)

2.1 ft.
(5:21)

0.2 ft.
(5:17)

12 1 2 3 4 5 6 7 8 9 10 11 noon 1 2 3 4 5 6 7 8 9 10 11 12

⊢——— 3.5 knots ebb ——— ⊢ 2.7 knots flood ⊣ ⊢— 2.7 knots ebb ——— ⊣ ⊢ 2.1 knots flood
s flood ⊣ ⊢——— 2.7 knots ebb ———⊣ ⊢ 2.4 knots flood ⊣ ⊢ 2 knots ebb ——— ⊢ 2.3 kn

THU SEP 14
dawn 5:53 sunrise 6:51 sunset 7:19 dark 8:17
moonrise 6:23 a.m. moonset 7:28 p.m.

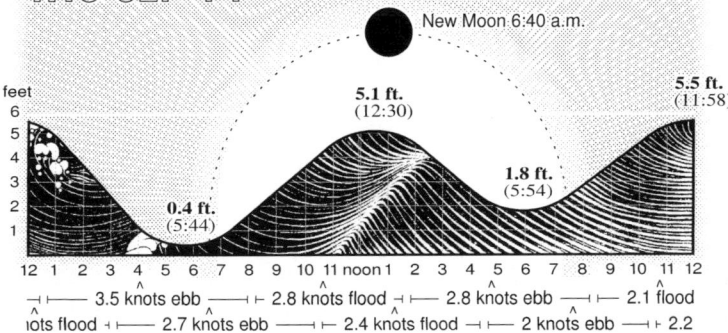

New Moon 6:40 a.m.

feet
6
5
4
3
2
1

5.5 ft.
(11:58)

5.1 ft.
(12:30)

1.8 ft.
(5:54)

0.4 ft.
(5:44)

12 1 2 3 4 5 6 7 8 9 10 11 noon 1 2 3 4 5 6 7 8 9 10 11 12

⊣ ⊢——— 3.5 knots ebb ——— ⊢ 2.8 knots flood ⊣ ⊢— 2.8 knots ebb ——— ⊣ ⊢— 2.1 flood
hots flood ⊣ ⊢——— 2.7 knots ebb ———⊣ ⊢ 2.4 knots flood ⊣ ⊢ 2 knots ebb ——— ⊢ 2.2

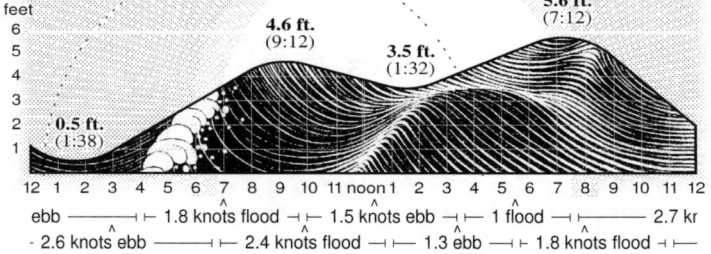

FRI SEP 8 dawn 5:48 sunrise 6:46 sunset 7:29 dark 8:26
moonrise 12:30 a.m. moonset 4:18 p.m.

North

feet

5.6 ft.
(7:12)

4.6 ft.
(9:12)

3.5 ft.
(1:32)

0.5 ft.
(1:38)

12 1 2 3 4 5 6 7 8 9 10 11 noon 1 2 3 4 5 6 7 8 9 10 11 12

ebb ─── ⊢ 1.8 knots flood ⊣ ⊢ 1.5 knots ebb ⊣ ⊢ 1 flood ⊣ ⊢ ── 2.7 kr
- 2.6 knots ebb ─── ⊢ 2.4 knots flood ⊣ ⊢ 1.3 ebb ⊣ ⊢ 1.8 knots flood ⊣ ⊢ ─

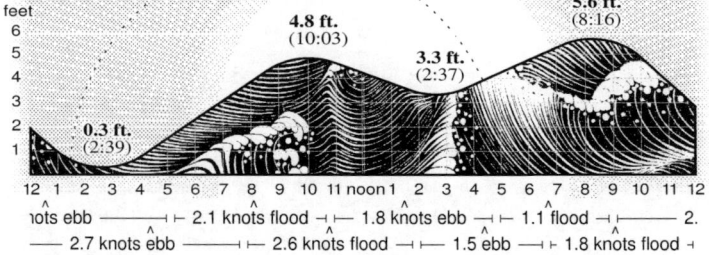

SAT SEP 9 dawn 5:49 sunrise 6:47 sunset 7:27 dark 8:25
moonrise 1:24 a.m. moonset 5:04 p.m.

feet

5.6 ft.
(8:16)

4.8 ft.
(10:03)

3.3 ft.
(2:37)

0.3 ft.
(2:39)

12 1 2 3 4 5 6 7 8 9 10 11 noon 1 2 3 4 5 6 7 8 9 10 11 12

ots ebb ─── ⊢ 2.1 knots flood ⊣ ⊢ 1.8 knots ebb ⊣ ⊢ 1.1 flood ⊣ ⊢ ── 2.
── 2.7 knots ebb ─── ⊢ 2.6 knots flood ⊣ ⊢ 1.5 ebb ⊣ ⊢ 1.8 knots flood ⊣

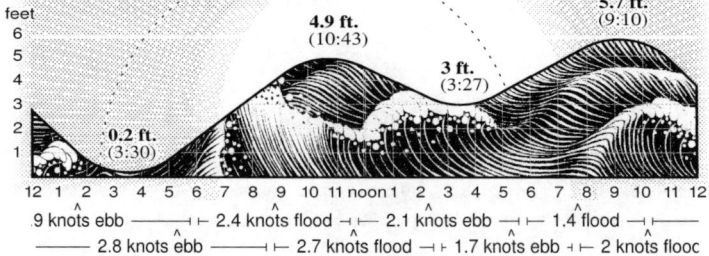

SUN SEP 10 dawn 5:50 sunrise 6:47 sunset 7:26 dark 8:23
moonrise 2:23 a.m. moonset 5:42 p.m.

feet

5.7 ft.
(9:10)

4.9 ft.
(10:43)

3 ft.
(3:27)

0.2 ft.
(3:30)

12 1 2 3 4 5 6 7 8 9 10 11 noon 1 2 3 4 5 6 7 8 9 10 11 12

.9 knots ebb ─── ⊢ 2.4 knots flood ⊣ ⊢ 2.1 knots ebb ⊣ ⊢ 1.4 flood ⊣ ⊢ ─
── 2.8 knots ebb ─── ⊢ 2.7 knots flood ⊣ ⊢ 1.7 knots ebb ⊣ ⊢ 2 knots flooc

MON SEP 4

dawn 5:44 sunrise 6:42 sunset 7:35 dark 8:33
moonset 12:07 p.m. moonrise 10:23 p.m.

Labor Day

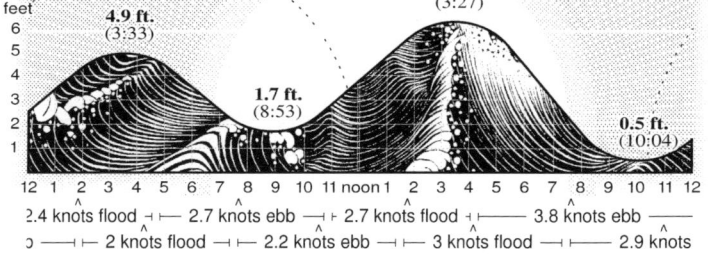

4.9 ft.
(3:33)

1.7 ft.
(8:53)

6.2 ft.
(3:27)

0.5 ft.
(10:04)

feet 6 5 4 3 2 1

12 1 2 3 4 5 6 7 8 9 10 11 noon 1 2 3 4 5 6 7 8 9 10 11 12

2.4 knots flood ⊣ ⊢ 2.7 knots ebb ⊣ ⊢ 2.7 knots flood ⊣ ⊢ 3.8 knots ebb ——
⊃ ⊢ 2 knots flood ⊣ ⊢ 2.2 knots ebb ⊣ ⊢ 3 knots flood ⊣ ⊢ 2.9 knots

TUE SEP 5

dawn 5:45 sunrise 6:43 sunset 7:33 dark 8:31
moonset 1:16 p.m. moonrise 10:59 p.m.

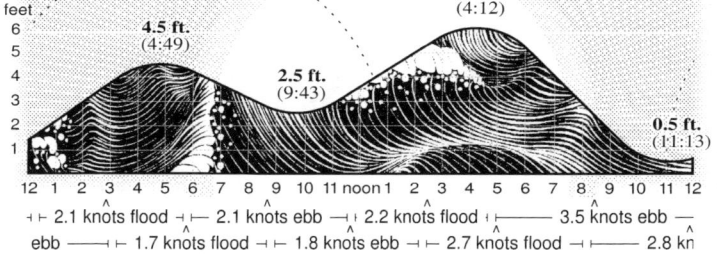

4.5 ft.
(4:49)

2.5 ft.
(9:43)

6 ft.
(4:12)

0.5 ft.
(11:13)

feet 6 5 4 3 2 1

12 1 2 3 4 5 6 7 8 9 10 11 noon 1 2 3 4 5 6 7 8 9 10 11 12

⊣ ⊢ 2.1 knots flood ⊣ ⊢ 2.1 knots ebb ⊣ ⊢ 2.2 knots flood ⊣ ⊢ 3.5 knots ebb —
ebb —— ⊢ 1.7 knots flood ⊣ ⊢ 1.8 knots ebb ⊣ ⊢ 2.7 knots flood ⊣ ⊢ 2.8 kn

WED SEP 6

dawn 5:46 sunrise 6:44 sunset 7:32 dark 8:30
moonset 2:23 p.m. moonrise 11:41 p.m.

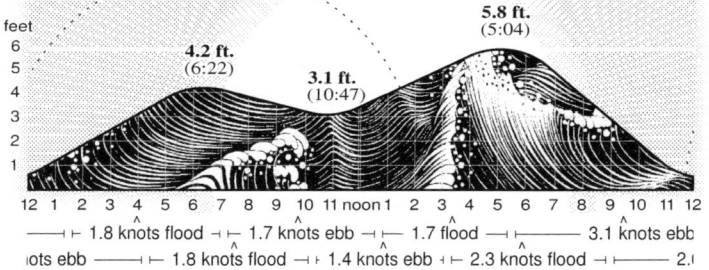

4.2 ft.
(6:22)

3.1 ft.
(10:47)

5.8 ft.
(5:04)

feet 6 5 4 3 2 1

12 1 2 3 4 5 6 7 8 9 10 11 noon 1 2 3 4 5 6 7 8 9 10 11 12

—— ⊢ 1.8 knots flood ⊣ ⊢ 1.7 knots ebb ⊣ ⊢ 1.7 flood ⊣ ⊢ 3.1 knots ebb
⊃ts ebb —— ⊢ 1.8 knots flood ⊣ ⊢ 1.4 knots ebb ⊣ ⊢ 2.3 knots flood ⊣ ⊢ 2.(

THU SEP 7

dawn 5:47 sunrise 6:45 sunset 7:30 dark 8:28
moonset 3:24 p.m.

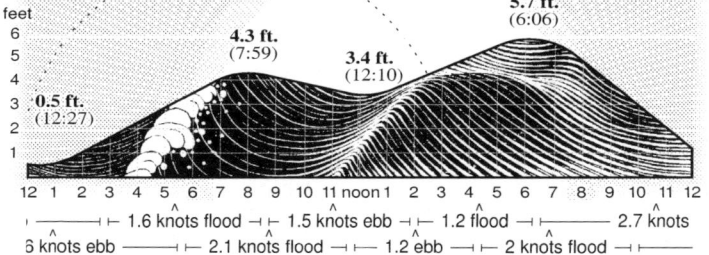

5.7 ft.
(6:06)

4.3 ft.
(7:59)

3.4 ft.
(12:10)

0.5 ft.
(12:27)

feet 6 5 4 3 2 1

12 1 2 3 4 5 6 7 8 9 10 11 noon 1 2 3 4 5 6 7 8 9 10 11 12

⊣ —— ⊢ 1.6 knots flood ⊣ ⊢ 1.5 knots ebb ⊣ ⊢ 1.2 flood ⊣ ⊢ 2.7 knots
⊃ knots ebb —— ⊢ 2.1 knots flood ⊣ ⊢ 1.2 ebb ⊣ ⊢ 2 knots flood ⊣ ⊢

FRI SEP 1

dawn 5:41 sunrise 6:40 sunset 7:39 dark 8:38
moonset 8:30 a.m. moonrise 8:55 p.m.

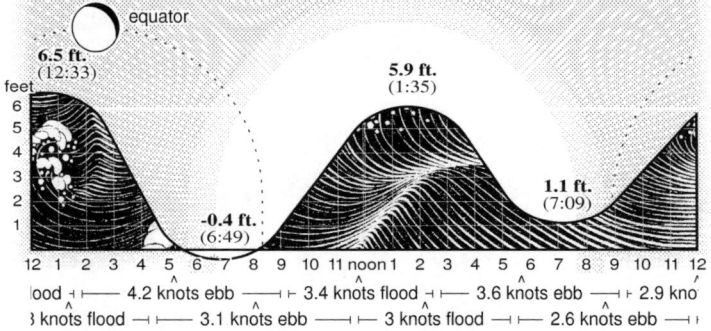

equator

6.5 ft.
(12:33)

5.9 ft.
(1:35)

feet

1.1 ft.
(7:09)

-0.4 ft.
(6:49)

12 1 2 3 4 5 6 7 8 9 10 11 noon 1 2 3 4 5 6 7 8 9 10 11 12

lood ⊣ ├── 4.2 knots ebb ──→ ├ 3.4 knots flood ⊣ ├── 3.6 knots ebb ──→ ├ 2.9 kno
3 knots flood ⊣ ├── 3.1 knots ebb ──→ ├── 3 knots flood ⊣ ├── 2.6 knots ebb ──→ ├

SAT SEP 2

dawn 5:42 sunrise 6:41 sunset 7:38 dark 8:36
moonset 9:44 a.m. moonrise 9:22 p.m.

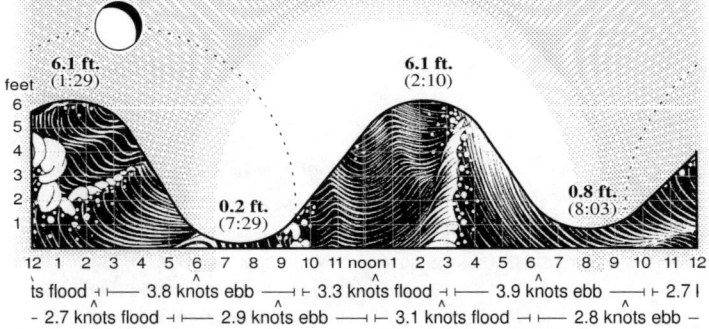

6.1 ft.
(1:29)

6.1 ft.
(2:10)

feet

0.2 ft.
(7:29)

0.8 ft.
(8:03)

12 1 2 3 4 5 6 7 8 9 10 11 noon 1 2 3 4 5 6 7 8 9 10 11 12

ts flood ⊣ ├── 3.8 knots ebb ──→ ├ 3.3 knots flood ⊣ ├ 3.9 knots ebb ──→ ├ 2.7 l
- 2.7 knots flood ⊣ ├── 2.9 knots ebb ──→ ├ 3.1 knots flood ⊣ ├── 2.8 knots ebb ─

SUN SEP 3

dawn 5:43 sunrise 6:42 sunset 7:36 dark 8:35
moonset 10:56 a.m. moonrise 9:51 p.m.

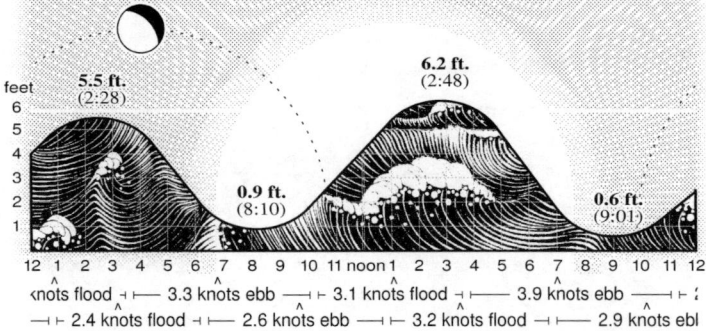

5.5 ft.
(2:28)

6.2 ft.
(2:48)

feet

0.9 ft.
(8:10)

0.6 ft.
(9:01)

12 1 2 3 4 5 6 7 8 9 10 11 noon 1 2 3 4 5 6 7 8 9 10 11 12

knots flood ⊣ ├── 3.3 knots ebb ──→ ├ 3.1 knots flood ⊣ ├── 3.9 knots ebb ──→ ├
⊣ ├ 2.4 knots flood ⊣ ├── 2.6 knots ebb ──→ ├ 3.2 knots flood ⊣ ├── 2.9 knots ebl

☿   ♃   ♀   Ⓜ

Supermoon The Aug 30th Full Super Blue Moon coincides with
its perigee, the closest the Moon comes to the Earth in its elliptic orbit.
The term supermoon has no precise astronomical definition as supermoon
is astrological in orgin. Astronomers can refer to this supermoon as
a perigean full moon or more precisely a perigee-syzgy Moon. This full
moon is notable as being a blue moon, the second full moon in a month.
Look for the planet **Saturn** 2 degrees North of the Moon.

MON AUG 28
dawn 5:37 sunrise 6:36 sunset 7:45 dark 8:44
moonset 3:18 a.m. moonrise 6:44 p.m.

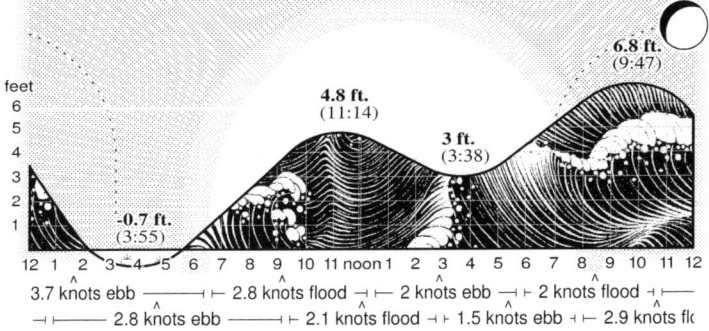

feet

6.8 ft.
(9:47)

4.8 ft.
(11:14)

3 ft.
(3:38)

-0.7 ft.
(3:55)

12 1 2 3 4 5 6 7 8 9 10 11 noon 1 2 3 4 5 6 7 8 9 10 11 12

3.7 knots ebb ⊢ 2.8 knots flood ⊣ ⊢ 2 knots ebb ⊣ ⊢ 2 knots flood ⊣ ⊢
⊣ ⊢ 2.8 knots ebb ⊣ ⊢ 2.1 knots flood ⊣ ⊢ 1.5 knots ebb ⊣ ⊢ 2.9 knots flo

TUE AUG 29
dawn 5:38 sunrise 6:37 sunset 7:44 dark 8:43
moonset 4:36 a.m. moonrise 7:24 p.m.

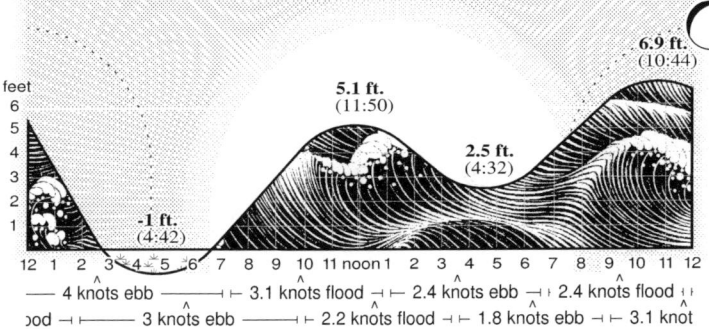

feet

6.9 ft.
(10:44)

5.1 ft.
(11:50)

2.5 ft.
(4:32)

-1 ft.
(4:42)

12 1 2 3 4 5 6 7 8 9 10 11 noon 1 2 3 4 5 6 7 8 9 10 11 12

⊢ 4 knots ebb ⊢ 3.1 knots flood ⊣ ⊢ 2.4 knots ebb ⊣ ⊢ 2.4 knots flood ⊣
ood ⊣ ⊢ 3 knots ebb ⊢ 2.2 knots flood ⊣ ⊢ 1.8 knots ebb ⊣ ⊢ 3.1 knot

WED AUG 30
dawn 5:39 sunrise 6:38 sunset 7:42 dark 8:41
moonset 5:56 a.m. moonrise 7:58 p.m.

perigee   Super Full Blue Moon 6:36 p.m.

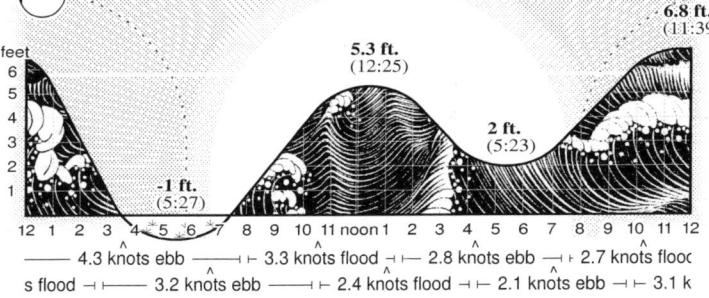

feet

6.8 ft.
(11:39)

5.3 ft.
(12:25)

2 ft.
(5:23)

-1 ft.
(5:27)

12 1 2 3 4 5 6 7 8 9 10 11 noon 1 2 3 4 5 6 7 8 9 10 11 12

⊢ 4.3 knots ebb ⊢ 3.3 knots flood ⊣ ⊢ 2.8 knots ebb ⊣ ⊢ 2.7 knots flood
s flood ⊣ ⊢ 3.2 knots ebb ⊢ 2.4 knots flood ⊣ ⊢ 2.1 knots ebb ⊣ ⊢ 3.1 k

THU AUG 31
dawn 5:40 sunrise 6:39 sunset 7:41 dark 8:40
moonset 7:15 a.m. moonrise 8:27 p.m.

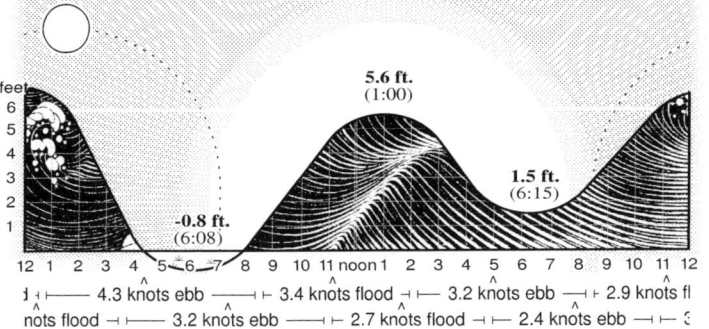

feet

5.6 ft.
(1:00)

1.5 ft.
(6:15)

-0.8 ft.
(6:08)

12 1 2 3 4 5 6 7 8 9 10 11 noon 1 2 3 4 5 6 7 8 9 10 11 12

⊣ ⊢ 4.3 knots ebb ⊢ 3.4 knots flood ⊣ ⊢ 3.2 knots ebb ⊣ ⊢ 2.9 knots fl
nots flood ⊣ ⊢ 3.2 knots ebb ⊢ 2.7 knots flood ⊣ ⊢ 2.4 knots ebb ⊣ ⊢ 3

FRI AUG 25

dawn 5:34 sunrise 6:34 sunset 7:49 dark 8:49
moonset 12:11 a.m. moonrise 3:53 p.m.

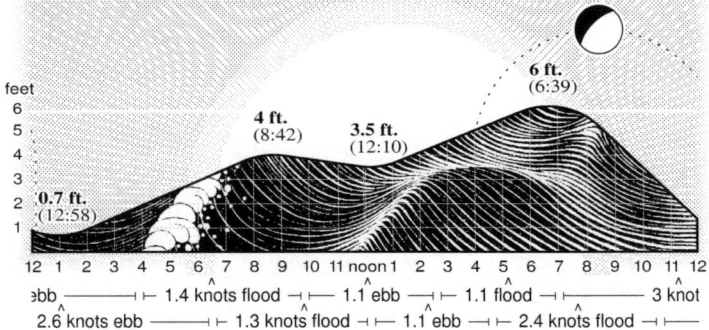

6 ft.
(6:39)

4 ft.
(8:42)

3.5 ft.
(12:10)

feet

0.7 ft.
(12:58)

12 1 2 3 4 5 6 7 8 9 10 11 noon 1 2 3 4 5 6 7 8 9 10 11 12

ebb ⊢—⊣ ⊢ 1.4 knots flood →⊣ ⊢ 1.1 ebb →⊣ ⊢ 1.1 flood → ⊢ ⊢————— 3 knot
2.6 knots ebb ————— ⊢ 1.3 knots flood →⊣ ⊢ 1.1 ebb →⊣ ⊢ 2.4 knots flood →⊣ ⊢—

SAT AUG 26

dawn 5:35 sunrise 6:35 sunset 7:48 dark 8:48
moonset 1:02 a.m. moonrise 4:58 p.m.

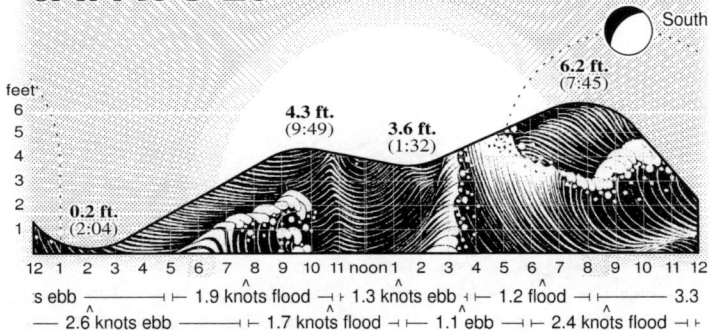

South

6.2 ft.
(7:45)

4.3 ft.
(9:49)

3.6 ft.
(1:32)

feet

0.2 ft.
(2:04)

12 1 2 3 4 5 6 7 8 9 10 11 noon 1 2 3 4 5 6 7 8 9 10 11 12

s ebb ————— ⊢ 1.9 knots flood →⊣ ⊢ 1.3 knots ebb ⊣⊢ 1.2 flood →⊣ ⊢————— 3.3
——— 2.6 knots ebb ————— ⊢ 1.7 knots flood →⊣ ⊢ 1.1 ebb →⊣ ⊢ 2.4 knots flood →⊣ ⊢

SUN AUG 27

dawn 5:36 sunrise 6:36 sunset 7:47 dark 8:46
moonset 2:05 a.m. moonrise 5:56 p.m.

Saturn at opposition

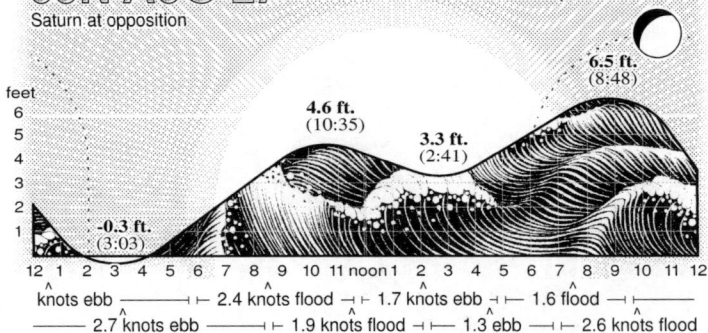

6.5 ft.
(8:48)

4.6 ft.
(10:35)

3.3 ft.
(2:41)

feet

-0.3 ft.
(3:03)

12 1 2 3 4 5 6 7 8 9 10 11 noon 1 2 3 4 5 6 7 8 9 10 11 12

knots ebb ————— ⊢ 2.4 knots flood →⊣ ⊢ 1.7 knots ebb ⊣⊢ 1.6 flood →⊣ ⊢—
——— 2.7 knots ebb ————— ⊢ 1.9 knots flood →⊣ ⊢ 1.3 ebb →⊣ ⊢ 2.6 knots flood

MON AUG 21

dawn 5:30 sunrise 6:31 sunset 7:55 dark 8:55
moonrise 11:27 a.m. moonset 10:30 p.m.

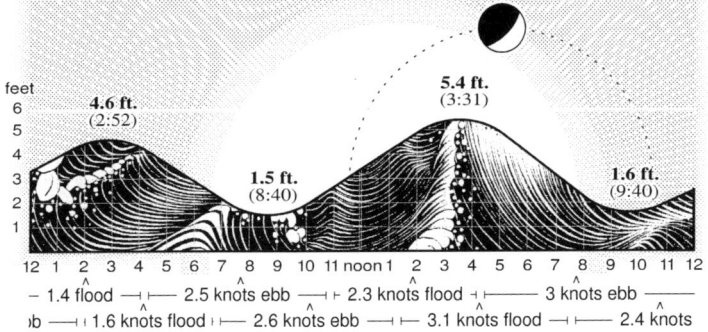

feet

4.6 ft.
(2:52)

5.4 ft.
(3:31)

1.5 ft.
(8:40)

1.6 ft.
(9:40)

12 1 2 3 4 5 6 7 8 9 10 11 noon 1 2 3 4 5 6 7 8 9 10 11 12

– 1.4 flood —| |— 2.5 knots ebb —| |– 2.3 knots flood –| |– 3 knots ebb —

)b —| |– 1.6 knots flood | |– 2.6 knots ebb —| |– 3.1 knots flood —| |– 2.4 knots

TUE AUG 22

dawn 5:31 sunrise 6:31 sunset 7:54 dark 8:54
moonrise 12:30 p.m. moonset 10:57 p.m.

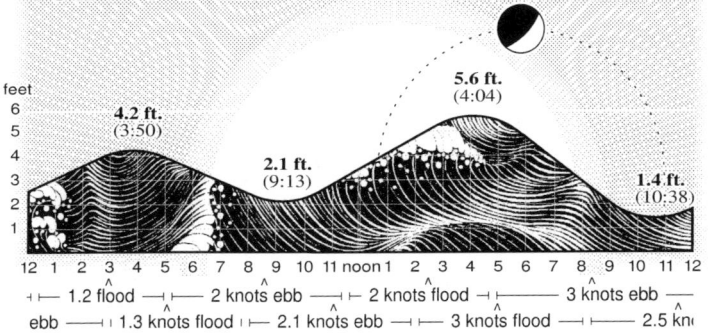

feet

4.2 ft.
(3:50)

5.6 ft.
(4:04)

2.1 ft.
(9:13)

1.4 ft.
(10:38)

12 1 2 3 4 5 6 7 8 9 10 11 noon 1 2 3 4 5 6 7 8 9 10 11 12

| |— 1.2 flood —| |— 2 knots ebb —| |– 2 knots flood —| |— 3 knots ebb —

ebb —| |– 1.3 knots flood | |– 2.1 knots ebb —| |– 3 knots flood —| |– 2.5 kn

WED AUG 23

dawn 5:32 sunrise 6:32 sunset 7:52 dark 8:52
moonrise 1:36 p.m. moonset 11:30 p.m.

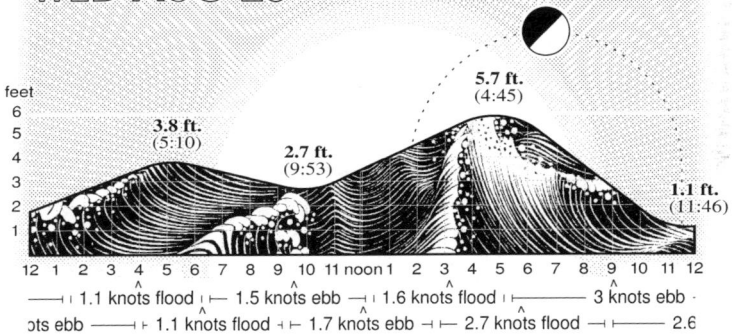

feet

3.8 ft.
(5:10)

5.7 ft.
(4:45)

2.7 ft.
(9:53)

1.1 ft.
(11:46)

12 1 2 3 4 5 6 7 8 9 10 11 noon 1 2 3 4 5 6 7 8 9 10 11 12

—| |– 1.1 knots flood | |– 1.5 knots ebb —| |– 1.6 knots flood | |— 3 knots ebb ·

)ts ebb —| |– 1.1 knots flood –| |– 1.7 knots ebb –| |– 2.7 knots flood —| |— 2.6

THU AUG 24

dawn 5:33 sunrise 6:33 sunset 7:51 dark 8:51
moonrise 2:44 p.m.

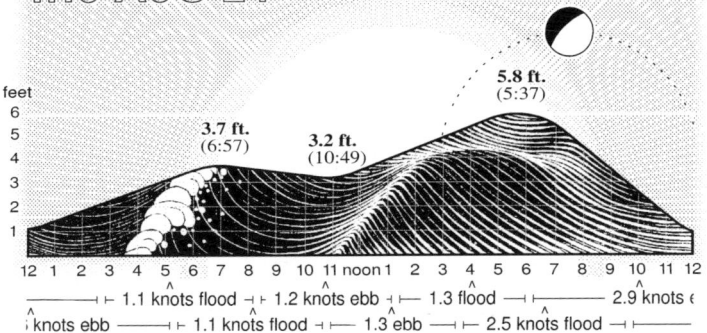

feet

3.7 ft.
(6:57)

3.2 ft.
(10:49)

5.8 ft.
(5:37)

12 1 2 3 4 5 6 7 8 9 10 11 noon 1 2 3 4 5 6 7 8 9 10 11 12

—| |– 1.1 knots flood –| |– 1.2 knots ebb –| |– 1.3 flood —| |— 2.9 knots e

 knots ebb —| |– 1.1 knots flood –| |– 1.3 ebb –| |– 2.5 knots flood —| |—

FRI AUG 18

dawn 5:27 sunrise 6:28 sunset 7:59 dark 9:00
moonrise 8:30 a.m. moonset 9:23 p.m.

Mars south Moon 2 degrees

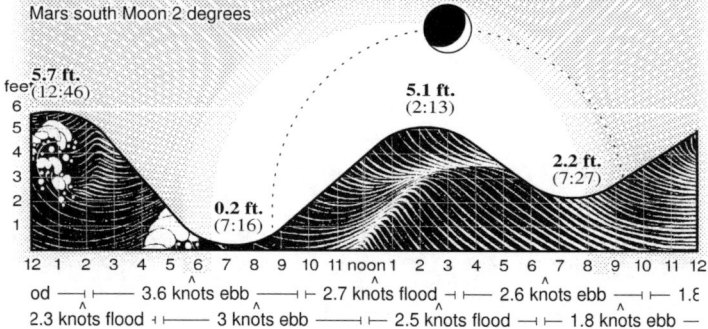

5.7 ft.
(12:46)
feet
6
5
4
3
2
1

5.1 ft.
(2:13)

2.2 ft.
(7:27)

0.2 ft.
(7:16)

12 1 2 3 4 5 6 7 8 9 10 11 noon 1 2 3 4 5 6 7 8 9 10 11 12

od ⊢ ⊢ 3.6 knots ebb ⊣ ⊢ 2.7 knots flood ⊣ ⊢ 2.6 knots ebb ⊢ ⊢ 1.8
2.3 knots flood ⊣ ⊢ 3 knots ebb ⊢ ⊢ 2.5 knots flood ⊣ ⊢ 1.8 knots ebb ⊢

SAT AUG 19

dawn 5:28 sunrise 6:29 sunset 7:58 dark 8:58
moonrise 9:28 a.m. moonset 9:44 p.m.

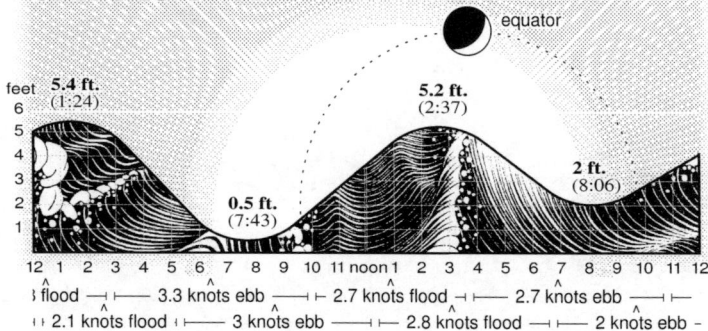

equator

feet **5.4 ft.**
(1:24)
6
5
4
3
2
1

5.2 ft.
(2:37)

2 ft.
(8:06)

0.5 ft.
(7:43)

12 1 2 3 4 5 6 7 8 9 10 11 noon 1 2 3 4 5 6 7 8 9 10 11 12

⊢ flood ⊣ ⊢ 3.3 knots ebb ⊢ ⊢ 2.7 knots flood ⊣ ⊢ 2.7 knots ebb ⊢ ⊢
⊢ 2.1 knots flood ⊣ ⊢ 3 knots ebb ⊢ ⊢ 2.8 knots flood ⊣ ⊢ 2 knots ebb ⊢

SUN AUG 20

dawn 5:29 sunrise 6:30 sunset 7:56 dark 8:57
moonrise 10:27 a.m. moonset 10:06 p.m.

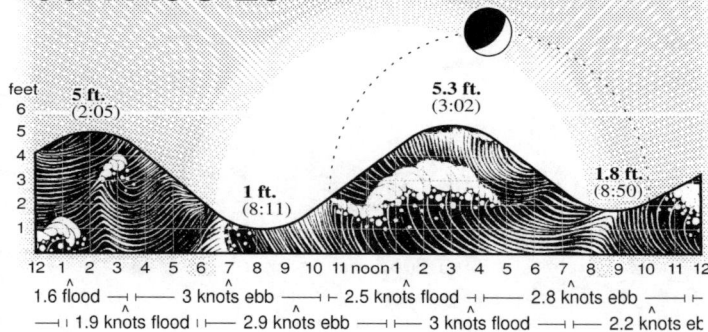

feet **5 ft.**
(2:05)
6
5
4
3
2
1

5.3 ft.
(3:02)

1.8 ft.
(8:50)

1 ft.
(8:11)

12 1 2 3 4 5 6 7 8 9 10 11 noon 1 2 3 4 5 6 7 8 9 10 11 12

1.6 flood ⊢ ⊢ 3 knots ebb ⊢ ⊢ 2.5 knots flood ⊣ ⊢ 2.8 knots ebb ⊢ ⊢
⊢ 1.9 knots flood ⊣ ⊢ 2.9 knots ebb ⊢ ⊢ 3 knots flood ⊢ ⊢ 2.2 knots et

Ⓢ   Ⓙ   Ⓥ   ⓜⓂ

MON AUG 14

dawn 5:22 sunrise 6:24 sunset 8:04 dark 9:06
moonrise 4:30 a.m. moonset 7:40 p.m.

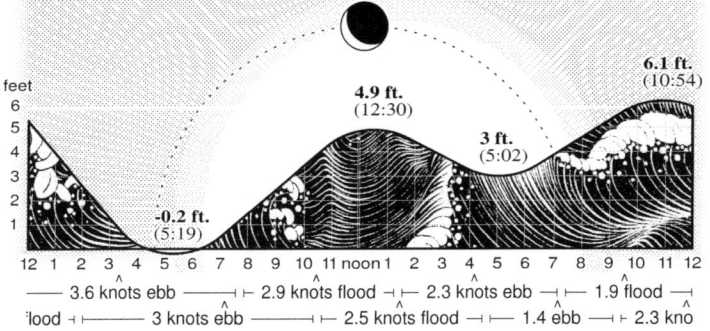

6.1 ft.
(10:54)

feet

4.9 ft.
(12:30)

3 ft.
(5:02)

-0.2 ft.
(5:19)

12 1 2 3 4 5 6 7 8 9 10 11 noon 1 2 3 4 5 6 7 8 9 10 11 12

⊢— 3.6 knots ebb ——⊣ ⊢ 2.9 knots flood ⊣ ⊢ 2.3 knots ebb ⊣ ⊢ 1.9 flood ⊣
flood ⊣ ⊢—— 3 knots ebb ——⊣ ⊢ 2.5 knots flood ⊣ ⊢ 1.4 ebb ⊣ ⊢ 2.3 kno

TUE AUG 15

dawn 5:24 sunrise 6:25 sunset 8:03 dark 9:04
moonrise 5:31 a.m. moonset 8:11 p.m.

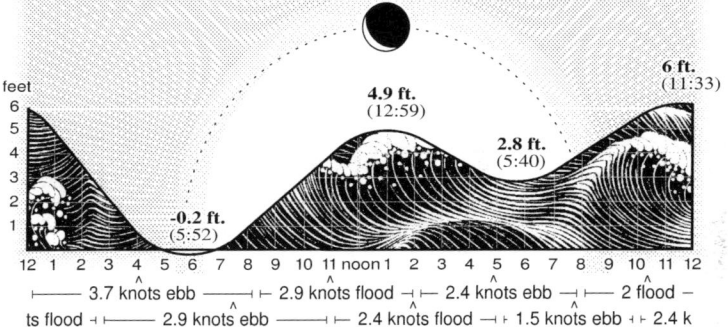

6 ft.
(11:33)

feet

4.9 ft.
(12:59)

2.8 ft.
(5:40)

-0.2 ft.
(5:52)

12 1 2 3 4 5 6 7 8 9 10 11 noon 1 2 3 4 5 6 7 8 9 10 11 12

⊢— 3.7 knots ebb ——⊣ ⊢ 2.9 knots flood ⊣ ⊢ 2.4 knots ebb ⊣ ⊢ 2 flood ⊣
ts flood ⊣ ⊢—— 2.9 knots ebb ——⊣ ⊢ 2.4 knots flood ⊣ ⊢ 1.5 knots ebb ⊣ ⊢ 2.4 k

WED AUG 16

dawn 5:25 sunrise 6:26 sunset 8:02 dark 9:03
moonrise 6:32 a.m. moonset 8:37 p.m.

New Moon 2:38 a.m.

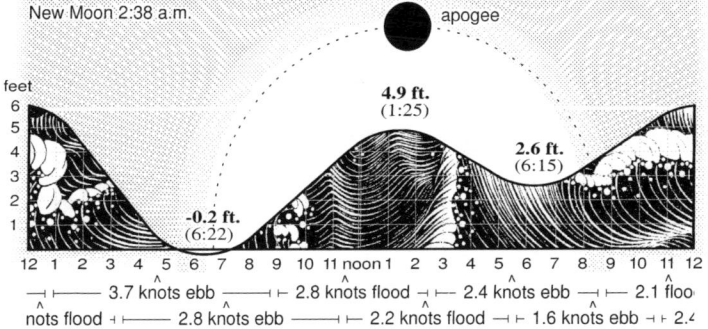

apogee

feet

4.9 ft.
(1:25)

2.6 ft.
(6:15)

-0.2 ft.
(6:22)

12 1 2 3 4 5 6 7 8 9 10 11 noon 1 2 3 4 5 6 7 8 9 10 11 12

⊣ ⊢— 3.7 knots ebb ——⊣ ⊢ 2.8 knots flood ⊣ ⊢ 2.4 knots ebb ⊣ ⊢ 2.1 floo
nots flood ⊣ ⊢—— 2.8 knots ebb ——⊣ ⊢ 2.2 knots flood ⊣ ⊢ 1.6 knots ebb ⊣ ⊢ 2.4

THU AUG 17

dawn 5:26 sunrise 6:27 sunset 8:00 dark 9:01
moonrise 7:31 a.m. moonset 9:01 p.m.

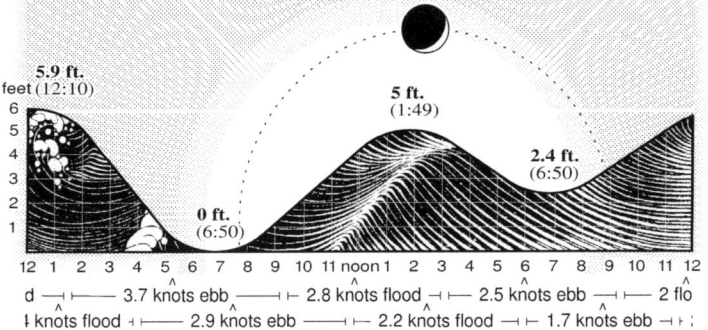

5.9 ft.
feet (12:10)

5 ft.
(1:49)

2.4 ft.
(6:50)

0 ft.
(6:50)

12 1 2 3 4 5 6 7 8 9 10 11 noon 1 2 3 4 5 6 7 8 9 10 11 12

d ⊣ ⊢— 3.7 knots ebb ——⊣ ⊢ 2.8 knots flood ⊣ ⊢ 2.5 knots ebb ⊣ ⊢ 2 flo
⊢ knots flood ⊣ ⊢—— 2.9 knots ebb ——⊣ ⊢ 2.2 knots flood ⊣ ⊢ 1.7 knots ebb ⊣ ⊢

FRI AUG 11

dawn 5:19 sunrise 6:22 sunset 8:08 dark 9:10
moonrise 1:45 a.m. moonset 5:29 p.m.

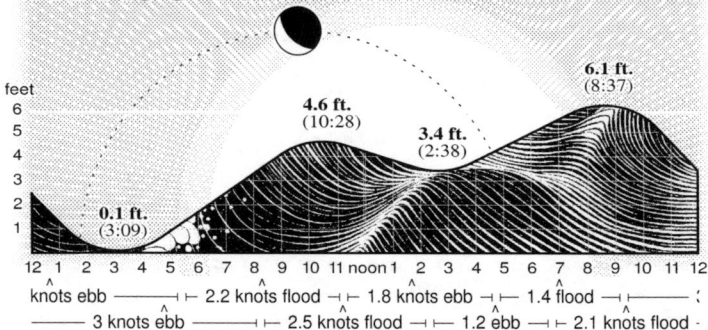

6.1 ft.
(8:37)

4.6 ft.
(10:28)

3.4 ft.
(2:38)

0.1 ft.
(3:09)

feet
6
5
4
3
2
1

12 1 2 3 4 5 6 7 8 9 10 11 noon 1 2 3 4 5 6 7 8 9 10 11 12

knots ebb ——— ⊢ 2.2 knots flood ⊣ ⊢ 1.8 knots ebb ⊣ ⊢ 1.4 flood ⊣ ⊢ ⋮
——— 3 knots ebb ———— ⊢ 2.5 knots flood ⊣ ⊢ 1.2 ebb ⊣ ⊢ 2.1 knots flood ⋅

SAT AUG 12

dawn 5:20 sunrise 6:23 sunset 8:06 dark 9:09
moonrise 2:35 a.m. moonset 6:20 p.m.

Perseids' Peak

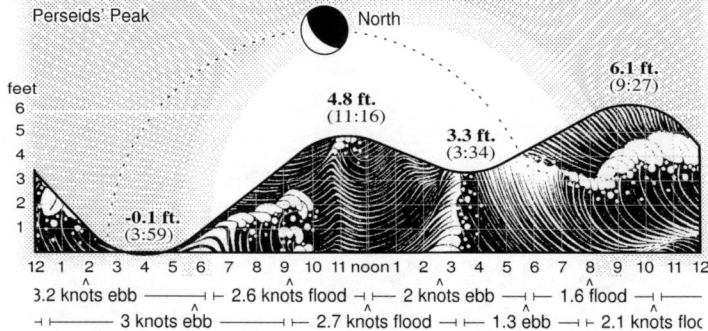

North

6.1 ft.
(9:27)

4.8 ft.
(11:16)

3.3 ft.
(3:34)

-0.1 ft.
(3:59)

feet
6
5
4
3
2
1

12 1 2 3 4 5 6 7 8 9 10 11 noon 1 2 3 4 5 6 7 8 9 10 11 12

3.2 knots ebb ——— ⊢ 2.6 knots flood ⊣ ⊢ 2 knots ebb ——— ⊢ 1.6 flood ⊣ ⊢
⊣ ⊢——— 3 knots ebb ———— ⊢ 2.7 knots flood ⊣ ⊢ 1.3 ebb ⊣ ⊢ 2.1 knots floc

SUN AUG 13

dawn 5:21 sunrise 6:24 sunset 8:05 dark 9:07
moonrise 3:31 a.m. moonset 7:04 p.m.

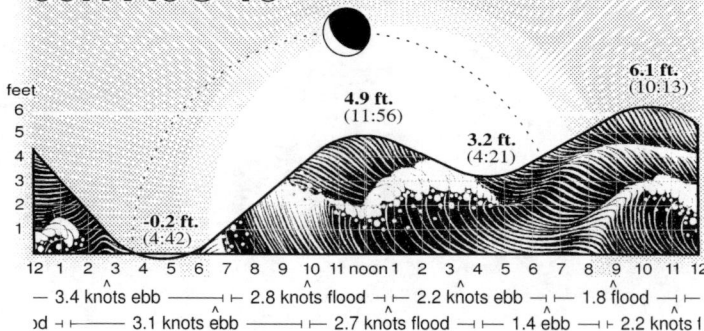

6.1 ft.
(10:13)

4.9 ft.
(11:56)

3.2 ft.
(4:21)

-0.2 ft.
(4:42)

feet
6
5
4
3
2
1

12 1 2 3 4 5 6 7 8 9 10 11 noon 1 2 3 4 5 6 7 8 9 10 11 12

— 3.4 knots ebb ——— ⊢ 2.8 knots flood ⊣ ⊢ 2.2 knots ebb ⊣ ⊢ 1.8 flood ⊣ ⊢
⋮d ⊣ ⊢——— 3.1 knots ebb ———— ⊢ 2.7 knots flood ⊣ ⊢ 1.4 ebb ⊣ ⊢ 2.2 knots f

Perseids Meteor Shower The Perseids in years past produced notable
showers of bight meteors at a peak hourly rate of up to 60 per hour. The
shower runs annually between Jul 27th to Aug 24th with this year's peak
on Aug 12th and morning of the 13th. The constellation Perseus, the
shower's radiant point, rises above the eastern horizon by 10:00 p.m. into
a dark sky provided by the early evening setting waning moon.

MON AUG 7
dawn 5:15 sunrise 6:18 sunset 8:12 dark 9:16
moonset 1:13 p.m. moonrise 11:52 p.m.

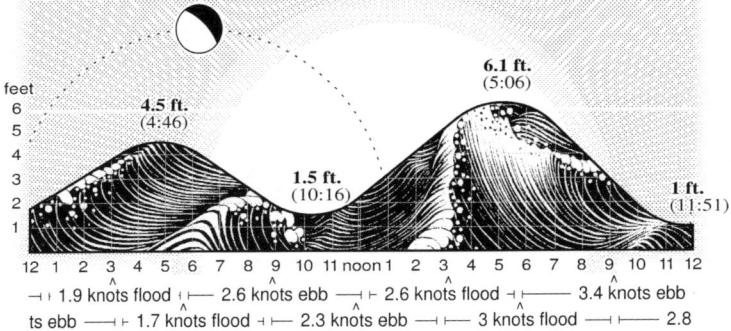

feet

4.5 ft.
(4:46)

6.1 ft.
(5:06)

1.5 ft.
(10:16)

1 ft.
(11:51)

12 1 2 3 4 5 6 7 8 9 10 11 noon 1 2 3 4 5 6 7 8 9 10 11 12

⊣ ⊢ 1.9 knots flood ⊣ ⊢— 2.6 knots ebb —⊢ 2.6 knots flood ⊣ ⊢— 3.4 knots ebb
ts ebb —⊢ 1.7 knots flood ⊣ ⊢ 2.3 knots ebb —⊣ ⊢ 3 knots flood —⊣ ⊢— 2.8

TUE AUG 8
dawn 5:16 sunrise 6:19 sunset 8:11 dark 9:14
moonset 2:21 p.m.

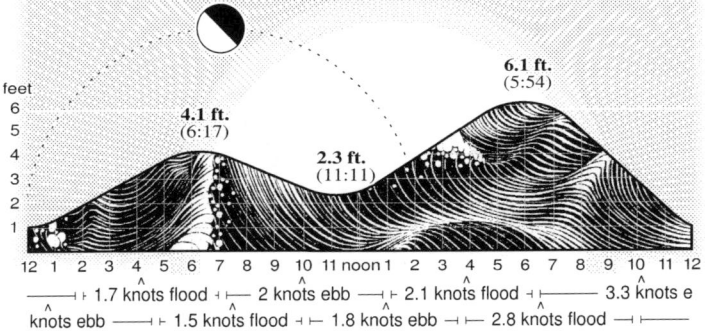

feet

6.1 ft.
(5:54)

4.1 ft.
(6:17)

2.3 ft.
(11:11)

12 1 2 3 4 5 6 7 8 9 10 11 noon 1 2 3 4 5 6 7 8 9 10 11 12

—⊣ ⊢ 1.7 knots flood ⊣ ⊢— 2 knots ebb —⊢ 2.1 knots flood ⊣ ⊢— 3.3 knots e
knots ebb —⊢ 1.5 knots flood ⊣ ⊢ 1.8 knots ebb —⊣ 2.8 knots flood —⊣ ⊢—

WED AUG 9
dawn 5:17 sunrise 6:20 sunset 8:10 dark 9:13
moonrise 12:24 a.m. moonset 3:28 p.m.

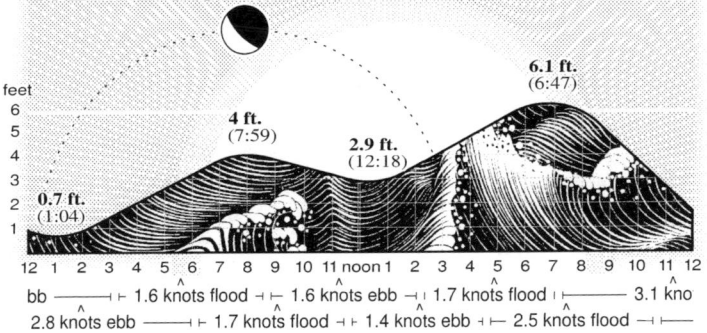

feet

6.1 ft.
(6:47)

4 ft.
(7:59)

2.9 ft.
(12:18)

0.7 ft.
(1:04)

12 1 2 3 4 5 6 7 8 9 10 11 noon 1 2 3 4 5 6 7 8 9 10 11 12

bb —⊣ ⊢ 1.6 knots flood ⊣ ⊢ 1.6 knots ebb —⊣ ⊢ 1.7 knots flood ⊣ ⊢— 3.1 kno
2.8 knots ebb —⊣ ⊢ 1.7 knots flood ⊣ ⊢ 1.4 knots ebb ⊣ ⊢ 2.5 knots flood —⊣ ⊢—

THU AUG 10
dawn 5:18 sunrise 6:21 sunset 8:09 dark 9:11
moonrise 1:02 a.m. moonset 4:31 p.m.

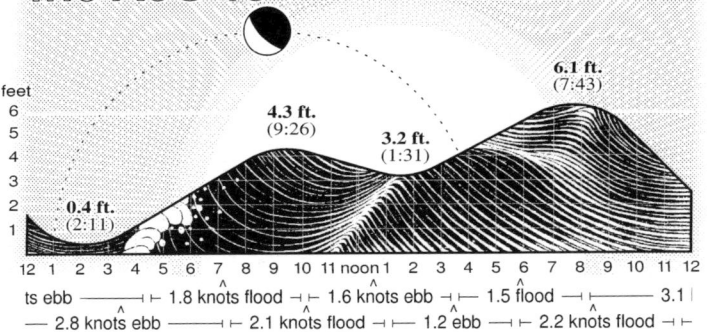

feet

6.1 ft.
(7:43)

4.3 ft.
(9:26)

3.2 ft.
(1:31)

0.4 ft.
(2:11)

12 1 2 3 4 5 6 7 8 9 10 11 noon 1 2 3 4 5 6 7 8 9 10 11 12

ts ebb —⊣ ⊢ 1.8 knots flood ⊣ ⊢ 1.6 knots ebb ⊣ ⊢ 1.5 flood ⊣ ⊢— 3.1 |
— 2.8 knots ebb —⊣ ⊢ 2.1 knots flood ⊣ ⊢ 1.2 ebb ⊣ ⊢ 2.2 knots flood ⊣ ⊢

FRI AUG 4

dawn 5:12 sunrise 6:16 sunset 8:16 dark 9:19
moonset 9:41 a.m. moonrise 10:30 p.m.

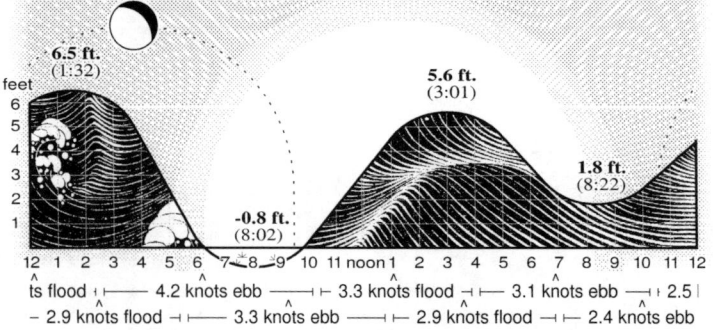

6.5 ft.
(1:32)

feet
6
5
4
3
2
1

5.6 ft.
(3:01)

1.8 ft.
(8:22)

-0.8 ft.
(8:02)

12 1 2 3 4 5 6 7 8 9 10 11 noon 1 2 3 4 5 6 7 8 9 10 11 12

ts flood ⊦—— 4.2 knots ebb ——⊢ 3.3 knots flood —⊣ ⊢ 3.1 knots ebb —⊣ ⊦ 2.5 ⊦
– 2.9 knots flood —⊣ ⊢—— 3.3 knots ebb ——⊣ ⊢ 2.9 knots flood —⊣ ⊢ 2.4 knots ebb

SAT AUG 5

dawn 5:13 sunrise 6:17 sunset 8:15 dark 9:18
moonset 10:54 a.m. moonrise 10:56 p.m.

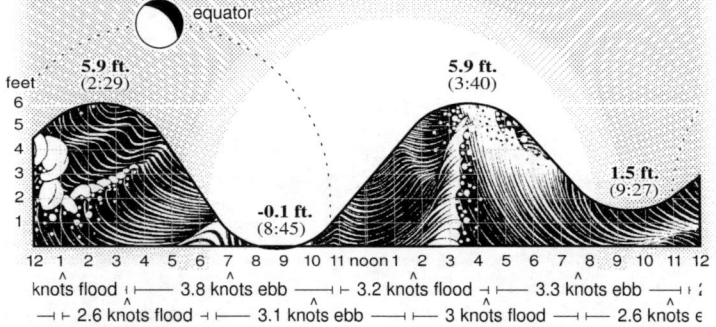

equator

5.9 ft.
(2:29)

feet
6
5
4
3
2
1

5.9 ft.
(3:40)

1.5 ft.
(9:27)

-0.1 ft.
(8:45)

12 1 2 3 4 5 6 7 8 9 10 11 noon 1 2 3 4 5 6 7 8 9 10 11 12

knots flood ⊦—— 3.8 knots ebb ——⊢ 3.2 knots flood —⊣ ⊢—— 3.3 knots ebb ——⊣ ⊦ 2
—⊣ ⊢ 2.6 knots flood —⊣ ⊢—— 3.1 knots ebb —— ⊢—— 3 knots flood —⊣ ⊢ 2.6 knots ε

SUN AUG 6

dawn 5:14 sunrise 6:18 sunset 8:13 dark 9:17
moonset 12:04 p.m. moonrise 11:23 p.m.

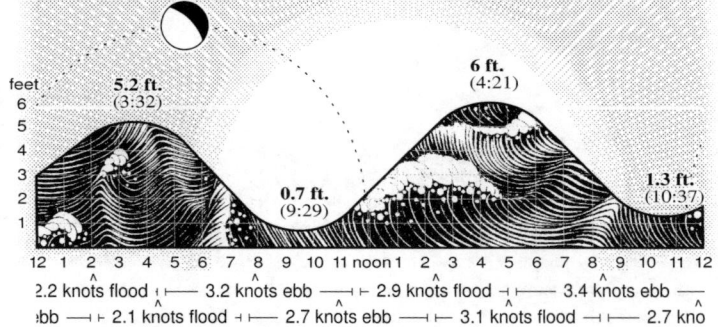

5.2 ft.
(3:32)

feet
6
5
4
3
2
1

6 ft.
(4:21)

1.3 ft.
(10:37)

0.7 ft.
(9:29)

12 1 2 3 4 5 6 7 8 9 10 11 noon 1 2 3 4 5 6 7 8 9 10 11 12

2.2 knots flood ⊦—— 3.2 knots ebb ——⊢ 2.9 knots flood —⊣ ⊢—— 3.4 knots ebb ——
ebb —— ⊢ 2.1 knots flood —⊣ ⊢— 2.7 knots ebb —⊣ ⊢—— 3.1 knots flood —⊣ ⊢ 2.7 kno

Ⓢ   Ⓙ   Ⓜ

MON JUL 31

dawn 5:08 sunrise 6:12 sunset 8:20 dark 9:24
moonset 4:29 a.m. moonrise 8:09 p.m.

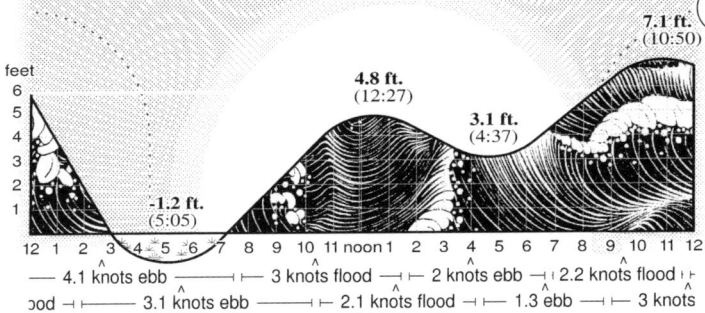

7.1 ft.
(10:50)

feet

4.8 ft.
(12:27)

3.1 ft.
(4:37)

-1.2 ft.
(5:05)

12 1 2 3 4 5 6 7 8 9 10 11 noon 1 2 3 4 5 6 7 8 9 10 11 12

— 4.1 knots ebb ——— ⊢ 3 knots flood ⊣ ⊢ 2 ebb ⊣⊢ 2.2 knots flood ⊢

ood ⊣ ⊢—— 3.1 knots ebb ——— ⊢ 2.1 knots flood ⊣ ⊢ 1.3 ebb —⊣ ⊢ 3 knots

TUE AUG 1

dawn 5:09 sunrise 6:13 sunset 8:19 dark 9:23
moonset 5:46 a.m. moonrise 8:54 p.m.

perigee

Full Moon 11:32 a.m.

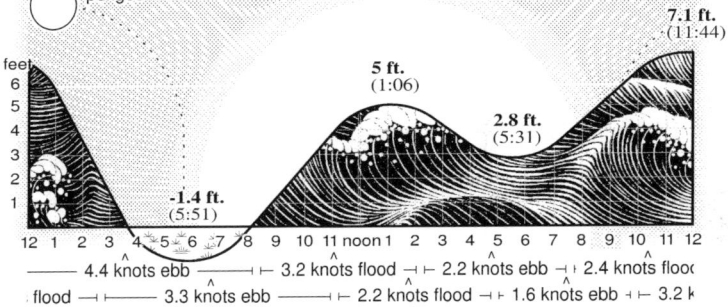

7.1 ft.
(11:44)

feet

5 ft.
(1:06)

2.8 ft.
(5:31)

-1.4 ft.
(5:51)

12 1 2 3 4 5 6 7 8 9 10 11 noon 1 2 3 4 5 6 7 8 9 10 11 12

—— 4.4 knots ebb ——— ⊢— 3.2 knots flood —⊣ ⊢ 2.2 knots ebb ⊣ ⊢ 2.4 knots flood

flood —⊣ ⊢—— 3.3 knots ebb ——— ⊢ 2.2 knots flood ⊣ ⊢ 1.6 knots ebb ⊣ ⊢ 3.2 k

WED AUG 2

dawn 5:10 sunrise 6:14 sunset 8:18 dark 9:22
moonset 7:07 a.m. moonrise 9:31 p.m.

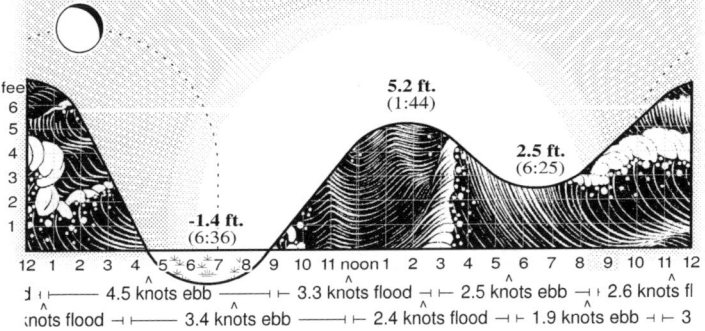

feet

5.2 ft.
(1:44)

2.5 ft.
(6:25)

-1.4 ft.
(6:36)

12 1 2 3 4 5 6 7 8 9 10 11 noon 1 2 3 4 5 6 7 8 9 10 11 12

d ⊢ ⊢—— 4.5 knots ebb ——— ⊢ 3.3 knots flood ⊣ ⊢ 2.5 knots ebb ⊣ ⊢ 2.6 knots fl

knots flood ⊣ ⊢—— 3.4 knots ebb ——— ⊢ 2.4 knots flood ⊣ ⊢ 1.9 knots ebb ⊣ ⊢ 3

THU AUG 3

dawn 5:11 sunrise 6:15 sunset 8:17 dark 9:21
moonset 8:26 a.m. moonrise 10:02 p.m.

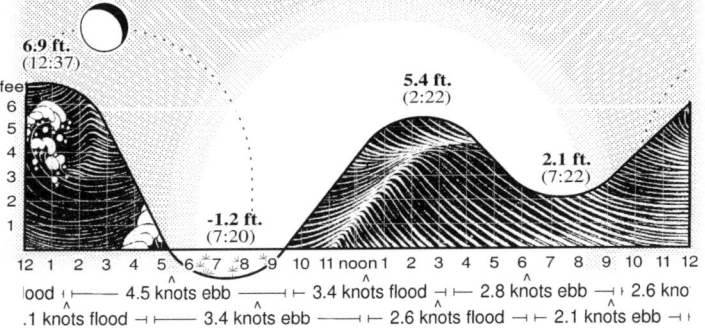

6.9 ft.
(12:37)

feet

5.4 ft.
(2:22)

2.1 ft.
(7:22)

-1.2 ft.
(7:20)

12 1 2 3 4 5 6 7 8 9 10 11 noon 1 2 3 4 5 6 7 8 9 10 11 12

lood ⊢ ⊢—— 4.5 knots ebb ——— ⊢ 3.4 knots flood ⊣ ⊢ 2.8 knots ebb ⊣ ⊢ 2.6 kno

.1 knots flood ⊣ ⊢—— 3.4 knots ebb ——— ⊢ 2.6 knots flood ⊣ ⊢ 2.1 knots ebb ⊣ ⊢

FRI JUL 28

dawn 5:04 sunrise 6:10 sunset 8:22 dark 9:28
moonset 1:34 a.m. moonrise 5:01 p.m.

Delta Aquarids Peak

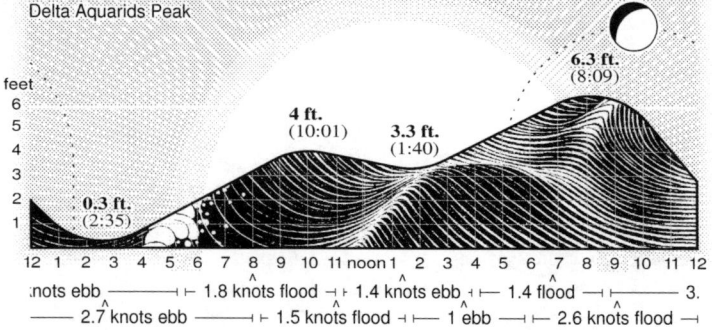

feet

6
5
4
3
2
1

4 ft.
(10:01)

3.3 ft.
(1:40)

6.3 ft.
(8:09)

0.3 ft.
(2:35)

12 1 2 3 4 5 6 7 8 9 10 11 noon 1 2 3 4 5 6 7 8 9 10 11 12

:nots ebb ——— ⊢ 1.8 knots flood ⊣ ⊢ 1.4 knots ebb ⊣ ⊢ 1.4 flood ⊣ ⊢ 3.
——— 2.7 knots ebb ——— ⊢ 1.5 knots flood ⊣ ⊢ 1 ebb ⊣ ⊢ 2.6 knots flood ⊣

SAT JUL 29

dawn 5:05 sunrise 6:11 sunset 8:21 dark 9:27
moonset 2:21 a.m. moonrise 6:11 p.m.

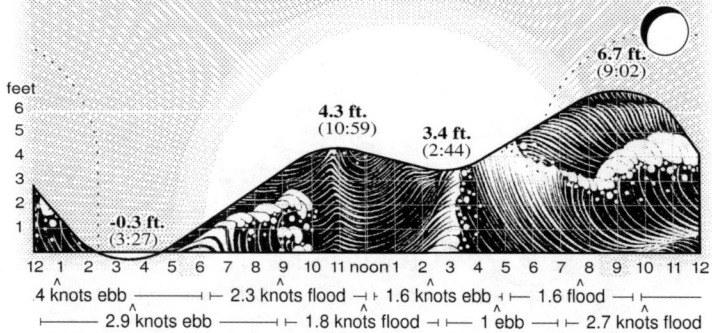

feet

6
5
4
3
2
1

4.3 ft.
(10:59)

3.4 ft.
(2:44)

6.7 ft.
(9:02)

-0.3 ft.
(3:27)

12 1 2 3 4 5 6 7 8 9 10 11 noon 1 2 3 4 5 6 7 8 9 10 11 12

4 knots ebb ——— ⊢ 2.3 knots flood ⊣ ⊢ 1.6 knots ebb ⊣ ⊢ 1.6 flood ⊣ ⊢
⊢——— 2.9 knots ebb ——— ⊢ 1.8 knots flood ⊣ ⊢ 1 ebb ⊣ ⊢ 2.7 knots flood

SUN JUL 30

dawn 5:06 sunrise 6:12 sunset 8:21 dark 9:25
moonset 3:19 a.m. moonrise 7:15 p.m.

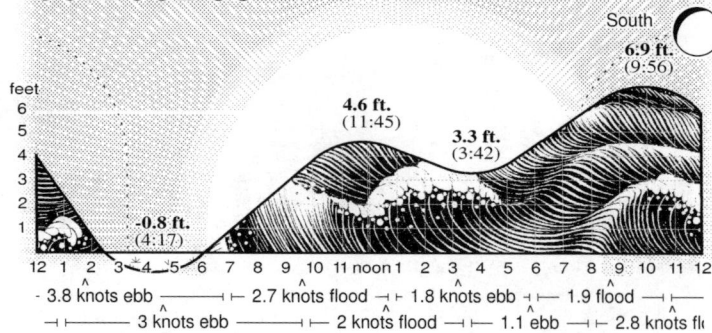

South

feet

6
5
4
3
2
1

4.6 ft.
(11:45)

3.3 ft.
(3:42)

6.9 ft.
(9:56)

-0.8 ft.
(4:17)

12 1 2 3 4 5 6 7 8 9 10 11 noon 1 2 3 4 5 6 7 8 9 10 11 12

- 3.8 knots ebb ——— ⊢ 2.7 knots flood ⊣ ⊢ 1.8 knots ebb ⊣ ⊢ 1.9 flood ⊣ ⊢
⊣ ⊢——— 3 knots ebb ——— ⊢ 2 knots flood ⊣ ⊢ 1.1 ebb ⊣ ⊢ 2.8 knots fl⸱

Delta Aquarids Meteor shower The shower is active between Jul 12th -
Aug 23rd and has produced up to 20 meteors per hour at peak. This year's
peak falls on the night of Jul 28th and the following morning. The waxing
to Full Moon will compete with this year's shower until it sets at
approximately 2:00 a.m. on the 29th with the shower's radiant point, the
constellation Aquarius, in the southern sky.

MON JUL 24
dawn 5:00 sunrise 6:07 sunset 8:26 dark 9:32
moonrise 12:34 p.m.

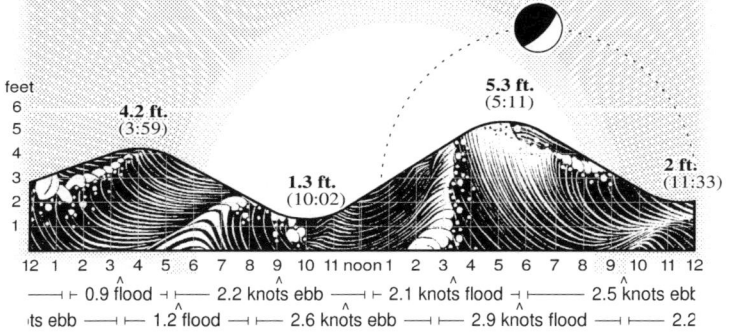

4.2 ft.
(3:59)

5.3 ft.
(5:11)

1.3 ft.
(10:02)

2 ft.
(11:33)

feet
6
5
4
3
2
1

12 1 2 3 4 5 6 7 8 9 10 11 noon 1 2 3 4 5 6 7 8 9 10 11 12

├─┤ ├ 0.9 flood ┤ ├── 2.2 knots ebb ──┤ ├ 2.1 knots flood ┤ ├──── 2.5 knots ebb

ts ebb ──┤ ├── 1.2 flood ──┤ ├── 2.6 knots ebb ──┤ ├── 2.9 knots flood ──┤ ├── 2.2

TUE JUL 25
dawn 5:01 sunrise 6:08 sunset 8:25 dark 9:31
moonset 12:02 a.m. moonrise 1:36 p.m.

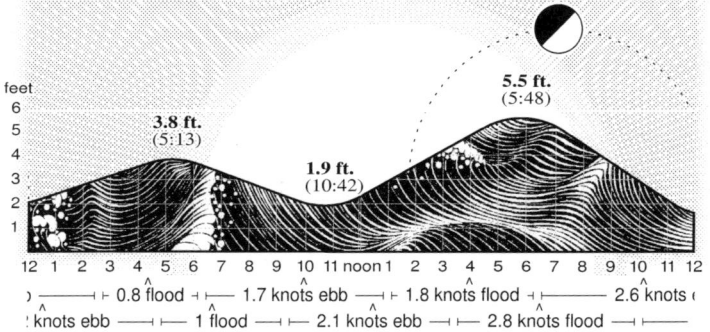

3.8 ft.
(5:13)

5.5 ft.
(5:48)

1.9 ft.
(10:42)

feet
6
5
4
3
2
1

12 1 2 3 4 5 6 7 8 9 10 11 noon 1 2 3 4 5 6 7 8 9 10 11 12

) ──┤ ├ 0.8 flood ┤ ├── 1.7 knots ebb ──┤ ├ 1.8 knots flood ┤ ├──── 2.6 knots

: knots ebb ──┤ ├── 1 flood ──┤ ├── 2.1 knots ebb ──┤ ├── 2.8 knots flood ──┤ ├──

WED JUL 26
dawn 5:02 sunrise 6:08 sunset 8:24 dark 9:30
moonset 12:28 a.m. moonrise 2:41 p.m.

Conjunction Venus & Mercury

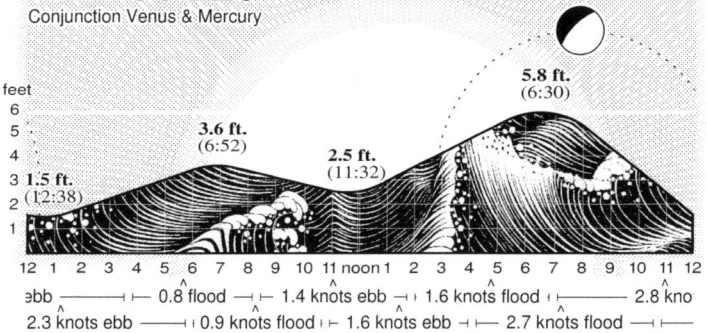

5.8 ft.
(6:30)

3.6 ft.
(6:52)

2.5 ft.
(11:32)

1.5 ft.
(12:38)

feet
6
5
4
3
2
1

12 1 2 3 4 5 6 7 8 9 10 11 noon 1 2 3 4 5 6 7 8 9 10 11 12

ebb ──────┤ ├ 0.8 flood ──┤ ├ 1.4 knots ebb ──┤ ├ 1.6 knots flood ┤ ├──── 2.8 kno

2.3 knots ebb ──────┤ ├ 0.9 knots flood ┤ ├ 1.6 knots ebb ──┤ ├ 2.7 knots flood ──┤ ├──

THU JUL 27
dawn 5:03 sunrise 6:09 sunset 8:23 dark 9:29
moonset 12:58 a.m. moonrise 3:50 p.m.

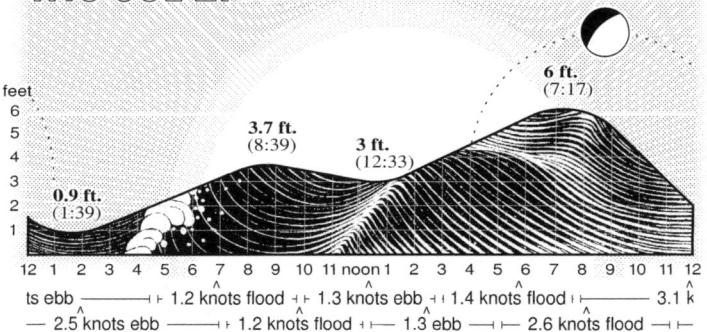

6 ft.
(7:17)

3.7 ft.
(8:39)

3 ft.
(12:33)

0.9 ft.
(1:39)

feet
6
5
4
3
2
1

12 1 2 3 4 5 6 7 8 9 10 11 noon 1 2 3 4 5 6 7 8 9 10 11 12

ts ebb ──────┤ ├ 1.2 knots flood ┤ ├ 1.3 knots ebb ┤ ├ 1.4 knots flood ┤ ├──── 3.1 k

── 2.5 knots ebb ──────┤ ├ 1.2 knots flood ┤ ├── 1.3 ebb ──┤ ├ 2.6 knots flood ──┤ ├──

FRI JUL 21 dawn 4:57 sunrise 6:04 sunset 8:28 dark 9:35
moonrise 9:38 a.m. moonset 10:56 p.m.

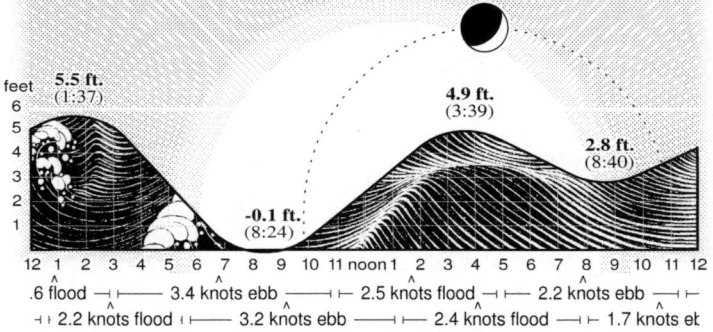

feet

5.5 ft.
(1:37)

4.9 ft.
(3:39)

2.8 ft.
(8:40)

-0.1 ft.
(8:24)

12 1 2 3 4 5 6 7 8 9 10 11 noon 1 2 3 4 5 6 7 8 9 10 11 12

.6 flood ⊢⊣ ⊢— 3.4 knots ebb —⊣ ⊢ 2.5 knots flood —⊣ ⊢ 2.2 knots ebb —⊣ ⊢
⊣ 2.2 knots flood ⊢—— 3.2 knots ebb ——⊣ ⊢ 2.4 knots flood —⊣ ⊢ 1.7 knots et

SAT JUL 22 dawn 4:58 sunrise 6:05 sunset 8:27 dark 9:34
moonrise 10:36 a.m. moonset 11:18 p.m.

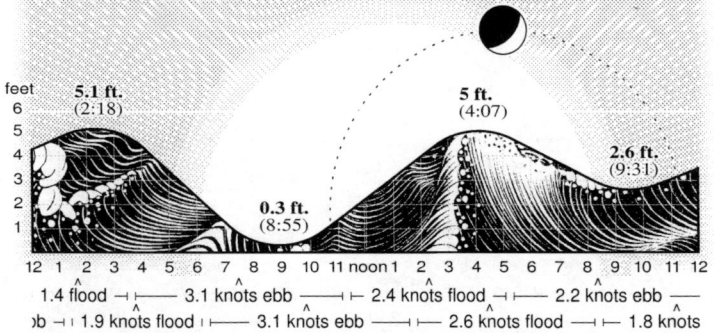

feet

5.1 ft.
(2:18)

5 ft.
(4:07)

2.6 ft.
(9:31)

0.3 ft.
(8:55)

12 1 2 3 4 5 6 7 8 9 10 11 noon 1 2 3 4 5 6 7 8 9 10 11 12

1.4 flood —⊣ ⊢— 3.1 knots ebb ——⊣ ⊢ 2.4 knots flood —⊣ ⊢ 2.2 knots ebb ——
⊢b —⊣ 1.9 knots flood ⊢—— 3.1 knots ebb ——⊣ ⊢ 2.6 knots flood —⊣ ⊢ 1.8 knots

SUN JUL 23 dawn 4:59 sunrise 6:06 sunset 8:26 dark 9:33
moonrise 11:34 a.m. moonset 11:39 p.m.

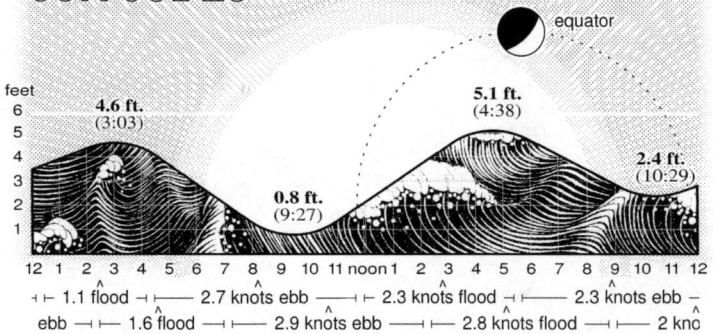

equator

feet

4.6 ft.
(3:03)

5.1 ft.
(4:38)

2.4 ft.
(10:29)

0.8 ft.
(9:27)

12 1 2 3 4 5 6 7 8 9 10 11 noon 1 2 3 4 5 6 7 8 9 10 11 12

⊣ ⊢ 1.1 flood —⊣ ⊢— 2.7 knots ebb ——⊣ ⊢ 2.3 knots flood —⊣ ⊢—— 2.3 knots ebb –
ebb —⊣ ⊢— 1.6 flood —⊣ ⊢— 2.9 knots ebb ——⊣ ⊢ 2.8 knots flood —⊣ ⊢— 2 kno

⊘   Ⓙ   Ⓥ Ⓜ
                      ⓜ

MON JUL 17
dawn 4:53 sunrise 6:01 sunset 8:30 dark 9:38
moonrise 5:37 a.m. moonset 9:03 p.m.

New Moon 11:32 a.m.

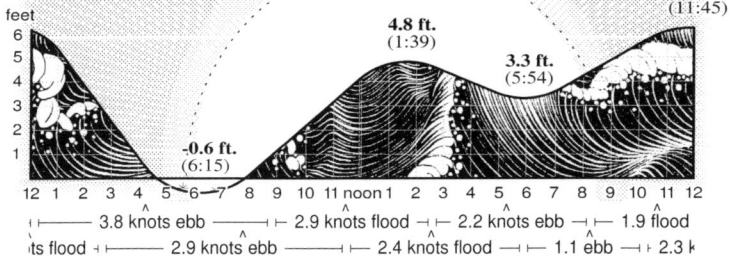

6.2 ft.
(11:45)

feet

4.8 ft.
(1:39)

3.3 ft.
(5:54)

-0.6 ft.
(6:15)

12 1 2 3 4 5 6 7 8 9 10 11 noon 1 2 3 4 5 6 7 8 9 10 11 12

3.8 knots ebb ⊢ 2.9 knots flood ⊢ 2.2 knots ebb ⊣ 1.9 flood
ts flood ⊣ 2.9 knots ebb ⊢ 2.4 knots flood ⊣ 1.1 ebb ⊣ 2.3 k

TUE JUL 18
dawn 4:54 sunrise 6:02 sunset 8:30 dark 9:37
moonrise 6:37 a.m. moonset 9:38 p.m.

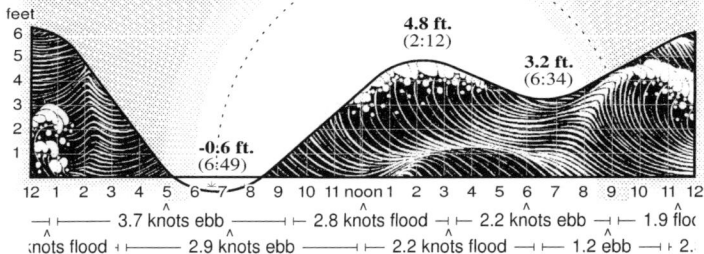

feet

4.8 ft.
(2:12)

3.2 ft.
(6:34)

-0.6 ft.
(6:49)

12 1 2 3 4 5 6 7 8 9 10 11 noon 1 2 3 4 5 6 7 8 9 10 11 12

3.7 knots ebb ⊢ 2.8 knots flood ⊣ 2.2 knots ebb ⊣ 1.9 floo
knots flood ⊣ 2.9 knots ebb ⊢ 2.2 knots flood ⊣ 1.2 ebb ⊣ 2.

WED JUL 19
dawn 4:55 sunrise 6:03 sunset 8:29 dark 9:37
moonrise 7:38 a.m. moonset 10:08 p.m.

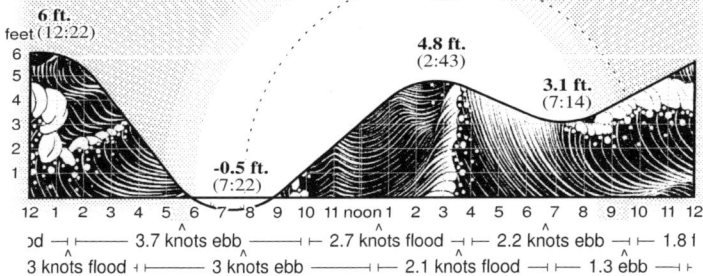

6 ft.
feet (12:22)

4.8 ft.
(2:43)

3.1 ft.
(7:14)

-0.5 ft.
(7:22)

12 1 2 3 4 5 6 7 8 9 10 11 noon 1 2 3 4 5 6 7 8 9 10 11 12

ood ⊣ 3.7 knots ebb ⊢ 2.7 knots flood ⊣ 2.2 knots ebb ⊣ 1.8 f
3 knots flood ⊣ 3 knots ebb ⊢ 2.1 knots flood ⊣ 1.3 ebb ⊣

THU JUL 20
dawn 4:56 sunrise 6:04 sunset 8:29 dark 9:36
moonrise 8:38 a.m. moonset 10:33 p.m.

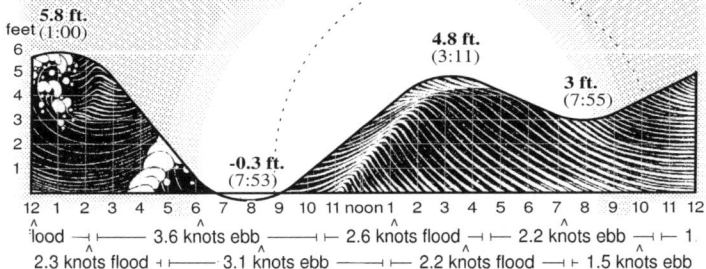

apogee

5.8 ft.
feet (1:00)

4.8 ft.
(3:11)

3 ft.
(7:55)

-0.3 ft.
(7:53)

12 1 2 3 4 5 6 7 8 9 10 11 noon 1 2 3 4 5 6 7 8 9 10 11 12

flood ⊣ 3.6 knots ebb ⊢ 2.6 knots flood ⊣ 2.2 knots ebb ⊣ 1
2.3 knots flood ⊣ 3.1 knots ebb ⊢ 2.2 knots flood ⊣ 1.5 knots ebb

FRI JUL 14

dawn 4:51 sunrise 5:59 sunset 8:32 dark 9:40
moonrise 3:03 a.m. moonset 6:36 p.m.

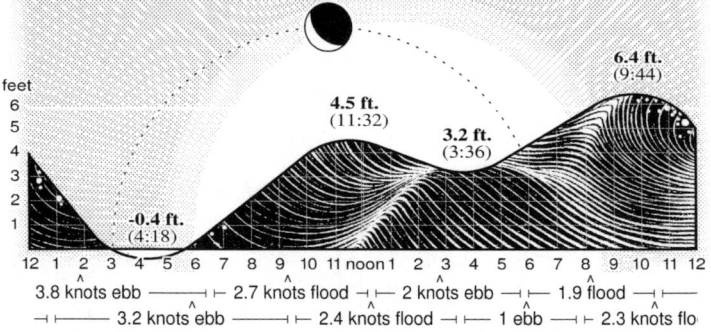

6.4 ft.
(9:44)

feet
6
5
4
3
2
1

4.5 ft.
(11:32)

3.2 ft.
(3:36)

-0.4 ft.
(4:18)

12 1 2 3 4 5 6 7 8 9 10 11 noon 1 2 3 4 5 6 7 8 9 10 11 12

3.8 knots ebb ———— ⊢ 2.7 knots flood ⊣ ⊢ 2 knots ebb ⊣ ⊢ 1.9 flood ⊣ ⊢
⊣ ⊢— 3.2 knots ebb ———— ⊢ 2.4 knots flood ⊣ ⊢ 1 ebb ⊣ ⊢ 2.3 knots flo

SAT JUL 15

dawn 4:52 sunrise 6:00 sunset 8:32 dark 9:40
moonrise 3:48 a.m. moonset 7:33 p.m.

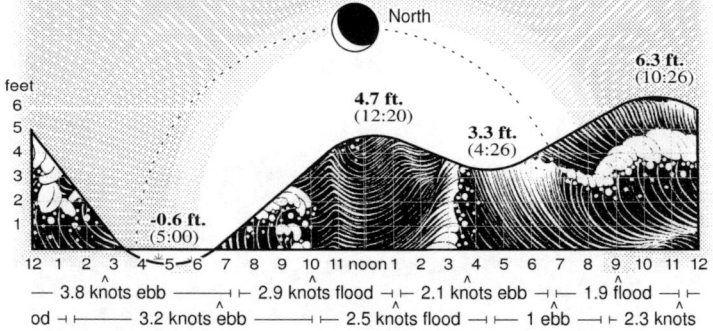

North

6.3 ft.
(10:26)

feet
6
5
4
3
2
1

4.7 ft.
(12:20)

3.3 ft.
(4:26)

-0.6 ft.
(5:00)

12 1 2 3 4 5 6 7 8 9 10 11 noon 1 2 3 4 5 6 7 8 9 10 11 12

— 3.8 knots ebb ———— ⊢ 2.9 knots flood ⊣ ⊢ 2.1 knots ebb ⊣ ⊢ 1.9 flood ⊣ ⊢
od ⊣ ⊢——— 3.2 knots ebb ———— ⊢ 2.5 knots flood ⊣ ⊢ 1 ebb ⊣ ⊢ 2.3 knots

SUN JUL 16

dawn 4:53 sunrise 6:01 sunset 8:31 dark 9:39
moonrise 4:40 a.m. moonset 8:22 p.m.

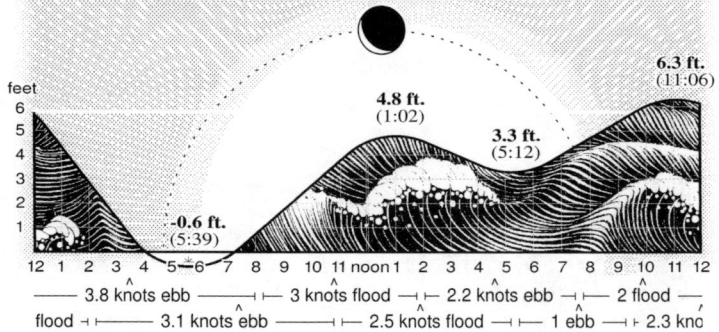

6.3 ft.
(11:06)

feet
6
5
4
3
2
1

4.8 ft.
(1:02)

3.3 ft.
(5:12)

-0.6 ft.
(5:39)

12 1 2 3 4 5 6 7 8 9 10 11 noon 1 2 3 4 5 6 7 8 9 10 11 12

——— 3.8 knots ebb ———— ⊢ 3 knots flood ⊣ ⊢ 2.2 knots ebb ⊣ ⊢ 2 flood —
flood ⊣ ⊢——— 3.1 knots ebb ———— ⊢ 2.5 knots flood ⊣ ⊢ 1 ebb ⊣ ⊢ 2.3 kno

MON JUL 10

dawn 4:47 sunrise 5:57 sunset 8:34 dark 9:43
moonrise 12:55 a.m. moonset 2:15 p.m.

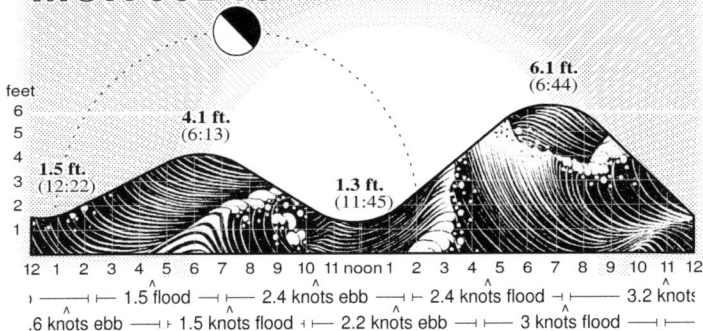

feet

6.1 ft.
(6:44)

4.1 ft.
(6:13)

1.5 ft.
(12:22)

1.3 ft.
(11:45)

12 1 2 3 4 5 6 7 8 9 10 11 noon 1 2 3 4 5 6 7 8 9 10 11 12

⊢ — 1.5 flood → ⊢ — 2.4 knots ebb — → ⊢ — 2.4 knots flood → ⊢— 3.2 knots
.6 knots ebb → ⊢ 1.5 knots flood ⊣ ⊢ — 2.2 knots ebb — → ⊢ — 3 knots flood — → ⊢—

TUE JUL 11

dawn 4:48 sunrise 5:57 sunset 8:33 dark 9:42
moonrise 1:21 a.m. moonset 3:22 p.m.

Jupiter south Moon 2 degrees

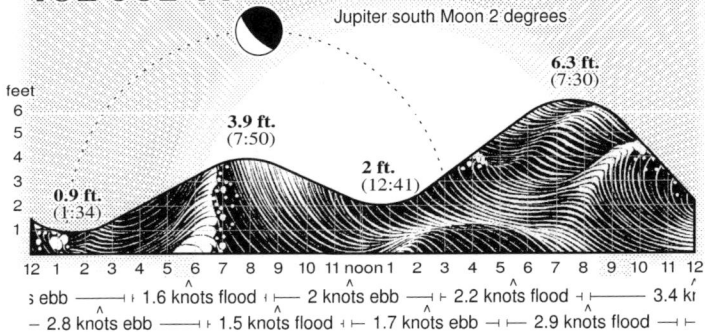

feet

6.3 ft.
(7:30)

3.9 ft.
(7:50)

2 ft.
(12:41)

0.9 ft.
(1:34)

12 1 2 3 4 5 6 7 8 9 10 11 noon 1 2 3 4 5 6 7 8 9 10 11 12

s ebb → ⊢ — 1.6 knots flood ⊣ ⊢ — 2 knots ebb — → ⊢ 2.2 knots flood → ⊢— 3.4 kr
— 2.8 knots ebb — → ⊢ 1.5 knots flood ⊣ ⊢ — 1.7 knots ebb — → ⊢ 2.9 knots flood — → ⊢ —

WED JUL 12

dawn 4:49 sunrise 5:58 sunset 8:33 dark 9:42
moonrise 1:50 a.m. moonset 4:29 p.m.

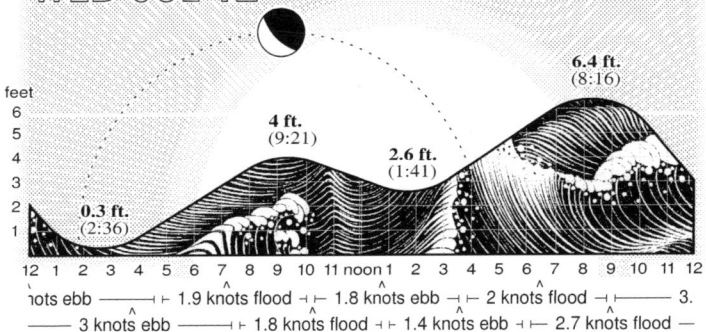

feet

6.4 ft.
(8:16)

4 ft.
(9:21)

2.6 ft.
(1:41)

0.3 ft.
(2:36)

12 1 2 3 4 5 6 7 8 9 10 11 noon 1 2 3 4 5 6 7 8 9 10 11 12

nots ebb ——— ⊢ 1.9 knots flood ⊣ ⊢ 1.8 knots ebb → ⊢ 2 knots flood ⊣ ⊢— 3.
—— 3 knots ebb ——— ⊢ 1.8 knots flood ⊣ ⊢ 1.4 knots ebb ⊣ ⊢ 2.7 knots flood —

THU JUL 13

dawn 4:50 sunrise 5:59 sunset 8:32 dark 9:41
moonrise 2:24 a.m. moonset 5:34 p.m.

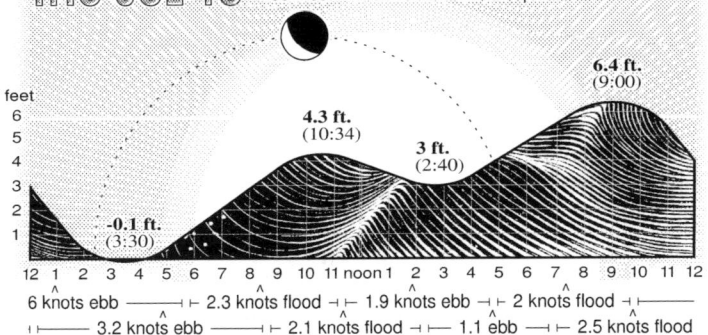

feet

6.4 ft.
(9:00)

4.3 ft.
(10:34)

3 ft.
(2:40)

-0.1 ft.
(3:30)

12 1 2 3 4 5 6 7 8 9 10 11 noon 1 2 3 4 5 6 7 8 9 10 11 12

6 knots ebb ——— ⊢ 2.3 knots flood ⊣ ⊢ 1.9 knots ebb → ⊢ 2 knots flood ⊣ ⊢—
⊢ —— 3.2 knots ebb ——— ⊢ 2.1 knots flood ⊣ ⊢ — 1.1 ebb — → ⊢ 2.5 knots flood

FRI JUL 7

dawn 4:45　sunrise 5:55　sunset 8:35　dark 9:44
moonset 10:47 a.m.

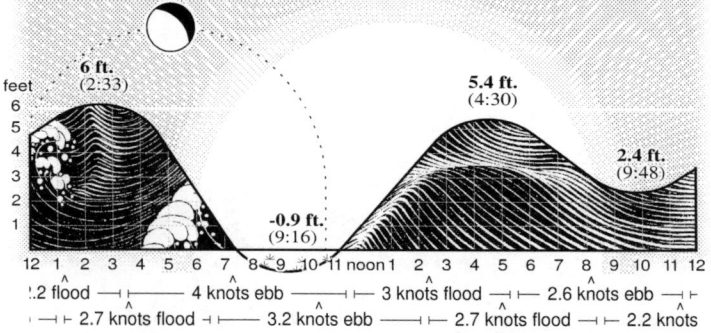

feet

6 ft.
(2:33)

5.4 ft.
(4:30)

2.4 ft.
(9:48)

-0.9 ft.
(9:16)

12　1　2　3　4　5　6　7　8　9　10　11　noon　1　2　3　4　5　6　7　8　9　10　11　12

1.2 flood ⊢ ⊢ 4 knots ebb ⊢ ⊢ 3 knots flood ⊣ ⊢ 2.6 knots ebb ⊣ ⊢

⊣ ⊢ 2.7 knots flood ⊣ ⊢ 3.2 knots ebb ⊢ ⊢ 2.7 knots flood ⊣ ⊢ 2.2 knots

SAT JUL 8

dawn 4:46　sunrise 5:55　sunset 8:34　dark 9:44
moonrise 12:03 a.m.　moonset 11:59 a.m.

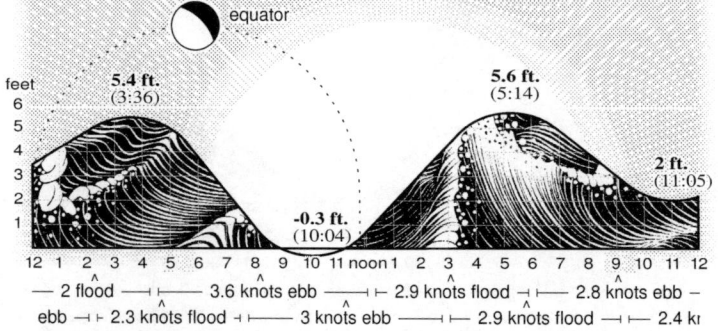

equator

feet

5.4 ft.
(3:36)

5.6 ft.
(5:14)

2 ft.
(11:05)

-0.3 ft.
(10:04)

12　1　2　3　4　5　6　7　8　9　10　11　noon　1　2　3　4　5　6　7　8　9　10　11　12

— 2 flood ⊢ ⊢ 3.6 knots ebb ⊢ ⊢ 2.9 knots flood ⊣ ⊢ 2.8 knots ebb —

ebb ⊢ ⊢ 2.3 knots flood ⊣ ⊢ 3 knots ebb ⊢ ⊢ 2.9 knots flood ⊣ ⊢ 2.4 kr

SUN JUL 9

dawn 4:47　sunrise 5:56　sunset 8:34　dark 9:43
moonrise 12:29 a.m.　moonset 1:08 p.m.

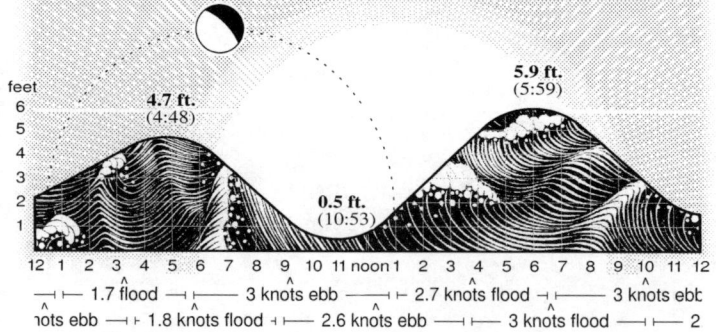

feet

4.7 ft.
(4:48)

5.9 ft.
(5:59)

0.5 ft.
(10:53)

12　1　2　3　4　5　6　7　8　9　10　11　noon　1　2　3　4　5　6　7　8　9　10　11　12

⊣ ⊢ 1.7 flood ⊣ ⊢ 3 knots ebb ⊢ ⊢ 2.7 knots flood ⊣ ⊢ 3 knots ebb

knots ebb ⊢ ⊢ 1.8 knots flood ⊣ ⊢ 2.6 knots ebb ⊢ ⊢ 3 knots flood ⊢ ⊢ 2

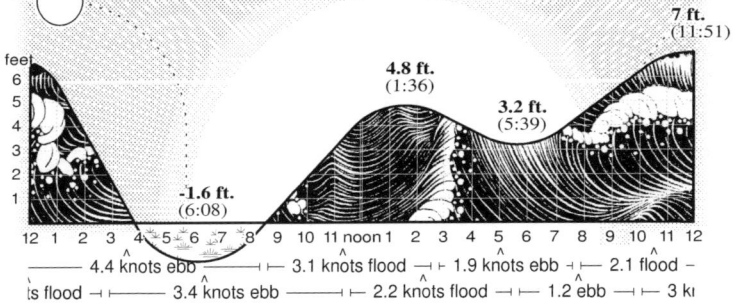

MON JUL 3

dawn 4:43 sunrise 5:53 sunset 8:36 dark 9:46
moonset 5:42 a.m. moonrise 9:32 p.m.

Full Moon 4:39 a.m.

7 ft.
(11:51)

4.8 ft.
(1:36)

3.2 ft.
(5:39)

feet
6
5
4
3
2
1

-1.6 ft.
(6:08)

12 1 2 3 4 5 6 7 8 9 10 11 noon 1 2 3 4 5 6 7 8 9 10 11 12

⊢— 4.4 knots ebb ——⊣ ⊢ 3.1 knots flood ⊣ ⊢ 1.9 knots ebb ⊣ ⊢ 2.1 flood –

ts flood ⊣ ⊢—— 3.4 knots ebb ——⊣ ⊢ 2.2 knots flood ⊣ ⊢ 1.2 ebb ⊣ ⊢ 3 k₁

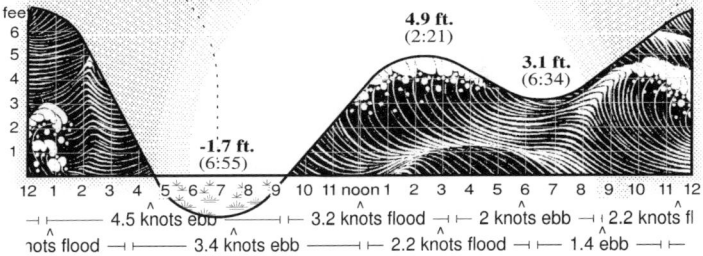

TUE JUL 4

dawn 4:43 sunrise 5:53 sunset 8:35 dark 9:45
moonset 6:56 a.m. moonrise 10:21 p.m.

perigee   Independence Day

4.9 ft.
(2:21)

3.1 ft.
(6:34)

feet
6
5
4
3
2
1

-1.7 ft.
(6:55)

12 1 2 3 4 5 6 7 8 9 10 11 noon 1 2 3 4 5 6 7 8 9 10 11 12

⊢ ⊢—— 4.5 knots ebb ——⊣ ⊢ 3.2 knots flood ⊣ ⊢ 2 knots ebb ⊣ ⊢ 2.2 knots fl

nots flood ⊣ ⊢—— 3.4 knots ebb ——⊣ ⊢ 2.2 knots flood ⊣ ⊢ 1.4 ebb ⊣ ⊢

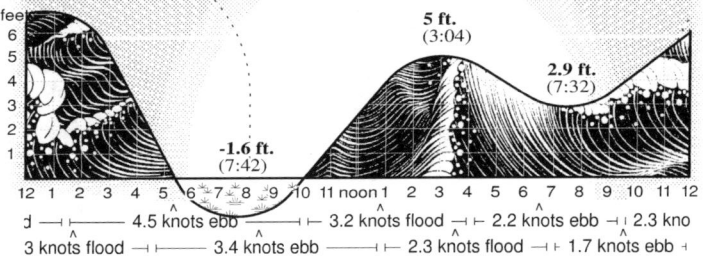

WED JUL 5

dawn 4:44 sunrise 5:54 sunset 8:35 dark 9:45
moonset 8:14 a.m. moonrise 11:01 p.m.

6.9 ft.
(12:42)

feet
6
5
4
3
2
1

5 ft.
(3:04)

2.9 ft.
(7:32)

-1.6 ft.
(7:42)

12 1 2 3 4 5 6 7 8 9 10 11 noon 1 2 3 4 5 6 7 8 9 10 11 12

d ⊢ ⊢—— 4.5 knots ebb ——⊣ ⊢ 3.2 knots flood ⊣ ⊢ 2.2 knots ebb ⊣ ⊢ 2.3 kno

3 knots flood ⊣ ⊢—— 3.4 knots ebb ——⊣ ⊢ 2.3 knots flood ⊣ ⊢ 1.7 knots ebb ⊣

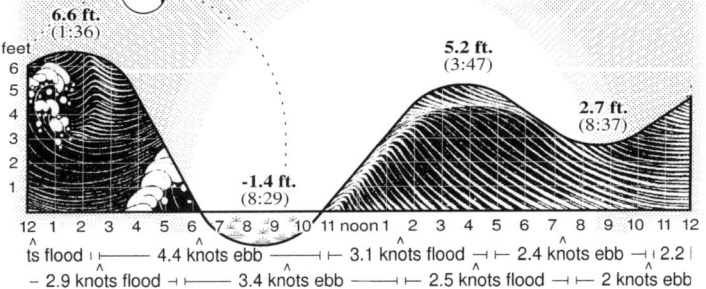

THU JUL 6

dawn 4:44 sunrise 5:54 sunset 8:35 dark 9:45
moonset 9:32 a.m. moonrise 11:34 p.m.

Earth at Aphelion 1:07 p.m.

6.6 ft.
(1:36)

feet
6
5
4
3
2
1

5.2 ft.
(3:47)

2.7 ft.
(8:37)

-1.4 ft.
(8:29)

12 1 2 3 4 5 6 7 8 9 10 11 noon 1 2 3 4 5 6 7 8 9 10 11 12

ts flood ⊢ ⊢—— 4.4 knots ebb ——⊣ ⊢ 3.1 knots flood ⊣ ⊢ 2.4 knots ebb ⊣ ⊢ 2.2 ⊢

– 2.9 knots flood ⊣ ⊢—— 3.4 knots ebb ——⊣ ⊢ 2.5 knots flood ⊣ ⊢ 2 knots ebb

FRI JUN 30

dawn 4:41 sunrise 5:51 sunset 8:36 dark 9:46
moonset 3:02 a.m. moonrise 6:11 p.m.

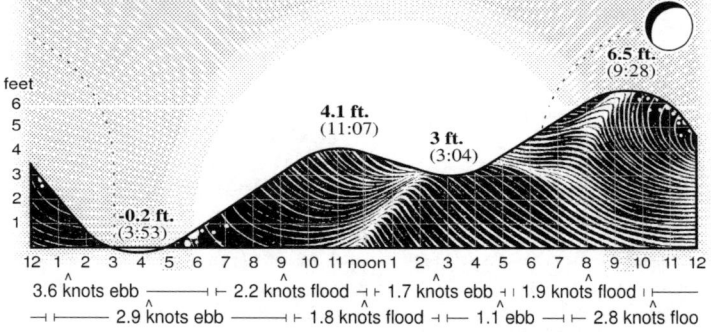

6.5 ft.
(9:28)

feet

4.1 ft.
(11:07)

3 ft.
(3:04)

-0.2 ft.
(3:53)

12 1 2 3 4 5 6 7 8 9 10 11 noon 1 2 3 4 5 6 7 8 9 10 11 12

3.6 knots ebb ──── ├ 2.2 knots flood ┤ ├ 1.7 knots ebb ┤ ├ 1.9 knots flood │ ├──
┤ ├──── 2.9 knots ebb ──── ├ 1.8 knots flood ┤ ├ 1.1 ebb ┤ ├ 2.8 knots floo

SAT JUL 1

dawn 4:41 sunrise 5:52 sunset 8:36 dark 9:46
moonset 3:44 a.m. moonrise 7:24 p.m.

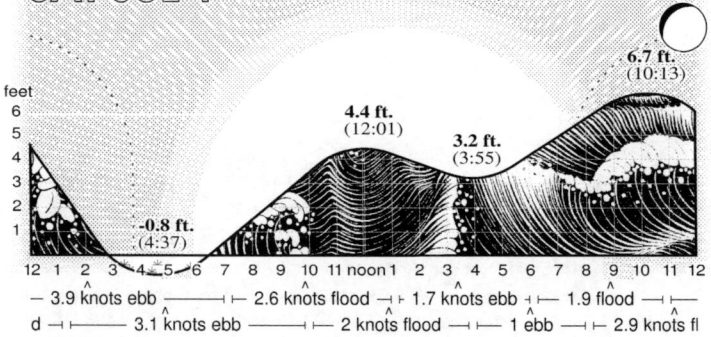

6.7 ft.
(10:13)

feet

4.4 ft.
(12:01)

3.2 ft.
(3:55)

-0.8 ft.
(4:37)

12 1 2 3 4 5 6 7 8 9 10 11 noon 1 2 3 4 5 6 7 8 9 10 11 12

─ 3.9 knots ebb ──── ├ 2.6 knots flood → ├ 1.7 knots ebb ┤ ├ 1.9 flood ── ┤
d ─┤ ├──── 3.1 knots ebb ──── ├ 2 knots flood ─┤ ├── 1 ebb ──┤ ├─ 2.9 knots fl

SUN JUL 2

dawn 4:42 sunrise 5:52 sunset 8:36 dark 9:46
moonset 4:37 a.m. moonrise 8:32 p.m.

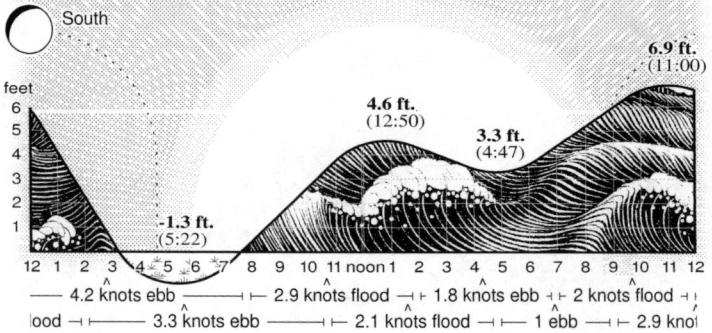

South

6.9 ft.
(11:00)

feet

4.6 ft.
(12:50)

3.3 ft.
(4:47)

-1.3 ft.
(5:22)

12 1 2 3 4 5 6 7 8 9 10 11 noon 1 2 3 4 5 6 7 8 9 10 11 12

──── 4.2 knots ebb ──── ┤ ├ 2.9 knots flood ─┤ ├ 1.8 knots ebb ┤ ├ 2 knots flood ─┤ │
lood ─┤ ├──── 3.3 knots ebb ──── ┤ ├ 2.1 knots flood ─┤ ├── 1 ebb ──┤ ├─ 2.9 knot

MON JUN 26   dawn 4:39 sunrise 5:50 sunset 8:36 dark 9:46
moonset 1:14 a.m. moonrise 1:44 p.m.

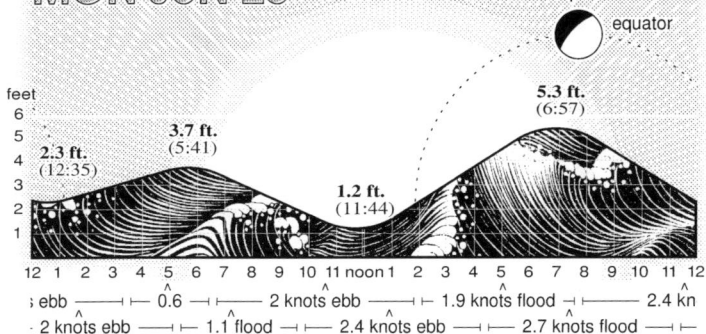

equator

feet
6
5
4
3
2
1

2.3 ft.
(12:35)

3.7 ft.
(5:41)

1.2 ft.
(11:44)

5.3 ft.
(6:57)

12 1 2 3 4 5 6 7 8 9 10 11 noon 1 2 3 4 5 6 7 8 9 10 11 12

; ebb ⊢— 0.6 —⊣ ⊢ 2 knots ebb ——⊣ ⊢ 1.9 knots flood ⊣⊢ —— 2.4 kn

· 2 knots ebb ——⊣ ⊢ 1.1 flood ⊣ ⊢ 2.4 knots ebb ⊣ ⊢ 2.7 knots flood ——⊣ ⊢

TUE JUN 27   dawn 4:39 sunrise 5:50 sunset 8:36 dark 9:46
moonset 1:37 a.m. moonrise 2:45 p.m.

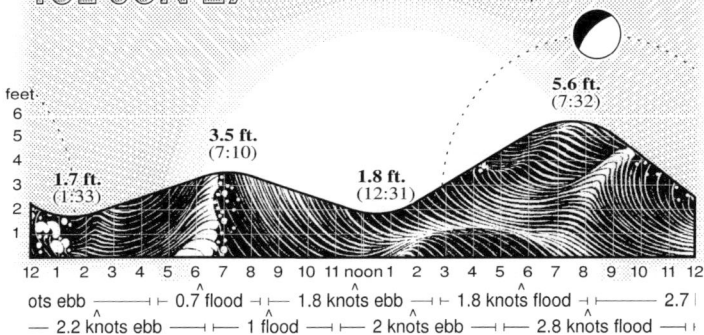

feet
6
5
4
3
2
1

1.7 ft.
(1:33)

3.5 ft.
(7:10)

1.8 ft.
(12:31)

5.6 ft.
(7:32)

12 1 2 3 4 5 6 7 8 9 10 11 noon 1 2 3 4 5 6 7 8 9 10 11 12

ots ebb ——⊣ ⊢ 0.7 flood ⊣ ⊢ 1.8 knots ebb ⊣ ⊢ 1.8 knots flood ⊣⊢ —— 2.7

— 2.2 knots ebb ——⊣ ⊢ 1 flood ⊣ ⊢ 2 knots ebb ⊣ ⊢ 2.8 knots flood ——⊣

WED JUN 28   dawn 4:40 sunrise 5:50 sunset 8:36 dark 9:46
moonset 2:01 a.m. moonrise 3:50 p.m.

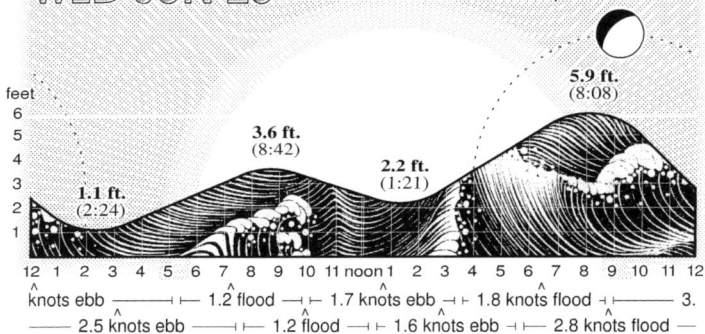

feet
6
5
4
3
2
1

1.1 ft.
(2:24)

3.6 ft.
(8:42)

2.2 ft.
(1:21)

5.9 ft.
(8:08)

12 1 2 3 4 5 6 7 8 9 10 11 noon 1 2 3 4 5 6 7 8 9 10 11 12

knots ebb ——⊣ ⊢ 1.2 flood ⊣⊢ 1.7 knots ebb ⊣⊢ 1.8 knots flood ⊣⊢ —— 3.

— 2.5 knots ebb ——⊣ ⊢ 1.2 flood ⊣ ⊢ 1.6 knots ebb ⊣ ⊢ 2.8 knots flood —

THU JUN 29   dawn 4:40 sunrise 5:51 sunset 8:36 dark 9:46
moonset 2:29 a.m. moonrise 4:59 p.m.

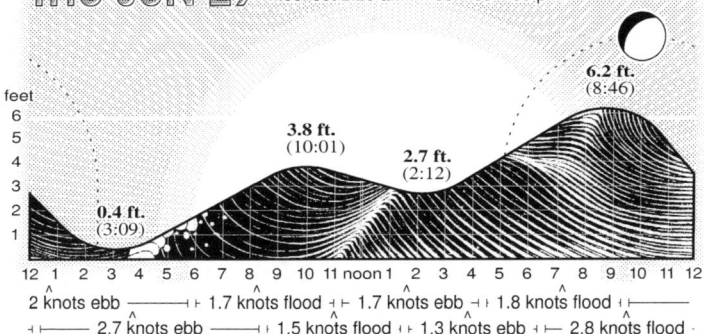

feet
6
5
4
3
2
1

0.4 ft.
(3:09)

3.8 ft.
(10:01)

2.7 ft.
(2:12)

6.2 ft.
(8:46)

12 1 2 3 4 5 6 7 8 9 10 11 noon 1 2 3 4 5 6 7 8 9 10 11 12

2 knots ebb ——⊣ ⊢ 1.7 knots flood ⊣⊢ 1.7 knots ebb ⊣⊢ 1.8 knots flood ⊣⊢

⊣ ⊢ 2.7 knots ebb ——⊣ ⊢ 1.5 knots flood ⊣⊢ 1.3 knots ebb ⊣⊢ 2.8 knots flood ·

FRI JUN 23 dawn 4:38 sunrise 5:49 sunset 8:36 dark 9:46
moonset 12:05 a.m. moonrise 10:47 a.m.

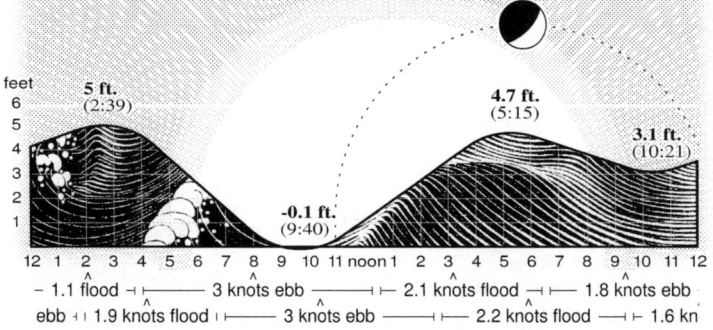

feet

5 ft.
(2:39)

4.7 ft.
(5:15)

3.1 ft.
(10:21)

-0.1 ft.
(9:40)

12 1 2 3 4 5 6 7 8 9 10 11 noon 1 2 3 4 5 6 7 8 9 10 11 12

– 1.1 flood ⊣ ⊢——— 3 knots ebb ——— ⊢– 2.1 knots flood –⊣ ⊢– 1.8 knots ebb

ebb ⊣⊢ 1.9 knots flood ⊣ ⊢——— 3 knots ebb ——— ⊢– 2.2 knots flood —⊣ ⊢– 1.6 kn

SAT JUN 24 dawn 4:38 sunrise 5:49 sunset 8:36 dark 9:46
moonset 12:30 a.m. moonrise 11:46 a.m.

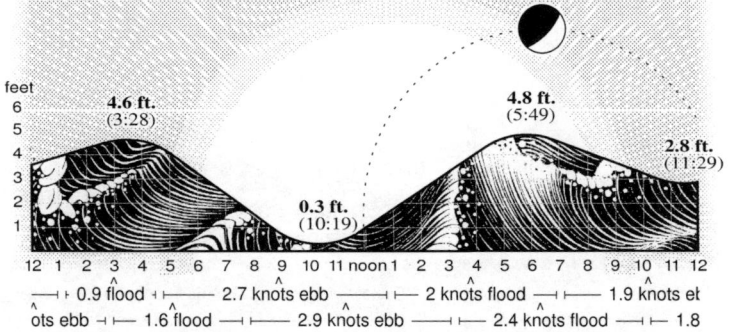

feet

4.6 ft.
(3:28)

4.8 ft.
(5:49)

2.8 ft.
(11:29)

0.3 ft.
(10:19)

12 1 2 3 4 5 6 7 8 9 10 11 noon 1 2 3 4 5 6 7 8 9 10 11 12

⊢– 0.9 flood ⊣ ⊢— 2.7 knots ebb ——— ⊢— 2 knots flood —⊣ ⊢— 1.9 knots et

ots ebb ⊣ ⊢– 1.6 flood —⊣ ⊢— 2.9 knots ebb ——— ⊢— 2.4 knots flood —⊣ ⊢– 1.8

SUN JUN 25 dawn 4:39 sunrise 5:49 sunset 8:36 dark 9:46
moonset 12:52 a.m. moonrise 12:44 p.m.

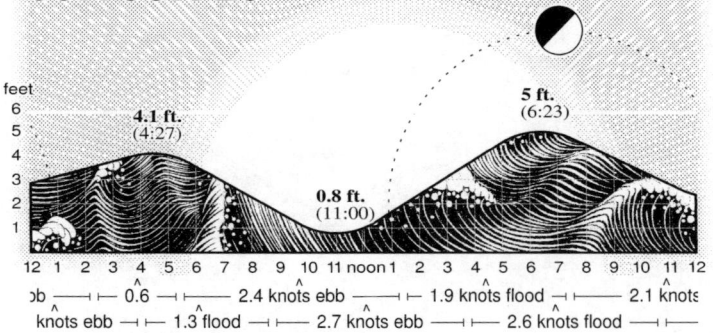

feet

4.1 ft.
(4:27)

5 ft.
(6:23)

0.8 ft.
(11:00)

12 1 2 3 4 5 6 7 8 9 10 11 noon 1 2 3 4 5 6 7 8 9 10 11 12

ɔb ⊢— 0.6 ⊣ ⊢— 2.4 knots ebb ——— ⊢– 1.9 knots flood –⊣ ⊢— 2.1 knots

knots ebb —⊣ ⊢– 1.3 flood —⊣ ⊢— 2.7 knots ebb ——— ⊢— 2.6 knots flood —⊣ ⊢—

Summer Solstice On the 21st the north pole will be tilted toward
the Sun at its most northernmost position in the sky. This marks the
beginning of summer in the northern hemisphere and the longest day of
the year. copyright 2022 Pacific Publishers, L.L.C. WWW.TIDELOG.COM

MON JUN 19
dawn 4:37 sunrise 5:48 sunset 8:35 dark 9:45
moonrise 6:47 a.m. moonset 10:25 p.m.

Juneteenth

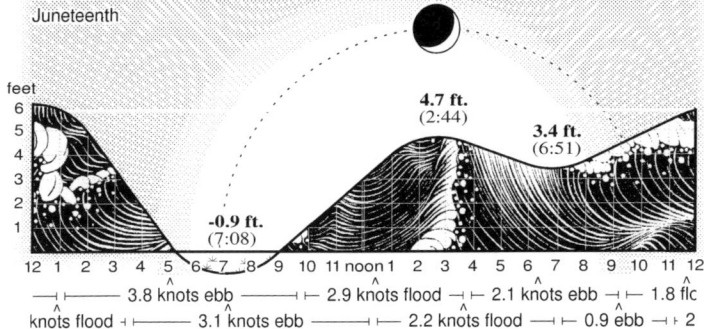

feet

4.7 ft.
(2:44)

3.4 ft.
(6:51)

-0.9 ft.
(7:08)

12 1 2 3 4 5 6 7 8 9 10 11 noon 1 2 3 4 5 6 7 8 9 10 11 12

⊢—— 3.8 knots ebb ——⊢ ⊢— 2.9 knots flood —⊣ ⊢ 2.1 knots ebb —⊣ ⊢ 1.8 flc

knots flood ⊣ ⊢——— 3.1 knots ebb ——— ⊢—— 2.2 knots flood —— ⊢ 0.9 ebb ⊣ ⊢ 2

TUE JUN 20
dawn 4:37 sunrise 5:48 sunset 8:35 dark 9:46
moonrise 7:45 a.m. moonset 11:04 p.m.

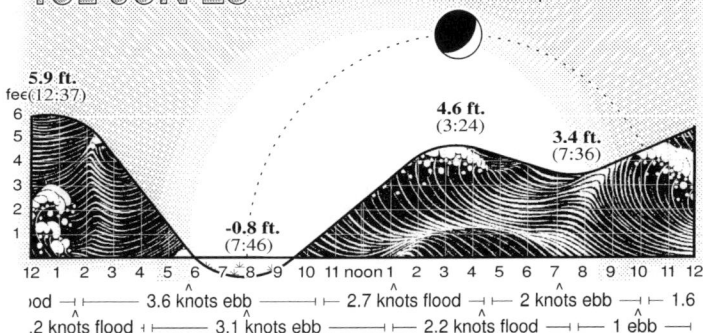

5.9 ft.
feet (12:37)

4.6 ft.
(3:24)

3.4 ft.
(7:36)

-0.8 ft.
(7:46)

12 1 2 3 4 5 6 7 8 9 10 11 noon 1 2 3 4 5 6 7 8 9 10 11 12

ood ⊢—— 3.6 knots ebb ——⊢ ⊢— 2.7 knots flood —⊣ ⊢ 2 knots ebb —⊣ ⊢ 1.6

.2 knots flood ⊣ ⊢——— 3.1 knots ebb ——— ⊢—— 2.2 knots flood —— ⊢ 1 ebb ⊣

WED JUN 21
dawn 4:37 sunrise 5:48 sunset 8:35 dark 9:46
moonrise 8:46 a.m. moonset 11:37 p.m.

Summer Solstice 7:58 a.m.

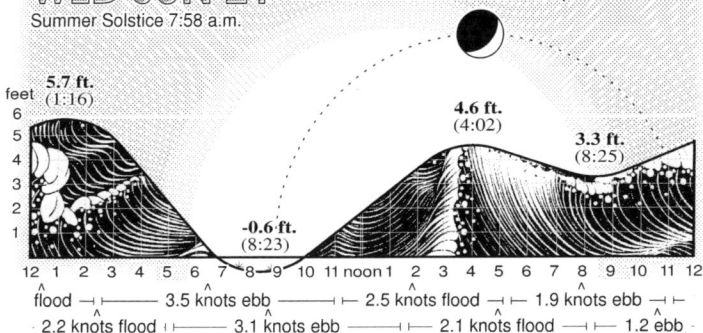

5.7 ft.
feet (1:16)

4.6 ft.
(4:02)

3.3 ft.
(8:25)

-0.6 ft.
(8:23)

12 1 2 3 4 5 6 7 8 9 10 11 noon 1 2 3 4 5 6 7 8 9 10 11 12

flood ⊣ ⊢— 3.5 knots ebb ——⊢ ⊢— 2.5 knots flood —⊣ ⊢ 1.9 knots ebb —⊣ ⊢⊢

2.2 knots flood ⊢ ⊢——— 3.1 knots ebb ——— ⊢—— 2.1 knots flood —⊣ ⊢ 1.2 ebb ⊣

THU JUN 22
dawn 4:38 sunrise 5:48 sunset 8:35 dark 9:46
moonrise 9:47 a.m.

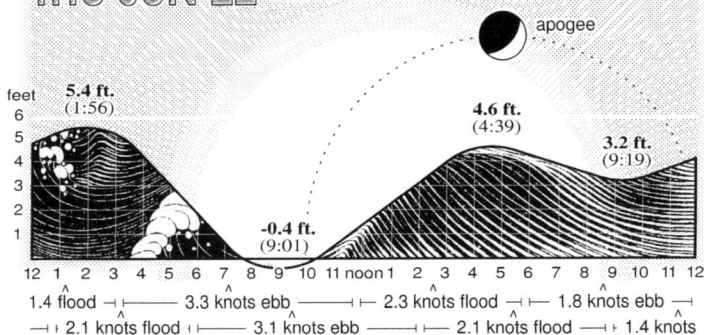

apogee

5.4 ft.
feet (1:56)

4.6 ft.
(4:39)

3.2 ft.
(9:19)

-0.4 ft.
(9:01)

12 1 2 3 4 5 6 7 8 9 10 11 noon 1 2 3 4 5 6 7 8 9 10 11 12

1.4 flood ⊣ ⊢— 3.3 knots ebb ——⊢ ⊢— 2.3 knots flood —⊣ ⊢ 1.8 knots ebb —⊣

⊣ ⊢ 2.1 knots flood ⊢ ⊢——— 3.1 knots ebb ——— ⊢—— 2.1 knots flood —⊣ ⊢ 1.4 knots

FRI JUN 16 dawn 4:37 sunrise 5:47 sunset 8:34 dark 9:45
moonrise 4:23 a.m. moonset 7:42 p.m.

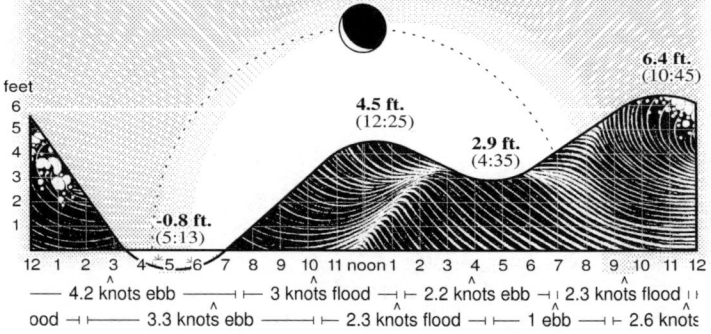

feet

6.4 ft.
(10:45)

4.5 ft.
(12:25)

2.9 ft.
(4:35)

-0.8 ft.
(5:13)

12 1 2 3 4 5 6 7 8 9 10 11 noon 1 2 3 4 5 6 7 8 9 10 11 12

— 4.2 knots ebb — ⊢ 3 knots flood — ⊢ 2.2 knots ebb — ⊣ 2.3 knots flood ⊢
ood — ⊢ 3.3 knots ebb — ⊢ 2.3 knots flood — ⊣ 1 ebb — ⊢ 2.6 knots

---

SAT JUN 17 dawn 4:37 sunrise 5:48 sunset 8:34 dark 9:45
moonrise 5:04 a.m. moonset 8:43 p.m.

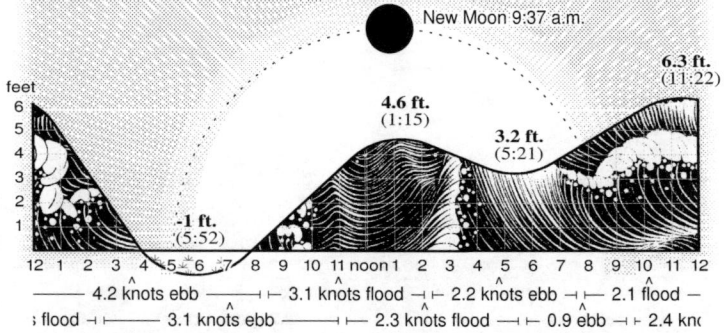

New Moon 9:37 a.m.

feet

6.3 ft.
(11:22)

4.6 ft.
(1:15)

3.2 ft.
(5:21)

-1 ft.
(5:52)

12 1 2 3 4 5 6 7 8 9 10 11 noon 1 2 3 4 5 6 7 8 9 10 11 12

— 4.2 knots ebb — ⊢ 3.1 knots flood — ⊢ 2.2 knots ebb — ⊣ 2.1 flood —
s flood — ⊢ 3.1 knots ebb — ⊢ 2.3 knots flood — ⊣ 0.9 ebb — ⊢ 2.4 kno

---

SUN JUN 18 dawn 4:37 sunrise 5:48 sunset 8:35 dark 9:45
moonrise 5:52 a.m. moonset 9:38 p.m.

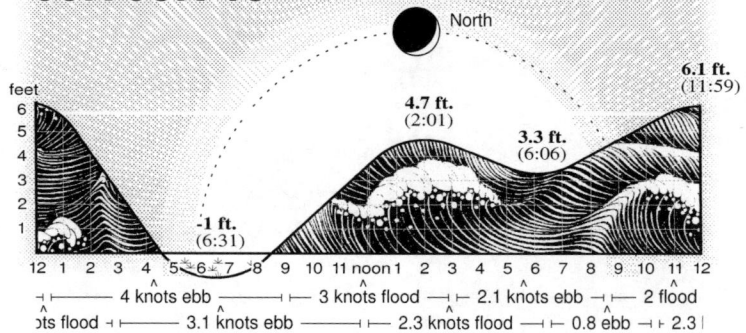

North

feet

6.1 ft.
(11:59)

4.7 ft.
(2:01)

3.3 ft.
(6:06)

-1 ft.
(6:31)

12 1 2 3 4 5 6 7 8 9 10 11 noon 1 2 3 4 5 6 7 8 9 10 11 12

⊣ — 4 knots ebb — ⊢ 3 knots flood — ⊢ 2.1 knots ebb — ⊣ — 2 flood —
ots flood — ⊢ 3.1 knots ebb — ⊢ 2.3 knots flood — ⊣ 0.8 ebb — ⊢ 2.3 l

MON JUN 12
dawn 4:37 sunrise 5:47 sunset 8:32 dark 9:43
moonrise 2:25 a.m. moonset 3:15 p.m.

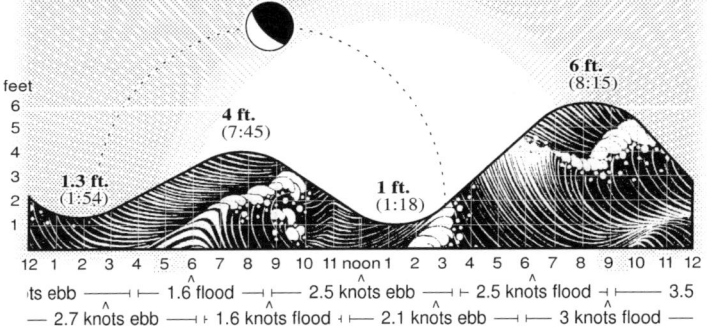

feet

6 ft.
(8:15)

4 ft.
(7:45)

1.3 ft.
(1:54)

1 ft.
(1:18)

12 1 2 3 4 5 6 7 8 9 10 11 noon 1 2 3 4 5 6 7 8 9 10 11 12

ts ebb ——⊢ 1.6 flood ——⊢ 2.5 knots ebb ——⊢ 2.5 knots flood —⊢—— 3.5
— 2.7 knots ebb ——⊢ 1.6 knots flood ⊢ 2.1 knots ebb —⊢ 3 knots flood —

TUE JUN 13
dawn 4:37 sunrise 5:47 sunset 8:33 dark 9:43
moonrise 2:51 a.m. moonset 4:22 p.m.

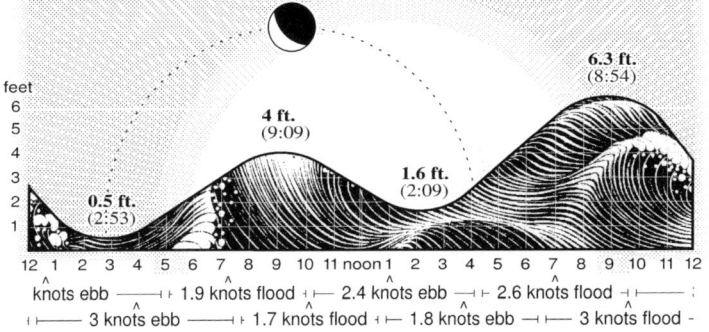

feet

6.3 ft.
(8:54)

4 ft.
(9:09)

1.6 ft.
(2:09)

0.5 ft.
(2:53)

12 1 2 3 4 5 6 7 8 9 10 11 noon 1 2 3 4 5 6 7 8 9 10 11 12

knots ebb ——⊢ 1.9 knots flood ⊢ 2.4 knots ebb —⊢ 2.6 knots flood ⊣⊢——
⊢—— 3 knots ebb ——⊢ 1.7 knots flood ⊣⊢ 1.8 knots ebb —⊢ 3 knots flood -

WED JUN 14
dawn 4:37 sunrise 5:47 sunset 8:33 dark 9:44
moonrise 3:18 a.m. moonset 5:29 p.m.

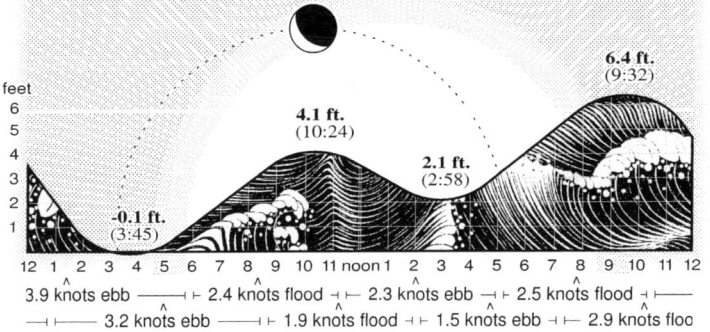

feet

6.4 ft.
(9:32)

4.1 ft.
(10:24)

2.1 ft.
(2:58)

-0.1 ft.
(3:45)

12 1 2 3 4 5 6 7 8 9 10 11 noon 1 2 3 4 5 6 7 8 9 10 11 12

3.9 knots ebb ——⊢ 2.4 knots flood ⊣⊢ 2.3 knots ebb —⊢ 2.5 knots flood ⊣⊢——
—⊣—— 3.2 knots ebb ——⊢ 1.9 knots flood ⊣⊢ 1.5 knots ebb ⊣⊢ 2.9 knots floo

THU JUN 15
dawn 4:37 sunrise 5:47 sunset 8:34 dark 9:44
moonrise 3:48 a.m. moonset 6:36 p.m.

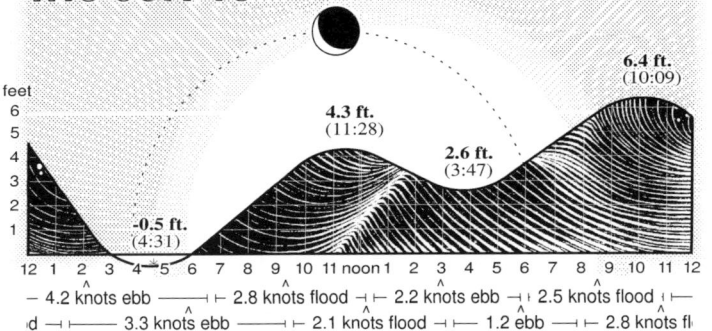

feet

6.4 ft.
(10:09)

4.3 ft.
(11:28)

2.6 ft.
(3:47)

-0.5 ft.
(4:31)

12 1 2 3 4 5 6 7 8 9 10 11 noon 1 2 3 4 5 6 7 8 9 10 11 12

— 4.2 knots ebb ———⊢ 2.8 knots flood ⊣⊢ 2.2 knots ebb ⊣⊢ 2.5 knots flood ⊣⊢—
d ⊣⊢—— 3.3 knots ebb ———⊢ 2.1 knots flood ⊣⊢ 1.2 ebb —⊣⊢ 2.8 knots fl

FRI JUN 9 dawn 4:38 sunrise 5:48 sunset 8:31 dark 9:41
moonrise 1:03 a.m. moonset 11:48 a.m.

Saturn north Moon 3 degrees

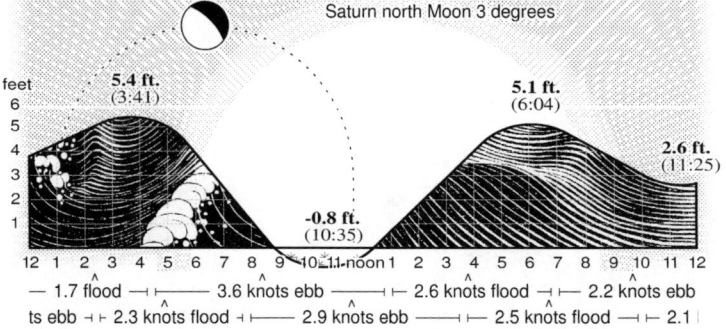

feet

5.4 ft.
(3:41)

5.1 ft.
(6:04)

2.6 ft.
(11:25)

6
5
4
3
2
1

12 1 2 3 4 5 6 7 8 9 10 11 noon 1 2 3 4 5 6 7 8 9 10 11 12

— 1.7 flood — ⊢ — 3.6 knots ebb ——— ⊢ 2.6 knots flood — ⊢ — 2.2 knots ebb

ts ebb ⊣ ⊢ 2.3 knots flood ⊣ ⊢—— 2.9 knots ebb ——— ⊢ 2.5 knots flood — ⊢ 2.1 ⊢

-0.8 ft.
(10:35)

SAT JUN 10 dawn 4:37 sunrise 5:48 sunset 8:31 dark 9:42
moonrise 1:33 a.m. moonset 12:59 p.m.

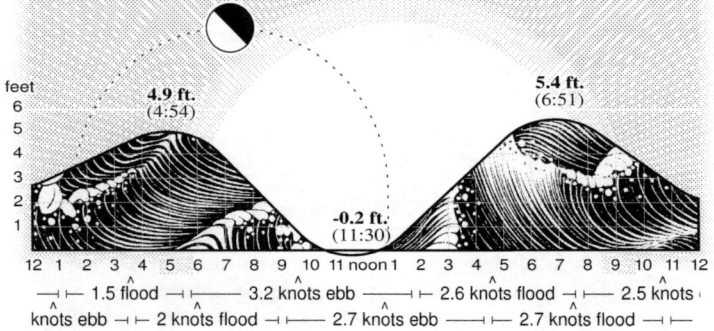

feet

4.9 ft.
(4:54)

5.4 ft.
(6:51)

6
5
4
3
2
1

12 1 2 3 4 5 6 7 8 9 10 11 noon 1 2 3 4 5 6 7 8 9 10 11 12

—⊢ 1.5 flood — ⊣ ⊢ — 3.2 knots ebb ——— ⊢ 2.6 knots flood — ⊢ — 2.5 knots ⊢

knots ebb ⊣ ⊢ 2 knots flood — ⊣ ⊢— 2.7 knots ebb ——— ⊢ 2.7 knots flood — ⊢ —

-0.2 ft.
(11:30)

SUN JUN 11 dawn 4:37 sunrise 5:47 sunset 8:32 dark 9:42
moonrise 2:00 a.m. moonset 2:08 p.m.

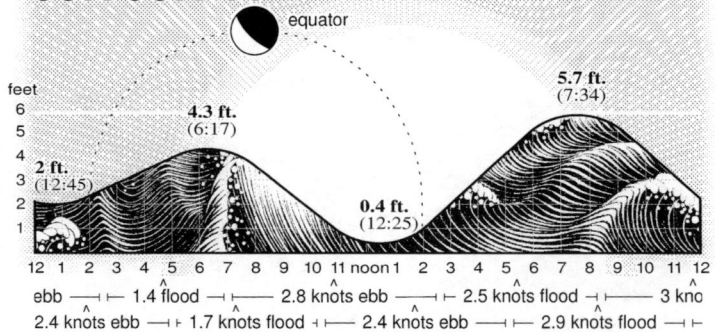

equator

feet

5.7 ft.
(7:34)

4.3 ft.
(6:17)

2 ft.
(12:45)

6
5
4
3
2
1

12 1 2 3 4 5 6 7 8 9 10 11 noon 1 2 3 4 5 6 7 8 9 10 11 12

ebb —— ⊢ 1.4 flood — ⊣ ⊢ — 2.8 knots ebb ——— ⊢ 2.5 knots flood — ⊣ ⊢—— 3 kno ⊢

2.4 knots ebb —— ⊢ 1.7 knots flood ⊣ ⊢—— 2.4 knots ebb ——— ⊢ 2.9 knots flood — ⊢ —

0.4 ft.
(12:25)

MON JUN 5
dawn 4:39 sunrise 5:48 sunset 8:29 dark 9:38
moonset 6:55 a.m. moonrise 10:50 p.m.

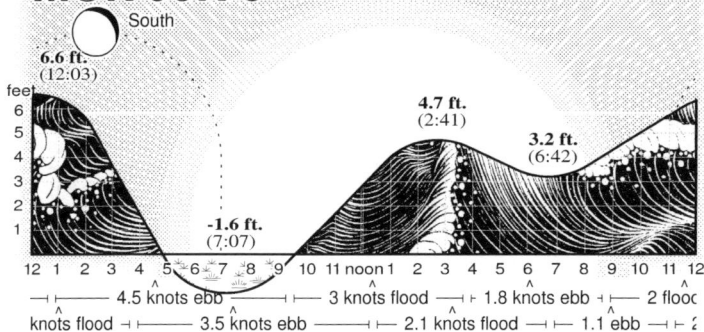

South

6.6 ft.
(12:03)

feet
6
5
4
3
2
1

4.7 ft.
(2:41)

3.2 ft.
(6:42)

-1.6 ft.
(7:07)

12 1 2 3 4 5 6 7 8 9 10 11 noon 1 2 3 4 5 6 7 8 9 10 11 12

├─┤ 4.5 knots ebb ──────┤ ├─ 3 knots flood ─┤ ├ 1.8 knots ebb ┤ ├ 2 flood
knots flood ┤ ├──── 3.5 knots ebb ────── ├─ 2.1 knots flood ─┤ ├─ 1.1 ebb ─┤ ├ 2

TUE JUN 6
dawn 4:39 sunrise 5:48 sunset 8:29 dark 9:39
moonset 8:03 a.m. moonrise 11:44 p.m.

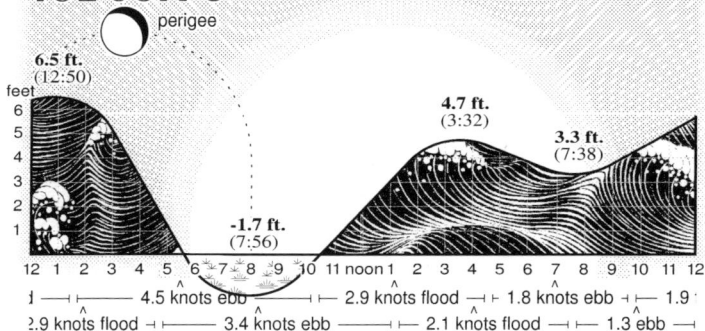

perigee

6.5 ft.
(12:50)

feet
6
5
4
3
2
1

4.7 ft.
(3:32)

3.3 ft.
(7:38)

-1.7 ft.
(7:56)

12 1 2 3 4 5 6 7 8 9 10 11 noon 1 2 3 4 5 6 7 8 9 10 11 12

┤ ──── 4.5 knots ebb ── ┤ ├─ 2.9 knots flood ─┤ ├ 1.8 knots ebb ┤ ├ 1.9
2.9 knots flood ┤ ├──── 3.4 knots ebb ────── ├─ 2.1 knots flood ─┤ ├─ 1.3 ebb ─┤

WED JUN 7
dawn 4:38 sunrise 5:48 sunset 8:30 dark 9:40
moonset 9:17 a.m.

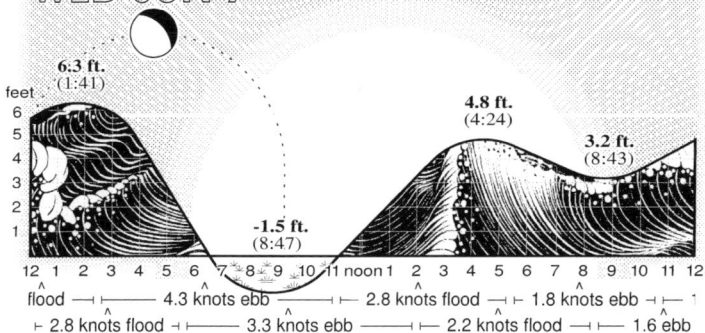

6.3 ft.
(1:41)

feet
6
5
4
3
2
1

4.8 ft.
(4:24)

3.2 ft.
(8:43)

-1.5 ft.
(8:47)

12 1 2 3 4 5 6 7 8 9 10 11 noon 1 2 3 4 5 6 7 8 9 10 11 12

flood ─┤ ├─── 4.3 knots ebb ──── ┤ ├─ 2.8 knots flood ─┤ ├ 1.8 knots ebb ┤ ├ 1
├ 2.8 knots flood ┤ ├──── 3.3 knots ebb ────── ├─ 2.2 knots flood ─┤ ├─ 1.6 ebb ─

THU JUN 8
dawn 4:38 sunrise 5:48 sunset 8:30 dark 9:40
moonrise 12:27 a.m. moonset 10:33 a.m.

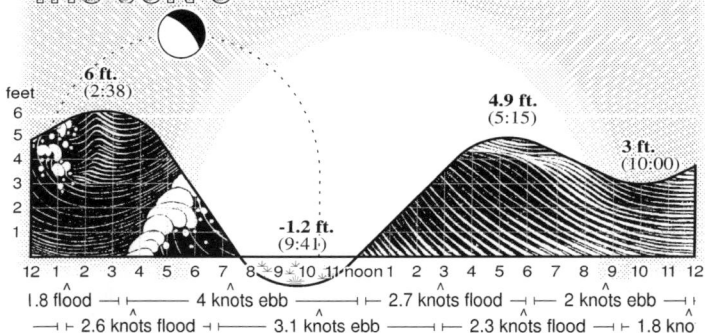

6 ft.
(2:38)

feet
6
5
4
3
2
1

4.9 ft.
(5:15)

3 ft.
(10:00)

-1.2 ft.
(9:41)

12 1 2 3 4 5 6 7 8 9 10 11 noon 1 2 3 4 5 6 7 8 9 10 11 12

1.8 flood ─┤ ├── 4 knots ebb ──── ┤ ├─ 2.7 knots flood ─┤ ├ 2 knots ebb ─┤ ├
─┤ ├ 2.6 knots flood ┤ ├──── 3.1 knots ebb ────── ├─ 2.3 knots flood ─┤ ├ 1.8 kno

FRI JUN 2
dawn 4:40 sunrise 5:49 sunset 8:27 dark 9:36
moonset 4:33 a.m. moonrise 7:22 p.m.

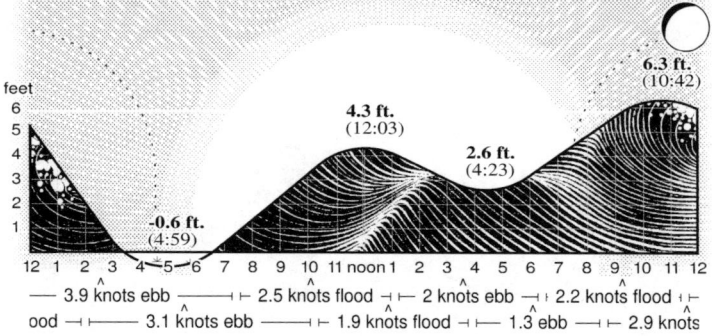

6.3 ft.
(10:42)

4.3 ft.
(12:03)

2.6 ft.
(4:23)

feet
6
5
4
3
2
1

-0.6 ft.
(4:59)

12 1 2 3 4 5 6 7 8 9 10 11 noon 1 2 3 4 5 6 7 8 9 10 11 12

— 3.9 knots ebb ——— ⊢ 2.5 knots flood ⊣ ⊢ 2 knots ebb ⊣ ⊢ 2.2 knots flood ⊣ ⊢
ood ⊣ ⊢——— 3.1 knots ebb ——— ⊢ 1.9 knots flood ⊣ ⊢ 1.3 ebb ⊣ ⊢ 2.9 knots

SAT JUN 3
dawn 4:40 sunrise 5:49 sunset 8:27 dark 9:37
moonset 5:10 a.m. moonrise 8:35 p.m.

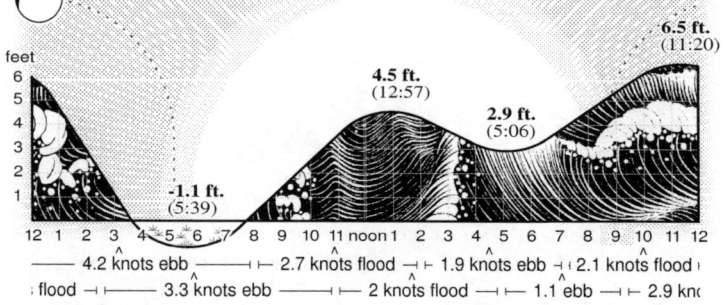 Full Moon 8:42 p.m.

6.5 ft.
(11:20)

4.5 ft.
(12:57)

2.9 ft.
(5:06)

feet
6
5
4
3
2
1

-1.1 ft.
(5:39)

12 1 2 3 4 5 6 7 8 9 10 11 noon 1 2 3 4 5 6 7 8 9 10 11 12

— 4.2 knots ebb ——— ⊢ 2.7 knots flood ⊣ ⊢ 1.9 knots ebb ⊣ ⊢ 2.1 knots flood ⊣
flood ⊣ ⊢——— 3.3 knots ebb ——— ⊢ 2 knots flood ⊣ ⊢ 1.1 ebb ⊣ ⊢ 2.9 kno

SUN JUN 4
dawn 4:39 sunrise 5:49 sunset 8:28 dark 9:38
moonset 5:57 a.m. moonrise 9:46 p.m.

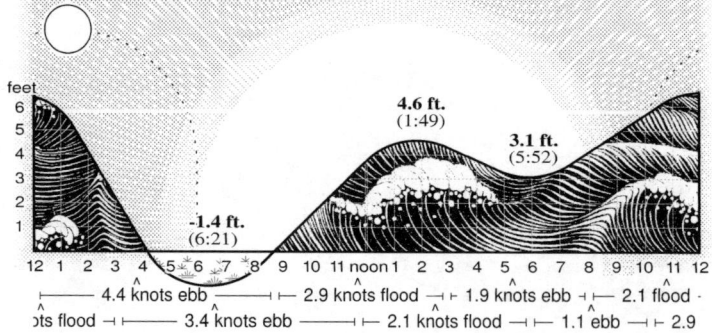

4.6 ft.
(1:49)

3.1 ft.
(5:52)

feet
6
5
4
3
2
1

-1.4 ft.
(6:21)

12 1 2 3 4 5 6 7 8 9 10 11 noon 1 2 3 4 5 6 7 8 9 10 11 12

⊢ 4.4 knots ebb ——— ⊣ ⊢ 2.9 knots flood ⊣ ⊢ 1.9 knots ebb ⊣ ⊢ 2.1 flood ·
ots flood ⊣ ⊢——— 3.4 knots ebb ——— ⊢ 2.1 knots flood ⊣ ⊢ 1.1 ebb ⊣ ⊢ 2.9

Venus greatest eastern elongation On June 4th, Venus will be at its
eastern elongation providing an ideal opportunity to view a bright Venus
at its highest point above the western horizon shortly after sunset.

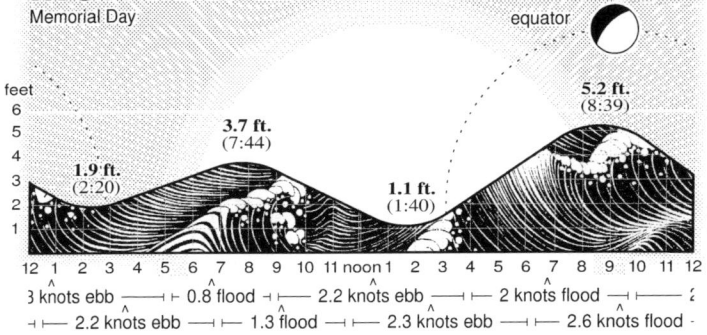

MON MAY 29

dawn 4:43 sunrise 5:51 sunset 8:24 dark 9:33
moonset 2:50 a.m. moonrise 2:57 p.m.

Memorial Day

equator

feet
6
5
4
3
2
1

1.9 ft.
(2:20)

3.7 ft.
(7:44)

1.1 ft.
(1:40)

5.2 ft.
(8:39)

12 1 2 3 4 5 6 7 8 9 10 11 noon 1 2 3 4 5 6 7 8 9 10 11 12

3 knots ebb ⟶ ⊢ 0.8 flood ⊣ ⟶ 2.2 knots ebb ⟶ ⊢ 2 knots flood ⟶ ⊢ 2
⊣ ⊢ 2.2 knots ebb ⟶ ⊢ 1.3 flood ⟶ ⊢ 2.3 knots ebb ⟶ ⊢ 2.6 knots flood ⁃

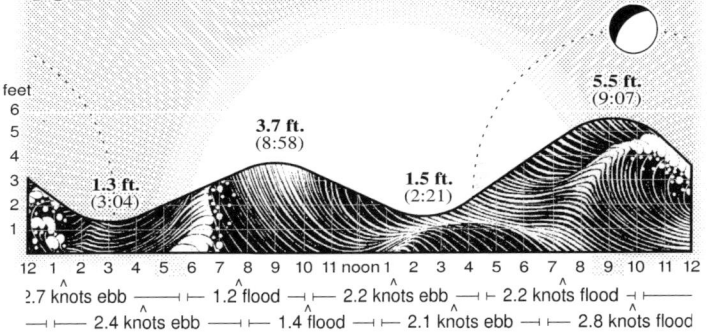

TUE MAY 30

dawn 4:42 sunrise 5:50 sunset 8:25 dark 9:34
moonset 3:12 a.m. moonrise 3:58 p.m.

feet
6
5
4
3
2
1

1.3 ft.
(3:04)

3.7 ft.
(8:58)

1.5 ft.
(2:21)

5.5 ft.
(9:07)

12 1 2 3 4 5 6 7 8 9 10 11 noon 1 2 3 4 5 6 7 8 9 10 11 12

2.7 knots ebb ⟶ ⊢ 1.2 flood ⟶ ⊢ 2.2 knots ebb ⟶ ⊢ 2.2 knots flood ⊣ ⊢
⟶ ⊢ 2.4 knots ebb ⟶ ⊢ 1.4 flood ⟶ ⊢ 2.1 knots ebb ⟶ ⊢ 2.8 knots flood

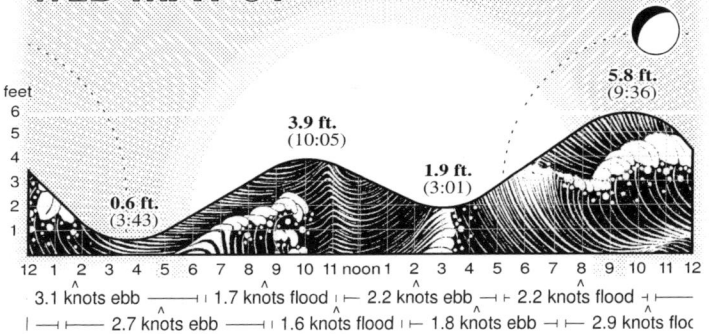

WED MAY 31

dawn 4:41 sunrise 5:50 sunset 8:26 dark 9:34
moonset 3:36 a.m. moonrise 5:02 p.m.

feet
6
5
4
3
2
1

0.6 ft.
(3:43)

3.9 ft.
(10:05)

1.9 ft.
(3:01)

5.8 ft.
(9:36)

12 1 2 3 4 5 6 7 8 9 10 11 noon 1 2 3 4 5 6 7 8 9 10 11 12

3.1 knots ebb ⟶ ⊢ 1.7 knots flood ⊢ ⟶ 2.2 knots ebb ⟶ ⊢ 2.2 knots flood ⊣ ⊢
⊢ ⟶ ⊢ 2.7 knots ebb ⟶ ⊢ 1.6 knots flood ⊢ ⟶ 1.8 knots ebb ⟶ ⊢ 2.9 knots floc

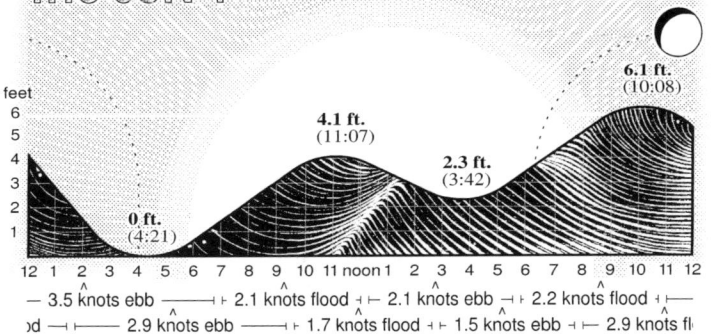

THU JUN 1

dawn 4:41 sunrise 5:50 sunset 8:26 dark 9:35
moonset 4:02 a.m. moonrise 6:10 p.m.

feet
6
5
4
3
2
1

0 ft.
(4:21)

4.1 ft.
(11:07)

2.3 ft.
(3:42)

6.1 ft.
(10:08)

12 1 2 3 4 5 6 7 8 9 10 11 noon 1 2 3 4 5 6 7 8 9 10 11 12

⟶ 3.5 knots ebb ⟶ ⊢ 2.1 knots flood ⊣ ⊢ 2.1 knots ebb ⟶ ⊢ 2.2 knots flood ⊣ ⊢
od ⟶ ⊢ 2.9 knots ebb ⟶ ⊢ 1.7 knots flood ⊢ ⊢ 1.5 knots ebb ⊣ ⊢ 2.9 knots fl

FRI MAY 26
dawn 4:45 sunrise 5:52 sunset 8:22 dark 9:30
moonset 1:37 a.m. moonrise 11:57 a.m.

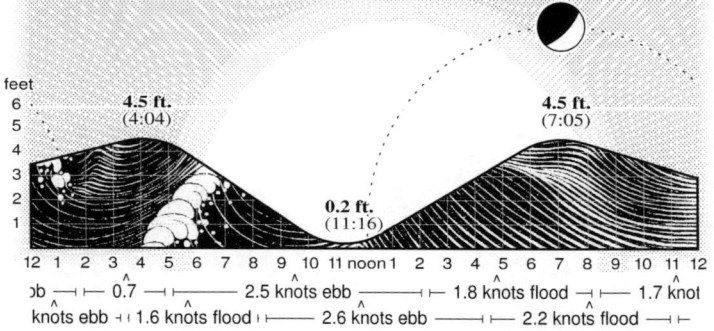

feet

4.5 ft.
(4:04)

4.5 ft.
(7:05)

0.2 ft.
(11:16)

12 1 2 3 4 5 6 7 8 9 10 11 noon 1 2 3 4 5 6 7 8 9 10 11 12

ɔb ⊢—⌃0.7—⊣ ⊢——2.5 knots ebb——⊣ ⊢—1.8 knots flood—⊣ ⊢—1.7 knot
knots ebb ⊣⊦1.6 knots flood⊦ ⊢——2.6 knots ebb——⊣ ⊢—2.2 knots flood—⊣ ⊢⊢

SAT MAY 27
dawn 4:44 sunrise 5:52 sunset 8:23 dark 9:31
moonset 2:04 a.m. moonrise 12:57 p.m.

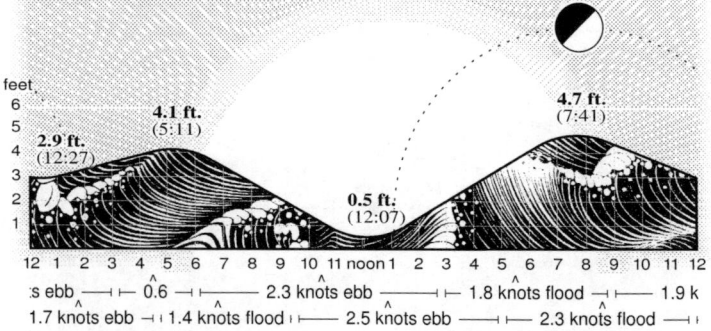

feet

4.1 ft.
(5:11)

4.7 ft.
(7:41)

2.9 ft.
(12:27)

0.5 ft.
(12:07)

12 1 2 3 4 5 6 7 8 9 10 11 noon 1 2 3 4 5 6 7 8 9 10 11 12

s ebb ⊢—⌃0.6—⊣ ⊢——2.3 knots ebb——⊣ ⊢—1.8 knots flood—⊣ ⊢—1.9 k
1.7 knots ebb ⊣⊦1.4 knots flood⊦ ⊢——2.5 knots ebb——⊣ ⊢—2.3 knots flood—⊣ ⊢

SUN MAY 28
dawn 4:43 sunrise 5:51 sunset 8:23 dark 9:32
moonset 2:28 a.m. moonrise 1:57 p.m.

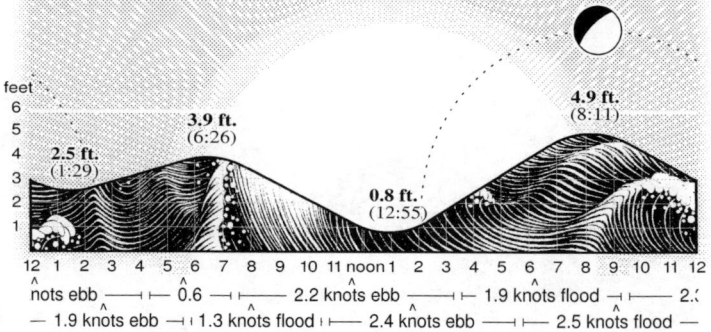

feet

3.9 ft.
(6:26)

4.9 ft.
(8:11)

2.5 ft.
(1:29)

0.8 ft.
(12:55)

12 1 2 3 4 5 6 7 8 9 10 11 noon 1 2 3 4 5 6 7 8 9 10 11 12

nots ebb ⊢—⌃0.6—⊣ ⊢——2.2 knots ebb——⊣ ⊢—1.9 knots flood—⊣ ⊢—2.3
— 1.9 knots ebb —⊣⊦1.3 knots flood⊦ ⊢——2.4 knots ebb——⊣ ⊢—2.5 knots flood—

Ⓢ   Ⓙ   Ⓥ Ⓜ
    ⓜ

MON MAY 22 dawn 4:48 sunrise 5:55 sunset 8:19 dark 9:26
moonrise 8:00 a.m. moonset 11:45 p.m.

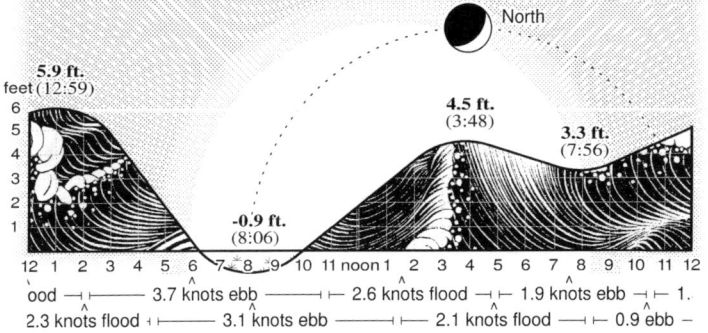

North

5.9 ft.
feet (12:59)
6
5
4
3
2
1

4.5 ft.
(3:48)

3.3 ft.
(7:56)

-0.9 ft.
(8:06)

12 1 2 3 4 5 6 7 8 9 10 11 noon 1 2 3 4 5 6 7 8 9 10 11 12

ood ⊣ ⊢— 3.7 knots ebb —— ⊢ 2.6 knots flood ⊣ ⊢ 1.9 knots ebb ⊣ ⊢ 1.
2.3 knots flood ⊣ ⊢— 3.1 knots ebb —— ⊣ ⊢ 2.1 knots flood —— 0.9 ebb –

TUE MAY 23 dawn 4:47 sunrise 5:54 sunset 8:20 dark 9:27
moonrise 8:56 a.m.

Venus south Moon 2 degrees

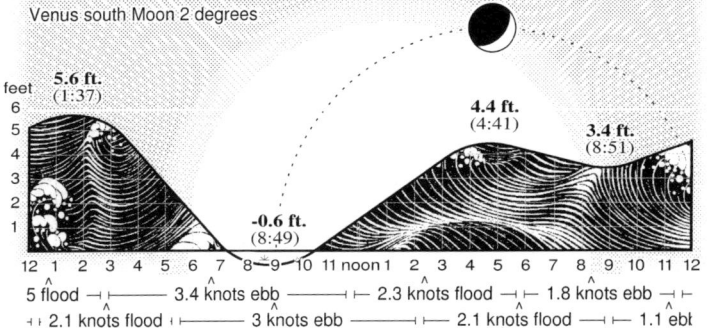

5.6 ft.
(1:37)
feet
6
5
4
3
2
1

4.4 ft.
(4:41)

3.4 ft.
(8:51)

-0.6 ft.
(8:49)

12 1 2 3 4 5 6 7 8 9 10 11 noon 1 2 3 4 5 6 7 8 9 10 11 12

5 flood ⊣ ⊢— 3.4 knots ebb —— ⊣ ⊢ 2.3 knots flood ⊣ ⊢ 1.8 knots ebb ⊣ ⊢
⊣ ⊢ 2.1 knots flood ⊣ ⊢— 3 knots ebb —— ⊣ ⊢ 2.1 knots flood —— 1.1 ebt

WED MAY 24 dawn 4:46 sunrise 5:54 sunset 8:20 dark 9:28
moonset 12:29 a.m. moonrise 9:56 a.m.

Mars south Moon 4 degrees

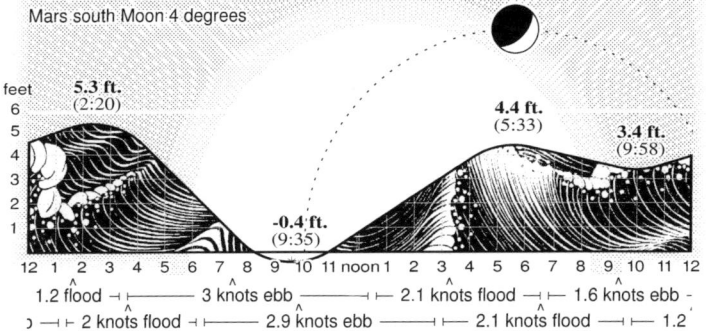

5.3 ft.
(2:20)
feet
6
5
4
3
2
1

4.4 ft.
(5:33)

3.4 ft.
(9:58)

-0.4 ft.
(9:35)

12 1 2 3 4 5 6 7 8 9 10 11 noon 1 2 3 4 5 6 7 8 9 10 11 12

1.2 flood ⊣ ⊢— 3 knots ebb —— ⊣ ⊢ 2.1 knots flood ⊣ ⊢ 1.6 knots ebb –
⊃ ⊣ ⊢ 2 knots flood ⊣ ⊢— 2.9 knots ebb —— ⊣ ⊢ 2.1 knots flood —— 1.2

THU MAY 25 dawn 4:45 sunrise 5:53 sunset 8:21 dark 9:29
moonset 1:06 a.m. moonrise 10:57 a.m.

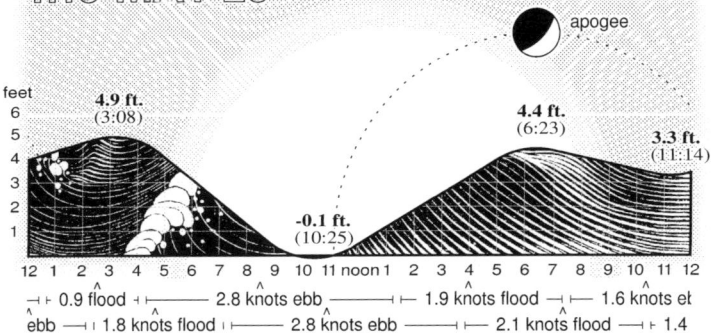

apogee

4.9 ft.
(3:08)
feet
6
5
4
3
2
1

4.4 ft.
(6:23)

3.3 ft.
(11:14)

-0.1 ft.
(10:25)

12 1 2 3 4 5 6 7 8 9 10 11 noon 1 2 3 4 5 6 7 8 9 10 11 12

⊣ ⊢ 0.9 flood ⊣ ⊢— 2.8 knots ebb —— ⊣ ⊢ 1.9 knots flood ⊣ ⊢ 1.6 knots et
ebb —— ⊣ 1.8 knots flood ⊣ ⊢— 2.8 knots ebb —— ⊣ ⊢ 2.1 knots flood —— 1.4

FRI MAY 19

dawn 4:51 sunrise 5:57 sunset 8:16 dark 9:23
moonrise 5:48 a.m. moonset 8:48 p.m.

New Moon 8:53 a.m.

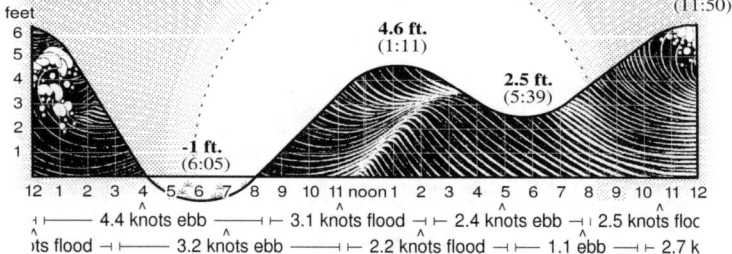

6.3 ft.
(11:50)

feet

4.6 ft.
(1:11)

2.5 ft.
(5:39)

-1 ft.
(6:05)

12 1 2 3 4 5 6 7 8 9 10 11 noon 1 2 3 4 5 6 7 8 9 10 11 12

⊢ 4.4 knots ebb ⟶ ⊢ 3.1 knots flood ⊣ ⊢ 2.4 knots ebb ⟶ ⊢ 2.5 knots floo

ts flood ⊣ ⊢ 3.2 knots ebb ⟶ ⊢ 2.2 knots flood ⊣ ⊢ 1.1 ebb ⟶ ⊢ 2.7 k

SAT MAY 20

dawn 4:50 sunrise 5:56 sunset 8:17 dark 9:24
moonrise 6:26 a.m. moonset 9:53 p.m.

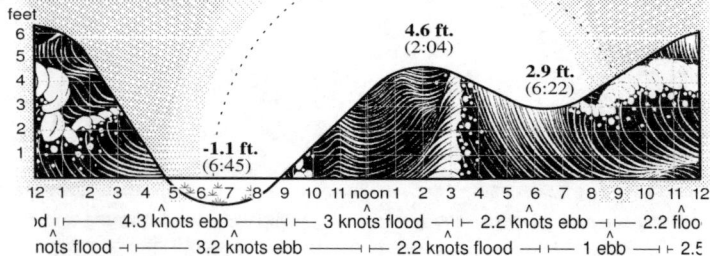

feet

4.6 ft.
(2:04)

2.9 ft.
(6:22)

-1.1 ft.
(6:45)

12 1 2 3 4 5 6 7 8 9 10 11 noon 1 2 3 4 5 6 7 8 9 10 11 12

od ⊢ 4.3 knots ebb ⟶ ⊢ 3 knots flood ⊣ ⊢ 2.2 knots ebb ⊣ ⊢ 2.2 floo

nots flood ⊣ ⊢ 3.2 knots ebb ⟶ ⊢ 2.2 knots flood ⊣ ⊢ 1 ebb ⟶ ⊢ 2.5

SUN MAY 21

dawn 4:49 sunrise 5:55 sunset 8:18 dark 9:25
moonrise 7:10 a.m. moonset 10:53 p.m.

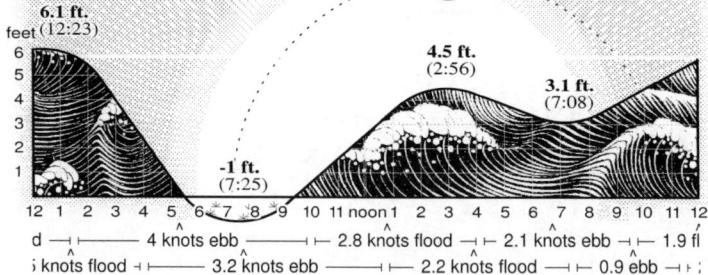

6.1 ft.
feet (12:23)

4.5 ft.
(2:56)

3.1 ft.
(7:08)

-1 ft.
(7:25)

12 1 2 3 4 5 6 7 8 9 10 11 noon 1 2 3 4 5 6 7 8 9 10 11 12

d ⟶ ⊢ 4 knots ebb ⟶ ⊢ 2.8 knots flood ⊣ ⊢ 2.1 knots ebb ⊣ ⊢ 1.9 fl

5 knots flood ⊣ ⊢ 3.2 knots ebb ⟶ ⊢ 2.2 knots flood ⟶ ⊢ 0.9 ebb ⟶ ⊢

Ⓢ Ⓙ Ⓥ Ⓜ
ⓜ

MON MAY 15
dawn 4:55 sunrise 6:00 sunset 8:13 dark 9:19
moonrise 3:56 a.m. moonset 4:16 p.m.

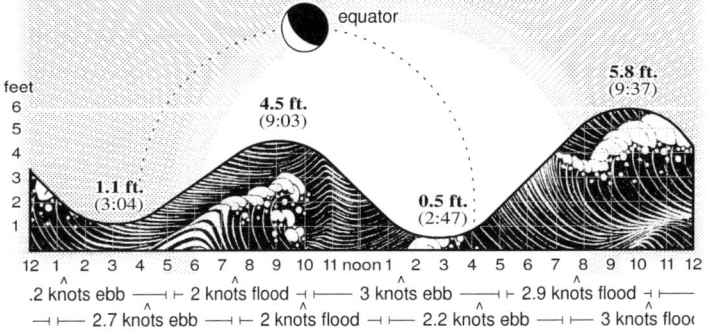

equator

feet

5.8 ft.
(9:37)

4.5 ft.
(9:03)

1.1 ft.
(3:04)

0.5 ft.
(2:47)

12 1 2 3 4 5 6 7 8 9 10 11 noon 1 2 3 4 5 6 7 8 9 10 11 12

.2 knots ebb ——ᐱ—⊢ 2 knots flood ᐱ—ᐣ—⊢ 3 knots ebb ——ᐱ—⊢ 2.9 knots flood ᐱ—⊢—
—ᐣ—⊢ 2.7 knots ebb ——⊢ 2 knots flood ᐱ—ᐣ—⊢ 2.2 knots ebb ——ᐱ—⊢ 3 knots flood

TUE MAY 16
dawn 4:54 sunrise 5:59 sunset 8:14 dark 9:20
moonrise 4:21 a.m. moonset 5:24 p.m.

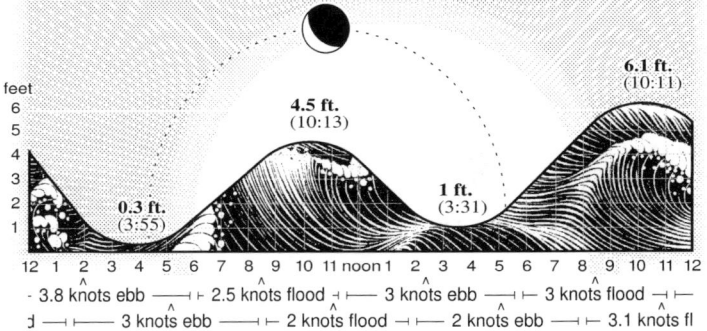

feet

6.1 ft.
(10:11)

4.5 ft.
(10:13)

0.3 ft.
(3:55)

1 ft.
(3:31)

12 1 2 3 4 5 6 7 8 9 10 11 noon 1 2 3 4 5 6 7 8 9 10 11 12

- 3.8 knots ebb ——ᐱ—⊢ 2.5 knots flood ᐱ—ᐣ—⊢ 3 knots ebb ——ᐱ—⊢ 3 knots flood ᐱ—⊢—
—ᐣ—⊢ 3 knots ebb ——ᐱ—⊢ 2 knots flood ᐱ—ᐣ—⊢ 2 knots ebb ——ᐱ—⊢ 3.1 knots fl

WED MAY 17
dawn 4:53 sunrise 5:58 sunset 8:15 dark 9:21
moonrise 4:47 a.m. moonset 6:32 p.m.

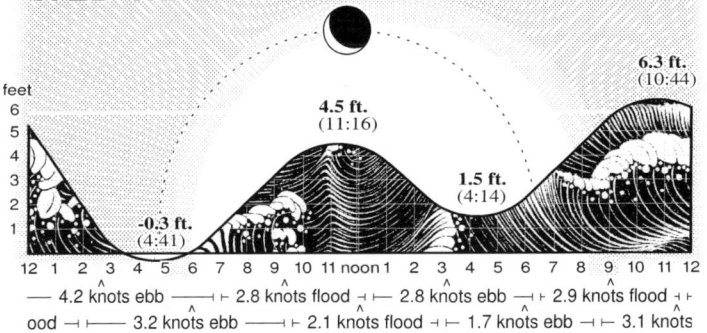

feet

6.3 ft.
(10:44)

4.5 ft.
(11:16)

-0.3 ft.
(4:41)

1.5 ft.
(4:14)

12 1 2 3 4 5 6 7 8 9 10 11 noon 1 2 3 4 5 6 7 8 9 10 11 12

—— 4.2 knots ebb ——ᐱ—⊢ 2.8 knots flood ᐱ—ᐣ—⊢ 2.8 knots ebb ——⊢ 2.9 knots flood ᐱ—⊢
ood ᐱ—ᐣ—⊢ 3.2 knots ebb ——ᐱ—⊢ 2.1 knots flood ᐱ—ᐣ—⊢ 1.7 knots ebb ——ᐱ—⊢ 3.1 knots

THU MAY 18
dawn 4:52 sunrise 5:58 sunset 8:15 dark 9:22
moonrise 5:16 a.m. moonset 7:41 p.m.

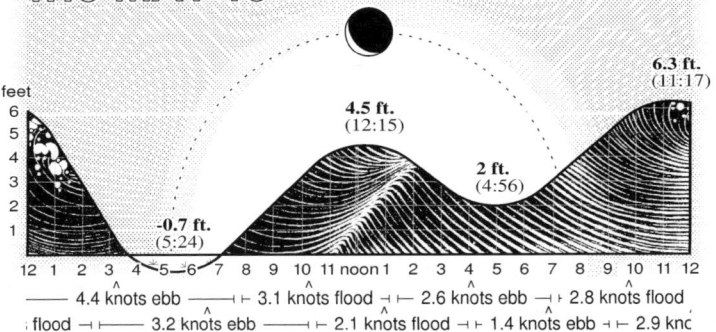

feet

6.3 ft.
(11:17)

4.5 ft.
(12:15)

-0.7 ft.
(5:24)

2 ft.
(4:56)

12 1 2 3 4 5 6 7 8 9 10 11 noon 1 2 3 4 5 6 7 8 9 10 11 12

—— 4.4 knots ebb ——ᐱ—⊢ 3.1 knots flood ᐱ—ᐣ—⊢ 2.6 knots ebb ——ᐱ—⊢ 2.8 knots flood
: flood ᐱ—ᐣ—⊢ 3.2 knots ebb ——⊢ 2.1 knots flood ᐱ—ᐣ—⊢ 1.4 knots ebb ᐱ—⊢ 2.9 knc

FRI MAY 12

dawn 4:58 sunrise 6:03 sunset 8:10 dark 9:15
moonrise 2:28 a.m. moonset 12:44 p.m.

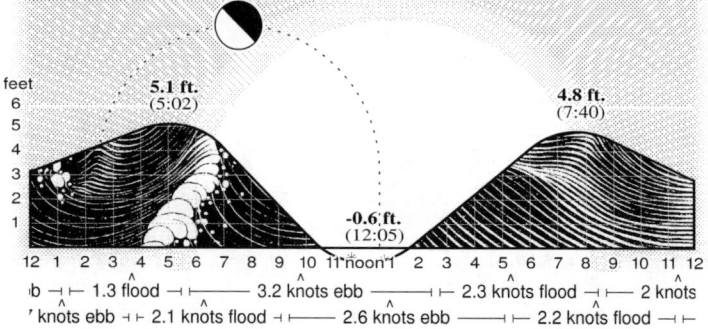

feet

5.1 ft.
(5:02)

4.8 ft.
(7:40)

-0.6 ft.
(12:05)

12 1 2 3 4 5 6 7 8 9 10 11 noon 1 2 3 4 5 6 7 8 9 10 11 12

b ⊣ ⊢ 1.3 flood ⊣ ⊢ 3.2 knots ebb ⊣ ⊢ 2.3 knots flood ⊣ ⊢ 2 knots
' knots ebb ⊢ 2.1 knots flood ⊣ ⊢ 2.6 knots ebb ⊣ ⊢ 2.2 knots flood ⊣ ⊢

SAT MAY 13

dawn 4:57 sunrise 6:02 sunset 8:11 dark 9:16
moonrise 3:01 a.m. moonset 1:57 p.m.

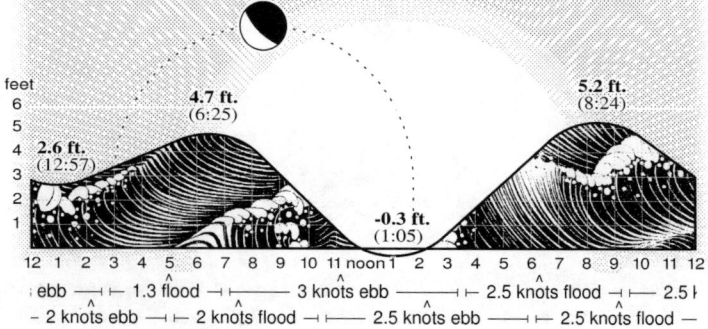

feet

4.7 ft.
(6:25)

5.2 ft.
(8:24)

2.6 ft.
(12:57)

-0.3 ft.
(1:05)

12 1 2 3 4 5 6 7 8 9 10 11 noon 1 2 3 4 5 6 7 8 9 10 11 12

: ebb ⊣ ⊢ 1.3 flood ⊣ ⊢ 3 knots ebb ⊣ ⊢ 2.5 knots flood ⊣ ⊢ 2.5 ⊢
~ 2 knots ebb ⊣ ⊢ 2 knots flood ⊣ ⊢ 2.5 knots ebb ⊣ ⊢ 2.5 knots flood ⊢

SUN MAY 14

dawn 4:56 sunrise 6:01 sunset 8:12 dark 9:17
moonrise 3:29 a.m. moonset 3:07 p.m.

Comets Panstarrs & Linear

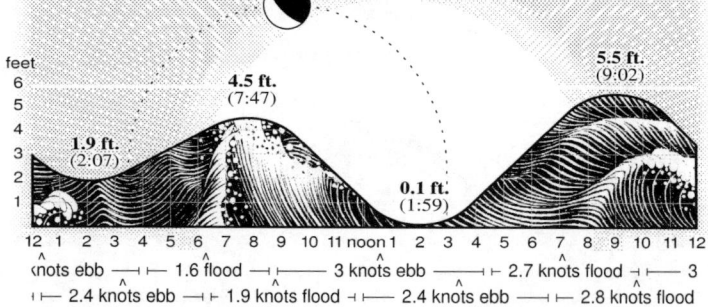

feet

4.5 ft.
(7:47)

5.5 ft.
(9:02)

1.9 ft.
(2:07)

0.1 ft.
(1:59)

12 1 2 3 4 5 6 7 8 9 10 11 noon 1 2 3 4 5 6 7 8 9 10 11 12

knots ebb ⊣ ⊢ 1.6 flood ⊣ ⊢ 3 knots ebb ⊣ ⊢ 2.7 knots flood ⊣ ⊢ 3
⊢ 2.4 knots ebb ⊣ ⊢ 1.9 knots flood ⊣ ⊢ 2.4 knots ebb ⊣ ⊢ 2.8 knots flood

Comets Panstarrs and Linear The comets 364P/Panstarrs and 237P/ Linear on May 14th will be at their periodic perihelion passage at .80 AU and 1.99 AU from the Sun, respectively. AU or astronomical unit is the approximate mean distance between the Earth and Sun. It is likely, the comet Panstarrs will be the most visible in the sky since at .80 AU distance, its coma and tail should be glowing brightly. Typically, a comet has to be within 1.4 AU - roughly the distance Mars is from the Sun - in order for the Sun to heat the comet's icy center and create the comet's coma and tail. copyright 2022 Pacific Publishers, L.L.C. WWW.TIDELOG.COM